Signature SERIES

ADVANCED MICROSOFT® WORD 2000

Desktop Publishing

Joanne Arford
College of DuPage
Glen Ellyn, Illinois

Judy Burnside
College of DuPage
Glen Ellyn, Illinois

Nita Rutkosky
Pierce College at Puyallup
Puyallup, Washington

Contributing Authors

Nancy Stanko
College of DuPage
Glen Ellyn, Illinois

Stella Styrczula
College of DuPage
Glen Ellyn, Illinois

EMCParadigm

Senior Editor	Sonja Brown
Developmental Editor	Mary Verrill
Copyeditor	David Dexter
Cover Designer	Chris Vern Johnson
Art Director	Joan D'Onofrio
Text Designer	Jennifer Wreisner
Desktop Production	Desktop Solutions
Proofreader	Laura M. Nelson Publishing Services
Testers	Rebecca Pepper, Nancy Weber
Indexer	Terry Casey

Publishing Team—George Provol, Publisher; Wesley Lawton, Executive Editor; Janice Johnson, Director of Product Development; Lori Landwer, Marketing Manager; Shelley Clubb, Electronic Design and Production Manager.

Registered Trademarks—Microsoft, Windows, PowerPoint, Outlook, and the MOUS icon are registered trademarks of Microsoft Corporation in the United States and other countries. IBM is a registered trademark of IBM Corporation.

Library of Congress Cataloging-in-Publication Data
        Rutkosky, Nita Hewitt.
                Advanced Microsoft Word 2000 : desktop publishing / Nita Hewitt Rutkosky, Joanne
        Marschke Arford, Judy Dwyer Burnside.
                  p.   cm. -- (Signature series)
                Includes index.
                ISBN 0-7638-0246-8 (text + CD-ROM)
                1. Microsoft Word. 2. Word processing. I. Arford, Joanne Marschke. II. Burnside,
        Judy Dwyer. III. Title. IV. Signature series (Saint Paul, Minn.)

Z52.5.M52 R868 2000
652.5'5369—dc21   99-051939

Text + CD-ROM package, ISBN 0-7638-0246-8, Order Number 04334

© 2000 by Paradigm Publishing Inc.
              Published by **EMC**Paradigm
              875 Montreal Way
              St. Paul, MN 55102
              (800) 535-6865
              E-mail: **educate@emcp.com**
              Web Site: www.emcp.com

Care has been taken to provide accurate and useful information about the Internet capabilities of Microsoft Word 2000. However, the authors, editor, and publisher cannot accept any responsibility for Web, e-mail, newsgroup, or chatroom subject matter nor content, nor for consequences from any application of the information in this book, and make no warranty, expressed or implied, with respect to the book's content.

Printed in the United States of America

10   9   8   7   6   5   4   3   2

Contents

Unit 2 Preparing Promotional Documents, Web Pages, and PowerPoint Presentations ▓ 185

Introduction

Advanced Microsoft® Word 2000: Desktop Publishing by Joanne Arford, Judy Burnside, and Nita Rutkosky addresses the expanded desktop publishing features of Microsoft Word 2000. This textbook primarily focuses on advanced Word 2000 features with an emphasis on desktop publishing terminology and concepts. Word 2000 and other Office 2000 integrated applications, such as PowerPoint, allow the desktop publisher to create professional-looking documents in an efficient manner. Desktop publishing greatly reduces the cost of publishing documents, combines the roles of page designer and typesetter, offers immediate results, and allows control of production from start to finish.

Text Pedagogy

Advanced Microsoft Word 2000: Desktop Publishing is designed for students who are proficient in word processing. This textbook assumes that students are using a custom or full installation of Microsoft Word 2000, as part of Office 2000 Professional Edition, in a computer lab or home study setting.

Most of the key desktop publishing concepts addressed in this textbook are presented in chapter 1. Reinforcement and applications of these key concepts are presented in the remaining chapters. The applications are designed to develop skills in critical thinking, decision making, and creativity. Many applications in this textbook are designed to reinforce collaborative learning in planning, designing, and evaluating business documents. In numerous applications, basic information is given for a task just as it may be given in a real life situation.

If the student wishes to build a portfolio of documents for course requirements or job applications, particular exercises are identified for this purpose. Exercises that can contribute to the student's portfolio are identified by a "portfolio" icon.

Emphasis on Visual Learning

Microsoft Office 2000 programs such as Word operate within the Windows operating system, a graphical user interface (GUI) that provides a visually oriented environment by using icons to represent program features. This textbook also emphasizes a graphical environment with icons that represent specific learning components.

In keeping with Windows' graphical environment, figures that illustrate numerous steps done at the computer are labeled with "bubble" callouts corresponding to the steps. The student can easily follow the steps by seeing the exact spot on the computer screen where a certain action is required on their part.

Structure of the Text

The text contains three units with a total of 11 chapters. Each chapter contains the following elements:

- Performance Objectives
- List of desktop publishing terms with definitions in the margins
- List of Word 2000 features used

- Introductory overview of chapter concepts and features
- DTP Pointers in the margin to reinforce concepts
- Hands-on exercises within each chapter to demonstrate key concepts and features
- Chapter Summary
- Commands Review
- Thinking Offline (short answer review)
- Working Hands-On (computer applications)
- Creative Activity (additional applications promoting collaborative learning and critical thinking as well as individual creativity)

In addition, each unit ends with Performance Assessments that evaluate students' mastery of both the desktop publishing concepts and software skills presented in the unit.

Industry Standards from the SCANS Commission

The Secretary's Commission on Achieving Necessary Skills (SCANS) standards emphasize the integration of competencies from the areas of information, technology, basic skills, and thinking skills. The concepts and applications material in this book have been designed to coordinate with and reflect this important interdisciplinary emphasis. In addition, learning assessment tools implement the SCANS standards. For example, the end-of-chapter exercises called Working Hands-On reinforce acquired skills while providing practice in decision-making and problem solving. Performance Assessments at the end of each unit offer simulation exercises that require students to demonstrate their understanding of the major skills and technical features taught in the unit's chapters within the framework of creativity, decision making, and writing. Optional exercises related to SCANS standards are included in the Performance Assessments and in selected Working Hands-On assessments.

Primary Program Outcomes

Students who successfully complete this course will have achieved the following competencies:

- Identify the design concepts of focus, balance, proportion, contrast, directional flow, consistency, and color.
- Evaluate documents for the use of basic design concepts.
- Integrate basic layout and design concepts, using the desktop publishing features of Microsoft Word 2000, to enhance the readability of multiple-page, portrait or landscape documents such as letterheads, business cards, personal documents, flyers, brochures, promotional documents, presentational materials, and newsletters.
- Produce and enhance business and personal documents with variable page layouts using standardized type and graphic design techniques along with Word templates and clip art.
- Use Microsoft Word 2000 to manage desktop publishing files and document templates.
- Publish Word documents in a variety of formats, including PowerPoint presentations and Web pages.

Completing Computer Exercises

Advanced Microsoft® Word 2000: Desktop Publishing is packaged with a student CD-ROM that contains keyed documents and extra graphics that students will use to complete various exercises. These exercise files are located in individual folders on the student CD-ROM that correspond to the chapter numbers in which the exercises are located, as indicated by an icon on the first page of each chapter.

Chapter 01

The most efficient and easiest way to use the student CD is to copy all of the files into their own folder on the hard drive or network file server. When you need a specific file, open the file from that folder, rather than taking it from the student CD. However, students may also choose to open files directly from the student CD and save them to the hard drive or a 3-1/2 inch floppy disk.

Use the hard drive, a 3-1/2 inch floppy disk, a zip disk (and zip drive), or a rewriteable CD (and CD-RW drive) to save and back up documents that are in progress or complete. If you plan to save to floppy disk, have several blank disks handy at all times since the completed exercise files tend to be quite large. Your instructor may suggest that you delete specific exercises once they have been turned in and graded. Check with your instructor for file backup and deletion procedures.

Understanding File Extensions

File names with extensions such as *.doc*, *.dot*, *.ppt*, and *.htm* are frequently used throughout this textbook. A filename extension identifies the file format of the associated file. The filename extensions referred to in this textbook and their corresponding file formats are as follows:

Extension	File Format
.doc	Microsoft Word document
.dot	Word template
.bmp	Windows Bitmap
.htm or .html	Hypertext Markup Language (HTML)
.gif	Graphics Interchange Format (GIF)
.jpg	Joint Picture Experts Group (JPEG)
.ppt	Microsoft PowerPoint presentation
.pot	PowerPoint template
.wmf	Windows Metafile

By default, file name extensions do not automatically display. To display file name extensions, complete the following steps:

1. At the Windows 95 or 98 desktop, double-click the My Computer icon.
2. Click <u>V</u>iew, Folder <u>O</u>ptions, and then select the View tab.
3. Remove the check mark from the *Hide file extensions for known file types* check box.
4. Click OK.
5. Close the My Computer dialog box.

As you work through the desktop publishing information and exercises, you need to be aware of the following important points:

*   All default formatting settings, such as fonts, margin settings, line spacing, and justification; toolbars; templates; and folders used in this textbook are based on the assumption that none of the original defaults have been customized after installation.

- Instructions for all features and exercises emphasize using the mouse. Where appropriate, keyboard or function key presses are added as an alternative.
- As you complete the exercises, view the completed figure that follows each exercise to see what the document should look like.
- Be aware that the final appearance of your printed documents depends on the printer you use to complete the exercises. Your printer driver may be different from the printer driver used for the exercises in this textbook. For example, not all printer drivers interpret line height the same, nor do they all offer the same font selections. Consequently, you may have to make some minor adjustments when completing the exercises in this book. For instance, if you have to select an alternate font from the one called for in the instructions, you may need to change the type size to complete the exercise in the space allotted. You may also need to adjust the spacing between paragraphs or specific blocks of text. As a result, your documents will look slightly different from what you see in this text. As you will find in the chapters that follow, creating desktop published documents is a constant process of making small adjustments to fine-tune the layout and design.

System Requirements

Whether you are using Word 2000 within the Microsoft Office 2000 Professional Edition or the Small Business Edition, the following information is important to your success in completing the exercises in this textbook. For best results, a full installation of Microsoft Office or Microsoft Word 2000 is recommended. Installation of the Microsoft Office 2000 Professional Edition is assumed. These are the basic system requirements and recommendations:

- Personal computer with a Pentium I (or later) processor.
- Microsoft Windows 95 or 98 operating system.
- At least 32 megabytes (MB) of memory.
- 250 MB or more free hard disk space for software installation.
- Super VGA, 256-color monitor.
- A double- or quad-speed CD-ROM drive.
- A 1.44 MB (3-1/2 inch) floppy disk drive for backup.
- Microsoft Mouse or other compatible pointing device.
- 9600 or higher baud modem (28,000 baud or higher recommended).
- 4 MB or more of free disk space at all times for temporary files.
- Laser printer or high quality inkjet printer supported by Windows 95 or 98; color printer preferred.
- Internet access to fully complete the exercises in chapter 8.
- Microsoft PowerPoint 2000 installed to complete the exercises in chapter 9.

Learning Components That Accompany This Text

The following products for instructors and students correspond to this text and enhance its teaching possibilities. These products can be ordered by contacting an EMC/Paradigm Publishing Customer Care representative by phone at (800) 535-6865 or via e-mail at educate@emcp.com and supplying the order number as follows:

Instructor's Guide with CD-ROM for Advanced Microsoft Word 2000: Desktop Publishing, Signature Series, order number 41334. The Instructor's Guide contains suggested course syllabi, assignment sheets, and grade sheets; comprehensive unit tests and answers to use for final exams; and Supplemental Performance Assessments with model answers. For each chapter, the Instructor's Guide also provides teaching hints for concepts and hands-on exercises in the text. The Instructor's CD-ROM contains everything found in the printed Instructor's Guide plus model answer files for exercises.

Test Bank for Advanced Microsoft Word 2000: Desktop Publishing, Signature Series, order number 59334. The Paradigm Test Generator is a full-featured test creation program that offers instructors a wide variety of options for generating and editing tests. Instructors can create custom tests that include questions from the existing test bank as well as new questions that can be added. The test bank provided on this disk offers approximately 450 questions that range in difficulty and discrimination levels. All the standard question types plus graphic- and procedure-oriented items are included.

Unit *one*

CREATING BUSINESS AND PERSONAL DOCUMENTS

Chapter 01

Understanding the Desktop Publishing Process

1

PERFORMANCE OBJECTIVES

Upon successful completion of chapter 1, you will be able to evaluate design elements in a desktop published document for the appropriate use of focus, balance, proportion, contrast, directional flow, consistency, color, and page layout.

DESKTOP PUBLISHING TERMS

Thumbnail sketch	Contrast	Consistency
Focus	White space	Color
Balance	Legibility	Gutter
Symmetrical design	Directional flow	Page layout
Asymmetrical design	Alignment	Grid
Proportion	Z pattern	

WORD FEATURES USED

Open as Read-Only
Viewing multiple pages

Defining Desktop Publishing

Since the 1970s, computers have been an integral part of the business environment. Businesses use computers and software packages to perform a variety of tasks. For many years, the three most popular types of software purchased for computers were word processing, spreadsheet, and database. The introduction of the laser printer and the inkjet printer, with their abilities to produce high-quality documents, in black and white as well as in color, led to the growing popularity of another kind of software called desktop publishing.

Desktop publishing involves using desktop publishing software, such as Microsoft Publisher 2000, or word processing software with desktop publishing capabilities, such as Microsoft Word 2000. Desktop publishing allows the user to produce professional-looking documents for both office and home use. The phrase "desktop publishing," coined by Aldus Corporation president Paul Brainard, means that publishing can now literally take place at your desk.

Until the mid-1980s, graphic design depended almost exclusively on design professionals. But desktop publishing software changed all that by bringing graphic design into the office and home. Faster microprocessors, larger storage capacity, improved printer capabilities, an increased supply of clip art, CD-ROMs, and access to the Internet continue to expand the role of desktop publishing. Everything from a flyer to a newsletter to a Web page can be designed, created, and produced at your own computer.

In traditional publishing, several people may be involved in completing a publication project, thus increasing the costs and the time needed to complete the project. With the use of desktop publishing software, one person may be performing all of the tasks necessary to complete a project, greatly reducing the costs of publishing documents. The two approaches, however, do have a great deal in common. Both approaches involve planning the project, organizing content, analyzing layout and design, arranging design elements, typesetting, printing, and distributing the project.

Desktop publishing can be an individual or a combined effort. As an individual effort, desktop publishing produces immediate results and offers you the ability to control the production from beginning layout and design to the end result—printing and distribution. However, desktop publishing and traditional publishing work well together. A project may begin on a desktop, where the document is designed and created, but an illustrator may be commissioned to create some artwork, and the piece may be sent to a commercial printer for printing and binding.

This book is designed to help those who possess an advanced skill level of Microsoft Word but who have little or no design experience. Today's office support staff are increasingly being required to create more sophisticated documents with little or no background on how to design a visually appealing document that still gets the message across to the reader. Home users are also finding the need to create similar professional-looking documents, whether it be for a home business, an organization, or personal use.

Initiating the Desktop Publishing Process

The process of creating a publication begins with two steps—planning the publication and creating the content. During the planning process, the desktop publisher must decide on the purpose of the publication and the intended audience. When creating the content, the desktop publisher must make sure that the publication's intended message is conveyed to the reader.

Planning the Publication

Initial planning is probably one of the most important steps in the desktop publishing process. During this stage, the following items must be addressed:

- **Clearly identify the purpose of your communication.** The more definite you are about your purpose, the easier it will be for you to organize your material into an effective communication. Are you trying to provide information? Are you trying to sell a product? Are you announcing an event?

- **Assess your target audience.** Who will read your publication? Are they employees, co-workers, clients, friends, or family? What will your target audience expect from your publication? Do they expect a serious, more conservative approach, or an informal, humorous approach?

DTP POINTERS
Consider your audience when planning your publication.

- **Determine in what form your intended audience will be exposed to your message.** Will your message be conveyed in a brochure as part of a packet of presentation materials for a company seminar? Or will your message take the form of a newspaper advertisement, surrounded by other advertisements? Will your message be in the form of a business card that is to be distributed when making sales calls? Or will your message be tacked on a bulletin board?

- **Decide what you want your readers to do after reading your message.** Do you want your readers to ask for more information? Do you want some kind of a response? Do you want your readers to be able to contact you in person or over the telephone?

- **Collect examples of effective designs.** Keep a design idea folder. Put copies of any designs that impress you into your idea folder. These designs may include flyers, promotional documents, newsletters, graphic images, interesting type arrangements, and the like. Look through your idea folder every time you begin a new project. Let favorite designs serve as a catalyst for developing your own ideas.

Creating the Content

The most important goal in desktop publishing is to get the message across. Design is important because it increases the visual appeal of your document, but content is still the most important consideration. Create a document that communicates the message clearly to your intended audience.

In analyzing your message, identify your purpose and start organizing your material. Establish a hierarchy of importance among the items in your communication. Consider what items will be the most important to the reader, what will attract the reader's attention, and what will spark enough interest for the reader to go on. Begin to think about the format or layout you want to follow. (Check your idea folder!) Clear and organized content combined with an attractive layout and design contributes to the effectiveness of your message.

Designing the Document

If the message is the most significant part of a communication, why bother with design? A well-planned and relevant design sets your work apart from others, and it gets people to read your message. Just as people may be judged by their appearance, a publication may be judged by its design. Design also helps organize ideas so the reader can find information quickly and easily. Whether you are creating a business flyer, letterhead, or newsletter, anything you create will look more attractive, more professional, and more convincing if you take a little extra

DTP POINTERS
Take the time to design!

time to design it. As in the planning stages, you must still consider the purpose of the document, the target audience, and the method of distribution. In addition, consider the following factors:

- What is the feeling the document is meant to elicit?
- What is the most important information and how can it be emphasized so that the reader can easily identify the purpose of the document?
- What different types of information are to be presented and how can these elements be distinguished, yet kept internally consistent?
- How much space is available?

Answering these questions will help you determine the design and layout of your communication.

An important first step in planning your design and layout is to prepare a thumbnail sketch. A *thumbnail sketch* is a miniature draft of the document you are attempting to create. As you can see in figure 1.1, thumbnail sketches let you experiment with alternative locations for such elements as graphic images, ruled lines (horizontal or vertical lines), columns, and borders.

Thumbnail Sketch

A rough sketch used in planning a layout and design.

figure
1.1

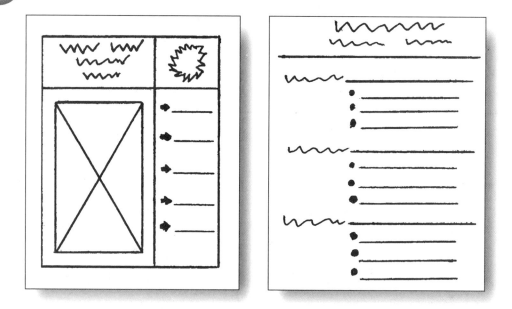

A good designer continually asks questions, pays attention to details, and makes well-thought-out decisions. Consider examples A and B in figure 1.2. Which example attracts your attention, entices you to read on, looks convincing, and would most likely encourage you to take action?

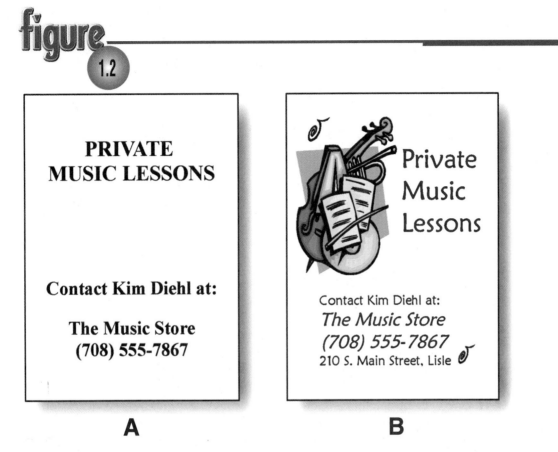

figure 1.2

A

> PRIVATE
> MUSIC LESSONS
>
> Contact Kim Diehl at:
>
> The Music Store
> (708) 555-7867

B

> Private
> Music
> Lessons
>
> Contact Kim Diehl at:
> *The Music Store*
> *(708) 555-7867*
> 210 S. Main Street, Lisle

Overdesigning is one of the most common tendencies of beginning desktop publishers. The temptation to use as many of the desktop publishing features as possible in one document is often difficult to resist. However, design elements should be used to communicate, not decorate. To create a visually attractive and appealing publication, start with the same classic design concepts professional designers use as guidelines. These concepts include focus, balance, proportion, contrast, directional flow, consistency, and color.

Creating Focus

The *focus* or focal point on a page is an element that draws the reader's eyes. Focus is created by using elements that are large, dense, unusual, and/or surrounded by white space. Two basic design elements used to create focus in a document are:

- Titles, headlines, and subheads created in larger, bolder, and often contrasting, typefaces
- Graphic elements such as ruled lines, clip art, photographs, illustrations, logos, or images created with a draw program or scanned into the computer

Creating Focus with Titles, Headlines, and Subheads

In business or in home use, you will find titles, headlines, and subheads in reports, procedure manuals, newsletters, term papers, etc. Untrained desktop publishers often create publications that are essentially typewritten documents

Focus
An element used to attract the reader's eyes.

DTP POINTERS
A well-designed headline attracts the reader's attention.

that happen to be set in proportional type. However, the choice of typeface, type size, and positioning are highly flexible. Used correctly, these features can create focus on the page even in a text-intensive document.

In a text-only document, primary focus is usually created by using large or bold type for titles and headings, surrounded by enough white space to contrast with the main text. *White space* is the background where no text or graphics are located. The amount of white space around a focal element can enhance its appearance and help to balance other design elements on the page. When creating titles/headlines, keep the following points in mind:

White Space
Background space with no text or graphics.

- State your title or headline in a precise, yet easily understood manner.
- Select typefaces that are readable. *Legibility* is of utmost importance. Readers must be able to clearly see and read the individual letters in the headline/title.
- Size your title or headline in proportion to its importance relative to the surrounding text.
- Set your title or headline in a larger type size so the reader immediately knows the nature of the publication.

Legibility
The ease with which individual characters are recognized.

Your selection of an appropriate font (typeface, type size, and type style), the alignment of the text, and the horizontal and vertical white space surrounding the text affect the impact of your headline/title as a focal element in your document. A well-designed headline attracts the reader's attention. It can play a big part in whether a reader continues reading your publication.

In any type of communication—a semi-annual report, company newsletter, advertising flyer, or brochure—subheads can be used to provide a secondary focal element. While headlines are designed to attract the reader's attention, the subheads may be the key to luring the reader in. Subheads provide order to your text and give the reader further clues about the content of your publication. Subheads also allow the reader to zero in on a specific area of interest. Content divided by subheads visually breaks up large blocks of text and appears more manageable to the reader's eye. Like titles and headlines, subheads need to be concise, legible, easy to understand, and consistently formatted throughout the entire document. Appropriate font selection, spacing above and below the subhead, length, and alignment must be taken into consideration.

DTP POINTERS
Subheads provide order to your text and give the reader further clues about the content of your publication.

Evaluating the Use of Titles and Subheads

Look at document A in figure 1.3. Does any particular location on the page attract your attention? You might say the title attracts your attention slightly, but there are no elements that really stand out. Now look at document B in the same figure. Why is this document an improvement over document A? Now look at document C. Are your eyes drawn to a certain spot on the page? Does the title attract your attention more so than in document A and B? Why? What about the subheads? Do they stand out? Does the material appear more organized? Not only is this a dramatic improvement over document A, but a much stronger design statement than document B. The title, set in a larger and bolder type, serves as a primary focal point. An important question is immediately answered for the reader; namely, what is this all about? What area of the page are your eyes drawn to next? Notice how the subheads, set in a type bolder and larger than the body text but smaller than the heading, provide secondary focal points on the page. You would probably agree that document C is much more visually appealing than documents A or B. Notice how the consistent font selection in all the subheads makes the document's organization readily apparent to the reader.

figure 1.3

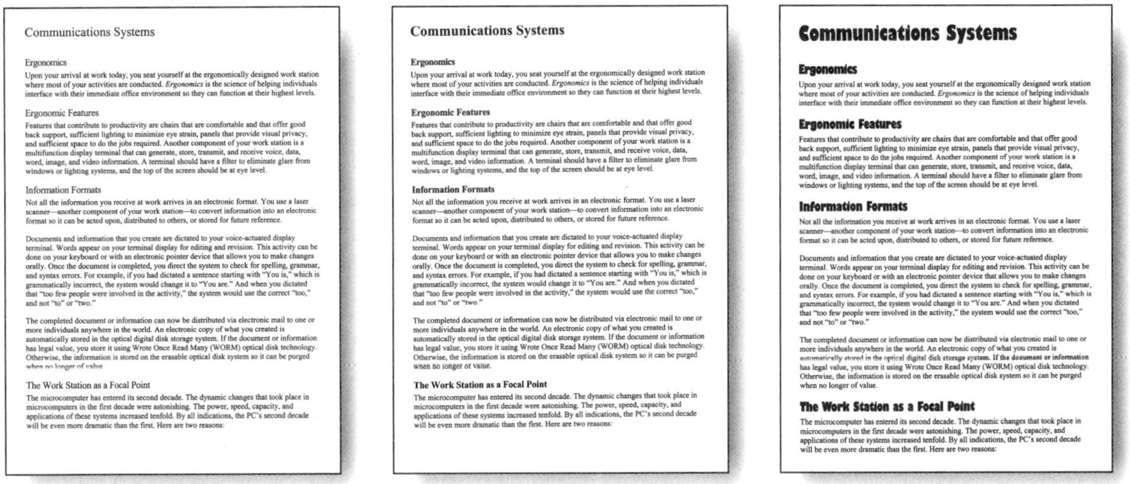

Communications Systems

Ergonomics

Upon your arrival at work today, you seat yourself at the ergonomically designed work station where most of your activities are conducted. *Ergonomics* is the science of helping individuals interface with their immediate office environment so they can function at their highest levels.

Ergonomic Features

Features that contribute to productivity are chairs that are comfortable and that offer good back support, sufficient lighting to minimize eye strain, panels that provide visual privacy, and sufficient space to do the jobs required. Another component of your work station is a multifunction display terminal that can generate, store, transmit, and receive voice, data, word, image, and video information. A terminal should have a filter to eliminate glare from windows or lighting systems, and the top of the screen should be at eye level.

Information Formats

Not all the information you receive at work arrives in an electronic format. You use a laser scanner—another component of your work station—to convert information into an electronic format so it can be acted upon, distributed to others, or stored for future reference.

Documents and information that you create are dictated to your voice-actuated display terminal. Words appear on your terminal display for editing and revision. This activity can be done on your keyboard or with an electronic pointer device that allows you to make changes orally. Once the document is completed, you direct the system to check for spelling, grammar, and syntax errors. For example, if you had dictated a sentence starting with "You is," which is grammatically incorrect, the system would change it to "You are." And when you dictated that "too few people were involved in the activity," the system would use the correct "too," and not "to" or "two."

The completed document or information can now be distributed via electronic mail to one or more individuals anywhere in the world. An electronic copy of what you created is automatically stored in the optical digital disk storage system. If the document or information has legal value, you store it using Wrote Once Read Many (WORM) optical disk technology. Otherwise, the information is stored on the erasable optical disk system so it can be purged when no longer of value.

The Work Station as a Focal Point

The microcomputer has entered its second decade. The dynamic changes that took place in microcomputers in the first decade were astonishing. The power, speed, capacity, and applications of these systems increased tenfold. By all indications, the PC's second decade will be even more dramatic than the first. Here are two reasons:

A

Communications Systems

Ergonomics

Upon your arrival at work today, you seat yourself at the ergonomically designed work station where most of your activities are conducted. *Ergonomics* is the science of helping individuals interface with their immediate office environment so they can function at their highest levels.

Ergonomic Features

Features that contribute to productivity are chairs that are comfortable and that offer good back support, sufficient lighting to minimize eye strain, panels that provide visual privacy, and sufficient space to do the jobs required. Another component of your work station is a multifunction display terminal that can generate, store, transmit, and receive voice, data, word, image, and video information. A terminal should have a filter to eliminate glare from windows or lighting systems, and the top of the screen should be at eye level.

Information Formats

Not all the information you receive at work arrives in an electronic format. You use a laser scanner—another component of your work station—to convert information into an electronic format so it can be acted upon, distributed to others, or stored for future reference.

Documents and information that you create are dictated to your voice-actuated display terminal. Words appear on your terminal display for editing and revision. This activity can be done on your keyboard or with an electronic pointer device that allows you to make changes orally. Once the document is completed, you direct the system to check for spelling, grammar, and syntax errors. For example, if you had dictated a sentence starting with "You is," which is grammatically incorrect, the system would change it to "You are." And when you dictated that "too few people were involved in the activity," the system would use the correct "too," and not "to" or "two."

The completed document or information can now be distributed via electronic mail to one or more individuals anywhere in the world. An electronic copy of what you created is automatically stored in the optical digital disk storage system. If the document or information has legal value, you store it using Wrote Once Read Many (WORM) optical disk technology. Otherwise, the information is stored on the erasable optical disk system so it can be purged when no longer of value.

The Work Station as a Focal Point

The microcomputer has entered its second decade. The dynamic changes that took place in microcomputers in the first decade were astonishing. The power, speed, capacity, and applications of these systems increased tenfold. By all indications, the PC's second decade will be even more dramatic than the first. Here are two reasons:

B

Communications Systems

Ergonomics

Upon your arrival at work today, you seat yourself at the ergonomically designed work station where most of your activities are conducted. *Ergonomics* is the science of helping individuals interface with their immediate office environment so they can function at their highest levels.

Ergonomic Features

Features that contribute to productivity are chairs that are comfortable and that offer good back support, sufficient lighting to minimize eye strain, panels that provide visual privacy, and sufficient space to do the jobs required. Another component of your work station is a multifunction display terminal that can generate, store, transmit, and receive voice, data, word, image, and video information. A terminal should have a filter to eliminate glare from windows or lighting systems, and the top of the screen should be at eye level.

Information Formats

Not all the information you receive at work arrives in an electronic format. You use a laser scanner—another component of your work station—to convert information into an electronic format so it can be acted upon, distributed to others, or stored for future reference.

Documents and information that you create are dictated to your voice-actuated display terminal. Words appear on your terminal display for editing and revision. This activity can be done on your keyboard or with an electronic pointer device that allows you to make changes orally. Once the document is completed, you direct the system to check for spelling, grammar, and syntax errors. For example, if you had dictated a sentence starting with "You is," which is grammatically incorrect, the system would change it to "You are." And when you dictated that "too few people were involved in the activity," the system would use the correct "too," and not "to" or "two."

The completed document or information can now be distributed via electronic mail to one or more individuals anywhere in the world. An electronic copy of what you created is automatically stored in the optical digital disk storage system. If the document or information has legal value, you store it using Wrote Once Read Many (WORM) optical disk technology. Otherwise, the information is stored on the erasable optical disk system so it can be purged when no longer of value.

The Work Station as a Focal Point

The microcomputer has entered its second decade. The dynamic changes that took place in microcomputers in the first decade were astonishing. The power, speed, capacity, and applications of these systems increased tenfold. By all indications, the PC's second decade will be even more dramatic than the first. Here are two reasons:

C

Creating Focus with Graphic Elements

Graphic elements provide focus on a page and can enhance the overall appearance of a publication. Various graphic elements that can be effectively used to establish focus in your document include the following:

- fonts (typefaces in varying sizes, styles, and colors)
- reverse text (traditionally defined as a black background with white text; see chapter 6)
- drop caps (the first letter of the first word in a paragraph, set into the paragraph; often set in a larger type size and contrasting typeface; see chapter 6)
- ruled lines (horizontal or vertical lines of varying sizes and thickness; see chapter 3)
- clip art
- watermarks (a lightened version of an image; see chapter 2)
- illustrations
- photographs
- charts
- graphs
- diagrams
- tables
- pull quotes (used in newsletters, newspapers, and magazines; defined as a direct phrase, summarizing statement, or important point associated with the body text; see chapter 11)
- sidebars (used in newsletters, newspapers, and magazines; defined as a block of information or a related story that is set off from the body text in some type of a graphics box; see chapter 11)

When considering using a graphic element as a focal point, remember the following three points:

- Legibility is just as important with graphic elements as it is with titles and subheads. Graphic elements should support the message in your text and not interfere with its readability in any way.

- Communicate; don't decorate. Let your message dictate the use of graphic elements. Does the graphic element enhance your message or does it overshadow your message? Is it relevant, meaningful, and appropriate? Do not use it just for the sake of using it.

- Less is best. Simplicity rules. Owning a CD-ROM with 10,000 clip art images does not mean that you should find as many pictures as you can to insert into your document. One simple, large, and effective graphic image provides more impact than using several smaller images. Your goal is to provide focus. Too many images create visual confusion for the reader.

If all other factors are equal, publications containing graphic elements will be noticed and perused before text-only publications. The open house announcement shown in figure 1.4 uses a high contrast clip art image as a major focal point. "Tuscany Realty" and "Open House" stand out as focal points but not quite as strong as the black and white image. Varying the type size and type style helps to organize the remaining information and to provide minor focal points on the page.

figure 1.4

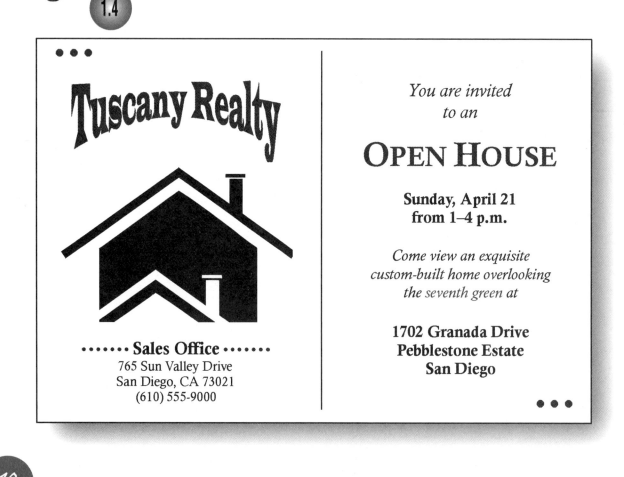

Creating Balance

Balance is attained by equally distributing the weight of various elements, such as blocks of text, graphic images, headings, ruled lines, and white space on the page. Balance can be described as either symmetrical or asymmetrical.

Balance
The equal distribution of design elements on a page.

Symmetrical Balance

A *symmetrically balanced design* contains similar elements of equal proportion or weight on the left and right sides and top and bottom of the page. Symmetrical balance is easy to achieve because all elements are centered on the page. If you were to fold a symmetrically designed document in half vertically (in other words, along its vertical line of symmetry), you would see that both halves of the document basically contain the same elements. To better visualize the concept of symmetrical balance, look at the shapes in the top half of figure 1.5. The squares, representing identical graphic elements, are positioned on the left and right sides of the page. The rectangle, representing a block of text, is centered in between the two squares. Notice the dotted line, representing a vertical line of symmetry, splitting the design in half. It is easy to see that the elements on both sides of the dotted line are equal in weight and proportion because they are exactly the same. Now look at the example of a symmetrically designed letterhead in the bottom half of figure 1.5. If you were to extend that same line of symmetry down through the sample letterhead, you would see that the design elements are equally distributed on both sides of the page.

Symmetrical Design
Balancing similar elements equally on a page (centered alignment).

figure 1.5

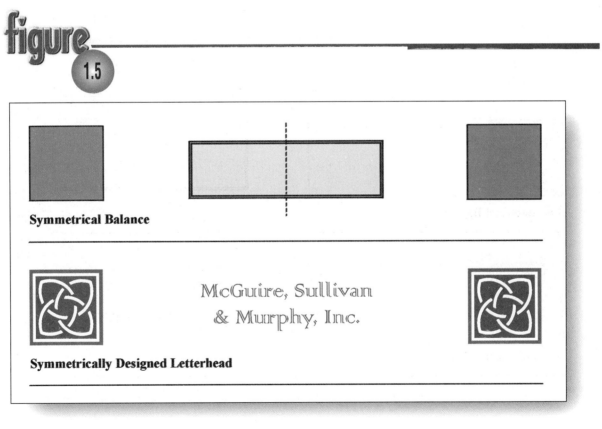

Symmetrical Balance

McGuire, Sullivan & Murphy, Inc.

Symmetrically Designed Letterhead

Asymmetrical Balance

Asymmetrical Design
Balancing contrasting
elements on a page.

Symmetrical balance is easy to identify and to create. However, contemporary design favors asymmetrical balance. An *asymmetrically balanced design* uses different design elements of varying weights and/or proportions to achieve balance on a page. Asymmetrical design is more flexible and visually stimulating than symmetrical design. Look at the shapes in the top half of figure 1.6. Notice the dotted line (the line of vertical symmetry) that divides the page in half. Do both sides match? Are there similar or identical elements on both sides? Even without the dotted line, you can easily see that both sides do not match. Therefore, you immediately know that this is not a symmetrical design. However, just because the design is not symmetrical, does not automatically mean that it is asymmetrical. Remember, the key to asymmetrical design is achieving a visual balance on the page using dissimilar or contrasting elements. Look back at the shapes and the white space surrounding the shapes in figure 1.6. Even though they are not the same and are not centered, would you agree that a visual balance is achieved on the page? The darker, more dense square and its surrounding white space on the left half of the page are balanced by the longer, less dense rectangle and its surrounding white space on the right half of the page. Now look at how those same shapes are converted into the design elements used in the sample letterhead in the bottom half of figure 1.6. Here, balance is achieved with dissimilar design elements resulting in an effective asymmetrical design.

figure 1.6

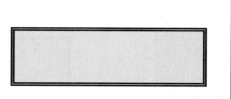

Asymmetrical Balance

McGuire, Sullivan & Murphy, Inc.

Asymmetrically Designed Letterhead

For another example, note the shapes and the line of vertical symmetry in the top half of figure 1.7. You obviously can tell that both sides do not match, and, therefore, this design is not symmetrical. But remember the key question—is visual balance achieved? View the sample letterhead in the bottom half of figure 1.7. Notice how the shapes in the top half of the figure translate into this asymmetrical design. When trying to achieve balance in your documents, consider the shape, size, and density of your blocks of text and/or graphic images and translate that information into shapes. Experiment, experiment, and experiment some more with those shapes to create a visually stimulating, balanced design.

figure
1.7

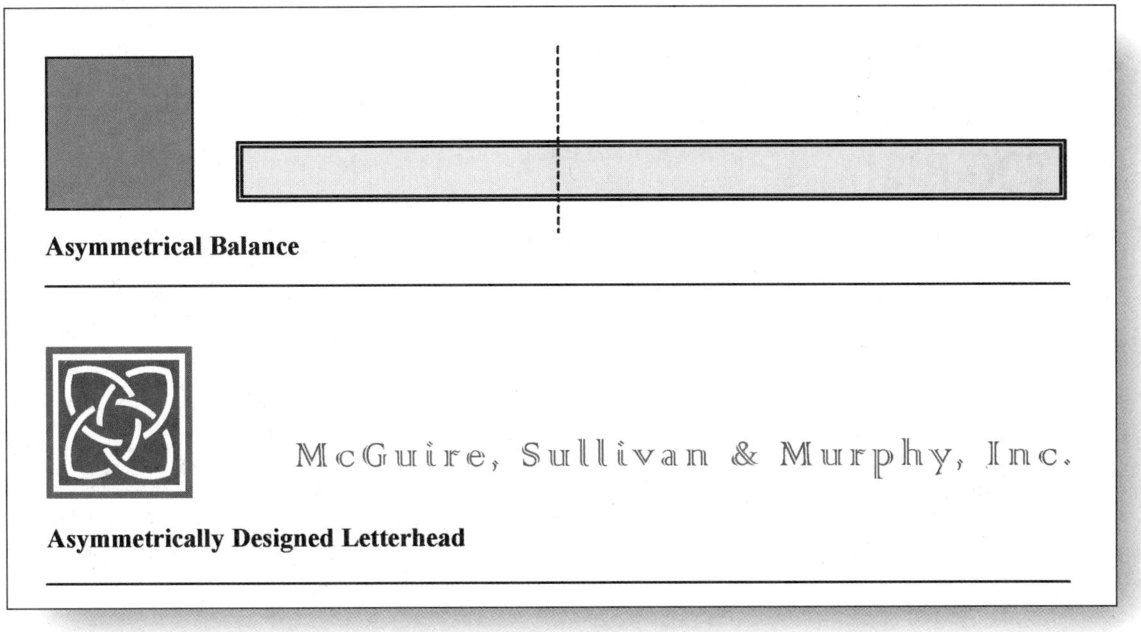

Asymmetrical Balance

McGuire, Sullivan & Murphy, Inc.

Asymmetrically Designed Letterhead

Multipage documents add another dimension to the challenge of achieving balance. Since balance must be achieved among the elements on more than one page, it is essential that you look at type and graphics in terms of each two-page unit, or spread, which is a set of pages facing each other.

Providing Proportion

When designing a communication, think about all the individual parts as they relate to the document as a whole. Readers tend to view larger elements as more important. Readers also are more likely to read a page where all the elements are in *proportion* to one another. When incorporating the concept of proportion into your documents, consider the following points:

Proportion
Sizing elements in relation to their relative importance and to each other.

• Size design elements, whether text or graphics, in proportion to their relative importance to the message.

• Size design elements so they are in proportion to each other.

Decide which elements in your document are the most important in conveying your message. Decide which elements are the second most important, and so on. Then proportionally size the visual elements in your publication according to their priority. This way you can make sure your readers see the most important information first. Appropriate typeface and type size selection for headlines, subheads, and body text can set the proportional standards for a document.

Evaluating Proportion

When viewing the documents in figure 1.8, look at the headline size in proportion to the body text. Think about this relationship when selecting the type size for titles/headlines and body text. When selecting the type size for subheads, consider how the subhead relates proportionally to the headline and to the body text.

figure
1.8

TOO BIG!

When designing a communication, think about all the individual parts as they relate to the document as a whole. Readers tend to view larger elements as more important.

Proportionally size the visual elements in your publication according to their importance. This way you can make sure your readers see the most important information first.

Readers also are more likely to read a page where all the elements are in proportion to one another. Appropriate typeface and type size selection for headlines, subheads, and body text can set the proportional

TOO SMALL!

When designing a communication, think about all the individual parts as they relate to the document as a whole. Readers tend to view larger elements as more important.

Proportionally size the visual elements in your publication according to their importance. This way you can make sure your readers see the most important information first.

Readers also are more likely to read a page where all the elements are in proportion to one another. Appropriate typeface and type size selection for headlines, subheads, and body text can set the proportional standards for a document.

JUST RIGHT!

When designing a communication, think about all the individual parts as they relate to the document as a whole. Readers tend to view larger elements as more important.

Proportionally size the visual elements in your publication according to their importance. This way you can make sure your readers see the most important information first.

Readers also are more likely to read a page where all the elements are in proportion to one another. Appropriate typeface and type size selection for headlines, subheads, and body text can set the proportional standards for a document.

Sizing Graphic Elements to Achieve Proportion

Sizing of graphic elements is also important in maintaining proportion among all the design elements on a page. For instance, look at illustration A in figure 1.9. The size of the musical graphic image visually tells the reader that it is the most important item on the page. But should it be? As discussed earlier in this chapter, the message that you want to get across to the reader always takes top priority. The graphic image in illustration A may be relevant, but it is overpowering the message rather than supporting it. The image is definitely out of proportion to its relative importance in the message.

Now take a look at illustration B in figure 1.9. The musical image is too small to be effective. Looking at the document as a whole, the image is out of proportion to the remaining elements. What is your reaction to illustration C in figure 1.9? Look at the individual elements as they relate to the whole document. All of the design elements appear to be in proportion to each other and to their ranking of importance in the intended message.

figure

1.9

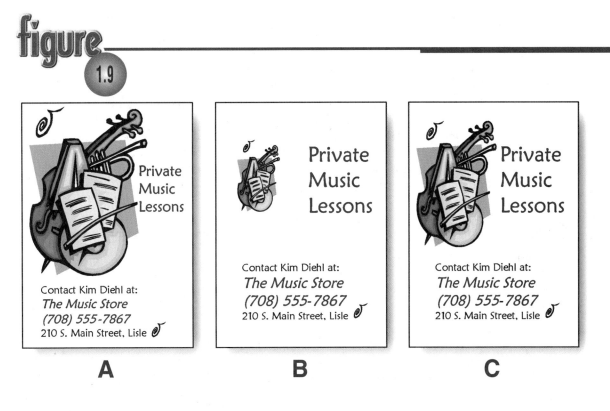

A   **B**   **C**

Using White Space to Achieve Proportion

White space is also important in sizing design elements proportionately on your page. Keep the following pointers in mind:

- Margins that are too narrow create a typing line that looks long in relation to the surrounding white space.
- Too much white space between columns makes the line length look short.
- Too little space between columns makes the text harder to read.
- Excess white space between lines of text creates gaps that look out of proportion to the type size.
- Not enough white space between lines of text makes the text hard to read.

Proportion must be achieved consistently throughout your whole project. A whole, integrated, unified look is established when elements are in proportion to one another.

Creating Contrast

Contrast is the difference between different degrees of lightness and darkness on the page. Text with a low level of contrast gives an overall appearance of gray to your page. Consider using strong contrast to achieve some emphasis or focus on your page. A high level of contrast is more visually stimulating and helps to draw your target audience into the document. Contrast is also used as an organizational aid so that the reader can distinctly identify the organization of the document and easily follow the logical flow of information. Headlines and subheads set in larger and denser type can help to create contrast on an otherwise "gray" page.

Contrast
The difference in the degrees of lightness and darkness on a page.

DTP POINTERS
Add contrast by setting headings and subheads in larger, denser type.

Achieving Contrast with Text

Take a look at illustrations A and B in figure 1.10. Which document grabs your attention? Why? In illustration A, some contrast is achieved with a larger type size for the name, bold side headings, and the use of a ruled line. However, the contrast is weak in comparison to illustration B. Strong contrast in illustration B is achieved by using a thicker sans serif typeface in a larger size and bolder style for the name and the side headings. The job title information was also formatted in the same way. A contrasting serif typeface was used for the remainder of the text and heavier ruled lines were added to divide each section of the resume. Not only is illustration B more eye-catching, but the reader can identify the purpose and organization of the document at a glance.

figure
1.10

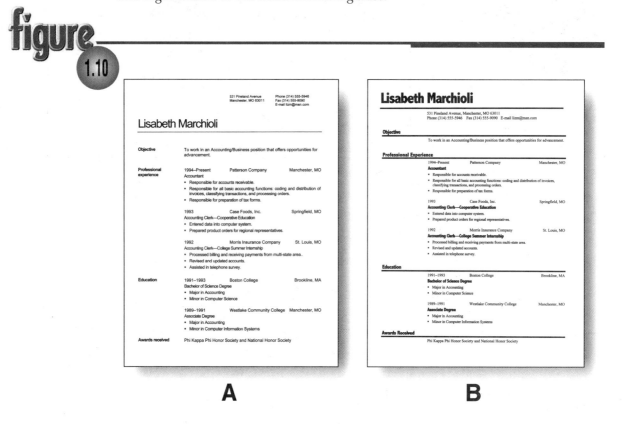

A   B

Achieving Contrast with Graphic Elements

DTP POINTERS
Make contrasting elements strong enough to be noticed.

High contrast graphics can create a powerful image or focal point. Depending on the colors used in the image, a color graphic can provide great contrast. A solid black image against a solid white background produces a sharp contrast, as illustrated by the housetop image in figure 1.4. A graphic image in varying shades of gray or a watermark can produce contrast on a lower level. Ruled lines in various weights, whether gray shaded or 100% black, can also provide visual contrast when used alone, as part of a heading, or as a visual separator in your text, as illustrated in figure 1.10 B.

DTP POINTERS
Use bullets to organize information and add visual contrast.

Special characters used as bullets to define a list of important points, such as, ■, ▼, ◆, ✓, ✦, ✇, ✧, ❦, ▶, 🖑, ♫, 🎥, ◈, ☏, ✂, and ◈, not only serve as organizational tools, but also contribute visual contrast to your page. Placing these special characters in a bolder and larger type size provides a higher level of contrast. Notice the flag bullets used in figure 1.14 in the next section.

Achieving Contrast with White Space

White space is an important tool in achieving contrast. A more open and light feeling is projected with the increased use of white space on a page. A more closed and darker feeling is projected when use of white space is limited. Think of white space as the floor space in a room. The more furniture and accessories in the room, the more closed or crowded the room becomes. Rearranging or removing some of the furniture can provide more floor space, producing an open, lighter feeling. Your page design, like a room, may need to have some elements rearranged or removed to supply some visually contrasting white space. See how too many design elements (accessories) are crowding the white space (floor space) in figure 1.11 A. Notice in illustration B how eliminating and rearranging some of the design elements to create more white space makes for a more open and lighter design.

DTP POINTERS
Use plenty of white space to convey an open, light feeling.

figure
1.11

A

B

Achieving Contrast with Color

The use of color in a heading, a logo, a graphic image, a ruled line, or as a background can also add to the contrast level on a page. When using more than one color, select colors that provide a pleasing contrast, not colors that provide an unpleasant conflict. In addition, consider whether the color(s) being used increases or decreases the legibility of your document. Color may look nice, but it will confuse the reader if there is not enough contrast to easily identify the text. Look at the examples in figure 1.12. In illustration A, the color of the text and the color of the background are not different enough, making the text barely legible. As you can see in illustration B, the stark contrast between the color of the text and the color of the background makes the text very easy to read. Use high contrast for the best legibility.

figure
1.12

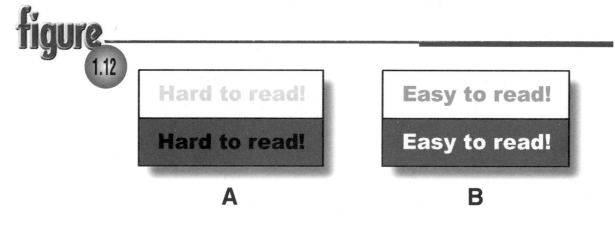

A   B

Creating Directional Flow

Directional Flow

Positioning elements to draw the reader's eyes through the document.

Smooth *directional flow* in a document is established by organizing and positioning elements in such a way that the reader's eyes are drawn through the text and to particular words or images that the designer wishes to emphasize. By nature, graphics and display type (larger than 14 points) act as focal elements that attract the eye as it scans a page. Focal elements may include a well-designed headline, logo, subheadings, graphic image, ruled lines, boxes with text inside, charts, reverse text, or a shaded background. Look back at figure 1.10 B. The title and side headings, set in a larger and bolder type, and the ruled lines not only create focal points and provide contrast on the page, but they also serve as directional markers. The reader knows when to start and stop and what comes next. When trying to establish the directional flow of your document, you must:

DTP POINTERS

Rank information according to its importance in conveying the intended message.

- organize your information into groups of closely related items and then rank the groups in order of importance
- decide on how to emphasize the most important information
- position related items close to each other on the page
- use left or right alignment to establish a stronger visual connection between all the elements on your page
- position elements so that the reader is drawn into the document and then directed through the document

Organizing Your Information Visually

DTP POINTERS

Position related items close to each other on the page.

Organize your information by grouping items that are related to each other. Place the related items close to each other so the reader views the group as one unit rather than as separate pieces. For example, a subheading should be close to the paragraph that follows it so the reader recognizes the relationship between the two. Dates, times, and locations are frequently grouped close together because of the relationship of when? where? and at what time? Titles and subtitles should be positioned close to each other because of their obvious relationship. What happens when there is little or no organization to the information in a document? Look at illustration A, figure 1.13. Besides being very boring and uninviting to read, do you find it difficult to tell what this is really about, when it's going to take place, at what time, etc.? Now look at illustration B. What has changed in B that did not exist in A? The larger and bolder headings and the watermark are very obvious changes. But what really happened here is that information that was related to each other was grouped together. You now see each presentation and its accompanying information as a single unit. Since each presentation unit is formatted exactly the same and is separated from the other units by the same amount of white space, you, as the reader, automatically establish a connection between the units; in this case, a set of individual presentations that make up the "Healthy Heart Series." The information at the bottom of the page is grouped close together because it is related to each other also. However, this information is set off from the rest of the information by a larger amount of white space and different formatting. This way the reader knows it is different from the information about the presentations. Yes, it has a relationship with the information that precedes it, but it is a much broader relationship.

figure

1.13   *Slide Master*

A   **B**

Ranking Elements

Once you have organized your information into groups of related items, decide which information plays the most important role in conveying your message and then emphasize that information. For example, the purpose of the flyer in illustration B in figure 1.13 is to inform readers of a series of presentations, their dates, times, and locations. Consequently, the presentation titles are important. They are emphasized in a larger and bolder typeface so the reader is drawn into the document and knows at a glance what this is all about. In addition to using a contrasting larger and bolder type as emphasis (or focus), you can use color, a logo, clip art, photographs, ruled lines, bullets, boxes with text inside, reverse text, drop caps, a shaded background, a chart etc.

Recognizing the Z Pattern

Z Pattern

When scanning a page, the eye tends to move in a Z pattern.

Directional flow in a strictly symmetrical design (all elements centered) is limited to movement down the visual center of the page, producing a very static design. On the other hand, a more dynamic directional flow can be created by using an asymmetrical design. To accomplish this, think of how your eyes naturally scan a page. When scanning a page, the eye tends to move in a Z pattern. The eye begins at the upper left corner of the page, moves to the right corner, then drops down to the lower left corner, and finally ends up in the lower right corner of the page. In text-intensive publications such as magazines, newspapers, and books, visual landmarks are frequently set in these positions. In an advertisement, the lower right corner is often where important information, such as a company name, address, and phone number, is placed.

Evaluating Directional Flow

The flyer shown as illustration A in figure 1.14 positions elements on the page to provide smooth directional flow down the page. The title, serving as the focal element, is located in the upper left corner of the page, where the reader's eye is most likely to look first. The reader's eyes are drawn across the page to the sun image then down towards the block of text delineated by the bulleted items. The flag bullets organize the information while leading the eyes through the text. The title "Computer Information Workshops and Trade Fair" draws the reader's eyes to the lower left corner of the page. The block of text including the name of the college and the address draws the eyes across to the right side where the eyes naturally expect a document to end. Look at illustration B to help you visualize the Z pattern in this document. Remember that the Z pattern is only a guideline. Some designs may contain modified versions of the Z pattern. However, since there are no hard-and-fast rules, not all designs fit exactly into this pattern.

figure 1.14

A   **B**

Choosing Visual Alignment

The way you choose to position and align text and/or graphics on a page greatly influences the directional flow in a document. One of the keys to creating dynamic directional flow and producing professional looking documents is *alignment*. Center alignment is fine for when you are trying to achieve a more formal look, as in a wedding invitation, but tends to be dull and boring in other types of documents. Break away from the center alignment habit! Experiment with using a strong left or right alignment as a way to visually connect different elements on your page. Look back at figure 1.11. See what a dramatic difference it made to use a strong left alignment in illustration B as opposed to illustration A. Notice the strong visual connection between all elements on the left side of the page even though some elements may not be close to each other. Let's look at a more simple example of how strong alignment can improve the looks of a document. The centered alignment used in the report cover shown in illustration A in figure 1.15 is very typical because it is the easiest to create. By just changing the alignment to left as shown in illustration B, the document takes on a more professional look. All elements are visually connected on the left side even though some elements are separated by a lot of white space. Your eyes do not have to bounce around as much trying to find the beginning of each line as they do with centered alignment in illustration A. Strong alignment can also be achieved using right alignment as shown in illustration C.

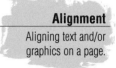

Alignment
Aligning text and/or graphics on a page.

DTP POINTERS
Save center alignment for formal, conservative documents.

DTP POINTERS
Use a strong left or right alignment to visually connect elements on a page.

figure
1.15

Grant County	Grant County	Grant County
Medical Benefits Plan	**Medical Benefits Plan**	**Medical Benefits Plan**
Administered by: Southport Benefits	Administered by: Southport Benefits	Administered by: Southport Benefits
September 1, 2001	**September 1, 2001**	**September 1, 2001**
A	**B**	**C**

Evaluating Alignment

Some alignment adjustments may not be quite as noticeable as those in figure 1.11 or figure 1.15. For example, look at illustration A in figure 1.16. What alignment adjustments could be made to improve the looks of this flyer? Now look at illustration B. The heavier dotted red lines identify the areas that could be improved by a strong left and right alignment. The lighter dotted red lines identify the areas that could benefit from horizontal alignment. Look at illustration C to see how these alignment corrections affect this document. The WordArt heading, the bulleted items, the title of the event and the date, time, and registration information were all vertically aligned on the left side. The sun image, the sailboat image, the title of the event, and the location of the event were all vertically aligned on the right side. The lighter dotted red lines indicate the horizontal alignment adjustments. The sailboat image is horizontally lined up with the last bulleted item. The two blocks of text at the bottom of the page were lined up horizontally both at the top and the bottom. See how alignment adjustments, large or small, can affect the professional quality of your document. As a general guideline, do not mix alignments on a page, throughout a series of pages, or among a series of documents. There is nothing wrong with elements aligning both on the left and the right at the same time, but avoid having some elements left aligned and some other elements right-aligned and/or centered.

figure
1.16

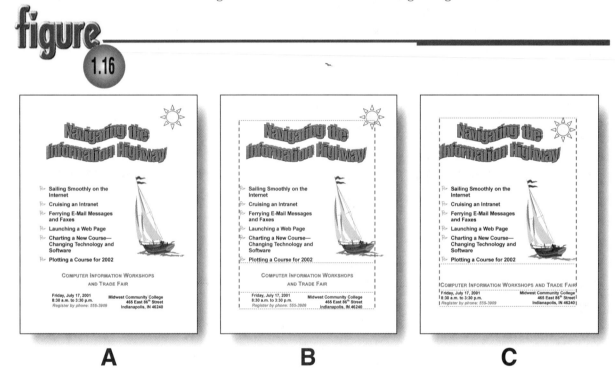

A   **B**   **C**

Headers and footers, text that appears repetitively at the top or bottom of each page, also contribute to directional flow in a publication. Chapter name, chapter number, title of a report, and page numbering are common items included in headers or footers. These page identifiers direct the reader to specific locations in a document.

Establishing Consistency

Uniformity among specific design elements establishes a pattern of *consistency* in your document. Inconsistency can confuse and frustrate the reader. Reader frustration can lead to a reduction in your readership. To avoid this, design elements such as margins, columns, typefaces, type sizes, spacing, alignment, and color should remain consistent throughout a document to achieve a degree of unity. In any document, whether single-page or multipage, consistent elements help to integrate all the individual parts into a whole unit. Additionally, in

Consistency
Uniformity among design elements.

multipage publications such as manuals, reports, or newsletters, consistency provides the connecting element between the pages. Repetitive, consistent elements can also lend identity to your documents and provide the reader with a sense of familiarity.

DTP POINTERS
Use of repetitive, consistent elements establishes unity within a document.

Consistent elements are evident in many of the figures in this chapter. In illustration B, figure 1.10, the same typeface is used for the heading, side headings, and the job titles. The side headings are all formatted in the same type size as are the job titles. Ruled lines of the same weight are used to separate each section. Finally, the typeface and type size of the remaining text is the same. Consider the flyer in illustration B, figure 1.16. Consistency is achieved by using the same color blue in the heading, the bullets, the water below the sailboat image, the title of the event, and the phone number. Additional consistent elements in the flyer include the left alignment, the flag bullets, the spacing between the bullets, the typeface used for the text, and the margins.

DTP POINTERS
Inconsistency confuses and frustrates the reader.

Use consistent elements when designing separate business documents for the same company or person, such as a business card, a letterhead, and an envelope. Look at the documents in figure 1.17. The consistent elements are very obvious. You know immediately that all three documents are associated with the same company which serves to reinforce the company's identity.

figure
1.17

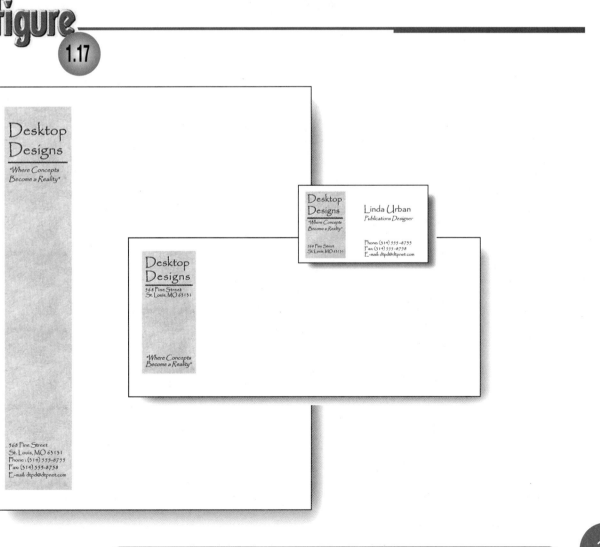

Evaluating Consistency

As mentioned previously, the use of consistent elements in multipage documents provides the visual connection between all the pages in the document. Consistency not only establishes unity within a section or chapter (or a newsletter, or an advertisement), but it also establishes unity among the sections or chapters (or a series of newsletters or advertisements). See how the consistent elements used in the manual pages displayed in figure 1.18 contribute to the unified appearance of this document. Notice how the green color scheme is carried throughout the pages of the manual, including the cover page. The same typeface is used for the cover, the headers, the section headings, and the subheadings. A different typeface is used for the body text and kept consistent throughout the document. Additionally, a thin horizontal line is repeated in the header that appears on every page except the cover.

figure
1.18

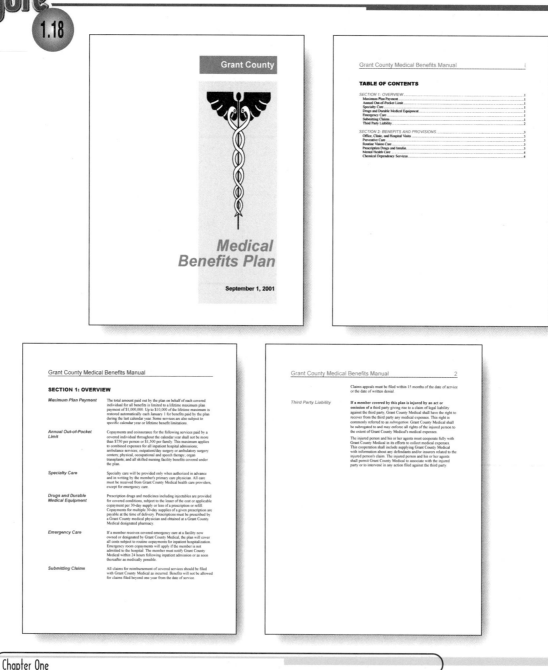

If you plan to insert a graphic image into your document, use the graphic to provide you with some ideas for consistency. For example, the globe/plane/mailbox graphic in the postcard in figure 1.19 provided the idea for the consistent color scheme used in this document. The arrow pointing to the mailbox slot inspired the use of a dotted line and arrow pointing to the new address. To add to the consistency and to create some visual interest, the arrow was repeated as a consistent element in the return address box and in the delivery address section. Did you notice how three rectangles were cleverly arranged to resemble a mailbox in the return address section of the postcard? You, too, can be this creative, given time and lots and lots of practice! One word of advice—since consistent elements are repetitive elements, keep it simple and distinct. Too much of a good thing can be very distracting!

figure **1.19**

Our New Address:
Debbie & Mike Law
53 Hidden Cove
Sarasota, FL 34230

Gail & Mike Zinn
1308 Linden Court
Cleveland, OH 44118

We've Moved!

Our New Address:

Debbie & Mike Law
53 Hidden Cove
Sarasota, FL 34230

Using Color

Color is a powerful tool in communicating a message and portraying an image. Color can even elicit an emotional response from the reader. Color on a page can help organize ideas and highlight important facts. Publications that use color appropriately have a professional look. In figure 1.18, you can see how the color green is used to create focus, to add emphasis, to provide organization to the text, and to serve as a consistent element throughout the document.

Using Color Graphics and Text Elements

Word provides many ways of inserting color into your documents. You may use graphic pictures, borders, backgrounds, bullets, and lines of a specific design and color. You may also create your own color shapes, lines, borders, text boxes, and text. For instance, look at illustration A, figure 1.20. This manual cover has a nice strong right alignment and related items are grouped close together. However, by putting the text in a text box and adding a gray shaded background as in illustration B, the various text elements have a stronger visual connection to each other and the manual cover becomes more visually appealing. Using various shades of gray is an easy way to get some "color" into your document even if you don't have a color printer! Now for adding some real color to that manual cover, look at illustration C. The manual cover has evolved into a very professional looking document! Obvious color changes include the white text set on a green background (reverse text) and the title set in green text. Of course, the graphic image adds additional color to the cover, as does the shaded background. For a very well-thought out use of color, take another look at figure 1.19. Notice that the colorful graphic image provided the catalyst for the creation of the blue shaded text boxes, the teal border, the teal and orange rectangle shapes, the orange dotted line, and the orange arrow shapes.

figure 1.20

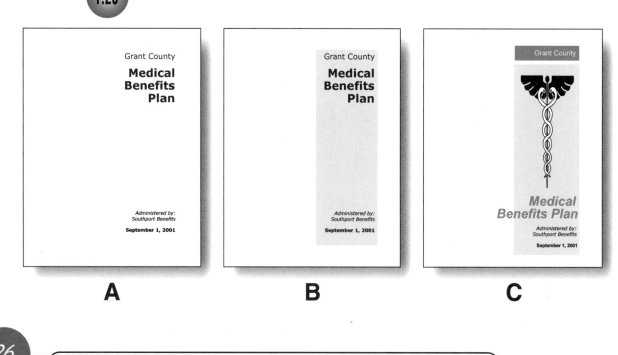

A   B   C

Using Colored Paper

If a color printer is not available, consider using color paper to complement your publication. Color paper can match the tone or mood you are creating in your document. Orange paper used for a Halloween flyer, as in figure 1.21, is an inexpensive alternative to color graphics and text. Your audience will recognize the theme of the flyer by associating the paper color with the event. The color paper provides contrast and adds vitality and life to the publication.

figure
1.21 *Slide Master*

Using Preprinted Stationery

You can also turn plain white documents into colorful, attention-grabbing documents by purchasing preprinted letterheads, envelopes, brochures, or presentation packets from paper supply companies or your local office supplies store. Color, emphasis, and contrast can all be achieved through an assortment of colorful page borders, patterned and solid color papers, as well as gradient color, marbleized, and speckled papers. Many of these paper suppliers provide free catalogs and offer inexpensive sample paper packets.

Printing Options

Even though laser printers have become more affordable, the color laser printer remains rather expensive. A less expensive, but very good, alternative is the ink jet color printer. The printer uses a color ink cartridge(s) to produce the color. The copy may be slightly damp when first removed from the printer. The resolution can be improved by using specially designed ink jet paper. Some ink jet printers are capable of achieving near-photographic quality with a resolution of 1440 dpi (dots per inch).

Another option for color is to send your formatted copy to a commercial printer for color printing. You can get almost any color you want from a commercial printer, but it can add significantly to the cost of your project. Always check out the prices and your budget first!

Guidelines for Using Color

Here are a few guidelines to follow when using color in documents:

DTP POINTERS
Use color sparingly.

- Use color sparingly—less is best! Limit your use of colors to two or three, including the color of the paper.
- Color can be used to identify a consistent element.
- Do not let color overpower the words. Color can add emphasis and style, but the message is most important!
- Do not set text in light colors—it is too difficult to read. Black text is still the easiest to read.
- Avoid changing all text to one color such as red. It is harder to read and the whole "color" of the document is changed.
- Use light colors for shaded backgrounds or watermarks.
- Use color to communicate, not decorate!

Evaluating Documents Using the Document Analysis Guide

Up to this point, you have learned the importance of carefully planning and designing your publication according to the desktop publishing concepts of focus, balance, proportion, contrast, directional flow, consistency, and color. In exercise 1, you will evaluate the document illustrated in figure 1.22 using a Document Analysis Guide, which can be printed from your student CD. The Document Analysis Guide is a tool used to evaluate design concepts in selected documents. In addition, a Document Evaluation Checklist can be printed from your student CD. This tool serves as a way for you to evaluate your progress during the planning and creation stages of your document and is directed toward the finished product. The Document Evaluation Checklist will be used in units 2 and 3. Both forms will be used to analyze your own documents, existing commercial publications, and/or other students' desktop publications.

Opening a Document as Read-Only

In Word, opening a document as "Read-Only" eliminates the risk of saving over the original copy of a document. A document opened as read-only may be read, printed, or edited. However, when a read-only document is saved with the Save command, Word displays the message, *This file is read-only*. Click OK for Word to lead you to the Save As dialog box so you can enter a new name for the document. This option protects the original copy of a document from being saved with any changes. You will use this feature when you open the *Document Analysis Guide* and the *Document Evaluation Checklist* to complete exercises in this textbook.

Saving Documents

SAVE! SAVE! SAVE! AND SAVE SOME MORE! Creating desktop published documents involves many steps and, often, a lot of experimentation. Frequently save your work so you always have a recent version to fall back on and to avoid losing it if a power or system failure occurs.

Evaluating a Document

Evaluate the flyer illustrated in figure 1.22 by completing the following steps:

1. Open Document Analysis Guide.doc, located on your student CD, as a read-only document by completing the following steps:
   a. Access the Open dialog box.
   b. At the Open dialog box, click the CD drive in the Look in list box that contains the desired document.
   c. At the Open dialog box, right-click the filename of the document that you want to open as read-only.
   d. From the drop-down menu that displays, click Open Read-Only.
2. Print one copy of the Document Analysis Guide.
3. Close Document Analysis Guide.doc.
4. Turn to figure 1.22 in your textbook.
5. Complete an analysis of the flyer in figure 1.22 by writing short answers to the questions in the Document Analysis Guide.
6. When completed, fill in the exercise number, located at the top of the guide, as c01ex01.

figure

1.22

Exercise 1

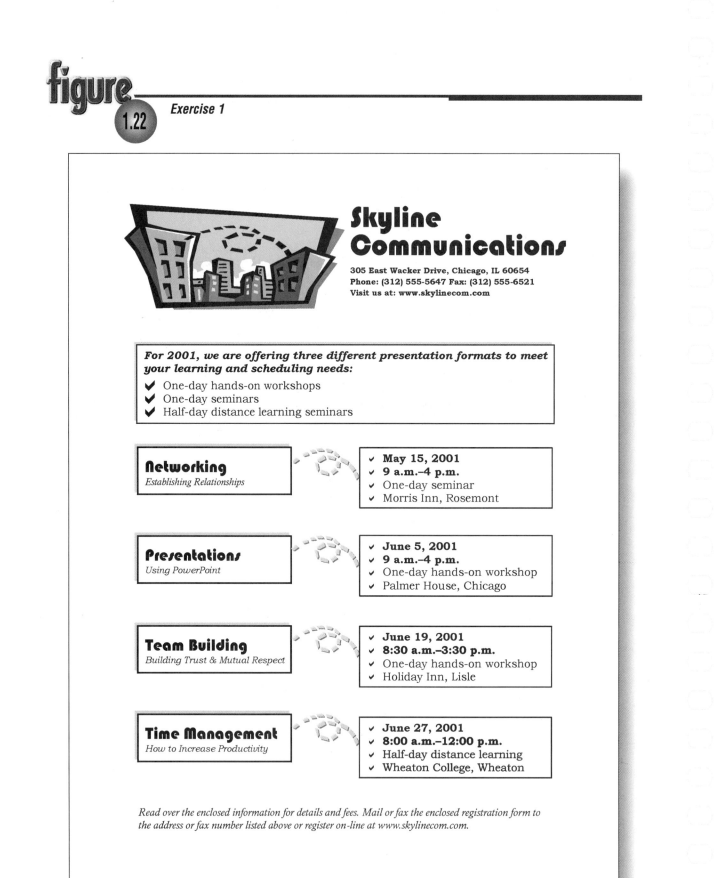

Skyline Communications

305 East Wacker Drive, Chicago, IL 60654
Phone: (312) 555-5647 Fax: (312) 555-6521
Visit us at: www.skylinecom.com

For 2001, we are offering three different presentation formats to meet your learning and scheduling needs:
- One-day hands-on workshops
- One-day seminars
- Half-day distance learning seminars

Networking
Establishing Relationships

- May 15, 2001
- 9 a.m.–4 p.m.
- One-day seminar
- Morris Inn, Rosemont

Presentations
Using PowerPoint

- June 5, 2001
- 9 a.m.–4 p.m.
- One-day hands-on workshop
- Palmer House, Chicago

Team Building
Building Trust & Mutual Respect

- June 19, 2001
- 8:30 a.m.–3:30 p.m.
- One-day hands-on workshop
- Holiday Inn, Lisle

Time Management
How to Increase Productivity

- June 27, 2001
- 8:00 a.m.–12:00 p.m.
- Half-day distance learning
- Wheaton College, Wheaton

Read over the enclosed information for details and fees. Mail or fax the enclosed registration form to the address or fax number listed above or register on-line at www.skylinecom.com.

Creating a Page Layout

Establishing Margins

Determining page margins is one of the first steps in designing a *page layout*. Using wider margins is an excellent way to add white space or breathing room around text and graphics. To apply an asymmetrical design to your document, experiment with using unequal margins to create a more interesting use of white space. The width of your margins is also dependent on the type size you have chosen to use. Large type sizes demand wider margins. To create a unified appearance throughout a multipage document, use the same margin settings throughout your entire publication.

In addition to establishing margins for your page layout, you also need to consider the amount of text needed to express your message, the paper size desired, and the number of pages you plan to use. If you are producing a multipage publication, remember that basic elements such as margins, headers and footers, page numbers, and borders should stay consistent from page to page.

Viewing a Multipage Document

Typically, when you work at a computer, you are creating and viewing one page at a time. In designing a page layout for a multipage document, think in terms of what is called a two-page spread or a two-page layout. Pages that are viewed opposite each other when opened, as in a book or brochure format, need to be looked upon as one unit. Remember that your readers will see both pages at the same time so certain elements must remain consistent.

In Word 2000, you can view your document in a two-page spread. To do this, make sure the viewing mode is Print Layout View, then click the Zoom button on the Standard toolbar. At the drop-down menu that displays, click Two Pages. The pages appear in reduced size, but you should be able to see placement of elements, the use of white space, and certain consistencies (or inconsistencies!) between the two pages.

Word also lets you view more than two pages at a time. To do this, click View, then Zoom. At the Zoom dialog box, select Many Pages. Click the monitor icon under Many Pages and then click the page icon representing the number of pages you want to display. If you point to one of the page icons and click and drag the mouse to the right or down and to the right, you can extend the number of pages offered. The Preview box shows the number of pages that will be displayed horizontally and vertically across the screen at one time. Click OK when done.

Using Columns

In planning a page layout, a column format is commonly used. Laying out text in columns adds visual interest and makes the text easier to read. A standard two-column layout contains two columns of equal width, while a standard three-column layout contains three equal columns as illustrated in figure 1.23. The *gutter*, which is the space between columns, creates additional contrasting white

Page Layout
Arranging all elements on a page.

DTP POINTERS
Use the same margin settings throughout your entire publication.

Gutter
The white space between columns.

space and serves as a separator between the columns. Keep these guidelines in mind when formatting text into columns:

- Text in full justification needs more column space than left-justified text.
- Text created in a larger type size demands more space between the columns than text in a smaller type size.
- Long lines of text are difficult to read because the eye can get lost reading along the line or trying to get to the next line. As a general rule, lines should be under 70 characters long but no less than 30 characters in length.
- In portrait orientation (when the paper's short side is the top of the paper), use no more than three columns on standard-sized paper.
- With a landscape orientation (when the paper's long side is the top of the paper), you can use four or five columns on standard-sized paper.

The centered one-column layout is commonly used for more formal, conservative documents such as letters, a financial report, a legal document, or a wedding invitation. Multicolumn layouts, whether equal or unequal, are often used for such items as sales brochures, advertisements, résumés, and newsletters.

Grid

The underlying structure of a document.

In determining the exact placement of columns and varying elements on the page, a *grid* is a helpful tool in visualizing the underlying structure of a document. In some software programs, a grid appears on the screen as a nonprinting framework to assist you in laying out the page. In Word, you can draw a table to serve as an underlying grid. You can also draw a grid on a sheet of paper using a ruler and pencil. Notice the grid illustrated in figure 1.23. A grid consists of vertical and horizontal lines to be used as a guide in the placement of elements on the page. A grid enables you to be consistent with the location of elements and the size of columns. The number of columns actually used does not have to match the number of columns in the grid as long as the underlying framework is maintained. For example, look at figure 1.23 and notice the column layout with the compass graphic and the grid lines in the background. Even though you may only see two columns, the underlying three-column structure is still maintained by

figure

1.23

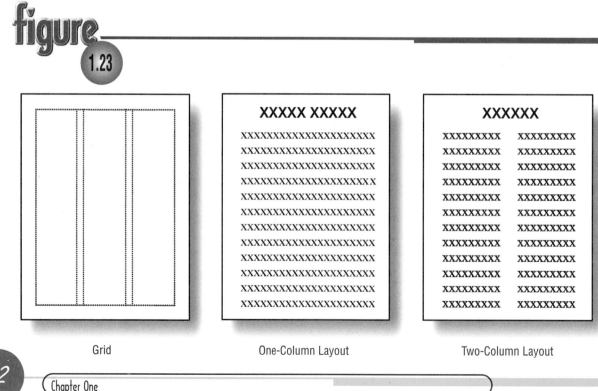

Grid

One-Column Layout

Two-Column Layout

Figure 1.23 continued

XXXXXX

Three-Column Layout

XXXXXX

Three-Column Layout (Left column equal to twice the width of the third column—notice the extended grid)

XXXXXX

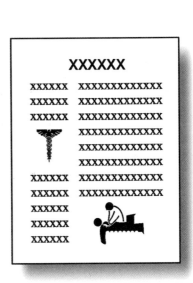

Three-Column Layout (Right column equal to twice the width of the first column)

XXXXXX

Three-Column Layout with graphic image spanning three columns

XXXXXX

Two-Page Spread with a standard three-column format on the first page and a variation of the three-column format on the second page

Piano Concert
September 16, 2001
Arts Center

making the left column twice as wide as the right column. Consequently, this type of layout is also referred to as a three-column layout. A variation of this layout, also shown in figure 1.23, makes the right column twice the width of the left column.

As a general rule, do not use more than one column layout in a document. If you choose to use a three-column layout, then stick to that layout throughout the rest of your document. However, you may mix variations of the same column layout. The two-page spread (or layout) shown in figure 1.23 demonstrates how a standard three-column layout can be mixed with a variation of the three-column layout because the underlying three-column structure is still maintained.

Using Word 2000 in Desktop Publishing

Word 2000 is a highly visual program providing an efficient means of editing and manipulating text and graphics to produce professional-looking documents and Web pages. Some of the desktop publishing features include a wide variety of fonts and special characters; drawing capabilities, text and graphics color options, charting, and text design capabilities; graphics, graphics manipulation, and image editing tools; predesigned templates; template wizards; and much more. In addition, Word 2000 includes the capability of creating and designing Web pages to be placed on an intranet or the Internet.

Putting It All Together

Design can be learned by studying well-designed publications and by experimenting. Analyze what makes a specific design and layout visually appealing and unique and try using the same principles or variations in your publications. Take advantage of the special design and layout features that Word 2000 has to offer. Take time to design. Layout and design is a lengthy process of revising, refining, and making adjustments. And above all else, EXPERIMENT! View each document in terms of focus, balance, proportion, contrast, directional flow, consistency, and use of color. Ask the opinion of your peers, fellow workers, etc. and listen to their feedback. The final judge is the reader, so always look at your document from the reader's perspective.

DTP POINTERS
Experiment with different layouts and designs.

The rest of the chapters in this book will take you through the steps for creating specific business and personal desktop publishing applications, such as letterheads, business cards, flyers, brochures, postcards, Web pages, presentations, and newsletters. In addition to step-by-step directions for completing the applications using Word 2000, each project will introduce guidelines relevant to that document type as well as reinforce the design concepts introduced in this chapter.

Remember: Take the time to design!
              Communicate; don't decorate!
              Less is best!
              Readability is the key!

exercise 2

Creating a Portfolio

Begin a "job-hunting" portfolio of the documents you will create in the exercises and assessments throughout this book. Exercises marked with the portfolio icon should be included in your portfolio. These documents have been chosen to show a prospective employer a wide range of your desktop publishing skills. You may also include any additional documents from the chapter and unit assessments. Since the assessments are less structured than the exercises, your creativity can really shine.

You will create a title page for your portfolio in the Unit 3 Performance Assessments. As an optional assignment, you may create a table of contents after completing Unit 3. Your instructor will determine a due date and any other specific requirements for your portfolio. If possible, purchase plastic protector sheets for your documents and a binder to hold them.

chapter summary

➤ When creating a publication, clearly define your purpose, assess your target audience, decide the format in which your audience will see your message, and decide what outcome you are expecting.

➤ Effective design involves planning and organizing content. Decide what items are most important to the reader. Design concepts such as focus, balance, proportion, directional flow, consistency, and the use of color are essential to creating a visually attractive publication that presents information in a logical, organized manner.

➤ Focus can be created by using large and/or bold type, such as for titles and subheads; by using graphic elements, such as ruled lines, clip art, and photographs; and by using color for emphasis.

➤ Balance on a page is created by equally distributing the weight of elements on a page in either a symmetrical or asymmetrical manner. Symmetrical design (all elements centered) balances similar elements of equal weight and proportion on the left and right sides and the top and bottom of the page. Asymmetrical design balances contrasting elements of unequal proportion and weight on the page.

➤ In establishing a proportional relationship among the elements on a page, think about all the parts as they relate to the total appearance. Proportionally size the visual elements in your publication according to their relative importance to the intended message.

➤ Contrast is the difference between varying degrees of lightness and darkness on the page. A high level of contrast is more visually stimulating and helps to draw your target audience into the document. Contrast is also used as an organizational aid so that the reader can distinctly identify the organization of the document and easily follow the logical flow of information.

➤ Directional flow can be produced by grouping related elements and placing them close to each other on the page, by using a consistent alignment to establish a visual connection between the elements on a page, and by positioning elements in such a way that the reader's eyes are drawn through the text and to particular words or images that the designer wishes to emphasize.

- Including consistent elements in a document such as margins, columns, typefaces, type sizes, spacing, alignment, and color, helps to provide a sense of unity within a document or among a series of documents. Repetitive, consistent elements can also lend identity to your documents.

- Use color on a page to help organize ideas; emphasize important information; provide focus, contrast, directional flow, and consistency; and to establish or reinforce an identity.

- In determining page layout, consider the width of the margins, the amount of text in the message, the desired length of the publication, and the desired paper size.

- Pages that are viewed opposite each other when opened, as in a book or brochure format, need to be looked upon as one unit.

- Most documents are laid out in some type of a column format ranging from one column to several columns.

commands review

	Mouse/Keyboard
Open document as Read-Only	File, Open, right-click the desired filename, then click Open Read-Only
Viewing multiple pages	View, Zoom, Many pages, then click the monitor button below and select the number of pages to be displayed

thinking offline

Terms: Match the terms with the correct definitions by writing the letter of the term on the blank line in front of the correct definition.

- Ⓐ Asymmetrical
- Ⓑ Balance
- Ⓒ Consistency
- Ⓓ Contrast
- Ⓔ Color
- Ⓕ Directional flow
- Ⓖ Focal point
- Ⓗ Grid
- Ⓘ One-column
- Ⓙ Proportion
- Ⓚ Symmetrical
- Ⓛ Thumbnail sketch
- Ⓜ Alignment
- Ⓝ White space

_____ 1. Areas in a document where no text or graphics appear.

_____ 2. Type of balance achieved by evenly distributing similar elements of equal weight on a page.

_____ 3. A method used to establish a strong visual connection between elements on a page.

_____ 4. Use this design technique to help organize ideas, highlight important information, provide focus and consistency, and to reinforce an organization's identity.

_____ 5. The underlying structure of a page layout.

_____ 6. Positioning elements in such a way that the reader's eyes are drawn through the text and to particular words or images that the designer wishes to emphasize.

_____ 7. An element that draws the reader's eye to a particular location in a document.

_____ 8. A preliminary rough draft of the layout and design of a document.

_____ 9. Uniformity among specific design elements in a publication.

_____ 10. The sizing of various elements so that all parts relate to the whole.

_____ 11. Contemporary design in which contrasting elements of unequal weight and proportion are positioned on a page to achieve balance.

_____ 12. The difference between varying degrees of lightness and darkness on the page.

_____ 13. Common page layout used for more formal, conservative documents.

Assessment 1

In this assessment, you will begin a presentation project. The purpose of this assignment is to provide you with experience in planning, organizing, creating, and making a class presentation using Microsoft Word or PowerPoint. Specific instructions are provided for you in the document named Presentation.doc located on your student CD. To print this document, complete the following steps:

1. Open Presentation.doc as read-only from your student CD.
2. Print one copy and then close Presentation.doc.

Begin researching a topic for your presentation. You may compose and create a presentation on a desktop publishing or Web publishing article or concept, a Word or PowerPoint desktop publishing or Web publishing feature(s) or process used to create a specific document, or an instructor-approved topic that you would like to share with your class. You may consider using any of the topics presented in this textbook. Include any Word or PowerPoint tips or techniques you may have discovered while creating your presentation. Use any one of the many desktop publishing, Word, and PowerPoint resources available at your local library or bookstore. Your instructor will notify you of a scheduled date for your presentation.

Assessment 2

The "information highway" is littered with many well-designed and poorly-designed documents. Looking critically at as many publications as possible will give you a sense of what works and what does not. In this skill assessment, find three different examples of documents—flyers, newsletters, résumés, brochures, business cards, announcements, certificates, etc. Evaluate these documents according to the desktop publishing concepts discussed in this chapter using the Document Analysis Guide located on your student CD. To do this, complete the following steps:

1. Open Document Analysis Guide.doc as read-only from your student CD.
2. Print three copies of this form and then close Document Analysis Guide.doc.
3. Complete the evaluation forms and attach the corresponding form to the front of each example document. Write the exercise number as c01sa02 on the front of each form.

Assessment 3

In this assessment, you will evaluate a poorly designed flyer according to the items listed on the Document Analysis Guide located on your student CD. On a separate piece of paper, list three suggestions to improve this flyer.

1. Open as read-only Document Analysis Guide.doc on your student CD.
2. Print one copy, then close Document Analysis Guide.doc.
3. Open as a read-only document Cleaning Flyer.doc on your student CD.
4. Print one copy and then close Cleaning Flyer.doc.
5. Complete the Document Analysis Guide and name the exercise c01sa03. List your three suggestions for improvement on the back of the form.

CREATIVE ACTIVITY

You have been asked to create flyers for the situations described below. Draw two thumbnail sketches, using lines, boxes, and rough drawings to illustrate the placement of text and graphics on the page. You decide how to include focus, balance, proportion, contrast, white space, directional flow, and consistency in your thumbnail sketches. Be sure to consider the purpose and target audience for each situation. Designate areas in your sketches for such items as time, date, location, and response information. Label your sketches as c01ca01.

Situation 1: Annual office golf outing

Situation 2: Software training seminar

Chapter 02

Preparing Internal Documents

PERFORMANCE OBJECTIVES

Upon successful completion of chapter 2, you will be able to produce internal business documents such as a conference sign, handout cover sheet, fax cover sheet, memo, and agenda with a variety of typefaces, type styles, type sizes, and special symbols.

DESKTOP PUBLISHING TERMS

Ascenders	Legibility	Sans serif
Baseline	Luminescence	Saturation
Cap height	Monospaced	Serif
Descenders	Pitch	Typeface (Font)
Em dash	Point size	Type style
En dash	Proportional	x-height
Hue	Readability	Watermark

WORD FEATURES USED

AutoFormat	Image Control	Templates
Behind Text	Smart Quotes	Text Boxes
Borders and Shading	Special Characters	Watermark
Bullets and Numbering	Tables	Wizards
Header and Footer		

Understanding Basic Typography

A document created on a typewriter generally contains uniform characters and spacing. A typeset document may contain characters that vary in typeface, size, and style and that are laid out on the page with variable spacing.

In this chapter, you will produce internal business documents using Word's Template feature along with producing and formatting your own business documents. An important element in the creation of internal business documents is the font used to format the text. To choose a font for a document, you need to understand basic typography and the terms that apply.

As you learned in chapter 1, when you plan your document, consider the intent of the document, the audience, the feeling the document is to elicit, and the important information that should be emphasized. Make sure the headlines, graphics, and choice of typography work together to support the message.

Before selecting the type specifications to be used in a document, a few terms used in desktop publishing need to be defined. Terms that are used to identify the type specifications are typeface, type size, and type style.

Choosing a Typeface

Typeface

A set of characters with a common design and shape.

A *typeface* is a set of characters with a common general design and shape (Word refers to typeface as *font*.) One of the most important considerations in establishing a particular mood or feeling in a document is the typeface. For example, a decorative typeface may be chosen for invitations or menus, while a simple block-style typeface may be chosen for headlines or reports. Choose a typeface that reflects the content, your audience expectations, and the image you want to project.

Baseline

An imaginary horizontal line on which type characters rest.

There are characteristics that distinguish one typeface from another. Type characters rest on an imaginary horizontal line called the *baseline*. From this baseline, parts of type may extend above the baseline and/or below the baseline. Figure 2.1 illustrates the various parts of type.

figure
2.1   *Parts of Type*

Cap height

The distance between the baseline and the top of capital letters.

x-height

Height of the font's lowercase x.

SERIF   ASCENDER

CAP HEIGHT ⟨Desktop Publishing⟩ x-HEIGHT

DESCENDER

Ascender

The parts of a lowercase character that rise above the x-height.

The *x-height* is the height of the main body of the lowercase characters and is equivalent to the lowercase *x*. The *cap height* is the distance between the baseline and the top of capital letters. *Ascenders* are the parts of lowercase characters that rise above the x-height, and *descenders* are parts of characters that extend below the baseline. *Serifs* are the small strokes at the ends of characters.

Descender

The parts of a lowercase character that extend below the baseline.

Typefaces are either *monospaced* or *proportional*. A monospaced typeface allots the same amount of horizontal space for each character and is rarely used in professional publications. Courier is an example of a monospaced typeface. Proportional typefaces allow a varying amount of space for each character. For example, the lowercase letter *i* takes up less space than an uppercase *M*. Also, different proportional typefaces take up different amounts of horizontal space. The same sentence in Times New Roman, for example, takes up less horizontal space when set in the same size Century Gothic.

Proportional typefaces are divided into two main categories: *serif* and *sans serif*. A serif is a small stroke at the edge of a character. Traditionally, a serif typeface is more readable (easier to read in blocks of text) and is used with documents that are text intensive, such as business letters, manuals, or reports. Serifs help move the reader's eyes across the page.

A sans serif typeface does not have serifs (*sans* is French for *without*). Sans serif typefaces are generally more *legible* (higher character recognition), and are often used for headlines and advertisements that are not text intensive.

In modern designs, sans serif typefaces may also be used for body text, but avoid using more than seven or eight words per line; using bold, italics, outlining or shadowing; or using a long line length. Figure 2.2 shows examples of serif and sans serif typefaces.

When using a proportional typeface, space once after end-of-sentence punctuation and after a colon. Proportional typeface is set closer together and extra white space at the end of a sentence or after a colon is not needed.

Monospaced
Same amount of character spacing for each character in a typeface.

Proportional
Varying amount of space for each character in a typeface.

Serif
A small stroke at the end of a character.

Sans serif
Without a small stroke at the end of a character.

Legible
Typefaces with higher character recognition.

DTP POINTERS
Use Word's Replace feature to find ending punctuation with two spaces and replace with one.

figure 2.2

Serif and Sans Serif Typefaces

Serif Typefaces	Sans Serif Typefaces
Bookman Old Style	Arial
Garamond	Eurostile
Goudy Old Style	**Haettenschweiler**
Modern No. 20	**Impact**
Rockwell	Lucida Sans
Times New Roman	Tahoma

Applying Desktop Publishing Guidelines

Desktop publishing includes general guidelines, or conventions, that provide a starting point for designing documents. Use moderation in choosing typefaces and type sizes—two fonts and three different font sizes are usually adequate for most publications. Too many typefaces and styles give the document a disorderly appearance, confuse the reader, and take away from the content of the document.

DTP POINTERS
Use a sans serif font for headings.

Font design may be harmonious, conflicting, or contrasting as shown in figure 2.3. A harmonious design is calm and formal. This design is desirable, but not exciting. A formal invitation may be created using one font and include other design elements (borders, graphics, and symbols) that have the same qualities as the font. Italic, bold, and varying font sizes may be applied to the font to add interest.

Conflicting font design exists when two or more typefaces are used on the same page, and they are too similar. The fonts are different, but not different enough to tell them apart easily. Using conflicting fonts should be avoided.

Contrasting fonts may create focus and attract the reader's eyes. Contrasting design may be achieved through varying the font size, weight, appearance, and color. For instance, if one typeface is light and airy, choose a thick black or dark gray font to go with it. If one typeface is small, make the other one large. Avoid creating weak contrasts, such as using a script font with an italic effect, or a large type size with a slightly larger font.

figure 2.3 *Harmonious, Conflicting, and Contrasting Font Designs*

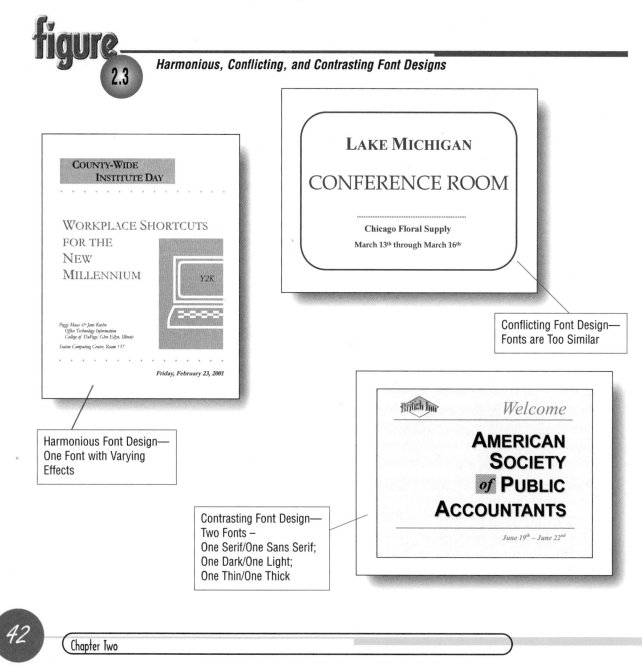

Additionally, use fonts that compliment the message of your document. Figure 2.4 displays fonts that match the mood and tone of your message.

figure 2.4 *Fonts That Match the Tone of Your Message*

Calling All Students!	**Braggadocio**
25th Anniversary	*Brush Script MT Italic*
Four Corners Art Gallery	*Matura MT Script Cap*
FUNFEST '97	**Impact**
DESIGN 2000	DESDEMONA
Antique Auction	Colonna MT
Line Dancing Classes Available	Playbill

Choosing a Type Size

Type size (font size) is defined by two categories: *pitch* and *point size*. Pitch is a measurement used for monospaced typefaces; it reflects the number of characters that can be printed in 1 horizontal inch. (For some printers, the pitch is referred to as cpi, or *characters per inch.* for example, the font Courier 10 cpi is the same as 10-pitch Courier.)

   Proportional typefaces can be set in different sizes. The size of proportional type is measured vertically in units called *points* (measured vertically from the top of the ascenders to the bottom of the descenders). A point is approximately 1/72 of an inch. The higher the point size selected, the larger the characters. Figure 2.5 shows Garamond and Arial typefaces in a variety of point sizes.

Pitch
The number of characters that can be printed in 1 horizontal inch.

Point size
A vertical measurement; a point is approximately 1/72 of an inch.

DTP POINTERS
When using a proportional font, do not use the spacebar to align text.

figure 2.5 *Varying Point Sizes in Garamond and Arial*

8-point Garamond	8-point Arial
12-point Garamond	12-point Arial
18-point Garamond	18-point Arial
24-point Garamond	24-point Arial

Choosing a Type Style

Type style
Variations of the basic type design including regular or normal, bold, and italic.

Within a typeface, characters may have a varying style. There are four main categories of type styles: normal (for some typefaces, this may be referred to as *light, black, regular, or roman*), bold, italic, and bold italic.

Choosing Fonts

The printer that you are using has built-in fonts. These fonts can be supplemented with cartridges and/or soft fonts. The types of fonts you have available with your printer depend on the type of printer you are using, the amount of memory installed with the printer, and the supplemental fonts you have.

Soft fonts are available as software on disk or CD-ROM. Before you can use soft fonts, the fonts must be installed. Many TrueType soft fonts were installed with Microsoft Office 2000. Additional fonts are available as a shared resource from other Windows-based software programs already installed on your hard drive.

DTP POINTERS
Substitute a different font if a particular font is not available.

If your printer does not support a font or size you are using to format your text, Word may substitute the closest possible font and size. If the textbook calls for a particular font and you do not have this font, select a similar one.

Changing Fonts

DTP POINTERS
Do not use less than 10 pt. type in large areas of text.

Fonts can be changed at the Font dialog box as shown in figure 2.6, at the Formatting toolbar as shown in figure 2.7, or at a shortcut menu that displays when clicking the right mouse button on any text in a document. In Word 2000, the default font is 12-point Times New Roman. To change this default setting, click Format and Font. At the Font dialog box, select the new defaults you want to use, then click the Default button located in the bottom left corner. At the dialog box stating that the change will affect all new documents based on the NORMAL template, click Yes. Font selections made within a document through the Font dialog box will override the default font settings for the current document only.

figure
2.6

Font Dialog Box

Choose a typeface in this list box. Use the scroll bar at the right side of the box to view various typefaces available.

Choose a type style in this list box. The options in the box may vary depending on the typeface selected.

Choose a type size in this list box; or, select the current measurement in the top box and then key the desired measurement.

figure

2.7

Font Drop-Down List on the Formatting Toolbar

Changing Font Size

To change a Font size at the Font dialog box, select a point size from the Size drop-down list or key a specific point size in the Size text box. The Size drop-down list displays common increments ranging from 8 to 72 points. However, you may key a point size not listed. For instance, to create a font size of 250 points, position the arrow pointer on the number immediately below Size, click the left mouse button, and then key 250.

To change a font size on the Formatting toolbar, click the down arrow at the right of the Font Size list box and left click on the desired point size or key an increment not listed. (*Hint:* press the Tab key or press Enter after keying the point size in the Font List box—the increment will remain when you move your insertion point back into the document screen.)

The point size of selected text can also be increased by one point by pressing Ctrl +]. The shortcut key combination to decrease the point size is Ctrl + [.

Changing Font Style

At the Font dialog box, select a font style from the list that displays below the Font style list box. As you select different typefaces, the list of styles changes in the Font style list box.

Selecting Underlining

In desktop publishing, underlining text has become somewhat dated. In place of underlining, consider enhancing your text with italics, bold, a different font size, all caps, or small caps.

Changing Effects

The Effects section of the Font dialog box contains a variety of options that can be used to create different character formatting, such as Strikethrough, Double strikethrough, Superscript, Subscript, Shadow, Outline, Emboss, Engrave, Small caps, All caps, and Hidden. To choose an effect, click the desired option. The text in the Preview box will reflect the change. If the text already exists, select the text before applying these formatting options.

DTP POINTERS
Use italics or small caps to emphasize text instead of all caps or underline.

Preparing Internal Documents

45

Also consider using the following keyboard shortcuts for applying font formatting:

Boldface	Ctrl + B
Italicize	Ctrl + I
Underline	Ctrl + U
Underline words only	Ctrl + Shift + W
Double underline	Ctrl + Shift + D
All caps	Ctrl + Shift + A
Small caps	Ctrl + Shift + K
Toggle capitalization	Shift + F3
Subscript	Ctrl + =
Superscript	Ctrl + Shift + =
Hidden text	Ctrl + Shift + H
Apply Symbol font	Ctrl + Shift + Q
Clear font formatting	Ctrl + Spacebar

Changing Font Color

Font Color

In Word 2000, you are not limited to just the 40 colors displayed on the color palette. You may make additional choices by clicking the More Colors button at the bottom of the color palette as shown in figure 2.8. At the Standard tab, 124 colors are available, as well as 15 shades of gray.

Font Color Palette

2.8

Standard Tab at the Colors Dialog Box

2.9

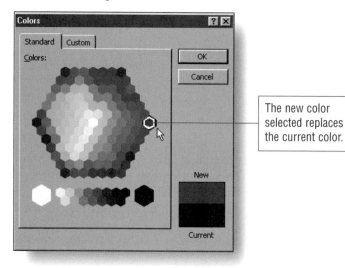

The new color selected replaces the current color.

At the Custom tab, you may choose from 16 million colors. In addition, you may create your own custom colors at the Custom tab shown in figure 2.10. To start creating a custom color, click a color in the <u>C</u>olors box, then by dragging the slider to the left/right or up/down, you may change the *luminescence*, which is the brightness of the color; the *hue*, which is the color itself; and the *saturation*, which is the color's intensity. Of course, using the 3-digit settings in the Hue, <u>S</u>at, and <u>L</u>um list boxes can be more precise.

Additionally, you may use the Custom tab to approximately match a color, such as R:65, G:100, B:10 (Red, Green, and Blue). In chapter 5, you will match font colors to colored graphics by using this method. Also, you may copy a color from one object to another using the Format Painter.

Luminescence
The brightness of a color.

Hue
The color itself.

Saturation
The color's intensity.

figure 2.10

Custom Tab at the Colors Dialog Box

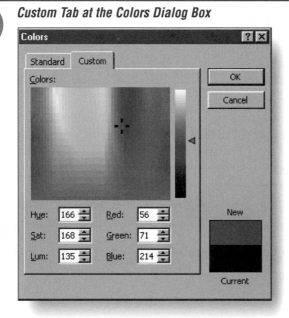

Animating Text

Animation effects can be added to text, such as a blinking background, a shimmer, or sparkle. To add an animation effect, select the text, display the font dialog box with the Te<u>x</u>t Effects tab selected, click the desired effect, and then close the Font dialog box. Animation effects added to text display in the screen but do not print.

In exercise 1, assume you are working at the British Inn and you have been asked to create a sign, which will be posted in the lobby welcoming the American Society of Public Accountants to your inn for a conference. Consider printing the sign on 24 lb. bond stock paper and placing it in an acrylic frame or sign stand for all the conference attendees to see.

Figure 2.11 illustrates how the sign was created in Word. Text boxes are used to easily position the text on the screen. The text box fill and line colors are changed to *No Fill* and *No Line* so that one box can overlap another. The border around the picture is a Rectangle AutoShape and the lines were drawn using the Line button on the Drawing toolbar. Additionally, a graphic border, or a Border or Page Border from the Borders and Shading dialog box may be used to create the border for a document. Graphics can be inserted more easily into these borders.

DTP POINTERS
Use a logo for continuity and recognition.

figure

2.11

Using Text Boxes to Create a Sign

Notice the font contrast—one thin serif font and one thick sans serif font. Text boxes will be covered in chapter 3. The logo, an AutoShape and WordArt combination, reinforces British Inn's identity as shown in figure 2.12.

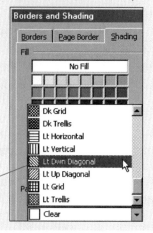

exercise

Formatting a Sign for a Conference

1. Open Sign 01.doc located on your student CD.
2. Save the document with Save <u>A</u>s to your hard drive or a floppy disk and name it c02ex01, Sign.
3. Select *Welcome* and change the font to 60-point Times New Roman bold, italic, and add the color Gray-50%. *(Hint: Each word of text is created in a separate text box.)*
4. Select *American* and change the font to 65-point Arial, bold, shadow, small caps, and add the color Indigo (located in first row and second column from the right).
5. Select *Society* and change the font as instructed in step 4. *(Hint: Use the Format Painter.)*
6. Select *Public* and change the font as instructed in step 4.
7. Select *Accountants* and change the font as instructed in step 4.
8. Select *of* and change the font to 48-point Times New Roman, bold, italic, and change the color to Indigo.
9. Change the shading in the box containing *of* by completing the following steps:
   a. With the text deselected, select the box (eight sizing handles will display).
   b. Click F<u>o</u>rmat and then <u>B</u>orders and Shading.
   c. At the <u>S</u>hading tab, click the down arrow at the right of the St<u>y</u>le list box in the Patterns section, scroll downward, and then select *Lt Dwn Diagonal*. (Make sure *Automatic* displays in the <u>C</u>olor list box.)

Borders and Shading

| Borders | Page Border | Shading |

Fill

No Fill

Dk Grid
Dk Trellis
Lt Horizontal
Lt Vertical
Lt Dwn Diagonal
Lt Up Diagonal
Lt Grid
Lt Trellis

Clear

Step 9c

     d. Click OK or press Enter.

10. Select *June 19...* and change the font to 22-point Times New Roman bold, italic, and color Gray-50%.

11. Change the color of the horizontal line below *Welcome* by completing the following steps:

     a. Double-click the horizontal line.

     b. At the Format AutoShape dialog box, select the Colors and Lines tab.

     c. Click the down arrow at the right of the Color list box in the Line section, then select Red in the first column and third row.

     d. Click OK or press Enter.

12. Change the color of the horizontal line below *Accountants* as instructed in step 11c.

13. Change the color of the border surrounding the text by completing the following steps:

     a. Double-click the border.

     b. At the Format AutoShape dialog box, click the down arrow at the right of the Color list box in the Line section and select Indigo in the first row and second column from the right, then click the down arrow at the right of Style list box and select the 3 pt. line.

     c. Click OK or press Enter.

14. Add the textured fill by completing the following steps:

     a. Double-click the border.

     b. At the Format AutoShape dialog box, click the down arrow at the right of the Color list box in the Fill section.

     c. Click the Fill Effects button on the color palette.

     d. Choose the Texture tab in the Fill Effects dialog box and select *Newsprint* in the first column and row.

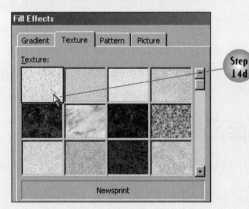

     e. Click OK twice.

15. Save the document again with the same name c02ex01, Sign.

16. Print and then close c02ex01, Sign.

figure
2.12 *Exercise 1*

Adding Symbols and Special Characters to a Document

Symbols and special characters can be used to add interest and originality to documents. Sometimes it is the small touches that make a difference, such as adding a symbol (◈) at the end of an article in a newsletter, enlarging a symbol (Υ) and using it as a graphic element on a page, or adding a special character (©) to clarify text. Interesting symbols can be found in such fonts as (normal text), Monotype Sorts, Wingdings, Wingdings 2, Wingdings 3, and Webdings. Special characters may include an em dash (—), en dash (–), copyright character (©), registered trademark character (®), ellipses (…), and nonbreaking hyphens.

To insert a symbol as shown in figure 2.13, display the Symbol dialog box from the Insert menu, select the Symbols tab, select a font, double-click on the desired symbol or press Insert, then click the Close button. To insert a special character, follow the same steps except choose the Special Characters tab and choose a desired Character.

In addition, symbols and special characters may be added to the AutoCorrect feature, which will automatically insert the desired symbol when using a specific keyboard command. Symbols may also be copied to the clipboard and pasted when needed.

figure 2.13 *Inserting a Symbol*

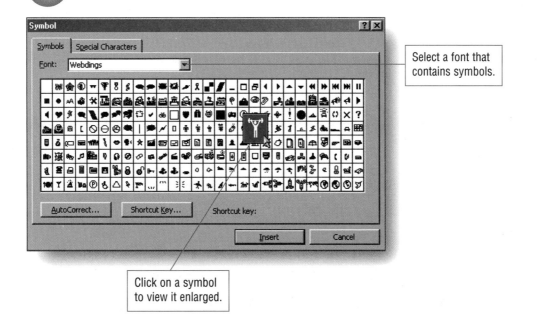

Select a font that contains symbols.

Click on a symbol to view it enlarged.

Creating Em and En Dashes

Two symbols that are used with proportional type include the em and en dashes. An *em dash* (—) is as long as the point size of the type and is used in text to indicate a pause in speech. An *en dash* (–) indicates a continuation, such as 116–133 or January–March, and is exactly one-half the width of an em dash. Besides inserting em and en dashes using the Symbol dialog box, you may insert an em dash at the keyboard by pressing Alt + Ctrl + Num - or an en dash by pressing Ctrl + Num - . Additionally, the AutoCorrect feature includes an option that will automatically create an em and en dash.

Em dash
A dash that indicates a pause in speech; the dash is as wide as the point size of the font used.

En dash
A dash that indicates a continuation; the dash is exactly one-half the width of an em dash.

DTP POINTERS
Use em and en dashes with proportional typefaces.

Using Smart Quotes

DTP POINTERS
Use vertical quotation marks only to indicate measurements.

In typesetting, the open quotation mark is curved upward (") and the close quotation mark is curved downward ("). In typesetting, the straight quotes are used to indicate inches (") or feet (').

The Smart Quote Feature will automatically choose the quote style that is appropriate if it is keyed in error. The Smart Quote option is turned on or off at the AutoFormat As You Type and AutoFormat tabs at the AutoCorrect dialog box.

Using Special Characters and Contrasting Fonts in Design

DTP POINTERS
Contrasting fonts create interest in a document.

Consider the designs in figure 2.14 and the effects these interesting fonts could have on a target audience. The designs incorporate many desktop publishing concepts, such as using contrasting fonts—thin and thick fonts, light and dark font color, serif and sans typefaces, ornate and plain appearance; using a variety of colors for focus; creating fonts in proportion to each other; and incorporating directional flow.

figure
2.14 *Creating Interesting Designs with Fonts*

In exercise 2, assume you are working at Kendall Community College and you are creating a cover for a workshop handout as shown in figure 2.15.

exercise 2

Creating a Cover for a Workshop Handout

1. Open *Cover 01.doc* located on your student CD.
2. Save the document with Save As to your hard drive or a floppy disk and name it c02ex02, Cover.
3. Format the text as shown in figure 2.15 by completing the following steps:
   a. Select *Microsoft* and change the font to 26-point Garamond bold.
   b. Add the registered trademark symbol (®).
   c. Apply superscript to the (®) symbol.
   d. Select *Word 2000* and change the font to 48-point Garamond bold.
4. Create the gray dots shown in figure 2.15 by completing the following steps:
   a. Click in the area directly below *Word 2000* to access the text box that will contain the gray dots, then position the insertion point inside the box.
   b. Click Insert and then Symbol.
   c. At the Symbol dialog box with the Symbols tab selected, make sure *Wingdings* displays in the Font list box.
   d. Click the dot (●) symbol in the eighth column from the right in the third row.
   e. Click the Insert button and then click Close.
   f. Press the F4 (Repeat) key fifteen times.
   g. Position your insertion point between the first and second (●) and press Tab. Continue pressing the Tab key between each symbol.
5. Format the rest of the cover text by completing the following steps:
   a. Select *MOUS Certification Training* and change the font to 34-point Wide Latin, shadow, and small caps.
   b. Select *Testing* (in another text box) and format as directed in step 5a.
   c. Select the *ampersand* (&) symbol and change the font to 135-point Times New Roman and the font color Gray-25%, then drag the text box similar to figure 2.15. *(Hint: Hold down the Shift key and use the arrow keys to select text where text boxes overlap.)*
   d. Select *Kendall Community College* and change the font to 22-point Garamond bold italic.
   e. Select *425 DeSoto Blvd., Des...* and *Academic Testing...* and change the font to 18-point Garamond italic.

f. Select *Authorized Testing Center* and change the font to 16-point Garamond bold italic.

6. Position the insertion point in the AutoShape box at the right of *MOUS Certification...* (the insertion point will display about one inch from the top of the box) and insert the mouse (🖱) symbol found in the *Wingdings* font in the fourth column from the right in the top row.

7. Select the symbol and change the font size to 290 points. *(Hint: Hold down the Shift key and use the arrow keys to select text where text boxes overlap.)*

8. Add shading to the text box containing the (🖱) symbol by completing the following steps:

    a. Double-click the border of the AutoShape box.

    b. At the Format AutoShape dialog box, click the down arrow at the right of C̲olor in the Fill section, and then click the F̲ill Effects button.

    c. At the Fill Effects dialog box, choose the Pattern tab, and then select the third pattern (Light downward diagonal) in the first row. (Make sure the F̲oreground is black and the B̲ackground is white.) Click OK twice.

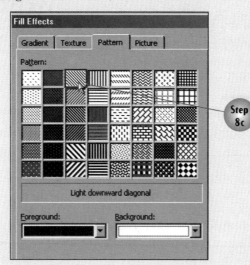

9. Drag to position any text boxes similar to figure 2.15.

10. Save the document again with the same name c02ex02, Cover.

11. Print and then close c02ex02, Cover. (If a prompt mentions that the margins are outside the printable area, click Y̲es.)

figure
2.15 *Exercise 2*

Microsoft®
Word 2000

MOUS
CERTIFICATION
TRAINING
&
TESTING

Kendall Community College
425 DeSoto Blvd., Des Moines, Iowa

Academic Testing Lab, Room 402B, Saxton Computer Center

KCC
Authorized Testing Center

Creating Documents Using Templates and Wizards

Every document created in Word is based on a template. When you create a
document at a clear document screen, you are using the default template. This
default template, called the Normal.dot template, contains formatting instructions
to use 12-point Times New Roman as the font, English (U.S.) as the language,

character spacing scaled to 100%, flush left alignment, single spacing, Widow/Orphan control, and body text as the default outline level.

A template may include several components, such as styles, text, graphics, AutoText entries, and macros. Depending on the type of document that is being created, templates often have additional styles. For instance, the Contemporary Fax template includes styles for the return address, document label, fax header, emphasis, body text, and slogan. If you position the insertion point within the return address, the Style box on the Formatting toolbar displays *Return Address* as shown in figure 2.16. You may override any style by changing the text formatting or by modifying the style itself. Styles are discussed in greater detail in chapter 6.

Style Box on the Formatting Toolbar

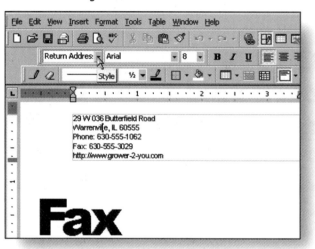

Word includes nearly 30 templates that you may choose from for documents you are most likely to create. These templates include agendas, brochures, business reports, calendars, directories, fax cover sheets, invoices, letters, manuals, memos, newsletters, press releases, purchase orders, theses, and Web pages. In addition, if you installed Office 2000 using a Custom installation and selected the option to include the Small Business Tools, or if you installed the Office 2000 Small Business Edition, you may have access to two additional template tabs named *Direct Mail Manager* and *Business Planner Templates*. The Direct Mail Manager tab contains a Flyer Wizard, Letter Wizard, Postcard Wizard, and Sample Form Letter template. These wizards help you create mail merge main documents such as flyers, letters, and postcards, using direct marketing techniques. Business Planner is a customizable small business reference program that incorporates business planning tools and templates with practical information about running a business. The templates help you create everyday business documents and spreadsheets.

Access the templates by clicking <u>F</u>ile, then <u>N</u>ew. The templates are organized on different tabs in the New dialog box. Many of the templates are formatted consistently using three designs—Contemporary, Elegant, and Professional. These designs make it easy to build a consistent set of documents.

Besides basic document templates, Word includes template Wizards. Wizards walk you through a series of steps in which you add or select information to set up formatting, content, and layout of your document.

Customizing Templates

When customizing a template to meet your specific needs, remember to apply the basic design concepts discussed in chapter 1. Always begin a document with the end in mind. Plan your text carefully to achieve your desired results without unnecessary wording or formatting. If you replace the existing fonts in a template, be sure the fonts increase the readability of the text. *Readability* is the ease with which a person can read and understand groups of words.

Readability
The ease with which a person can read and understand groups of words.

Templates and wizards can help you create great-looking documents. But if you do not want your documents to look like "one size fits all," or if you want more variety in your formatting, consider some of the following suggestions for a customized template (an example is shown in figure 2.17). Many of the features listed below will be discussed in greater detail in later chapters.

DTP POINTERS
Avoid "one size fits all" formatting by customizing to fit your needs.

- Change fonts, font styles, font sizes, font colors, and font effects
- Use expanded, condensed, lowered, or raised character spacing
- Use reverse text
- Add more or less leading (white space between the lines)
- Add fill color and fill effects—gradient, texture, or pattern
- Add text box shading, shadows, or 3-D
- Insert special characters and symbols
- Create unique bullets
- Add borders and shading
- Add graphics, photos, drawing objects, or scanned images
- Use drop caps
- Add a company logo
- Create a watermark
- Use unique column layout and specialized tables
- Include links to other documents
- Add AutoText entries
- Include Backgrounds and Themes
- Add form fields that fit your needs

figure
2.17

Customized Template

To save a document as a template that is based on an existing template:

1. Click File and then New.
2. Select the tab containing the template you want to use.
3. At the New dialog box, choose the Template option in the Create New section.
4. Double-click the template you want to use.
5. Name the template (Word will automatically assign the extension *.dot*).
6. Save your template to either the hard drive or to a floppy disk.

To save a document as a template:

1. Choose Save As from the File menu.
2. In the Save as type: list box, select *Document Template* (**.dot*).
3. Next time you want to use it, choose New from the File menu, and then double-click your template.

Changing File Locations

By default, Word saves a template document in a *Templates* subfolder within the Microsoft Office program. In a setting, such as a school or business, where more than one person uses the same computer, consider changing the location where Word saves template documents. For example, in the next exercise, you will specify the *DTP Templates* folder on your disk as the location where Word is to save template documents as shown in exercise 3. To change the file location, you would complete these steps:

1. At a clear document screen, click Tools and then Options.
2. At the Options dialog box, click the File Locations tab.
3. At the Options dialog box with the File Locations tab selected, click *User templates* in the File types list box.
4. Click the Modify button.
5. At the Modify Location dialog box, specify the desired folder in the Look in list box, and then click OK.
6. Click OK to close the Options dialog box.

In exercise 3, assume you are working for Butterfield Gardens, a nursery and gardening supply company. Frequently, you send and receive faxes directly from your computer. To reinforce your company's identity and save time, you are going to customize a fax cover sheet (include a logo), save it as a template, and reuse it as needed. The fax template provides the convenience of a "fill in the blanks" form, which makes it easy for the sender/recipient to enter data. To fill in areas containing this text, "Click **here** and type," click and then key text between the brackets. Select any placeholder text in the template, and then key your desired text. (*Hint*: Read the placeholder text first—sometimes it will provide helpful tips.)

In addition, you will create a folder on your (A:) drive and direct Word to save your templates there. (*Hint*: If you have access to a scanner, scan a copy of your signature and save it as a graphic that can be added to your fax.)

DTP POINTERS
Read the placeholder text in each template.

exercise 3

Customizing a Fax Cover Sheet Template

1. At a clear document screen, create a folder on drive A for your templates by completing the following steps:
   a. Insert a floppy disk in drive A.
   b. Click the Open button on the Standard toolbar, click the down arrow at the right of the Look in list box, and select the *3-1/2 Floppy* (*A:*) drive.
   c. At the Open dialog box, click the Create New Folder button (third button from the right).
   d. At the New Folder dialog box, key **DTP Templates** in the Name text box.
   e. Click OK or press Enter.

f.   At the Open dialog box, click the Close button (X).
2. Specify the DTP Templates folder on your floppy disk as the location where Word is to save template documents by completing the following steps:
   a.   Insert your disk (containing the *DTP Templates*) in drive A.
   b.   At a clear document screen, click Tools and then Options.
   c.   At the Options dialog box click the File Locations tab.
   d.   At the Options dialog box with the File Locations tab selected, click *User templates* in the File types list box.
   e.   Click the Modify button.
   f.   At the Modify Location dialog box, click the down arrow at the right of the Look in list box and then click *3-1/2 Floppy (A:)*.
   g.   Double-click the *DTP Templates* folder.
   h.   Click OK to close the Modify Location dialog box.
   i.   Click Close at the Options dialog box.

Options | ? X
View | General | Edit | Print | Save | Spelling & Grammar
Track Changes | User Information | Compatibility | File Locations

File types: | Location:
Documents | C:\My Documents
Clipart pictures | A:\
User templates | C:\...\Microsoft\Templates
Workgroup templates |
User options |
AutoRecover files | C:\...\Application Data\Microsoft\...
Tools | C:\...\MICROSOFT OFFICE\OFFICE
Startup | C:\...\Microsoft\Word\STARTUP

Modify...

Step 2c
Step 2d
Step 2e

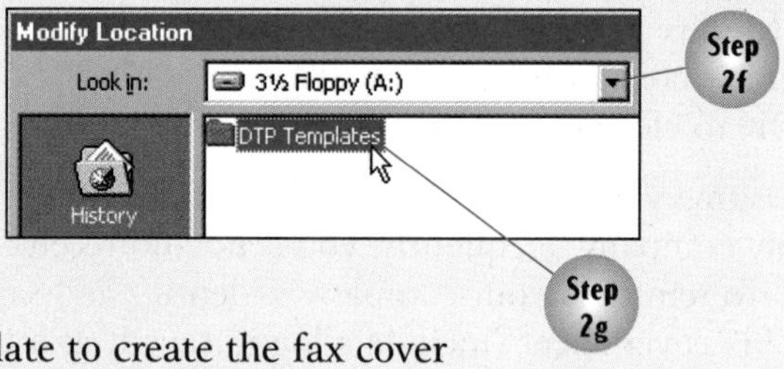

Modify Location
Look in: | 3½ Floppy (A:)
DTP Templates
History

Step 2f
Step 2g

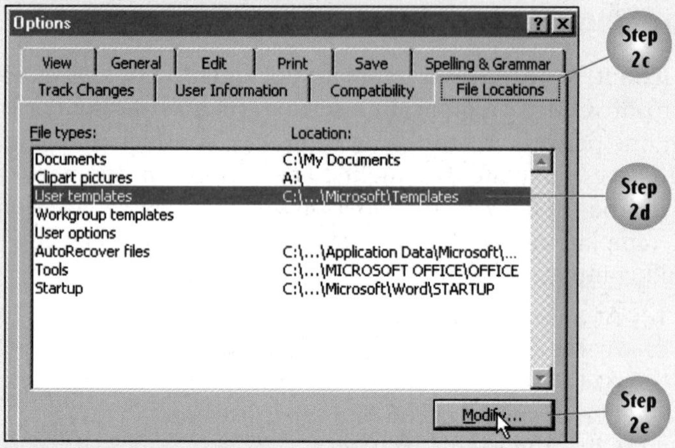

3. Use the Professional Fax template to create the fax cover sheet in figure 2.18 by completing the following steps:
   a.   Click File and then New.
   b.   At the New dialog box, click the Letters & Faxes tab.
   c.   Make sure that Template is selected in the Create New section and then double-click the Professional Fax icon.

Create New
○ Document   ● Template
OK   Cancel

Step 3c

   d.   At the fax template screen, click File and then Save As.
   e.   In the File name: text box, key **c02ex03, BG Fax**.
   f.   Make sure *DTP Templates* displays in the Save in: text box. (Consult your instructor whether you should save to the hard drive or to a floppy disk.)
   g.   Click Save.
   h.   Customize the fax design by completing the following steps:
      1)   Change the Zoom to 100%, click inside the brackets for the return address, and then key:

29 W 036 Butterfield Road
Warrenville, IL 60555
Phone: 630-555-1062
Fax: 630-555-3029
http://www.grower-2-you.com

      2)   Select the text you keyed in step 3h1 and change the font size to **10** points.
      3)   Select *Company Name Here*, click the Center align button on the Formatting toolbar, and then key **Butterfield Gardens**.
   i.   Add a logo by completing the following steps:
      1)   Position the insertion point at the beginning of the first paragraph of body text.

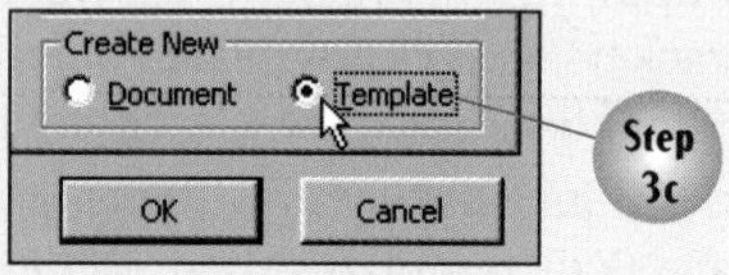

2) Change the Zoom to Whole Page.
3) Click Insert, point to Picture, and then click From File.
4) At the Insert Picture dialog box, make sure the drive where the student CD is located displays in the Look in: list box.
5) Double-click *BGLogo.tif*.
6) Double-click the image to access the Format Picture dialog box.
7) At the Format Picture dialog box, select the Layout tab, and click In front of text. This permits you to move the image. (*Hint*: In Word 2000 a clip art image defaults to *In line with text*.)

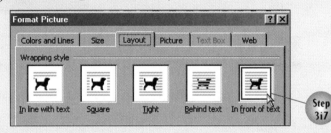

8) Select the Size tab and change the Height to 1.5 inches in the Size and rotate section. (If the Lock aspect ratio is turned on, the Width will automatically display in proportion to the height.) Click OK or press Enter.
9) Drag and drop the image to position it above the horizontal line at the bottom of the fax cover; see figure 2.18. (The customized template could be saved at this point before any specific text is inserted, but for our textbook use, you will continue keying the text.)
   j. Change the Zoom to 75%.
   k. Key the text in the brackets as shown in figure 2.18.
   l. Read the body placeholder text, then select the text to the right of *Comments* and replace it with the text in figure 2.18. Do not select and replace *Comments*.
4. Save the template again with the same name c02ex03, BG Fax.dot.
5. Print and then close c02ex03, BG Fax.dot.
6. Remove c02ex03, BG Fax.dot from the New dialog box by completing the following steps:
   a. Click File and New.
   b. At the New dialog box with the General tab selected, *right-click* on the *c02ex03, BG Fax.dot* icon.
   c. At the shortcut menu that displays, click the Delete option.
   d. At the Confirm File Delete message, click Yes.
   e. Click Cancel to close the New dialog box.
7. Return *DTP Templates* to the default location by completing the following steps:
   a. At the document screen, click Tools and Options.
   b. At the Options dialog box, click the File Locations tab.
   c. At the Options dialog box with the File Locations tab selected, click *DTP Templates* in the File types list box.
   d. Click the Modify button.
   e. At the Modify Location dialog box, change to the default *DTP Templates* folder. (If the default location was blank, select any text currently displayed in the Folder name text box and then press the Delete key.)
   f. Click OK or close the Modify Location dialog box.
   g. Click OK to close the Options dialog box.
   h. Click File and New.
   i. At the New dialog box with the General tab selected, double-click *c02ex03, BG Fax*.
Hint: Check with your instructor to determine if you should change the locations for future exercises.

figure

2.18

Exercise 3

29 W 036 Butterfield Road
Warrenville, IL 60555
Phone: 630-555-1062
Fax: 630-555-3029
http://www.grower-2-you.com

Butterfield Gardens

Fax

To:	P. Manich Floral Distribution	**From:**	Floyd Rogers
Fax:	618-555-7823	**Pages:**	2
Phone:	618-555-7720	**Date:**	7/8/01
Re:	Annual and perennial flowers	**CC:**	J. J. Whitman, Midwest Sales

☐ **Urgent**   ☐ **For Review**   ☐ **Please Comment**   X **Please Reply**   ☐ **Please Recycle**

● **Comments:** Please review the completed purchase order and confirm the availability of the flowers by return fax. The last shipment was beautiful!

Thank you for your prompt service.

Butterfield GARDENS

Adding a Watermark for Visual Appeal

Watermark
A lightened graphic or text displayed behind text on a page.

A *watermark* is a lightened version of an image, which enables you to superimpose legible text above it. For example, you may use a watermark when you want a graphic, such as a company logo, or text, to display in the background of a printed page. Traditionally, a watermark is a design impressed in high-quality paper stock. This design can be seen more clearly when the paper is held up to the light.

Using Word Layers in Documents

In exercise 4, you will customize a memo template by adding a watermark for visual appeal and corporate identity. A basic understanding of the unique layering of text, pictures, and drawing objects in Word will be helpful in understanding how to create watermarks in documents.

Word has three basic layers—the *foreground layer, text layer,* and the *background layer.* Word layers are illustrated in figure 2.19. In addition to these basic layers, each drawing object created in Word is placed in an individual layer in the foreground layer. Every time you add another object, it is drawn in the layer on top of the previous layer. This stacking is similar to a stack of cards as shown in figure 2.20.

figure
2.19   *Word Layers*

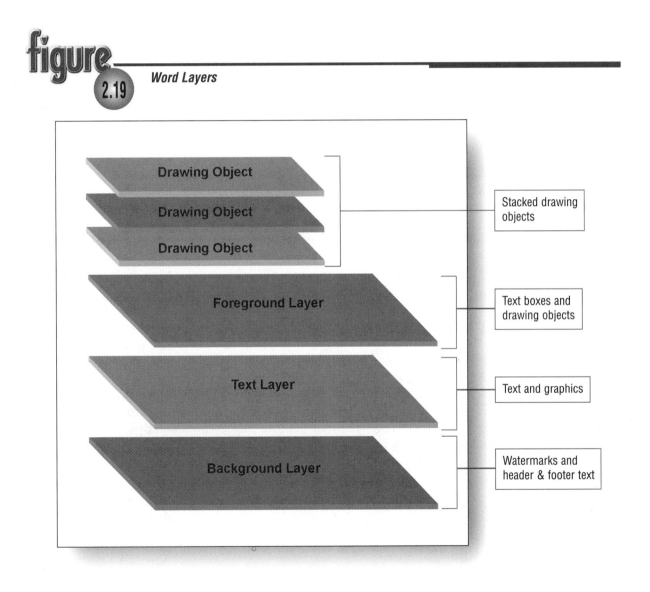

figure

2.20 *Layered Objects Are Similar to a Stack of Cards*

Objects are stacked in layers like a deck of cards. The first object created is on the bottom, and the last object is at the top.

Figure 2.21 illustrates Word's unique layering process. Document text and pictures exist in the middle layer or *text layer*. This layer is the one you may be most accustomed to working with in word processing. In Word 2000, graphics default to *In line with text* and anchor to a paragraph. The exception is clip art that is dragged and dropped from the Clip Gallery—the image will float over text.

Word also includes the *foreground layer* above the text layer where text boxes and drawing objects display by default. Drawing objects include AutoShape forms, rectangles, ovals, WordArt, lines, 3D objects and shadowed objects. All of these objects created with buttons on the Drawing toolbar can be drawn in a document containing text. By default, the object will display above the text layer, covering the text.

The third layer is the *background layer*, where pictures, text boxes, and drawing objects may be sent behind the document text. Objects and pictures may be sent behind text by accessing each respective dialog box or toolbar. Text created in a header or footer or images inserted into the Header and Footer pane automatically exist in the *background layer*.

figure
2.21
Word Layers in a Document

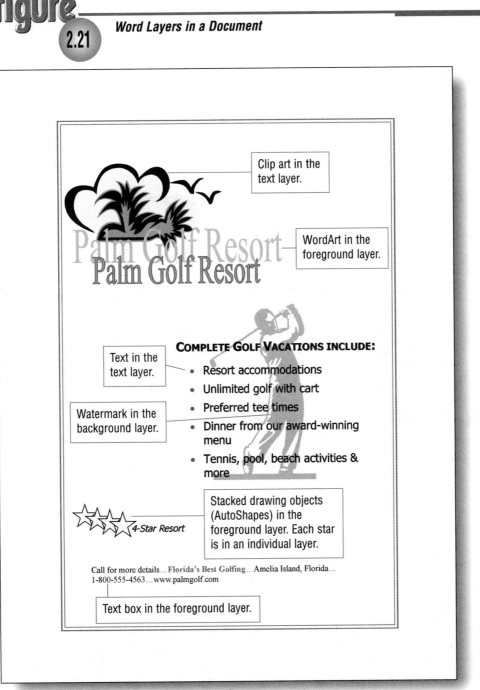

Clip art in the text layer.

WordArt in the foreground layer.

Palm Golf Resort

Text in the text layer.

Watermark in the background layer.

COMPLETE GOLF VACATIONS INCLUDE:

- Resort accommodations
- Unlimited golf with cart
- Preferred tee times
- Dinner from our award-winning menu
- Tennis, pool, beach activities & more

Stacked drawing objects (AutoShapes) in the foreground layer. Each star is in an individual layer.

4-Star Resort

Call for more details…Florida's Best Golfing…Amelia Island, Florida…
1-800-555-4563…www.palmgolf.com

Text box in the foreground layer.

Inserting Images

To insert a clip art image, click Insert, point to Picture, and then click Clip Art or From File. At the Insert ClipArt dialog box with the Pictures tab selected (see figure 2.22), click a category in the category list box. To insert a clip art image in the document, click the desired clip art, and then click the Insert Clip Art button at the top of the callout side menu that displays. Remove the Insert ClipArt dialog box by clicking the Close button (X) located in the upper right corner of the dialog box.

Insert
Clip Art

Another method for displaying the ClipArt dialog box is to click the Insert Clip Art button on the Drawing toolbar.

figure

2.22

Insert ClipArt Dialog Box

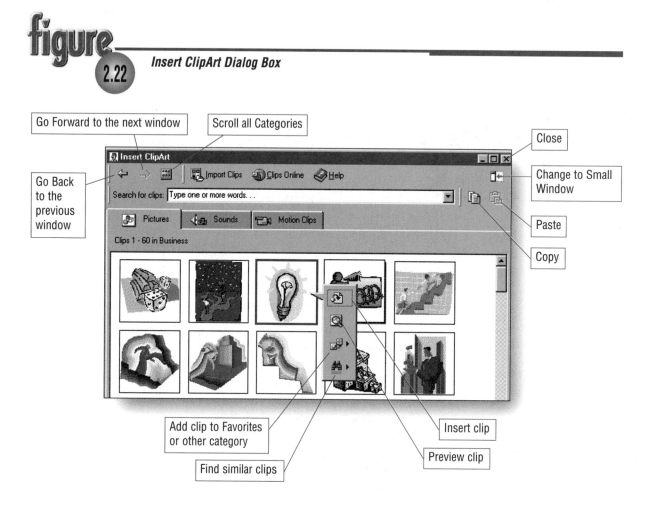

Go Forward to the next window

Scroll all Categories

Close

Go Back to the previous window

Change to Small Window

Paste

Copy

Add clip to Favorites or other category

Find similar clips

Insert clip

Preview clip

Sizing and Moving Images

Once an image is inserted in a document, it can be sized using the white sizing handles that display around a selected clip art image. To change the size of an image, select it, position the mouse pointer on a sizing handle until the pointer turns into a double-headed arrow ⊹. Hold down the left mouse button, drag the sizing handle in or out to decrease or increase the size of the image, and then release the mouse button. Use the sizing handles in the corners to change the height and width at the same time and in proportion to each other.

To move a clip art image you must first select the image, make sure the Picture toolbar displays (see figure 2.23), and then click the Text Wrapping button on the Picture toolbar. Choose a text wrapping style, such as In Front of Text or Behind Text, then select the image and move it.

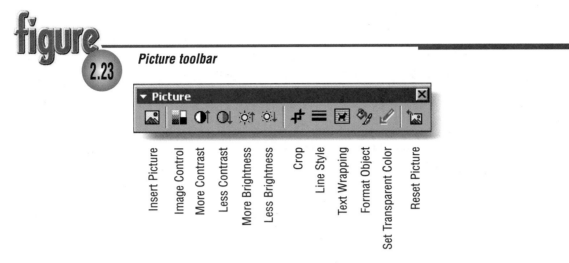

figure
2.23

Picture toolbar

Insert Picture
Image Control
More Contrast
Less Contrast
More Brightness
Less Brightness
Crop
Line Style
Text Wrapping
Format Object
Set Transparent Color
Reset Picture

Selecting the Watermark Option

To reduce the shading of a picture, display the Picture toolbar, click the Image Control button, and then select Watermark from the drop down list. This option automatically reduces the brightness of the image to 85% and the contrast to 15%.

If the watermark is a drawing object, you may reduce the shading by either choosing a lighter Fill Color or Fill Effect, or double-clicking the object to access the AutoShape dialog box and selecting Semitransparent in the Fill section of the Colors and Lines tab. If the object is a WordArt object, simply select a lighter color at the Format WordArt dialog box.

Inserting Watermarks in a Document

Basically there are two methods for creating watermarks in Word documents. One method uses the Header and Footer feature, which automatically positions the image behind the text layer. The other method suggests that you send the image behind the text layer.

Creating a Watermark in a Header and Footer

One of the easiest ways to create a watermark, which will appear on every page of your document, is to insert the image or text you want to use as the watermark into a header or footer. Placing the watermark into a header or footer automatically positions the object in the appropriate layer below the text layer.

Creating a watermark in a header and footer:

1. Click View, then Header and Footer.
2. Click Insert, point to Picture, and then click Clip Art or From File.
3. Display the Insert ClipArt dialog box, select the picture you want, and then click the Insert Clip Art button. Close the Insert ClipArt dialog box.
4. Click once on the image to select it (make sure the Picture toolbar displays).
5. Click the Text Wrapping button and select In Front of Text or Behind Text to change the default *in line* option. (In Front of Text or Behind Text will allow you to move the image freely around the screen.)

6. Drag a corner-sizing handle to size the image proportionally.
7. Drag the four-headed arrow to move the image.
8. Click the Image Control button on the Picture toolbar and select Watermark.
9. Click the Close button on the Header and Footer toolbar.

Creating a watermark by sending it behind:

1. Click Insert, point to Picture, and then click Clip Art or From File.
2. Display the Insert ClipArt dialog box, select the picture you want, and then click the Insert Clip Art button. Close the Insert ClipArt dialog box.
3. Select the image, click the Image Control button on the Picture toolbar, and then click Watermark.
4. Click the Text Wrapping button on the Picture toolbar and select Behind Text. (If the clip art displays in front of the text, repeat this step.)
5. Resize and move the image.

Troubleshooting Watermarks

If a document is created with text boxes, rectangles, or other AutoShape boxes, the boxes may obstruct the view of the watermark below them. If this should occur, click the Fill Color button on the Drawing toolbar and select No Fill. Also, click the Line Color button and select No Line.

If you use a text box, rectangle, or other AutoShape as a container or border for a document, the graphics you select may fill the entire area of the text box or shape. When using graphics and watermarks in signs or other documents created with a border around them, you may find it helpful to use a Page Border or a Border from the Borders and Shading dialog box to serve as the border around a document.

If the watermark is a drawing object, select the Layout tab at the Format AutoShape dialog box and select Semitransparent or choose a lighter color for the fill.

To use text as a watermark, use a light font color or create a WordArt object and select the Semitransparent option at the Format WordArt dialog box.

Inserting Bullets

Bullets

Bullets may be inserted in a document at the Bullets and Numbering dialog box or with the Bullets button on the Formatting toolbar. To display the Bullets and Numbering dialog box, click Format and then Bullets and Numbering. The Bullets and Numbering dialog box contains three tabs: Bulleted, Numbered, and Outline Numbered. If you click the Customize button at the right side of the dialog box, the Customize Bulleted List dialog box displays. At this dialog box, you can select a different Bullet character, Font, and Bullet.

The bullet and text positions can also be changed. For instance, to insert a different bullet character, click the Customize button, click the Bullet button, and then select a character at the Symbol dialog box. Change the size and color of the bullet by clicking the Font button.

DTP POINTERS
Use bullets to organize a list.

DTP POINTERS
Use special characters or customized bullets to add interest and contrast.

In exercise 4 assume you are an employee at Chicago Mercy Hospital. In this exercise you will customize a memo for the hospital with a watermark.

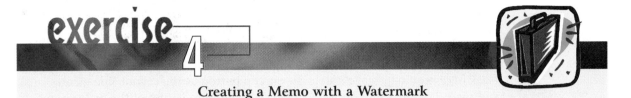

exercise 4

Creating a Memo with a Watermark

1. At a clear document screen, create the memo shown in figure 2.24 by completing the following steps:
   a. Open Medical Memo.doc located on your student CD.
   b. Save the document with Save As to your hard drive or a floppy disk and name it c02ex04a, Watermk.
   c. Click the Show/Hide button on the Standard toolbar to turn on nonprintable characters.
   d. Select *Memorandum* and change the font to 34-point Colonna MT (or a similar font), in Violet (third row and second from the right), with Shadow effect, and then key **Chicago Mercy Hospital Memo**.
   e. Change the line style and color of the line above the memo text by completing the following steps:
      1) Position the insertion point anywhere in the subject line (Re:), click Format, and then Borders and Shading.
      2) At the Borders tab, scroll downward in the Style list box and select the three-line style.
      3) Change the Color to Violet in the third row and second from the right.
      4) Make sure the Width displays at 1/2 pt.
      5) Make sure the bottom line is selected in the Preview box, and then click OK or press Enter.
   f. Select the gray-shaded circle on the left side of the memo and press Delete.
   g. Add bullets to the listed text by completing the following steps:
      1) Select the text beginning with *Necessary operative forms…* and ending with *Anesthesiologist has reviewed….*
      2) Click Format and Bullets and Numbering.
      3) At the Bullets and Numbering dialog box, select the Bulleted tab.
      4) Choose any one of the bullets displayed, and then click Customize.
      5) At the Customize Bulleted List dialog box, click the Bullet button.
      6) At the Symbol dialog box, click the down arrow at the right of the Font list box, and then choose *Wingdings*.
      7) Click the checkmark symbol in the last row and fourth column from the right and then click OK.
      8) Make sure the Bullet position is set at 0.75 inch.
      9) Make sure the Text position is set at 1 inch.
      10) Click OK or press Enter. (If a hollow bullet displays, select the checkmark again.)
   h. Create the medical watermark in figure 2.24 by completing the following steps:
      1) Display the Drawing and Picture toolbars.
      2) Click View and Header and Footer.
      3) Change the Zoom to 50% and scroll downward until the first few paragraphs of text displays.

4) Click <u>I</u>nsert, point to <u>P</u>icture, and then click <u>C</u>lip Art.

5) At the Insert ClipArt dialog box, click the *Healthcare and Me...* category in the category list box. Scroll (through several screens) until you find the image shown in figure 2.24.

Step 1h5

6) Click once on the image, click the Insert clip button at the callout side menu, and then click the Close button (X) in the upper right corner of the dialog box.

7) Select the picture, click the Text Wrapping button on the Picture toolbar, and select <u>I</u>n Front of

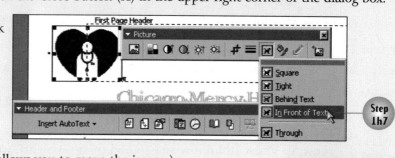

Step 1h7

Text. (This allows you to move the image.)

8) Resize and move the image similar to figure 2.24.

9) Select the picture, click the Image Control Button on the Picture toolbar, and then click <u>W</u>atermark.

10) Click the <u>C</u>lose button on the Header and Footer toolbar.

Step 1h9

2. View the document at Print Preview.

3. Save the memo with the same name c02ex04a, Watermk.

4. Print c02ex04a, Watermk.

5. Remove the watermark created in c02ex04a, Watermk and create another watermark using the Behin<u>d</u> Text option by completing the following steps:

   a. Click <u>V</u>iew and <u>H</u>eader and Footer.

   b. Select the heart/doctor image and press Delete.

   c. Click <u>C</u>lose on the Header and Footer toolbar.

   d. Position the insertion point at the beginning of the first paragraph of text.

   e. Display the Insert ClipArt dialog box, click the *Healthcare and Me...* category in the category list box. Scroll until you find the image shown in figure 2.25.

   f. Click once on the image, click the Insert clip button at the callout side menu, and then click the Close button (X) in the upper right corner of the dialog box.

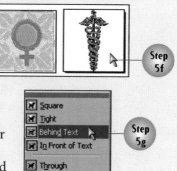

Step 5f

   g. Select the image, click the Text Wrapping button on the Picture toolbar, and then click <u>I</u>n Front of Text (this allows you to move the image easily).

   h. Resize and position the image similar to figure 2.25.

   i. Click the Image Control button on the Picture toolbar and click <u>W</u>atermark.

   j. Click the Text Wrapping button and then click Behin<u>d</u> Text. *(Hint: If you need to resize or move the watermark image after sending it behind text, click the Select Objects button on the Drawing toolbar to access the image.)*

Step 5g

6. View the document at Print Preview.

7. Save with Save <u>A</u>s and name the document c02ex04b, Watermk.

8. Print and then close c02ex04b, Watermk.

figure
2.24
Exercise 4, Steps 1–4

Chicago Mercy Hospital Memo

To: Fred Médard

From: Juliette Danner

Date: May 17, 2001

Re: PREOPERATIVE PROCEDURES

At the last meeting of the medical team, concern was raised about the structure of preoperative procedures. In light of recent nationwide occurrences in some city hospitals, members of the team decided to review written procedures to determine if additional steps should be added. A meeting of the surgical team has been set for Tuesday, May 22. Please try to arrange surgical schedules so a majority of the surgical team can attend this meeting.

Please review the following items to determine where each should be positioned in a preoperative surgical checklist:

- ✔ Necessary operative forms are signed—admissions and consent for surgery.
- ✔ Blood tests have been completed.
- ✔ Blood type is noted in patient chart.
- ✔ Surgical procedure has been triple-checked with patient and surgical team.
- ✔ All allergies are noted in patient chart.
- ✔ Anesthesiologist has reviewed and initialed patient chart.

I am confident that the medical team will discover that the preoperative checklist is one of the most thorough in the region. Any suggestions made by the medical team will only enhance a superior checklist.

xx:c02ex04a, Watermk

CONFIDENTIAL

figure

2.25

Exercise 4, Steps 5–8

Chicago Mercy Hospital Memo

To: Fred Médard

From: Juliette Danner

Date: May 17, 2001

Re: PREOPERATIVE PROCEDURES

At the last meeting of the medical team, concern was raised about the structure of preoperative procedures. In light of recent nationwide occurrences in some city hospitals, members of the team decided to review written procedures to determine if additional steps should be added. A meeting of the surgical team has been set for Tuesday, May 22. Please try to arrange surgical schedules so a majority of the surgical team can attend this meeting.

Please review the following items to determine where each should be positioned in a preoperative surgical checklist:

✔ Necessary operative forms are signed—admissions and consent for surgery.
✔ Blood tests have been completed.
✔ Blood type is noted in patient chart.
✔ Surgical procedure has been triple-checked with patient and surgical team.
✔ All allergies are noted in patient chart.
✔ Anesthesiologist has reviewed and initialed patient chart.

I am confident that the medical team will discover that the preoperative checklist is one of the most thorough in the region. Any suggestions made by the medical team will only enhance a superior checklist.

xx:c02ex04b, Watermk

CONFIDENTIAL

Preparing an Agenda

Before a meeting in a business, an agenda is generally prepared that includes such information as the name of the group or department holding the meeting; the date, time, and location of the meeting; and the topics to be discussed during the meeting. In Word, an agenda can be created with the Agenda Wizard or created at a clear document screen in a table. A customized agenda may be saved as a template to save you time and effort.

Agendas created with the Agenda Wizard may be sent through e-mail and fax connections. An agenda created at a clear document screen may be sent to an e-mail recipient or fax recipient by clicking File, then Send to. An example of an agenda created with the Agenda Wizard is shown in figure 2.26.

figure 2.26

Sample Agenda Using the Agenda Wizard

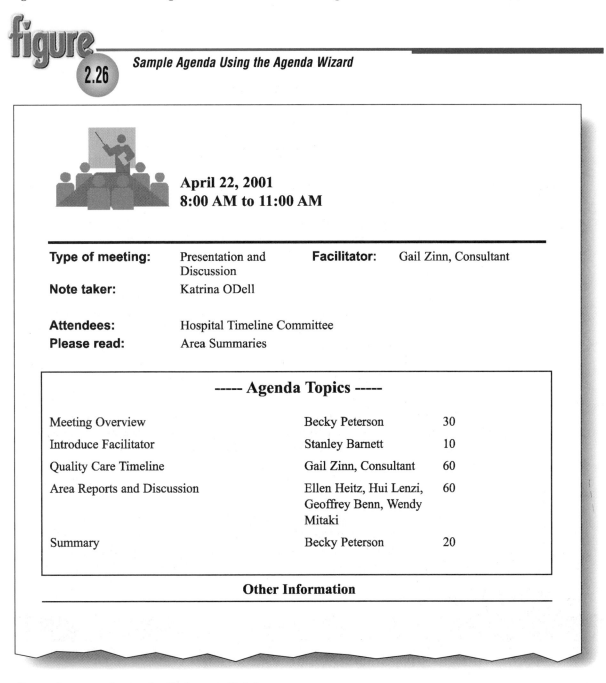

April 22, 2001
8:00 AM to 11:00 AM

Type of meeting:	Presentation and Discussion	**Facilitator:**	Gail Zinn, Consultant
Note taker:	Katrina ODell		

Attendees: Hospital Timeline Committee
Please read: Area Summaries

----- Agenda Topics -----

Meeting Overview	Becky Peterson	30
Introduce Facilitator	Stanley Barnett	10
Quality Care Timeline	Gail Zinn, Consultant	60
Area Reports and Discussion	Ellen Heitz, Hui Lenzi, Geoffrey Benn, Wendy Mitaki	60
Summary	Becky Peterson	20

Other Information

Creating an Agenda Using a Table

Besides using the Agenda Wizard, an agenda may be prepared at a clear document screen with side-by-side columns, which are similar to parallel columns. Word does not include a parallel column feature where text is grouped across a page in rows. However, the same effect can be accomplished by using a table to format an agenda as shown in figure 2.27.

figure

2.27

Sample Agenda Using a Table

CHICAGO MERCY HOSPITAL

QUALITY CARE PROJECT

❖ AGENDA ❖

9:00 – 9:30 a.m.	Call to order and introduction of new project members.	Becky Peterson, Chair
9:00 – 9:30 a.m.	Presentation of project mission statement.	Stanley Barnett

Insert Table

A table can be created with the Insert Table button (eighth button from the right) on the Standard toolbar or the T_able option from the Menu bar. To create the agenda in figure 2.28, create a table with three columns and seven rows. The number of rows will depend on the number of entries in your agenda.

Entering Text in a Table

Information in a table is keyed in cells. A *cell* is the intersection between a row and a column. With the insertion point positioned in a cell, key or edit text as you would normal text. Move the insertion point to other cells with the mouse by positioning the arrow pointer in the desired cell, then clicking the left mouse button. If you are using the keyboard, press Tab to move the insertion point to the next cell or press Shift + Tab to move the insertion point to the previous cell. If you want to move the insertion point to a tab stop within a cell, press Ctrl + Tab.

If the insertion point is located in the last cell of the table and you press the Tab key, Word adds another row to the table. If you have added too many rows to your table, select the unwanted rows then press Delete. When all the information has been entered into the cells, move the insertion point below the table and, if necessary, continue keying the document, or save the document in the normal manner.

Assume you are an employee at Chicago Mercy Hospital and you are preparing an agenda for a project meeting. This agenda will be sent as an e-mail attachment to all the project members. If your class has e-mail access, create the document in exercise 5 and send it to a recipient in your class as an e-mail attachment.

exercise 5

Preparing an Agenda with a Table

1. At a clear document screen, create the agenda shown in figure 2.28 by completing the following steps:
   a. Open Agenda 01.doc located on your student CD.
   b. Save the document with Save _As to your hard drive or a floppy disk and name it c02ex05, Agenda.
   c. Click the Show/Hide button on the Standard toolbar to display nonprinting characters.

d. Format the heading text by completing the following steps:
   1) Position the insertion point at the right margin (right alignment).
   2) Change the font to 30-point Colonna MT (or a similar font), small caps, shadow, in Violet (second color from right in the third row of the color palette), then key **Chicago Mercy Hospital**. Press Enter.
   3) Change the font to 18-point Arial bold, small caps, in Violet (turn off shadow), then key **Quality Care Project**, press Enter, and then key **Agenda**.
   4) Change the font to 12-point Book Antiqua (turn off bold, small caps, and change the font color to Automatic).
   5) Press Enter three times and change the alignment to Align Left.
e. Create a table format for the agenda text by completing the following steps:
   1) Click Table, point to Insert, then click Table.
   2) At the Insert Table dialog box, change the Number of columns to **3**.
   3) Change the Number of rows to **7**.
   4) Click OK or press Enter.
f. With the insertion point positioned inside the first cell, format the table by completing the following steps:
   1) Click Table, point to Select, and then click Table.
   2) Click Table and then Table Properties.
   3) At the Table Properties dialog box, select the Table tab, and then click Center in the Alignment section.
   4) Click the Options button.
   5) At the Table Options dialog box, change the Left and Right Margins to **0.1** inch. Click OK or press Enter.
   6) Select the Row tab, click the check box at the left of Specify height, and key **0.75** inch. Make sure the Row height is **At least**.
   7) Select the Cell tab and click Center in the Vertical Alignment section.
   8) Select the Column tab, click the check box at the left of Preferred width, and key **2** inches in the Preferred width text box.
   9) Click the Next Column button twice, make sure you are in the second column, change the Preferred width of Column 2 to **2.8** inches, and then click the Next Column button.
   10) Change the Preferred width of Column 3 to **2** inches.
   11) Click OK or press Enter.
g. Select the first row and change the font to 14-point Book Antiqua bold, small caps (Ctrl + Shift + K), and Center align.
h. Position the insertion point inside the first cell and key **Time**; press Tab and key **Topic**; press Tab and key **Discussion Leaders**; then press Tab.
i. Change the alignment to Left align, press the space bar once, key **9:00 – 9:30 a.m.** in the first cell, and then press Tab. (Add a space before a single digit number to align the times. Insert an en dash between the times and add a space before and after the en dash.)
j. Key **Call to order and introduction of new project members.**, then press Tab.
2. Continue keying the text and pressing Tab until the agenda is completed as shown in figure 2.28.
3. Apply a predesigned format to the table by completing the following steps:
   a. With the insertion point positioned inside the table, click Table, and then click Table AutoFormat.

b. At the Table AutoFormat dialog box, scroll down at the Formats list box and select *Contemporary*.

c. Click OK or press Enter.

4. View the agenda at Print Preview.

5. Save the agenda again with the same name c02ex05, Agenda.

6. Print and then close c02ex05, Agenda.

figure
2.28

Exercise 5

CHICAGO MERCY HOSPITAL
QUALITY CARE PROJECT
AGENDA

TIME	TOPIC	DISCUSSION LEADERS
9:00 – 9:30 a.m.	Call to order and introduction of new project members.	Becky Peterson, Chair
9:30 – 10:00 a.m.	Presentation of project mission statement.	Stanley Barnett
10:00 – 11:00 a.m.	Determination of project goals and timelines.	Katrina O'Dell, Geoffrey Benn, and Wendy Mitaki
11:00 – 11:45 a.m.	Brainstorming on public relations activities.	Ellen Heitz and Hui Lenzi
11:45 – 12:00 Noon	Scheduling of next project meeting.	Becky Peterson, Chair
12:00 Noon	Adjournment.	Becky Peterson, Chair

chapter summary

- A font consists of three characteristics: typeface, type style, and type size.
- The term typeface refers to the general design and shape of a set of characters.
- The typeface used in a document establishes a particular mood or feeling.
- Characteristics that distinguish one typeface from another include x-height, cap height, height of ascenders, depth of descenders, and serifs.
- A serif is a small stroke on the edge of characters. A sans serif typeface does not have serifs.
- Typefaces are either monospaced or proportional. Monospaced typefaces allot the same amount of horizontal space to each character, while proportional typefaces allot a varying amount to each character.
- Pitch is the number of characters that can be printed in one horizontal inch.
- Point size is a vertical measurement and is approximately 1/72 of an inch. The higher the point size chosen, the larger the characters.
- Printer fonts are the built-in fonts and the supplemental fonts that are available to your printer. Supplemental fonts can be added to your printer in cartridge form or as soft fonts.
- The Font Color feature has been expanded to include 40 colors on the color palette, 124 colors and 15 shades of gray at the Standard tab, and an option to mix your own colors at the Custom tab of the Colors dialog box.
- At the Custom tab of the Colors dialog box, you can change the *luminescence*, which is the brightness of the color; the *hue*, which is the color itself; and the *saturation*, which is the color's intensity. You can also change the values of <u>R</u>ed, <u>G</u>reen, and <u>B</u>lue.
- Readability is the ease with which a person can read and understand groups of words.
- For text set in a proportional typeface, space once after end-of-sentence punctuation.
- Special symbols can be inserted in a document at the Symbol dialog box with the <u>S</u>ymbols tab or the S<u>p</u>ecial Characters tab selected.
- The Fax Wizard helps you send a fax through your computer.
- Text boxes may be used to position text in a document. To prevent overlapping text boxes, select No Line and No Fill.
- An em dash (—) is as long as the point size of the type and is used in text to indicate a pause in speech.
- An en dash (–) indicates a continuation, such as 116–133 or January–March, and is exactly one-half the width of an em dash.
- Bullets can be inserted in a document at the Bullets and Numbering dialog box or with the Bullets button on the Formatting toolbar.
- In typesetting, the open quotation mark is curved upward (") and the close quotation mark is curved downward ("). In typesetting, the straight quotes are used to indicate inches (") or feet (').
- Word provides a number of templates that can be used to produce a variety of documents. The default template document is Normal.dot.

➤ Many of the templates are formatted consistently using three designs—Contemporary, Elegant, and Professional.

➤ A watermark is a lightened image that can be added to a document to add visual interest.

➤ One of the easiest ways to create a watermark in Word is to insert the watermark into a header or footer.

➤ Another method to create a watermark is to insert a picture into a document, select the Watermark option at the Image Control, and then select the Behind Text option.

➤ Word contains an agenda template that may be used to prepare an agenda for a meeting. The agenda may be customized and saved as a separate template.

➤ Tables may be used when formatting an agenda into side-by-side columns.

➤ The Table Properties dialog box includes options to change table size, alignment, and text wrap; row height; column width; and cell size and vertical alignment.

commands review

Mouse/Keyboard

Font dialog box	Format, Font; or press Ctrl + D
New dialog box	File, New; or press Ctrl + N
Header and Footer	View, Header and Footer
Borders and Shading dialog box	Format, Borders and Shading
Insert ClipArt dialog box	Click Insert, point to Picture, click Clip Art
Watermark	Click View, then Header and Footer. Insert a picture, select In Front of Text (image is movable), resize and move the image, click Image Control on the Picture toolbar, then select Watermark. Close Header and Footer pane. Or, insert picture, change Text Wrapping to In Front of Text (image is movable), resize and move, click Watermark from Image Control, click Behind Text.
Symbol dialog box	Insert, Symbol
AutoFormat	Tools, AutoCorrect, AutoFormat tab
Bullets and Numbering dialog box	Format, Bullets and Numbering
Insert Table dialog box	Click Table, point to Insert, click Table

Matching: Match the terms with the correct definitions by writing the letter of the term on the blank line in front of the correct definition.

- Ⓐ Baseline
- Ⓑ Monospaced
- Ⓒ Serif
- Ⓓ Descenders
- Ⓔ Point
- Ⓕ Cap height
- Ⓖ Point size
- Ⓗ x-height
- Ⓘ En dash
- Ⓙ Proportional
- Ⓚ Type style
- Ⓛ Sans serif
- Ⓜ Typeface
- Ⓝ Ascenders
- Ⓞ Em dash

_____ 1. A set of characters with a common design and shape.

_____ 2. Imaginary horizontal line on which text rests.

_____ 3. Height of the main body of the lowercase characters and equivalent to the lowercase x.

_____ 4. Distance between the baseline and the top of capital letters.

_____ 5. Parts of lowercase characters that rise above the x-height.

_____ 6. Parts of characters that extend below the baseline.

_____ 7. A special character that is used in a duration of time or continuation.

_____ 8. A small stroke at the edge of characters.

_____ 9. A typeface that does not contain serifs.

_____ 10. Approximately 1/72 of an inch.

_____ 11. Varying style of a typeface, including bold and italic.

_____ 12. A special symbol that is used to indicate a pause in speech.

True/False: Circle the letter T if the statement is true; circle the letter F if the statement is false.

T F 1. Proportional typefaces allot the same amount of horizontal space for each character in a typeface.

T F 2. Text boxes may be used to position text in a document.

T F 3. When text is set in a proportional typeface, space once after punctuation.

T F 4. The default template document is the Main template.

T F 5. Click the New Blank Document button on the Standard toolbar to display the New dialog box.

T F 6. A watermark exists in the text layer of a document.

T F 7. You can specify a certain row height at the Table Properties dialog box.

T F 8. Press the Tab key to move the insertion point to the next cell in a table.

Assessment 1

As an employee at Horizon Travel, prepare a sign announcing an anniversary sale on a travel package to London. Include the following specifications:

1. Create the sign in landscape orientation.
2. Include a graphic or photo (if you wish, you may use the image as a watermark).
3. Use a border or lines to organize and add interest to the sign.
4. Choose an appropriate font and font size for ease in reading the text.
5. Compose the message using the following information:
    a. Horizon Travel is celebrating 25 years of making memories
    b. 25% discount on room rates at Oxford Inn, in the heart of the Theatreland
    c. Airfare at a 25% discount
    d. Complimentary bottle of champagne
    e. Offer valid from July 1, 2001 to August 31, 2001
    f. Subject to availability
6. Save the sign and name it c02sa01, Sign.
7. Print and then close c02sa01, Sign.

Assessment 2

Assume you are the coordinator of High School Articulation at Kendall Community College, and in coordination with the local school districts, you have put together an agenda for a District Wide Institute Day.

1. At a clear document screen, create an agenda similar to figure 2.29 using the Agenda Wizard and include the following specifications:
    a. Access the Agenda Wizard.
    b. At the Agenda Wizard, include the following information:
        1) Select the Boxes style for your agenda.
        2) Date: February 24, 2001
        3) Time: 9:00 AM
        4) Title: District Wide Institute Day
           Education to Careers—Learning to Earning
        5) Location: Kendall Community College
        6) Headings: Type of meeting and Special notes
        7) Names: Facilitator, Attendees, Resource persons
        8) Agenda Topics: see figure 2.29.
        9) Form for minutes? No
    c. Fill in after Wizard is finished:
        1) Type of meeting: Workshops
        2) Facilitator: Shirley Thompson
        3) Attendees: All District 203 and 204 teachers, staff, and administrators
        4) Resource persons: Pat Donofrio, Coordinator, High School Articulation, Kendall Community College, (515) 555-8611
        5) Customize the agenda with an appropriate graphic, watermark, or symbol. (Figure 2.29 is an example—be creative!)

6) Change at least one font and add a coordinating font color.
7) *Kendall Community College* and the logo were created in a footer—create your own logo for the college (use WordArt, a symbol, or graphic—be creative!)
8) Shading is optional.
2. Save the document and name it c02sa02, Agenda.
3. Print and then close c02sa02, Agenda.

figure

2.29

Assessment 2

DISTRICT WIDE INSTITUTE DAY
Education to Careers—Learning to Earning
February 24, 2001
9:00 AM to 3:00 PM
Kendall Community College

Type of meeting:	Workshops	**Facilitator:**	Shirley Thompson

Attendees: All District 203 and 204 teachers, staff, and administrators

----- **Agenda Topics** -----

Workplace Shortcuts for the New Millennium	Peggy Maas	60
Communication Skills	Greg White	60
Distance Learning	Nancy Stanko	60
Internet Usage in Schools and Careers	Ron Kapper	60
Work-Based Learning	Nancy Weber	60
Building Partnership and Support	Andrew Agtey	60

Other Information

Resource persons: Pat Donofrio, Coordinator, High School Articulation, Kendall Community College, (515) 555-8611

Special notes:

KCC KENDALL COMMUNITY COLLEGE

Assessment 3

As an employee at Chicago Mercy Hospital, you have been asked to send a memo to Audra Schöenbeck with an addition to next week's newsletter.

1. Choose one of the Memo templates in Word.
2. Save the memo as a template (check with your instructor if you should save the template to the hard drive or to a floppy disk.) Name the template c02sa03, CMH Memo.
3. Key the heading text below: Use the (normal text) font for the character symbols. Date: **March 13, 2001**; To: **Audra Schöenbeck**; From: **Marcus Cañete**; Subject: **Healthy Heart Week**
4. Insert Memo Text.doc located on your student CD.
5. Customize the memo and include the following specifications:
   a. Use a sans serif font in the heading and a serif font in 12 points for the body text.
   b. Format the memo text appropriately.
   c. Use three font effects to emphasize text in the document.
   d. Insert appropriate bullets.
   e. Insert an appropriate watermark.
6. Save the memo template again with the same name (c02sa03, CMH Memo).
7. Print and then close c02sa03, CMH Memo.

CREATIVE ACTIVITY

Situation: You work for a desktop publisher called Desktop Designs located at 4455 Jackson Drive, Raleigh, NC 27613. You have been asked by your supervisor to develop a press release describing the services performed by Desktop Designs. A customized sample press release is shown in figure 2.30. Use a Word template to create this press release and include the following information in your own words:

- Desktop Designs has been operating in the Raleigh area for over 12 years.
- The employees of Desktop Designs have over 30 years of combined graphics design and typesetting experience.
- The company provides a variety of services, including creating personal documents such as cover letters, résumés, invitations, programs, cards, envelopes and labels; creating business documents such as letterheads, envelopes, business cards, forms, logos, and slides; and creating promotional and marketing documents such as newsletters, flyers, and brochures.
- The company is open Monday through Saturday from 7:00 a.m. to 6:00 p.m.

After creating the press release, save it and name it c02ca01, Press. Print and then close c02ca01, Press.

figure **2.30** *Sample Press Release*

CHICAGO MERCY HOSPITAL

708 North 42nd Street
Chicago, IL 63209
Phone 312-555-2200
Fax 312-555-2086

Press Release

Contact: Your Name
Phone: (312) 555-2205

FOR IMMEDIATE RELEASE
9 AM EDT, March 13, 2001

NEW PEDIATRICS WING

Chicago, Illinois—Chicago Mercy Hospital announces a $3-million project to build a pediatrics wing on the north side of the hospital. Construction will begin at the end of this month and will be completed by the end of the year. The new wing will include 50 patient rooms and 10 family rooms, a children's physical therapy unit, and three operating rooms equipped with the latest medical technology. In a recent interview, Terry Kasuski, chief executive officer for Chicago Mercy, stated, "The construction of the new pediatrics wing reflects our strong commitment to providing the highest possible quality medical care to children in our community."

-End-

Chapter 03

Creating Letterheads, Envelopes, and Business Cards

3

PERFORMANCE OBJECTIVES

Upon successful completion of chapter 3, you will be able to produce letterheads, envelopes, and business cards using Word features such as text boxes, ruled lines, WordArt, and templates.

DESKTOP PUBLISHING TERMS

Templates	Exact placement	Consistency
Line styles	Kerning	Weight
Ruled lines	Tracking	

WORD FEATURES USED

Anchor	Text boxes	Character spacing
Fonts	Format text box	WordArt
Letter template	Horizontal and vertical	AutoText
Letter Wizard	lines	Envelopes and Labels
Template folder	Borders and shading	Business card label
Drawing toolbar	Automatic kerning	definition
Click and type	Manual kerning	

In this chapter, you will produce business letterheads, envelopes, and business cards using your own design and creative skills as well as Word's Template feature. Although Word provides a variety of letter templates to choose from, they do not meet the needs of all situations. Information on how to customize an existing template and how to create your own design and layout from scratch are presented in this chapter. Ruled lines, kerning (the spacing between specific pairs of letters), and tracking (character spacing), along with Word's Envelopes and Labels, Text Box, and AutoText features, are also discussed.

Identifying the Purpose of Letterheads

In planning a letterhead design, think about its purpose. While the content of a letter may vary, the purpose of any letterhead is generally the same—to convey information, to establish an identity, and to project an image.

Conveying Information

Consider all the necessary information you want to include in your letterhead. Also, consider what items your readers expect to find in your letterhead. Although the information provided may vary, letterheads commonly contain the following:

- Name of company or organization
- Logo
- Address
- Shipping or mailing address, if different from street address
- Telephone number, including area code (include actual numbers if your phone number incorporates a catchy word as part of the number; include extra phone numbers, such as a local number and/or an 800 number, if any)
- Fax number, including area code
- E-mail address
- Internet or Web address
- Marketing statement or company slogan

The information in a letterhead supplies the reader with a means of contacting you in person, by phone, by e-mail, or by regular mail. Leaving out an important component in your letterhead can affect your company's business and project a careless attitude.

Establishing an Identity

DTP POINTERS
A letterhead conveys information, establishes an identity, and projects an image.

A business identity is often initiated through written communication. For example, a buyer from one company may write to another company inquiring about a certain product or asking for a price list; a real estate agent may send out a letter explaining his or her services to residents in surrounding communities; or, a volunteer organization may send letters to local businesses soliciting their support. Whatever the reason for the letter, a letterhead with a specific design and layout helps to establish an organization's identity. When readers are exposed to the same pattern of consistent elements in a letterhead over a period of time, they soon begin to establish a certain level of familiarity with the organization's name, logo, colors, etc. A letterhead is recognizable and identifiable.

You can further emphasize an organization's identity by using some of the design elements from a letterhead in other business documents. If you don't want to create your own design, many direct mail paper suppliers offer a whole line of attractively designed color letterheads, along with coordinating envelopes, business cards, brochures, postcards, note cards, disk labels, and more. All you have to do is plan the layout of the letterhead text to complement the existing design and then print on the preprinted papers. Purchasing a coordinating line of preprinted papers can save on the high costs of professional designing and printing. It also provides a convenient way to establish your identity among your readers. Some paper suppliers offer a sample kit of their papers for purchase at a reasonable price. This is a great opportunity to see and feel the papers and to test some of them in your printer.

Projecting an Image

Along with establishing an identity, think about the image that identity projects to your readers. Is it appropriate? As mentioned in chapter 1, assess your target audience. Who are they? What is their background, education, age, etc. What image do you want your readers to form in their minds about your company, business, or organization? What does their experience tell them to expect?

Look at the two different letterheads in figure 3.1. Without knowing any other supporting details, what image do you form in your mind about each of these hospitals? Why? The top letterhead projects a more fun, casual, somewhat juvenile, not-so-professional image while the bottom letterhead certainly conveys a more serious, businesslike attitude. Which image do you, as the reader, expect from a hospital? Even though the projected image may not be an accurate representation of either of the hospitals, it is the image that is presented to the reader and, therefore, it carries a lot of impact. On the other hand, giving your readers what they expect can sometimes lead to boredom. Your challenge is to create a design that gives the readers what they expect and, at the same time, sets your letterhead apart from the rest.

figure
3.1

What Image Do Each of These Letterheads Project?

St. Mary's Hospital

203 South Jefferson
Chicago, IL 63208
Phone: 312.555.6820
Fax: 312.555.6821

Mercy Hospital

**780 North 42ⁿᵈ Street
Chicago, IL 63209
Phone: 312.555.2035
Fax: 312.555.2086**

DTP POINTERS
Printing on high-quality
paper presents a
professional image

Printing your letterhead on high-quality paper may add to the cost, but it certainly presents a more professional image. An off-white, ivory, cream, or gray paper is a better choice than plain white. You may have to go to a commercial printer to purchase this kind of paper. Many print shops let you buy paper by the sheet, along with matching envelopes.

Using Word's Letterhead Templates

Template
A predesigned document
used as a basis for other
documents.

As discussed in chapter 2, Word includes a variety of predesigned *template* documents, including letterheads. At the New dialog box, select the Letters & Faxes tab to display the following Word letter templates:

- Letter Wizard.wiz (Helps you create a letter)
- Contemporary Letter.dot
- Elegant Letter.dot
- Professional Letter.dot

DTP POINTERS
Templates can provide the
framework for creating
customized documents.

The descriptive names of the letterhead templates coordinate with the descriptive names for the memo, fax, report, and resume templates provided by Word. This is an easy way for you to establish identity and consistency among both your internal and external business documents.

DTP POINTERS
Establish identity and
consistency among your
internal and external
business documents.

The body of a template document may contain some valuable user information. For example, when you select the Contemporary Letter from the New dialog box, the body of the letter contains a brief paragraph that includes the following sentence: *For more details on modifying this letter template, double-click* ✉. When you double-click the envelope icon, the letter is replaced with a completed sample letter. The body of this sample letter provides more specific information on how to use the existing template and how to customize the letterhead for your own use.

Using the Letter Wizard

Word provides a Letter Wizard that guides you through the steps for creating a single business or personal letter using the Contemporary, Professional, or Elegant Letter template or any other letter template that you may have created. The difference between accessing the letter templates directly through the New dialog box versus the Letter Wizard is that the wizard allows you to make various decisions on the letter style, the recipient and sender information, the wording used in the salutation and the closing, and the inclusion of specialized letter elements before the letter even displays on the screen. In addition, the Letter Wizard gives you the opportunity to make an envelope or label for the letter being created.

In certain documents that are constructed with a Wizard, such as letters, memos, and faxes, you may find that your name and/or address (or whoever is listed as the designated user of the computer) may be inserted automatically. This is the result of Word using specific information that is stored in User Information. The User Information feature is a way to store the name, initials, and address of the primary user of your Word program. For example, the Letter Wizard uses the Name listed in User Information in any of the letter closings it helps you create. However, it does not use this information if you select one of the letter templates from the New dialog box instead of using the Letter Wizard to create your letter. Word uses the Mailing Address from User Information as the default return address on envelopes. The Initials are used in conjunction with Word's Annotation feature—a feature that lets you leave notes to yourself or others in your document. To change or delete User Information, select <u>T</u>ools, <u>O</u>ptions, then click the User Information tab.

Customizing the Letter

After constructing a document with a wizard or template, the existing template document can be customized once it is displayed at the document screen. Any changes made only affect the document displayed on the screen, leaving the template available in its original format. Complete exercise 1 to create a Contemporary letter using the Letter Wizard. You will then customize the letter by changing the shading of some of the graphic elements included in the template.

exercise 1

Creating a Contemporary Letter with the Letter Wizard

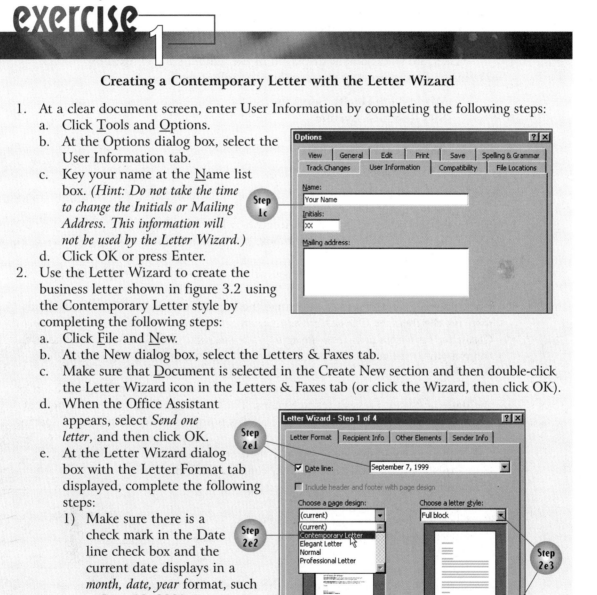

1. At a clear document screen, enter User Information by completing the following steps:
   a. Click Tools and Options.
   b. At the Options dialog box, select the User Information tab.
   c. Key your name at the Name list box. *(Hint: Do not take the time to change the Initials or Mailing Address. This information will not be used by the Letter Wizard.)*
   d. Click OK or press Enter.
2. Use the Letter Wizard to create the business letter shown in figure 3.2 using the Contemporary Letter style by completing the following steps:
   a. Click File and New.
   b. At the New dialog box, select the Letters & Faxes tab.
   c. Make sure that Document is selected in the Create New section and then double-click the Letter Wizard icon in the Letters & Faxes tab (or click the Wizard, then click OK).
   d. When the Office Assistant appears, select *Send one letter*, and then click OK.
   e. At the Letter Wizard dialog box with the Letter Format tab displayed, complete the following steps:
      1) Make sure there is a check mark in the Date line check box and the current date displays in a *month, date, year* format, such as June 10, 2001.
      2) Click the arrow in the Choose a page design list box and select *Contemporary Letter*.
      3) Make sure *Full block* displays as the letter style; then click Next>.

f. With the Recipient Info tab displayed, complete the following steps:
    1) In the Recipient's name text box, key **Mr. George Peraza**.
    2) In the Delivery address text box, key the following:

    > **Assistant Director, Health Services**
    > **Mercy Hospital**
    > **780 North 42nd Street**
    > **Chicago, IL 63209**

    3) In the Salutation section, select *Business,* and then click <u>N</u>ext>.
    4) With the Other Elements tab displayed and no options checked, click <u>N</u>ext>.
g. With the Sender Info tab displayed, complete the following steps:
    1) Make sure your name is displayed in the <u>S</u>ender's name text box.
    2) In the <u>R</u>eturn address text box, key the following:

    > **WorldWide Health Services**
    > **893 Renquist Avenue**
    > **Chicago, IL 65068**
    > **Phone: (312) 555-7350**
    > **Fax: (312) 555-4098**

    3) In the Closing section, click the down arrow to the right of the Complimentar<u>y</u> closing list box; select *Yours truly,* as the closing.
    4) In the <u>J</u>ob title text box, key **Director of Human Resources**.
    5) In the <u>W</u>riter/typist initials text box, key your initials in lowercase.
    6) Click <u>F</u>inish.
h. When the Office Assistant asks if you would like to do more with the letter, click Cancel.
i. Click <u>F</u>ile, Page Set<u>u</u>p and then change the bottom margin to 0.5 inch. If Word displays the message *One or more margins are set outside the printable area of the page. Choose the Fix button to increase the appropriate margins.*, click <u>F</u>ix. Word will adjust the margin to the minimum amount allowed by your printer; then click OK or press Enter.
j. With the letter displayed on the screen, position the insertion point to the left of the date, and then press Enter five times. The spacing will be more than normal because the *Date* style, which is active at this point, includes 13 points of spacing after each paragraph.
k. Select the return address in the upper right corner and change the font to Copperplate Gothic Bold and the text color to Dark Blue.
l. Change the color of the vertical dotted line by completing the following steps:
    1) Click <u>V</u>iew and then <u>H</u>eader and Footer.
    2) Select the dotted line (a text box appears) and change the text color to Dark Blue.

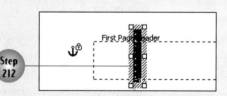

m. Insert the company name on top of the gray shaded rectangle (which is an AutoShape inserted in the header pane) by completing the following steps:
    1) Position the mouse pointer in the shaded rectangle until it displays as an arrow with a four-headed arrow attached; then right-click one time to display a shortcut menu.
    2) Click Add Te<u>x</u>t.

3) Change the font to 24-point Copperplate Gothic Bold and the text color to Dark Blue; then key **WorldWide Health Services**. (The text will not completely fit in the box; the size will be adjusted next.)

n. Change the size of the AutoShape rectangle by completing the following steps:

1) With the rectangle still selected, click <u>F</u>ormat and Aut<u>o</u>Shape (or double-click the AutoShape border).

2) At the AutoShape dialog box, select the Size tab. In the Size and rotate section, change the H<u>e</u>ight to 0.48 inch and make sure the Wi<u>d</u>th displays as 7.5 inches.

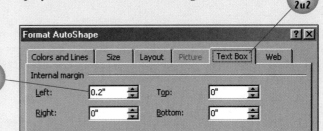

3) Click OK or press Enter.

o. Click <u>C</u>lose on the Header and Footer toolbar.

p. Position the insertion point to the right of the date and press Enter once to increase the spacing between the date and inside address.

q. Select the one paragraph of body text; then key the three paragraphs as displayed in figure 3.2, pressing Enter one time between paragraphs.

r. Position the insertion point after your reference initials and then key :**c03ex01, Letter**.

s. Select all of the text in the letter from the date through the end of the reference line; then change the font to 11-point Book Antiqua.

t. Insert the slogan on top of the shaded rectangle (which is an AutoShape inserted in the footer pane) located at the bottom of the page by completing the following steps:

1) Click <u>V</u>iew, then <u>H</u>eader and Footer.
2) Click the Switch Between Header and Footer button on the Header and Footer toolbar.
3) Position the mouse in the shaded rectangle until it displays as an arrow with a four-headed arrow attached; then right-click one time.
4) Click Add Te<u>x</u>t.
5) Change the font to 11-point Book Antiqua Bold Italic, the text color to Dark Blue; then key **Serving those in need around the globe**!.
6) Click F<u>o</u>rmat, <u>P</u>aragraph, and change the Spacing <u>B</u>efore to 12 points. Click OK.

u. Adjust the distance between the slogan and the dotted line by completing the following steps:

1) Click in the dotted line to display the text box surrounding it.
2) Double-click the text box border (or click F<u>o</u>rmat, then Aut<u>o</u>Shape); then select the Text Box tab at the Format AutoShape dialog box.
3) In the Internal margin section, change the <u>L</u>eft option to 0.2 inch.
4) Click OK or press Enter.

v. Change the color of the dotted line by selecting it and changing the text color to Dark Blue. Click <u>C</u>lose on the Header and Footer toolbar.

w. Save the completed letter and name it c03ex01, Letter.

x. Print and then close c03ex01, Letter.

figure

3.2

Exercise 1

WORLDWIDE HEALTH SERVICES
893 RENQUIST AVENUE
CHICAGO, IL 65068
PHONE: (312) 555-7350
FAX: (312) 555-4098

WORLDWIDE HEALTH SERVICES

August 25, 2001

Mr. George Peraza
Assistant Director, Health Services
Mercy Hospital
780 North 42nd Street
Chicago, IL 63209

Dear Mr. Peraza:

Thank you for your inquiry about employment opportunities at WorldWide Health Services. We appreciate your interest in our company.

Although your background is impressive, we currently have no openings that match your skills and qualifications. We will keep your résumé on file for six months for review should we have an opening for which you are qualified.

Again, thank you for your interest. Best wishes for success in your career search.

Yours truly,

Your Name
Director of Human Resources

xx:c03ex01, Letter

Serving those in need around the globe! •

Evaluating Your Customized Letterhead

Can you see how the concepts of focus, balance, proportion, contrast, directional flow, consistency, and color are used in the letter you just created from exercise 1 (see figure 3.2)? The shaded rectangle, containing the company name, acts as a focal point, provides contrast, and draws the reader's eyes to the natural starting position for reading (upper left corner of the page), initiating the directional flow in the letter. The reader is able to readily identify the name of the company, which is set in 24-point Copperplate Gothic Bold, Dark Blue. The company name and the shaded rectangle continue the directional flow by drawing the reader's eyes to the right side of the page. The globe watermark acts as a secondary focal point that draws the eyes back over to the left side of the page and to the body text. The shaded rectangle located in the bottom left corner of the page leads the reader down to the bottom of the page and over to the right. The horizontal dotted line provides a finishing touch, leading the reader to the bottom right corner of the page. Can you visualize a form of the Z directional flow pattern in this letter's design and layout? Consistent elements are exemplified by the repeated use of the same typeface and color in the return address, company name, and slogan; the shaded rectangles; and the dark blue of the dotted lines. This letter utilizes several examples of asymmetrical design. The vertical dotted line at the top left of the page and the accompanying white space help to balance the block of text containing the return address and phone and fax numbers. Also note that the white space provided by the wider left margin and the globe watermark extending into the left margin counterbalance the larger block of letter text. In addition, the horizontal dotted line and the surrounding white space located at the bottom of the page help to balance out the weight of the gray shaded rectangle containing the slogan.

Word's template documents are definitely an easy and convenient way to create a variety of professional-looking documents, but they cannot meet the needs of all people, companies, or organizations in all situations. However, templates can serve as the framework for creating customized documents and new templates. Remember, a document created from a template can be individualized (as in exercise 1), a new template can be created from an existing document, an existing template can be edited permanently, or a whole new template can be created from scratch.

Designing Your Own Letterhead

Designing your own letterhead lets you create your own identity and image while cutting costs at the same time. In upcoming exercises, you will have the chance to create a letterhead from scratch and to convert the letterhead into a template.

Smaller businesses and newly created businesses may not have the financial resources to purchase a letterhead designed by a graphic designer and created by a commercial printer. With the lower-cost laser and ink jet printers available today and your Word software, you can create professional-looking letterheads economically. In addition, when working with a commercial printer, you would probably be required to meet a minimum purchase order. If you produce your own letterhead, you can print any amount you need and save yourself the upfront costs of purchasing a large number of letterheads. Also, as long as you have a supply of paper, your letterhead is always only a few keystrokes away. Second sheets to go along with your letterhead are readily available, too. All things considered, designing and producing your own letterhead is a cost-effective alternative to having it created through an outside source.

Designing and producing your own letterhead takes some time and practice. When you have completed the planning stage for your letterhead and you are actually ready to "create" the design, get out pencil and paper and make some thumbnail sketches. This is a great way to experiment with layout and design.

Incorporating Design Concepts in a Letterhead

When creating thumbnail sketches and, ultimately, your letterhead, think of the following design concepts, as presented in chapter 1:

- **Focus:** What is the focal point(s) in your letterhead? What is the most important information? What is the least important information? Is there more than one focal element? If so, is there a natural progression from one to the other?

- **Balance:** Is your layout and design symmetrical with similar elements distributed evenly on the page, such as a horizontally centered layout? Or is it asymmetrical with dissimilar elements distributed unevenly on the page in such a way as to balance one another out?

- **Proportion:** Are design elements sized in proportion to their relative importance to the intended message? Are the design elements sized in proportion to one another? Is the type size of the company name in proportion to the company logo? To the other letterhead information? To the type size that will be used for the body text? Is the letterhead in proportion to the space left to create the letter? Your letterhead should not take up any more than 2 inches at the top of the page, preferably less.

- **Contrast:** Are there varying degrees of lightness and darkness? Is there enough contrast to make it noticeable, or is it too weak? Is there enough surrounding white space assigned to darker elements on the page? Does the typeface used in the letterhead provide a complementary contrast to the typeface that will be used in the body text? Does the use of color provide a pleasing contrast?

- **Directional flow:** Are related items grouped and positioned close to each other? Does the type of alignment used establish a visual connection between items on the page? Are the design elements strategically placed to create a natural flow of information? Is the reader able to logically progress from the more important information to the less important information? Do text, special characters, ruled lines, and graphic images direct the flow rather than impede the flow of information?

- **Consistency:** What are the consistent elements of your page layout and design? Is a particular typeface consistently used in your letterhead even though it may vary in type size, type style, or color? Is one color repeated sparingly to emphasize important or distinctive elements (called "spot" color)? Is there some repeating element that ties the letterhead to subsequent pages, such as a ruled horizontal line that is repeated as a footer on each page?

- **Color:** Does the use and intensity of color relate proportionally to the importance of the item? Is color used sparingly to provide emphasis and contrast? Does the color used meet readers' expectations for the mood, tone, and image of your organization and your message?

Using the Click and Type Feature to Position Design Elements

Word's Click and Type feature can be used to quickly insert text, graphics, tables, or other items into a blank area of a document. Change to Print Layout View and then double-click in a blank area. Click and Type automatically adds the formatting necessary to position the insertion point where you double-clicked the mouse button. For example, if you double-click in a blank area that is approximately 4 inches from the left margin, Word sets a left tab at that position and places the insertion point at that location as if you had set the tab position and pressed the Tab key manually. If you double-click in a blank area below text, Word automatically inserts returns and places the insertion point at that location.

Changing Paragraph Alignment with Click and Type

The Click and Type feature also may be used to change paragraph alignment. To do this, hover the I-beam pointer near the left margin, the center of the page, or the right margin. The I-beam pointer will display with short horizontal lines representing the different alignments as displayed in figure 3.3. Double-click when you see the correct alignment displayed. The insertion point will be placed in the correct location, and the corresponding alignment will be activated on the Formatting toolbar.

figure

3.3

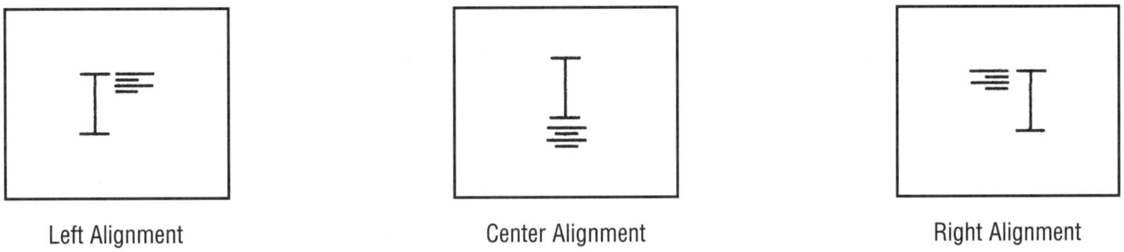

Left Alignment	Center Alignment	Right Alignment

Assessing the Limitations of Click and Type

The Click and Type feature, the Enter key, the space bar, and the Tab key are all ways of placing the insertion point on the page at different locations, but they may not give you the exact location desired for positioning design elements in desktop publishing. For example, pressing the Enter key one time after a line of text or a design element may not allow enough vertical white space, but pressing Enter two times may allow too much white space. Adjustments to the spacing before and after a paragraph (or hard return) can be made more specifically at the Paragraph dialog box; however, paragraph spacing adjustments only affect vertical spacing of text and have no effect on graphic elements. The space bar and the Tab function in Word can place text in specific locations horizontally across the page, but have no effect on the positioning of graphic elements or vertical placement. The Click and Type feature, while useful, is limited also because it automatically inserts tabs, returns, or horizontal alignment formatting to position the insertion point in a specific location.

Using Text Boxes to Place Text at Exact Locations on a Page

A text box is used as a container for text and/or graphics. Text boxes are extremely useful in desktop publishing because text and/or graphics enclosed in a text box can be dragged to any position on the page using the mouse, or *exact* horizontal and vertical locations can be specified. Almost anything that can be inserted into a Word document, such as text, tables, worksheets, pictures, or other objects, can be placed into a text box. (Exceptions include a page break, column break, section break, or text formatted into columns.) A text box can also be inserted into a document as a placeholder for a photograph or illustration to be inserted at a later date. The text box feature lets you keep text and graphics together, makes text flow around other text or graphics, allows you to layer text and/or graphics, enables you to align design elements on a page, allows just the right amount of white space around elements, and helps fit text and other design elements into a specific amount of space (called copy fitting) on a page.

Understanding Text Box Characteristics

A text box is created in the drawing layer and is considered a drawing object. Like any other object in Word (lines, AutoShapes, WordArt, and some graphics images) a text box can be placed above or below the main text (which is created in the text layer) in a Word document. Text can be wrapped around a text box in a variety of ways, the direction of the text can be changed, and text boxes can also be linked (discussed in chapter 11). Text boxes, as well as other Word objects, can be formatted by using options from the Drawing toolbar, such as applying 3-D effects, shadows, border styles and colors, fills, and backgrounds. Text boxes can also be formatted by accessing the Format Text Box dialog box. A text box does not automatically expand to the amount or size of text, table, picture, or object that is being inserted. For example, if you key more text than can fit in the text box, only the part of the text that fits within the text box size will be visible. Text that has been keyed in the text box will not be lost even if it is not visible; simply adjust the size of the text box.

Turning on the Drawing Toolbar

You must turn on Word's Drawing toolbar to create text boxes. To turn on the display of the toolbar, choose one of the following methods:

Drawing

- Click the Drawing button on the Standard toolbar.
- Choose <u>V</u>iew, <u>T</u>oolbars, click Drawing (this inserts a check mark in the check box); then click OK or press Enter.
- Position the arrow pointer in any gray area of any currently displayed toolbar, click the right mouse button, and then click Drawing from the drop-down menu.

When you select the Drawing toolbar, the toolbar appears at the bottom of the screen above the Status bar. The Drawing toolbar and the names of each button are shown in figure 3.4.

figure
3.4
Drawing Toolbar

Inserting a Text Box

You can insert a text box by using the Insert, Text Box command from the Insert menu or by using the Text Box button on the Drawing toolbar. Either method will change the arrow pointer to crosshairs and automatically change the view to Print Layout View. Position the crosshairs where you want the top left corner of the text box to appear, hold down the left mouse button, drag the outline of the text box to the location where you want the lower right corner of the text box to appear, and then release the mouse button. After the mouse button is released, an empty box with a hatched border will appear. As an alternative, simply position the crosshairs and click the left mouse button one time and Word will insert a one-inch square text box.

Text Box

Inserting Text Box Contents

After a text box has been inserted, the insertion point is automatically positioned within the text box so that you can enter text, insert a picture, insert an Excel worksheet, or add whatever is needed. To edit text in a text box, simply position the I-beam within the text box at the desired location and click once. You can also insert existing text into a text box. If you keyed some text and then decide to place the text in a text box, simply select the desired text and then click the Text Box button on the Drawing toolbar.

Setting Internal Margins in a Text Box

By default, a text box has left and right internal margins of 0.1 of an inch, and top and bottom internal margins of 0.05 of an inch. These margins can be adjusted to increase or decrease the distance between the contents of the text box and the text box borders. To do this, select the desired text box, click Format, Text Box, or double-click the text box border, and then select the Text Box tab. At the Text Box tab, as shown in figure 3.5, change the left, right, top, and bottom internal margins as desired.

figure
3.5

Text Box Tab Displayed from the Format Text Box Dialog Box

Format Text Box

Colors and Lines | Size | Layout | Picture | Text Box | Web

Internal margin

Left: 0.1"   Top: 0.05"

Right: 0.1"   Bottom: 0.05"

Format Callout...   Convert to Frame...

OK   Cancel

Sizing a Text Box

A text box (or object) must first be selected before the size can be changed. To do this, position the I-beam pointer within the text box, and then click the left mouse button. This selects the text box and adds sizing handles (white squares) to the text box borders. The following two methods may be used to size a text box:

- **Using the Mouse:** Select the text box (or object) and then position the mouse pointer on a sizing handle until it turns into a double-headed arrow. Hold down the left mouse button, drag the outline of the text box toward or away from the center of the object until it is the desired size, and then release the mouse button. To maintain the proportions of the existing text box dimensions, use one of the corner sizing handles to change both the width and the height at the same time. This method is easy but sometimes limiting when trying to make very precise adjustments.

- **Using the Format Text Box Dialog Box:** Select the text box (or object), point the mouse pointer at the text box border until it turns into a four-headed arrow, double-click (or right-click the text border), and then select Format Text Box from the shortcut menu; or select the line first and then choose Format, Text Box. At the Format Text Box dialog box, choose the Size tab. In the Size and rotate section, key the desired measurements for the width and height of the text box. As an alternative to putting in specific measurements in the Size and rotate section, you can enter width and height measurements as a percentage of the original size of the text box in the Scale section. If you want to change the height and width settings in relation to each other, select the Lock aspect ratio option in the Scale section. Using the Format Text Box dialog box for sizing allows you to precisely adjust the size of the text box.

Positioning a Text Box at an Exact Location on a Page

DTP POINTERS
Change the display to whole page when repositioning a text box.

One of the biggest advantages to using a text box is the ability to easily position the text box anywhere on the page in a document. When positioning a text box on a page, changing Zoom to Whole Page is helpful so that you can see the entire page on the screen. If you want to move a text box to a different page in a multipage document, choose Zoom from the View menu, and then change the Many pages option (as discussed in chapter 1) to display the desired configuration of pages. Select the text box, position it, and then return the view back to your preferred document view. You can use one of the following three methods (or in combination) to position a text box:

- **Using the Mouse:** Position the I-beam pointer inside the text box border (or object) until it displays as an arrow with a four-headed arrow attached. Hold down the left mouse button, drag the outline of the object to the new location, and then release the mouse button. This method is easy but sometimes limiting when trying to make very precise adjustments.

- **Using the Keyboard:** Select the text box (or object) and then press one of the arrow keys (left, right, up, or down). This method is very useful when you want to make slight adjustments to the position of the text box.

- **Using the Format Text Box Dialog Box:** Select the text box (or object), point the mouse pointer at the text box border until it turns into a four-headed arrow, double-click (or right-click the text border), and then select Format Text Box from the shortcut menu; or select the text box first and choose Format, Text Box. At the Format Text Box dialog box, choose the Layout tab. In the Horizontal Alignment section, you may choose left, center, or right alignment, or set your own specifications. To set other placement specifications, make sure Other is selected and click the Advanced button. At the Advanced Layout dialog box, select the Picture Position tab. In the Horizontal section, make sure Absolute position is selected, and then key in the desired measurement in the corresponding text box. In the to the left of: list box, select the point (Margin, Page, Column, or Character) from which you want to horizontally position the selected line. Follow the same process with the Vertical section. This method allows more precise control over the placement of an object. For example, the settings in figure 3.6 indicate that the selected line will be positioned horizontally 2.5 inches from the left edge of the page and 1.2 inches below the top edge of the page.

figure

3.6

Advanced Layout Dialog Box

Copying a Text Box

If you want to make an exact copy of a text box so you can place it in a different location, position the insertion point inside the text box border until the I-beam turns into an arrow with a four-headed arrow attached. Hold down the left mouse button and hold down the Ctrl key while dragging a copy of the text box to a new location.

Anchoring a Text Box

All objects, including text boxes, are automatically anchored or attached to the paragraph closest to the object. With the object selected and nonprinting symbols displayed (click the Show/Hide ¶ button on the Standard toolbar), an *anchor* symbol will display to the left of the paragraph to which the object is anchored as shown in figure 3.7. If a text box is repositioned, the anchor moves to the paragraph closest to the text box. The following points clarify the anchoring concept:

- A text box always appears on the same page as the paragraph to which it is anchored. By default, the text box moves with the paragraph to which it is anchored.

- If you do not want the text box (or object) to move with the paragraph to which it is anchored, double-click the text box border to access the Format Text Box dialog box. Select the Layout tab and click Advanced. At the Advanced Layout dialog box, make sure the Picture tab is selected, and then remove the check mark from the Move object with text check box.

- To always keep the object on the same page as the paragraph to which it is anchored, access the Advanced Layout dialog box, and click the Lock anchor check box to insert a check mark. This feature allows the object to be moved any place on the same page as the paragraph to which it is anchored, but not to another page. If the paragraph is moved to another page, the object can then be moved to that page also.

- For an object to remain stationary at a specific location on a page regardless of the text that surrounds it, access the Advanced Layout dialog box. Enter specific measurements at the Absolute position options in the Horizontal and Vertical sections and make corresponding selections at the to the left of: and below: list boxes. Last, remove the check mark from the Move object with text check box.

figure

3.7

Anchor Symbol Associated with the Selected Text Box

Wrapping Text Around a Text Box

By default, a text box displays in the layer above or "in front of" text as illustrated in figure 3.9. If you want text to wrap around a text box, first select the text box, then display the Format Text Box dialog box, and then click the Layout tab. Several wrapping options are available as explained in figure 3.8 and illustrated in figure 3.9.

Text Box Wrapping Style Options

The Wrapping styles offered at the Format Text Box dialog box Layout tab include:
- In Line with text: The object is placed in the text layer at the insertion point in a line of text. This wrapping style is not available with text boxes.
- Square: Text wraps around all four sides of the selected text box or object.
- Tight: Text wraps tightly around the shape of an object rather than the box holding the object. (This style is more apparent when applied to a shape other than a square or rectangle.) After you select Tight, you can adjust the dotted wrapping perimeter by clicking the Text Wrapping button on the Picture toolbar and then clicking Edit Wrap Points. Drag the dotted line or sizing handles to reshape the wrapping perimeter.
- Behind text: Text wrapping is removed and the text box (object) is placed in its own layer behind the text layer in the document. To access an object behind text, click the Select Objects button on the Drawing toolbar, then position the mouse pointer over the object until it turns into an arrow with a four-headed arrow attached. Click the left mouse button to select the text box (object).
- In front of text: Text wrapping is removed and the text box (object) is placed in front of text in its own layer. This is the default setting.

The Advanced Layout dialog box, accessed by clicking the Advanced button at the Layout tab and then selecting the Text Wrapping tab, offers additional wrapping styles and associated options:
- Through: This option is the same as Tight. Text not only wraps around the shape of an object, but it also flows through any open areas of the object box. This option may produce a visible change with certain graphic images, but no changes will occur when applied to a text box.
- Top & bottom: Text wraps around the top and bottom of the text box (object) but not on both sides. Text stops at the top of the text box (object) and restarts on the line below the object.

The Wrap text section at the Text Wrapping tab in the Advanced Layout dialog box operates in conjunction with the Wrapping style section and offers:
- Both sides: Text wraps on both sides of the text box.
- Left: Text wraps along the left side of the text box but not on the right side.
- Right: Text wraps along the right side of the text box but not on the left side.
- Largest side: Text wraps along the largest side of the object. This does not produce any changes when applied to a text box.

The Text Wrapping tab also provides a Distance from text section. In this section, you can set the distance between the edges of the text box and the surrounding text. The choice made in the Wrapping style section determines which measurements may be changed.

Text wrapping style may also be selected by clicking the Text Wrapping button on the Picture toolbar. The wrapping styles available from the drop-down menu that displays include Square, Tight, Behind Text, In Front of Text, Top and Bottom, Through, and Edit Wrap Points.

figure 3.9

Text Box Wrapping Style Examples

Text boxes are extremely useful in desktop publishing because text and/or graphics enclosed in a text box can be dragged to any position on the page using the mouse, or precise locations can be spe xt Box dialog box. Almost anything that can be inserted into a Word document, such as text, tables, worksheets, pictures, or other objects, can be placed into a text box. (Exceptions include a page break, column break, section break, or text formatted into columns.) A text box can also be inserted into a document as a placeholder for a photograph or illustration to be inserted at a

Top and Bottom

later date. The text box feature lets you keep text and graphics together, makes text flow around other text or graphics, allows you to layer text and/or graphics, enables you to align design elements on a page, allows just the right amount of white space around elements, and helps fit text and other design elements into a specific amount of space (called copy fitting) on a page.

A text box is used as a container for text and/or graphics. A text box is created

in the drawing layer. and is considered a drawing object. Like any other object in Word (lines, AutoShapes, WordArt, and some graphics images) a text box can be placed above or below the **Square** main text (which is created in the text layer) in a Word document. Text can be wrapped around a text box in a variety of ways, the direction of the text can be changed, and text boxes can also be linked (discussed in chapter 11). Text boxes, as well as other Word objects, can be formatted by using options from the Drawing toolbar, such as applying 3-D effects, shadows, border styles and colors, fills, and backgrounds. Text boxes can also be formatted by accessing the Format Text Box dialog box. A text box does not automatically expand to the amount or size of text, table, picture, or object that is being inserted. For example, if you key more text than can fit in the text box, only the part of the text that fits within the text box size will be visible. Text that has been keyed in the text box will not be lost even if it is not visible; simply adjust the size of the text box.

Square, Left (side) only

Text boxes are extremely useful in desktop publishing because text and/or graphics enclosed in a text box can be dragged to any position on the page using the mouse, or precise horizontal and vertical locations can be specified Text Box dialog box. Almost anything that can be inserted into a Word document, such as text, tables, worksheets, pictures, or other objects, can be placed into a text box. (Exceptions include a page break, column break, section break, or text formatted into columns.) A text box can also be inserted into a document as a placeholder for a photograph or illustration to be inserted at a

Square, Right (side) only

later date. The text box feature lets you keep text and graphics together, makes text flow around other text or graphics, allows you to layer text and/or graphics, enables you to align design elements on a page, allows just the right amount of white space around elements, and helps fit text and other design elements into a specific amount of space (called copy fitting) on a page.

A text box is used as a container for text and/or graphics. A text box is created in the drawing layer. and is considered a drawing object. Like any other object in

Removing a Text Box

To remove a text box and its contents, select the text box, and then press the Delete key.

Customizing a Text Box

By default, a text box has a black single-line border around all sides and contains white background fill as displayed in figure 3.7. However, a text box can be customized in a variety of ways, including changing style and color of the border and changing the background fill color.

Changing the Text Box Border

DTP POINTERS
Customize borders by changing the line style, thickness, color, and location.

The following methods, along with your own imagination, can be used to customize the border of a text box (object):

- **To add, remove, or change the color of a text box border:** Select the text box, then click the Line Color arrow on the Drawing toolbar to display the line color palette (or click F̲ormat, Text Box, then select the Colors and Lines tab.) Select a color from the line color palette or select the M̲ore Line Colors command to pick from an extended selection of standard colors or to create your own custom colors. Select P̲atterned Lines to add a pattern to the text box border. Choose No Line to remove a border from a text box (object).

Line Color

- **To change the style and thickness of a text box border:** Select the text box (or object), then click the Line Style button on the Drawing toolbar to display the line style palette. Select the desired line style and thickness. To further refine the line style and weight of your text box border, select M̲ore Lines to display the Colors and Lines tab of the Format Text Box dialog box. You may also choose from a selection of dashed lines by clicking the Dash Style button on the Drawing toolbar.

Line Style

Dash Style

- **To add shadow box effects to a text box border:** Select the text box (or object), click the Shadow button on the Drawing toolbar. Select a shadow design from the shadow palette that displays. Click the S̲hadow Settings command to display the Shadow Settings toolbar. Use the four Nudge Shadow buttons to move the shadow in small increments either closer to the shape or farther away. Use the Shadow Color button to change the color of the shadow, and use the Shadow On/Off button to add or remove the shadow effect.

Shadow

- **To add a three-dimensional look to a text box (or object):** Select the text box, and then click the 3-D button on the Drawing toolbar. Select from the choices offered on the 3-D options palette. To customize any of the 3-D options, click the 3̲-D Settings option to display the 3-D Settings toolbar. Use the buttons on this toolbar for turning 3-D on or off and changing the tilt, depth, direction, and light source.

3D

Changing the Fill

You can use the following methods to fill a text box or any drawing object with solid or gradient (shaded) colors, a pattern, a texture, or a picture:

- **To add solid color background fill:** Select the desired text box, then check the color of the stripe on the Fill Color button on the Drawing toolbar. If the stripe is the fill color you want, simply click the Fill Color button. To select a different fill color, click the arrow to the right of the Fill Color button to display the Fill Color palette and select the desired color. If you don't see the color you want, click M̲ore Fill Colors to display the Colors dialog box. Click a color on the Standard tab, or click the Custom tab to mix your own color. Click OK or press Enter. Word saves the custom color you select in the Standard tab or the Custom tab and places it in its own color block in the Fill Color palette in a new row above the M̲ore Fill Colors command. You can also find these same color options by selecting the Colors and Lines tab in the Format Text Box dialog box, and clicking the C̲olor list box in the Fill Section.

Fill Color

- **To add gradient (a single color that fades gradually to another color) background fill:** Select the text box (or object) and then click the arrow to the right of the Fill Color button on the Drawing toolbar. Select Fill Effects, and then select the Gradient tab at the Fill Effects dialog box. (Or you can click Format, Text Box, Colors and Lines tab, Fill Effects.) In the Colors section of the Gradient tab, select One color to produce a single color gradient that gradually fades to black or white; then choose the color you want from the Color 1 list box. Drag the slider on the Dark/Light slider bar towards Dark to make the selected color fade to black or towards Light to make the color fade to white. Use the Two colors option to produce gradient shading that gradually fades from one color to another color. Use the Preset option to select from a list of predesigned gradient fills. In the Shading styles section, select the desired style of gradient shading, and then select the desired variation of the shading style in the Variants section. Click OK or press Enter. See examples of different gradient colors, shading styles, and variations in figure 3.10.
- **To add textured background fill:** Select the text box (or object); then access the Fill Effects dialog box. Select the Texture tab, then click the desired texture sample in the Texture section. Click OK or press Enter. At the Texture tab, click Other Texture to be able to access other texture or background files you may have stored on disk.
- **To add a pattern to background fill:** Select the text box (or object), then access the Fill Effects dialog box. Select the Pattern tab, then click the desired pattern block in the Pattern section. Click the Foreground list box to select a color for the dots, dashes, lines, waves, etc., of the pattern. Click the Background list box to select a color for the spaces between the dots, dashes, lines, waves, etc. Click OK or press Enter.
- **To add a picture for background fill:** Select the text box (or object), then access the Fill Effects dialog box. Select the Picture tab, then click the desired picture in the Picture section. Click OK or press Enter. At the Picture tab, click Select Picture to be able to access other picture files you may have stored on disk.

figure 3.10

Examples of Gradient Color and Shading Styles

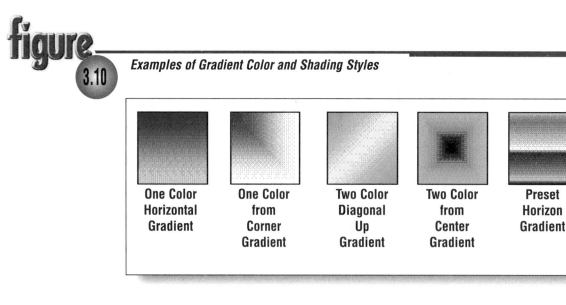

| One Color Horizontal Gradient | One Color from Corner Gradient | Two Color Diagonal Up Gradient | Two Color from Center Gradient | Preset Horizon Gradient |

Creating Horizontal and Vertical Ruled Lines
Using Word's Drawing Toolbar

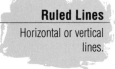

In Word, you may create horizontal and/or vertical lines anywhere on a page using the Line feature on the Drawing toolbar. As with text boxes, you can adjust the size, position, color, and shading of lines drawn with the Drawing toolbar. In typesetting, these horizontal and vertical lines are called *rules, ruling lines, or ruled lines* to distinguish them from lines of type.

Horizontal and vertical ruled lines are used in a document to guide readers eyes across and/or down the page, to separate one section of text from another, to separate columns of text, or to add visual interest. Remember that ruled lines act as boundaries to the surrounding text. A thicker line serves as more of a barrier than a thinner line. For example, a thin vertical line separating columns of text tends to keep the reader's eyes from jumping over to the next column. Alternately, a thicker ruled line between columns tends to tell the reader that the information in one column is entirely separate from the information in the next column. Keep this same idea in mind when considering using ruled lines with headings. Ruled lines can be placed above the heading rather than below the heading. This way the reader definitely knows that the heading belongs to the text that follows it. In addition, when using ruled lines, be consistent in their purpose and their appearance.

Ruled Lines
Horizontal or vertical lines.

DTP POINTERS
Ruled lines act as boundaries to surrounding text.

Drawing Horizontal and Vertical Lines

To insert a horizontal or vertical line using the Drawing toolbar, click the Line button (the fifth button from the left), then position the crosshairs where you want the line to begin. To create a perfectly straight horizontal or vertical line, hold down the Shift key and the left mouse button, drag the mouse horizontally or vertically to the location where you want the line to end, and then release the mouse button and the Shift key. (Ragged or imperfect lines are created when the Shift key is not pressed during the drawing process.) To create horizontal or vertical arrow lines, follow the same basic procedure but click the Arrow button (the sixth button from the left) on the Drawing toolbar instead of the Line button. To display the crosshairs continuously to draw additional lines, double-click on the Line (or Arrow) button, and then draw any number of lines. Click the Line (or Arrow) button again to discontinue line drawing.

Line

Arrow

Sizing Horizontal and Vertical Lines

Sizing a line created with the Drawing toolbar is similar to sizing a text box. Select the line to be sized, position the mouse pointer on either sizing handle until it turns into a double-headed arrow (hold down the Shift key if you want a straight line), drag the cross hairs in the appropriate direction until the line is the desired length, and then release the left mouse button. For more precise measurements, select the line (or object), double-click the left mouse button (or select the line first, and then select Format, AutoShape). At the Format AutoShape dialog box, select the Size tab. In the Size and rotate section, key the desired length of the line in the Width list box.

Positioning Horizontal and Vertical Lines

Horizontal and vertical lines may be positioned in the same way a text box is positioned. Select the line, and then use the mouse, the arrow keys on the keyboard, or the options at the Format AutoShape dialog box Layout tab or the Advanced Layout dialog box.

Anchoring Horizontal and Vertical Lines

Lines created from the Drawing toolbar are automatically anchored or attached to the paragraph closest to the object. Refer to the previous section in this chapter, "Anchoring a Text Box," for clarification on the relationship between a line (or object) and the paragraph to which it is anchored.

Deleting Horizontal and Vertical Lines

To remove a line created with the Drawing toolbar, select the line, then press the Delete key.

Customizing Horizontal and Vertical Lines

Weight and Style

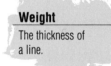

Weight
The thickness of a line.

Line Style

Dash Style

Arrow Style

In typesetting, the thickness of a line, called its *weight*, is measured in points. Word defaults to a line thickness of 3/4 of a point. To change the style or weight of a line, select the line first. You can then select different styles and weights of solid lines from the Line Style palette that displays when you click the Line Style button (the fifteenth button from the left) on the Drawing toolbar. Click the Dash Style button (the sixteenth button from the left) on the Drawing toolbar to choose from various styles of dashed lines or click the Arrow Style button (the seventeenth button from the left) to choose from a variety of arrow lines that begin and/or end with arrows, circles, or diamond shapes.

To have more control over the style of your lines (solid, dashed, or arrow), you can select <u>M</u>ore Lines from the Line Style palette or <u>M</u>ore Arrows from the Arrow Style palette to display the Format AutoShape dialog box. (You may also double-click the line you want to edit or select the line first, and then click F<u>o</u>rmat, <u>A</u>utoShape.) From this dialog box with the Colors and Lines tab chosen, you can increase or decrease the point measurement by 0.25 of a point by using the up or down arrows in the <u>W</u>eight list box or you can key in any desired measurement into the list box. It is not necessary to key "pt" when keying a weight measurement. Figure 3.11 shows several styles of horizontal ruled lines at varying point sizes (weights). To draw several lines of the same style and weight, double-click the Line or Arrow button first, as mentioned above.

figure

3.11 *Varying Weights and Styles of Lines*

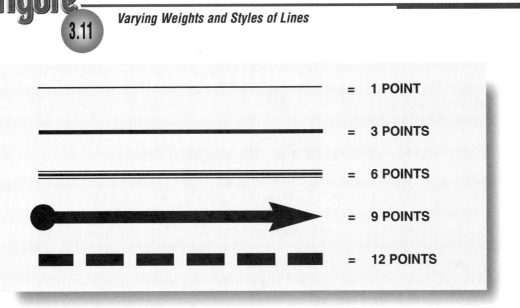

Color

Changing the color of a horizontal or vertical line created from the Drawing toolbar is done the same way as changing the color of a text box border. Refer to the previous section in this chapter, Changing the Text Box Border, under the heading Customizing a Text Box.

Shadow and 3-D Effects

Shadow and 3-D effects can be applied to lines just as they can with text boxes. Refer to the previous section in this chapter, Customizing a Text Box.

Creating Horizontal Lines Using the Borders Toolbar

Word's Borders feature can be used to add horizontal or vertical lines in headers and/or footers, as well as to any other text. Every paragraph you create in Word contains an invisible frame. (Remember that a paragraph may contain text or it may only consist of a hard return.) A border can be added to the invisible frame that exists around a paragraph or to specific sides. Consequently, you can add a border above and/or below a paragraph to create a horizontal line, or you can add a border to the left and/or right sides of a paragraph to create a vertical line that is equal to the length of the paragraph. A ruled line created with the borders feature stays with the paragraph that was current when the feature was applied.

To create a border on the top or sides of your paragraph, you may use the Border button on the Formatting toolbar. The Border button icon changes according to the most recent border position selected. To change the position of the border, click the arrow to the right of the Border button, and then select the desired border location. For example, to insert a horizontal line above the current

Border

paragraph select the Top Border option. To add a border to more than one paragraph, select the paragraphs first and then click the desired option. You can further customize lines created with the Border button by choosing Format, then Borders and Shading. At the Borders and Shading dialog box, options exist to change the border settings, the border line style, the border line color, the border line width, the border location, and the distance between any border and text.

This feature is useful in headers and footers. You can easily add a line below text in a header or add a line above text in a footer. This line acts as a graphic element that separates the header/footer text from the rest of the text and adds visual appeal to the document.

Using the Borders Feature vs. the Drawing Toolbar

Creating horizontal and vertical lines with the Borders feature is very limiting. Horizontal lines are limited in size by the right and left margins and to the weights offered in the Borders and Shading dialog box. Vertical lines are limited to the length of a paragraph or selected paragraphs. You have much more flexibility when creating lines with the Drawing toolbar. The Draw program has the ability to create both custom horizontal and vertical lines at any location on a page, whereas lines created with the Borders features may only be placed above, below, to the left, or to the right of a paragraph.

In exercise 2, you will create a letterhead using a text box that is inserted in the header and footer layer in the left margin space. Inserting it in this layer is a safeguard against users who might inadvertently make a change in the letterhead. Placing the letterhead in the header and footer layer will result in the letterhead appearing on all subsequent pages, which is not appropriate for a multipage letter. To eliminate the letterhead on subsequent pages, the header will be created as a Different first page header. This option tells Word that this header is to be used for the first page only. Subsequent pages may have a different header if desired.

**Creating a Letterhead Using a Customized Text Box
and Customized Horizontal Line**

1. At a clear document screen, create the letterhead shown in figure 3.12 by completing the following steps:
    a. Change the left margin to 2.5 inches and the right margin to 1 inch.
    b. Insert a text box for the company letterhead by completing the following steps:

1) Click <u>V</u>iew, then <u>H</u>eader and
Footer to display the Header
pane. (The letterhead text box is
going to be inserted in the
header and footer layer. This
way you can prevent other users
from inadvertently changing the
letterhead.)

2) Click the Zoom button on the
Standard toolbar; then select
Whole Page.

3) Display the Drawing
toolbar; then click the
Text Box button on the Drawing
toolbar. Position the crosshairs
in the upper left corner of the
page and click and drag to draw
a text box in the left margin
approximately the same size as
that shown in figure 3.12. (The
text box will be specifically sized
and positioned in the next few
steps.)

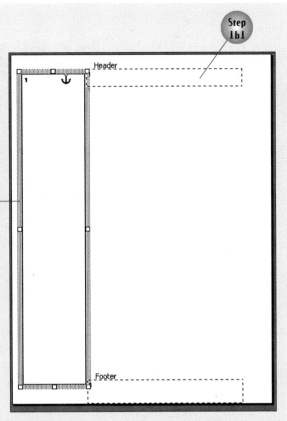

c. Size and position the text box by
completing the following steps:

1) Double-click the text box border to display the Format Text Box dialog box.

2) Select the Size tab and then change the height of the text box to 10 inches
and the width to 1.8 inches.

3) Select the Layout tab, and then click the <u>A</u>dvanced button to display the
Advanced Layout dialog box. In the Horizontal section, change the Absolute
po<u>s</u>ition to 0.3" <u>t</u>o the left of Page. In the Vertical section, change the
Absolute po<u>s</u>ition to 0.5" belo<u>w</u> Page. (Select the <u>t</u>o the left of and belo<u>w</u>
options first before changing the measurements.)

4) Click OK to close the Advanced Layout dialog box and then click OK again to
close the Format Text Box dialog box.

d. Insert the textured fill and remove the text box borders by completing the following steps:

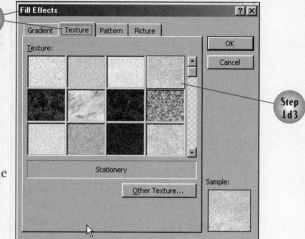

1) With the Format Text Box dialog box still displayed, click the Colors and Lines tab.

2) In the Fill section, click the Color list box, click Fill Effects, and then click the Texture tab in the Fill Effects dialog box.

3) In the Texture section, click the last texture block from the left in the first row. *Stationery* will display as the name of the texture below the texture selections.

4) Click OK or press Enter to close the Fill Effects dialog box.

5) In the Line section, click the Color list box, and then click No Line.

6) Click OK again to close the Format Text Box dialog box.

e. Insert and format the text box contents by completing the following steps:

1) Use the Zoom button on the Standard toolbar to change the view to at least 75%.

2) Click once inside the text box to position the insertion point inside the text box, and then key the following text, pressing Enter at the end of every line except the last line:

> **Desktop**
> **Designs**
> **"Where Concepts Become a Reality"** (let text wrap)
> **568 Pine Street**
> **St. Louis, MO 63131**
> **Phone: (314) 555-8755**
> **Fax: (314) 555-8758**
> **E-mail: dtpd@dtpnet.com**

Select all the text just entered; then change the font to Papyrus Bold and the text color to Teal.

3) Select Desktop Designs, display the Font dialog box, change the type size to 29-point, and then apply Emboss from the Effects section. Click OK.

4) Position the insertion point within the word *Desktop*, and click Format, then Paragraph. At the Paragraph dialog box, change the spacing Before the paragraph to 28 points and the Line Spacing to Exactly At: 30 points. Click OK.

5) Position the insertion point within the word *Designs* and change the spacing after the paragraph to 4 points.

6) Select the slogan *"Where Concepts Become a Reality,"* display the Font dialog box, change the type size to 12 points, change the type style to Bold Italic, and then apply Emboss from the Effects section. Click OK.

7) With the slogan still selected, access the Paragraph dialog box; then change the Spacing After: to 470 points and the Line Spacing to Exactly At: 17 points. Click OK.

8) Select the address, phone number, fax number, and E-mail address. *(Hint: To select all of the text, including the text that is not visible, position the insertion point at the beginning of the address, hold down the Shift key, and then press Ctrl + End.)*

9) Change the font size to 10.5 points; access the Paragraph dialog box and then change the line spacing to Exactly 14 points.

   f. Insert the horizontal line under the company name by completing the following steps:

1) Click the Line button on the Drawing toolbar; then position the crosshairs under *Designs*. Hold down the Shift key; then click and drag the crosshairs to the right to create a straight horizontal line the approximate length of the horizontal line shown in figure 3.12.

   g. Customize the horizontal line by making the following changes at the Format AutoShape dialog box (double-click the line to access this dialog box):

1) Select the Colors and Lines tab; change the weight of the line to 2 points and the color of the line to Violet.

2) Select the Size tab and change the width of the line to 1.6 inches.

3) Select the Layout tab; then click the Advanced button. At the Advanced Layout dialog box, change the horizontal position to .41 inches to the left of the page and the vertical position to 1.97 inches below the page. (*Hint*: Change the to the left of and below options first.)

4) Click OK to close the Advanced Layout dialog box, then click OK again to close the Format AutoShape dialog box.

   h. Click Close on the Header and Footer toolbar. (Due to the wide left margin setting, the insertion point is located an appropriate distance to the right of the text box in the text layer so that letter text may be entered at a later date.)

   i. Use Print Preview to view the entire document.

2. Save the letterhead and name it c03ex02, ddltrhead.

3. Print and then close c03ex02, ddltrhead.

figure 3.12 *Exercise 2*

Evaluating the Letterhead

Review the letterhead created in exercise 2. What is the focus? Is the design symmetrical or asymmetrical? How is balance achieved on the page? Are the type sizes in proportion to each other? Does the type size indicate a logical order of importance? How is directional flow established? Are related items grouped together? What elements provide contrast? If color was used, was it used effectively? Can you identify any consistent elements? Are any elements out of alignment? Continually asking yourself these kinds of questions will help develop your sense of design and layout.

Refining Letter and Word Spacing

Certain refinements such as kerning and tracking make your letterhead or any other document look more professional.

Kerning Character Pairs

The process of decreasing or increasing the white space between specific character pairs is called *kerning*. Generally, the horizontal spacing of typefaces is designed to optimize body text sizes (9- to 13-point). At larger sizes, the same relative horizontal space appears "loose," especially when uppercase and lowercase letters are combined. Kerning visually equalizes the space between specific characters and is generally used only on headlines and other blocks of large type (14-point and larger). However, it may sometimes be used to fit text in a certain amount of space or to achieve special effects. Figure 3.13 illustrates common character pairs that are affected by using the kerning feature. As you can see, kerning results in minor but visually important adjustments.

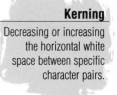

Kerning
Decreasing or increasing the horizontal white space between specific character pairs.

DTP POINTERS
Kern when the type size exceeds 14 points.

Examples of Character Pair Kerning

WA (kerned)	Ta (kerned)
WA (not kerned)	Ta (not kerned)
Ty (kerned)	Vi (kerned)
Ty (not kerned)	Vi (not kerned)

Using Automatic or Manual Kerning

In Word, kerning can be accomplished automatically or character pairs may be selected and kerned manually.

Automatic Kerning

When automatic kerning is turned on, Word adjusts the space between certain pairs of letters above a specific point size. Not all character pairs are affected with automatic kerning. The shape and design of characters in a typeface affects whether certain combinations of character pairs will be affected by automatic kerning. For example, some common character pairs that may be automatically kerned are Ta, To, Ty, Vi, and WA. The amount of space that is adjusted for specific character pairs is defined in a kerning table, which is part of the printer definition. The printer definition is a preprogrammed set of instructions that tells the printer how to perform various features. Word contains printer definitions for hundreds of printers. When a printer is selected during the installation of Word, a file containing the particular printer definition is copied to the folder specified for printer files. Word has defined kerning tables for True Type and Adobe Type Manager fonts only. You may want to print some of the character pairs listed in figure 3.13 as kerned and not kerned in large point sizes (14-point and larger) to see if your printer definition supports kerning. To turn on automatic kerning, access the Font dialog box, then select the Character Spacing tab as displayed in figure 3.14. Click the check box to the left of the Kerning for fonts option to insert a check mark. In the Points and above text box, use the up and down arrows to specify the minimum point size for kerning to take effect; or key the desired point size.

If the text to be kerned has not been keyed yet, there is no need to select the text first. If you want to kern existing text, select the text to be kerned. The best way to incorporate kerning into entire documents is to modify the Normal style to include automatic kerning. Styles are discussed in greater detail in chapter 6.

figure
3.14

Character Spacing Tab Displayed at the Font Dialog Box

Font	? X

Font | Character Spacing | Text Effects

Scale: [100% ▼]

Spacing: [Expanded ▼] By: [1 pt ▲▼]

Position: [Normal ▼] By: [▲▼]

☑ Kerning for fonts: [16 ▲▼] Points and above

Preview

Times New Roman

This is a TrueType font. This font will be used on both printer and screen.

Default...   OK   Cancel

Manual Kerning

If you choose to kern letters manually, you make the decision as to which letters to kern. Manual kerning is especially helpful if you need to increase or decrease space between letters to improve legibility, to create a special effect, or to fit text in a specific amount of space. As a word of caution, do not sacrifice legibility when making kerning adjustments. To manually kern a specific pair of letters, select the pair of characters you want to kern, then access the Font dialog box, Character Spacing tab. Click the Spacing list box; then select Expanded (if you want to increase the spacing between the selected character pair) or Condensed (if you want to decrease the spacing). In the By: list box, click the up or down arrows to specify the amount of space the selected character pair is to be increased or decreased. Manual kerning can provide very accurate results; however, it can be very tedious. For example, compare the normal text to the manually kerned text in figure 3.15. The S and the A were selected and the character spacing was condensed. This then led to minor character spacing adjustments between some of the other letters and several printings to achieve the desired result.

figure 3.15

Normal Text and Manually Kerned Text

RIDE SAFE, INC. (Normal)

RIDE SAFE, INC. (Manually Kerned)

Tracking Text

In traditional typesetting, equally reducing or increasing the horizontal space between all characters in a block of text is called *tracking*. Tracking affects all characters, while automatic kerning affects only specific character pairs as determined by your printer definition and manual kerning involves selected character pairs only. The purpose of tracking is the same as kerning: to produce more attractive, easy-to-read type. In addition, you can use tracking to create unusual spacing for a specific design effect or possibly to fit text into a certain amount of space. However, be extremely cautious about tracking body text. Even though condensing the character spacing allows more text in the same amount of space, the text appears more dense and can be more difficult to read.

> **Tracking**
> Equally reducing or increasing the horizontal space between all characters in a selected block of text.

In Word, tracking is virtually the same as manual kerning because both processes involve condensing or expanding character spacing at the Font dialog box. Whereas manually kerning involves adjusting the character spacing of selected character pairs, tracking involves adjusting the character spacing of a selected block of text, such as a heading, a subheading, a phrase, etc. Figure 3.16 specifies what occurs with each character spacing option that is available in the Character Spacing tab at the Font dialog box.

figure 3.16

Character Spacing Options

Normal	The default setting chosen by the program or the printer as the best spacing between words and letters.
Condensed	Condenses the spacing between all characters in a block of text by subtracting the amount of space specified in the By: box from the current letter spacing.
Expanded	Expands the spacing between all characters in a block of text by adding the amount of space specified in the By: box to the current letter spacing.

DTP POINTERS
Kern and track headings and subheadings.

When condensing or expanding the character spacing of a phrase of text, the spaces between the words are condensed or expanded as well. However, the amount of space specified between characters and the amount of space specified between words does not have to be the same. The headings shown in figure 3.17 are all set in a 24-point type size. The first heading in each pair is set at the default character spacing of Normal. The character spacing for the text in the second heading of each pair was condensed by 1 point and the space between each word was condensed by 0.5 points. Notice how condensing the character spacing by the same amount affects different typefaces. You must decide if the character spacing is appropriate. Is it easy to read? Are all letters easily identifiable? Does it look too close together or too far apart?

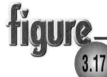

figure 3.17 ***Tracking Examples: Normal Text Followed by Text with Condensed Character Spacing***

DESKTOP PUBLISHING IN WORD

DESKTOP PUBLISHING IN WORD

Desktop Publishing In Word

Desktop Publishing In Word

Desktop Publishing In Word

Desktop Publishing In Word

Desktop Publishing In Word

Desktop Publishing In Word

Desktop Publishing In Word

Desktop Publishing In Word

Figure 3.18 provides an example of a heading that has also been tracked. The difference with this heading is that the character spacing has been expanded by 7 points to produce a special effect.

figure
3.18
Tracking Example with Expanded Character Spacing

Desktop Publishing in Word

Re-evaluating the Letterhead from Exercise 2

The letterhead produced in exercise 2 (see figure 3.12) looks good, but there are some minor adjustments that could be made. For example, left alignment was used for all the text in the text box. The left alignment is most noticeable with the address, phone, fax, and e-mail information at the bottom of the text box. However, the left alignment is less noticeable with the text located at the top of the text box because the company name and the slogan take up most of the width of the text box. Because the text looks off-center, someone may wonder if a mistake was made—was the text really supposed to be centered? To solve this problem, you will make minor character spacing adjustments to the letterhead created in exercise 2.

In exercise 3, you will also save the letterhead as a template. Since your letterhead helps to establish an identity for your organization, it will probably stay the same for quite a long period of time. Converting your letterhead into a template ensures that your letterhead is always available in its original form. If you mistakenly rearrange the letterhead while keying the letter content, you can open the original template to start anew. For more efficiency, you can even include styles, AutoText entries, field codes, macros, and more in your template letterhead.

DTP POINTERS
Consider creating a template of your letterhead.

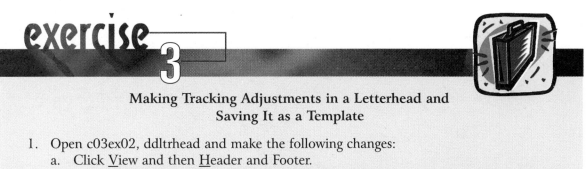

exercise
3

Making Tracking Adjustments in a Letterhead and
Saving It as a Template

1. Open c03ex02, ddltrhead and make the following changes:
   a. Click <u>V</u>iew and then <u>H</u>eader and Footer.
   b. In the letterhead text box in the Header and Footer pane, adjust the character spacing by completing the following steps:

1) Select *Designs;* and display the Font dialog box.
2) Select the Character Spacing tab. Change the <u>S</u>pacing: to Expanded and make sure the <u>B</u>y: list box displays 1 pt. Click OK or press Enter.

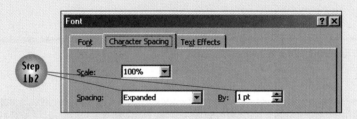

3) Select *"Where Concepts Become a Reality"* and expand the character spacing to 1pt as in the previous step.

  c. Save the letterhead as c03ex03, ddltrhead.

  d. Close the Header and Footer toolbar, and then print c03ex03, ddltrhead.

  e. Before saving the letterhead as a template, select a font for the body of the letter and insert an automatically updated date field by completing the following steps:

    1) With the insertion point at the top of the document, select the paragraph symbol to the right of the insertion point and then change the font to 12-point Book Antiqua.

    2) Insert an automatically updated date field by completing the following steps:

      a) Press Enter six or seven times so the insertion point is located approximately 2 inches from the top of the page.

      b) Click <u>I</u>nsert, then Date and <u>T</u>ime.

      c) At the Date and Time dialog box, select the appropriate date format for a business letter (third from the top in the <u>A</u>vailable formats: list box).

      d) Click in the <u>U</u>pdate automatically check box to turn this feature on.

      e) Click OK or press Enter.

2. Save the letterhead as a template by completing the following steps:

  a. Click <u>F</u>ile, Save <u>A</u>s, then change the Save as <u>t</u>ype: option to Document Template.

  b. Change the folder location in the Save <u>i</u>n: list box to the template folder that you created in chapter 2. (Most likely the location is A:*DTP Templates*.)

  c. Name the file ddtemplate.

3. Close ddtemplate.

figure
3.19
Exercise 3

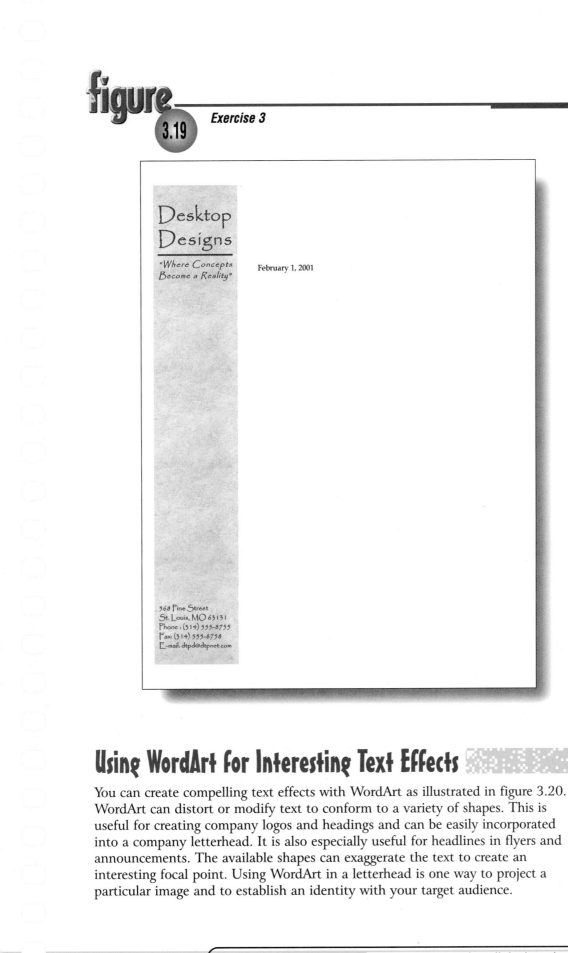

Using WordArt for Interesting Text Effects

You can create compelling text effects with WordArt as illustrated in figure 3.20. WordArt can distort or modify text to conform to a variety of shapes. This is useful for creating company logos and headings and can be easily incorporated into a company letterhead. It is also especially useful for headlines in flyers and announcements. The available shapes can exaggerate the text to create an interesting focal point. Using WordArt in a letterhead is one way to project a particular image and to establish an identity with your target audience.

figure
3.20

Examples of WordArt Objects

Creating a WordArt Object

Insert
WordArt

To create a WordArt object, click the Insert WordArt button on the Drawing toolbar; or click <u>I</u>nsert, point to <u>P</u>icture, and then click <u>W</u>ordArt; or click the Insert WordArt button on the WordArt toolbar. At the WordArt Gallery dialog box, double-click the desired WordArt style. At the Edit WordArt Text dialog box with the words *Your Text Here* selected, key the text to be included in your WordArt object in the <u>T</u>ext box. Press the Enter key if your WordArt object is to include more than one line of text.

The WordArt toolbar appears automatically whenever you select a WordArt object. Figure 3.21 illustrates the WordArt toolbar. You may also display the WordArt toolbar by right-clicking any toolbar displayed on the screen and then clicking WordArt. The WordArt toolbar enables you to edit text; change the WordArt style and/or shape; and change alignment, color, color effects, size, position, wrapping style, rotation, vertical text position, letter height, and character spacing (kerning and tracking).

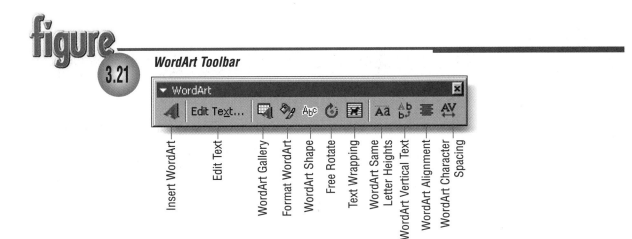

figure
3.21

WordArt Toolbar

Insert WordArt | Edit Text | WordArt Gallery | Format WordArt | WordArt Shape | Free Rotate | Text Wrapping | WordArt Same Letter Heights | WordArt Vertical Text | WordArt Alignment | WordArt Character Spacing

Changing the Shape of a WordArt Object

If you decide you want a different shape for your WordArt object, click the
WordArt Shape button (fifth button from the left) on the WordArt toolbar.
The WordArt Shape button opens up a palette of approximately forty shapes as
shown in figure 3.22. Some shapes produce different results depending on how
many lines of text and spaces you key into the text entry box in WordArt.
When you are deciding on which shape to use, experiment with several to find
the right effect. You may want to experiment with various fonts, font sizes,
colors, and color effects to find the right combination for your text. As a
cautionary note, make sure your WordArt object is readable.

WordArt
Shape

Adding Enhancements

As with any other objects such as text boxes, lines, AutoShapes and pictures, you
can size, move, copy, add fill shading or color, add or remove a border, and add
shadow or 3-D effects to a WordArt object by using options from the Drawing
toolbar or the Format WordArt dialog box. The Format WordArt button on the
WordArt toolbar opens the Format WordArt dialog box where you can change the
fill color of the letters or add gradient, texture, pattern or picture fill. You can
change the color, style, and weight of the borders surrounding the letters
depending on the options selected. Additionally, you can change the height,
width, and rotation of the object depending on the options you select at the
Format WordArt dialog box.

Format
WordArt

figure
3.22

WordArt Shape Palette

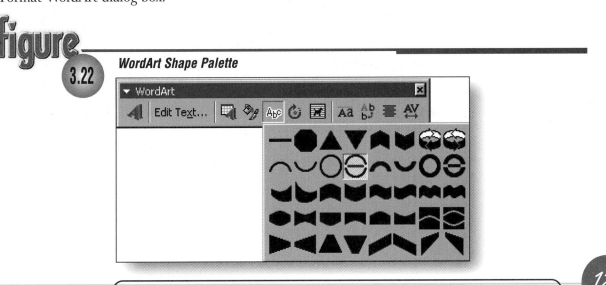

exercise 4

Creating a Letterhead Using WordArt and Text Boxes

1. At a clear document screen, create the letterhead shown in figure 3.23 by completing the following steps:
   a. Change the top margin to 0.5 inch, the bottom margin to 0.55 inch, and the left and right margins to 1 inch.
   b. Create the WordArt company logo by completing the following steps:
      1) Display the Drawing toolbar and click the Insert WordArt button on the Drawing toolbar.
      2) At the WordArt Gallery dialog box in the Select a WordArt style section, click the second style from the left in the second row; then click OK or press Enter.
      3) At the Edit WordArt Text dialog box with *Your Text Here* selected, key the following, pressing Enter as indicated:

         Carlucci (press Enter)
         & (press Enter)
         Associates

      4) Change the font to Bookman Old Style, turn on bold, and click OK.
      5) With the WordArt object selected in your document, click the WordArt Shape button on the WordArt toolbar.
      6) Select the fourth shape from the left in the second row, labeled as *Button (Curve)*.

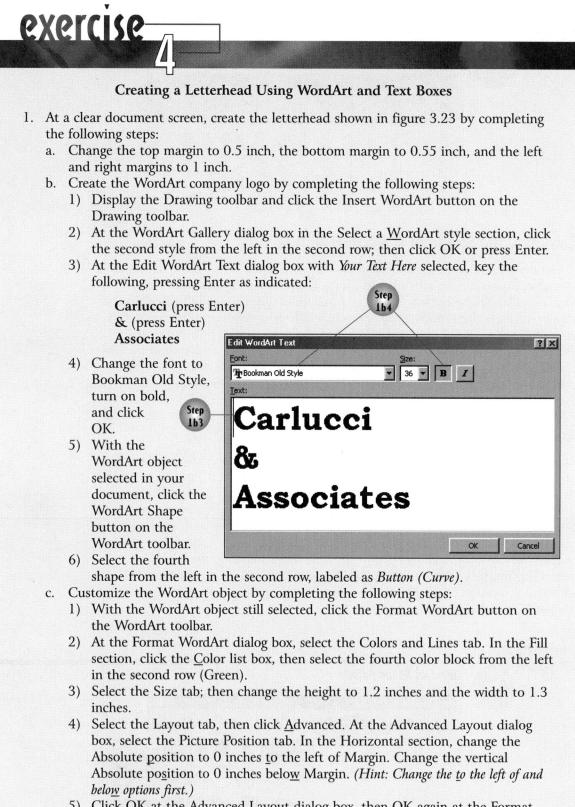

   c. Customize the WordArt object by completing the following steps:
      1) With the WordArt object still selected, click the Format WordArt button on the WordArt toolbar.
      2) At the Format WordArt dialog box, select the Colors and Lines tab. In the Fill section, click the Color list box, then select the fourth color block from the left in the second row (Green).
      3) Select the Size tab; then change the height to 1.2 inches and the width to 1.3 inches.
      4) Select the Layout tab, then click Advanced. At the Advanced Layout dialog box, select the Picture Position tab. In the Horizontal section, change the Absolute position to 0 inches to the left of Margin. Change the vertical Absolute position to 0 inches below Margin. *(Hint: Change the to the left of and below options first.)*
      5) Click OK at the Advanced Layout dialog box, then OK again at the Format WordArt dialog box.

6) Click the Shadow button on the Drawing toolbar, then click Shadow Settings. At the Shadow Settings toolbar, change the shadow to Gray-40%. Click Close.

d. Insert the horizontal line by completing the following steps:
1) Click the Line button on the Drawing toolbar.
2) Draw a straight line (hold down the Shift key) to the right and center of the WordArt object. Make the line approximately the same length as the line in figure 3.23.

e. Customize the horizontal line by completing the following steps:
1) Double-click the line to display the Format AutoShape dialog box.

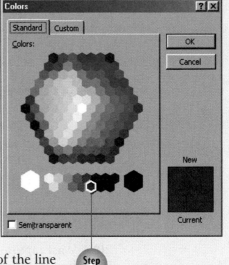

2) Click the Colors and Lines tab. In the Line section, click the Color list box; then select More Colors. At the Colors dialog box, make sure the Standard tab is selected and then select the dark gray color located in the bottom row, third from the right in the black, gray, white color block section. Click OK.
3) Change the weight of the line to 2.5 pt.
4) Select the Size tab and change the width of the line to 5.3 inches.
5) Select the Layout tab; then click Advanced. At the Advanced Layout dialog box, change the horizontal position of the line to 2.5 inches to the left of the page and change the vertical position to 1.02 inches below the page. *(Hint: Change to the left of and below options first.)*
6) Click OK at the Advanced Layout dialog box; then click OK again at the Format AutoShape dialog box.

f. Insert and customize the text box containing Marketing Specialists by completing the following steps:
1) Click the Text Box button on the Drawing toolbar; then draw a text box approximately 1/2 inch by 2-1/2 inches in the approximate position indicated in figure 3.23.
2) Customize the text box at the Format Text Box dialog box by completing the following steps:
   a) Double-click one of the text box borders (or click Format, then Text Box) to display the Format Text Box dialog box.
   b) Select the Colors and Lines tab. In the Fill section, click the arrow to the right of the Color list box; then select No Fill. In the Line section, click the arrow to the right of the Color list box; then select No Line.
   c) Click the Size tab; then change the height to 0.35 inch and the width to 2.7 inches.
   d) Click the Layout tab, then Advanced. At the Advanced Layout dialog box, change the horizontal position of the line to 5.18 inches to the left of the page. Change the vertical position to 0.66 inches below the page. *(Hint: Change the to the left of and below options first.)*
   e) Click OK at the Advanced Layout dialog box, then OK again at the Format Text Box dialog box.
3) Insert and format the text box contents by completing the following steps:

a) Click once inside the text box to position the insertion point.
b) Key **Marketing Specialists**.
c) Select the text just entered, change the alignment to right, and then change the font to 16-point Lucida Sans, Demibold Italic. Change the color to Green and then apply Small caps.

4) Insert a text box that will contain the address, phone and fax numbers, and the e-mail address in the approximate location as shown in figure 3.23.

5) Customize the text box as follows:
a) Change the fill and line color of the text box to No Fill and No Line.
b) Change the height of the text box to 0.8 inches and the width to 2.21 inches.
c) Change the horizontal position of the text box to 5.69 inches to the left of the page and the vertical position to 1.02 inches below the page. *(Hint: Change the to the left of and below options first.)*

6) Click once inside the text box to position the insertion point. Change the alignment to right, then change the font to 8-point Lucida Sans, Demibold Roman, and the text color to dark gray. (Click More Colors from text color palette. At the Standard tab in the Colors dialog box, select the dark gray color located in the bottom row, third from the right in the black, gray, white color block section.)

7) Key the following text pressing Enter where indicated:

> **2021 Washington Street** (press Enter)
> **Providence, Rhode Island 02890** (press Enter)
> **Phone: (401) 555-3595** (press Enter)
> **Fax: (401) 555-3593**
> **E-mail: jcarlucci@carlucci.com**

g. Create and customize the text box that will contain the slogan at the bottom of the page by completing the following steps:
1) Insert a text box that is the same approximate size and in the same approximate location as the text box containing the slogan shown in figure 3.23.
2) Remove the text box borders.
3) Change the fill color to 25%-Gray (the last color block on the right in the fourth row of the line color palette).
4) Change the height of the text box to 0.3 inch and the width to 6.5 inches.
5) Change the horizontal alignment of the text box so that it is centered across the page. Change the vertical alignment to 10.09 inches below the page. *(Hint: Change the below option first.)*

h. Insert and format the text box contents by completing the following steps:
1) Click once inside the text box to position the insertion point; then key **Over 25 years' experience in developing successful marketing plans.**
2) Select the text just entered, access the Font dialog box, and make the following changes:
a) Change the font to 11-point Bookman Old Style, Italic, and the color to Green.
b) Select the Character Spacing tab, then expand the character spacing by 1 pt.
c) Click OK or press Enter.
3) Change the paragraph alignment to center.

2. Save the letterhead and name it c03ex04, Carlucci ltrhead.
3. Print and then close c03ex04, Carlucci ltrhead.

Note: This letterhead could have been created in the header/footer pane as the letterhead was in exercise 2. Additionally, this letter could have been saved as a template.

figure
3.23   *Exercise 4*

Creating Envelopes

Let your company's letterhead be the starting point for the design of your other business documents. An envelope designed in coordination with a letterhead is another way of establishing your identity with your target audience. Using some of the same design elements in the envelope as in the letterhead contributes to continuity and consistency among your documents. These same elements can be carried over into memos, faxes, business cards, invoices, and brochures.

DTP POINTERS
Use your company's letterhead as the starting point for the design of your other business documents.

As in a letterhead, there is certain information that must be included on the front of an envelope so your correspondence reaches its intended destination. The necessary information includes the following items:

Return Address:

- Logo
- Name
- Address
- Mailing address if different

- Optional: Company motto or slogan
- Optional: Telephone and fax number (include area code)

Recipient's Address:

- Name
- Title (only if you really know it)
- Company name
- Street address

- City, State, ZIP (check a ZIP Code directory if necessary)
- Optional: Postal Bar Code

Designing Your Own Envelope

DTP POINTERS
Consider the actual size of the design area.

DTP POINTERS
Use consistent elements to establish a visual connection between your envelope and letterhead.

If you decide to design your own envelope, consider the size of the envelope to be used. Any design elements will most likely be located on the left side of the envelope, concentrated in the upper left corner. Hence, your design area is much smaller than that of a letterhead.

When planning your design, remember that the envelope design does not have to be an exact replica of the letterhead. Select enough common elements to establish a visual link between the two documents. For example, using the same typeface and type styles in a smaller type size and repeating a graphic element on a smaller scale may be just enough to establish that link. Size the fonts used on the envelope so they are in proportion to those used in the letterhead. Restrain from making the design too large or overpowering. The design should not interfere in any way with the recipient's name and address. Be aware that the postal sorting equipment reads an envelope both from left to right and bottom to top at the same time. The "reader" is searching for an address and will respond first to the darkest item that includes numbers. Therefore, if you position the return address in the upper left corner of the envelope, the reader will first encounter the delivery address before it finds the return address. Check with your local post office for any mailing restrictions on placing text or design elements on the front of an envelope.

Using Word's Envelope Feature

Word's envelope feature makes creating professional-looking envelopes easy and inexpensive. You can create a blank envelope that already contains appropriate formatting for margins and a text box in the mailing address position. First you must add a blank envelope to a document and then add your own design and return address. To do this, at a clear screen click Tools, Envelopes and Labels, and then select the Envelopes tab at the Envelopes and Labels dialog box. Click the Options button. Select the Envelope Options tab and make sure the desired envelope size is displayed at the Envelope size list box. If not, change to the desired size, then click OK. At the Envelopes and Labels dialog box, click Add to Document. Word adds the envelope to the beginning of the current active document (which is usually a blank document). Word numbers the envelope as page 0 and the blank page as page 1. When you print your envelope, print the current page only to avoid sending a blank piece of paper through the printer.

Checking Printing Options

Word determines the feed method for envelopes and the feed form that is best suited to your printer as shown in the Feed section of the Envelopes and Labels dialog box (with the Envelopes tab selected). If this method does not work for your printer, choose the correct feed method and feed form at the Envelope Options dialog box with the Printing Options tab selected. Feed methods are visually displayed at this dialog box. You can also determine if the envelope is fed into the printer face up or face down.

In addition to including text in any available font, a clip art image, a company logo, a graphic created using Word's drawing tools, or an image created using WordArt can be included as part of your envelope design. If you are taking the time to design an envelope, convert it to a template as in the following exercise, so you can use it over and over again.

exercise 5

Designing and Creating an Envelope Template
Using the Envelope Feature

1. At a clear document screen, create an envelope design, as shown in figure 3.24, to coordinate with the Desktop Design letterhead created in exercise 2, by completing the following steps:
   a. Create the envelope by completing the following steps:
      1) Click Tools, Envelopes and Labels, and then the Envelopes tab at the Envelopes and Labels dialog box.
      2) Select and delete any text that displays in the Delivery address text box.
      3) If a default address appears in the Return address text box, click the Omit check box to insert a check mark, or select and delete the address.
      4) Make sure a business size envelope appears in the Preview box; then click Add to Document to insert a blank envelope form in your document. The screen will display with the insertion point in the return address position. The page number in the status line will display as Page 0. A blank page will also be included following the envelope because the envelope was added to a clear document screen.

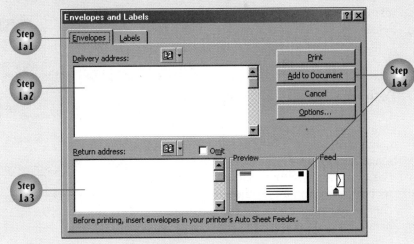

5) With the insertion point in the upper left corner, change the left margin to 0.4 inch. If Word prompts you that your printer will not accept this measurement, choose <u>F</u>ix to accept the minimum margin setting as determined by Word.

b. Insert a text box for the return address design by completing the following steps:
   1) Click the Zoom button on the Standard toolbar and select Page Width.
   2) Display the Drawing toolbar, click the Text Box button on the Drawing toolbar, and then draw a text box on the left side of the envelope that is approximately the same size and in the same location as that shown in figure 3.23.

c. Customize the text box at the Format Text Box dialog box by completing the following steps:
   1) Display the Format Text Box dialog box by double-clicking one of the text box borders, or click F<u>o</u>rmat and Text B<u>o</u>x.
   2) Select the Colors and Lines tab and make the following changes:
      a) In the Fill section, click the <u>C</u>olor list box, <u>F</u>ill Effects, and then the Texture tab in the Fill Effects dialog box.
      b) In the <u>T</u>exture section, click the last texture block from the left in the first row. The texture name, *Stationery*, will display below the texture selections.
      c) Click OK or press Enter to close the Fill Effects dialog box.
      d) In the Line section, click the C<u>o</u>lor list box and then No Line.
   3) Select the Size tab and change the height of the text box to 3.2 inches and the width to 1.45 inches.
   4) Select the Layout tab and change the horizontal alignment to left. Click <u>A</u>dvanced and change the vertical position to 0.45 inches below the page at the Advanced Layout dialog box. *(Hint: Change the belo<u>w</u> option first.)*
   5) Click OK to close the Advanced Layout dialog box; then OK again to close the Format Text Box dialog box.

d. Insert and format the text box contents by completing the following steps:
   1) Click once inside the text box to position the insertion point.
   2) Key the following text, pressing Enter at the end of every line except the last line *(Hint: The longer lines will wrap.)*:

   Desktop
   Designs
   568 Pine Street
   St. Louis, MO 63131
   "Where Concepts Become a Reality"

   3) Select all the text just entered; then change the font to Papyrus Bold and the text color to Teal.
   4) Select *Desktop Designs*, access the Font dialog box, change the type size to 22 points, and then apply <u>E</u>mboss from the Effects section.
   5) With the company name still selected, click F<u>o</u>rmat, then <u>P</u>aragraph. At the Paragraph dialog box, change the Li<u>n</u>e Spacing to Exactly <u>A</u>t: 26 points.
   6) Position the insertion point within the word *Desktop* and change the spacing before the paragraph to 4 points.

Paragraph ? X

Indents and Spacing | Line and <u>P</u>age Breaks

Alig<u>n</u>ment: [Left ▼]   Outline level: [Level 2 ▼]

Indentation
   <u>L</u>eft: [0"]   S<u>p</u>ecial: [(none) ▼]   B<u>y</u>: [▲▼]
   <u>R</u>ight: [0"]

Spacing
   <u>B</u>efore: [4 pt ▲▼]   Li<u>n</u>e spacing: [Exactly ▼]   <u>A</u>t: [26 pt ▲▼]
   Aft<u>e</u>r: [0 pt ▲▼]

Step 1d6   Step 1d5

7) Select the word *Designs,* expand the character spacing by 1 point at the Font dialog box, and then change the spacing after the paragraph to 8 points at the Paragraph dialog box.

8) Select the address, change the type size to 9 point, and then access the Paragraph dialog box and change the line spacing to exactly 10 points.

9) Position the insertion point in the last line of the address; then change the spacing after the paragraph to 108 points.

10) Select the slogan *"Where Concepts Become a Reality,"* access the Font dialog box, change the type size to 11 points, change the font style to Bold Italic, and apply <u>E</u>mboss from the Effects section. (To select the slogan, position the insertion point at the beginning of the slogan, hold down the Shift key and press Ctrl + End.)

11) With the slogan still selected, access the Paragraph dialog box and then change the line spacing to exactly 12 points.

e. Insert the horizontal line under the company name by completing the following steps:

1) Click the Line button on the Drawing toolbar, hold down the Shift key, and then draw a line below *Designs* that is the same approximate length as the horizontal line shown in figure 3.24.

2) Customize the horizontal line by making the following changes at the Format AutoShape dialog box:

a) Double-click the line to access the Format AutoShape dialog box.

b) Select the Colors and Lines tab; change the weight of the line to 2 points and the color of the line to Violet.

c) Select the Size tab and change the width of the line to 1.27 inches.

d) Select the Layout tab; then click the <u>A</u>dvanced button. At the Advanced Layout dialog box, change the horizontal position to 0.49 inch to the left of the page and the vertical position to 1.35 inches below the page.

e) Click OK to close the Advanced Layout dialog box and then OK again to close the Format AutoShape dialog box.

f. Use Print Preview to view the completed envelope.

2. Save the letterhead and name it c03ex05, ddenvelope.

3. Print c03ex05, ddenvelope (current page only).

4. Save your envelope as a template by completing the following steps:

a. Add placeholder text to indicate placement of the mailing address by completing the following steps:

1) Click the Show/Hide ¶ button on the Standard toolbar to turn on the display of nonprinting characters. Click the paragraph symbol located in the mailing address area to display a frame (similar to a text box) reserved for the mailing address. (This frame exists when an envelope is produced using the Envelopes and Label feature.)

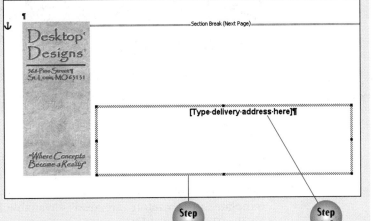

2) Key **[Type delivery address here]**.

3) Use Print Preview to view the entire envelope.

b. Save your envelope as a template by completing the following steps:
1) Click File and Save As, and then change the Save as type: option to Document Template.
2) Change the folder location in the Save in: list box to the template folder that you created in chapter 2. (Most likely the location is A:\DTP Templates)
3) Name the envelope template ddenvelope, and click Save.
4) Close the envelope template.

figure
3.24
Exercise 5

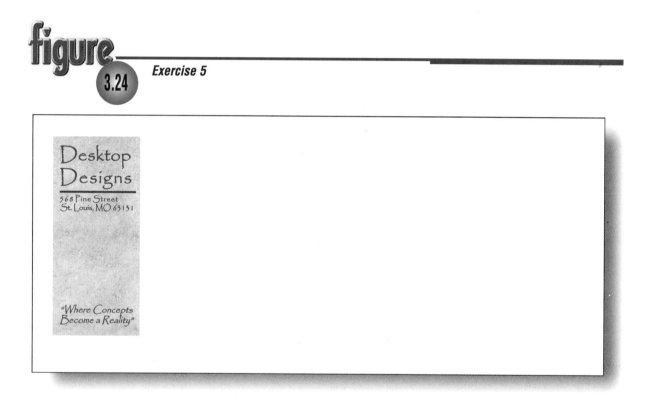

Using AutoText to Store and Reuse Text and Graphics

AutoText allows you to quickly and easily store and reuse commonly used text and/or graphics, including any associated formatting, and to insert them into documents whenever you need them. Associated formatting may include such items as font selections, text color, paragraph spacing, text boxes, graphic images, and the like. The AutoText feature is useful for items such as a company logo, company name, addresses, lists, standard text, a closing to a letter, or any other text and/or graphics that you use on a frequent basis or that would take too much time to recreate. By default, AutoText entries are saved as part of the Normal template and, therefore, are always available for future use in all documents based on the Normal template.

Creating an AutoText Entry

To create and save an AutoText entry, key the desired text, apply any formatting, and/or insert any graphics or objects. Select the text and/or graphics you want to store as an AutoText entry. If any paragraph formatting is applied to the text, make sure you include the paragraph mark with the selected text. To make sure the paragraph mark is included, turn on the display of nonprinting characters before selecting the text. Click Insert, point to AutoText, and then click New. At the Create AutoText dialog box, either accept the default name assigned to the AutoText entry or key a new short name. If you plan to create, insert, or edit several AutoText entries, display the AutoText toolbar to save time. Position the arrow pointer anywhere within a toolbar that is currently displayed on the screen; then right-click. Select AutoText from the toolbar drop-down list. After selecting the desired text and/or graphics, click New on the AutoText toolbar to access the Create AutoText dialog box.

Inserting an AutoText Entry

An AutoText entry can be inserted into a document by using two different shortcut methods. To use the first shortcut method, key the name given to the AutoText entry and then press the shortcut key F3. The AutoText entry will immediately appear in your document at the location of the insertion point.

The second shortcut method works only if an AutoText entry name contains at least four characters. Once you have keyed the first four letters of an AutoText entry name, Word suggests the complete word or phrase in a small yellow box (called an AutoText Complete tip) displayed above the current line of typing. When the suggestion appears, press Enter or F3 to accept Word's suggestion or continue keying to ignore the suggestion. If the AutoText Complete tip does not display after keying the first four characters of an AutoText entry name, click Insert, point to AutoText, and then click AutoText to display the AutoCorrect dialog box. In the AutoText tab, click the check box to the left of Show Auto Complete tip for AutoText and dates to insert a check mark and then click OK. Once this feature is activated, it remains active during all future working sessions unless you deactivate the feature by removing the check mark.

An AutoText entry can also be inserted by choosing Insert, pointing to AutoText, and then clicking AutoText. At the AutoCorrect dialog box with the AutoText tab selected, click the name of the AutoText entry in the list box; then click Insert.

Editing an AutoText Entry

An AutoText entry can be edited by inserting the entry in a document, making any necessary changes, then saving it again with the same AutoText entry name. When Word asks if you want to redefine the AutoText entry, choose Yes.

Deleting an AutoText Entry

An AutoText entry can be removed from the AutoCorrect dialog box. To do this, display the AutoText tab in the AutoCorrect dialog box, select the entry name from the AutoText entry list box, and then click the Delete button. In a classroom lab setting, check with your instructor about deleting AutoText entries after you are finished with them. Deleting them would allow other students the opportunity to create their own entries with the same names.

Creating Business Cards

Business cards eliminate the unprofessional and sometimes awkward scribbling of your name, address, and telephone number on a piece of paper whenever you want to leave your name with a business contact. A business card represents you and your company or organization and projects an organized, professional image. A business card is one of your best marketing opportunities.

DTP POINTERS
Using coordinating design elements in your business documents establishes identity and consistency.

A business card usually includes your name, title, company or organization name, address, telephone number, fax number, and e-mail address. You can also include a one-sentence description of your business, business philosophy, or slogan. To further establish your identity and to stay consistent with other business documents such as letterheads, envelopes, etc., include the same company logo or symbol in reduced size. Also, continue to use the same typefaces and colors used in your other business documents. Most business cards are created with sans serif typefaces because the characters are easier to read. The type sizes vary from 12 to 14 points for key words and 8 to 10 points for telephone and fax numbers. Vary the appearance by using bold, italics, or small caps.

Business cards should be printed on high-quality cover stock paper. Specially designed full-color papers and forms for creating business cards more easily and professionally are available at office supply stores and paper companies. Printing your own business cards saves you the expense of having to place a large minimum order with an outside printer. This is especially helpful to a new small business. You may decide to design your own card and then take it to a professional printer to be printed in large quantities. Be sure to call the printer first to confirm that your Word file will be acceptable.

Using Word's Labels Feature to Create Business Cards

Although Word does not include a template for creating business cards, you can use Word's business card label definition to design and create your own business cards. You can also use the business card label definition to create membership cards, name tags, coupons, place holders, or friendly reminders. The label definition will produce 10 business cards—two columns of labels with five rows in each column. The columns and rows are automatically set up in a Word table. Each label is actually a cell in the table.

When creating business cards, you can use the Avery standard 5371 or 8371 Business Card label definition. The only difference between these two label product numbers occurs in the actual product when you purchase these brand-name items at an office supply store—the 5371 is made to be used in a laser printer and the 8371 is made to be used in an ink jet printer. In both cases, the business card will be 3-1/2 by 2 inches and the sheet containing the business cards will be 8-1/2 by 11 inches.

You will create 10 business cards in exercise 6 using the Avery 5371 Business Card label definition. You will first use the Labels feature to create a business card that will be saved as an Auto Text entry. Because several objects (text boxes and a line) are used to construct the business card, you will use Word's object grouping feature to treat the multiple objects as a single object. You will then use the Envelopes and Labels feature and the AutoText feature to create a full sheet of business cards.

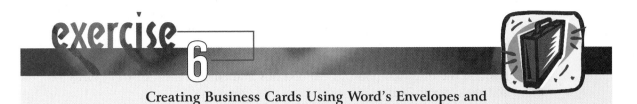

exercise 6

Creating Business Cards Using Word's Envelopes and Labels Feature and AutoText Feature

1. At a clear document screen, create the AutoText entry to be used to produce the business cards shown in figure 3.25 by completing the following steps:
   a. Insert a blank sheet of labels by completing the following steps:
      1) Click Tools and then Envelopes and Labels. Select the Labels tab and click Options.
      2) At the Label Options dialog box, select *Avery standard* in the Label products list box; then select *5371-Business Card* from the Product number list box. Click OK or press Enter.

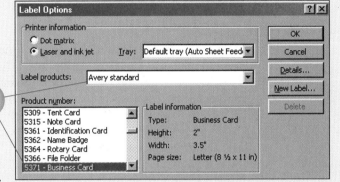

      3) At the Envelopes and Labels dialog box, delete any text that may appear in the Address list box.
      4) At the same dialog box, make sure Full page of the same label is selected; then click New Document.
   b. If the table gridlines do not display, click Table and Show Gridlines.
   c. Insert the text box that will contain the company name, slogan, and address by completing the following steps:
      1) Click the Zoom arrow on the Standard toolbar and change the display to Page Width.
      2) Display the Drawing toolbar and click the Text Box button.
      3) Position the crosshairs in the upper left corner of the first label (or cell) and draw a text box that is approximately the same size and in the same approximate location as the Desktop Designs text box shown in figure 3.25.
   d. Customize the text box by completing the following steps:
      1) Double-click the text box border to display the Format Text Box dialog box (or click Format and Text Box).
      2) Select the Colors and Lines tab. In the Fill section, click the Color list box, click Fill Effects, then the Texture tab in the Fill Effects dialog box. In the Texture section, and click the last texture block from the left in the first row. The texture name, *Stationery*, will display below the texture selections. Click OK or press Enter to close the Fill Effects dialog box.
      3) In the Line section, click the Color list box, and then click No Line.
      4) Select the Size tab and change the height of the text box to 1.8 inches and the width to 1.22 inches.
      5) Select the Layout tab; then click the Advanced button to display the Advanced Layout dialog box. Change the horizontal position to 0.15 inch to the left of the page and the vertical position to 0.1 inch below the page. *(Hint: Change the to the left of and below options first.)* Click OK.

6) Select the Text Box tab and change the left and right margins to 0.05 inch. Click OK.

e. Insert and format the text box contents by completing the following steps:
1) Position the insertion point in the text box and change the font to Papyrus and the color to Teal.
2) Key the following text, pressing Enter at the end of every line except the last line: *(Hint: Extend the height of the text box when necessary to see the text as you are keying it in. It will be resized later.)*

> **Desktop**
> **Designs**
> **"Where Concepts Become a Reality"** (let text wrap)
> **568 Pine Street**
> **St. Louis, MO 63131**

3) Select *Desktop Design* and change the font size to 20 points. Apply bold and apply Emboss at the Font dialog box.
4) Position the insertion point within *Desktop* and change the spacing before the paragraph to 2 points and the line spacing to exactly 20 points at the Paragraph dialog box.
5) Select *Designs* and expand the character spacing by 0.8 point and change the spacing after the paragraph to 1 point.
6) Select *"Where Concepts Become a Reality,"* change the font to 9-point, and then apply italics.
7) With the slogan still selected, change the spacing after the paragraph to 24 points and the line spacing to exactly 12 points at the Paragraph dialog box.
8) Select the address, city, state, and ZIP code, change the font size to 8 points, apply bold, and change the line spacing to exactly 10 points.
9) Double-click the text box border, select the Size tab, then change the height back to 1.8 inches.

f. Insert the horizontal line by completing the following steps:
1) Click the Line button on the Drawing toolbar and position the crosshairs under *Designs*. Hold down the Shift key and draw a straight horizontal line the same approximate length and in the same approximate location as that shown in figure 3.25.

g. Customize the horizontal line by making the following changes at the Format AutoShape dialog box (double-click the line to access this dialog box):
1) Select the Colors and Lines tab; change the weight of the line to 1.75 points and the color of the line to Violet.
2) Select the Size tab and change the width of the line to 1.07 inches.
3) Select the Layout tab; then click the Advanced button. At the Advanced Layout dialog box, change the horizontal position to 0.23 inches to the left of the page and the vertical position to 0.89 inch below the page. *(Hint: Change the to the left of and below options first.)*
4) Click OK to close the Advanced Layout dialog box and click OK again to close the Format AutoShape dialog box.

h. Insert and customize the text box that will contain the business person's name, title, phone number, fax number, and e-mail address by completing the following steps:
1) Draw a text box to the right of the first text box that is approximately 1.5 inches by 2 inches.

2) Double-click one of the text box borders to display the Format Text Box dialog box and make the following changes:
   a) Select the Colors and Lines tab and change the line color to No Line.
   b) Select the Size tab and change the height of the text box to 1.57 inches and the width to 1.8 inches.
   c) Select the Layout tab and click the Advanced button. At the Advanced Layout dialog box, change the horizontal position to 1.58 inches to the left of the page and the vertical position to 0.34 inch below the page. *(Hint: Change the to the left of and below options first.)*
   d) Click OK to close the Advanced Layout dialog box and click OK again to close the Format AutoShape dialog box.

i. Insert and format the text box contents by completing the following steps:
   1) Position the insertion point inside the text box; then key the following text, pressing Enter at the end of every line except the last line:

   Linda Urban
   Publications Designer
   Phone: (314) 555-8755
   Fax: (314) 555-8758
   E-mail: urban@dtpd.com

   2) Select all the text just entered and change the font to Papyrus, Teal.
   3) Select *Linda Urban*, change the type size to 17 point, turn on bold, and apply the Emboss effect from the Font dialog box.
   4) Select *Publications Designer*, change the type size to 10 point, and apply italics.
   5) Select both the name and title and change the line spacing to exactly 15 points.
   6) Position the insertion point within the title only and change the spacing after the paragraph to 43 points.
   7) Select the phone, fax, and e-mail address, change the type size to 10 point, apply bold, and then change the line spacing to exactly 11 points. *(Hint: To select the text, position the insertion point to the left of* Phone:*, hold down the Shift key, then press Ctrl + End.)*

j. To save the business card as an AutoText entry, the objects (the text boxes and the horizontal line) in the business card must be grouped together so they can be treated as one unit. Group the objects by completing the following steps:
   1) Select the text box that contains the company name.
   2) Hold down the Shift key and select the horizontal line. (The text box should still be selected.)
   3) Hold down the Shift key again and select the remaining text box. (All objects should be selected.)
   4) Click Draw on the Drawing toolbar and click Group. (Sizing handles should display on all four sides of the business card.)

Step 1j3

Step 1j1

Step 1j2

Desktop'
Designs
*Where Concepts·
Become a Reality*¶

568 Pine Street¶
St. Louis, MO 63151·

Linda·Urban¶
Publications·Designer¶

Phone:·(314)·555-8755¶
Fax:·(314)·555-8758¶
E-mail:·urban@dtpnet.com·

k. Save the business card (now an object) as an Auto Text entry by completing the following steps:

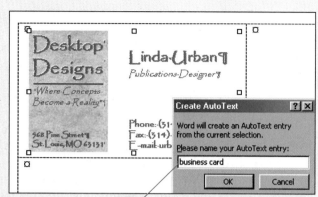

1) With the business card selected, click Insert, point to AutoText, and then click New.

2) At the Create AutoText dialog box, key **business card**, and then click OK or press Enter.

l. Save the object (the business card) as a Word document so that you can always go back to this point if your AutoText entry is deleted. Name the document ddbusiness card.

m. Close ddbusiness card.

n. Create a full sheet of business cards using your business card AutoText entry by completing the following steps:

1) Click Tools and then Envelopes and Labels. Make sure the Labels tab is selected and click Options.

2) At the Label Options dialog box, select *Avery standard* in the Label products list box, and then choose *5371-Business Card* from the Product number list box. Click OK or press Enter.

3) At the Envelopes and Labels dialog box, delete any text that may appear in the Address list box, and then key **business card** and press F3.

Step 1n3

4) At the same dialog box, make sure Full page of the same label is selected, and then click New Document. A full sheet of business cards will display on your screen.

Step 1n4

5) Use Print Preview to make sure your document will print correctly. Depending on your printer's unprintable zone and the margins set in the business card's label definition, the printing on the bottom row of the business cards may be cut off. One easy way to avoid this is to fool your printer into thinking your document is going to be printed on a longer piece of paper. To do this, complete the following steps:

a) Click File, click Page Setup, and then select the Paper Size tab.

b) In the Paper Size list box, select Legal and click OK. Word may prompt you that *One or more margins are set outside the printable area of the page.* If so, click Ignore.

2. Save the full sheet of business cards with the name c03ex06, Business card.

3. Print and then close c03ex06, Business card. Printing the business cards on a sheet of business cards made especially for your type of printer is preferable. If you print the business cards on plain paper, you may want to print the table grid lines as shown in figure 3.25. To print the grid lines, complete the following steps:
   a. Click Table, point to Select, and then click Table.
   b. Click Format, Borders and Shading, and then select the Borders tab.
   c. In the Setting section, click All.
   d. In the Style list box, click the fourth line choice (the dashed line) from the top.
   e. Click OK.

figure

3.25

Exercise 6

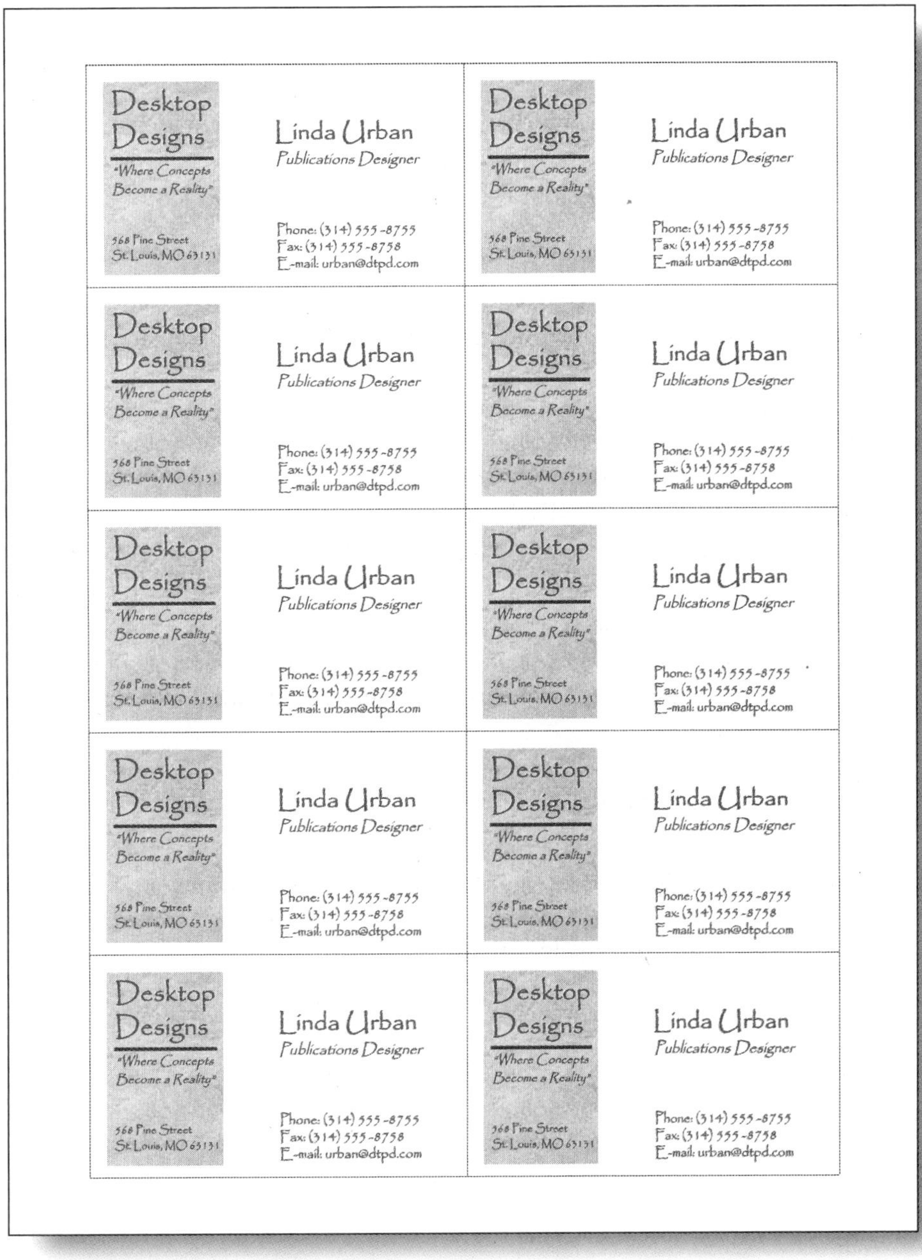

chapter summary

➤ A letterhead contains a specific design and layout that helps establish an organization's identity with a target audience. Designing and producing your own letterhead can be a less costly alternative to having it designed and produced through a professional printer.

➤ A number of letter templates are available, including Contemporary, Elegant, and Professional. A Letter Wizard is also available that guides you through the creation of a business letter.

➤ The Click and Type feature allows you to click in any blank area of the screen and positions the insertion point at that location along with automatically inserting associated formatting such as tabs and paragraph returns. This feature also lets you position the insertion point so that text to be keyed will be left-, right-, or centered-aligned.

➤ A text box is used as a container for text and/or graphics. Text boxes are extremely useful in desktop publishing because text and/or graphics can be placed at exact horizontal and/or vertical locations on the page. They can also serve as placeholders for items such as illustrations and photos.

➤ Ruled lines act as boundaries to the surrounding text. Ruled lines can be used in a document to create a focal point, draw the eye across or down the page, separate columns and sections, or add visual appeal.

➤ An existing template document can be customized once it is displayed at the document screen. Any changes made only affect the document displayed on the screen, leaving the template available in its original format.

➤ A new template can be created from any existing Word document. Saving documents, such as letterheads or envelopes, as template documents ensures that they are always available to use over again and thus increases efficiency and productivity.

➤ Kerning is the process of decreasing or increasing the white space between specific character pairs and is used on headlines and other blocks of large type.

➤ Tracking is the equal reduction or enlargement of the horizontal space between all characters in a block of text.

➤ WordArt can be used to distort or modify text in a variety of interesting shapes. Use WordArt to create company logos, letterheads, headlines, and headings in flyers and announcements.

➤ When creating a design for an envelope, select enough common elements so that a link is established in the viewer's eyes between the letterhead and the envelope.

➤ Use the AutoText feature to save and insert frequently-used text and/or graphics.

➤ Business cards are another way to establish identity among a target audience. Establish an identifying connection between a business card and a letterhead by repeating some of the design elements from the letterhead.

commands review

	Mouse/Keyboard
New dialog box to access a template	Click File, New; select desired tab
Letter Wizard	Click File, New, Letters & Faxes tab
User Information	Click Tool, Options, User Information tab
Change font	Click Format, Font; or click the Font list box, Font Size list box, and/or character formatting buttons on the Formatting toolbar
Display Drawing toolbar	Click Drawing button on Standard toolbar; or right-click Standard toolbar, select Drawing; or click View, Toolbars, and then Drawing
Format AutoShape dialog box	Select object, click Format and AutoShape; or double-click the object
Border a paragraph	Position insertion point, click Border button or arrow on Formatting toolbar; or click Format, Borders and Shading, and Borders tab
Create Header/Footer	Click View, Header and Footer, click Switch Between Header and Footer to display Footer pane
Insert a text box	Click Text Box button on Drawing toolbar, position crosshairs, click and drag to draw box
Format Text Box dialog box	Select text box, click Format and Text Box; or double-click the text box border
Kerning (character spacing between specific pairs of characters)	Click Format, Font, Character Spacing tab, Kerning for fonts, and enter Points and above
Tracking (character/letter spacing)	Click Format, Font, Character Spacing tab, Spacing, enter point By: amount in point increments
Create a WordArt object	Click the WordArt button on the Drawing toolbar; or click Insert, point to Picture, and then click WordArt
Envelopes and Labels dialog box	Click Tools, Envelopes and Labels, and select Envelopes or Labels tab
Symbol dialog box	Insert, Symbol
Create AutoText entry	Click Insert, point to AutoText, and then click New
Insert an AutoText entry	Key AutoText entry name and press F3; or click Insert, point to AutoText, and then click AutoText

thinking offline

Terms: In the space provided at the left, indicate the correct term.

_____ 1. This feature guides you through the steps for creating a business letter using any of the available letter templates.

_____ 2. This term refers to the decreasing or increasing of white space between specific character pairs.

_____ 3. In typesetting, the thickness of a line is called its weight and is measured in this.

_____ 4. A customized horizontal or vertical ruled line can be created using this feature.

_____ 5. This term refers to the equal reduction or enlargement of the horizontal space between all characters in a block of text.

_____ 6. Use this feature to position the insertion point in a blank area of the document or to change paragraph alignment for text to be keyed.

_____ 7. Turn on kerning for specific point sizes and above at this dialog box.

_____ 8. This feature allows you to store commonly used text and/or graphics along with their formatting.

_____ 9. Use this type of paper size definition when designing and creating your own business cards.

Concepts: Answer the following questions in the space provided.

1. What is the purpose of a letterhead?

2. What information might be contained in a letterhead?

3. Define the User Information feature. What other Word features does it affect?

4. When creating your own letterhead, design concepts such as focus, balance, and proportion should be considered. What are some other design concepts that should be considered?

5. Name two methods of creating ruled lines in Word. Explain advantages or disadvantages of using one method over the other.

6. Explain the various ways a text box may be customized.

Assessment 1

1. You have decided to open your own restaurant. Design a letterhead for your business that will be used for a mailing to introduce it to the community and for all your future business correspondence. Include the following information:

Company Name:	You decide on the name depending on the picture/graphic that you incorporate into your design.
Name of Owner:	Use your own name and include Owner or Proprietor as your title.
Slogan:	You decide on a slogan.
Address:	**250 San Miguel Boulevard** **Mission Viejo, CA 92691**
Phone:	**(714) 555-8191**
Fax:	**(714) 555-8196**

2. Create thumbnail sketches of your restaurant's letterhead by incorporating the following elements:
    a. An asymmetrically balanced design.
    b. Appropriate and proportional typeface, type size, and type style selections.
    c. Turn on kerning and use tracking (condensing or expanding character spacing), if necessary, for a desired effect.
    d. Some suggestions for graphics and layout:
        (1) Include one of the clip art images found in the Food and Dining category at the Clip Art Gallery in your letterhead. Use the image to inspire you on a theme and a color scheme. (You may use any other relevant clip art that is available to you.)
        (2) Create a restaurant logo using WordArt and/or AutoShapes.
        (3) Include a ruled horizontal or vertical line.
        (4) Include consistent elements such as typeface, color, alignment, repetitive symbol or graphic element, etc.
        (5) Group related items close to each other.
        (6) Use color (sparingly) if a color printer is available.
        (7) Make sure your letterhead is not too large.
        (8) Use special characters if appropriate.
3. Save the document and name it c03sa01, Restaurant ltrhd.
4. Print c03sa01, Restaurant ltrhd.
5. Save your letterhead as a document template in your template folder on your hard drive or a floppy disk and name it restaurant ltrhd. Close Restaurant ltrhd.
6. As a self-check for your design, print a copy of Document Analysis Guide.doc from your student CD and answer the questions on the form. Name the exercise c03sa01, Restaurant ltrhd.
7. Attach the Document Analysis Guide to the hard copy of the letterhead.

Assessment 2

1. Design an envelope to be used with the restaurant letterhead created in assessment 1. Include some consistent elements that demonstrate continuity from the letterhead to the envelope. Include the following specifications:
   a. Create thumbnail sketches of your proposed envelope design.
   b. At a clear editing window, use the automatic envelope feature and add the envelope to the blank document.
   c. Use the same typeface(s) as in your letterhead. Pay attention to size and proportion.
   d. Turn on automatic kerning and adjust character spacing if necessary.
   e. Use the same color scheme in the envelope as in your letterhead.
2. Save your envelope as a template and name it (your name) Restaurant env.
3. Close (your name) Restaurant env.
4. Access your envelope template and insert your own name and address in the mailing address area.
5. Save the document and name it c03sa02, Restaurant env.
6. Print and then close c03sa02, Restaurant env.

Assessment 3

1. Create a page of business cards to coordinate with the restaurant letterhead and envelope created in assessments 1 and 2. Even though a business card does not have to be an exact replica of your letterhead, include some consistent identifying elements that link the two documents together. Include the following specifications when creating the business cards:
   a. Create thumbnail sketches of your proposed business card design and layout.
   b. Use the Labels feature and the Avery 5371 (or 8371) business card label definition.
   c. Use the same typeface(s) used in your letterhead. You decide on size and proportion.
   d. Kern and track if necessary.
   e. If you used color in your letterhead, use it here also.
   f. Create an AutoText entry that will work easily in the Envelope and Labels feature. If you have difficulty using the AutoText entry in the Envelopes and Labels feature, you may have to add a blank sheet of label forms to a clear document screen, create the business card in the first label form, and then copy it to the rest of the labels.
2. Save and name the business cards as c03sa03, Restaurant buscard.
3. Print and then close c03sa03, Restaurant buscard.

CREATIVE ACTIVITY

Find an example of a letterhead from a business, school, or volunteer organization. Redesign the letterhead using the desktop publishing concepts learned so far. On a separate sheet, key the changes you made and explain why you made those changes. Evaluate your letterhead using the Document Analysis Guide (Document Analysis Guide.doc) located on your student CD. Name the revised letterhead c03ca01. Submit a thumbnail sketch, the original letterhead (or a copy), the revised letterhead, and the Document Analysis Guide.

Chapter 04

Creating Personal Documents

P E R F O R M A N C E   O B J E C T I V E S

Upon successful completion of chapter 4, you will be able to create compact disc covers, calendars, personal address labels, personal stationery and envelopes on odd-sized paper, and certificates.

DESKTOP PUBLISHING TERMS

Balance	Grouping	Kerning
Character spacing	Stacking	Form
Color	Unprintable Zone	

WORD FEATURES USED

AutoShapes	Form fields	Tables
Calendar Wizard	Group and ungroup	Text boxes
Drawing toolbar	Page Border	Text fields
Envelopes and Labels	Pictures	Watermark
Fill effects	Tabs	

In this chapter, you will produce personal documents using Word's templates and wizards, and create and format your own personal documents. You will use other Word features such as tables, text boxes, and labels to produce compact disc covers, calendars, address labels, personal stationery, and certificates. In addition, you will apply basic desktop publishing concepts of planning document content, maintaining consistency, and achieving balance through the use of pictures, symbols, text, lines, color, and borders.

While you are creating the documents in this chapter, consider how you can apply what you have learned to create other personal documents such as invitations, greeting cards, tickets, bookmarks, recipe cards, bookplates, change-of-address cards, thank you cards, personal note cards, and even birth announcements. Sample personal documents are displayed in figure 4.1.

figure
4.1

Sample Personal Documents

Personal Cards

Invitation

Bookplate

Bookplate

Personalized Calendar

Change of Address Card

Invitation

Creating a Compact Disc Cover

Standard diskette labels and compact disc labels are used to catalog the contents of a disk/disc. If you were to purchase a new computer today, you may have the option to purchase a CD-ROM, CD-R, DVD-ROM, CD-RW, and/or Zip Drive. Each storage medium is associated with a particular label and/or additional elements to identify the contents. A Zip disk stores about 70 times the capacity of a traditional floppy and looks very similar to a standard floppy disk. Therefore, an Avery standard diskette label measuring 2-3/4 by 2-3/4 inches may be customized and used to identify the contents of the disk.

The rewriteable CD-ROM and CD-RW discs store about 650 MB of data and measure approximately 4-3/4 inches diameter and may be identified using a label on the disc cover (sometimes called a jewel case). Word includes an Avery label definition (#5824) for a CD front and back label measuring 4-1/2 by 4-1/2 inches. However, this label does not fit the case precisely and does not include a spine, which identifies the disc when stored on edge. You can make your own CD label and spine by creating tables and text boxes, adding borders around them, and then inserting graphics and lines.

Creating a Spine Label

To create a spine label, first design a text box (cell), then rotate the text from horizontal to vertical as shown in figure 4.2. To rotate the text, complete the following steps:

1. Position the insertion point in the cell where you want to rotate the text.
2. Click Format and then Text Direction.
3. At the Text Direction—Table Cell dialog box, select a text direction button that represents the desired effect, then click OK.

figure
4.2
Rotated Text in a Table

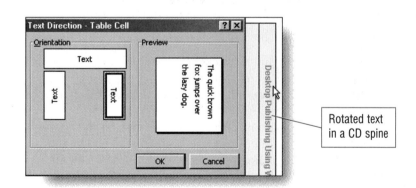

Rotated text in a CD spine

Creating Horizontal Lines that Align

Basically, there are four methods for creating horizontal lines that align:

1. Using the underscore key;
2. Using tabs with the underline command;
3. Using a tab leader; and
4. Using the Grid feature.

Using the underscore key to create lines is inefficient for long blanks and offers little control for aligning one line below another.

To draw lines quickly and control their alignment, use tabs with the Underline command. For instance, type the text (example: Name), turn Underline on, click on the ruler to set a custom tab where you want the blank to end, press Tab, then turn Underline off. (If used within a table, remember to press Ctrl + Tab to insert a Tab within a cell.)

The third method uses a tab leader. Choose Format and then Tabs. Set left tabs for the beginning of each data label and for each blank's end point. For each "end point" tab, select leader #4, the underline style, then click OK. Now after typing a label, press Tab (or Ctrl + Tab if used within a table) to insert the following blank line. This method will be used in exercise 2 for creating lines to hold file names and other information on the back of the CD case.

A fourth method uses the Grid feature. By default, objects (for example, *lines*) you draw are lined up against the nearest gridlines, making it easier to align multiple objects consistently.

Assume you recently purchased a computer with a CD-RW disk drive and as a student in a desktop publishing class, you will prepare a jewel case cover for a CD that will contain your completed documents. In exercise 1, you will create a CD label using a table and save the label as a template for use in creating additional customized CD labels.

exercise 1

Creating a Compact Disc Label

1. At a clear document window, create the CD label in figure 4.3 using a table by completing the following steps:
   a. Click Table, point to Insert, and then click Table.
   b. Create a table with 1 column and 1 row.
   c. Position the insertion point inside the table, click Table, and then click Table Properties.
   d. At the Table Properties dialog box, click the Center option in the Alignment section of the Table tab, and then click the Borders and Shading button.
   e. At the Borders and Shading dialog box, choose the Borders tab, and then click the Box button in the Setting section. Make sure a single 1/2 point black line displays around the table.
   f. Choose the Shading tab and click the More Colors button.

g. At the Standard tab, select the Ivory color located below the center white hexagon; then click OK. Click OK again to close the Borders and Shading dialog box.

h. Choose the Row tab, click the check box at the left of Specify height: in the Size section, and key **4.75** inches. The Row height should display *At least*.

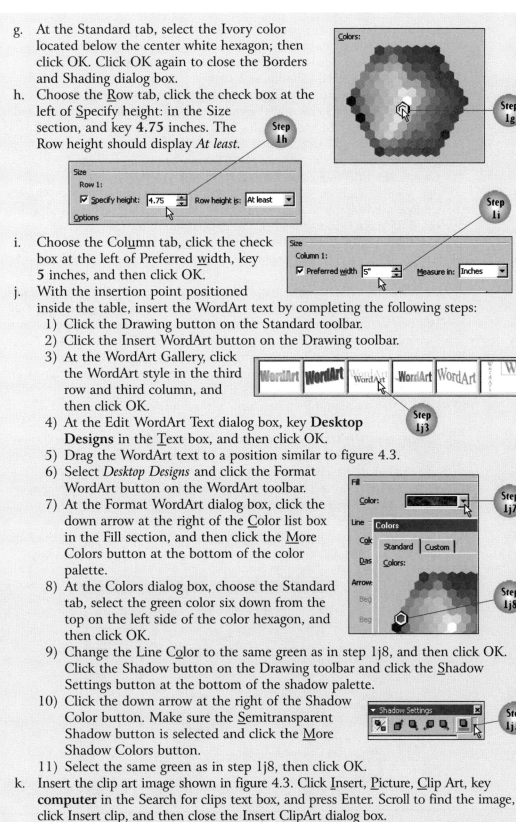

i. Choose the Column tab, click the check box at the left of Preferred width, key **5** inches, and then click OK.

j. With the insertion point positioned inside the table, insert the WordArt text by completing the following steps:
   1) Click the Drawing button on the Standard toolbar.
   2) Click the Insert WordArt button on the Drawing toolbar.
   3) At the WordArt Gallery, click the WordArt style in the third row and third column, and then click OK.
   4) At the Edit WordArt Text dialog box, key **Desktop Designs** in the Text box, and then click OK.
   5) Drag the WordArt text to a position similar to figure 4.3.
   6) Select *Desktop Designs* and click the Format WordArt button on the WordArt toolbar.
   7) At the Format WordArt dialog box, click the down arrow at the right of the Color list box in the Fill section, and then click the More Colors button at the bottom of the color palette.
   8) At the Colors dialog box, choose the Standard tab, select the green color six down from the top on the left side of the color hexagon, and then click OK.
   9) Change the Line Color to the same green as in step 1j8, and then click OK. Click the Shadow button on the Drawing toolbar and click the Shadow Settings button at the bottom of the shadow palette.
   10) Click the down arrow at the right of the Shadow Color button. Make sure the Semitransparent Shadow button is selected and click the More Shadow Colors button.
   11) Select the same green as in step 1j8, then click OK.

k. Insert the clip art image shown in figure 4.3. Click Insert, Picture, Clip Art, key **computer** in the Search for clips text box, and press Enter. Scroll to find the image, click Insert clip, and then close the Insert ClipArt dialog box.

l. Select the image, click the Text Wrapping button on the Picture toolbar, click In Front of Text, and then move and size the image similar to figure 4.3.

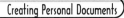

m. Create another table for the back of the CD case by completing the following steps:
   1) Press Ctrl + Enter to create a hard page break. (Look at the Status Bar to make sure your insertion point is located on the second page.)
   2) Create a table with 2 columns and 1 row.
   3) At the Table Properties dialog box, click the Center option in the Alignment section of the Table tab, and then click the Borders and Shading button.
   4) At the Borders and Shading dialog box, make sure a single 1/2 point black line displays in and around the table (select All), and add the same Ivory shading as used on the front of the CD case label.
   5) Choose the Row tab, click the check box at the left of Specify height: in the Size section, and key **4.65** inches. The Row height should display *At least.*
   6) Choose the Column tab, click the check box at the left of Preferred width, key **5.35** inches, and then click the Next Column button.
   7) Key **0.18** inch in the Column 2 Preferred width text box.
   8) Choose the Cell tab, select Center in the Vertical alignment section, and then click OK.
   9) Click the Text Box button on the Drawing toolbar, drag the crosshairs into the first cell, and create a text box approximately **1-1/2″** Height by **3-1/2″** Width. (Verify the measurements at the Format Text Box dialog box, on the Size tab.)
   10) Click the Center align button on the Formatting toolbar, change the font to 12-point Arial bold, italic, press Enter, and then key **Your name**. Press Enter twice, turn off italic, and then key **Course name and number**.
   11) Press Enter twice and then key **Your e-mail address**. Press Enter twice, turn on italic, and then key the **Current date**.
   12) Double-click the text box, choose the Colors and Lines tab at the Format Text Box dialog box, click the down arrow at the right of Color in the Fill section, and then click the Fill Effects button.
   13) Click the radio button to the left of Two Colors and select the same green color used in step 1j8 in the Color 1 list box.
   14) At the Color 2 list box, select the same ivory color used in step 1g.
   15) Click the Diagonal down Shading style, select the first variant in the Variants section, and then click OK.

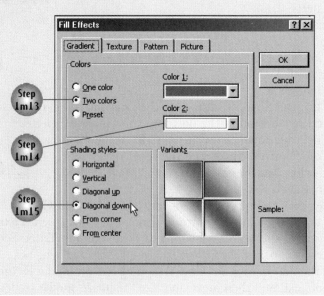

16) Click the down arrow at the right of Color in the line section and select *No Line*.

17) Click OK again to close the Format Text Box dialog box.

18) Position the text box similar to figure 4.3.

n. Create horizontal lines, to be used for file names and information, above the text box by completing the following steps:

1) At the Tabs dialog box, create a Left Tab at **0.5** inch and a Left Tab with a single line Leader (#4) at **4.5** inches, and then click OK.

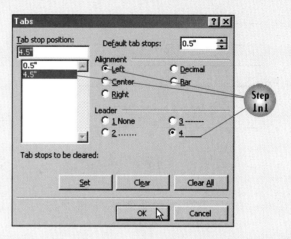

Step 1n1

2) Position the insertion point in the first cell, and press Enter three times.

3) Press Ctrl + Tab twice, and then press Enter twice. (A horizontal line should display from the first tab to the next tab.)

4) Repeat step 1n3 five more times to create a total of 6 lines.

o. Create the text in the spine of the CD case by completing the following steps:

1) Position the insertion point in the spine text box; click Format and then Text Direction.

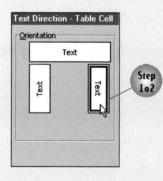

Step 1o2

2) At the Text Direction—Table Cell dialog box, select the right vertical box in the Orientation section; then click OK.

3) Click the Center align button on the Formatting toolbar.

4) Change the font to 12-point Arial bold in the same green used in step 1j8, and then key **Desktop Publishing Using Word 2000**.

2. View the labels in Print Preview.

3. Save the document as a template and name it c04ex01, CD.dot.

4. Print and then close c04ex01, CD.dot.

5. Cut out the front and back of the CD label along the borderlines, fold at the left border to create the spine, and then insert each label in the front and back of the CD case.

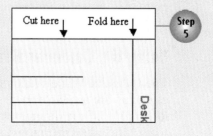

Step 5

figure

4.3

Exercise 1

Desktop Designs
Desktop Designs

Desktop Publishing Using Word 2000

Your Name

Course name and number

Your e-mail address

Date

Creating a Personal Calendar

A calendar can be one of the most basic tools of organization in your everyday life. No desk at home or at work is complete without a calendar to schedule appointments, plan activities, and serve as a reminder of important dates and events.

A calendar may also be used as a marketing tool in promoting a service, product, or program. For example, a schedule of upcoming events may be keyed on a calendar to serve as a reminder to all the volunteers working for a charitable organization, or the calendar may be sent to prospective donors to serve as a daily reminder of the organization.

You will customize your own calendar using Word's Calendar Wizard in exercise 2. If you want to create your own calendar from scratch without the help of the Calendar Wizard, you may want to start by creating a table.

Using the Calendar Wizard

The Calendar Wizard helps you create monthly calendars. Three basic styles of calendars are available: Boxes and borders, Banner, and Jazzy. See figure 4.4 for an illustration of the different styles. In addition, other customizing options in the wizard include: Portrait or Landscape orientation, placeholder for a picture, and starting and ending months.

figure
4.4
Calendar Wizard Template Types

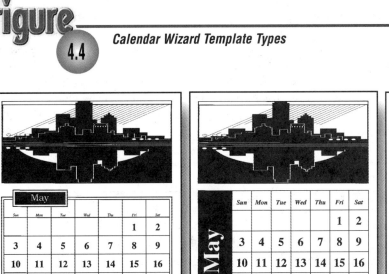

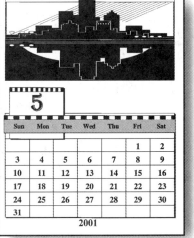

BOXES AND BORDERS   **BANNER**   **JAZZY**

To access the Calendar Wizard, click File, then New. Choose the Other Documents tab and double-click the Calendar Wizard icon. Proceed with making choices from the prompts built into the template. Continue clicking the Next> button to advance to the next screen. Click Finish when the calendar is complete.

Adding, Removing, or Replacing a Picture in a Calendar

The default picture used in the Calendar Wizard is *Cityscpe.wmf.* This picture is inserted in a placeholder, so you can easily replace it with a different image. After using the Calendar Wizard, select the existing picture and press Delete. To replace the image, click Insert, then Picture, or Insert, then Object, depending on the source of your graphic. (A photo would look great!)

DTP POINTERS
Use scanned photos of family, friends, or pets in your personalized documents.

Entering Information into a Calendar

To enter information, click where you want to insert the text, then start keying. To move between different dates in the calendar, press Tab to move forward and press Shift + Tab to move to the previous date. Remember that the calendar template is formatted in a table. Click the Center align button on the Formatting toolbar to center text within a cell. Select rows or columns and apply different styles if you are not satisfied with the default ones, or customize the styles to fit your specific needs. *(Hint: Turn on the Show/Hide button to view formatting symbols.)*

Adding a Shape to a Calendar

You can automatically create a variety of shapes by using the AutoShapes tools on the Drawing toolbar. The AutoShapes menu contains several categories of shapes. In addition to lines, there are basic shapes, block arrows, flowchart elements, stars and banners, and callouts. One of the star shapes (16-Point Star) was selected to show emphasis and draw attention to an important fact, as shown in figure 4.5. In addition, yellow fill was added for impact. Text was added to the shape by selecting the star shape, right-clicking the mouse, and then clicking the Add Text option as shown in figure 4.6.

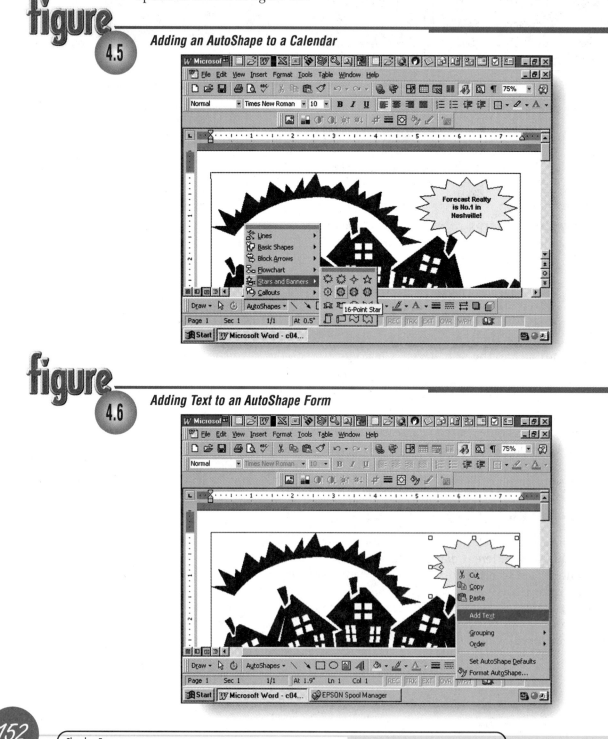

figure 4.5

Adding an AutoShape to a Calendar

figure 4.6

Adding Text to an AutoShape Form

To draw an AutoShape, click A̲utoShapes on the Drawing toolbar, point to a category, and then click the shape you want. Click in the document to add the shape at its default size, or drag it to the size you want. Notice in figure 4.7 the yellow adjustment handle in the AutoShape form. Many AutoShapes have adjustment handles you can drag to adjust a unique aspect of the shape.

figure 4.7

Dragging an Adjustment Handle to Reshape an AutoShape Object

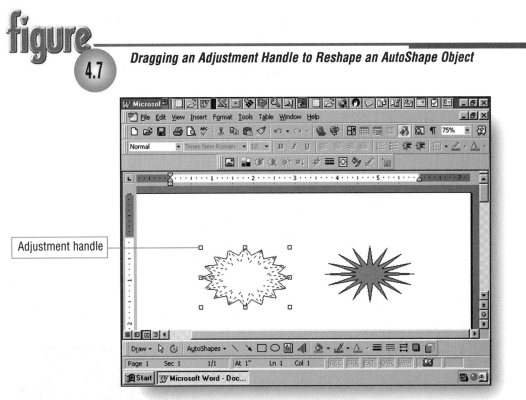

Adjustment handle

Troubleshooting Calendars

If the bottom line of your document does not print, you may have to make adjustments to your document to compensate for the unprintable zone of your particular printer. The *unprintable zone* is an area where text will not print; this area varies with each printer. For instance, if the bottom line of the calendar created in exercise 2 does not print properly, increase or decrease the top and/or bottom margins, or use a smaller font size, or rewrite some of the text. If the margins cannot be changed, experiment with moving the text up or reducing the length of the document. Another option is to draw a line using the Line tool on the Drawing toolbar.

Unprintable Zone
An area where text will not print.

If you choose to draw a horizontal line to fix the side of a calendar that will not print, you may want to deselect the S̲nap objects to grid option at the Grid feature. To access the Grid controls, click the D̲raw button on the Drawing toolbar. Choose G̲rid to open the Drawing Grid dialog box. You can input new values for both the Horizontal and V̲ertical Spacing. Word automatically aligns objects to this invisible grid, with each square in the grid set to 0.13″ by 0.13″. You can turn the grid off, make the gridlines visible, or even specify where on the page you want the grid to begin. Figure 4.8 illustrates the Grid dialog box, where you may turn on or off the S̲nap object to grid option. If you turn the grid feature off, you may move lines closer to other intersecting lines or objects.

 **figure**
4.8

Grid Dialog Box

> Remove the check mark to turn the Grid feature off.

Drawing Grid

Snap to
☑ Snap objects to grid
☐ Snap objects to other objects

Grid settings
Horizontal spacing: `0.13`
Vertical spacing: `0.13`

Grid origin
☑ Use margins
Horizontal origin: `1.18"`
Vertical origin: `1.38"`

☐ Display gridlines on screen
☐ Vertical every:
Horizontal every: `3`

[Default...] [OK] [Cancel]

In exercise 2, assume that a friend of yours owns a small real estate office in your hometown and you occasionally volunteer your time to help with desktop publishing projects. Create a calendar that will be given to prospective homebuyers and sellers.

exercise 2

Customizing a Calendar

1. Use the *Calendar Wizard* to create a calendar by completing the following steps:
   a. Click File and then New.
   b. At the New dialog box choose the Other Documents tab.
   c. Select Document in the Create New section, and then double-click the Calendar Wizard icon.
   d. At the Start screen, click Next.
   e. At the Style screen, select the Banner style, and then click Next.
   f. At the Direction & Picture screen, select Portrait, and then select Yes to leave room for a picture. Click Next.
   g. At the Date Range screen, select February and 2001 in the Start Month, End Month, and Year list boxes. Then, click Next.
   h. At the Finish screen, click Finish.
   i. If the Office Assistant appears, click the Add, remove, or replace picture option. Read the Office Assistant's advice, and then click OK.

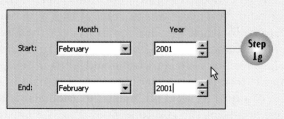

	Month	Year	
Start:	February	2001	
End:	February	2001	

Step 1g

j. Click the Enter information into the calendar option. Read the Office Assistant's advice, and then click OK.

k. Click the Cancel button to remove the Office Assistant.

2. Save the calendar with Save <u>A</u>s and name it c04ex02, Realty.

3. Replace the picture in the calendar by completing the following steps:

a. Display the Drawing toolbar.

b. At the document window, select and then delete the placeholder picture, *Cityscpe.wmf*. (You will know the picture has been selected when eight black sizing handles display inside the border of the picture. Be careful not to select the rectangular AutoShape instead of the picture. The AutoShape should remain once the picture has been deleted. If you accidentally remove the rectangle, you can undo the deletion by clicking the Undo button on the Standard toolbar.)

c. With the insertion point positioned inside the rectangle, insert the image shown in figure 4.9. Click <u>I</u>nsert, <u>P</u>icture, <u>C</u>lip Art, key **winter** in the Search for clips text box, and press Enter. Scroll to find the image, click Insert clip, and then close the Insert ClipArt dialog box.

4. Insert text near calendar dates by completing the following steps:

a. Select all of the rows in the calendar (table) except for the first row, which contains the days of the week. (Include the blank cells, too.)

b. Click the down arrow at the right of the Style button on the Formatting toolbar, and then select Normal (10 pt) from the list. (The calendar dates will display in 10 points allowing space in the cells to add text.)

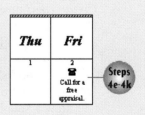

c. Select all of the rows, including the first row, and click the Center align button on the Formatting toolbar.

d. Deselect the rows by clicking anywhere in the calendar.

e. Position the insertion point to the right of February 2; then press Enter.

f. Click <u>I</u>nsert and then <u>S</u>ymbol.

g. Choose the <u>S</u>ymbols tab and change the Font to *Wingdings*.

h. Click the telephone symbol in the first row and the ninth column.

i. Click <u>I</u>nsert, then Close.

j. Press Enter and then key **Call for a free appraisal.**

k. Select the telephone symbol and change the font size to 14 points.

l. Position the insertion point to the right of February 12; then press Enter twice.

m. Key **Abraham Lincoln's Birthday**.

n. Position the insertion point to the right of February 14, then press Enter.

o. Insert the heart symbol located in the Symbol font in the fifth row and the third column from the right; then press Enter.

p. Click the down arrow at the right of the Font Color button on the Standard toolbar and select Red; then key **Valentine's Day**.

q. Select the heart symbol and change the font color to red and the font size to 16 points.

r. Key **President's Day** on February 19.

s. Key **George Washington's Birthday** on February 22 (change the font size to 9 points).

t. Key **Join our tour of homes at 10:00 a.m.** on February 27.

5. Key the text at the bottom of the calendar in figure 4.9 by completing the following steps:

a. Select the last row of blank cells, click T<u>a</u>ble, and then click <u>M</u>erge Cells.

b.   Deselect the cell; then press Enter.

c.   Turn kerning on at 14 points.

d.   Click Format, Paragraph, and key **6 pt** in the Before text box in the Spacing section. Click OK.

e.   Key **Predicting a Successful Move for You...**; then press Enter.

f.   Key **450 South Ashton Avenue ❖ Nashville ❖ TN 37201-5401**; then press Enter. (The ❖ symbol is located in the fourth row and third column of the Wingdings Font list box.)

g.   Key **(901) 555-1000 ❖ Fax (901) 555-6752 ❖ E-mail Forecst@msn.com**.

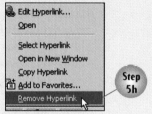

h.   Right-click on the hyperlink text, click Hyperlink, and then click Remove Hyperlink. The e-mail address should remain, but the hyperlink (blue text and underline) should be removed.

i.   Select *Predicting...* and change the font to 16-point Brush Script MT.

j.   Select the last two lines, *450 South Ashton...* and *(901) 555-1000...* and change the font to 10-point Times New Roman.

k.   Select the text box containing the year 2001, click Format, Borders and Shading, and then select the Shading tab.

l.   Select Green in the fifth row and fourth column of the Fill color palette and click OK.

m.   Click the Center align button on the Formatting toolbar.

n.   Click anywhere on *February* in the rotated text box, and then click the Center align button on the Formatting toolbar.

6.   Create the AutoShape form at the top of the calendar by completing the following steps:

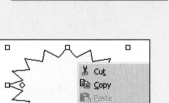

a.   Click the AutoShapes button on the Drawing toolbar, point to Stars and Banners, and then click the shape in the second row (16-Point Star).

b.   Drag the crosshairs to the top of the calendar and draw a shape in a size similar to figure 4.9; then release the left mouse button.

c.   Select the shape, click the down arrow to the right of the Fill Color button on the Drawing toolbar, and select Yellow.

d.   Select the shape, right-click the mouse, and then select Add Text.

e.   Click the Center align button on the Formatting toolbar.

f.   Change the font to 13-point Arial bold; then key **Forecast Realty is No. 1 in Nashville!**. (You may need to change the font size and position to fit the text inside your shape or adjust the size of the shape.)

g.   Select the shape, click the Shadow button on the Drawing toolbar, and select *Shadow Style 1* in the first row and the first column.

7.   Create the WordArt text at the bottom of the graphic by completing the following steps:

a.   Click the Insert WordArt button on the Drawing toolbar.

b.   At the WordArt Gallery, select the style displayed in the third row and fourth column.

c. At the Edit WordArt text dialog box, select 44-point Broadway and key **Forecast Realty** in the Text box. Click OK or press Enter.

d. Click the Format WordArt button on the WordArt toolbar, and change the Fill Color and Line Color to Green. (Make any necessary adjustments so that the document looks similar to figure 4.9.)

8. Save the document with the same name, c04ex02, Realty.
9. Print and then close c04ex02, Realty.

figure 4.9 ***Exercise 2***

Forecast Realty is No. 1 in Nashville!

Forecast Realty

February

2001

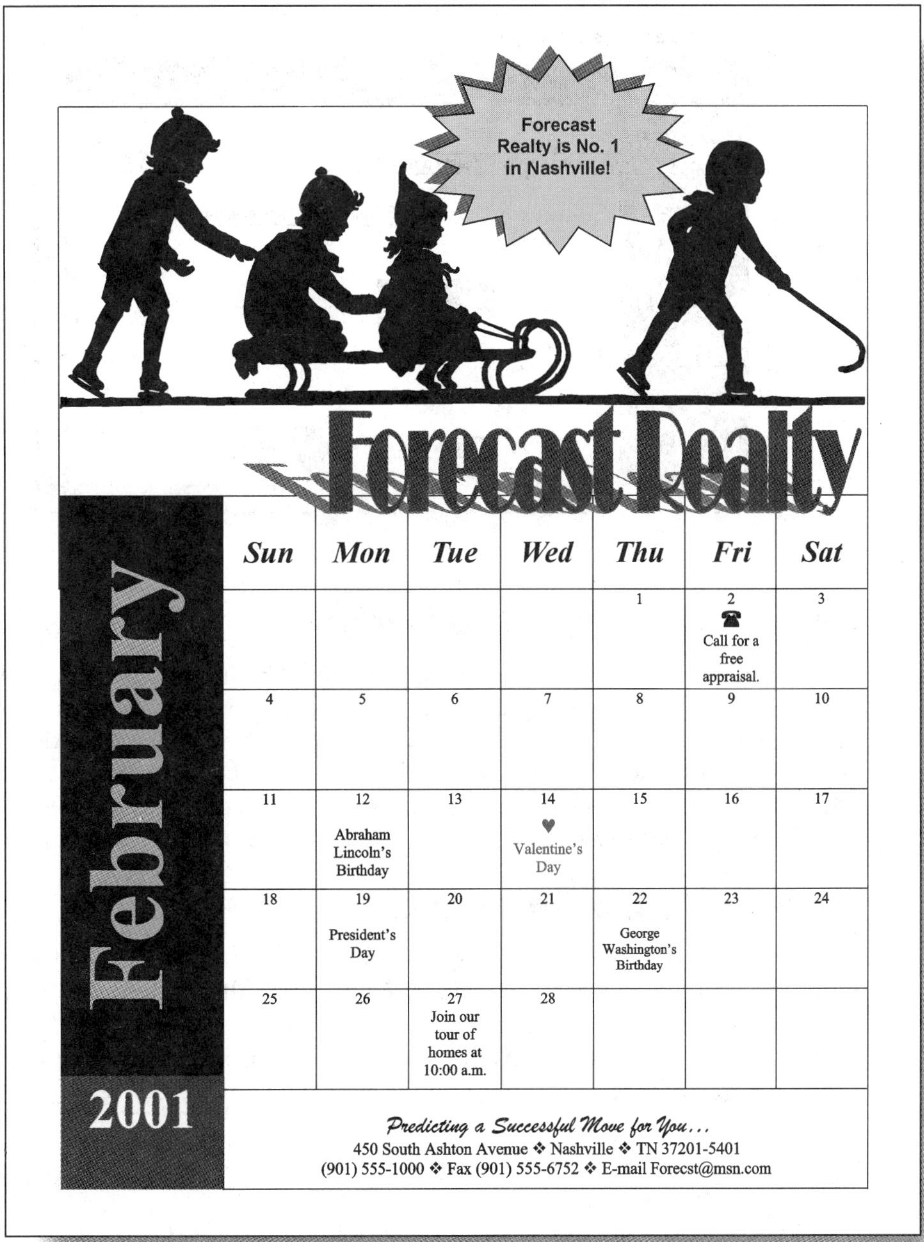

Sun	Mon	Tue	Wed	Thu	Fri	Sat
				1	2 ☎ Call for a free appraisal.	3
4	5	6	7	8	9	10
11	12 Abraham Lincoln's Birthday	13	14 ♥ Valentine's Day	15	16	17
18	19 President's Day	20	21	22 George Washington's Birthday	23	24
25	26	27 Join our tour of homes at 10:00 a.m.	28			

Predicting a Successful Move for You...
450 South Ashton Avenue ❖ Nashville ❖ TN 37201-5401
(901) 555-1000 ❖ Fax (901) 555-6752 ❖ E-mail Forecst@msn.com

Arranging Drawing Objects to Enhance Personal Documents

See figure 4.10 for suggestions on enhancing a calendar. A brief explanation of each feature follows figure 4.10.

figure
4.10

Arranging Drawing Objects in a Calendar (From Help)

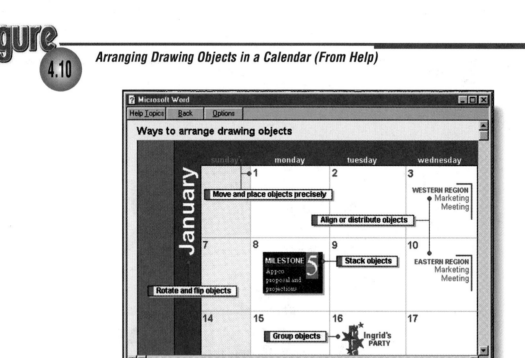

Moving and Placing Objects Precisely

To move a drawing object, click the object and then drag it when the mouse pointer becomes a four-headed arrow, or use the arrow keys on the keyboard. To use the keyboard to move an object, click the object, and then hold down the Ctrl key as you press the arrow key on the keyboard that corresponds to the direction you want to move the object. You may want to deselect the Snap objects to Grid option to more easily move the object closer to other design elements.

Aligning or Distributing Objects

You can align two or more drawing objects relative to each other by their left, right, top, or bottom edges or by their center (vertically) or middle (horizontally) as shown in figure 4.11. To align objects, click the Draw button on the Drawing toolbar, point to Align or Distribute, and then select one of the options listed, such as Align Left, Align Center, Align Right, Align Top, etc.

Aligning Objects

4.11

Order	▶
▦ Grid...	
Align or Distribute ▶	
Rotate or Flip ▶	
Change AutoShape ▶	
Set AutoShape Defaults	

▐	Align Left
♣	Align Center
⊒	Align Right
⑪	Align Top
◫	Align Middle
◫	Align Bottom

Stacking Objects

When you draw an object on top of another, you create an overlapping stack. Objects automatically stack in individual layers as you add them to a document. You see the stacking order when objects overlap. The top object covers a portion of objects beneath it, as discussed in chapter 2.

You may overlap as many drawing objects as you want and then rearrange them in the stack by clicking the D<u>r</u>aw button on the Drawing toolbar, pointing to O<u>r</u>der, then selecting one of the options listed, such as Bring to Fron<u>t</u>, Send to Bac<u>k</u>, etc. If you lose an object in a stack, you can press Tab to cycle forward or Shift + Tab to cycle backward through the objects until it is selected.

Grouping Objects

Grouping objects combines the objects as a single unit. To group drawing objects, hold the Shift key as you click each object, click the Draw button on the Drawing toolbar, and then click <u>G</u>roup. Alternatively, you can click the right mouse button, point to <u>G</u>rouping, and then click <u>G</u>roup. When objects have been grouped, sizing handles should appear around the new unit, as shown in figure 4.12, and not around each individual object.

Grouping
Combining objects as a single unit.

Grouping Text Boxes

4.12

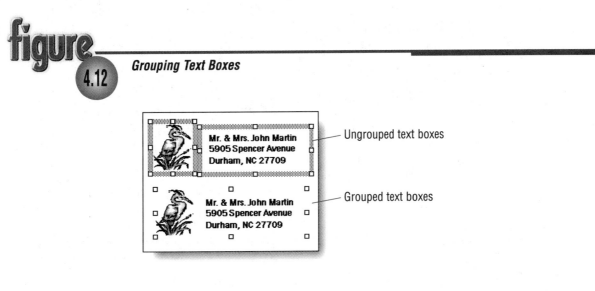

Rotating and Flipping Objects

To rotate or flip objects, select the object or grouped objects, then click the D<u>r</u>aw button on the Drawing toolbar, point to Rotate or Fli<u>p</u>, and click the option you want. You can also use the Free Rotate button on the Drawing toolbar. Generally, you cannot rotate or flip clip art images; however, if you ungroup and then group the images (they become drawing objects), you can usually rotate them.

Creating Personal Return Address Labels

Return address labels are convenient and cost efficient to use at home as well as at the office. Whether you are paying a huge stack of bills, addressing holiday cards, or volunteering to mail a hundred PTA newsletters, the convenience of having preprinted return labels is worth the little time it takes to create them. You can create your own return labels using Word's label feature. Word includes a variety of predefined label definitions that coordinate with labels that can be purchased at office supply stores.

When purchasing labels, be careful to select the appropriate labels for your specific printer. Labels are available in sheets for laser and ink jet printers. Carefully follow the directions given with your printer to insert the forms properly into the printer.

Return labels can be created using two different methods—creating labels individually and copying them using the label feature or creating labels using a data source and Word's merge feature. In exercise 3, you will create labels using a label definition and insert a picture. Merge will be used in a later chapter.

exercise 3

Personal Return Address Labels with a Graphic

1. At a clear document window, create the return address labels in figure 4.13 by completing the following steps:
   a. Display the Drawing toolbar.
   b. Click <u>T</u>ools, then <u>E</u>nvelopes and Labels.
   c. Select the <u>L</u>abels tab.
   d. Click the <u>O</u>ptions button.
   e. At the Label Options dialog box, select 5160 Address in the Product n<u>u</u>mber: list box.
   f. Make sure the Printer information is correct for your specific printer and then click OK or press Enter.
   g. At the Envelopes and Labels dialog box, click the New <u>D</u>ocument button.
   h. If gridlines of the labels (cells) do not display, click T<u>a</u>ble, then Show <u>G</u>ridlines.
   i. Position the insertion point in the first label (cell) and click the Text Box button on the Drawing toolbar.
   j. Drag the crosshairs into the first label and create a text box approximately 0.7″ in H<u>e</u>ight and 0.7″ in Wi<u>d</u>th. (Verify these settings by clicking F<u>o</u>rmat, then Text B<u>o</u>x.)
   k. At the Format Text Box dialog box, select the Layout tab. Make sure In <u>f</u>ront of text displays in the Wrapping style section.

l. Select the Text Box tab and change the internal margins to **0** inch in each of the margin text boxes; then click OK or press Enter.

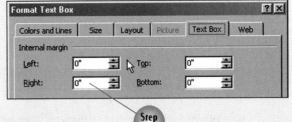

Step 1l

m. With the insertion point positioned in the text box, click Insert, point to Picture, and then click Clip Art.

n. At the Insert Picture dialog box, choose the *Animals* category and insert the *bird* clip art image shown in figure 4.13 or insert a clip art image of your choosing.

o. To remove the border around the text box, select the text box, click the down arrow at the right of the Line Color button on the Drawing toolbar, and select No Line.

p. Click the Text Box button on the Drawing toolbar and drag the crosshairs in the first label and to the right of the text box containing the picture.

q. Create the text box to measure approximately **0.65** inch in Height and **1.65** inches in Width. (Verify the settings at the Format Text Box dialog box.)

r. At the Format Text Box dialog box, select the Text Box tab and change the internal margins to **0** inch in each of the margin text boxes.

s. Select the Layout tab and make sure In front of text displays in the Wrapping style section, then click OK or press Enter.

t. With the insertion point positioned in the text box, change the font to 10-point Franklin Gothic Medium, and then key **Mr. & Mrs. John Martin** (press Enter) **5905 Spencer Avenue** (press Enter) **Durham, NC 27709**, or key your name and address.

Step 1t

u. Remove the border around the text box.

v. Group the two text boxes by completing the following steps:

1) Click the text box containing the picture, hold down the Shift key, and click the text box containing the address.

2) Click the Draw button on the Drawing toolbar.

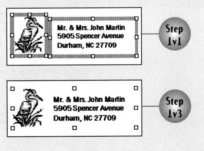

Step 1v1

Step 1v3

3) Click Group. (Sizing handles should display around the new unit.)

w. Copy the grouped text box to the second and third labels in the first row by completing the following steps:

1) Click the grouped text box, hold down the Ctrl key, and drag a copy of the box to the second label. (If the box displays slightly above the label, click the box and drag it down into the label.)

2) The arrow pointer should display with a + symbol to indicate a copy.

3) Release the mouse and a copy should display in the second label.

4) Drag and drop another copy of the grouped text box into the third label.

x. Copy the first row of labels by completing the following steps:

1) Position the insertion point in the first cell (label) in the first row of labels, click Table, point to Select, and then click Row.

2) Click Edit and then Copy.

3) Position the insertion point in the first label in the second row, click <u>E</u>dit and then <u>P</u>aste Rows.
4) Press the F4 key (the Repeat key repeats the last command).
5) Continue pressing the F4 key to copy the picture and address text to the remaining labels on the page.
y. When you have one complete page of labels, select any blank labels that may display on another page, click T<u>a</u>ble, point to <u>D</u>elete, and then click <u>R</u>ows.
2. Use Print Preview to make sure your document will print correctly.
3. Save the document with Save <u>A</u>s and name it c04ex03, Labels.
4. Print and then close c04ex03, Labels. (If possible, print the labels on an Avery 5160 sheet of labels.)

Edit	View	Insert	Format	Tools

↶ <u>U</u>ndo Move Object				Ctrl+Z
✂ Cu<u>t</u>				Ctrl+X
📋 <u>C</u>opy				Ctrl+C
📋 Paste Rows				Ctrl+V
Select A<u>l</u>l				Ctrl+A
🔍 <u>F</u>ind...				Ctrl+F

Step 1x3

figure

4.13

Exercise 3

Creating Personal Stationery on Odd-Sized Paper

Personal documents may include personalized note cards, stationery, and envelopes. A favorite clip art image, personal logo, distinctive color assortment, scanned image, or monogrammed text may be used to illustrate your unique style and personality. In exercise 4, you will create personal stationery and a matching envelope on custom-sized paper. Print the stationery on high-quality 24 lb. bond stock.

Notice the sample personal documents displayed in figure 4.14 and think about how you would create your own personalized documents.

figure
4.14

Samples of Personalized Documents

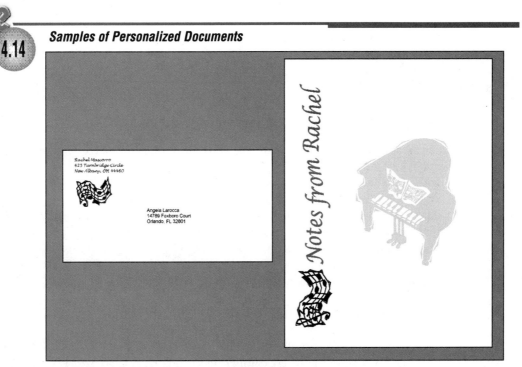

Personal Stationery

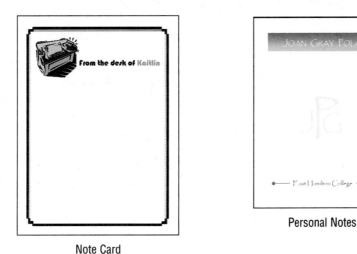

Note Card

Personal Notes

Inserting an AutoText Entry on an Envelope

To automatically include a graphic logo on all envelopes you print, you can save the graphic, including its position on the envelope, as an AutoText entry named **EnvelopeExtra1**. You can define up to two EnvelopeExtra AutoText entries. For instance, if you want Word to automatically insert additional text such as promotional text or a slogan each time you print an envelope, you can create another entry called **EnvelopeExtra2**. If you do not want the AutoText entry to print, simply delete it from the AutoText tab at the AutoCorrect dialog box.

Assume you want to create your own personal stationery and envelopes. Complete exercise 4 to learn how to do this using an odd-sized paper and envelope definition. You may use your name and address in place of *Susan Howard*. After you are finished, remember to change the paper and envelope sizes back to the default settings and delete the AutoText entry.

exercise 4

Creating Personal Stationery and an Envelope

1. At a clear document window, create the stationery in figure 4.15 by completing the following steps:
    a. Click File and then Page Setup.
    b. At the Page Setup dialog box, choose the Paper Size tab, click the down arrow at the right of the Paper size list box, and then select *Executive 7 1/4 × 10 1/2 in* (another good choice may be *Statement 5 1/2 × 8 1/2 in*).
    c. Make sure Portrait is selected.
    d. Choose the Margins tab, change all the margins to 1 inch, and then click OK.
    e. Insert the image shown in figure 4.15. Click Insert, Picture, Clip Art, key **opportunity** in the Search for clips text box, and then press Enter. Scroll to find the image, click Insert clip, and then close the Insert ClipArt dialog box.
    f. Display the Picture and Drawing toolbars.
    g. Select the image, click the Text Wrapping button on the Picture toolbar, and then click In Front of Text.
    h. Size and position the image as shown in figure 4.15. (Reduce the size by approximately 25 percent.)
    i. Click the Text Box button on the Drawing toolbar, drag the crosshairs into the document window, and create a text box that is approximately **0.5** inch in Height and **2.2** inches in Width.
    j. Position the insertion point in the text box, change the font to 22-point Bauhaus 93, and key **Susan Howard** (or your name if you prefer).
    k. Change the text box fill to No Fill.
    l. Change the text box line color to No Line.
    m. Drag the text box to position it similar to figure 4.15. (This is stacking.)

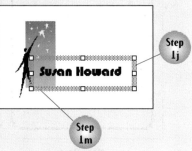

n. Click the AutoShapes button on the Drawing toolbar, point to Stars and Banners, and then click the *5-Point Star* in the first row and last column.

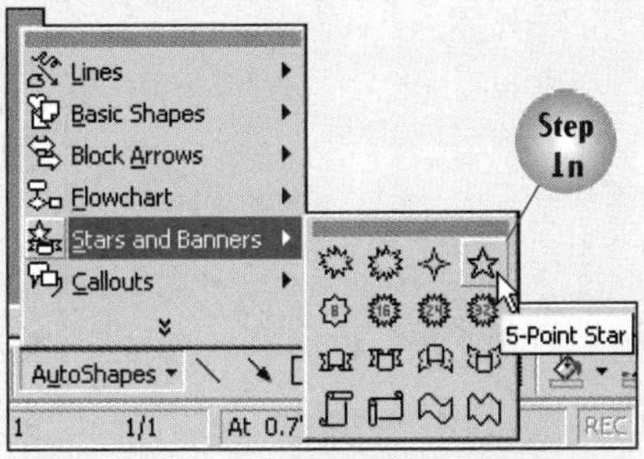

o. Drag the crosshairs to the right of the graphic and draw a small star.

p. Select the star and change the fill color to Light Yellow.

q. Select the star, click the Shadow button on the Drawing toolbar, and then click *Shadow Style 13* in the fourth row and first column.

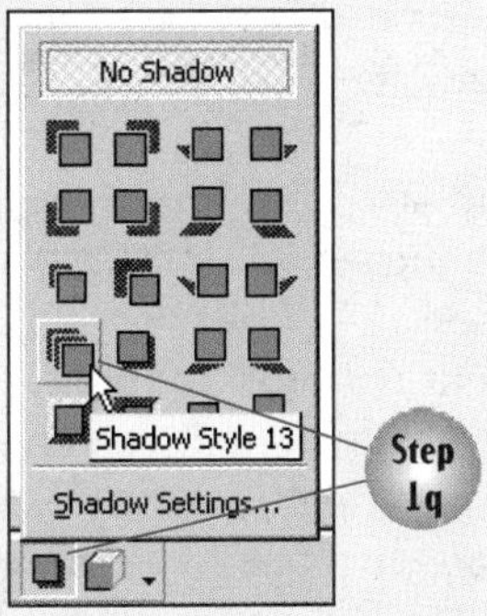

r. Select the star again, hold down the Ctrl key, and drag and drop two copies of the star; then position all three stars as shown in figure 4.15.

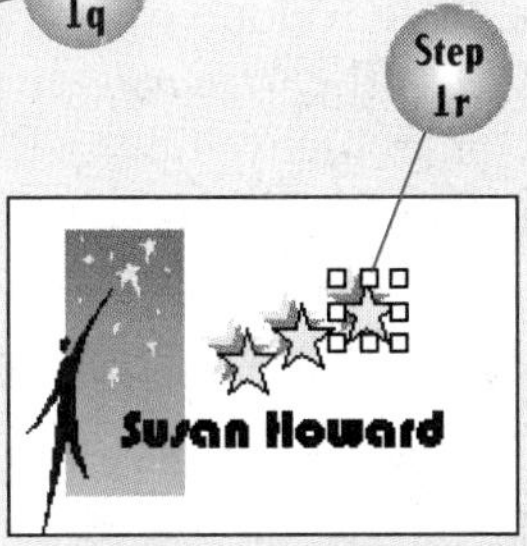

s. Group the design elements as one unit by completing the following steps:

1) Select the graphic, hold down the Shift key, select the text box containing *Susan Howard*, and then select each star.

2) Click the Draw button on the Drawing toolbar, and then click Group. (Eight sizing handles should display around all the design elements.)

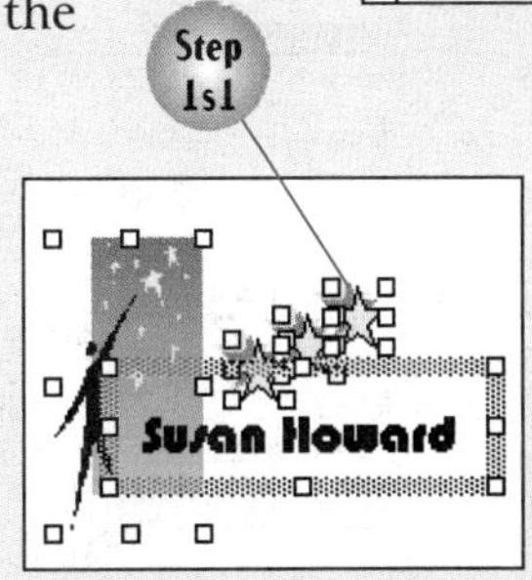

2. Save the document with Save As and name it c04ex04, Personal.

3. Create an AutoText entry that automatically inserts a graphic on the envelope by completing the following steps:

a. Click the New Blank Document button on the Standard toolbar.

b. Click Tools and then Envelopes and Labels.

c. At the Envelopes and Labels dialog box, click Options at the Envelopes tab.

d. Select the Envelope Options tab.

e. Click the down arrow at the right of the Envelope size list box and select *Monarch (3 7/8 × 7 1/2 in)*. Click OK.

f. Delete any text inside the Return address text box. Click Add to Document at the Envelopes tab.

g. Insert the image shown in figure 4.15. Click <u>I</u>nsert, <u>P</u>icture, <u>C</u>lip Art, key **opportunity** in the Search for clips text box, and then press Enter. Scroll to find the image, click Insert clip, and then close the Insert ClipArt dialog box.

h. Select the image and click the Text Wrapping button on the Picture toolbar.

i. Click <u>I</u>n Front of Text and position as shown in figure 4.15.

j. Select the image, click <u>I</u>nsert, point to <u>A</u>utoText, and then click <u>N</u>ew.

k. At the Create AutoText dialog box, key **EnvelopeExtra1** and then click OK. (Word automatically inserts the image each time it prints an envelope—you will delete the AutoText entry at the end of the exercise.)

l. Close the document without saving it.

4. At the c04ex04, Personal document screen, create the envelope by completing the following steps:

a. Access the *Monarch* envelope by completing steps 3b–3e. (If you do not have a Monarch envelope, select the standard No. 10 envelope.)

b. At the <u>E</u>nvelopes tab, key **Mr. John Sullivan** (press Enter), **6201 Essex Court** (press Enter), **Fort Wayne, IN 46801** in the <u>D</u>elivery address text box.

c. Click the <u>O</u>ptions button, click the <u>F</u>ont button in the Delivery address section, change the font to 17-pt. Bauhaus 93, and turn on kerning at 12 points. Click OK.

d. In the <u>R</u>eturn address text box, key **Susan Howard** (press Enter), **2534 Countryside Court** (press Enter), **Rochester Hills, MI 48306**. (Make sure there is not a check mark in the O<u>m</u>it check box.)

e. Click the <u>O</u>ptions button, click the <u>F</u>ont button in the Return address section, change the font to 11-pt. Bauhaus 93, and then click OK twice.

f. Click <u>A</u>dd to Document.

5. Save the document again with the same name (c04ex04, Personal).

6. Print and then close c04ex04, Personal. (You will print the letter and the envelope.)

7. Delete the AutoText entry, *EnvelopeExtra1*, by completing the following steps:

a. Click <u>I</u>nsert, point to <u>A</u>utoText, and then click AutoTe<u>x</u>t.

b. Scroll down until you find *EnvelopeExtra1*, select it, click <u>D</u>elete, and then click Close.

figure

4.15   *Exercise 4*

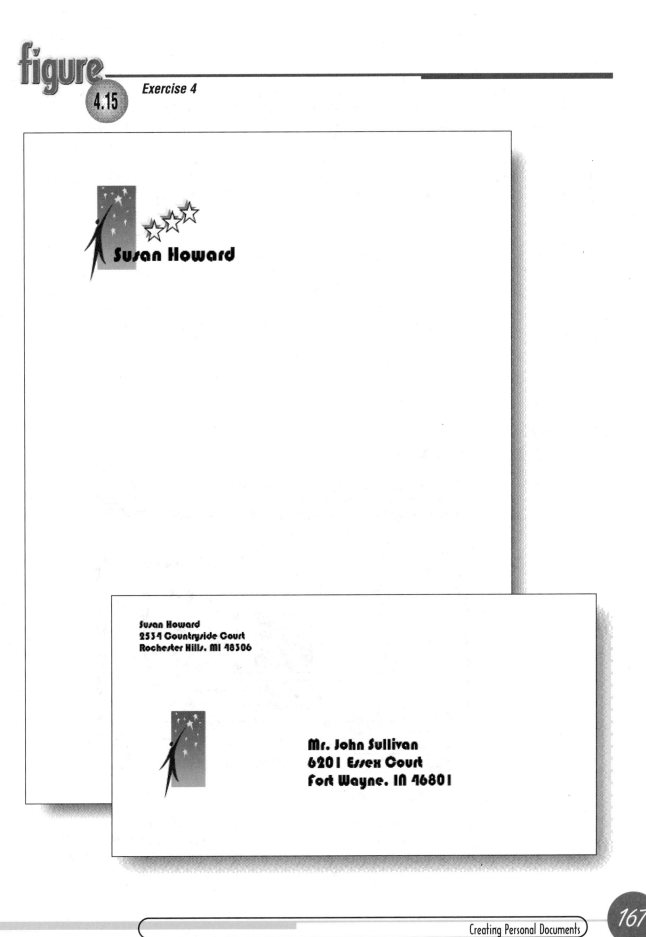

Creating a Certificate

Certificates are generally used to show recognition and promote excellence. Some other suggested uses for certificates include: diplomas, coupons, warranties, special event awards, program completion awards, and special-offer documents.

When printing your certificate, consider using an appropriate choice of high-quality 24 lb. uncoated bond stock or parchment paper in conservative colors, such as natural, cream, off-white, light gray, or any light marbleized color. In addition, consider using preprinted borders, ribbons, seals, and jackets, which are generally available through many mail-order catalogs and office supply stores.

DTP POINTERS
Use high-quality paper in conservative colors for business certificates.

DTP POINTERS
Preprinted papers add interest and professional appearance.

Adding a Page Border

Word provides page borders that range from simple to highly ornate. When planning the layout and design of your certificate, choose a border that best complements the content and purpose of your certificate.

DTP POINTERS
Use an appropriate border.

You can add a picture border (such as a row of ice cream cones) to any or all sides of each page in a document. To see the different kinds of page borders available, click Format, Borders and Shading, then select the Page Border tab. You may use one of the standard line borders and select different colors and widths, or click the down arrow at the right of the Art list box and choose more elaborate designs, as shown in figure 4.16.

Selecting a Page Border

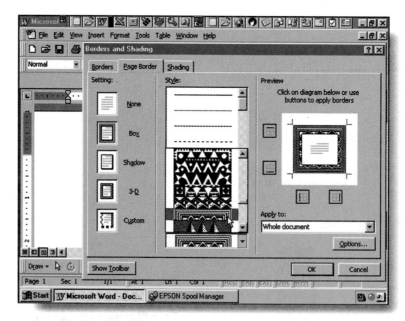

Changing Page Border Margins

Most printers cannot print to the edge of a page, especially at the bottom of the page. If a page border does not print, click the down arrow at the right of the Measure from: list box in the Borders and Shading Options dialog box, and select *Text* as shown in figure 4.17. Also, experiment with changing your document margins.

figure
4.17 *Borders and Shading Options*

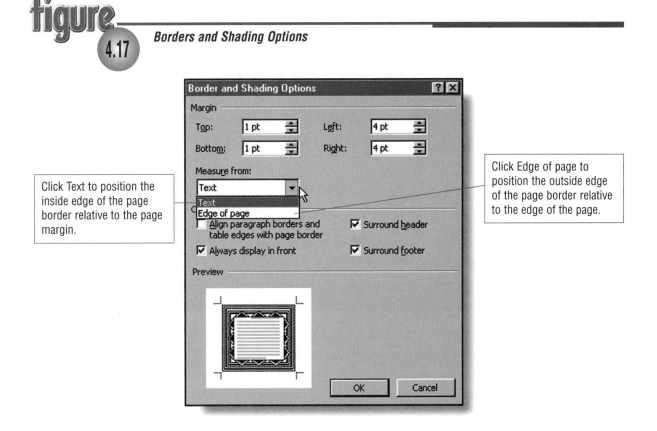

Click Text to position the inside edge of the page border relative to the page margin.

Click Edge of page to position the outside edge of the page border relative to the edge of the page.

Inserting Text Fields

Whether creating a client survey form for your company's marketing and research department, or creating an award certificate for volunteers at your local hospital, using form fields in your templates saves time and effort. In Word, a *form* is a protected document that includes fields where information is entered. A form document contains *form fields* that are locations in the document where one of three things is performed: text is entered (text field), a check box is turned on or off, or information is selected from a drop-down list. Basically three steps are completed in creating a form document:

1. Design the structure and enter the text that will appear in your document or template.
2. Insert form fields prompting the user to insert information at the keyboard.
3. Save the document as a protected document or template.

In exercise 5, assume you are a volunteer at Edward Hospital and you have offered to create an award certificate template. In this certificate, you will use the Forms toolbar, as shown in figure 4.18, and insert basic text fields.

Form
A protected document that includes form fields.

Form Fields
Locations in a document when text is entered, a check box is turned on or off, or a drop-down list is accessed.

figure
4.18

Forms Toolbar

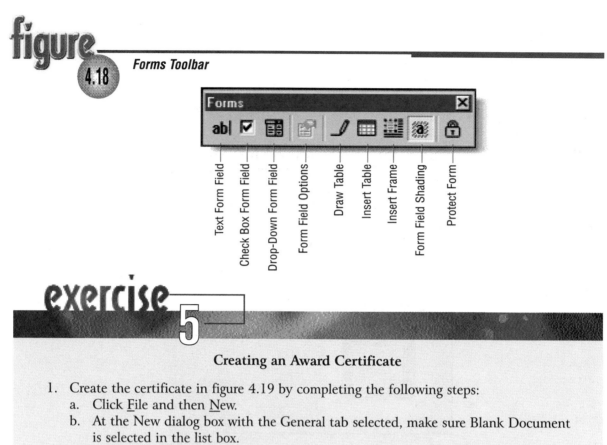

Text Form Field
Check Box Form Field
Drop-Down Form Field
Form Field Options
Draw Table
Insert Table
Insert Frame
Form Field Shading
Protect Form

exercise 5

Creating an Award Certificate

1. Create the certificate in figure 4.19 by completing the following steps:
   a. Click File and then New.
   b. At the New dialog box with the General tab selected, make sure Blank Document is selected in the list box.
   c. Click Template in the Create New section located at the bottom right corner of the dialog box. Click OK or press Enter.
   d. Display the Drawing and Picture toolbars.
   e. Select Landscape orientation at the Page Setup dialog box, and make sure the Top and Bottom margins are set at 1 inch and the Left and Right margins are set at 1.25 inches.
   f. Create the page border in figure 4.19 by completing the following steps:
      1) Click Format and then Borders and Shading.
      2) Select the Page Border tab.
      3) Click the down arrow at the right of the Art list box and select the border displayed in figures 4.16 and 4.19.
      4) Key **31 pt** in the Width text box.
      5) Click the Options button and then click the down arrow at the right of the Measure from: list box and select *Text*.
      6) Key **4 pt** in each of the four margin text boxes.
      7) Click OK and then click OK again to close the Borders and Shading dialog box.
   g. With the insertion point positioned inside the page border, click Insert and File; then insert the file Award.doc from your student CD.

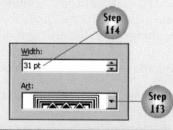

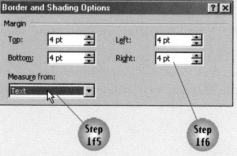

h. Select the entire document by pressing Ctrl + A; then turn on kerning at 14 points.
i. Select the following text and apply the listed formatting:

Community Service Award	42-point Matura MT Script Capitals with shadow
Awarded to	14-point Arial bold italic
XXX	24-point Britannic Bold
As an expression of...	12-point Arial
Your commitment of time...	12-point Arial
Presented by	14-point Arial bold italic
Edward Hospital...	22-point Britannic Bold in small caps with spacing expanded by 1.5 points
YYY	14-point Arial bold italic
Stephen, Ameeta, Joseph, Laurel...	12-point Arial

j. Change the Zoom to Page width.
k. Draw the signature lines in the award by completing the following steps:
1) Click the Line button on the Drawing toolbar.
2) Position the crosshairs above Stephen P. Becker, M.D.
3) Hold down the Shift key and drag the crosshairs to create a single line that is approximately 3.25 inches in length; then release the left mouse button. (Verify the length at the Format AutoShape dialog box.)
4) Select the line, hold down the Ctrl key, and then drag and drop a copy of the line above each of the names.

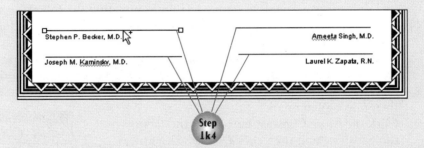

Step 1k4

l. Align the four lines by completing the following steps:
1) Select the line above Stephen P. Becker, M.D., hold down the Shift key, and select the line above Joseph M. Kaminsky, M.D.
2) Click the Draw button on the Drawing toolbar, point to Align or Distribute, and then click Align Left.

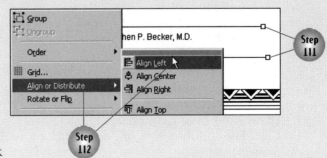

Step 1l1

Step 1l2

3) Align the remaining lines by following steps similar to l(1) and l(2); however, click Align Right.
4) Align the lines horizontally by following steps similar to l(1) and l(2).

m. Create two text fields to replace XXX and
   YYY in the document by completing the
   following steps:
1) Display the Forms toolbar.
2) Select XXX and click the Text Form Field
   button (first button from the left) on the
   Forms toolbar.
3) Click the Form Field Options button
   (fourth button from the left) on the
   Forms toolbar.
4) Key **Insert recipient's name** in the
   D̲efault text: text box.

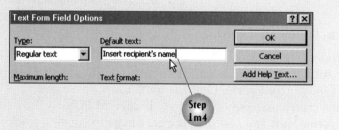

5) Click the down arrow at the right of the Text f̲ormat list box, select *Title case*,
   and then click OK or press Enter.
6) Select YYY and follow steps similar to steps m(2) and m(3), then key **Insert a**
   date in February in the text field. Close the Forms toolbar.
n. Create the heart watermark in figure 4.19 by completing the following steps:
1) Insert the heart clip art image shown in figure 4.19. Click I̲nsert, Picture, C̲lip
   Art, key **heart** in the Search for clips text box, and then press Enter. Scroll to
   find the image, click Insert clip at the pop-up menu, and then close the Insert
   ClipArt dialog box. (If the heart image is not available, choose another.)
2) Select the picture, click the Image Control button on the Picture toolbar, and
   then select W̲atermark.
3) Click the More Contrast button on the Picture
   toolbar twice and then click the Less Brightness
   button three times.
4) Click the Text Wrapping button and then click
   In̲ Front of Text.
5) Size and position the heart similar to figure 4.19.
6) Click the Text Wrapping button and then click
   Behin̲d Text.

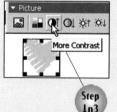

2. Save the template with Save A̲s and name it (Your name), Award.dot. (Ask your
   instructor if you should save the template to the hard drive or to a floppy disk, *DTP*
   Templates folder.)
3. Close (Your name), Award.dot.
4. Click F̲ile and then N̲ew or double-click on (your name), Award.doc if saved on your
   floppy disk.
5. Double-click (Your name), Award.dot. (Make sure D̲ocument is selected in the Create
   New section.)
6. Click the first text field and key **Grace Chu**. Click the next text field and key
   February 16, 2001.
7. Save the document with Save A̲s and name it c04ex05, Award.
8. Print and then close c04ex05, Award.

figure

4.19 *Exercise 5*

Community Service Award

Awarded to

Grace Chu

As an expression of your volunteer efforts for National Healthy Heart Month.
Your commitment of time, energy, and dedicated service is greatly appreciated.

Presented by

EDWARD HOSPITAL CARDIOVASCULAR INSTITUTE

February 16, 2001

Stephen P. Becker, M.D.   Ameeta Singh, M.D.

Joseph M. Kaminsky, M.D.   Laurel K. Zapata, R.N.

chapter summary

➤ Fill effects are added to documents for impact and focus.

➤ To draw lines quickly and to control their alignment, use tabs with the Underline command.

➤ Word provides a Calendar Wizard that guides you through the steps of creating monthly calendars in either portrait (narrow) or landscape (wide) orientation.

➤ Watermarks, pictures, special characters, shading, and text can be added to a calendar to enhance its appearance and add to its effectiveness. Reducing the shading of a watermark in a calendar improves the readability of the calendar text.

➤ AutoShape forms are added to documents to emphasize important facts. Text and fill can be added to an AutoShape form.

➤ Many AutoShape forms have adjustment handles you can drag to adjust a unique aspect of the shape.

➤ Adjustments may be necessary in the size and position of document elements to compensate for the unprintable zone of a particular printer.

➤ Deselect the Snap objects to Grid option to more easily move an object closer to another object.

➤ You can move objects precisely by holding down the Ctrl key as you press an arrow key on the keyboard.

➤ Objects automatically stack in individual layers as you add them to a document. You see the stacking order when objects overlap—the top object covers a portion of the objects beneath it.

➤ Grouping objects combines the objects into a single unit.

➤ You can align two or more drawing objects relative to each other by their left, right, top, or bottom edges or by their centers (vertically) or middles (horizontally).

➤ Selecting a predefined label definition at the Envelopes and Labels dialog box creates address labels.

➤ Use the F4 key to repeat a previous command.

➤ A page border can be added to any or all sides of a page.

➤ Form fields are added to documents or templates to allow the user to efficiently insert variable information.

commands review

	Mouse/Keyboard
Picture	Insert, Picture, Clip Art or From File
File	Insert, File
Text Box	Text Box button on Drawing toolbar
Watermark	View, Header and Footer, Insert Picture, Image Control, Watermark or Insert Picture, In Front of Text, Image Control, Watermark, Behind Text
WordArt	Insert, Picture, WordArt
Group	Draw, Group
AutoText	Insert, AutoText, New
Labels	Tools, Envelopes and Labels
Page Border	Format, Borders and Shading, Page Border tab
Align	Draw, Align or Distribute
Form Fields	View, Toolbars, Forms toolbar

True/False: Circle the letter T if the statement is true; circle the letter F if the statement is false.

T F 1. The Expanded Spacing option at the Font dialog box adjusts the vertical space between lines of text.

T F 2. Modifications made to a calendar template will be reflected in all calendars created with that template.

T F 3. Text can be rotated in a text box or in a cell in a table.

T F 4. Tabs and leaders may be used to create lines that vertically align.

T F 5. A text field is a form field where the user is prompted to enter text.

T F 6. A watermark image may be inserted into a calendar through a built-in prompt within the Calendar Wizard.

T F 7. Use the F2 key to repeat a command.

T F 8. Objects and text may not be grouped into a single unit.

T F 9. A picture or text may be added to an envelope by inserting an AutoText entry.

T F 10. The Shadow option may not be applied to AutoShape objects.

Concepts: Answer the following questions in the space provided.

1. How do you add borders and shading to a table?

2. How do you create a page border?

3. How do you insert, position, and modify a watermark?

4. How do you rotate text in a table?

5. How do you select several drawing objects and group the objects?

Assessment 1

You have volunteered to help your daughter's tennis coach prepare a calendar for the team's activities in June. Figure 4.20 is a sample calendar using a watermark for emphasis—use your own design ideas! Include the following specifications:

- Using the Calendar Wizard, choose a calendar style.
- Select a desired page orientation at the Calendar Wizard.
- Choose to leave room for a picture at the Calendar Wizard if you decide to use a clip art image, photo, or scanned image. Choose not to leave room for a picture if you decide to use a watermark.
- Select June 2001 for the calendar date.
- Use appropriate fonts, font sizes, font styles, and font colors.
- Include the text in figure 4.20.
- If you wish to add shading to cells in the table structure, click Format, Borders and Shading, and then select the Shading tab. Select a color in the Fill palette or select a Style and/or Color in the Patterns section. Make sure Cell displays in the Apply to list box. Click OK.
- Save the document and name it c04sa01, Tennis.
- Print and then close c04sa01, Tennis.

figure

4.20

Sample Calendar

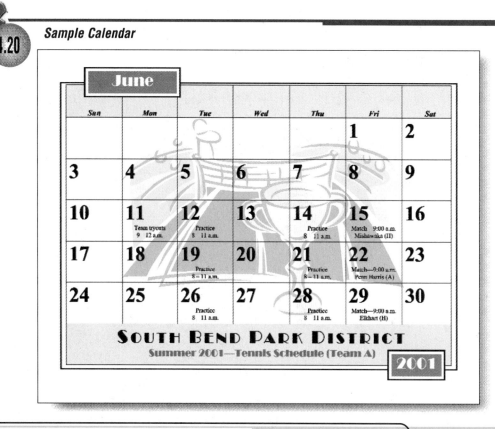

Assessment 2

1. Create the change-of-address card in figure 4.21 by following the handwritten specifications; however, use your name and address and send the card to a friend.
2. Access the Envelopes and Labels feature and choose a postcard definition that measures 4″ × 6″.
3. Insert the clip art image shown in figure 4.21. Click <u>I</u>nsert, <u>P</u>icture, <u>C</u>lip Art, key **mailing** in the Search for clips text box, and then press Enter. Scroll to find the image, click Insert clip at the pop-up menu, and then close the Insert ClipArt dialog box.
4. Use the Papyrus font or a similar font if this one is not available.
5. The triangle-shaped object is a <u>F</u>lowchart A<u>u</u>toShape object.
6. Draw three connecting lines using the Line button on the Drawing toolbar, change the Line Style to 2 1/4 pt Square Dot, and change the Line Color to Light Orange.
7. Save the document as c04sa02, Address.
8. Print and then close c04sa02, Address.

figure

4.21

Change of Address Card

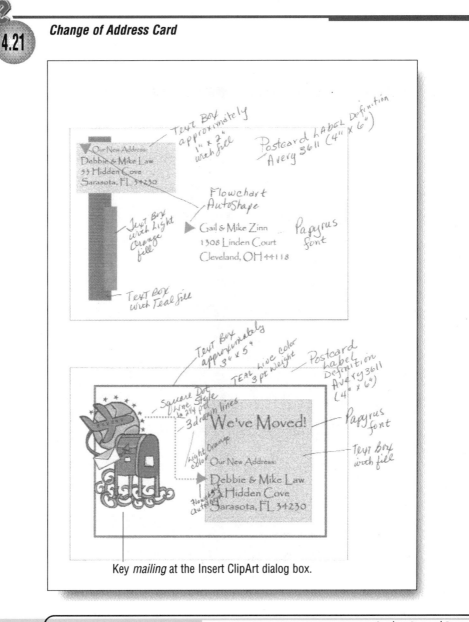

Key *mailing* at the Insert ClipArt dialog box.

Assessment 3

1. Create a sheet of personal return address labels using your name and address. Include a picture of your choice. Use the Avery Standard 5160 Address label definition. Size the picture and address to fit into the label dimensions. You may use the method explained in chapter 2 (*business cards*) or use the method explained in this chapter.
2. Save the address labels as c04sa03, Labels.
3. Print and then close c04sa03, Labels.

CREATIVE ACTIVITY

1. Find an example of a calendar, certificate, award, just moved postcard, personal invitation, or any other type of personal document.
2. Recreate the example, improving it with appropriate font selections and enhancements—a picture, watermark, page border, or special characters. Be sure to apply appropriate desktop design concepts to the layout of your document—draw a thumbnail first!
3. Save your document as c04ca01, Redo and then print and close c04ca01, Redo.
4. Attach the original document to your recreated document.

Performance Assessments

Unit 01 PA

CREATING BUSINESS AND PERSONAL DOCUMENTS

Assessment One

Your employer, First Trust Bank, will be closed July 4 in observance of the national holiday. Please prepare a sign notifying the bank's customers that the bank will not be open and post the sign in the lobby where it can be clearly seen. Complete the following steps:

1. Open Sign02 located on your student CD and copy it to your hard drive or a floppy disk.
2. Format the sign using appropriate fonts and font sizes.
3. Insert a relevant photo, clip art, or symbol to draw attention to the message.
4. Save the document as u01pa01, Sign.
5. Print and then close u01pa01, Sign.

Assessment Two

1. At a clear document screen, create the letterhead as illustrated in figure U1.2. Use the following list of specifications to help you in the creation process:
   a. Change the top margin to 0.5 inch, the bottom margin to 0.55 inch, and the left and right margins to 1 inch.
   b. Display the Insert ClipArt dialog box and search for clips using the keyword *airplanes*. Scroll through the selections until you find the airplane graphic shown in figure U1.2. You may have to search through several windows of clipart before finding this graphic.
   c. Format the picture so that it is horizontally aligned at the left margin and vertically aligned at the top margin.
   d. Create the arrows that lead to the company name by completing the following steps:
      1) Select the airplane image, click D<u>r</u>aw on the Drawing toolbar, and then click <u>U</u>ngroup.
      2) Click outside of the image to deselect all of the image segments.
      3) Click the Select Objects button on the Drawing toolbar and then draw a box around the arrow image.

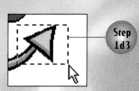

Step 1d3

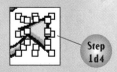
Step 1d4

4) Release the mouse button and all three segments should be selected.
5) With all of the segments selected, click the D<u>r</u>aw button on the Drawing toolbar, and then click <u>G</u>roup.
6) Select the arrow (which is now one unit), hold down the Ctrl key, and then drag a copy of the arrow to the right.
7) Continue copying the arrow image five more times.
8) Size, position, and rotate the arrows using figure U1.2 as a guide. You may need to make some additional adjustments after the company name has been inserted.

e. Click the Select Objects button on the Drawing toolbar and draw a box around the entire airplane image. Do not include the additional six arrows. Click D<u>r</u>aw on the Drawing toolbar and then click <u>G</u>roup so that the image becomes one unit instead of separate segments.

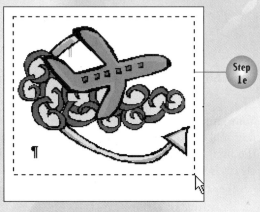
Step 1e

f. Insert the company name by completing the following steps:
1) Insert a text box in the upper right hand corner.
2) With the insertion point within the text box, change the font to 28-point Cooper Black.
3) Customize the text color by changing the H<u>ue</u> to 143, the <u>S</u>at to 201,and the <u>L</u>um to 95.
4) Set a right tab to align with the inside edge of the text box.
5) Press the Tab key, key **Penny**, and then press Enter.
6) Press the Tab key, key **Wise**, and then press Enter.
7) Key **Travel** as the last line of the company name.
8) Size the text box so that the boundaries are as close to the text as possible. View the document in Print Preview to make sure that no text is partially cut off.
9) Display the Format Text Box dialog box, horizontally align the text box with the right margin, and then vertically align the text box with the top margin.

g. If necessary, make adjustments to the size and position of the arrows in relation to the company name.

h. Create a text box and insert the address and contact information located at the bottom of the letterhead by completing the following steps:
1) Create a text box at the bottom of the page that approximately extends from margin to margin.
2) With the insertion point within the text box, change the font to 10-point Cooper Black and customize the font color as in step 1e3.
3) Set a right tab to align with the inside edge of the text box.
4) Press the Tab key, key **Phone: 630.555.3777**, and then press Enter.
5) Key **1960 Middleton Drive**, press the Tab key, and then key **Fax: 630.555.3780**. Press Enter.

6) Key **Lombard, IL 60147**, press the Tab key, and then key **E-mail: Pwise@att.net**.

7) Size the text box as close to the text as possible without cutting any text off. Use Print Preview to make sure all of the text is visible.

8) Position the text box more specifically after making the lines as indicated in the next steps.

   i.   Create the vertical and horizontal orange lines by completing the following steps:

1) Using the Line button on the Drawing toolbar, draw a line below the text box.

2) Customize the color of the line by changing the H<u>u</u>e to 28, the <u>S</u>at to 255, and the <u>L</u>um to 124.

3) Change the weight of the line to 1-1/2 pt.

4) Size the line using figure U1.2 as your guide.

5) Create a vertical line that is the same approximate size and in the same approximate location as the orange vertical line in figure U1.2.

6) Make sure the line weight is 1-1/2 pt.

7) Change the line color to orange as in step 1g2.

8) Position the line so that it is perpendicular to the horizontal line. Use figure U1.2 as your guide.

9) Adjust the position of the text box in relation to the horizontal and vertical lines.

10) Pay attention to aligning the information within the text box on the left and right sides so that it is in alignment with the right and left sides of the letterhead design at the top of the page.

2. Save the completed letter and name it u01pa02, Travel ltrhd.

3. Print and then close u01pa02, Travel ltrhd.

Optional: Using the same travel theme, create your own design using the company name, address, and contact information as in figure U1.2.

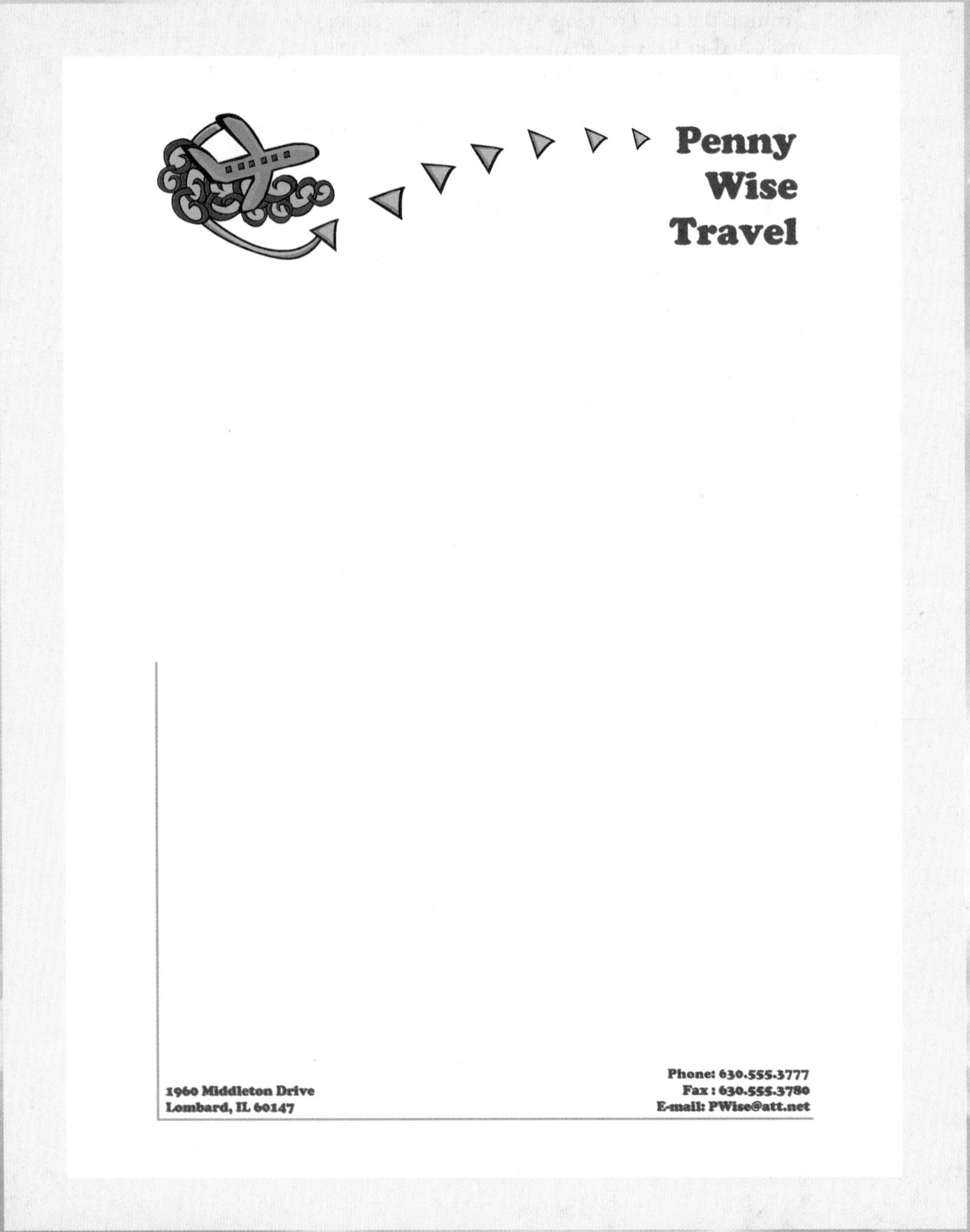

Penny
Wise
Travel

1960 Middleton Drive
Lombard, IL 60147

Phone: 630.555.3777
Fax : 630.555.3780
E-mail: PWise@att.net

Figure U1.2 • Assessment 2

Assessment Three

1. You work for a company named Design 2000 that specializes in ergonomically designed offices. Your company works hard to create designs that provide maximum worker comfort. Create a letterhead and envelope for Design 2000. Include the following information in your letterhead design:

Slogan	=	(Make up a slogan for your company.)
Address	=	**300 Sun Drive**
	=	**Tucson, AZ 96322**
Phone	=	**304.555.2344**
Fax	=	**304.555.2345**

2. Include the following specifications in your letterhead and envelope design:
   a. Create a thumbnail sketch or sketches of your proposed letterhead and envelope design and layout.
   b. Create an asymmetrical design.
   c. Incorporate appropriate and proportional typefaces, type sizes, and type styles. Consider using the WordArt feature.
   d. Turn on kerning for fonts 14 points and above.
   e. Use tracking (condensing or expanding character spacing) if necessary or to create a special effect.
   f. You may use text boxes, a graphic image, watermarks, horizontal or vertical ruled lines, special characters, etc., if appropriate.
   g. Use some color if a color printer is available.
   h. Save the letterhead and name it u01pa03, letterhead.
   i. Evaluate your design for the concepts of focus, balance, proportion, contrast, directional flow, consistency, and the use of color.
   j. Make sure related information is positioned close to each other.
   k. Avoid center alignment; aim for a strong left or right alignment.
   l. With the letterhead still displayed on the screen, create a coordinating envelope by completing the following steps:
      1) Display the Envelopes and Labels dialog box with the Envelopes tab selected.
      2) Delete any text in the Delivery Address and Return Address text boxes.
      3) Display the Envelope Options dialog box (with the Envelope Options tab selected) and make sure the Envelope size list box displays Size 10 (4-1/8 x 9-1/2 inches).
      4) Add the envelope to your document (your letterhead) and create a design that contains the company name and return address for Design 2000. Incorporate some of the same design elements as your letterhead. You decide if you want to include the slogan in your design.
3. Save the document containing the envelope and name it u01pa03, Ltr&env.
4. Print and then close u01pa03, Ltr&env.

Optional: Print a copy of Document Analysis Guide.doc located on your student CD-ROM and use it to evaluate your finished document.

Assessment 4

four

Create your personal calendar for the month of December (current year) using the Calendar Wizard and include the following specifications:

- If you have access to a scanner or digital camera, include a photograph of yourself, a family member, pet, or special scenery. Otherwise, include any appropriate clip art image or photograph from the Clip Gallery or the Web.
- Include four noteworthy events, meetings, parties, etc. on the calendar.
- Include at least two symbols.
- Experiment with a variety of fonts and font sizes until you achieve the look you want for your calendar.
- Save the calendar and name it u01pa04, Calendar.
- Print and then close u01pa04, Calendar.

Unit two

PREPARING PROMOTIONAL DOCUMENTS, WEB PAGES, AND POWERPOINT PRESENTATIONS

Chapter 05

Creating Promotional Documents

PERFORMANCE OBJECTIVES

Upon successful completion of chapter 5, you will be able to produce promotional documents such as flyers and announcements using Word's Tables and Borders toolbar, Picture toolbar, Drawing toolbar, Microsoft Word Picture editor, and WordArt along with text boxes, pictures, lines, AutoShapes, 3-D boxes, shadow boxes, and borders.

DESKTOP PUBLISHING TERMS

Announcement	Fill	Nudge
Bitmap	Flyer	Scale
Crop	Metafile	Thumbnail sketch

WORD FEATURES USED

AutoShapes	Group	Scale
Align or distribute	Ungroup	Size
Character spacing	Line color	Tables and Borders
Drawing objects	Microsoft Word Picture	toolbar
Drawing toolbar	Picture toolbar	Text boxes
Fill color	Rotate	WordArt
Fill effects		

In this chapter, you will produce flyers and announcements for advertising products, services, events, and classes using your own design and layout ideas with Word's desktop features. First, you will review basic desktop publishing concepts for planning and designing promotional documents. Then, you will incorporate fonts, graphics, borders, and objects into your documents to increase their appeal. Finally, more complex and powerful features such as WordArt, Microsoft Word Picture, and the tools on the Drawing and Picture toolbars will be introduced.

Creating Flyers and Announcements

Flyer

Promotional document used to advertise a product or service that is available for a limited amount of time.

A *flyer* is generally used to advertise a product or service that is available for a limited amount of time. Frequently, you may find flyers stuffed in a grocery bag; attached to a mailbox, door handle, or windshield; placed in a bin near an entrance; or placed on a countertop for customers to carry away. The basic goal of a flyer is to communicate a message at a glance, so the message should be brief and to the point. For the flyer to be effective, the basic layout and design should be free of clutter—without too much text or too many graphics. Use white space generously to set off an image or text and to help promote good directional flow.

Announcement

Promotional document used to inform an audience of an upcoming event.

An *announcement* informs an audience of an upcoming event. An announcement may create interest in an event but not necessarily promote a product or service. For instance, you may have received an announcement for course offerings at your local community college or an announcement of an upcoming community event, sporting event, concert, race, contest, raffle, or a new store opening that informs and creates interest, but does not promote the event.

Planning and Designing Promotional Documents

As stated in chapter 1, planning your document is a basic desktop publishing concept that applies to flyers and announcements as well as to other publications. Most important, always prepare a thumbnail sketch, which is like thinking on paper, before beginning a project. Clearly define your purpose and assess your target audience. For instance, consider your audience when choosing type sizes—the older your audience, the larger the print might need to be. Besides assessing your needs and your approach, consider your budget as well. Flyers and announcements are generally considered one of the least expensive means of advertising.

DTP POINTERS

Consider your audience when choosing type sizes.

Successful promotional documents attract the reader's attention and keep it. Consider how you can attract the reader's eye: by using eye-catching headlines, displaying graphics that create impact, or using color for emphasis or attention. People generally look at the graphics first, then they read the headline, and finally they look at the logo for company identity. The logo may be placed low on the page to anchor the message.

DTP POINTERS

The upper left corner is usually read first.

Using a Table for Layout

DTP POINTERS

Prepare a thumbnail sketch.

Use a thumbnail sketch as a tool to guide you in creating documents. In addition, you may draw a table to block off areas of the page to reflect the layout you have sketched in your thumbnail. Figure 5.1 shows how a table can serve as a framework for an announcement.

Align Top Left

Tables provide an efficient means for aligning text and objects using options on the Tables and Borders toolbar such as Align Top Left, Align Top Center, Align Top Right, Align Center Left, Align Center, Align Center Right, Align Bottom Left, Align Bottom Center, Align Bottom Right as shown in figure 5.2. You will learn how to create an announcement in a table in exercise 1.

To create a table for the announcement in figure 5.1, complete the following steps:

figure
5.1
Using a Table to Create an Announcement

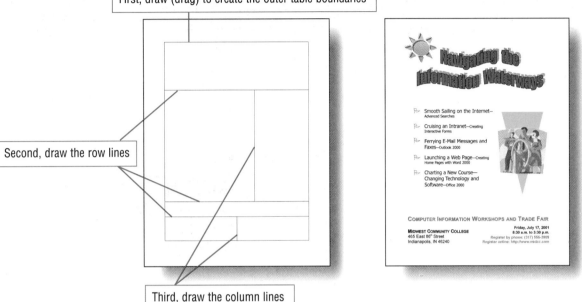

First, draw (drag) to create the outer table boundaries

Second, draw the row lines

Third, draw the column lines

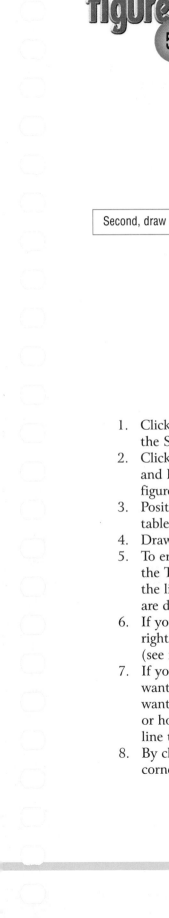

1. Click the Tables and Borders button (ninth button from the right) on the Standard toolbar.
2. Click the Draw Table button (first button from the left) on the Tables and Borders toolbar. (The arrow pointer will display as a pen—see figure 5.2 for the Tables and Borders toolbar.)
3. Position the pen in the upper-left corner, and then drag to create a table.
4. Draw lines by clicking and dragging.
5. To erase lines, click the Eraser button (second button from the left) on the Tables and Borders toolbar (see figure 5.2). Drag the eraser along the line you want to erase. Remember to turn the Eraser off when you are done.
6. If you do not want borders on your table, click the down arrow at the right of the Outside Borders button on the Tables and Borders toolbar (see figure 5.2), then click the No Border button.
7. If you want to change the cell width or length, drag the boundary you want to change. (Position the insertion point on the boundary line you want to change; when the insertion point displays as either two vertical or horizontal lines with up/down or left/right pointing arrows, drag the line to a new location.)
8. By clicking and dragging the *Table Move Handle* icon in the upper-left corner of the table, you can move the table to a new location.

Draw Table

Eraser

Outside Borders

figure

5.2

Tables and Borders Toolbar and the Aligning Palette

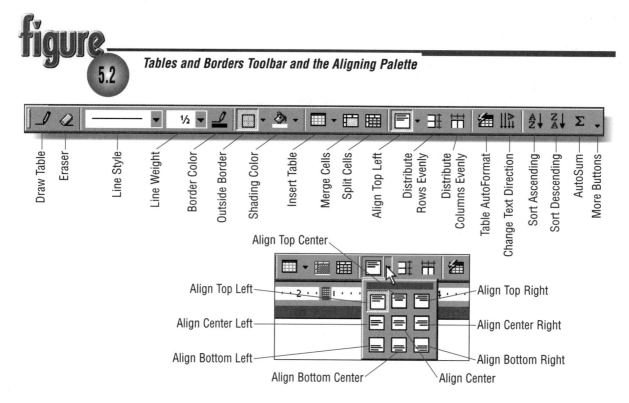

Using Text for Focus

DTP POINTERS
White space creates a clean page that is easy to read.

Flyers and announcements provide tremendous opportunities to be creative. To grab attention, consider using BIG graphics, uncommon typefaces, asymmetrical design, and plenty of white space. Figure 5.3 illustrates a flyer that attracts attention through the use of various fonts and font attributes.

figure

5.3

Sample Flyer (All Text)

Once you have finished a document, look at the document from a distance to make sure that the important information is dominant. Also, look through a newspaper or magazine to find ads that grab your attention and prompt you to act. Study the designs and apply what you have learned to your own documents.

Using WordArt in Announcements and Flyers

WordArt can distort or modify text to create a variety of shapes. This is useful for creating company logos and headings. It is especially useful for headlines in flyers and announcements. The shapes can exaggerate the text to draw in an audience. Many flyers that advertise sales use this feature to emphasize a discount and persuade an audience to act on this message.

Consider the impact that text can have, as shown in figure 5.4. The name of the font used in this example is Impact and when used with a WordArt shape in a green color, you can imagine the impact this heading will have—big savings! Wise use of text in publications can have a forceful effect on how the message is communicated. A flyer with a large, colorful headline is an eye-catching way to announce an event or advertise a product or service.

figure 5.4 *WordArt for Emphasis*

40-pt. Impact with Shadow Style 4

WordArt changes ordinary text into graphic objects, and since WordArt is based on text, fonts are very important in creating interesting text designs. The fonts that are available in WordArt applications include Windows fonts, Word program fonts, printer fonts, and any other soft fonts you may have added to your computer. Refer to chapter 3 for additional information on WordArt.

Using Graphics for Emphasis

Graphics can add excitement to and generate enthusiasm for a publication. A well-placed graphic can transform a plain document into a compelling visual document. However, it is effective only if the image relates to the subject of the document.

DTP POINTERS
Leave plenty of white
space around a graphic.

DTP POINTERS
Do not overuse clip art;
use one main visual
element per page.

Before selecting a graphic, decide what your theme or text will be. If you are deciding among many graphics, select the simplest. A simple graphic demands more attention and has more impact; too many graphics can cause clutter and confusion. Use a graphic to aid in directional flow. Also, use a generous amount of white space around a graphic. Use a thumbnail sketch as a tool to help you make decisions on position, size, and design.

Also consider using clip art as a basis for your own creations. Combine clip art images with other clip art images, then crop, size, or color different areas of the combined image to create a unique look. Alternatively, you may include photographs in your flyers or announcements. Word and Office come with their own clip art gallery; if you have a version of Office that includes Microsoft Publisher, this gallery will contain over 10,000 clip art and photo images. If you have a version that includes Microsoft PhotoDraw 2000, you have numerous opportunities to create interesting pictures.

Downloading Graphics from the Web

Keep in mind that if you have access to the Internet, you can add to your clip art, photographs, videos, and sound clips collection by downloading images and clips from Microsoft's Web site as shown in figure 5.5.

figure

5.5

Microsoft Clip Gallery Live

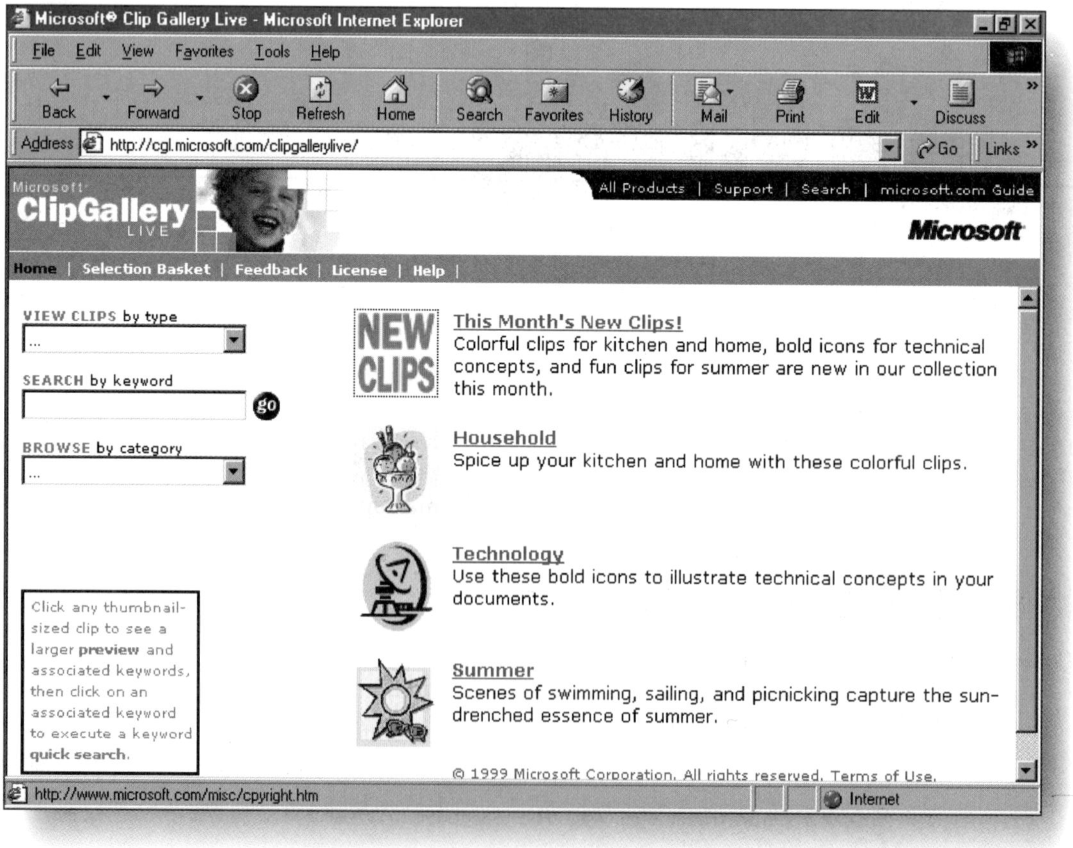

The following partial list of search engines will help you locate graphics on the Web. Key **clipart** (one word) at each search text box:

- Alta Vista (www.altavista.com)
- HotBot (www.hotbot.com)
- Yahoo (www.yahoo.com)
- Lycos (www.lycos.com)

You can easily download images from the Web by completing the following steps:

1. Access the Internet.
2. Open Word 2000, click Insert, point to Picture, and then click Clip Art.
3. At the Insert ClipArt dialog box, click the Clips Online button as shown in figure 5.6.
4. Select the clip you wish to download by clicking in the check box at the right of the clip as shown in figure 5.7.
5. To download the clip immediately, click the animated down arrow next to the clip or click the hyperlink at the top of the screen as shown in figure 5.7. The clip you select from Microsoft Clip Gallery Live is automatically added to the Clip Gallery in the *Downloaded Clips* category at the Insert ClipArt dialog box.

figure
5.6
Connecting to Web for More Clips

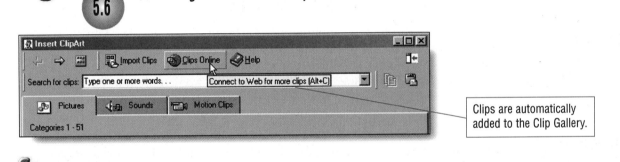

Clips are automatically added to the Clip Gallery.

figure
5.7
Downloading a Clip from the Web

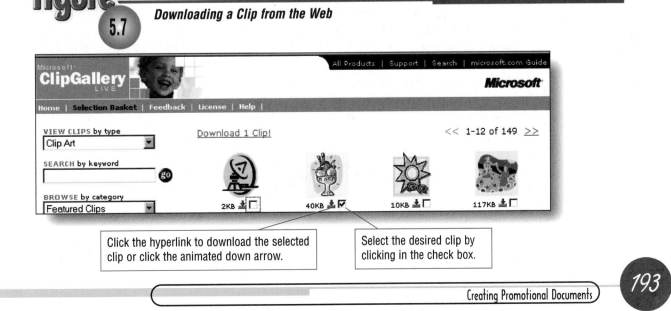

Click the hyperlink to download the selected clip or click the animated down arrow.

Select the desired clip by clicking in the check box.

In addition, clip art software provides inexpensive clip art images on CD-ROM. Consider Corel Gallery 1,000,000 *(www.corel.com)* and ClickArt 200,000 Image Pak *(www.broderbund.com)*. These products change rapidly so check the Web sites for the latest updates.

You can also download any graphic you see on the Web. Move your mouse pointer over an image and right-click. You get a shortcut menu where one of the options is Save Image As (or Save Picture As). At the Save As dialog box, select a folder, name the file, and click Save.

Inserting Clip Art from a Scanner or Digital Camera

You can insert images directly from a scanner or digital camera, without using an additional applet such as Microsoft Photo Editor. Word utilizes the scanner or digital camera drivers that you install, as long as they comply with the TWAIN interface. To insert a picture from a scanner or digital camera, complete the following steps:

1. Make sure the scanner or digital camera is properly connected. Place the image in the scanner if you are using a scanner.
2. Click Insert, point to Picture, and then click From Scanner or Camera.
3. Choose the source from the Device drop-down box.
4. Select the desired resolution: Web Quality or Print Quality.
5. Click Insert, and Word captures the image and inserts it in your document.

Using Color in Promotional Documents

DTP POINTERS
Use color consistently in a document.

Color is a powerful tool in communicating information. The colors you choose should reflect the nature of the business you represent. Someone in an artistic line of work may use bolder, splashier colors than someone creating documents for a business dealing with finane. In addition, men and women often respond differently to the same color. Always identify your target audience in planning your documents and think about the impact color will have on your audience.

DTP POINTERS
Use spot color to attract the reader's eyes.

Choose one or two colors for a document and stick with them to give your page a unified look. Add "spot color" in your document by using color only in specific areas of the page. Also, pick up a color from your graphic in your text.

Many flyers and announcements are printed on either white or color paper and duplicated on a copy machine to help keep costs down. A color printer or color copier adds to the cost but can help the appeal of the document. If you are using a color printer, limit the color to small areas so it attracts attention but does not create visual confusion.

DTP POINTERS
Color can create a mood.

As an inexpensive alternative to printing in color, use color paper or specialty papers to help get your message across, as stated in chapter 1. Specialty papers are predesigned papers used for brochures, letterheads, postcards, business cards, certificates, etc., and can be purchased through most office supply stores or catalog paper supply companies. Be sure to choose a color that complements your message and/or matches the theme of your document—orange for harvest or fall, green for spring, yellow for summer, blue for water and sky, and so on.

Understanding Desktop Publishing Color Terms

When working in desktop publishing and using Word 2000 you may encounter terms used to explain color. Here is a list of color terms along with definitions:

- *Balance* is the amount of light and dark in a picture.
- *Brightness* or *value* is the amount of light in a color.
- *Contrast* is the amount of gray in a color.
- A *color wheel* is a device used to illustrate color relationships.
- *Complementary colors* are colors directly opposite each other on the color wheel, such as red and green, which are among the most popular color schemes.
- *CYMK* is an acronym for cyan, yellow, magenta, and black. A color printer combines these colors to create different colors.
- *Dither* is a method of combining several different-colored pixels to create new colors.
- *Gradient* is a gradual varying of color.
- *Grayscale* is a range of shades from black to white.
- *Halftone* is a process of taking basic color dots (including black) and combining them to produce many other colors. Your printer driver can use a halftone setting to produce more shades of color.
- *Hue* is a variation of a primary color, such as green-blue.
- *Luminosity* is the brightness of a color, that is, of the amount of black or white added to a color. The larger the luminosity number, the lighter the color.
- *Pixel* is each individual dot of color in a picture or graphic.
- *Resolution* is the number of dots that make up an image on a screen or printer—the higher the resolution, the denser the number of dots and "higher resolution" of the print.
- *Reverse* is a black background and white foreground, or white type against a colored background.
- *RGB* is an acronym for red, green, and blue. Each pixel on your computer monitor is made up of these three colors.
- *Saturation* is the purity of a color. A color is completely pure, or saturated, when it is not diluted with white. Red, for example, has a high saturation.

exercise 1

Creating an Announcement Using a Table

As an employee of Midwest Community College, you are responsible for preparing advertisements for new courses and workshops sponsored by the college. Create the announcement in a table format.

1. At a clear document screen, create the announcement in figure 5.8 by completing the following steps (you will create a table similar to figure 5.1):
   a. Change all the margins to 0.75 inch and change the Zoom to Whole page.
   b. Click the Tables and Borders button (ninth button from the right) on the Standard toolbar.

c. Click the Draw Table button (first button from the left) on the Tables and Borders toolbar. The arrow pointer will display as a pen. Position the pen in the upper-left corner, then drag to create the outer boundary lines of a table approximately 1 inch from all edges of the page. The lines should be similar to the illustration below. (Use your horizontal and vertical ruler bars to guide you.)

d. Position the pen approximately 2 inches below the top boundary line of the table and draw a horizontal line by clicking and dragging.

e. Position the pen approximately 2 inches above the bottom boundary line of the table and draw another horizontal line by clicking and dragging.

f. Position the pen approximately 3/4 inch below the line created in step 1e, and then draw another horizontal line by clicking and dragging.

g. In the center section, position the pen approximately 2-1/2 inches from the right boundary line and draw a vertical line by clicking and dragging.

h. In the bottom section, position the pen at the approximate center of the last row, then draw a vertical line by clicking and dragging.

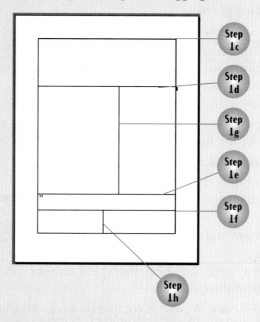

Step 1c
Step 1d
Step 1g
Step 1e
Step 1f
Step 1h

i. Click the Draw Table button to turn this feature off.

j. Change the Zoom to Page Width.

2. Insert the announcement text by completing the following steps:

a. Position the insertion point in the first cell and insert the Navigating.doc file located on your student CD. Select the WordArt text and drag it to the center of the cell.

b. Position the insertion point in the first cell of the second row of the table and insert the Sailing.doc file located on your student CD. Click the down arrow at the right of the Align Top Left button (eighth button from the right) on the Tables and Borders toolbar and select Align Center Left.

c. Position the insertion point in the second cell in the second row of the table and insert the photograph shown in figure 5.8. Click Insert, point to Picture, click Clip Art, key **sailing** in the Search for clips: text box, and then press Enter. Scroll to find the photo, click the Insert clip button, and then close the Insert ClipArt dialog box. Size the image similar to Figure 5.8.

d. With the image selected, center the image by clicking the Align Center button on the Tables and Borders toolbar.

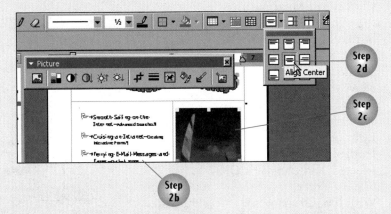

e. Position the insertion point in the cell in the third row of the table, then insert Trade Fair.doc located on your student CD. Make sure that the text is centered horizontally and vertically in the cell.

f. Position the insertion point in the first cell in the fourth row and insert Midwest.doc located on your student CD. Center the text vertically.

g. Position the insertion point in the second cell in the fourth row and insert Register.doc located on your student CD. Center the text vertically.

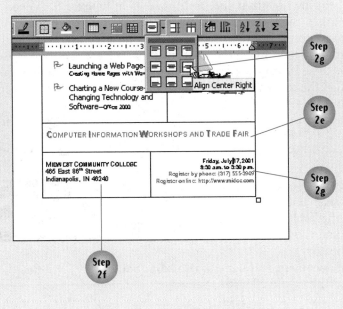

3. Create the AutoShape object in figure 5.8 by completing the following steps:
   a. Display the Drawing toolbar.
   b. Click the AutoShapes button on the Drawing toolbar, point to Basic Shapes, and then click the Sun shape in the sixth row.
   c. Drag the crosshairs to the top left of the table and draw the Sun shape similar to figure 5.8.
   d. Add a gradient fill to the Sun shape by completing the following steps:
      1) Select the sun shape, click the down arrow at the right of the Fill Color button on the Drawing toolbar, and then click the Fill Effects button.
      2) At the Fill Effects dialog box, choose the Gradient tab, and then select One color.
      3) Click the down arrow at the right of the Color 1 list box and select Gold in the fourth row and second column.
      4) Move the slider below Color 1 to the approximate center between Dark and Light, make sure the first Horizontal variant is selected, and then click OK or press Enter.
      5) With the sun shape still selected, click the Shadow button on the Drawing toolbar, and then select Shadow Style 13 in the fourth row and first column.

   e. View your announcement at Print Preview. Drag any boundary line in the table if the cells are not sized and positioned as in figure 5.8. (When you click on a line in a table, the arrow pointer should display as two vertical bars with two arrows pointing to the left and right or as two horizontal bars pointing to top and bottom; drag to move the line, and then release the left mouse button when you are satisfied with the position.) If the flyer displays too high or low on the page, change the top and/or bottom margins to help center the flyer vertically on the page.
4. With the insertion point positioned in the table, click Table, point to Select, and then click Table. Click the down arrow at the right of the Borders button (sixth button from the left) on the Tables and Borders toolbar, and then select the No Border button.
5. Save the document and name it c05ex01, Sailing.
6. Print and then close c05ex01, Sailing.

figure
5.8

Exercise 1

Adding Lines, Borders, and Special Effects to Text, Objects, and Pictures

As discussed in chapter 3, ruled lines can be used in a document to create a focal point, draw the eye across or down the page, separate columns and sections, or add visual appeal. Borders are generally used to frame text or an image with more than one side. Shading can be added to the background of a table, a paragraph, or selected text, or used as fill in a drawing object. Examples of lines, borders, shading, shadow, and 3-D effects are displayed in figure 5.9.

figure 5.9

Sample Lines, Borders, and Shading

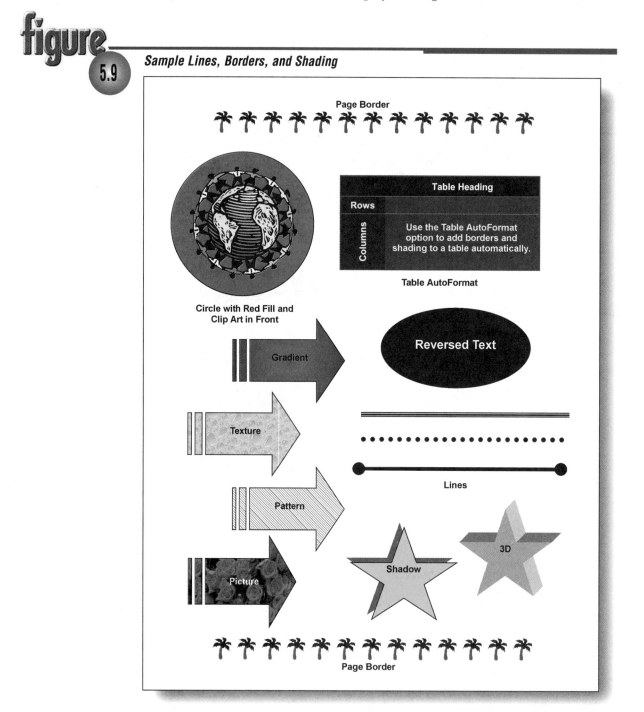

Adding Lines and Borders

You can add a border to any or all sides of a table, a paragraph, or selected text in a document. You can add a page border or an art border (such as a row of trees) to any or all sides of each page or section in a document. You can also add borders to text boxes, pictures, and imported pictures.

Rules and/or borders can be drawn using the Line button or the Rectangle button on the Drawing toolbar, clicking the Border button on the Tables and Borders toolbar or the Formatting toolbar, or using the Borders and Shading dialog box from the Format menu.

In addition, graphic borders are available in Word 2000 (check your version) and accessed as any other clip art at the Insert ClipArt dialog box. These graphic borders are found in the *Borders & Frames* category as shown in figure 5.10.

figure

5.10 *Sample Borders and Frames from the ClipArt Gallery*

Adding Lines and Borders to Tables

All tables default to a single 1/2 pt. black solid-line border that prints. To add a line or customized border to a table, display the Tables and Borders toolbar as shown in figure 5.2. Select the cells where you want the line or border to appear, then click any one or more of the following buttons to customize the line or border: Line Style, Line Weight, Border Color, and/or the Border button. If you prefer drawing the line or border, use the Draw Table button. Alternatively, you can use the Table AutoFormat command to add borders and shading to a table automatically.

To add a border to a table, click anywhere in the table. To add borders to specific cells, select only those cells, including the end-of-cell mark.

Adding a Page Border

Word provides page borders that range from simple to highly ornate. Choose the art border that best complements the content of your document. Refer to chapter 4 for additional information on the Page Border option in the Borders and Shading dialog box.

Adding Fill to Design Elements

You can add shading to the background of a table, a paragraph, or selected text. Shading added to drawing objects—including a text box or an AutoShape—is called a *fill*. You can fill drawing objects with solid or gradient (shaded) colors, a pattern, a texture, or a picture.

To add a picture as fill, such as the example in the announcement in figure 5.11, select the Picture tab at the Fill Effects dialog box and then click the Select Picture button. At the Select Picture dialog box, make sure your desired photo or clip art file displays in the Look in: list box, then click OK or press Enter.

Alternatively, you may select a photograph or clip art at the Insert ClipArt dialog box, right-click on the image, and then click Copy from the drop-down list. This copies the image to the clipboard. Proceed with accessing the Fill Effects dialog box, select the Picture tab, click the Select Picture button, and then paste the image into the list box at the Select Picture dialog box. Finally, select the file and click Insert. The clip art images in Office 2000 Professional Edition are identified by numbers, such as ph02829j. Right-click on an image at the Insert ClipArt dialog box, click Clip Properties, and record the number if you want to access it later.

exercise 2

**Creating an Announcement with
AutoShapes and Picture Fill**

Assume you are working part-time at the Brighton Health & Fitness Center while attending classes at a local community college. Prepare an announcement promoting a new summer program. The location of the photos may vary; substitute the images if necessary.

1. At a clear document screen, create the announcement in figure 5.11 by completing the following steps:

a. Open Health.doc located on your student CD.
b. Save the document with Save As and name it c05ex02, Health.
c. Turn on the Hide/Show ¶ feature.
d. Display the Drawing toolbar.
e. Select *Healthy choices point to Healthy lives...*, change the font to 36-pt. Papyrus bold, and then select *point* and apply italics. Turn on kerning at 14 points.
f. Position the insertion point in the text box below *Healthy choices...* and insert Cardio.doc located on your student CD.
g. Select the Cardio.doc text, right align the text, then change the font to 14-point Arial, select *Summer Cardio Mix* and change the point size to 16 points and apply bold.
h. Remove the border around the text box containing the Cardio.doc text.
i. Select the text in the text box below *Summer Cardio Mix* and change the alignment to Center. (The text box contains the text *Brighton Health...*)
j. Select *Brighton Health & Fitness Center*, change the font to 22-point Bauhaus 93 in Green.
k. Select the address and phone number, change the font to 14-point Arial in Green.
l. Select the text box containing *Brighton...*, change the fill to *No Fill* and the Line Color to *No Line*.
m. Position the insertion point in the text box behind the *Brighton* text, and insert the symbol in figure 5.11 by completing the following steps:
   1) Click Insert and then Symbol.
   2) Choose the Symbols tab, select the Webdings Font, and then select the 'Y' symbol in the fourth row and tenth from the right. (This symbol is a logo for Brighton.)

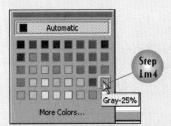

Step 1m4

   3) Click Insert and then Close.
   4) Select the 'Y' symbol and change the point size to 175 points and the color to Gray-25%. (Position the text box as shown in figure 5.11.)
   5) Change the Line Color of the text box to *No Line*.
n. Create the arrows by completing the following steps:
   1) Click the AutoShapes button on the Drawing toolbar, point to Block Arrows, and click the Striped Right Arrow in the fifth row and first column.

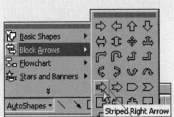

Striped Right Arrow

Step 1n1

   2) Drag the crosshairs to create an arrow similar to those in figure 5.11.
   3) Copy the arrow twice to create a total of three arrows.
   4) Add the picture fill by completing the following steps:
     a) Select the first arrow, click down arrow at the right of the Fill Color button on the Drawing toolbar, and then click the Fill Effects button.
     b) At the Fill Effects dialog box, select the Picture tab, and then click the Select Picture button.
     c) Insert graphic **ph02829j** (vegetable photo shown at the right) by completing one of the following paths:
       i) With the C drive displayed in the Look in list box, C:\Program Files\Microsoft Office\Clipart\Standard\Stddir4\ph02829j; or
       ii) With Office 2000 disc 2 in the CD drive, D:\Pfiles\MsOffice\Clipart\ Standard\Stddir4\ph02829j. Click Insert and OK to close the Fill Effects dialog box. *(Hint: An alternative is to key **vegetables** at the Insert ClipArt dialog box, scroll to find the photo, copy it to the clipboard, close the ClipArt*

dialog box, make sure the AutoShape is selected, click the Fill Color button on the Drawing toolbar, click the Fill Effects button, select the Picture tab, click the Select Picture button, make sure the A drive displays in the Look in list box, right-click in a blank area of the Select Picture list box and click Paste. Select the photo file and click Insert. Click OK to close the Fill Effects dialog box.)

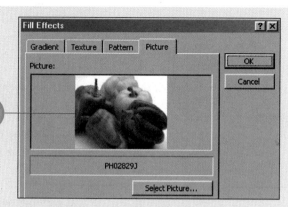

Step 1n4c

d) Insert graphics **ph02827j** and **ph01458j** by following the steps given in the previous step. *(Hint: Key **fruit** and then key **run** at the Insert ClipArt dialog box.)*

e) Position the arrows similar to those shown in figure 5.11.

o. View the document in Print Preview and make any necessary adjustments.

2. Save the document with the same name, c05ex02, Health.

3. Print and then close c05ex02, Health.

figure 5.11

Exercise 2

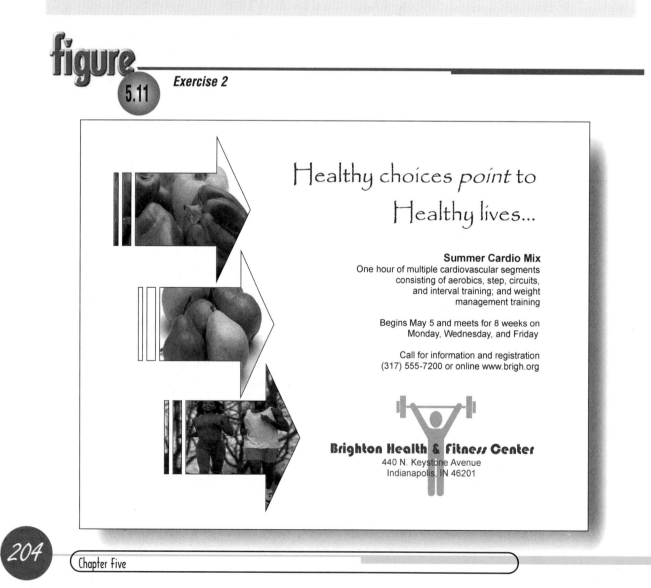

Matching Colors

To make your document look even more professional, match a color from an image used in your document to your font color as shown in figure 5.12. To match colors, ungroup the clip art image, select a segment that contains the color you want to use, write down the values for the Hue, Sat, and Lum, along with the settings for Red, Green, and Blue, which are found in the Custom tab of the Colors dialog box, then use the same values to color your fonts and/or other drawing objects.

figure
5.12
Matching Colors

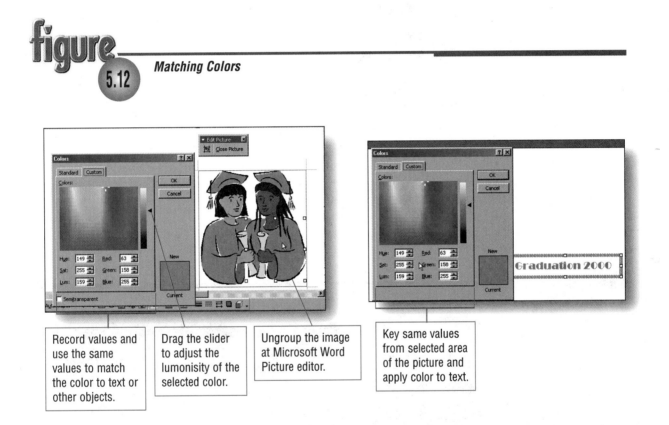

Record values and use the same values to match the color to text or other objects.

Drag the slider to adjust the lumonisity of the selected color.

Ungroup the image at Microsoft Word Picture editor.

Key same values from selected area of the picture and apply color to text.

Adding Special Effects: Shadow and 3-D

You can add depth to lines, drawing objects, and some pictures by using the Shadow button (second button from the right) on the Drawing toolbar. To make adjustments to the shadow position, click Shadow Settings and then click the appropriate buttons on the Shadow Settings toolbar as shown in figure 5.13. You can add either a shadow or a 3-D effect to a drawing object, but not both.

Shadow Palette and Shadow Settings Toolbar

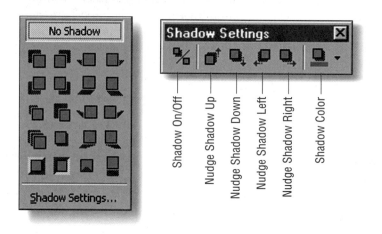

You can add a 3-D effect to lines, AutoShapes, and other drawing objects by clicking the 3-D button (last button) on the Drawing toolbar. You can modify any of the settings by clicking the 3-D Settings button, then selecting options to change color, angle, direction, etc., at the 3-D Settings toolbar as shown in figure 5.14. Experiment with these settings—you will be amazed by the possibilities.

3-D Effects and 3-D Settings Toolbar

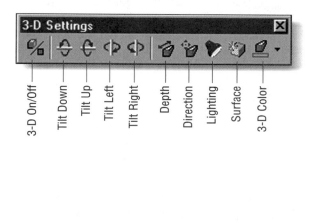

Using Microsoft Word Picture

The Edit tab of the Options dialog box controls which drawing or image editing program will open when you select an image to be edited. Typically, your choices will be Microsoft Word Picture as shown in figure 5.15 or Microsoft Photo Editor. Other editors may display depending on the Office version you are using and any other software you have installed.

figure

5.15

Choosing the Microsoft Word Picture Editor

Microsoft Word Picture is a graphic editor available within Word. If you do not have the original program where your graphic was created loaded on your computer, Word will place the image in a Microsoft Word Picture window where you can edit it.

Word recognizes a wide variety of picture formats dependent on the graphic filters installed with your program. Basically, there are two types of pictures:

- *bitmaps*, which cannot be ungrouped; and
- *metafiles*, which can be ungrouped, converted to drawing objects, and then edited by using tools on the Drawing toolbar.

Pictures created in bitmaps are made from a series of small dots that form shapes and lines. Many scanned pictures are bitmapped. Bitmaps cannot be edited in Microsoft Word Picture, but they can be scaled, cropped, and re-colored by using tools on the Picture toolbar. However, bitmaps can be edited in Microsoft Paint, Microsoft Photo Editor, Microsoft PhotoDraw 2000, or the program in which they were created. Most clip art is saved in metafile format (files named with a .wmf extension) and can be edited in Microsoft Word Picture.

After choosing the desired graphic editor at the Options dialog box, you can invoke the editor by selecting the image, right-clicking the mouse, and choosing Edit Picture from the shortcut menu. Once the picture has been edited, you can easily return to Microsoft Word Picture by simply double-clicking the image.

An ungrouped object in Microsoft Word Picture's special editing screen is shown in figure 5.16. While at the editing screen, an image can be grouped as one unit, ungrouped into separate components, rotated, re-colored, scaled, realigned, redesigned, and cropped. Figure 5.16 shows an image re-colored in Microsoft Word Picture using tools on the Drawing toolbar. You may also edit a picture by using the Format Picture or Format Object dialog boxes accessed through the Format menu. More than one component of an image can be selected and altered at the same time by holding down the Shift key while clicking to select each component.

To exit this screen and return to your document, click the Close Picture button on the Edit Picture toolbar or click File, then Close & Return to Document X.

Bitmaps
Pictures made up of small dots that form shapes and lines.

Metafiles
Graphic files that allow images to be ungrouped and edited in Microsoft Word Picture.

figure
5.16
Altering an Image in Microsoft Word Picture

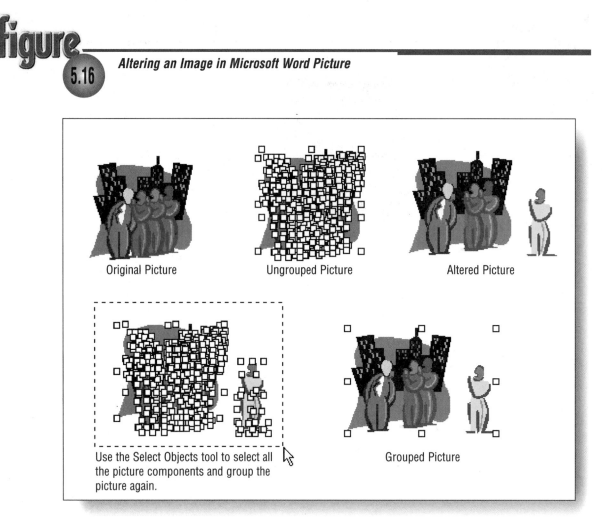

Original Picture

Ungrouped Picture

Altered Picture

Use the Select Objects tool to select all the picture components and group the picture again.

Grouped Picture

Creating a Flyer Using a Graphic Border

In exercise 3, you will create a flyer using a Word graphic border and insert text inside the border. Compare figure 5.17 to figure 5.18. Which flyer attracts your attention and pulls you in to read the text? Of course, figure 5.18 communicates more effectively because of the relevant graphic border and the varied typefaces, type styles, and type sizes. How many typefaces can you find in this document? (There are only two typefaces used in this flyer—Brush Script MT and Book Antiqua.) A graphic border is inserted into a document like any other picture.

figure
5.17
Flyer Before

Details by Design
Residential and Commercial Design

Think Spring!

Plan a new look for your home or office—complete
design service available

Space planning and consultation with trained professionals

Call today for an appointment
(614) 555-0898

25 W. Jefferson, Columbus, OH 43201

figure
5.18
Flyer After

Details by Design

*Residential and
Commercial
Design*

Think Spring!

Plan a new look for your home or
office—complete design service
available

Space planning and consultation with
trained professionals

Call today for an appointment
(614) 555-0898

25 W. Jefferson • Columbus, OH • 43201

exercise 3

Creating a Flyer Using a Graphic Border

Assume your neighbor is an interior decorator and you have offered to create a flyer advertising her company.

1. At a clear document screen, create the flyer in figure 5.19 by completing the following steps:
   a. Display the Drawing and Picture toolbars.
   b. Turn on kerning at 14 points and above.
   c. Open Graphic Border.doc located on your student CD.
   d. Double-click the graphic border and change the Height to 8.5 inches and the Width to 5.97 inches at the Format Picture dialog box, and then click OK or press Enter.
   e. Select the image and click the Center align button on the Formatting toolbar.
   f. Add color to the border by completing the following steps:
      1) Change the Zoom to Page Width.
      2) Select the graphic, right click, and select Edit Picture at the shortcut menu.
      3) Click to select the large flower, hold down the Shift key, and then click the small flower.
      4) Click the down arrow at the right of the Fill Color button on the Drawing toolbar, select Violet in the third row and the seventh column, and then deselect.

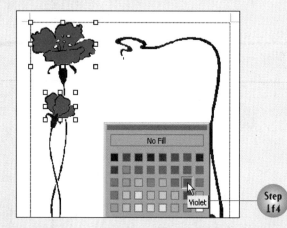

Step 1f4

   5) Hold down the Shift key as you select each section of the stem (may involve several selections), then click the down arrow to the right of the Fill Color button and select Green in the second row and the fourth column. Also, make sure the Line Color is Green.
   6) Click File and then Close & Return to Document#, or click the Close Picture button at the Edit Picture dialog box.
   g. Change the Zoom to Whole Page.
   h. Create a text box inside the graphic border by completing the following steps:
      1) Click the Text Box button on the Drawing toolbar.
      2) Drag the crosshairs inside the graphic border and draw a box near the inside edge of the graphic border.

3) Remove the border around the text box.

i. Position the insertion point inside the text box and key the following text in 12-point Times New Roman (change the Zoom to 75%):

Details by Design (press Enter)
Residential and (press Enter)
Commercial (press Enter)
Design (press Enter five times)
Think Spring! (press Enter twice)
Plan a new look for your home or office—complete design service available. (press Enter twice; use an em dash.)
Space planning and consultation with trained professionals. (press Enter five times)
Call today for an appointment. (press Enter)
(614) 555-0898 (press Enter twice)
25 W. Jefferson • Columbus, OH • 43201 Create the bullet symbol by pressing the Num Lock key on the keypad to turn it on, holding down the Alt key, keying **0149** on the keypad, and then turning off the Num Lock key.

j. Select *Details by Design* and then change the font to 36-point Brush Script MT with Shado<u>w</u>. Click the Align Right button on the Standard toolbar.

k. Select *Residential and Commercial Design*, and then change the font to 16-point Book Antiqua bold italic and the Font Color to Gray-50%. Click the Align Right button on the Formatting toolbar.

l. Position the insertion point before *Think Spring!* and press Ctrl + Shift + End to select to the end of the document. Click the Center align button on the Standard toolbar.

m. Select *Think Spring!* and change the font to 28-point Brush Script MT in Green.

n. Select the next two paragraphs and change the font to 14-point Book Antiqua.

o. Select *Call today for an appointment (614) 555-0898* and change the font to 14-point Book Antiqua bold italic.

p. Select *25 W. Jefferson • Columbus, OH • 43201* and change the font to 12-point Book Antiqua bold italic in Gray-50%.

q. Resize the text box if necessary.

2. View the document at Print Preview.

3. Save the document with Save <u>A</u>s and name it c05ex03, Border.

4. Print and then close c05ex03, Border.

figure

5.19

Exercise 3

Details by Design

Residential and
Commercial
Design

Think Spring!

Plan a new look for your home or
office—complete design service
available.

Space planning and consultation
available with trained professionals.

Call today for an appointment.
(614) 555-0898

25 W. Jefferson • Columbus, OH • 43201

Customizing Pictures Using the Picture Toolbar

When you select a picture that you have inserted into a document, the Picture
toolbar will appear with tools you can use to crop the picture, add a border to it,
or adjust its brightness and contrast, as shown in figure 5.20. If the Picture
toolbar does not appear, right-click the picture, and then click Show Picture
Toolbar on the shortcut menu.

figure 5.20

Picture Toolbar

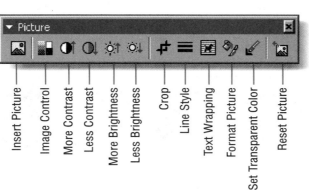

Insert Picture
Image Control
More Contrast
Less Contrast
More Brightness
Less Brightness
Crop
Line Style
Text Wrapping
Format Picture
Set Transparent Color
Reset Picture

Using the Insert Picture Button

To quickly insert a picture into your document, display the Picture toolbar and click the Insert Picture button (first button) on the Picture toolbar.

Using the Image Control Button

The Image Control button provides options to change the color of an image into varying shades of gray, black and white, or lightened to create a watermark as shown in figure 5.21.

Insert Picture

Image Control

figure 5.21

Image Control Options

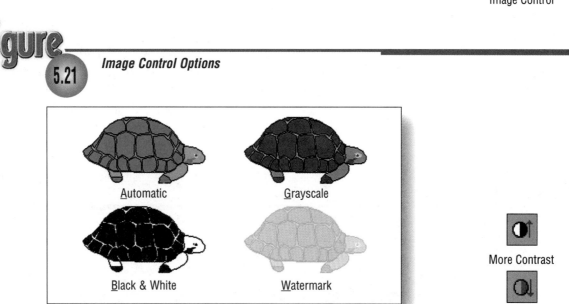

Automatic   Grayscale

Black & White   Watermark

Using the Contrast and Brightness Buttons

The Brightness options can darken or brighten a picture. Less contrast gives a grayer, "flatter" picture; more contrast means more black and white. See figure 5.22.

More Contrast

Less Contrast

More Brightness

Less Brightness

In addition, brightness and contrast can be altered at the Format Picture or Format Object dialog boxes. These options are found in the Image control section of the Picture or Object tab as slider or percentage settings.

figure

5.22

Contrast and Brightness Settings

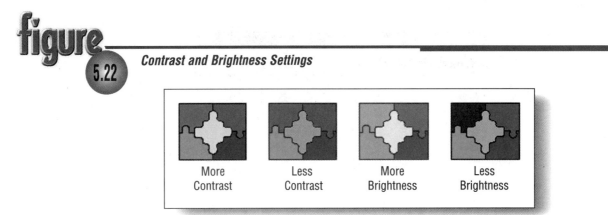

| More Contrast | Less Contrast | More Brightness | Less Brightness |

Using the Crop Button

Crop

To *crop* is to trim vertical and horizontal edges off of a picture as shown in figure 5.23. You can crop by using the cropping tool (seventh button from the left) on the Picture toolbar or by holding down the Shift key as you drag a sizing handle. Photos are usually cropped to focus attention on a particular area of a picture (for instance, a person's face).

Crop

To trim vertical and horizontal edges off a picture.

To use the cropping tool, select your image first, and then click the Crop button on the Picture toolbar. Position the cropping tool, which displays as two overlapping right angles, on one of the sizing handles, and then drag. The corner handles enable you to crop from two sides. The center handles cut away part of the picture. As you drag the sizing handles, you see a dotted-line box that represents the picture's new size and shape. The picture adjusts to the size and shape of the box when you release the mouse button.

You can also crop pictures using the Format Picture dialog box by keying specific increments in the Crop from text boxes. Click the Reset button to return to the original picture.

figure

5.23

Scaling and Cropping a Picture

Original Picture   Scaled Picture   Cropped Picture

Scaling or Resizing a Picture or Object

To *scale* a picture or object is to increase or decrease the size of an image proportionally or disproportionately, as shown in figure 5.23. To resize a picture or object, move the mouse over a sizing handle until it turns into a two-headed arrow. Drag a corner-sizing handle to scale a picture proportionally or drag a side handle to scale a picture disproportionately. Hold down the Ctrl key as you left-click and drag the mouse over a sizing handle and this will keep the image centered.

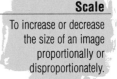

Scale
To increase or decrease the size of an image proportionally or disproportionately.

In addition, you can scale or size a picture at either the Format Object or Format Picture dialog boxes. If you want your picture to be a specific size, key increments in the He͟ight and Wi͟dth boxes in the Size and Rotate section. If you want to scale your picture by percentages, use the options in the Scale section, and enter percentages in the He͟ight and W͟idth boxes. To scale proportionally, select the Lock a͟spect ratio option. To scale in relation to the original size, select the R͟elative to original picture size option.

Using the Line Style Button

You can add a border around a picture by clicking the Line Style button on the Picture toolbar as shown in figure 5.24.

Line Style

figure

5.24   *Adding a Border to a Picture*

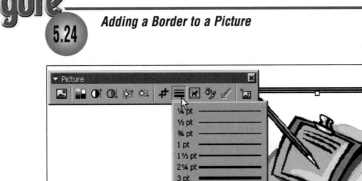

Using the Text Wrapping Button

You can place a picture anywhere in a document, even in a margin, and wrap text around it in many different ways. You can shape the text around the picture by editing the wrapping points as shown in figure 5.25. In addition, you can specify the amount of space between the picture and the text as illustrated and discussed in chapter 2.

Text Wrapping

figure
5.25

Using Wrapping Points

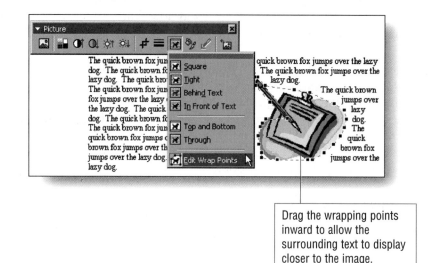

Drag the wrapping points inward to allow the surrounding text to display closer to the image.

Using the Format Picture Button

Format Picture

To quickly access the Format Picture dialog box, click the Format Picture button (third button from the right) on the Picture toolbar. If you edit a picture with Microsoft Word Picture by ungrouping and then grouping the image again, Word converts the picture to an object that can be altered using the tools on the Drawing toolbar.

Using the Transparent Color Button

Set Transparent Color

The Set Transparent Color button on the Picture toolbar offers a tool that can be used to alter colors in bitmap, GIF, and JPEG graphics, and in most clip art. You can make only one color transparent. When printed, transparent areas will be the same color as the paper they are printed on. In figure 5.26 an area of the picture was made transparent and another color was added by clicking the Fill Color button on the Drawing toolbar. In an electronic display, such as a Web page or a PowerPoint presentation, transparent areas will be the same color as the background.

figure

5.26 Using the Set Transparent Color Tool

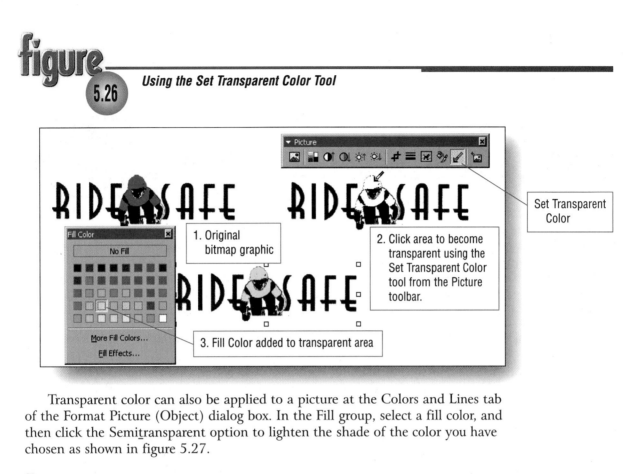

Set Transparent Color

1. Original bitmap graphic

2. Click area to become transparent using the Set Transparent Color tool from the Picture toolbar.

3. Fill Color added to transparent area

Transparent color can also be applied to a picture at the Colors and Lines tab of the Format Picture (Object) dialog box. In the Fill group, select a fill color, and then click the Semitransparent option to lighten the shade of the color you have chosen as shown in figure 5.27.

figure

5.27 Applying the Semitransparent Option to an AutoShape Object

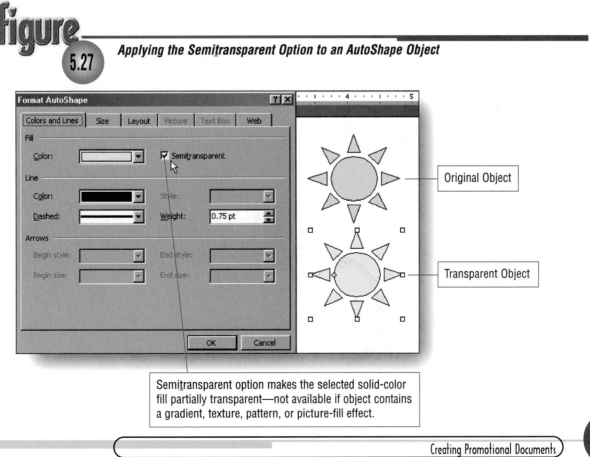

Original Object

Transparent Object

Semitransparent option makes the selected solid-color fill partially transparent—not available if object contains a gradient, texture, pattern, or picture-fill effect.

Using the Reset Button

Reset

The Reset Picture button returns the picture to its original configuration.

exercise 4

Creating a Flyer Promoting a Service

As an employee of the Edward Cardiovascular Institute, you will create a flyer promoting a new heart scan service. The flyer will incorporate an asymmetrical design in which the text will align off center. Contrast is achieved by using thick and thin fonts in serif and sans serif designs. Spot color is used to promote directional flow and reinforce the logo color. In addition, a dark red fill color is added to the clip art image to show continuity. The image will be resized, ungrouped, and regrouped in Microsoft Word Picture, and then rotated and cropped.

1. At a clear document screen, create the flyer in figure 5.28 by completing the following steps:
   a. Open Heart Scan.doc located on your student CD.
   b. Select *ANNOUNCING* and change the font to 20-pt. Tahoma in Dark Red and change the Character Spacing to Expanded <u>B</u>y 18 points. Turn on kerning at 14 points.
   c. Select *Ultra Fast* and change the font to 48-pt. Elephant and Expanded <u>B</u>y 3 points, then turn kerning on at 14 points. Select *Fast* and apply italics.
   d. Select *Heart Scan* and change the font to 48-pt. Elephant and Expanded <u>B</u>y 3 points, then turn kerning on at 14 points.
   e. Select *from the Edward Cardiovascular Institute* and change the font to 22-pt. Tahoma bold in Dark Red and turn kerning on at 14 points. Deselect the text.
2. Save the document with Save <u>A</u>s and name it c05ex04, Scan.
3. Customize a clip art image by completing the following steps:
   a. Display the Insert ClipArt dialog box, key **clock** at the Search for clips: list box, press Enter, scroll to find the image, click the Insert clip button, and then close the Insert ClipArt dialog box.
   b. Select the clock and change the text wrap to I<u>n</u> Front of Text.
   c. With the image still selected, right-click and select <u>E</u>dit Picture from the shortcut menu.

Step 3c

d. At the Word Picture editor, click the rust-colored circle in the top middle of the clock (ungroup the image if necessary), click the Fill Color button on the Drawing toolbar, click More Fill Colors, and then select the Custom tab. Write down the settings and then click OK or press Enter.

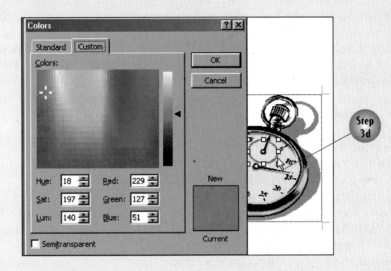

e. Reduce the Zoom to 50%, click the Select Objects button on the Drawing toolbar, and drag the arrow to create a dashed box around the image beginning at the top left corner and continuing to the bottom right corner, and then release the mouse (an ungrouped image should display). Next, click the Draw button on the Drawing toolbar and select Group.

f. Click the Free Rotate button on the Drawing toolbar, position the tool on the green dot in the upper-left corner, and drag downward slightly to rotate the clock to a position similar to figure 5.28. Click the Free Rotate button to turn it off.

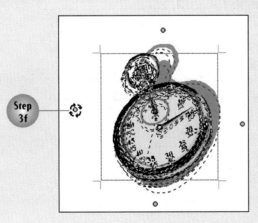

g. Close Microsoft Word Picture and return to the document.

h. With the image selected, click the Crop button on the Picture toolbar, position the cropping tool to the left middle sizing handle, and drag inward (see figure 5.28); then position the tool on the middle bottom sizing handle and drag upward. Click the Crop button to turn it off.

i. Select the image, size it, and then position it similar to figure 5.28.
j. With the image still selected, click the down arrow at the right of the Fill Color button on the Drawing toolbar and select Dark Red.

4. Format the remaining text by completing the following steps:
    a. Select *15 minutes, start to finish...* and change the font to 24-pt. Times New Roman bold and change the font color using the settings you recorded in step 3d. Remove the border around the text box.
    b. Select *Take it during your lunch hour.* Change the font to 18-pt. Times New Roman bold. Select *(And be back in time...)* and change the font to 12 pt. Times New Roman bold.
    c. Insert Scan.doc located on your student CD in the text box below the text in step 4b and remove the border around the text box.

5. Create the logo by completing the following steps:
    a. Click the AutoShapes button on the Drawing toolbar, point to Basic Shapes, and then select the Heart shape in the sixth row and first column. Drag the crosshairs to form a narrow heart shape as shown in figure 5.28.
    b. Fill the shape with the Dark Red fill color and add Shadow Style 13.
    c. Draw a text box to the right of the heart and key **EDWARD** (press Enter) **CARDIOVASCULAR** (press Enter) **INSTITUTE** in 12-pt. Tahoma bold, all caps, shadow, and in Dark Red, as shown in figure 5.28.
    d. Remove the border around the text box.
    e. Group the logo.

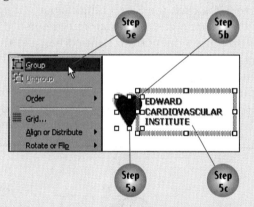

6. View the document in Print Preview and make any necessary adjustments.
7. Save the document with the same name, c05ex04, Scan.
8. Print and then close c05ex04, Scan.

figure
5.28
Exercise 4

Reviewing the Drawing Toolbar

The Drawing toolbar in figure 5.29 provides tools you can use to draw, manipulate, and format all kinds of drawing objects. A brief explanation of each tool follows. Additional information may be accessed from the <u>H</u>elp menu.

figure
5.29
Drawing Toolbar

Draw • | ⟋ | ⟍ | □ | ○ | Text Box | Insert WordArt | Insert Clip Art | Fill Color | Line Color | Font Color | Line Style | Dash Style | Arrow Style | Shadow | 3D | More Buttons

Draw — Select Objects — Free Rotate — AutoShapes — Line — Arrow — Rectangle — Oval — Text Box — Insert WordArt — Insert Clip Art — Fill Color — Line Color — Font Color — Line Style — Dash Style — Arrow Style — Shadow — 3D — More Buttons

Using the Draw Button

Draw ▼

Draw

The Draw menu has many shape adjustment commands, including grouping, ordering, using a grid, nudging, aligning, distributing, rotating, flipping, editing points, changing shape, and setting AutoShape defaults.

Using the Grouping, Ungrouping, and Regrouping Commands

When you group pictures or objects, they function as a single unit. Ungrouping a group releases the individual components from a whole unit. Ungrouping and regrouping the image converts the clip art image into an object, which can be edited using the Drawing tools. See figure 5.16 for examples of grouping and ungrouping.

Changing the Order of Pictures and Objects

When you create an object on top of another object, you create an overlapping stack. You can rearrange the stacked objects by using the Order command on the Draw menu. You can also stack groups and then change their stacking order as shown in figure 5.30.

Using the Grid Option

The drawing grid is an invisible grid of lines that aligns drawing objects and draws straight lines. It acts as a magnet, attracting your crosshairs as you draw lines at certain increments.

Using the Nudge Option

Nudge
To move something in small increments.

To nudge an object is to move it in small increments. Select the object you want to nudge, click Draw, point to Nudge, and then click the direction you want to nudge the object. You can also nudge an object by selecting it and pressing the arrow keys. Press Ctrl and the arrow keys to nudge an object in one-pixel increments.

figure
5.30 *Changing the Order of Objects*

Using the Align or Distribute Command

You can align two or more drawing objects relative to each other by the left, center, right, top, middle, or bottom edges, or distribute them equally vertically or horizontally as shown in figure 5.31.

figure
5.31 *Aligning Drawing Objects*

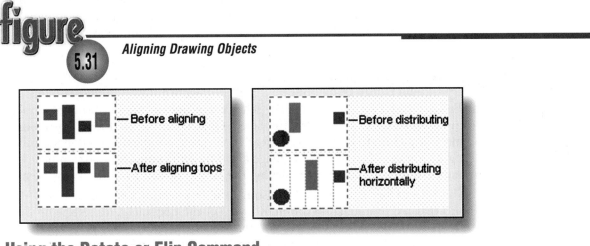

Using the Rotate or Flip Command

You can rotate a drawing object or group of drawing objects 90 degrees to the left or right, or flip a drawing object or group of drawing objects horizontally or vertically as shown in figure 5.32. Select the object, click Draw, point to Rotate or Flip, and then click the option you want to use. You can also click the Free Rotate tool on the Drawing toolbar.

Free Rotate   Rotate Left   Rotate Right   Flip Horizontal   Flip Vertical

Using the Text Wrapping Command

The Text Wrapping command provides options to change how text will wrap around an object, picture, or text box.

Using Edit Points

The Edit Points command on the Draw menu plots the points of your freehand drawing to enable you to modify it. You can point to any one of the editing points and drag it to a new location, altering the shape of your drawing.

Using the Change AutoShape Command

When you draw an AutoShape object in your document and decide you want to use a different shape, select the object, click Draw, point to Change AutoShape, and then select a different AutoShape. The new shape will automatically replace the old one.

Using the Select Objects Button

Select Objects

The Select Objects button enables the selection of one or more drawing objects as shown in figure 5.33. You can use the Select Objects button to draw a box around an object or picture to ungroup it, and after selecting a separate component and editing it, you can then group the image again by redrawing the selection box around the object or picture and clicking the Group option from the Draw menu.

The Select Objects command is also helpful in selecting text, objects, or pictures that are positioned in different layers of the document. To select the picture, position the Select Objects pointer over the picture and click to select it; then click the Select Objects button to deselect it when you are finished.

In addition, you can select several objects by holding down the Shift key as you select each object.

figure 5.33

Selecting Objects Using the Select Objects Button

Using the Free Rotate Button

You can rotate drawing objects to any degree by using the Free Rotate tool on the Drawing toolbar. Position the Free Rotate tool (circular arrow) over one of the green dots (rotation handles) that will display around the image, drag it in a desired direction, and then release the left mouse button as shown in figure 5.34.

Free Rotate

figure 5.34

Using the Free Rotate Button

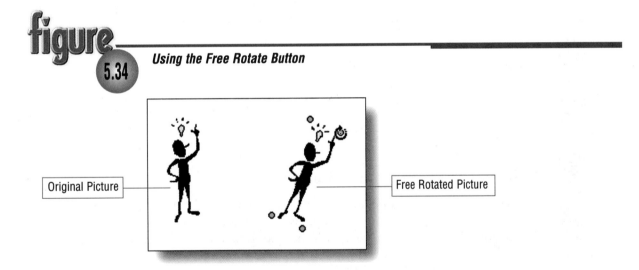

Original Picture

Free Rotated Picture

Using the AutoShapes Button

The AutoShapes button opens a menu of shapes in six categories as shown in figure 5.35. Each of the categories offers a variety of shapes. The More AutoShapes category takes you to the Clip Gallery.

AutoShapes

figure
5.35

A<u>u</u>toShapes Palettes

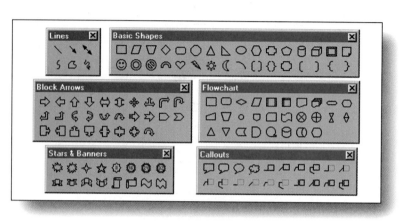

Line

Arrow

Using the Line, Arrow, Rectangle, and Oval Buttons

You can draw straight lines vertically, horizontally, or at 15, 30, 45, 60, 75, or 90 degree angles if you hold down the Shift key as you draw. Use the Arrow button to draw lines with arrowheads. The Shift key will cause the same effects as the Line button. If you hold down the Shift key as you draw a Rectangle shape, you will create a square. If you hold down the Shift key as you draw an Oval shape, you will create an ellipse or a circle.

Rectangle

Oval

Using the Text Box Button

Use the Text Box button to create a container for text, pictures, or objects. You can double-click a text box to quickly display the Format Text Box dialog box. Using the dialog box is an efficient way to make several formatting changes at once. Refer to chapter 3 for additional information and figures concerning text boxes.

Text Box

Insert WordArt

Using the Insert WordArt Button

With WordArt you can pour text into a shape, flip or stretch letters, condense or expand letter spacing, rotate or angle words, or add shading, colors, borders, or shadows to text. Refer to chapter 3 for additional information and samples.

Using the Insert ClipArt Button

Insert ClipArt

This button enables you to quickly access the Insert ClipArt dialog box. Clip art displays in the text layer; however, if the picture is dragged and dropped from the Clip Gallery as shown in figure 5.36, it will automatically display in the layer above the text layer and may easily be moved. As shown in figure 5.36, it is helpful to click the Change to Small Window button in the upper-right corner of the Insert ClipArt dialog box. This feature is particularly helpful when inserting pictures in cells.

figure
5.36

Dragging and Dropping a Picture from the ClipArt Gallery

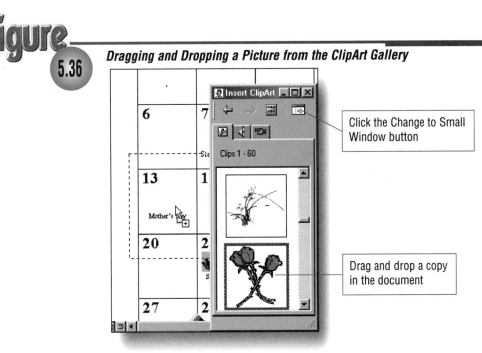

Click the Change to Small Window button

Drag and drop a copy in the document

Using the Fill Color Button

The Fill Color option fills a selected object with color, gradient, texture, pattern, or a picture as shown in figure 5.37.

Fill Color

figure
5.37

Examples of Fill Effects

| Gradient (Preset, Desert) | Texture (White Marble) | Pattern (Solid Diamond) | Picture (Dove.wmf) |

Line Color

Font Color

Line Style

Dash Style

Arrow Style

Using the Line Color, Font Color, Line Style, Dash Style, and Arrow Style Buttons

The Line Color button colors a selected line (or a line selected around a shape) or sets the default line color if no line is selected. The Font Color button colors the text for selected objects or sets the default if no font color is selected. The Line Style button changes the line width or sets the default if one has not been selected. The Dash Style button provides various types of dashes that can be used on different line styles and arrow styles. See figure 5.38 for examples created from each of these buttons.

figure 5.38

Examples of Line Colors, Font Colors, Line Styles, Dash Styles, and Arrow Styles

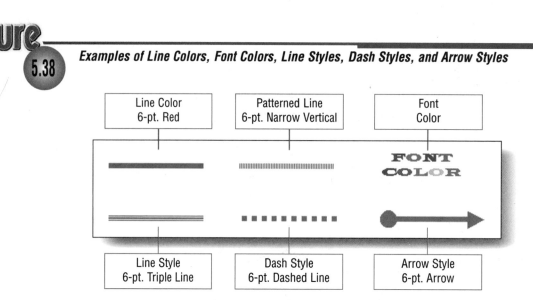

Using the Shadow Button

Shadow

The Shadow button adds a shadow style to a selected object. The Shadow tool was described in greater detail earlier in the chapter. Refer to figure 5.13 for the Shadow palette and the Shadow Settings toolbar. See figure 5.39 for examples of different shadow styles. The effects of the Shadow button make the images seem to lift off the page.

figure 5.39

Examples of Shadows

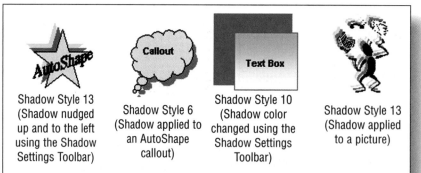

Using the 3-D Button

3-D

The 3-D button applies a three-dimension effect to a selected object or it sets the default if no object is selected. The 3-D Settings toolbar provides tools to make numerous adjustments to 3-D objects. You can tilt the shape up, down, left, or right to control its perspective. You can add depth, change the lighting source, or change the surface type to add additional effect. You can also change the color of the 3-D effect. See figure 5.40 for examples of enhanced 3-D objects.

figure

5.40

Examples of 3-D Effects

chapter summary

- ➤ Flyers and announcements are considered among the least expensive means of advertising. A flyer is generally used to advertise a product or service that is available for a limited amount of time. An announcement informs an audience of an upcoming event.

- ➤ When creating headlines for flyers or announcements, select typefaces that match the tone of the document and type sizes that stress important information.

- ➤ Graphics added to a flyer or announcement can add excitement and generate enthusiasm for the publication. A simple graphic demands more attention and has more impact than a complex one.

- ➤ Use color in a publication to elicit a particular feeling, emphasize important text, attract attention, organize data, and/or create a pattern in a document. Limit the color to small areas so it attracts attention but does not create visual confusion.

- ➤ In planning a flyer or announcement, use a table to organize text, graphics, and other design elements on the page.

- ➤ Borders and lines can be used in documents to aid directional flow, add color, and organize text to produce professional-looking results.

- ➤ Clip art images can be altered and customized using Microsoft Word Picture and/or using tools on the Picture toolbar.

- ➤ Clip art can be downloaded from the Microsoft Clip Gallery Live.

- ➤ Two basic graphic file formats include bitmap and metafile formats. Bitmapped graphics cannot be ungrouped. Metafile graphics can be ungrouped, converted to drawing objects, and then edited by using tools on the Drawing toolbar.

➤ Pictures and clip art are inserted with the *In line with text* text wrapping style applied.

➤ Use WordArt to distort or modify text to create a variety of shapes.

➤ Create your own shapes and images using Word's Drawing toolbar.

➤ Logos may be added to flyers and announcements to reinforce company identity or promote product recognition. The logo may be placed low on the page to anchor the message.

➤ With buttons on the Drawing toolbar, you can add fill color, gradient, pattern, texture, and a picture to an enclosed object; change thickness and color of the line that draws the object; and rotate, align, and change the position of the object.

➤ When objects overlap, use the Bring to Front and Send to Back options from the Draw menu. You can also move an object in front of or behind text and position an object in a stack.

➤ Using the Group option, you can group two or more objects or sections of an object together as a single object. You can also ungroup objects or sections of an object using the Ungroup option.

➤ After you ungroup a picture, the picture becomes an object, and then you can edit it by using options on the Drawing toolbar.

➤ With the drawing grid turned on, an object is pulled into alignment with the nearest intersection of grid lines.

➤ Selected items can be aligned using the Align or Distribute command from the Draw menu.

commands review

	Mouse/Keyboard
Table	Click Table, Draw Table; or click the Draw Table button on the Tables and Borders toolbar
WordArt	Click Insert, Picture, WordArt; click the Insert WordArt button on Drawing and WordArt toolbars
Microsoft Word Picture	Right-click picture, click Edit Picture; click Insert, Picture, New Drawing
Drawing Toolbar	Click Drawing button on Standard toolbar; right-click toolbar, click Drawing; or click View, Toolbars, Drawing
Picture Toolbar	Right-click on Standard toolbar, click Picture; or click View, Toolbars, Picture
AutoShapes	Click Insert, Pictures, AutoShapes; click the AutoShapes button on Drawing toolbar
Microsoft Clip Gallery Live	Access Internet Service Provider, access Word, click Insert, Picture, Clip Art, Clips Online; or access ISP, open Word, click Help, Office on the Web, Clip Art

thinking offline

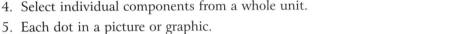

Matching: Match the terms with the correct definitions by writing the letter (or letters) of the term on the blank line in front of the correct definition.

- Ⓐ Announcement
- Ⓑ Flyer
- Ⓒ Group
- Ⓓ WordArt
- Ⓔ Tables and Borders toolbar
- Ⓕ Gradient
- Ⓖ Nudge
- Ⓗ Pixel
- Ⓘ Ungroup
- Ⓙ Drawing toolbar
- Ⓚ Picture toolbar
- Ⓛ Crop
- Ⓜ Logo
- Ⓝ Scale
- Ⓞ Resolution
- Ⓟ Contrast

_____ 1. With this Word feature, you can modify text to create a variety of shapes.

_____ 2. A gradual varying of color.

_____ 3. To trim vertical and horizontal edges off a picture.

_____ 4. Select individual components from a whole unit.

_____ 5. Each dot in a picture or graphic.

_____ 6. To increase or decrease the size of an image.

_____ 7. The number of dots that make up an image on a screen or printer.

_____ 8. This type of document communicates or informs an audience of an event.

_____ 9. This toolbar includes buttons that are used to create shapes, add fill and effects, access WordArt, add shadows, and apply 3-D effects.

_____ 10. A unique design that is composed of combinations of letters, words, shapes, or graphics and that serves as an emblem for an organization or a product.

_____ 11. This toolbar provides options to rotate text in a table.

_____ 12. To move an object in small increments.

True/False: Circle the letter T if the statement is true; circle the letter F if the statement is false.

T   F   1.   A complex graphic has more impact than a simple graphic.

T   F   2.   Generally, the upper-right side of a document is read first.

T   F   3.   To display the Drawing toolbar, click Tools, and then Draw.

T   F   4.   A grouped picture or object functions as a single unit.

T   F   5.   Bitmap pictures can be converted to drawing objects and customized using tools on the Drawing toolbar.

T   F   6.   To copy a picture, hold down the Shift key, select the picture, and then drag and drop the picture to another location.

T   F   7.   To draw a square shape using the Rectangle button on the Drawing toolbar, hold down the Ctrl key as you draw the shape.

T   F   8.   Pictures and clip art are inserted with the *In line with text* text wrapping style applied.

T   F   9.   Once objects have been grouped, they cannot be ungrouped.

T   F   10.   If you rotate an AutoShape containing text, the shape rotates but the text does not.

T   F   11.   Hold down the Shift key and select each object you want to align using the Align or Distribute command from the Draw menu.

T   F   12.   Text automatically wraps around all sides of a text box.

Assessment 1

As a parent of a high school senior, you have volunteered to serve on a committee to organize a senior celebration party at NNHS. Create a flyer similar to figure 5.41 asking for volunteers to sign up for this event. Include the following specifications:

1. Display the Insert ClipArt dialog box, key **graduation** in the Search for clips: text box, and then select the clip art shown in figure 5.41 or other appropriate pictures.
2. Match a color from the picture to the font color used in the headline.
3. Use WordArt in the headline.
4. Double-click the insertion point below the WordArt headline, and begin keying the text displayed in figure 5.41. (*Hint: Recall that* Click and type *enables you to double-click, and then start typing text or insert an item as usual. To turn this feature on, click Tools, Options, Edit tab, Enable click and type.*)
5. Set a Left tab at 1/2 inch and another Left tab at 6 inches with the #4 Leader at the Tabs dialog box. Key **Name:** and press the space bar once, then press Tab to create each line.

figure

5.41 — *Assessment 1*

Senior Celebration 2000

Senior Celebration is an end of the year and end of the high school career celebration that honors all the experience and accomplishments of the NNHS graduating seniors. The all-night party is a "gift" from the parents to their graduating seniors provided in a safe, alcohol- and drug-free setting.

Volunteer Sign-up

Name: _____

Address: _____

Phone: _____

Student's Name: _____

AREA OF INTEREST

☐ I would like to help plan an Area/Event.
   Area/Event of interest _____
☐ I would like to help set up *Senior Celebration*.
☐ I would like to work the night of *Senior Celebration*.
   I would like to work with these friends:

   _____

Please mail your completed form to Mary Jo Smith, 298 Jefferson Blvd., Naperville, IL 60540. If you have any questions, please call Mary Jo Smith (630) 555-5748.

6. Insert the checkbox symbol located in the fifth row and fourth column from the right of the Wingdings font at the Symbol dialog box. Press the Tab key after the first symbol, then press Shift + Enter to insert a new line command where another checkbox is not needed.
7. Save the document as c05sa01, Senior.
8. Print and then close c05sa01, Senior.

Assessment 2

You are working in the Dallas office of Universal Packaging Company. Your company is well known for its involvement in environmental issues. On April 21, several Dallas businesses will offer free seminars and distribute flyers, brochures, etc., in an effort to promote public awareness and involvement in Earth Day 2001. Complete the following task:

1. Create the document shown in figure 5.42 with the handwritten specifications.
2. Save the document and name it c05sa02, Earth.
3. Print and then close c05sa02, Earth.

figure

5.42 Assessment 2

Assessment 3

You have recently completed a desktop publishing class at local community college, and you are working part-time at Steinbock's Art and Frame Shoppe. Create a flyer for Steinbock's promoting their business. Include the following specifications:

1. Create a logo.
2. Use a photograph, clip art image, or Web free clip art.
3. Include the following text:

> **Steinbock's Art and Frame Shoppe**
> **Founded in 1970**
> **21 S. Main Street**
> **Naperville, IL 60540**
> **(630) 555-0372**
> **Daily, 9:30–5:00 or by appt.**
> **Thursday until 8 pm**
> **(Closed Sunday)**
> **Fine quality framing & matting**
> **More than 1000 frame choices**
> **Limited editions, originals, & reproductions**
> **Design assistance**
> **Enjoy our shoppe and a 20% new neighbor discount on your first order!**

4. Save the document and name it c05sa03, Art.
5. Print and then close c05sa03, Art.

CREATIVE ACTIVITY

Collect two examples of flyers and/or announcements and evaluate them according to the guidelines presented in the Document Evaluation Checklist.doc. Use any of the flyers and announcements that you started collecting in chapter 1. Include one example of a flyer or announcement that demonstrates one of these features: poor layout and design; no graphic or one that does not relate to the subject; poor use of fonts, sizes, and styles; or a message that is unclear. Complete the following steps:

1. Open Document Evaluation Checklist.doc located on your student CD.
2. Print two copies of the form.
3. Complete and attach an evaluation form to each publication.
4. Re-create one of the flyers incorporating your own ideas and formatting. You do not have to reconstruct the poor example. However, the poor example will show the greatest amount of improvement.
5. A few possible suggestions for enhancing your document are to include: appropriate fonts, sizes, and styles; reverse; WordArt; special characters; color paper; color graphics, watermarks, or text; horizontal or vertical lines; and/or borders, shadow, 3-D effects, and so on.
6. Create a thumbnail sketch first.
7. Save your document and name it c05ca01, Flyer.
8. Print and then close c05ca01, Flyer. Turn in the evaluation forms and examples along with c05ca01, Flyer. *(Hint: You may want to exhibit this remake in your portfolio.)*

Chapter 06

Creating Brochures

PERFORMANCE OBJECTIVES

Upon successful completion of chapter 6, you will be able to create brochures using a variety of page layouts and design techniques.

DESKTOP PUBLISHING TERMS

Parallel folds	Copyright	Reverse text
Right-angle folds	Normal Style	Screens
Dummy	Paragraph Style	Style
Newspaper columns	Character Style	Drop cap
Panels	Base Style	

WORD FEATURES USED

Paper size	Bullets and numbering	2 pages per sheet
Margins	Picture	Indents
Columns	Brochure template	Styles
Drawing toolbar	Paragraph spacing	Drop caps
Text boxes	Paragraph alignment	Tabs

In this chapter, you will be introduced to different methods for creating your own brochures. You will use the Columns feature, the Word brochure template, and the 2 pages per sheet feature to create brochures. Purpose, content, paper selection, brochure folds, page layout, design considerations, and desktop publishing concepts are also discussed.

Planning a Brochure

Clearly defining the purpose of your communication is a very important step in initiating the desktop publishing process. Consequently, defining purpose is as important to the creation of a brochure as it is to the creation of any other publication.

Defining the Purpose

The purpose of a brochure can be to inform, educate, promote, or sell. Identify the purpose in the following examples:

- A city agency mails brochures to the community explaining a local recycling program.
- A doctor displays brochures on childhood immunizations in the patient waiting room.
- A car salesperson hands out a brochure on a current model to a potential buyer.
- A new management consulting firm sends out brochures introducing its services.
- A professional organization mails brochures to its members about an upcoming conference.

If you found yourself thinking that some brochures have more than one purpose, you are correct. As examples, the goals of a brochure on childhood immunizations may be to inform and to educate; the goals of a brochure about a car model may be to inform and promote the sale of the car.

In addition, a brochure may be another means of establishing your organization's identity and image. Incorporating design elements from your other business documents into the design of your brochure reinforces your image and identity among your readers.

Determining the Content

Before creating the actual layout and design of your brochure, determine what the content will be. Try to look at the content from a reader's point of view. The content should include the following items:

- A clearly stated description of the topic, product, service, or organization
- A description of the people or company doing the informing, educating, promoting, or selling
- A description of how the reader will benefit from this information, product, service, or organization
- A clear indication of what action you want your audience to take after reading the brochure
- An easy way for readers to respond to the desired action, such as a fill-in form or detachable postcard

Determining the Size and Type of Paper

Brochures are usually printed on both sides of the page on an assortment of paper stocks. The paper stock may vary in size, weight, color, and texture, and it can also have defined folding lines.

Brochures can be folded in a number of different ways. The manner in which a brochure is folded determines the order in which the panels are set on the page and read by the recipient. The most common brochure fold is called a *letter fold*. It is also known as a *trifold* or *three-panel brochure*. The letter fold and other common folds, as shown in figure 6.1, are referred to as *parallel folds* because all of the folds

Parallel folds

All folds run in the same direction.

run in the same direction. *Right-angle folds* are created by pages that are folded at right angles to each other, such as the folds in a greeting card. Standard-size 8-1/2 by 11 inch (landscape orientation) paper stock can easily accommodate a letter fold, accordion fold, and single fold. Standard legal-size paper that is 8-1/2 by 14 inches can be used to create a brochure with a *map fold* or a *gate fold*. Different paper sizes can be used to create variations of these folds. In addition, folds do not always have to create equal panel sizes. Offsetting a fold can produce an interesting effect.

Right-angle folds
Folds created by pages folded at right angles to each other.

figure
6.1
Brochure Folds

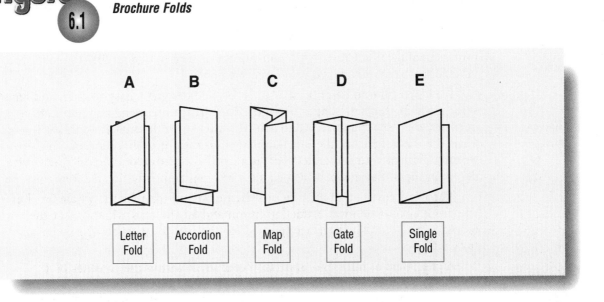

A	B	C	D	E
Letter Fold	Accordion Fold	Map Fold	Gate Fold	Single Fold

The type of paper selected for a brochure affects the total production cost. When selecting the paper stock for a brochure, consider the following cost factors:

- Standard-size brochures, such as a three-panel brochure created from 8-1/2 by 11-inch paper stock or a four-panel brochure created from 8-1/2 by 14-inch paper stock, are easily enclosed in a #10 business envelope.
- Standard-size brochures designed as self-mailers satisfy postal regulations and are, therefore, less costly to mail.
- Nonstandard-size paper stock may be more expensive to purchase and to mail.
- Heavier weight papers are more costly to mail.
- Higher quality paper stocks are more expensive to purchase.
- Color paper is more costly than standard white, ivory, cream, or gray.
- Predesigned paper stock is more expensive than plain paper stock.

Although cost is an important issue when choosing paper stock, you should also take into account how the brochure will be distributed, how often it will be handled, and the image you want to project. If you plan to design the brochure as a self-mailer, take a sample of the paper stock to the post office to see if it meets USPS mailing regulations. If you expect your target audience to keep your brochure for a period of time or to handle it often, plan to purchase a higher quality, heavier paper stock. By the same token, choose a paper within your budget that enhances the image you want to leave in the reader's mind.

If you intend to print the brochure yourself, run a sample of the paper you intend to use through your printer. Some papers are better suited for laser and ink jet printers than others. If you are unsure about what type of paper to purchase, take a master copy of your brochure to a printer for advice on the best type of paper for the situation. You can also take your printed brochure to a print shop and have it folded on their folding equipment.

Designing a Brochure

As with letterheads, envelopes, and business cards, designing your own brochure can be a cost-saving measure. It eliminates the cost of paying a professional designer and the cost of committing to a minimum order. In addition, if the information in your brochure needs to be updated, it can easily be changed. Although not as cost effective, you can design your own brochure and take it to a professional printer. Check with your printer or service bureau first to make sure your files are compatible with their requirements.

For a brochure to be noticed, it must be well designed, easy to read, and have some element that sets it apart from the pack. As in preparing any publication, consider your target audience and start drawing some thumbnail sketches. Consider the content of the brochure; any illustrations or graphics that might be a required part of your brochure, such as a logo or a picture of a product or service; and any colors that might be associated with your company, organization, or topic.

The front cover of a brochure sets the mood and tone for the whole brochure. The front cover title must attract attention and let the reader know what the brochure is about. The typeface selected for the title must reflect the image and tone intended.

DTP POINTERS
Vary the style of the typeface rather than changing typefaces.

A great deal of information is often contained within the confines of a brochure. Using one typeface for the brochure title, headings, and subheadings and another typeface for the body copy can provide visual contrast. Do not use more than two typefaces or the brochure will appear crowded, cluttered, and more difficult to read. To provide contrast within the brochure text, vary the style of the typeface rather than changing typefaces. Text can be set in all caps, small caps, shadow, outline, embossed, engraved, italics, reverse, bold, or color to achieve contrast. While text set in color can be an effective contrasting element, use it sparingly. Use it for titles, headings, subheadings, and small graphics elements such as bullets.

DTP POINTERS
Use bullets to organize text and improve directional flow.

Several elements can be used to direct the reader's eyes through a brochure. Subheadings set in color or in reverse text can be useful directional tools. A text box with a specific border can also be used to place items of importance. Horizontal and vertical ruled lines can be used as visual separators. A screen (a shaded area behind a block of text) can be used to emphasize and separate a block of text. Bullets or special characters can be used to aid directional flow.

Effective use of white space can separate items on the page. White space makes the copy more appealing and easier to read. Remember to allow for white space between the headings and body copy and among separate sections of the body copy.

Consistent elements are necessary to maintain continuity in a multipage brochure. Be consistent in your design and layout. Generally, do not mix landscape and portrait orientations within the same brochure. Format each panel in the same basic manner so the reader knows what to expect. Be consistent in the fonts used for headings, subheadings, and body copy.

Continuity can be maintained by emphasizing the same theme or style throughout the brochure. When evaluating a brochure for continuity, open the brochure and view it the way your readers would. Although the individual elements of each panel are important, viewing the design and layout as a whole unit is equally important. When you open a three-panel brochure, look at panels 1, 2, and 3 as a three-page spread. Does the design flow from one panel to the next? Do all three panels work together visually as a unit?

A visual, such as a clip art image, illustration, photograph, drawing, or other graphic can be a powerful tool. Although a visual may attract attention, it also delivers its own immediate message. It can turn a reader away before the intended message has even been read. When selecting visuals, select only those visuals that best enhance the intended message. Also, always find out about *copyright* restrictions before using any artwork. Often clip art software owners are allowed to use and publish the images contained in the software package; however, the clip art may not be resold in any manner. If you intend to use a drawing, clip art, scanned art, or photograph, find out the source and request permission from the copyright owner.

Copyright
Exclusive legal ownership of a literary, musical, or artistic work.

Understanding Brochure Page Layout

A brochure page (defined by the dimensions of the paper stock) is divided into sections called *panels*. At least one fold separates each panel. Folds create distinct sections to place specific blocks of text. For example, a three-panel or letter-fold brochure layout actually has six panels available for text—three panels on one side of the paper and three more panels on the other side. The way a brochure is folded determines the order in which the panels are read by the recipient. The correct placement of text depends on understanding this order. Look how the panels are labeled in the letter-fold page layout illustrated in figure 6.2. Panels 1, 2, and 3 are located on the inside of the brochure, counting left to right. Panel 4 is the page you see when the cover is opened. Panel 5 is the back of the folded brochure, which may be used for mailing purposes, if desired. Panel 6 is the cover of the brochure. The main content of the brochure is focused in panels 1, 2, and 3.

Panels
Sections separated by folds in a brochure page layout.

figure 6.2

Letter-Fold Panel Layout

PANEL 1 (inside)	PANEL 2 (inside)	PANEL 3 (inside)	PANEL 4 (first flap viewed when cover is opened)	PANEL 5 (back/ mailing)	PANEL 6 (cover)

Dummy

A mock-up that is positioned, folded, trimmed, and/or labeled as the actual publication.

To avoid confusion about the brochure page layout and the panel reference numbers, create a mock-up or *dummy* of your brochure. A dummy is folded in the same manner as the actual brochure and is particularly useful because brochures can be folded in a number of different ways. A dummy can be as simple or as detailed as you would like. If you only need a visual guide to make sure you are placing the correct text in the correct panel, make a simple dummy using the number of columns desired and label each panel as in figure 6.2. If you need to visualize the placement of text within each panel, the margins, and the white space between columns, make a more detailed dummy that includes very specific margin settings, column width settings, and settings for the spacing between columns.

A brochure or a dummy can be created using Word's Columns, Table, Text Box, or 2 pages per sheet feature (only applicable to single-fold brochures). For example, for a standard-sized three-panel brochure, the actual page size is 8-1/2 by 11 inches positioned in landscape orientation. The page is divided into three columns using the Columns feature, or into three columns and one row using the Table feature. Or, three text boxes can be sized and positioned on the page to represent three panels. Although each method has its advantages and disadvantages, the Columns feature requires the least adjustments. Consequently, having a solid understanding of the Columns feature is necessary to create a dummy or a template provided by Word for your brochure.

Setting Brochure Margins

The left and right margins for a brochure page are usually considerably less than those for standard business documents. Many printers will only allow a minimum of a 0.5 inch left or right side margin (depending on page orientation) because a certain amount of space is needed for the printer to grab the paper and eject it from the printer. If you set margins less than the minimum, Word prompts you with the following message: *One or more margins are set outside the printable area of the page. Select the Fix button to increase the appropriate margins.* Click Fix to set the margins to the printer's minimum setting. Check the new margin setting in the <u>M</u>argins tab of the Page Setup dialog box. If landscape is the selected paper orientation, the right margin will be the only margin "fixed" by Word because that is the side of the paper the printer grabs to eject the paper from the printer. When creating a brochure, adjust the opposite side margin to match the margin adjusted by Word. For example, the printer used to create the brochure exercises in this chapter will only allow a minimum of 0.55 inches for the right margin with landscape chosen as the paper orientation. Hence, you are directed to set the left and right margins at 0.55 inches. Alternately, the printer imposes minimum margin settings when portrait is the selected paper orientation. The bottom margin setting is affected the most because it is the last side of the paper to come out of the printer.

DTP POINTERS
Adjust margin settings to allow an adequate amount of white space on each side of the brochure page.

If you click <u>I</u>gnore as a response to Word's prompt to "fix" the margins, the program will ignore the printer's minimum requirement and accept whatever margins you have set. However, the printer will not print anything in its defined unprintable area, which will result in text that is cut off. Use Print Preview to view the results of setting margins that are less than the printer's minimum requirements.

Determining Column Widths

The widths of the panels in most brochures cannot all be equal. If equal panel sizes are used, the margins on some of the panels will appear uneven and the brochure folds will not fall properly in relation to the text. In addition, the thickness of the paper stock affects the amount of space taken up by the fold. To solve this problem, individually size the text columns, the space between the columns, and the margins within each panel to accommodate the appropriate placement of the text and the folds to achieve the desired result. You will have to experiment somewhat and make adjustments to find the appropriate column width and space between columns. *(Hint:* These suggestions give you a starting point from which to work but experiment by printing and folding the brochure and then fine-tuning any measurements.)

DTP POINTERS
Use unequal column widths in a brochure to accommodate appropriate placement of the text and folds.

Using panels 1, 2, and 3 of a letter-fold brochure as an example, as shown in figure 6.3, consider the following suggestions when setting column widths and the space between columns:

1. One way to determine the approximate width of each panel is to fold the brochure paper stock into the desired brochure fold configuration, which, in this example, is a letter-fold brochure. Measure the width of each panel. The width obtained will be approximate because a ruler cannot measure hundredths of an inch, but it will be a good starting point.
2. Establish the left and right margins for the whole page. One-half inch margin settings, or something close to that, are common. (See the section above on setting brochure margins.)
3. For panel 1, the left margin for the whole brochure page is also the left margin for the panel. Therefore, subtract the left margin setting from the total width of panel 1. From the remaining amount, estimate how much of that space is needed to allow for an appropriate column width for the text and for an appropriate amount of white space on the right side of the panel. For example, if panel 1 measures approximately 3.7 inches and the left page margin is 0.55 inches, subtract 0.55 inches

from 3.7 inches. From the 3.15 inches that remains, estimate how much of that space will be occupied by text and how much needs to be allotted for the right margin of panel 1 (i.e., the white space before the fold).

4. For panel 2, use the whole panel width to estimate an appropriate column width for the text and an appropriate amount of white space on the left and right sides of the panel. The column width in panel 2 will be wider than the column widths in panels 1 and 3.

5. For panel 3, the right margin for the whole brochure page is also the right margin for the panel. Therefore, subtract the amount of the right margin setting from the total width of the panel. From the remaining amount, determine an appropriate column width for the text and an appropriate amount of white space on the left side of the panel.

6. After establishing text column widths and the amount of white space in between for panels 1, 2, and 3, reverse the measurements for panels 4, 5, and 6. For example, panels 1 and 6 will be the same measurement, panels 2 and 5 will be the same, and panels 3 and 4 will be the same. (*Hint:* If you are using the Columns feature, you will need to insert a section break to vary the column formatting on the second page. See the section below, Varying Column Formatting within the Same Document. If you are using the Table feature, you will have to create another table for the second page of the brochure reversing the column measurements from panels 1, 2, and 3.)

7. Refer to figure 6.3 to see that the space between columns is actually divided by the fold, allowing white space on either side of the fold. In other words, the space between columns serves as the margins for two different panels. For example, the space between columns surrounding the first fold in figure 6.3 provides the white space (or margin) for the right side of panel 1 and the left side of panel 2.

8. Use the suggestions above to create a dummy. Insert random text in every panel and print. Fold the page as you would the brochure and check the amount of space between columns. Is the text positioned correctly within each panel? If not, adjust the space between columns and/or the column width settings and print again.

figure

6.3 *Column Width Guide for a Letter-Fold Brochure*

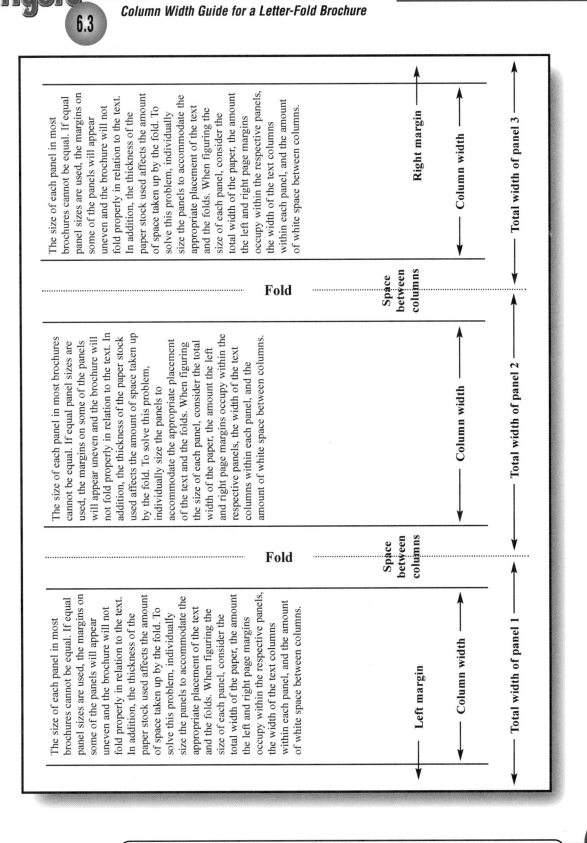

The size of each panel in most brochures cannot be equal. If equal panel sizes are used, the margins on some of the panels will appear uneven and the brochure will not fold properly in relation to the text. In addition, the thickness of the paper stock used affects the amount of space taken up by the fold. To solve this problem, individually size the panels to accommodate the appropriate placement of the text and the folds. When figuring the size of each panel, consider the total width of the paper, the amount the left and right page margins occupy within the respective panels, the width of the text columns within each panel, and the amount of white space between columns.

Right margin

Column width

Total width of panel 3

Fold

Space between columns

The size of each panel in most brochures cannot be equal. If equal panel sizes are used, the margins on some of the panels will appear uneven and the brochure will not fold properly in relation to the text. In addition, the thickness of the paper stock used affects the amount of space taken up by the fold. To solve this problem, individually size the panels to accommodate the appropriate placement of the text and the folds. When figuring the size of each panel, consider the total width of the paper, the amount the left and right page margins occupy within the respective panels, the width of the text columns within each panel, and the amount of white space between columns.

Column width

Total width of panel 2

Fold

Space between columns

The size of each panel in most brochures cannot be equal. If equal panel sizes are used, the margins on some of the panels will appear uneven and the brochure will not fold properly in relation to the text. In addition, the thickness of the paper stock used affects the amount of space taken up by the fold. To solve this problem, individually size the panels to accommodate the appropriate placement of the text and the folds. When figuring the size of each panel, consider the total width of the paper, the amount the left and right page margins occupy within the respective panels, the width of the text columns within each panel, and the amount of white space between columns.

Left margin

Column width

Total width of panel 1

The method used to create the white space between columns depends on the method used to create the columns, as explained in figure 6.4.

figure

6.4   *Methods Used to Create Spacing between Columns*

Method Used to Create Columns	Method Used to Create Spacing between Columns
Columns feature	At the Columns dialog box in the Width and spacing section, adjust the amount in the <u>S</u>pacing list box.
Table feature	Create blank columns in between the columns that contain the text for each panel.
Text Box feature	Size and position the text boxes containing the text for each panel, leaving the desired amount of white space between text boxes.
2 Pages per Sheet	Applicable only to single-fold brochures, white space is achieved by adjusting the margin settings.

Understanding Newspaper Columns

Newspaper columns

Text flows from the bottom of one column to the top of the next column.

The types of columns created by using the Columns feature are commonly referred to as *newspaper columns*. Newspaper columns are used for text in newspapers, newsletters, brochures, and magazines. Text in these types of columns flows continuously from the bottom of one column to the top of the next column, as shown in figure 6.5. When the first column on the page is filled with text, the insertion point moves to the top of the next column on the same page, and so on. When the last column on the page is filled with text, the insertion point moves to the beginning of the first column on the next page.

figure
6.5

Newspaper Columns

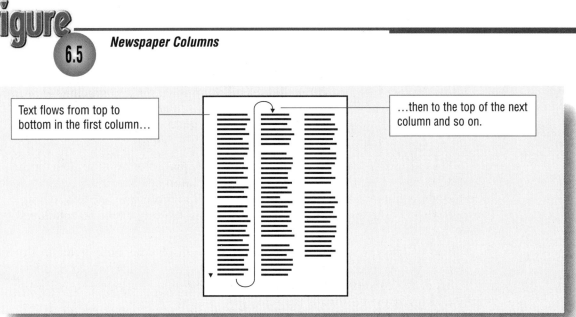

Text flows from top to bottom in the first column...

...then to the top of the next column and so on.

By default, all Word documents are automatically set up in a one-column format. However, a document can include as many columns as there is room for on the page. Word determines how many columns can be included based on the page width, the margin settings, the size of the columns, and the spacing between columns. Column formatting can be assigned to a document before the text is keyed or it can be applied to existing text.

Creating Newspaper Columns of Equal Width

Click the Columns button on the Standard toolbar to easily create newspaper columns of equal width. Hold down the left mouse button, drag the mouse down and to the right highlighting the desired number of column displays, and then release the mouse button. Even though only four column icons display, you can continue dragging toward the right to select a greater number of columns. The view will automatically change to the Print Layout View so you may view the columns side by side.

Columns

DTP POINTERS
Use Print Layout View to display columns side by side.

Columns of equal width can also be created at the Columns dialog box. (Click Format and Columns). By default, the Equal column width option contains a check mark. With this option selected, Word automatically determines column widths and the spacing between columns for the number of columns specified. The number of columns can be specified by selecting One, Two, or Three in the Presets section or by indicating the number in the Number of columns list box of the Columns dialog box. By default, columns are separated by 0.5 inches of space. This amount of space can be increased or decreased with the Spacing option in the Width and spacing section.

Creating Newspaper Columns of Unequal Width

Use the Columns dialog box to create columns of unequal width. To create columns of unequal width, complete the following steps:

1. Click Format and Columns.
2. At the Columns dialog box, select One, Two, Three, Left, or Right in the Presets section; or key the desired number of columns in the Number of columns text box.
3. Click the Equal column width check box to disable this option.
4. In the Width and spacing section, find the Col #(s) you want to change, and then enter the desired column widths and spacing between columns in the corresponding Width and Spacing text boxes.
5. Click OK or press Enter. Word automatically changes to Print Layout View so the column text is displayed side by side.

The Left and Right options will result in unequal columns of a predetermined width. If you select the Left option, the right column of text will be twice as wide as the left column of text. Select the Right option if you want the left column twice as wide. The options contain a preview box showing what the columns will look like.

The Width and Spacing section has room to display measurements for three columns. If you specify more than three columns, a vertical scroll bar displays to the left of the column numbers. To view other column measurements, click the down arrow at the bottom of the scroll bar.

Experiment with changing the width between columns so you can see how the changes affect the text in each panel. For example, in a letter-fold brochure column layout, increasing the space between columns 1 and 2 will cause the text in panel 2 to be shifted to the right, whereas, decreasing the space between columns 1 and 2 will cause the text in panel 2 to shift to the left.

DTP POINTERS
Be consistent when varying column widths within a document.

Using the Horizontal Scroll Bar to Adjust Column Settings

Once columns have been created, the width of the columns or the spacing between columns may be changed with the column markers on the horizontal ruler. To do this, make sure the horizontal ruler is displayed (View and Ruler). Position the arrow pointer in the middle of the left or right margin column marker on the horizontal ruler until it turns into a double-headed arrow pointing left and right. Hold down the left mouse button, drag the column marker to the left or right to make the column wider or narrower, and then release the mouse button. If the columns are of equal width, changing the width of one column changes the width of all columns and the corresponding space between columns. If the columns are of unequal width, changing the width of a column only changes that column and the corresponding white space.

Varying Column Formatting within the Same Document

By default, any column formatting you select is applied to the whole document. If you want to create different numbers or styles of columns within the same document, the document must be divided into sections. For example, if a document contains a title, you may want the title to span the top of all the columns rather than be included within the column formatting. To span a title across the tops of columns, key and format the title. Position the insertion point at the left margin of the first line of text to be formatted into columns and display the Columns dialog box. Select the desired number of columns, make any necessary column width and spacing changes, and then change the Apply to: option at the bottom of the Columns dialog box from *Whole document* to *This point forward*.

When *This point forward* is selected, a section break is automatically inserted in your document. Column formatting is applied to text from the location of the insertion point to the end of the document or until other column formatting is encountered.

In addition to the method just described, you can manually insert the section break before accessing the Columns dialog box by choosing Insert and Break. At the Break dialog box, select Continuous, click OK or press Enter, and then access the Columns dialog box.

If text that is formatted into columns is to be followed by text that is not formatted into columns, you must change the column format to one column and select the *This point forward* option. An alternate approach is to insert a section break through the Break dialog box and use the Columns button on the Standard toolbar to create one column.

Specific text in a document can be formatted into columns by first selecting the text and then using the Columns button on the Standard toolbar, or the options from the Columns dialog box.

Removing Column Formatting

To remove column formatting, position the insertion point in the section containing columns and change the column format to one column either by using the Columns button on the Standard toolbar or the Columns dialog box.

Inserting a Column, Page, or Section Break

When formatting text into columns, Word automatically breaks the columns to fit the page. At times, a column may break in an undesirable location or you may want a column to break in a different location. For example, a heading may appear at the bottom of the column, while the text that follows the heading begins at the top of the next column. You can insert a column break into a document to control where columns end and begin on the page.

DTP POINTERS
Make sure all column breaks are in appropriate locations.

To insert a column break, position the insertion point where you want the new column to begin, and then press Ctrl + Shift + Enter; or click Insert and Break. At the Break dialog box, click Column Break, and then click OK or press Enter.

If you insert a column break in the last column on a page, the column continues on the next page. If you want any other column on the page that is not the last column to continue on the next page, insert a page break. To do this, press Ctrl + Enter or click Insert, Break, and Page Break.

If you want to "even out" or balance the text in columns, insert a Continuous section break at the end of the last column. The text that follows the section break will continue to the top of the next column.

Moving the Insertion Point within and between Columns

To move the insertion point in a document using the mouse, position the I-beam pointer in the desired location, then click the left mouse button. If you are using the keyboard, the up and down arrow keys move the insertion point in the direction indicated. The left and right arrow keys move the insertion point in the direction indicated within the column and the insertion point follows the snaking pattern of newspaper columns—down one column and then to the top of the next column. Consequently, the mouse is most often the preferred method to move the insertion point in text formatted into columns.

To move the insertion point between columns using the keyboard, press Alt + Up arrow to move the insertion point to the top of the previous column or Alt + Down arrow to the top of the next column.

To familiarize you with the layout of panels in a letter-fold (or three-panel) brochure, you will create a simple dummy (three even columns with default spacing between the columns) in the following exercise. Measuring the panels and creating unequal column widths is not necessary in this case because you will only use the dummy as a guide to placing text in the correct panels. Remember, you can always make a more detailed dummy if necessary.

exercise 1

Creating a Dummy of a Letter-Fold Brochure Using the Columns Feature

1. At a clear document screen, create a dummy similar to the one illustrated in figure 6.2 by completing the following steps:
   a. Change to Print Layout view.
   b. Change the paper orientation to landscape at the Page Setup dialog box.
   c. Change to a three-column format by completing the following steps:
      1) Click Format and Columns.
      2) At the Columns dialog box, change the Number of columns to 3, or select Three (equal columns) in the Presets section of the Columns dialog box.
      3) Make sure the Equal column width check box contains a check mark and click OK to close the Columns dialog box.
   d. Insert the panel labels by completing the following steps:
      1) Change the paragraph alignment to Center.
      2) Key **PANEL 1**, press Enter, then key **(inside)** in the first panel (column 1).
      3) Click Insert and Break.
      4) At the Break dialog box, click Column Break and click OK.
      5) Using figure 6.2 as a guide, repeat steps d2 through d4 until all six panels are labeled.
   e. Print the three-panel brochure dummy by completing the following steps:
      1) Position the insertion point on the first page (panels 1, 2, and 3) by pressing Ctrl + Home.
      2) Click File and Print.
      3) At the Print dialog box, click Current Page and then click OK.
      4) Put the first printed page back in the printer so the second page can be printed on the back of the first page. (Experiment with your printer to position the paper correctly.)
      5) Position the insertion point on the second page (panels 4, 5, and 6) and print the current page.
   f. Fold the dummy as you would the real brochure and refer to the panel labels when creating the actual brochure to avoid confusion on the placement of text.
2. Save the dummy brochure to your hard drive or a floppy disk and name it c06ex01, Dummy.
3. Close c06ex01, Dummy.

You can use a procedure similar to exercise 1 to create a dummy using a table. Insert a table with five columns and one row—three columns for the panels and two columns for the space between the columns. Label the panels and then print the dummy.

A dummy can also be created with pencil and paper. Take a piece of the paper stock to be used and position it correctly (portrait or landscape). Fold the paper as the brochure will be folded and label each panel as shown in figure 6.2.

Using Reverse Text as a Design Element

Reverse text usually refers to white text set against a solid background (such as 100% black), as shown in the first example in figure 6.6. Reversing text is most effective with single words, short phrases such as headings, or special characters set in a large type size. Impact is also achieved by using *screens* (shading with lighter shades of gray or color) for the background fill. Solid areas of black, white, and varying shades of gray on a page give the visual effect of color, creating a dramatic effect with the use of only one color. In addition, interesting effects are achieved by reversing color text out of a solid, screened, gradient, or textured colored background fill and/or by varying the shape that contains the reverse text. As shown in figure 6.6, many different variations of reverse type can be created. Keep these examples in mind when you are trying to provide focus, balance, contrast, and directional flow in a document.

Reverse Text
White text set against a solid background.

figure 6.6

Reverse Text Examples

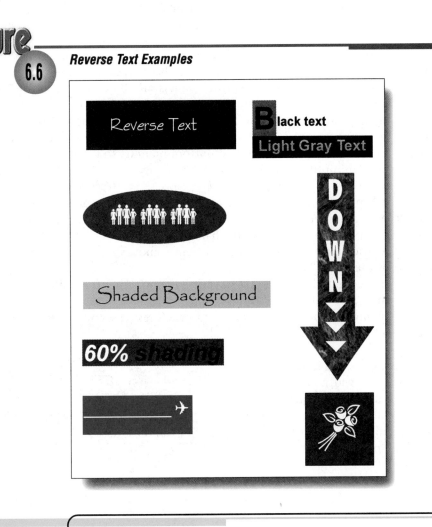

Text Box

One of the easiest ways to create reverse text is to use the Text box feature. To create traditional reverse text (solid black background with white text) using a text box, simply create a text box, change the fill to black, change the text color to white, and then key in the desired text. Or, you can create a reverse text effect using an AutoShape by selecting an AutoShape, adding text, and then adding background fill.

DTP POINTERS
Brochures involve many steps so SAVE often as you work.

In exercises 2 and 3, you will have the opportunity to create a letter-fold (or three-panel) brochure using three uneven newspaper columns and other formatting features such as text boxes to create reverse text, color, and bulleted lists. Remember to SAVE often! Creating even a simple brochure involves many steps. Save your document periodically as you are creating it to avoid any disasters—they happen to the best of us! Also, view your document frequently to assess the overall layout and design. Adjustments often need to be made that can affect other parts of the document not visible in the document window. The Page Width and Full Page options, accessible by clicking the Zoom button on the Standard toolbar, are useful for viewing a brochure layout during the creation process.

exercise 2

Creating Panels 1, 2, and 3 of a Letter-Fold Brochure
Using the Columns Feature and Reverse Text

1. Keep the dummy created in exercise 1 handy to visually guide you in the correct placement of text (or create a new dummy following the directions in exercise 1).
2. At a clear document screen, create the first three panels of a brochure, as shown in figure 6.7, by completing the following steps:
   a. Change the margins and the paper size according to the following specifications:
      1) Access the Page Setup dialog box Margins tab, change the left and right margins to 0.55 inch and the top and bottom margins to 0.5 inch. (Please click Fix if Word notifies you that one of the margin settings is within your printer's unprintable zone.)
      2) Select the Paper Size tab, make sure *Letter 8-1/2 × 11 in* displays in the Paper size list box, and then select Landscape in the Orientation section.
      3) Click OK or press Enter to close the dialog box.
   b. Turn on automatic kerning for font sizes 14 points and above at the Character Spacing tab of the Font dialog box.
   c. Set up the three-column brochure page layout by completing the following steps:
      1) Click Format and Columns.
      2) At the Columns dialog box, select Three in the Presets section or increase the number to 3 in the Number of columns option.
      3) Remove the check mark in the Equal column width check box.
      4) In the Width and spacing section, key the following amounts in the Width and Spacing text boxes for the columns indicated:

Width and spacing

Col #:	Width:	Spacing:
1:	2.78"	0.7"
2:	3"	0.7"
3:	2.72"	

☐ Equal column width

Step 2c4

Step 2c3

Col #	Width	Spacing
1	2.78	0.7
2	3.00	0.7
3	2.72	

     5) Click OK or press Enter.

d. Insert the file containing the brochure text by completing the following steps:

     1) Make sure the insertion point is positioned in the first column at the beginning of the document and click Insert and File.

     2) At the Insert File dialog box, change the Look in: list box to the drive containing your student CD, and then double-click Ride Safe Four Text.doc. Save the document and name it c06ex02, Panels 1,2,3.

     3) Select the whole document and change the font to 12-point Arial Rounded MT Bold.

e. Click the Zoom button on the Standard toolbar and change the view to 75% or Page Width.

f. Click the Show/Hide ¶ button on the Standard toolbar to display nonprinting characters, such as paragraph symbols and spaces.

g. Format the number 1 that displays at the top of the first panel (or column) of the brochure by completing the following steps:

     1) Select the number *1* and the paragraph symbol that follows it.

     2) Change the font size to 72-point.

     3) With the number and paragraph symbol still selected, click the Text Box button on the Drawing toolbar or click Insert and Text Box.

     4) Double-click the text box border and make the following changes at the Format Text Box dialog box:

         a) Select the Colors and Lines tab and change the fill color to Red.

         b) Select the Size tab and change the height of the text box to 1.3 inches and the width to 1.3 inches.

         c) Select the Layout tab and click Advanced. At the Advanced Layout dialog box, select the Picture Position tab and change the Horizontal Alignment to Left relative to Margin and the Vertical Alignment to Top relative to Margin.

         d) At the same dialog box, select the Text Wrapping tab and change the Wrapping style to Top and bottom.

         e) Click OK to close the Advanced Layout dialog box and click OK again to close the Format AutoText dialog box.

     5) With the text box still selected, add a shadow effect, adjust the line weight of the text box border, and center the number in the text box by completing the following steps:

         a) Click the Shadow button on the Drawing toolbar and select the first shadow style option in the fifth row *(Shadow Style 17)*.

         b) Click the Line Style button on the Drawing toolbar and change the line style to 3 pt.

         c) Click the Center alignment button on the Formatting toolbar.

h. Format the lead-in text below the number by completing the following steps:

     1) Position the insertion point to the left of *Before entering the street from your driveway or sidewalk:* and press Enter.

     2) Select *Before entering the street from your driveway or sidewalk:*, change the font size to 20-point, and turn on italics.

i. Create the red bullet list by completing the following steps:

     1) Position the insertion point to the left of *Stop.* and press Enter.

2) Select the text that starts with *Stop.* and ends with *Listen to be sure no traffic is approaching.* and change the font size to 22-point.

3) With the text still selected, click F_ormat and then Bullets and _Numbering. At the Bullets and Numbering dialog box, select the _Bulleted tab.

4) Click the first bullet option (first row, second column) and click Cus_tomize.

5) At the Customize Bulleted List dialog box, click a round bullet in the Bullet character section. If you don't see a round bullet, click Bullet and select a round bullet from a font, such as Wingdings, at the Symbol dialog box.)

Step 2i5

Step 2i6

Customize Bulleted List

Bullet character

Font...   Bullet...

Bullet position
Indent _at: 0"

Text position
Indent at: 0.3"

6) Click the F_ont button and change the S_ize to 32 points and change the Font _color to Red. Click OK to close the Font dialog box.

7) In the Bullet position section, change the Indent _at: to 0 inch. In the Text position section, change the I_ndent at: to 0.3 inch.

8) Click OK to close the Customize Bulleted List dialog box.

j. With the bulleted list selected, adjust the spacing between the bulleted items by changing the spacing after the paragraphs to 16 points at the Paragraph dialog box Indents and Spacing tab.

k. If the number 2 is not positioned at the top of column two, position the insertion point to the left of 2, and then click I_nsert and B_reak. At the Break dialog box, click C_olumn break.

l. Format the number 2 that displays at the top of the second panel (or column) in the same way as you formatted the number 1 in the first panel by referring to steps 2g1–5, with the following exceptions:

1) Change the fill color of the text box to Yellow.

2) At the Advanced Layout dialog box, change the Horizontal Absolute position to 4.03 inches _to left of Page. The Vertical Alignment will be the same (Top re_lative to Margin).

m. Format the lead-in text below the number 2 by completing the following steps:

1) Position the insertion point to the left of *At stop signs, stoplights, or other busy streets:* and press Enter.

2) Select *At stop signs, stoplights, or other busy streets:*, change the font size to 20-point, and turn on italics.

n. Create the yellow bulleted list by completing the following steps:

1) Position the insertion point to the left of *Stop.* and press Enter one time.

2) Select the text that starts with *Stop.* and ends *Listen and make sure the street is clear of traffic before crossing.* Change the font size to 22-point.

3) With the text still selected, display the Bullets and Numbering dialog box, and then select the _Bulleted tab. Select the red bulleted list, click Cus_tomize, and then click F_ont. Change the bullet color to Yellow, and then click OK twice.

o. Adjust the spacing between the bulleted items as in step 2j above.

p. If the number 3 is not positioned at the top of column three, insert a column break (as in step 2k) to the left of the number 3.

q. Format the number 3 that displays at the top of the third panel (or column) of the brochure in the same way as you formatted the numbers 1 and 2 by referring to steps 2g1–5, with the following exceptions:

1) Change the fill color of the text box to Green.

2) At the Advanced Layout dialog box, change the Horizontal Absolute position to 7.72 inches to left of Page. The Vertical Alignment will be the same (Top relative to Margin).

r. Format the lead-in text below the number 3 by completing the following steps:
1) Position the insertion point to the left of *Before turning, changing lanes, or swerving to avoid an obstacle:* and press Enter.
2) Select *Before turning, changing lanes, or swerving to avoid an obstacle:*, change the font size to 20-point and turn on italics.

s. Create the green bulleted list by completing the following steps:
1) Position the insertion point to the left of *Look back over your shoulder.* and press Enter one time.
2) Select the text that starts with *Look back over your shoulder.* and ends *Look again.* Change the font size to 22-point.
3) Follow step 2n3 to insert bullets; however, select the yellow bullet and change the color to Green.

t. Adjust the spacing between the bulleted items as in step 2j.

u. Below the bulleted list, position the insertion point to the left of 4 and insert a column break.

3. Save the brochure with the same name (c06ex02, Panels 1,2,3).
4. Print the first page of this exercise now, or print after completing exercise 3.
5. Close c06ex02, Panels 1,2,3.

figure

6.7

Exercise 2

Before entering the street from your driveway or sidewalk:

● Stop.

● Look left.

● Look right.

● Look left again.

● Listen to be sure no traffic is approaching.

At stop signs, stoplights, or other busy streets:

Stop.

Look left.

Look right.

Look left again.

Listen and make sure the street is clear of traffic before crossing.

Before turning, changing lanes, or swerving to avoid an obstacle:

● Look back over your shoulder.

● Be sure the road is clear of traffic.

● Signal.

● Look again.

In exercise 3, you will complete the brochure started in exercise 2. As in the previous exercise, uneven columns will be used to form the panels on the reverse side of the brochure. Refer to your dummy to see that panel 4 is on the reverse side of panel 3, panel 5 is the reverse side of panel 2, and panel 6 is the reverse side of panel 1. Consequently, panel 4 will be the same width as panel 3, panel 5 will be the same width as panel 2, and panel 6 will be the same width as panel 1. As you progress through the exercise, remember to save your document every 10 to 15 minutes.

Creating Panels 4, 5, and 6 of a Letter-Fold Brochure

1. At a clear document screen, open c06ex02, Panels 1,2,3.doc.
2. Save the document to your hard drive or floppy disk with Save <u>A</u>s and name it c06ex03, Ride safe brochure.
3. Create panels 4, 5, and 6 of the Ride Safe brochure shown in figure 6.8 by completing the following steps:
   a. Set the column formatting for the outside panels of the brochure by completing the following steps:
      1) Position the insertion point at the top of the second page of the brochure to the left of the number 4.
      2) Click Format and <u>C</u>olumns.
      3) At the Columns dialog box, make sure the number of columns is set to 3.
      4) Make sure there is no check mark in the <u>E</u>qual column width check box.
      5) In the Width and spacing section, enter the following amounts in the Wi<u>d</u>th and <u>S</u>pacing text boxes for the columns indicated. *(Hint: These settings are the opposite of panels 1, 2, and 3.)*

Col #	Width	Spacing
1	2.72	0.7
2	3.00	0.7
3	2.78	

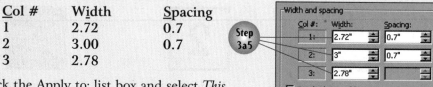
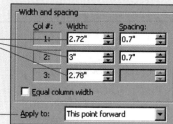

Step 3a5

Step 3a6

      6) Click the <u>A</u>pply to: list box and select *This point forward*. This automatically inserts a section break in the document along with the new column formatting.
      7) Click OK or press Enter.
   b. Format the number 4 in panel 4 in the exact same way as number 1 was formatted in exercise 2, steps 2g1-5.
   c. Format the lead-in text located below the number 4 by completing the following steps:
      1) Position the insertion point to the left of *Every time you go bicycling or in-line skating:* and press Enter.
      2) Select *Every time you go bicycling or in-line skating:*, change the font size to 20 pt, and turn on italics.
   d. Create the bulleted list by completing the following steps:
      1) Position the insertion point to the left of *Wear an ANSI, ASTM, or Snell certified helmet.* and press Enter one time.

2) Select *Wear an ANSI...* through *...appropriate protective gear!* and change the font size to 22 pt.
3) Insert bullets as you did for the bulleted items in panels 1, 2, and 3 (see step 2n3 in exercise 2). Make sure the bullet color is Red.

e. Adjust the spacing between the bulleted items as you did in panels 1, 2, and 3 (see step 2j in exercise 2).

f. Position the insertion point to the left of *Ride Safe is committed to educating children...* and insert a column break.

g. Format the text in panel 5 by completing the following steps:
1) With the insertion point at the top of panel 5, press Enter.
2) Select the paragraph that begins with *Ride Safe is committed to educating children...* and add a 1-pt red border at the Borders and Shading dialog box.
3) With the insertion point within the same paragraph, change the alignment to justified.
4) Position the insertion point to the left of the slogan *We want everyone to RIDE SAFE!* and change the spacing before the paragraph to 90 pt and the spacing after the paragraph to 162 pt at the Paragraph dialog box, Indents and Spacing tab.
5) Select *We want everyone to RIDE SAFE!* and make the following changes:
   a) Change the font size to 24 pt, change the color to Green, and then apply bold and italics.
   b) Change the paragraph alignment to Center.
6) Select *Call us today at 1-800-555-RIDE* and make the following changes:
   a) Change the font size to 20 points and change the font color to Yellow.
   b) Change the paragraph alignment to Center.
   c) Access the Borders and Shading dialog box and select the <u>S</u>hading tab. In the Fill section, select the black color block in the fourth row, first column. Click OK.
   d) Position the insertion point after the word *at*, delete the space, and press Enter to force the phone number down to the next line.

h. *The Ride Safe Four* title should be positioned at the top of panel 6. If not, insert a column break before the title.

i. Position the insertion point to the left of *RIDE SAFE, INC.* and press Enter.

j. Format the title by completing the following steps:
1) Select the title *The Ride Safe Four*, change the font to 40-point, and then change the paragraph alignment to Center.
2) Change where the lines break within the title by making the following changes:
   a) Position the insertion point after *The*, delete the space, and press Enter to force *Ride* down to the next line.
   b) Delete the space after *Ride* and press Enter.
   c) Delete the space after *Safe* and press Enter.
3) Select *Ride* in the title and change the color to Red.
4) Select *Safe* in the title and change the color to Yellow.
5) Select *Four* in the title and change the color to Green.
6) Select *The Ride Safe Four* and change the line spacing to exactly 40 points at the Paragraph dialog box.

k. To position the title correctly, insert and format a text box to contain the title by completing the following steps:
1) Select the title.

2) Click the Text Box button on the Drawing toolbar, or click Insert and Text Box.

3) Click and drag the bottom center sizing handle of the text box to display all of the text.

4) Double-click the text box border and make the following changes at the Format Text Box dialog box:

    a) Select the Colors and Lines tab and then change the line color to No Line.

    b) Select the Size tab and change the height of the text box to 2.62 inches and the width to 2 inches.

    c) Select the Layout tab and click Advanced. At the Advanced Layout dialog box, select the Picture Position tab, and then change the Horizontal Absolute position to 8.16 inches to the left of Page. Change the Vertical Alignment to Top relative to Margin.

    d) Select the Text Wrapping tab and change the Wrapping style to Top and bottom.

    e) Click OK to close the Advanced Layout dialog box, and click OK again to close the Format Text Box dialog box.

l. Format the company information below the title by completing the following steps:

1) Select *RIDE SAFE, INC.* only and change the font size to 14 pt.

2) Select the company name, address, and phone number and change the paragraph alignment to Center.

m. To position the company information correctly, insert and format a text box to contain this information by completing the following steps:

1) Click the Text Box button on the Drawing toolbar, or click Insert and Text Box, to insert a text box around the selected text.

2) Double-click the text box border and make the following changes at the Format Text Box dialog box:

    a) Select the Colors and Lines tab and then change the line color to No Line.

    b) Select the Size tab and change the height of the text box to 1 inch and the width to 2.2 inches.

    c) Select the Layout tab and click Advanced. At the Advanced Layout dialog box, select the Picture Position tab and change the Horizontal Absolute position to 8.09 inches to the left of Page. Change the Vertical Alignment to Bottom relative to Margin.

    d) Select the Text Wrapping tab and change the Wrapping style to Top and bottom.

    e) Click OK to close the Advanced Layout dialog box and click OK again to close the Format Text Box dialog box. (The text box will move to the bottom of the panel.)

n. Insert the stop sign image by positioning the insertion point under the text box containing *The Ride Safe Four,* access the Insert ClipArt dialog box, search for clips using the keywords *stop sign,* and then insert the stop sign image as shown in figure 6.8.

o. Size and position the stop sign by completing the following steps:

1) Double-click the image, or click Format and Picture, to display the Format Picture dialog box.

2) Select the Size tab and change the height of the picture to 2.87 inches and the width to 2.39 inches.

3) Select the Layout tab and make the following changes:

    a) Click In front of text in the Wrapping style section.

    b) Click <u>A</u>dvanced. At the Picture Position tab of the Advanced Layout dialog box, change the Horizontal Absolute position to 7.9 inches <u>t</u>o the left of Page. Change the Vertical Absolute po<u>s</u>ition to 3.88 inches belo<u>w</u> Page.

    c) Click OK to close the Advanced Layout dialog box, then click OK again to close the Format Picture dialog box.

4. Save the brochure with the same name (c06ex03, Ride safe brochure).

5. Print the first page of the brochure, reinsert the first page back in the printer, and then print the second page on the back of the first page. Refer to the directions for printing in exercise 1, if necessary.

6. Close c06ex03, Ride safe brochure.

figure

6.8

Exercise 3

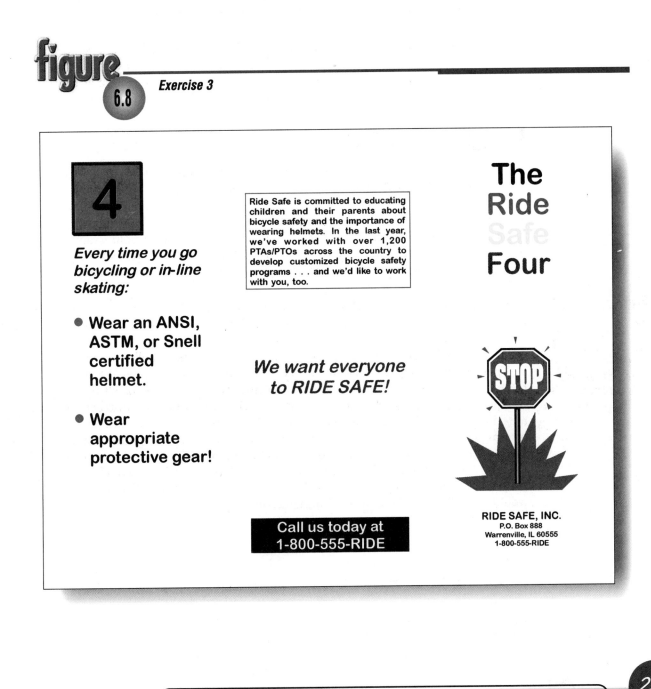

Evaluating a Brochure

When evaluating a brochure, be aware of the typeface, use of color, and consistency in design elements. Arial Rounded MT Bold was the only typeface used in the Ride Safe Four brochure shown in figures 6.7 and 6.8. The rounded, slightly juvenile nature of this typeface reflects the target audience. The typeface was varied by using different type sizes, italics, caps, and color. If the same title had been set in Times New Roman, the mood or tone would be much more businesslike and conservative. Which do you think would be more appealing to a target audience of school-aged bicyclists?

The text boxes containing the numbers 1 through 4 are set in different colors to make them stand out. These numbered squares direct the reader to important points. The round bullets also help to lead the reader's eyes down through the important points in each panel.

As you can see in figures 6.7 and 6.8, the red, yellow, and green color scheme, along with the stop sign image, reinforces the traffic safety theme of this brochure and provides consistency. In addition, consistent amounts of white space at the top and bottom of each panel and within each panel add to the continuity.

Formatting with Styles

Professional-looking documents generally require a great deal of formatting. Formatting within any document that uses a variety of headings, subheadings, and other design elements should remain consistent. Some documents, such as company newsletters, brochures, and manuals, may be created on a regular basis and require consistent formatting within the document as well as from issue to issue. You can save time and keystrokes by using Word's Style feature to store repetitive formatting and to maintain consistent formatting throughout your document.

Style

A group of defined formatting instructions that can be applied at one time to a whole document or to various parts of a document.

A *style* is a set of defined formatting instructions such as font, font size, bold, italic, paragraph spacing, tab settings, bullets, and numbering that can be applied to text in your document to quickly change its appearance. For example, a style can be created for the bulleted text in figures 6.7 and 6.8 that contains bullet instructions and paragraph spacing instructions. Every time you are ready to format the text to be bulleted, you can quickly apply the specific style and save yourself the time of repeating the same keystrokes for each item. Because formatting instructions are contained within a style, a style can be edited, automatically updating any occurrence of that style within a document. For instance, if you applied a style for the bulleted text in all four panels of the brochure that specified an 18-point font size and then decided to change the font size to 16 points, all you would need to do is edit the formatting instructions in the style and all of the bulleted text would be changed to 16 points at the same time.

Understanding the Relationship between Styles and Templates

As previously mentioned, Word bases a new blank document on the Normal template. By default, text that is keyed is based on *Normal Style*. This means that when you start keying in text, Word uses the font, font size, line spacing, text alignment, and other formatting instructions assigned to the Normal Style, unless you specify other formatting instructions.

Normal Style
A set of formatting instructions automatically applied to any text that is keyed unless other formatting instructions are specified.

When you access a clear document window, *Normal* displays in the Style list box located at the left side of the Formatting toolbar. If you click the down arrow to the right of the Style list box, you will see a total of five built-in styles immediately available for your use, as shown in figure 6.9. The style names are displayed as they would appear if applied to selected text. In addition to these styles, Word provides a large selection of other built-in styles. To view the styles that come with Word in the Style list box on the Formatting toolbar, hold down the Shift key and click the down arrow on the right side of the Style list box.

figure 6.9 *Style List Displayed on the Formatting Toolbar*

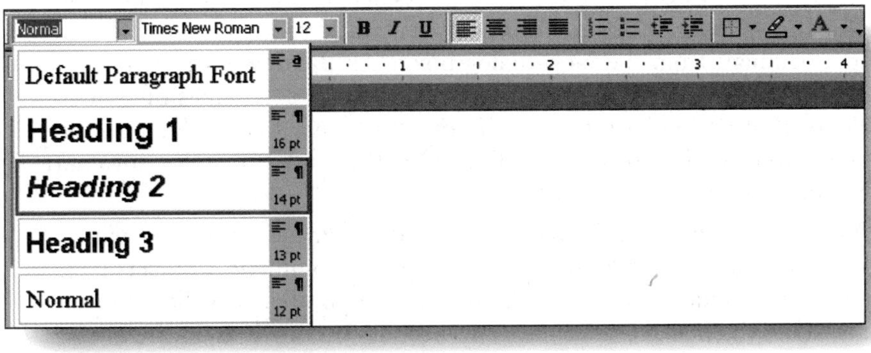

You can also view all available styles by choosing Format and Style. At the Style dialog box shown in figure 6.10, click the down arrow in the List box and select *All styles*. Select any style name from the Styles list box and a description of the formatting instructions contained in that style will be displayed in the Description section of the Style dialog box. As displayed in figure 6.10, the Description section tells you that the *Heading 1* style includes all the formatting instructions contained in the Normal style in addition to a font size instruction of 16-point Arial Bold, kerning at 16 pt, a paragraph spacing setting that will provide 12 points of spacing before and 3 points of spacing after the paragraph to which this style is applied, and a Keep with next paragraph instruction. (Level 1 refers to the level to which this style is automatically applied when using the Word's Outline feature.) An example of how the selected style will format text is also displayed in the Paragraph preview box.

figure 6.10

Style Dialog Box

Style Dialog Box (screenshot)

Styles:
- ¶ Endnote Text
- ¶ Envelope Address
- ¶ Envelope Return
- a FollowedHyperlink
- ¶ Footer
- a Footnote Reference
- ¶ Footnote Text
- ¶ Header
- Heading 1
- ¶ Heading 2
- ¶ Heading 3
- ¶ Heading 4
- ¶ Heading 5
- ¶ Heading 6
- ¶ Heading 7

List: All styles

Character preview: **Arial**

Description: Normal + Font: Arial, 16 pt, Bold, Kern at 16 pt, Space before 12 pt after 3 pt, Keep with next, Level 1

Organizer... New... Modify... Delete

Apply Cancel

Most of Word's built-in styles are available in any of its template documents. However, some of Word's template documents also contain additional styles depending on the type of document being created. If you choose a different template document from the New dialog box, click the down arrow to the right of the Style list box on the Formatting toolbar to display the names of styles available for that particular template. If you access the Style dialog box and select *Styles in use* from the List box, you will also see the names of styles automatically available for that particular template.

Word contains some styles that are applied automatically to text when you use certain commands. For example, if you use the command to insert page numbers, Word applies a certain style to the page number text. Some other commands for which Word automatically formats text with styles include headers, footers, footnotes, endnotes, indexes, and tables of contents.

Paragraph and Character Styles

Paragraph Style

A set of formatting instructions that applies to an entire paragraph.

Two types of styles exist in Word—paragraph styles and character styles. A *paragraph style* applies formatting instructions to the paragraph that contains the insertion point or to selected text. A paragraph style may include formatting instructions such as text alignment, tab settings, line indents, borders, paragraph spacing, numbers and bullets, and so on. As you know, the Normal Style is the default style automatically applied to all paragraphs unless you specify other formatting instructions. Paragraph styles are useful for formatting headings, subheadings, and bullet lists in a document.

Character Style

A set of formatting instructions that applies to selected text only.

A *character style* applies formatting to selected text within a paragraph. Character styles include options available at the Font dialog box such as font, font size, and font style (bold, underlining, and italics). Character styles are useful for formatting single characters, technical symbols, special names, or phrases. Characters within a paragraph can have their own style even if a paragraph style is applied to the paragraph as a whole.

In the Styles list (accessed through the Style dialog box or the Style box on the Formatting toolbar), paragraph styles are indicated by a ¶ symbol and character styles are preceded by an <u>a</u> symbol. To find out if a particular style has been applied to text, position the insertion point within the line or paragraph, and the style name will display in the Style box on the Formatting toolbar.

Applying Styles

A style can be applied before you key text, or it can be applied to text in an existing document. The most common methods of applying styles in Word include using the Style button on the Formatting toolbar and the Style command from the Format menu. To apply a style to existing text using the Style button on the Formatting toolbar, you would complete the following steps:

1. Position the insertion point in the paragraph to which you want the style applied, or select the text.
2. Click the down arrow to the right of the Style button on the Formatting toolbar.
3. Click the desired style name in the drop-down list to apply the style to the text in the document.

To apply a style using the Style command from the Format menu, you would complete the following steps:

1. Position the insertion point in the paragraph to which you want the style applied, or select the text.
2. Click F<u>o</u>rmat and <u>S</u>tyle.
3. At the Style dialog box, select <u>L</u>ist and *All styles*.
4. In the <u>S</u>tyles list box, double-click the desired style name or select the style name and click <u>A</u>pply.
5. If you want to apply the same style to different sections of text in a document, such as applying a heading style to all the headings, apply the style to the first heading. Then move the insertion point to each of the remaining headings and press F4, Word's Repeat key.

To apply a style before text is keyed, position the insertion point where formatting is to begin, and then select the desired style name from either the Style list accessed through the Style box on the Formatting toolbar or from the <u>S</u>tyle list box at the Style dialog box. If you apply a style before text is keyed, the style will affect any text you key after the style is applied, even if you begin a new paragraph. You must apply a different style to discontinue the first style.

Modifying and Updating an Existing Style

You can modify an existing style by changing the formatting instructions that it contains and then instructing Word to update the style to include the changes. When you modify a style, all text to which that style has been applied is changed accordingly. To modify a style using the Formatting toolbar, you would complete the following steps:

1. Open the document that contains the style that is to be changed.
2. Format the text to which the style has already been applied with the desired formatting changes.
3. Select the reformatted text.

4. Click the Style list box on the Formatting toolbar to select the current style name and Enter.
5. When the Modify Style dialog box displays, make sure *Update the style to reflect recent changes?* is selected and click OK or press Enter.

To modify a style at the Style dialog box, you would complete the following steps:

1. Open the document that contains the style that is to be changed.
2. Click Format and Style.
3. At the Style dialog box, select the style name you want to modify in the Styles list box, and then select Modify.
4. At the Modify Style dialog box, add or delete formatting options by choosing Format and then select the appropriate options.
5. When all changes are made, click OK or press Enter to close the Modify Style dialog box.
6. Close the Style dialog box.

The modified style is available to the current active document. If you would like the modified style to be available in a new document based on the active template (most likely this is the Normal template), click Add to template in the Modify Style dialog box to insert a check mark in the check box. For example, if the active template is the Normal template, the modified style is added to that template so that it will be available every time you create a document based on the Normal template.

Updating Styles Automatically

Styles can be updated manually as described in the previous section, or they can be updated automatically. When a style is set to update automatically, Word detects when you change the formatting of the text containing the style and automatically updates the style without displaying the Modify Style dialog box. All text formatted with that style is updated to match the formatting of the text you just changed. To update a style automatically, click Format and Style. In the Styles list box, select the desired style name and click Modify. At the Modify Style dialog box, click in the Automatically update check box to activate this option. Or you may select Automatically update the style from now on at the Modify Style dialog box that displays when you modify a style through the Style list box on the Formatting toolbar. Remove the check mark at the Modify Style dialog box if you no longer want the style to update automatically.

The disadvantage to having a style update automatically is that you cannot make formatting changes without the style being redefined. If this feature is not active, you can make a formatting change to specific text without the need to redefine the whole style.

Using Word's Brochure Template

As mentioned previously, a template serves as a foundation for creating a customized document. Word's Brochure template is a letter-fold (three-panel) brochure. When the Brochure template document is displayed on screen, it contains instructions and tips on how to create and customize the brochure. Note that the instructions and tips in this template must be deleted when keying the actual brochure content. The instructional text is formatted as text might appear in a brochure, including columns, headings, subheadings, cover title, and a cover graphic image. The formatting instructions for many parts of the brochure are contained in styles that are available to the Brochure template document.

In exercise 4, you will create panels 1, 2, and 3 of a brochure using the Brochure template as a base. You will insert a file containing the brochure text, change the column formatting to three unequal columns, and then format specific sections of the text using some of the predefined styles provided in the brochure template. In addition, you will then redefine some of the styles.

exercise 4

Creating Panels 1, 2, and 3 of a Brochure Using the Brochure Template

1. Create panels 1, 2, and 3 of the brochure shown in figure 6.11 using the Brochure.dot template by completing the following steps:
    a. Open the Brochure template by completing the following steps:
        1) Click File and New.
        2) At the New dialog box, select the Publications tab.
        3) Make sure Document is selected in the Create New section.
        4) Double-click Brochure in the Publications tab list box.
        5) Print a copy of the Brochure template and label as your dummy, or use the dummy you created in exercise 1.
    b. Select the whole document and delete all text and graphics. *(Hint: This will eliminate the second page; however, you will re-create the second page when needed.)*
    c. Click the Show/Hide ¶ button on the Standard toolbar so that nonprinting characters, such as paragraph symbols and style indicators, display on the screen. A *style indicator* is a small black square that usually appears to the left of the text where a style has been applied.
    d. Change the left and right margin settings to 0.55 inch. Leave the top and bottom margins as set. Adjust any of the margin settings if Word prompts you that the margin settings are within your printer's unprintable zone.
    e. Turn on automatic kerning for font sizes 14 pt and above at the Character Spacing tab of the Font dialog box.
    f. Change the column formatting to three columns of unequal width by completing the following steps:
        1) With the insertion point positioned at the top of the document, click Format and Columns.
        2) At the Columns dialog box, select Three in the Presets section or increase the number to 3 in the Number of columns option.
        3) Remove the check mark in the Equal column width check box.
        4) In the Width and spacing section, key the following amounts in the Width and Spacing text boxes for the columns indicated:

Col #	Width	Spacing
1	2.78	0.7
2	3.00	0.7
3	2.72	

5) Click OK or press Enter.

g. Make sure the insertion point is still at the top of the document and copy the contents of the file Volunteer Text.doc located on your student CD.

h. Apply the predefined styles provided in the Brochure template document to specific sections of text in the first panel (or column) of the brochure by completing the following steps:

1) With the insertion point at the beginning of the document, select <u>E</u>dit and Select A<u>l</u>l, or press Ctrl + A.

2) Click the down arrow at the right side of the Style list box located on the Formatting toolbar and select *Body Text* from the Style drop-down list. Use the vertical scroll bar in this drop-down menu to see all the style names listed. (The Body Text style will change the font for all the text in the document to 12-point Garamond. Since the majority of text in this brochure is to be formatted as Body Text, applying the style to the whole document will eliminate the need to frequently reapply this style.)

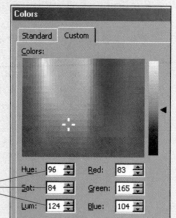

3) Click the Zoom button on the Standard toolbar and change the view to Page Width.

4) Format *Giving Is Its Own Reward. . .* by completing the following steps:

a) Press Ctrl + Home and position the insertion point anywhere within the title *Giving Is Its Own Reward. . . .*

b) Select *Heading 1* from the Style drop-down list similar to step 1h2 above.

c) Select the title, *Giving Is Its Own Reward. . .* , access the Font dialog box, and then change the font size to 27 points and turn on bold and small caps.

d) Change the font color to a custom green color by completing the following steps:

i) With the title still selected, use the Font Color button on the Standard toolbar, or the Font dialog box to access the Font Color palette, and then click More Colors.

ii) At the Colors dialog box, select the Custom tab.

iii) Change the H<u>ue</u> to 96, the <u>S</u>at to 84, and the <u>L</u>um to 124. *(Hint: The color will be a shade of green.)*

iv) Click OK to close the Colors dialog box.

e) With the title still selected, click once in the Style list box on the Formatting toolbar (*Heading 1* should be selected) and press Enter. Make sure <u>U</u>*pdate the style to reflect recent changes?* is selected and click OK to redefine the current style for future use.

5) Select the line that reads *As a volunteer, you will:*, apply the *Emphasis* style from the Style drop-down list, and then customize the font color by changing the H<u>ue</u> to 96, the <u>S</u>at to 84, and the <u>L</u>um to 124. *(Hint: The customized color may already be displayed on the Font Color button on the Formatting toolbar.)*

6) Select the list of items that begins with *Share your skills and talents* and ends with *Make a difference in other people's lives.* Keep the text selected during the following steps and apply bullets:

a) Select *List Bullet* from the Style drop-down list. If this style does not display in the Style drop-down list, click Format and Style. At the Style dialog box, click the List: list box and select *All styles*. Find the *List Bullet* style in the Styles: list box and click Apply.

b) Change the font size of the bulleted text to 12 points.

c) Access the Bullets and Numbering dialog box and select the Bulleted tab. Click the bullet option that displays *List Bullet* and click Customize.

d) At the Customized Bulleted List dialog box, select Font and customize the bullet font color by changing the Hue to 232, the Sat to 128, and the Lum to 163. (*Hint: The color will be a shade of pink.*)

e) Click OK to close the Colors dialog box, click OK to close the Font dialog box, and then click OK again to close the Customized Bulleted List dialog box.

f) Click once in the Style list box on the Formatting toolbar (*List Bullet* should be selected) and press Enter. Make sure <u>Update the style to reflect recent changes?</u> is selected and click OK to redefine the current style for future use.

7) Format *What Do Volunteers Do?* by completing the following steps:

a) Select the heading *What Do Volunteers Do?* and select *Heading 2* from the Style drop-down list.

b) With the heading still selected, display the Font dialog box and make the following changes:

i) Turn on bold and small caps.

ii) Change the font size to 15.5 points.

iii) Customize the font color by changing the Hue to 96, the Sat to 84, and the Lum to 124.

c) Change the color and weight of the line below the heading by completing the following steps:

i) Position the insertion point within the heading *What Do Volunteers Do?*, display the Borders and Shading dialog box, and make sure the Borders tab is selected.

ii) Click the Color: list box, click More Line Colors from the color palette, and then select the Custom tab. Change the Hue to 232, the Sat to 128, and the Lum to 163.

iii) Click OK to close the Colors dialog box.

iv) Click the Width: list box and select *2-1/4 pt* as the line weight.

v) Click the bottom border of the diagram in the Preview box to display a pink border and then click OK to close the Borders and Shading dialog box.

d) With the insertion point still within the heading, display the Paragraph dialog box, and then change the spacing Before the paragraph to 12 pt and make sure the spacing After is set to 3 pt at the Indents and Spacing tab.

e) Redefine the *Heading 2* style by following step 1h4e.

i. Position the insertion point at the beginning of the line of text that reads *Visitor Services* and insert a column break to move this text to the top of panel 2.

j. Apply predefined styles to the text in panel 2 by completing the following steps:

1) In panel 2, select the subheading *Visitor Services* and complete the following steps:

a) Apply the *Heading 7* style from the Style drop-down list.

b) Customize the font color by changing the Hue to 96, the Sat to 84, and the Lum to 124. (*Hint: The color may already be displayed on the Font Color button on the Formatting toolbar.*)

      c) Change the spacing after the paragraph to 6 points.

      d) Redefine the *Heading 7* style by following step 1h4e.

   2) Apply the *Heading 7* style to the subheading *Patient Services*.

k. Position the insertion point to the left of *Staff Services* and insert a column break.

l. Apply existing styles to format the text in panel 3 by completing the following steps:

   1) At the top of panel 3, apply the *Heading 7* style to the subheading *Staff Services*.

   2) Apply the *Heading 2* style to the heading *Who Can Volunteer?*

m. At the end of the paragraph that starts with *The volunteers at Edward Hospital range . . .*, press Enter twice.

n. Change the paragraph alignment to right, change the type size to 11 points, turn on italics, and then key **(Continued on back panel)**.

o. Press Enter and change the paragraph alignment to Left.

p. Position the insertion point at the beginning of the heading *About Edward Hospital . . .* and insert a column break.

q. Insert a text box and then insert and format the decorative symbols at the bottom of panel 1 by completing the following steps:

   1) Move the insertion point back to the bottom of panel 1 on the first page.

   2) Click the Text Box button on the Drawing toolbar and draw a text box that is the approximate size and in the same approximate location as the symbols shown in panel 1 in figure 6.11.

   3) Click Insert and Symbol, and then select the Symbols tab.

   4) Change the Font to Wingdings and double-click the ☙ symbol located in the fifth row, thirteenth column. Double-click the ❧ symbol immediately to the right (fifth row, fourteenth column) and click Close.

   5) Select the symbols just inserted, change the font size to 26 point, and then customize the font color by changing the Hue to 232, the Sat to 128, and the Lum to 163.

   6) Center the symbols in the text box by changing the paragraph alignment to center.

   7) Use the sizing handles to adjust the size of the text box so the symbols are completely visible.

r. Double-click the text box border and make the following changes to the text box at the Format Text Box dialog box:

   1) Click the Colors and Lines tab, and then change the line color to No Line.

   2) Click the Size tab and change the height to 0.5 inch and the width to 1 inch.

   3) Select the Layout tab and click Advanced. At the Advanced Layout dialog box, select the Picture Position tab, and then change the Horizontal Absolute position to 1.4 inches to the left of *Page*. Change the Vertical Alignment to *Bottom* relative to *Margin*.

   4) Click OK to close the Advanced Layout dialog box; click OK again to close the Format Text Box dialog box.

s. Copy the text box containing the decorative symbols at the bottom of panel 1 to the bottom of panel 3 by completing the following steps:

   1) Make sure the viewing mode is set to Page Width using the Zoom button on the Standard toolbar.

   2) Position the insertion point on one of the text box borders until it displays as a four-headed arrow. Hold down the Ctrl key and the left mouse button, drag an outline of the text box to the bottom of panel 3, and then release the left mouse button.

t. Adjust the position of the text box in panel 3 by making the following changes at the Format Text Box dialog box:

1) Double-click the text box border to display the Format Text Box dialog box.

2) Select the Layout tab and click Advanced. At the Advanced Layout dialog box, select the Picture Position tab and change the Horizontal Absolute position to 8.63 inches to the left of Page. Change the Vertical Alignment to Bottom relative to Margin.

3) Click OK to close the Advanced Layout dialog box; click OK again to close the Format Text Box dialog box.

u. Insert and format the clip art image at the bottom of panel 2 by completing the following steps:

1) Position the insertion point to the left of the column break.

2) Access the Insert ClipArt dialog box, select the *Healthcare and Medicine* category from the Pictures tab, and then insert the medical staff image shown in figure 6.11.

3) Double-click the clip art image to access the Format Picture dialog box and then complete the following steps:

a) Select the Size tab, click the Lock aspect ratio check box to remove the check mark, and then change the Height to 1.33 inches and the Width to 1.09 inches.

b) Select the Layout tab and click Advanced. At the Advanced Layout dialog box, select the Text Wrapping tab and change the wrapping style to Top and bottom.

c) Select the Picture Position tab. Change the Horizontal Absolute position to 4.02 inches to the left of Page. Change the Vertical Alignment to Bottom relative to Margin.

d) Click OK to close the Advanced Layout dialog box; click OK again to close the Format Picture dialog box.

v. Insert and format the text box that will contain the slogan to the right of the clip art image by completing the following steps:

1) Click the Text Box button on the Drawing toolbar and draw a text box that is the same approximate size and in the same approximate location as the text box containing the slogan at the bottom of panel 2 in figure 6.11.

2) Double-click one of the text box borders and make the following changes at the Format Text Box dialog box:

a) Select the Colors and Lines tab and then customize the color of the line in the Line section by changing the Hue: to 232, the Sat: to 128, and the Lum: to 163. Make sure the line weight is 0.75 pt.

b) Select the Size tab, change the height to 1.29 inches, and change the width to 1.85 inches.

c) Select the Layout tab and click Advanced. At the Advanced Layout dialog box, select the Picture Position tab and change the Horizontal Absolute position to 5.08 inches to the left of Page. Change the Vertical Absolute position to 6.68 inches below Page. Click OK to close the Advanced Layout dialog box.

d) Select the Text Box tab and change the left and right internal margins to 0.2 inch and the top and bottom internal margins to 0.02 inch.

e) Click OK to close the Format Text Box dialog box.

f) Make sure the clip art image and the text box are as close together and evenly aligned as shown in figure 6.11. If not, make adjustments to their horizontal and/or vertical positions at the Advanced Layout dialog box.

w. Insert and format the slogan by completing the following steps:
   1) Click inside the text box to position the insertion point and key "**Sharing Responsibility for Your Family's Health.**"
   2) Select *"Sharing Responsibility for Your Family's Health."* and change the font to 16-point Garamond, bold, italic.
x. Use Print Preview to view your document. Check carefully for the correct placement of text and design elements. Make any adjustments if necessary.

2. Save the brochure and name it c06ex04, Panels 1,2,3.
3. You may either print the first page of your brochure now or at the end of exercise 5.
4. Close c06ex04, Panels 1,2,3.

figure

6.11

Exercise 4

GIVING IS ITS OWN REWARD . . .

As an Edward Hospital volunteer, you will be involved in new experiences and challenges each day. Volunteering is a job that requires giving of yourself; your pay is in the form of personal reward.

As a volunteer, you will:

- Share your skills and talents
- Develop new interests
- Learn new skills
- Make new friends
- Grow in understanding and self-awareness
- Enjoy the satisfaction that comes from helping others
- Make a difference in other people's lives

WHAT DO VOLUNTEERS DO?

Edward Hospital offers volunteer opportunities in three different areas: visitor services, patient services, and staff services.

Visitor Services

At Edward Hospital, we stand by our motto, "Sharing Responsibility for Your Family's Health." We want to show our community that those are not just words, but the way Edward Hospital really operates. Often, a volunteer is the first and last person a hospital visitor encounters. We rely on our volunteers to provide accurate information while, at the same time, acting as goodwill ambassadors for the hospital.

Patient Services

Many volunteer positions involve direct interaction with patients. Many of our volunteers make a difference simply by lending a friendly ear or by performing a small favor when it is most needed and appreciated.

For those volunteers who are uncomfortable dealing directly with patients, there are many ways to help indirectly. Many Edward Hospital volunteers bring a smile to our patients' faces without ever seeing them. For instance, volunteers sew stuffed clowns to give to pediatric patients before surgery. We are always looking to our volunteers for new ideas to help make our patients' hospital stay as pleasant as possible.

"Sharing Responsibility for Your Family's Health."

Staff Services

Many volunteers draw on their past and present work experience to generously assist various hospital departments. Staff service volunteers play an important role in the hospital's team effort to provide cost-efficient, quality healthcare.

Volunteers offer their assistance in the following areas: Business Office, Central Distribution, Fitness Center, Women's Health Center, Employee Health, Human Resources, Laboratory, Edward Institute, Medical Library, Medical Records, Pharmacy, Preadmission Testing, and Surgery.

WHO CAN VOLUNTEER?

You must be at least 15 years of age to volunteer. We ask our volunteers to commit to a regular weekly schedule. It can be a few hours once a week or several hours each day. Volunteer opportunities are available seven days a week, days and evenings.

The volunteers at Edward Hospital range in age from teenagers to professionals to retirees, bringing a wealth of skill and experience to their volunteer positions.

(Continued on back panel)

In the following exercise, you will create panels 4, 5, and 6 to complete the brochure started in exercise 4. Remember to save periodically as you create the panels.

exercise 5

Creating Panels 4, 5, and 6 of a Brochure Using the Brochure Template

1. Open c06ex04, Panels 1,2,3.
2. Save the document to your hard drive or a floppy disk with Save As and name it c06ex05, Volunteer brochure.
3. Create panels 4, 5, and 6 of the brochure, as shown in figure 6.12, by completing the following steps:
   a. Set the column formatting for the outside panels of the brochure by completing the following steps:
      1) Position the insertion point at the top of the second page of the brochure to the left of *About Edward Hospital*.
      2) Access the Columns dialog box and make sure the number of columns is set to 3 and there is no check mark in the Equal column width check box.
      3) In the Width and spacing section, enter the following amounts in the Width and Spacing text boxes for the columns indicated. *(Hint: These settings are the opposite of the settings for panels 1, 2, and 3):*

Col #	Width	Spacing
1	2.72	0.7
2	3.00	0.7
3	2.78	

      4) Click the Apply to: list box and select *This point forward*. This automatically inserts a section break in the document along with the new column formatting.
      5) Click OK or press Enter.
   b. Apply styles to format the text in panel 4 by completing the following steps:
      1) Position the insertion point within the heading *About Edward Hospital . . .* and apply the *Heading 2* style.
      2) With the insertion point in the same line, access the Paragraph dialog box and change the paragraph spacing before the paragraph to 0 pt for this heading only. Do not redefine the style.
      3) Position the insertion point within the heading *Take The First Step . . .* and apply the *Heading 2* style.
   c. In the paragraph in panel 4 that starts with *For more information,* bold the text that reads *Cindy Bonagura, Volunteer Services Coordinator,* and customize the text color by changing the Hue: to 96, the Sat: to 84, and the Lum: to 124. Select the area code and phone number, turn on bold, and then repeat the customized color settings.
   d. Position the insertion point at the beginning of the line that reads *You can make a difference at Edward Hospital.* and insert a column break at this point.
   e. Position the insertion point at the top of panel 5 to the left of *You can make a difference . . . Volunteer today!* and press Enter three times.
   f. Format the text in panel 5 by completing the following steps:
      1) Select *You can make a difference at Edward Hospital.*, change the font size to 22 points, turn on bold, and then change the paragraph alignment to center.
      2) With the text still selected, change the spacing after the paragraph to 0 pt.

3) Format the line endings by making the following changes:
   a) Delete the space after *a* and press Enter.
   b) Delete the space after *at* and press Enter.
4) Position the insertion point within *Edward Hospital* (in the line above *Volunteer today!*) and change the spacing after the paragraph to 6 pt.
5) Select *Volunteer today!*, change the font size to 26 points, and then apply bold, italics, and emboss.
6) Center align the same line of text.
7) Add a green-shaded background and a pink border by completing the following steps:
   a) Select *You can make a difference at Edward Hospital. And Volunteer Today!*
   b) Access the Borders and Shading dialog box and then select the Shading tab. In the Fill section, customize the color by changing the Hue: to 93, the Sat: to 61, and the Lum: to 201.
   c) Select the Borders tab and customize the border color by changing the Hue: to 232, the Sat: to 128, and the Lum: to 163. *(Hint: The color should be pink.)*
   d) Change the Width option to 1 pt to change the weight of the line.
   e) In the Setting section, click the Box option to insert a pink border on all four sides of the selected text.
   f) Click OK to close the Borders and Shading dialog box.
8) With the insertion point still within *Volunteer today!*, change the spacing after the paragraph to 204 pt at the Paragraph dialog box.
9) Format the hospital name and address by completing the following steps:
   a) Select the hospital name and address, apply the *Heading 7* style.
   b) With the text still selected, change the paragraph alignment to center and the spacing after the paragraph (the selected text) to 0 points.
   c) Select the name of the hospital only and change the type size to 16 points.
   d) Do not redefine the style.

g. At the bottom of panel 5, position the insertion point below the address at the beginning of the line that reads *Edward Hospital* and insert a column break.

h. Insert the decorative symbols at the top and bottom of panel 5 by completing the following steps:
   1) Change the viewing mode to Two Pages using the Zoom button on the Standard toolbar.
   2) Copy the text box at the bottom of panel 1 or panel 3 to the top of panel 5. *(Hint: Hold down the left mouse button and the Ctrl key while dragging an outline of the text box to the top of panel 5.)*
   3) Copy the same text box to the bottom of panel 5.
   4) With the bottom text box still selected, double-click the text box border, select the Layout tab, and then click Advanced. At the Advanced Layout dialog box, select the Picture Position tab and change the Horizontal Absolute position to 4.98 inches to the left of Page. Change the Vertical Alignment to Bottom relative to Margin. Click OK to close the Advanced Layout dialog box; click OK again to close the Format Text Box dialog box.

i. Select the text box at the top of panel 5, change the horizontal position to match the position in the previous step, 3h4, and then change the Vertical Alignment to *Top* relative to *Margin*.

j. Insert the cover title and subtitle into a text box by completing the following steps:
   1) Select both the cover title and subtitle (*Edward Hospital* and *Volunteer Now . . . Giving Is Its Own Reward*).

2) Click the Text Box button on the Drawing toolbar to insert this text into a text box. The text box and text seem to disappear. Scroll down to the bottom of panel 6, and you will see the text box. Correct the position in the next step.

k. Display the Format Text Box dialog box and make the following changes:
  1) Double-click one of the text box borders to access the Format Text Box dialog box and select the Colors and Lines tab. Change the line color to No Line.
  2) Select the Size tab, change the height of the text box to 5.5 inches, and change the width to 3.4 inches.
  3) Select the Layout tab and click Advanced. At the Advanced Layout dialog box, select the Picture Position tab and change the Horizontal Absolute position to 7.5 inches to the left of Page. Change the Vertical Alignment to Top relative to Margin.
  4) Click OK to close the Advanced Layout dialog box; click OK again to close the Format Text Box dialog box.

l. Apply a style to the cover title on panel 6 and modify the style by completing the following steps:
  1) Change the view to Page Width using the Zoom button on the Formatting toolbar.
  2) Position the insertion point within the cover title *Edward Hospital* and apply the *Title Cover* style.
  3) Modify the applied style by completing the following steps:
    a) Select *Edward Hospital*, change the font size to 24 points, and then turn on bold and apply small caps.
    b) With the text still selected, customize the font color by changing the Hue: to 96, the Sat: to 84, and the Lum: to 124.
    c) Change the color of the border, insert a top border, and adjust the spacing between the borders and the text by completing the following steps:
  1) Access the Borders and Shading dialog box and click the Borders tab. Customize the border color by changing the Hue: to 232, the Sat: to 128, and the Lum: to 163.
  2) Change the Width of the line to 2-1/4 pt.
  3) In the Preview section, click the top side of the diagram to insert a pink top border. Click the bottom side of the diagram to replace the existing black border with a pink border. Make sure no border displays on the left or right side of the diagram.
  4) Click the Options button to display the Borders and Shading Options dialog box. In the From text section, change the Top option to 12 pt and the Bottom option to 7 pt to adjust the distance from the text to the borders.
  5) Click OK to close the Borders and Shading Options dialog box; click OK again to close the Borders and Shading dialog box.
  6) With the title still selected, click once in the Style list box on the Formatting toolbar, and then press Enter. Make sure *Update the style to reflect recent changes?* is selected and click OK to redefine the current style for future use.

m. Format the cover subtitle by completing the following steps:
  1) Select *Volunteer Now . . .* and make the following changes:
    a) Change the font size to 26 pt and turn on bold and italics.
    b) Customize the font color by changing the Hue: to 232, the Sat: to 128, and the Lum: to 163.
    c) Change the spacing before the paragraph to 48 pt. and the spacing after the paragraph to 42 pt.

2) Select *Giving Is Its Own Reward.*, change the font size to 40 points, turn on bold and italics, and then customize the font color by changing the H<u>ue</u>: to 96, the <u>S</u>at: to 84, and the <u>L</u>um: to 124.

3) Change the spacing after the paragraph to 0 pt.

4) Insert hard returns and delete any unnecessary spaces so that the line endings within *Giving Is Its Own Reward.* match the line endings as displayed in figure 6.12.

n. Insert the three medical staff clip art images by completing the following steps:

1) Press Ctrl + End to position the insertion point after the subtitle.

2) Display the Insert ClipArt dialog box, select the Healthcare and Medicine category from the Pictures tab, and then insert the medical staff image shown in figure 6.12.

3) Size and position the picture by completing the following steps:

a) Display the Format Picture dialog box and select the Size tab. Click the Lock <u>a</u>spect ratio check box to remove the check mark and then change the height of the image to 1.15 inches and the width to 0.83 inches.

b) Select the Layout tab, click S<u>q</u>uare as the Wrapping style, and then click <u>A</u>dvanced.

c) At the Advanced Layout dialog box, select the Picture Position tab, and then change the Horizontal Absolute position to 7.62 inches <u>t</u>o the left of Page. Change the Vertical Alignment to Bottom r<u>e</u>lative to Margin.

d) Click OK to close the Advanced Layout dialog box; click OK again to close the Format Picture dialog box.

4) Copy the same image two times to the right of the original image. *(Hint: Select the image first and hold down the Ctrl key and the left mouse button as you drag an outline of the picture to the right.)*

5) Position the copied images by completing the following steps:

a) Double-click the second image to display the Format Picture dialog box.

b) Select the Layout tab and click <u>A</u>dvanced. At the Advanced Layout dialog box, select the Picture Position tab and change the Horizontal Absolute position to 8.61 inches <u>t</u>o the left of Page. Change the Vertical Alignment to Bottom r<u>e</u>lative to Margin.

c) Click OK to close the Advanced Layout dialog box; click OK again to close the Format Picture dialog box.

d) Following similar steps to those above, horizontally position the third image by changing the Horizontal <u>A</u>lignment to Right r<u>e</u>lative to Margin and the Vertical Alignment to Bottom r<u>e</u>lative to Margin.

o. Use Print Preview to view your brochure. Carefully check your brochure for the correct placement of text and design elements. Make adjustments if necessary.

4. Save the brochure with the same name (c06ex05, Volunteer brochure).

5. Print both pages of the brochure using both sides of the paper.

6. Close c06ex05, Volunteer brochure.

figure **6.12** *Exercise 5*

Creating Styles

In exercises 4 and 5, you used some of Word's built-in styles and then modified and updated several of them. An alternative to modifying a style, especially if it involves many changes, is to create a brand new style. Creating a style by formatting the text first and then using the Style button on the Formatting toolbar is the easiest way to create a style. You can also create a new style through the Style dialog box.

When you create your own style, you must give it a name. The name must be unique and indicate what the style will accomplish so it is apparent when you view the Style list. Consider the following factors when naming a style:

- A style name can contain a maximum of 213 characters.
- A style name can contain spaces and commas.

- A style name is case-sensitive. Uppercase and lowercase letters can be used.
- Do not use a backslash (\), braces ({}), or semicolon (;) when naming a style.

To create a new style from existing text, you would complete the following steps:

1. Key a paragraph of text, such as a heading. *(Hint: Any text that ends in a hard return is considered a paragraph.)*
2. Format the text the way you want it to appear, such as changing the font, font size, applying color, paragraph spacing, and so on.
3. Position the insertion point within the paragraph that contains the desired formatting.
4. Click the Style box on the Formatting toolbar to select the current style name.
5. Type a new name and press Enter. The new style will be visible in the Style drop-down list from the Formatting toolbar as well as the Style dialog box.

The above method automatically defines the style as a paragraph style. You can use the Style dialog box to create both paragraph and character styles from existing text. To create a new style from existing text using the Style dialog box, complete the following steps:

1. Position the insertion point within the paragraph that contains the formatting. If you are creating a character style, select the text first.
2. Click Format and Style.
3. At the Style dialog box, click New.
4. At the New Style dialog box, key a name for the style in the Name text box.
5. Select the Style type option and specify whether you are creating a paragraph or character style.
6. If you want the style to be available to all new documents based on this template, click the Add to template check box.
7. Click OK or press Enter.
8. Click Close at the Style dialog box.

You may also create a style from scratch by assigning formatting instructions at the Style dialog box, rather than from existing text. To do this, complete the following steps:

1. Display the Style dialog box and click the New button.
2. At the New dialog box, name the style in the Name text box and indicate whether you are creating a paragraph or character style at the Style type option.
3. Click Format and select the desired options.
4. When all formatting has been selected, make sure the correct formatting instructions display in the Description section of the New Style dialog box, and then click the Close button.

When you select Format at the New Style dialog box, a drop-down list displays with the following formatting options: Font, Paragraph, Tabs, Border, Language, Frame, and Numbering. These options will display the associated dialog boxes as indicated by their names. Changes that you make at these dialog boxes will be included in the new style.

Creating a Style Based on an Existing Style

You may also use an existing style as a base for creating a new style. The existing style is known as the *base style*. The new style inherits all the formatting instructions included in the base style in addition to the formatting currently selected for the new style. If you make a change to the base style, the new style and any other related styles will reflect that change. For example, many of Word's predesigned styles are based on the Normal style. If you make a change to the Normal style, all styles based on the Normal style will be changed also. This may produce some unwanted results in your document if you applied any styles that were based on the Normal style. For this reason, avoid making changes to the Normal style.

You can create your own base styles for different elements of your document. For example, suppose you want 14-point Impact headings and 12-point Impact Italic subheadings in your document. You could create a new style that contains an Impact font instruction that will serve as the base style. You could then create two separate styles for the headings and subheadings that include the specific font size and font style choices. Each style would be based on the base style that includes the Impact font selection. If you decide later to change the font to Arial Rounded MT Bold, all you have to do is change the base style and the font will be changed in all the headings and subheadings. To create a style based on an existing style, display the Style dialog box and click New. At the New Style dialog box, change the Based on option to display the name of the existing style on which the new style will be based.

Following One Style with Another

In some situations, one set of formatting instructions is immediately followed by another set of formatting instructions. For instance, formatting for a heading is usually followed by formatting for body text. In Word, you can define one style to be immediately followed by another style. Pressing the Enter key after applying the first style will automatically apply the second style to the text that follows. For example, to define a heading style so that it is followed by a body text style, complete the following steps:

1. Create the body text style first using either the Style button on the Formatting toolbar or the Style dialog box. (Creating the style that is to follow another style first is the easiest.)
2. Create the heading style by displaying the Style dialog box and clicking New.
3. At the New Style dialog box, click the Down arrow at the Style for following paragraph option, and then select the body text style (created in step 1) from the drop-down list.
4. Click OK or press Enter.
5. Click Close at the Style dialog box.

Copying Individual Styles from Other Documents and Templates

When you work on a document, you may want to use a style that already exists in one of Word's templates or in a document you have created. For example, if you had to create some other promotional material for the Edward Hospital volunteer program (see figures 6.11 and 6.12), you could maintain consistency and reinforce the organization's identity by using the same heading and subheading styles that were used in the brochure in exercises 4 and 5.

In Word, the Organizer dialog box, as shown in figure 6.13, offers options for copying individual styles, in addition to macros, toolbars, and AutoText entries, from an existing document or template to another document or template. For instance, to copy the *Heading 1* style and the *Heading 2* style from *c06ex05, Volunteer brochure* to a document named *Volunteer fact sheet* using the Organizer dialog box, you would complete the following steps:

1. With the insertion point located in *Volunteer fact sheet*, click Format and Style.
2. At the Style dialog box, click Organizer and select the Styles tab. By default, the name of the current document displays above the list box on the left side of the Organizer dialog box and in the Styles available in list box, also on the left side of the dialog box. The list box shows a list of the styles available in that particular document. By default, *Normal* will display as the file name on the right side of the dialog box and the list box below will display the styles available in the Normal template.
3. On the right side of the dialog box, click Close File to change the command button to Open File, and click Open File.
4. Select *c06ex05, Volunteer brochure* and click Open or press Enter.
5. In the right list box for *c06ex05, Volunteer brochure*, select *Heading 1*, hold down the Shift key and select *Heading 2*. (Hint: Both style names should be selected as shown in figure 6.13.)
6. Click Copy. (The *Heading 2* and *Heading 7* styles will now be listed in the *Volunteer fact sheet* list box on the left side of the dialog box as shown in figure 6.13.)
7. Click Close.

Style Organizer Dialog Box

Organizer

Styles | AutoText | Toolbars | Macro Project Items

To volunteer fact sheet:

Default Paragraph Font
Normal

◀◀ Copy

Delete

Rename...

In c06ex05, volunteer brochure:

Header Even
Header First
Header Odd
Heading 1
Heading 2
Heading 3
Heading 4

Styles available in:

volunteer fact sheet (Document)

Styles available in:

c06ex05, volunteer brochure (Docume

Close File

Close File

Description

Close

A specific document does not have to be open for you to copy styles from one document or template to another. At the Organizer dialog box, you can select a different document name or template for each list box by clicking the Close File (or Close File) command button below either list box to change the command button to an Open File (or Open File) button. Click Open File (or Open File) and select the document or template you want to copy styles to or from.

The Styles Organizer dialog box can be confusing because the <u>C</u>opy button displays triangles pointing to the right, making you think that styles must be copied from the left side to the right side. However, styles can be copied from either side. If you select a style in the list box on the right, the triangles on the <u>C</u>opy button point to the left, as do the labels above each list box.

Removing a Style from Text

If you wish to remove a style immediately after applying it, click the Undo button on the Standard toolbar. When a style is removed, the style that was previously applied to the text is applied once again (usually this is the Normal style). Because only one style can be applied at a time to the same text, you can also remove a style from text by applying a new style.

Using Drop Caps as a Design Element

In publications such as magazines, newsletters, or brochures, a graphics feature called drop caps can be used to enhance the appearance of text. A *drop cap* is the first letter of the first word in a paragraph that is set in a larger font size and set into the paragraph. Drop caps identify the beginning of major sections or parts of a document.

Drop caps look best when set in a paragraph containing text set in a proportional font. The drop cap can be set in the same font as the paragraph text or it can be set in a complementary font. For example, a drop cap can be set in a sans serif font while the paragraph text is set in a serif font. A drop cap can be one character or the entire first word of a paragraph. A special character may be used as the first character in a paragraph and then formatted as a drop cap to create an interesting effect. The examples in figure 6.14 show some of the ways drop caps can be created and formatted. Practice restraint when using this design element or it can be distracting.

A drop cap can be applied only to existing text. To create a drop cap, you would complete the following steps:

1. Position the insertion point within the paragraph to be formatted with a drop cap. If you want to format the first word(s) or a special character as a drop cap, select the symbol or the word(s) first.
2. Click F<u>o</u>rmat and <u>D</u>rop Cap.
3. At the Drop Cap dialog box, select <u>D</u>ropped in the Position section to create a drop cap positioned into the paragraph with the remaining text wrapping around it; or select In <u>M</u>argin to create a drop cap that is positioned in the margin to the left of the paragraph (shown in the special character example in figure 6.14).
4. Click <u>F</u>ont in the Drop Cap dialog box to select the desired font for the drop cap letter only. This does not affect the remaining paragraph text.
5. Click the <u>L</u>ines to drop option to set the number of lines (from 1 to 10 lines) that the drop cap will be vertically positioned into the paragraph. This option affects both the height and width of the drop cap letter.
6. Click Distance from te<u>x</u>t to set the amount of distance the drop cap is positioned in relation to the paragraph text.
7. Click OK or press Enter.

Drop Cap
The first letter of the first word in a paragraph, formatted in a larger font size and positioned into the beginning of the paragraph.

DTP POINTERS
Use drop caps sparingly.

figure

6.14

Drop Cap Examples

drop cap looks best when set in a paragraph containing text set in a proportional font. The drop cap can be set in the same font as the paragraph text or it can be set in a complementary font. For example, a drop cap can be set in a sans serif font while the paragraph text is set in a serif font. A drop cap can be one character or the entire first word of a paragraph. A special character may be used as the first character in a paragraph and then formatted as a drop cap to create a visually interesting effect. *(The drop cap is set in Curlz MT with a green font color and shadow effect applied; the body text is set in High Tower Text.)*

drop cap looks best when set in a paragraph containing text set in a proportional font. The drop cap can be set in the same font as the paragraph text or it can be set in a complementary font. For example, a drop cap can be set in a sans serif font while the paragraph text is set in a serif font. A drop cap can be one character or the entire first word of a paragraph. A special character may be used as the first character in a paragraph and then formatted as a drop cap to create a visually interesting effect. *(The drop cap is set in Jokerman with a light blue font color; the body text is set in Comic Sans MS.)*

drop cap looks best when set in a paragraph containing text set in a proportional font. The drop cap can be set in the same font as the paragraph text or it can be set in a complementary font. For example, a drop cap can be set in a sans serif font while the paragraph text is set in a serif font. A drop cap can be one character or the entire first word of a paragraph. A special character may be used as the first character in a paragraph and then formatted as a drop cap to create a visually interesting effect. *(The drop cap and body text are both set in Maiandra GD.)*

drop cap looks best when set in a paragraph containing text set in a proportional font. The drop cap can be set in the same font as the drop cap can be set in a complementary font. For example, a drop cap can be set in a sans serif font while the paragraph text is set in a serif font. A drop cap can be one character or the entire first word of a paragraph. A special character may be used as the first character in a paragraph and then formatted as a drop cap to create a visually interesting effect. *(The drop cap is set in Engravers MT; the body text is set in Baskerville Old Face. Black shading was added to the frame through the Borders and Shading dialog box, and the text color was changed to white.)*

drop cap looks best when set in a paragraph containing text set in a proportional font. The drop cap can be set in the same font as the paragraph text or it can be set in a complementary font. For example, a drop cap can be set in a sans serif font while the paragraph text is set in a serif font. A drop cap can be one character or the entire first word of a paragraph. A special character may be used as the first character in a paragraph and then formatted as a drop cap to create a visually interesting effect. *(The drop cap is set in Vivaldi; the body text is set in High Tower Text. A red shadow border was added to the frame through the Borders and Shading dialog box.)*

 publications such as magazines, newsletters, or brochures, a graphics feature called *drop caps* can be used to enhance the appearance of text. A drop cap is the first letter of the first word in a paragraph that is set in a larger font size and set into the paragraph. Drop caps identify the beginning of major sections or parts of a document. *(The drop cap is set in Mercurius Script MT with a plum font color; the body text is set in Book Antiqua.)*

 In publications such as magazines, newsletters, or brochures, a graphics feature called *drop caps* can be used to enhance the appearance of text. A drop cap is the first letter of the first word in a paragraph that is set in a larger font size and set into the paragraph. Drop caps identify the beginning of major sections or parts of a document. *(The drop cap is from the Webdings character set; the body text is set in Verdana.)*

The drop cap is placed within a frame in your document. A frame is similar to a text box except that it is inserted in the text layer rather than the drawing layer. Although text boxes have replaced frames for the most part in the most recent versions of Word, the drop cap feature still uses a frame to enclose the text. You can customize the drop cap letter by selecting the letter within the frame and changing the font color and font style and adding special effects. You can also apply other formatting, such as borders and shading, to the frame itself.

Using Word's 2 Pages per Sheet Feature

Word 2000 has a feature that makes creating single fold brochures much easier. The 2 pages per sheet feature divides each physical page (not the text) in half as shown in figure 6.15, so that the printed page can be folded in half and used as a single-fold brochure or several pages can be folded and bound at the fold to create a booklet. Word displays and numbers each half page as a separate page. Any page formatting such as margins, paper size, and orientation can be applied to each half page. Headers and footers, page numbering, and page borders, can also be inserted.

To use the 2 pages per sheet feature, click File and Page Setup, select the Paper Size tab, and then select the paper size and orientation. Select the Margins tab and click the 2 pages per sheet check box. Enter the desired margin values. When you select the 2 pages per sheet feature, the name of some of the margin boxes will change depending on the orientation selected at the Paper Size tab. If you select portrait orientation, the Top and Bottom margin box names change to Outside and Inside. If you select landscape orientation, the Left and Right margin box names change to Outside and Inside. Refer to figure 6.15 to see where the outside and inside margins are located when portrait or landscape is selected.

figure

6.15 *2 Pages per Sheet*

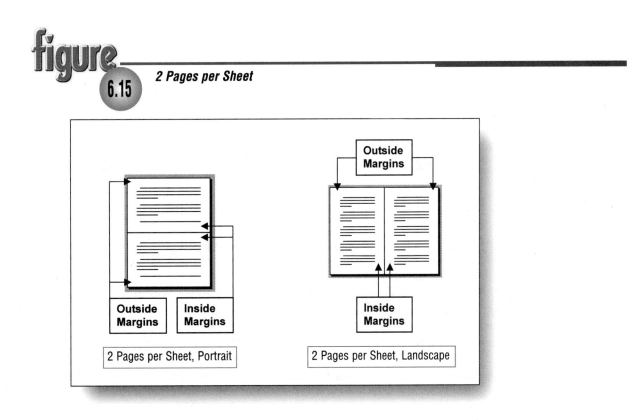

In exercise 6, you will create the inside panels of a single-fold brochure using various design and formatting techniques, including 2 pages per sheet, a drop cap, and styles.

exercise 6

Creating the Inside Panels of a Single-Fold Brochure Using Styles and a Drop Cap

1. Create a dummy for a single-fold brochure by taking a piece of standard size 8-1/2 by 11 inch paper, holding the long side up, and folding it in half. With a pen or pencil, label the panels on one side of the page as Panel 1 (Inside) and Panel 2 (Inside). Label the panels on the other side as Panel 3 (Back) and Panel 4 (Cover). Refer to the dummy when creating the brochure to ensure that you are keying the appropriate text in the correct location. Save your document periodically as you are working.

2. At a clear document screen, create the inside panels of a single-fold brochure, as shown in figure 6.16, by completing the following steps:
   a. Set up the 2 pages per sheet feature and change the margins and orientation by completing the following steps:
      1) Display the Page Setup dialog box, select the Paper Size tab, and then select Landscape as the orientation.
      2) In the bottom left section of the Margins tab, click 2 pages per sheet to insert a check mark.
      3) Select the Margins tab and change the top and bottom margins to 0.7 inch and the outside and inside margins to 0.55 inches. *(Hint: The outside and inside margin settings were chosen because of the unprintable zone associated with the printer that was used to create and print this brochure. If your printer will not allow you to use these same settings, change your margins accordingly, and then make any necessary adjustments to the settings so that your document basically matches figure 6.16.)*
      4) Click OK or press Enter to close the dialog box.
   b. Turn on automatic kerning for font sizes 14 points and above at the Character Spacing tab of the Font dialog box.
   c. With the insertion point located at the top of the document, copy the contents of the file Heart Text.doc located on your student CD.
   d. Format the drop cap paragraph by completing the following steps:
      1) Click the Show/Hide ¶ button on the Standard toolbar to display nonprinting symbols.
      2) Select the first paragraph and change the font to 16-point Arial Italic, Violet.
      3) With the insertion point within the paragraph (the text may still be selected), change the line spacing to 1.5 lines.
      4) Make sure the text is deselected, and the insertion point is within the same paragraph, and then click Format and Drop Cap.
      5) At the Drop Cap dialog box, select Dropped in the Position section.
      6) Click the Down arrow to the right of the Font list box and select Impact as the font.
      7) Make sure the Lines to drop option displays 3.
      8) Change the Distance from text to 0.1 inch, and click OK or press Enter.
      9) Make sure the frame around the drop cap is selected (black sizing handles will display), change the font color to Teal, and then turn on bold and turn off italics.
      10) Position the insertion point at the end of the same paragraph and press Enter.
   e. Format the first heading and create a style from the formatted heading by completing the following steps:

1) Select *Diabetes: The Latest News* and change the font to 16-point Impact Bold, Teal.

2) Display the Paragraph dialog box and select the Line and <u>P</u>age Breaks tab. In the Pagination section, click the check box to the left of Keep with ne<u>x</u>t so that the heading will always stay with the paragraph that follows and will not be separated by a column break or a page break. Click OK.

3) Create a style from the formatted heading by completing the following steps:

   a) Position the insertion point within the heading just formatted (the heading can still be selected). Click the Style list box on the Formatting toolbar to select the style name that is currently in the box.

   b) Key **teal heading** and press Enter. (This heading style name will display in the Style box and be added to the list of styles available for this brochure.)

Step
2e3b

f. Format the first subheading (day, date, name, and title) and create a style from the formatted subheading by completing the following steps:

   1) Select *Tuesday, March 9, 2001* and *Katherine Dwyer, M.D.*

   2) Change the font to 12-point Arial Bold Italic, Violet.

   3) Display the Paragraph dialog box, select the Line and <u>P</u>age Breaks tab, and then click the Keep with ne<u>x</u>t option to insert a check mark. Click OK.

   4) Create a style from the formatted subheading by completing the following steps:

      a) Position the insertion point within the subheading just formatted (the subheading can still be selected). Click the Style list box on the Formatting toolbar to select the style name that is currently in the box.

      b) Key **violet subheading** and press Enter. This subheading style name displays in the Style box and is added to the list of styles available for this brochure.

g. Format the body text and create a style from the formatted body text by completing the following steps:

   1) Select the paragraph that begins with *One of the best ways...* and ends with... *new medical recommendations.*

   2) Change the font to 12-point Arial, Violet.

   3) Change the spacing before the paragraph to 6 pt and the spacing after to 24 pt.

   4) Create a style from the formatted body text by completing the following steps:

      a) Position the insertion point within the paragraph just formatted (the paragraph can still be selected). Click the Style list box on the Formatting toolbar to select the style name that is currently in the box.

      b) Key **violet body text** and press Enter. This body text style name displays in the Style box and is added to the list of styles available for this brochure.

h. Position the insertion point within the heading *New Advances in Cardiac Surgery* and apply the *teal heading* from the Style drop-down list on the Formatting toolbar.

i. Select *Tuesday, March 23, 2001* and *Christine Johnson, M.D.* and apply the *violet subheading* from the Style drop-down list on the Formatting toolbar.

j. Position the insertion point within the paragraph that begins with *Advances in minimally invasive...* and ends with... *leads an informative discussion.*, and apply the *violet body text* from the Style drop-down list on the Formatting toolbar.

k. Move the insertion point to the top of the second page (panel 2) and apply the *teal heading*, the *violet subheading*, and the *violet body text* styles to the remaining headings, subheads, and body text (up to but not including *All lectures:...*), as shown in figure 6.16. *(Note: You can apply the teal heading style to all the headings by applying the first one, moving the insertion point to each heading, and then pressing F4. Repeat the process for the subheadings and body text.)*

l. Format the lecture information text at the bottom of panel 2 by completing the following steps:

   1) Select from *All lectures:* until the end of the document and change the font to 12-point Arial, Teal.

   2) Insert tabs to align the lecture information (time and location) as displayed in figure 6.16.

   3) Position the insertion point to the right of *Naperville, Illinois* and press Enter.

   4) Select the last paragraph and change the font style to italics.

   5) Select *FREE,* and change the color to Violet.

   6) Select *(630) 555-4941.* and change the color to Violet.

m. Insert the watermark (yellow heart image) by completing the following steps:

   1) Move the insertion point to the space below the first paragraph on the first page.

   2) Click the Zoom Control button on the Standard toolbar and change the viewing mode to Whole Page.

   3) Display the Insert ClipArt dialog box and search for clips under the keyword *heart.*

   4) Scroll through the selections until you find a black-and-white double heart that looks like the yellow heart shown in figure 6.16 and then insert the image. *(Hint: The heart image will probably be located within clips 121–180. If you cannot locate this image, close the Insert ClipArt dialog box. Click Insert, point to Picture, then click From File. Change the Look in list box to display the following location: C:\Program Files\Microsoft Office\ClipArt\Pub60Cor. Double-click So02439 to insert the heart image.)*

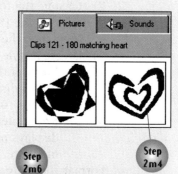

Step 2m4

   5) Select the heart image, click the Text Wrapping button on the Picture toolbar, and then click In front of text. *(Note: You will work with the image on top of the text until all necessary changes are made and then you will send it behind the text.)*

Step 2m6

   6) With the image still selected, display the Format Picture dialog box, and then select the Size tab. In the Scale section, click the Lock aspect ratio check box to remove the check mark. In the Size and Rotate section, size the image by changing the height to 5.91 inches and the width to 6.25 inches. Click OK.

Step 2m6

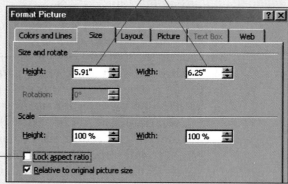

Step 2m7c

   7) Change the color of the heart to yellow by completing the following steps:

     a) Right-click the heart image and select Edit picture from the shortcut menu.

     b) Click the Zoom button on the Standard toolbar and adjust the view to 50%.

     c) Click the inner heart to select it, hold down the Shift key, and select the outer heart. Both hearts should show sizing handles.

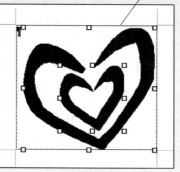

d) Click the Fill Color button on the Drawing toolbar and select Light Yellow (fifth row, third column from the left).

e) Click Close Picture on the Edit Picture toolbar to return to your document.

8) Position the image on the right side of the page so that it is approximately half visible. Try aligning the top center of the larger heart image along the right edge of the page. The bottom point of the heart is not a good alignment reference point because the image is asymmetrical. *(Hint: Only half of the image is visible, whether you are viewing your document in Print Layout View or Print Preview, but the remaining half of the image will print on the second page as shown in figure 6.16.)*

9) With the image still selected, click the Text Wrapping button on the Formatting toolbar and click Behind Text.

3. Save panels 1 and 2 of the brochure to your hard drive or floppy disk and name the project c06ex06, Panels 1,2.

4. Print and then close c06ex06, Panels 1,2. (You may wait until exercise 7 to print because panels 1 and 2 are printed as part of that exercise.)

Step 2m8

figure

6.16   Exercise 6

A fit heart can contribute to a long, healthy life for you and the ones you love. Join experts at the Edward Cardiovascular Institute to learn how to keep yours beating strong.

Diabetes: The Latest News

Tuesday, March 9, 2001
Katherine Dwyer, M.D.

One of the best ways to manage any medical condition is to keep abreast of the very latest information. Join endocrinologist Katherine Dwyer, M.D., for an up-to-the-minute discussion of the latest diabetes clinical trials, revised treatment guidelines, and new medical recommendations.

New Advances in Cardiac Surgery

Tuesday, March 23, 2001
Christine Johnson, M.D.

Advances in minimally invasive surgical procedures are helping patients get back to active, healthy lives more quickly—and more safely—than ever. Today, cardiac surgical procedures are marked by shorter hospital stays and recovery times, and lower costs. Learn more about these advances as Christine Johnson, M.D., leads an informative discussion.

Exercise—Is It the Fountain of Youth?

Tuesday, April 6, 2001
Joan Polak, M.D.

Everyone knows that exercise is good for your heart. Now, learn from a cardiologist exactly why it is good for you and what exercises provide the greatest benefits. Learn the specifics behind the "Just Do It" philosophy from Dr. Joan Polak.

Setting Up a Heart-Healthy Kitchen

Tuesday, April 20, 2001
Kaitlin Anzalone, Registered Dietitian

A great start to beginning a heart-healthy diet is doing a heart-check of your kitchen. Join us for practical tips and suggestions for setting up your kitchen.

Diabetes and Cardiovascular Disease

Tuesday, May 4, 2001
Wilma Schaenfeld, M.D.

During this session, we will discuss the clinical features of heart disease in the diabetic, as well as what you can do to reduce the likelihood of future problems.

All lectures: 7:00 to 8:30 p.m.
                 Edward Cardiovascular Institute
                 120 Spalding Drive
                 Naperville, Illinois

The talk is FREE, but because space is limited, please register by calling (630) 555-4941.

In exercise 7, you will create the back and cover (panels 3 and 4) of the heart brochure started in exercise 6. To make this brochure self-mailing, the back of the brochure will be used for mailing purposes. You will insert return address information and leave the rest of panel 3 blank with the assumption that mailing labels will be used. This exercise involves using the Text Direction feature to create the rotated return address, editing the heart image on the cover to change the fill color, and using text boxes to place text at specific locations on the page.

exercise 7

**Creating the Back (Panel 3) and Cover (Panel 4)
of a Single-Fold Brochure**

1. Open c06ex06, Panels 1,2.
2. Save the document to your hard drive or a floppy disk with Save As and name it c06ex07, Heart brochure.
3. Create panels 3 and 4 of the brochure shown in figure 6.17 by completing the following steps:
   a. Press Ctrl + End to move the insertion point to the end of the document and then press Ctrl + Enter to insert a hard page break.
   b. Create the text box and insert the return address located on the back of the brochure (panel 3) as illustrated in figure 6.17 by completing the following steps:
      1) With the insertion point positioned on panel 3, click the Text Box button on the Drawing toolbar and draw a text box toward the bottom of the page that is approximately 3-1/2 inches wide and 1-1/2 inches high. (The size and position of the text box will be adjusted later.)
      2) Key the following information in the format indicated:

      **EDWARD CARDIOVASCULAR INSTITUTE
      One ECI Plaza
      120 Spalding Drive, Suite 102
      Naperville, IL 60540-9865**

   c. Format the return address by completing the following steps:
      1) Select the text just entered, change the font to 10-point Arial and the color to Teal.
      2) Select *EDWARD CARDIOVASCULAR INSTITUTE* and apply bold.
      3) Rotate the position of the text by completing the following steps:
         a) Position the insertion point anywhere within the address.
         b) Click Format and Text Direction to display the Text Direction-Text Box dialog box.
         c) In the Orientation section, click the text direction selection that displays text pointing up and matches the direction of the text in figure 6.17.
         d) Click OK or press Enter.
   d. Display the Format Text Box dialog box and make the following changes:
      1) Select the Colors and Lines tab, change the line color to Violet, and then change the line weight to 2.25 pt.
      2) Select the Size tab and change the height to 2.9 inches and the width to 0.9 inch.
      3) Select the Layout tab and click Advanced. At the Advanced Layout dialog box, select the Picture Position tab and change the Horizontal Absolute position to 0.42 inch to the left of Page. Change the Vertical Absolute position to 5.15 inches below Page.

4) Select the Text Wrapping tab and change the wrapping style to Top and bottom.

5) Click OK to close the Advanced Layout dialog box; click OK again to close the Format Text Box dialog box.

e. Place the insertion point above the text box and double-click to position the insertion point there. *(Hint: The Click and Type feature should insert hard returns.)*

f. Press Ctrl + Enter to insert a hard page break. The text box should remain on panel 3.

g. Create the heart image on the front cover (panel 4) by completing the following steps:

1) Make sure the insertion point is positioned at the top of the cover page (panel 4).

2) Display the Insert ClipArt dialog box and search for clips under the keyword *heart*.

3) Scroll through the selections until you find a black-and-white heart image that looks like the heart image displayed in figure 6.17 and then insert the image. *(Hint: The heart image will probably be located within clips 121–180. If you cannot locate this image, try inserting the picture from file using the path C:\Program Files\Microsoft Office\ClipArt\Pub60Cor. The filename is So02437.)*

4) Use one of the corner sizing handles and make the picture larger so it is easier to see. You will size the picture more precisely later.

5) Change the color of the heart image by completing the following steps:

a) With the image still selected, right-click inside the heart image, and then click Edit Picture from the shortcut menu.

b) At Word's Picture editor window, click in the center of the heart to select the background rectangle, and then change the fill color to light yellow.

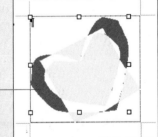

c) Click individual segments of the heart and change the fill color to either teal or violet to match the image in figure 6.17.

d) Click Close Picture on the Edit Picture toolbar to return to your document.

h. With the heart selected, right-click the image, select Format Object, and then make the following changes at the Format Object dialog box:

1) Select the Size tab, clear the Lock aspect ratio check box, and then change the height to 6.17 inches and the width to 4.6 inches.

2) Select the Layout tab and click Advanced. At the Advanced Layout dialog box, select the Text Wrapping tab, and then change the Wrapping style to Top and Bottom.

3) Select the Picture Position tab and change the Horizontal Alignment to *Right* relative to *Margin*. Change the Vertical Alignment to *Top* relative to *Margin*.

4) Click OK to close the Advanced Layout dialog box; click OK again to close the Format Object dialog box.

i. Create a text box inside the heart to hold the word *for* by completing the following steps:

1) Click the Text Box button on the Drawing toolbar and draw a text box in the approximate location of the word *for* as shown in figure 6.17.

2) Change the font to 26-point Impact, teal, and then key **for**.
3) Click the Fill Color button on the Drawing toolbar and click No Fill.
4) Click the Line Color button on the Drawing toolbar and click No Line.
5) Size the text box with the sizing handles so the text is completely visible, if necessary, and then position the text box with the mouse in the approximate position as displayed in figure 6.17.

j. Create a second text box that will contain the word *your* by completing the following steps:
1) Select the first text box containing *for*, hold down the Ctrl key, and then drag a copy of the text box to the approximate position of the word *your* in figure 6.17.
2) Select the word *for* and key **your**.
3) Size and position the text box as necessary.

k. Create a third text box that will contain the word *Heart's* by copying the second text box to the approximate position of the word *Heart's* in figure 6.17. Select *your*, change the font size to 60-point and the font color to Violet, and key **Heart's**. Size and position the text box as necessary.

l. Create a fourth text box that will contain the word *sake* by copying the second text box to the approximate position of the word *sake* in figure 6.17. Select *your* and key **sake**. Size and position the text box as necessary.

m. Check the vertical spacing between the text boxes against figure 6.17 and adjust accordingly.

n. Right-align all four text boxes by completing the following steps:
1) Hold down the Shift key and click each text box so that all four text boxes are selected simultaneously.
2) Click the D̲raw button on the Drawing toolbar, point to A̲lign or Distribute, and then click Align R̲ight.
3) With the four text boxes still selected, use the keyboard arrow keys to simultaneously adjust the position of the text boxes so they are located in the same approximate location as the corresponding words in figure 6.17.

o. Create a fifth text box to hold the *Spring 2001* by completing the following steps:
1) Click outside of the heart image to deselect the text boxes.
2) Click the Text Box button on the Drawing toolbar and draw a text box in the upper left corner of the page. *(Hint: Do not worry about the exact size or position at this time.)*
3) Change the font to 24-point Impact Italic, Violet, and then key **Spring 2001**.
4) Click the Line Color button on the Drawing toolbar and click No Line.
5) Size the text box with the mouse so that the text is visible.
6) Double-click the text box border to display the Format Text Box dialog box. Select the Layout tab and click A̲dvanced. At the Advanced Layout dialog box, select the Picture Position tab and change the Horizontal A̲lignment to *Left* r̲elative to *Margin*. Change the Vertical Alignment to *Top* r̲elative to *Margin*.

p. Create a sixth text box to hold the *Presented by:* information by completing the following steps:
1) Click the Text Box button on the Drawing toolbar and draw a text box below the heart image closer to the bottom of the page. *(Hint: Do not worry about the exact size or position at this time.)*
2) Change the font to Impact. Key **Presented by:**, press Enter, and then key **The Edward Cardiovascular Institute**.
3) Select *Presented by:* and change the font to 12-point Italic, Teal.
4) With the text still selected, display the Paragraph dialog box, and then change spacing after the paragraph to 6 pt.

5) Select *The Edward Cardiovascular Institute* and make the following changes:
   a) Display the Font dialog box Font tab and change the font to 20-point, Violet, Small caps.
   b) Select the Character Spacing tab and expand the spacing by 1 pt.
6) Click OK to close the Font dialog box.
7) Size the text box, if necessary, so all the text is visible.
8) Click the Line Color button and click No Line.
9) Double-click the text box border to display the Format Text Box dialog box. Select the Layout tab and click Advanced. At the Advanced Layout dialog box, select the Picture Position tab and change the Horizontal Alignment to *Left* relative to *Margin*. Change the Vertical Absolute position to *7.3* inches below *Page*.

4. Save the document with the same name (c06ex07, Heart brochure).
5. Print both pages of the brochure using both sides of the paper. Refer to the directions for printing in exercise 1, if necessary.
6. Close c06ex07, Heart brochure.

figure
6.17

Exercise 7

chapter summary

➤ A brochure can be used to inform, educate, promote, or sell. It can also be used to establish an organization's identity and image.

➤ The manner in which a brochure is folded determines the order in which the panels are set on the page. Folds create distinct sections in which to place blocks of text. The most common brochure fold is called a letter fold.

➤ A dummy can be created to help determine the location of information on the brochure page layout.

➤ Consistent elements are necessary to maintain continuity in a multi-page brochure.

➤ The easiest method of creating the page layout for a letter-fold brochure is to use the Columns feature; the easiest method for a single-fold brochure is to use the 2 pages per sheet feature.

➤ Column formatting can be varied within the same document by using section breaks to separate the sections that will be formatted with different column settings.

➤ Reverse text can be created in a document as a design element and usually refers to white text set against a solid black background. Reverse text can also be created with different colors for the text and the background, as well as shading.

➤ The front cover of a brochure sets the mood and tone for the whole brochure. The front cover title must attract attention and let the reader know what the brochure is about.

➤ Repetitive formatting that is used to maintain consistency in a single publication or among a series of documents can be applied to text by using a style.

➤ A style can be edited and any occurrence of the style in the document is automatically updated to reflect the changes.

➤ The Normal style from the Normal template is automatically applied to any text that is keyed, unless you specify other formatting instructions.

➤ Word provides two types of styles—character and paragraph. A character style applies formatting to selected text only. A paragraph style affects the paragraph that contains the insertion point or selected text.

➤ A drop cap is a design element in which the first letter of the first word in a paragraph is formatted in a larger font size and set into the beginning of the paragraph.

commands review

	Mouse/Keyboard
Change margins	File, Page Setup, Margins tab
2 pages per sheet	File, Page Setup, Margins tab, 2 pages per sheet
Columns dialog box	Format, Columns
Insert a column break	Insert, Break, Column Break; or Ctrl + Shift + Enter
Insert a page break	Insert, Break, Page Break; or Ctrl + Enter

Move insertion point between columns	Position I-beam pointer at desired location, click left button; or Alt + up arrow or Alt + down Arrow (toggles back and forth to top of previous column and to top of next column)
Character Spacing and Kerning	Format, Font, Character Spacing tab
Paragraph Borders and Shading dialog box	Format, Borders and Shading
Display Drawing toolbar	Click Drawing button on Standard toolbar; or right-click Standard toolbar, select Drawing; or View, Toolbars, select Drawing, and then press Enter
Draw a text box	Click the Text Box button on the Drawing toolbar, click and drag the crosshairs to draw a box
Insert existing text into a text box	Select text, click the Text Box button on the Formatting toolbar
Size a text box	Double-click the text box border, select the Size tab
Position a text box	Double-click the text box border, select the Layout tab, click Advanced
Format Text Box dialog box	Format, Text Box
Drop Cap dialog box	Format, Drop Cap
Insert Picture dialog box	Insert, Picture
Style dialog box	Format, Style
Style Organizer dialog box	Format, Style, Organizer, Styles tab
Font dialog box	Format, Font; or click the Font list box, Font Size list box, and/or Character formatting buttons on the Formatting toolbar
Format Object dialog box	Format, Object

Matching: Match the terms with the correct definitions by writing the letter of the term on the blank line in front of the correct definition.

Ⓐ Applying
Ⓑ Style
Ⓒ Character style
Ⓓ 2 pages per sheet
Ⓔ Drop cap
Ⓕ Dummy
Ⓖ Panels

Ⓗ Paragraph style
Ⓘ Parallel
Ⓙ Column break
Ⓚ Columns dialog box
Ⓛ Reverse text
Ⓜ All styles
Ⓝ Newspaper columns

_____ 1. Folds in a brochure that all run in the same direction.

_____ 2. The sections that divide a brochure page.

_____ 3. A mock-up of a brochure.

_____ 4. In this type of formatting, text flows from top to bottom in the first column, to the top of the next column, and so on.

_____ 5. Use this dialog box to create columns of unequal width.

_____ 6. This feature divides a physical page in half and may be used to create single-fold brochures.

_____ 7. Insert this (or these) into a document to control where columns end and begin on the page.

_____ 8. A set of formatting instructions saved with a name to be used repeatedly on different sections of text.

_____ 9. Select this at the Style dialog box to display all the available styles in Word.

_____ 10. The name for the first letter of the first word in a paragraph that is formatted in a larger font size and is set into the paragraph.

_____ 11. The name for white text set against a black background.

Concepts: Write your answers to the following questions in the space provided.

1. What is the purpose of creating a dummy before creating a brochure?

2. What is the biggest advantage of using styles?

3. What is the disadvantage of having Word automatically update your styles?

4. What styles could you create for the text in figure 6.7 to save time and keystrokes in the document creation process?

5. Explain the 2 pages per sheet feature. What does it do? What can it be used for? Explain the difference between choosing portrait or landscape with this feature.

6. How can drop caps and reverse text serve as design elements in a document?

Assessment 1

You are an involved and supportive member of the Newport Art League. Other members became aware of your desktop publishing skills and asked you to create a promotional brochure for the league. Anxious to show off your skills, you volunteer! Your target audience includes the general public, but more specifically artists, aspiring artists, art lovers, and those with a general interest in art. Your audience may also include both adults and children. Your purpose is to let your readers know what the art league has to offer. The content of your brochure will include information on annual art events, classes and workshops, membership, and volunteer opportunities.

In this assessment, you will create the inside panels of the Newport Art League's brochure. A sample solution of a complete brochure is provided in figures 6.18 and 6.19; however, you are to create your own design (using text located on your student CD). Include the following specifications in your brochure design.

1. You may create a letter-fold brochure or a single-fold brochure.
2. Include all the information contained in the file Art Text.doc located on your student CD.
3. Create a thumbnail sketch of your design.
4. Create a dummy to guide you in the placement of text.
5. Create styles for the headings, subheadings, and bulleted text. Create any additional styles if appropriate.
6. Use relevant graphics. A large selection of art-related graphics can be viewed by displaying the Insert ClipArt dialog box and searching for clips with the keyword *art*. Viewing these graphics may serve as an inspiration for the design and color scheme of your brochure.
7. Use a coordinated color scheme. Remember you can customize text colors to match a color(s) in a clip art image, or you can customize the color(s) of a clip art image to match a specific text color or coordinate colors within another image.
8. For margins, if you are going to create a letter-fold brochure, use the column measurements provided in exercises 2 and 3, or exercises 4 and 5. If you are going to create a single-fold brochure, use the 2 pages per sheet feature.
9. Use an appropriate typeface. Make sure all text is legible.
10. Insert column breaks when necessary.
11. Use the Paragraph dialog box to make adjustments to the spacing before and after paragraphs.
12. As you work, evaluate your design for the concepts of focus, balance, proportion, contrast, directional flow, consistency, and color.
13. Save the inside panels of the brochure and name it c06sa01, Panels.
14. Print and then close c06sa01, Panels.

figure
6.18 *Assessment 1*

SUPPORTING FINE ART

Art League Offerings

- Studio and Gallery Open to the Public

- Monthly Lectures and Demonstrations by Professional Artists

- Art Classes, Workshops, & Instruction

- Monthly Exhibits of Juried Fine Art in All Media

- Annual Student Art Show

- Waterfront Art Fair

- Annual Fine Arts Auction

- Annual Christmas Show & Sale

- "Sea and Sand"—Sculpture on the Waterfront by John Dwyer

ANNUAL ART EVENTS

Art for the New Millennium

Waterfront Art Fair
Juried Fine Arts Exhibition and Sale
September 13 & 14, 2000

Christmas Show & Sale
Fine Arts & Crafts
Guest Artists
**November 28, 2000 through
January 10, 2001**

34th Annual Fine Arts Auction
March 9, 2001

Student Art Show
Award Presentation and Open House
May 11, 2001

Membership

- Participate in all programs

- Exhibit work in the gallery

- Preference for workshops, classes, and demonstrations

CLASSES & WORKSHOPS

Classes

- Watercolors

- Pastels

- Oils

- Drawing and composition

- Framing

Class Schedule

Session I
   September 25–October 27, 2000
Session II
   January 15–February 16, 2001
Session III
   March 18–April 19, 2001

Regular Workshops

- Tuesday evening life drawing workshop at the Gallery, 7 p.m.

- Wednesday workshop at the Gallery, 12–4 p.m. All media.

Assessment 2

In this assessment, you will create the back panels of the brochure created in assessment 1. Include the following specifications:

1. Open c06sa01, Panels. Save the document to your hard drive or a floppy disk with Save As and name it c06sa02, Art brochure.
2. Referring to the dummy created in assessment 1, create the back panels of the art league brochure. A sample solution is provided in figure 6.19.
3. If you created a letter-fold brochure, remember to reverse the column settings for panels 4, 5, and 6. Make sure you select *This point forward* from the Apply to: list box at the Columns dialog box.
4. Apply any relevant styles created in assessment 1.
5. When creating the lines after Name, Address, Zip, and Phone, set a right tab at the position where the line is to end. When you need to insert a line, turn on underlining, press the Tab key, and then turn underlining off.

6. When creating the Zip and Phone lines, set a left tab where the Zip line is to end. Use underline as stated previously.
7. Use the Symbol dialog box to find a check box symbol.
8. Consider using a table to create the two columns of volunteer activities.
9. Make any adjustments to the spacing or positioning of text as you deem necessary.
10. Save the brochure document with the same name (c06sa02, Art brochure).
11. Print the first page of the brochure and then print the second page on the back of the first page. Fold your brochure and check the placement of text and images in relation to the folds. Make any adjustments as necessary to produce a professionally finished product.
12. Print a copy of the Document Evaluation Checklist located on your student CD. Evaluate your brochure using the checklist and make any additional adjustments if necessary.
13. Close c06sa02, Art brochure.

figure
6.19   Assessment 2

JOIN THE ART LEAGUE

Membership Application

Name: _____

Address: _____

Zip: _____ Phone: _____

Dues are payable June 1 for the year ending May 31.

☐ $5 Junior Membership (Jr./Sr. High)

☐ $24 Individual Membership

☐ $30 Family Membership

☐ $50 Contributing Membership

☐ $100 Supporting Membership

How would you like to participate in art league activities?

☐ Gallery   ☐ Committee
  volunteer   work

☐ Class instructor ☐ Workshops

☐ Exhibiting   ☐ Board member

Discover the artist in you!

Newport Art League
240 America's Cup Drive
Newport, RI 02040
Phone: (401) 555-2730
Fax: (401) 555-2732

Newport Art League

Studio & Art Gallery

Assessment 3

You are a member of a fundraising committee for a local charity. Pick a charity, plan an event to raise money, and create a brochure that promotes the charity and advertises the event.

1. Open Document Evaluation Checklist.doc located on your student CD and print one copy.
2. Use the Document Evaluation Checklist to analyze your brochure. Label the exercise as c06sa03.
3. Attach the completed form to the back of your brochure.

CREATIVE ACTIVITY

Visit a business and/or an organization and find examples of brochures. Places to look include a school or college, chamber of commerce office, travel agency, doctor's office, park district office, hotel lobby, or other publicly-accessed location. You will need four printed copies of the Document Evaluation Checklist.

a) Find two brochures that grab your attention. Use the Document Evaluation Checklist to help you identify the design elements that attracted you and made you want to pick up the two brochures. Write a short summary explaining what design elements are successful in each brochure and why.

b) Find two brochures that failed to grab your attention. Use the Document Evaluation Checklist to help you identify what is "wrong" with the two brochures. Write a short summary explaining the design problems in each brochure and discuss ways in which they could be improved.

c) Divide into small groups in class and share your findings with your group.

Chapter 07

Creating Specialty Promotional Documents

7

Using Resources in Desktop Publishing

By the time you reach this chapter, you will have accumulated a number of different examples of desktop publishing applications. As you know, studying the work of others is a great way to pick up pointers on layout and design, as well as interesting uses of fonts, color, text, and graphics. There are a number of published sources for useful project ideas, tips, and resources. Also, as mentioned earlier, paper supply companies offer pre-designed papers that are frequently available in catalogs; those catalogs may offer many helpful ideas for the layout and design of your documents.

Using Various Approaches to Creating Documents

You may have already realized that there are many different approaches to creating documents in Word. You must decide which approach is easiest for you to

295

remember and apply. Getting good at a skill takes a lot of practice and experimentation. You may begin thinking of other ways of creating documents that are more efficient or easier to adapt to your setting. Any one of the exercises presented in this chapter can be adapted to just about any personal or business situation. Although this text typically presents one or two different approaches to creating a document, there are usually many other ways to achieve the same results.

Creating Promotional Documents

Besides flyers and announcements, other promotional documents include tickets, enrollment forms, gift certificates, postcards, bookmarks, nametags, invitations, and business greeting cards. They become promotional documents when a business or organization name is visible or an item or service is mentioned for sale in a document.

Whether creating tickets for a charitable event, discount coupons for a grocery store, bookmarks promoting reading at a public library, or coasters advertising a local restaurant, Word's desktop publishing features combined with a little imagination can produce endless possibilities. Figure 7.1 illustrates other promotional documents created with the same basic design concepts and Word features used in most of the exercises in this chapter.

figure
7.1
Examples of Promotional Documents Created in Word

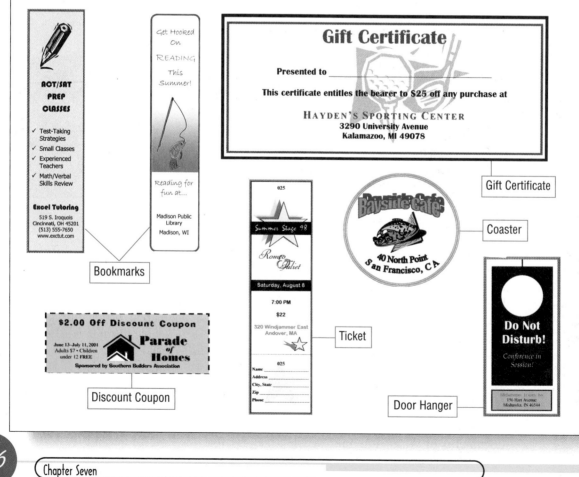

Web pages on the Internet can also be considered promotional in nature. The vast exposure of the World Wide Web provides endless possibilities for advertising products, services, research, data, and more, which may be presented on a company or corporation Web site. In chapter 8, you will learn how to design and lay out Web pages.

Using Tables to Create Promotional Documents

Tables are useful in desktop publishing because they offer options to format several objects consistently and predictably. Tables can give you precise control over layout. If your document needs to be separated by lines or has several areas that share a common border, tables can be a most efficient choice. However, tables require some planning before you use them in the layout of your document.

In exercise 1, you will use Word's table feature to format tickets and Word's SEQ fields to number the tickets and stubs sequentially.

Adding SEQ Fields for Numbering

You have probably worked with field codes before, although you may have not realized it. For instance, whenever you insert an automatic date, time, or page number, you are inserting field codes into your document. In the next exercise, you will create specific field codes that will produce desired results in your document. The field codes, formatted as { SEQ Identifier [Switches] }, will be used to enable sequential numbering in tickets and stubs. When working with syntaxes (see next page), you may use the Field dialog box as shown in figure 7.2, or you may key the necessary field codes directly into the document.

figure
7.2

Field Dialog Box

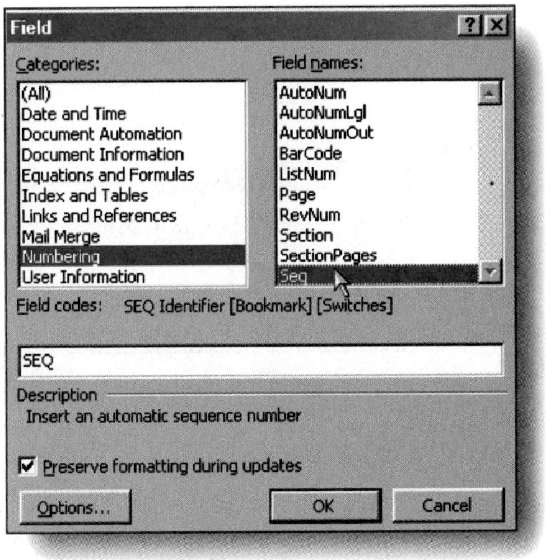

A *syntax* is a set of rules for entering field codes. Because the syntax for sequential numbering is relatively simple, you will key the necessary codes within the table format used to create the tickets and stubs in exercise 1. Keep the following syntax points in mind as you precisely key the required fields:

- Press Ctrl + F9 to produce the curly brackets around your insertion point. These curly brackets are called *field characters.*
- Press Alt + F9 to toggle field codes on/off.
- Leave one blank space after the left field character and before the right field character.
- The *identifier* is the name you will give the field, such as *TktNo* for ticket number.
- Leave one space between a switch and any parameters associated with the switch. A *switch* is a field instruction that changes the behavior or formatting of a field.
- If a field refers to a file name or specific text, enclose the text in quotation marks.
- To update a field, press F9.
- To update all the fields in a document, press Ctrl + A (select all), and then press F9.

As an active volunteer for Charlotte United Charities, you will create raffle tickets for a fundraiser. Each ticket will need a number printed twice—once on a ticket to serve as a claim ticket and once on a stub to be placed in a raffle. Print the tickets on 65 lb. uncoated cover stock or send a master copy of the ticket without the sequential numbering to a commercial printer to be copied, cut, numbered, and perforated.

exercise 1

Creating Tickets/Stubs with Sequential Numbering

1. At a clear document screen, create a table for the tickets in figure 7.3 by completing the following steps:
   a. Create a table with 2 columns and 4 rows.
   b. Select the entire table, click Table, and then click Table Properties.
   c. At the Table Properties dialog box, select the Row tab, click in the check box at the left of Specify height, and then change the setting to 2 inches. *Row height is* should display *At least.*
   d. Select the Column tab and key the column 1 width at **3.75** inches, click the Next Column button and change the column 2 width to **2.25** inches. Click OK or press Enter. *(Hint: You may have to click the Next Column button twice to get to the appropriate column.)*

e. Select the first column and change the right cell border to a dashed line at the Borders and Shading dialog box.

2. Save the document with Save <u>A</u>s and name it c07ex01, Raffle.

3. Insert the ticket and stub text by completing the following steps:

   a. Position the insertion point in the first cell in the first row and insert Raffle.doc located on your student CD.

   b. Position the insertion point in the second cell in the first row and insert Stub.doc located on your student CD.

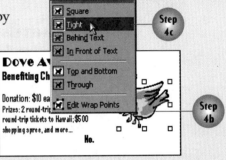

4. Insert the dove image by completing the following steps:

   a. Position the insertion point in the first cell of the first row and insert the dove image shown in figure 7.3. To find this image, access the Clip Gallery, key **dove** in the Search for clips: text box at the Insert ClipArt dialog box, press Enter, and then insert the image.

   b. Resize the clip art image similar to figure 7.3 by making it smaller.

   c. Select the dove, click the Text Wrapping button on the Picture toolbar, and then click <u>T</u>ight.

   d. Position the dove as shown in figure 7.3.

   e. Hold down the Ctrl key as you drag and drop a copy of the dove to the stub section of the ticket.

   f. Change the dove image in the stub into a watermark. Adjust the Contrast and Brightness if needed.

   g. Position the dove as shown in figure 7.3, click the Text Wrapping button, and then click Behin<u>d</u> Text.

5. Insert the sequential numbering by completing the following steps:

   a. Position the insertion point at the right of *No.* in the first cell in the first row and press the spacebar once.

   b. Press Ctrl + F9 (if needed, press Alt + F9 to display field codes). Within the braces, key: { **SEQ TktNo \# 000** }. Key the code *precisely* as shown. Do not key the braces.

   c. Position the insertion point at the right of *No.* in the second cell in the first row (stub), press the spacebar once, press Ctrl + F9, and then key { **SEQ TktNo \c \# 000** }.

   d. Select the first row and copy it to the clipboard.

   e. Position your insertion point in the next row and click Paste. (Press Alt + F9 if the field codes do not display.)

   f. Press F4 (repeat command) twice to create a total of 4 rows of tickets.

   g. Delete any empty rows that may appear on the next page.

h. Position the insertion point in the first cell and add **\r 101** (this is a switch) at the end of the field codes in the *first* cell only. The field codes in the first cell should display as

{ SEQ TktNo \# 000 \r 101 }

Step 5h

i. Position your insertion point anywhere in the table, press Ctrl + A to select everything, and then press F9 to update the fields. If the field codes are still on, press Alt + F9 to toggle the field codes off.

6. View your tickets in Print Preview.
7. Save the document again as c07ex01, Raffle.
8. Print and then close c07ex01, Raffle.

figure
7.3

Exercise 1

Dove Awards & Raffle	Name _____
Benefiting Charlotte Unified Charities	Address _____
Donation: $10 each or 3 for $25	City _____
Prizes: 2 round-trip tickets to London; 2 round-trip tickets to Hawaii; $500 shopping spree, and more...	State _____
No. 101	Phone _____
	No. 101

Dove Awards & Raffle	Name _____
Benefiting Charlotte Unified Charities	Address _____
Donation: $10 each or 3 for $25	City _____
Prizes: 2 round-trip tickets to London; 2 round-trip tickets to Hawaii; $500 shopping spree, and more...	State _____
No. 102	Phone _____
	No. 102

Dove Awards & Raffle	Name _____
Benefiting Charlotte Unified Charities	Address _____
Donation: $10 each or 3 for $25	City _____
Prizes: 2 round-trip tickets to London; 2 round-trip tickets to Hawaii; $500 shopping spree, and more...	State _____
No. 103	Phone _____
	No. 103

Dove Awards & Raffle	Name _____
Benefiting Charlotte Unified Charities	Address _____
Donation: $10 each or 3 for $25	City _____
Prizes: 2 round-trip tickets to London; 2 round-trip tickets to Hawaii; $500 shopping spree, and more...	State _____
No. 104	Phone _____
	No. 104

Building the Framework of a Form

One of the beginning steps in creating a form is to determine how the form will be completed—hard copy or online? Next, decide what information needs to be included in the form, and if there is an existing Word template that will fit your needs.

You will create a template from scratch by clicking New at the File menu and then selecting Templates in the Create New section. This form is created as a template so the original remains intact after an employee fills in the form. Information can only be keyed in the fields designated when the form was created.

The underlying structure of the form will be a table. You will draw a table for exercise 2 by using the Draw Table tool on the Tables and Borders toolbar. If you make a mistake, click the Eraser button, and drag to erase the lines you do not want.

Draw Table

Eraser

Adding Interactive Form Fields

The essential commands for creating and editing a form are grouped together on the Forms toolbar as discussed in chapter 4. The buttons on the Forms toolbar enable you to easily insert a text box, check box, or drop-down list.

Before you make the form available to users, protect it by clicking the Protect Form button on the Forms toolbar. Protection allows users to fill in the form, but prevents them from changing the form's layout. If you want to modify the form, click Protect Form again to unprotect the form.

Protect Form

If you save the template in exercise 2 to your hard drive, you will access it by clicking New at the File menu and double-clicking on the template in the specific tab where you saved it. Otherwise, you may access the template from the *DTP Templates* folder on your hard drive or floppy disk. In either case, if field codes display in the fill-in form fields as shown in figure 7.4, click Tools, click Options, and then remove the check mark at the left of *Field codes* at the View tab. The Field Shading option should display *Always*. The shading will display, but will not print.

figure
7.4

Completing a Forms Document

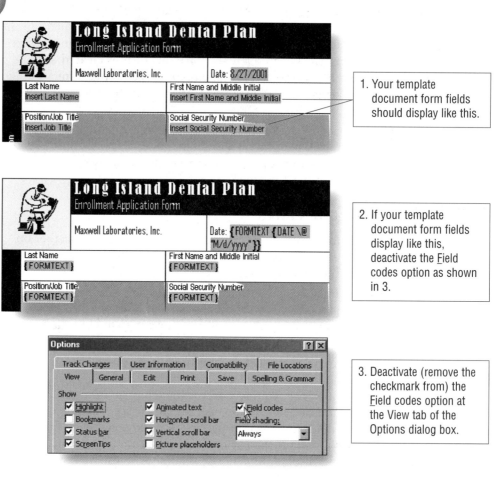

1. Your template document form fields should display like this.

2. If your template document form fields display like this, deactivate the Field codes option as shown in 3.

3. Deactivate (remove the checkmark from) the Field codes option at the View tab of the Options dialog box.

Whenever you are working in a form template document, press the Tab key to move to the next form field and Shift + Tab to move to a preceding form field. Press the spacebar to insert an X in a check box form field, click the down arrow at the right of the drop-down form field, and then click the desired choice.

As an employee in Human Resources at Maxwell Laboratories, you will create an enrollment application for employees interested in participating in the company's new dental plan. Maxwell employees will access the form via the company Intranet, so prepare the form for online completion.

exercise 2

Creating a Form

1. At a clear document screen, create the form in figure 7.5 by completing the following steps:
   a. Click File and New.
   b. At the New dialog box with the General tab selected, click Template in the Create New section, and then double-click Blank Document.
   c. Insert Dental.doc located on your student CD. The basic table structure has been created.
   d. Save the document and name it c07ex02, Dental.dot. (Consult your instructor if you should save the template to a floppy disk or to the hard drive.)
   e. Position the insertion point in the first cell in the first row and insert the dentist image shown in figure 7.5. Key **dentist** at the Search for clips: text box in the Insert ClipArt dialog box.
   f. Select the image and center it vertically and horizontally in the cell.
   g. Position the insertion point in the top cell to the right of the dentist image, and at the Borders and Shading dialog box, change the shading to Black. The text should automatically reverse to White. Make sure *Cell* is selected in the Apply to: list box.
   h. Press the spacebar once after *Date:* and insert a date code by clicking Insert, Date and Time. Select the fourth

   > **Long·Island·Dental·Plan¶**
   > Enrollment·Application·Form¤
   >
   > ¶
   > Maxwell·Laboratories,·Inc.¤   ¶ Date:·{ TIME·\@·"M/d/yyyy" }·¤

   Step 1f   **Step 1g**   **Step 1h**

   code from the top and make sure the option to Update automatically is selected. (The date command is actually a field code { TIME \@ "M/d/yyyy" }; press Alt + F9 to turn the field code off if necessary.)
   i. Position the insertion point in the first column of the table (the text is rotated). Key **Applicant Information** and then change the shading of the cell to Black. The text should automatically reverse to White.
   j. Display the Forms toolbar.
2. Insert field codes, that will prompt the applicant to fill in information, by completing the following steps:
   a. Position the insertion point below *Last Name*, click the Text Form Field button (first button) on the Forms toolbar, and make sure the Form Field Shading button (second button from the right) is active.
   b. Click the Form Field Options button on the Forms toolbar.

   Step 2c

   c. At the Text Form Field Options dialog box, make sure *Regular text* displays in the Type text box, key **Insert Last Name** in the Default text text box, and make sure *Unlimited* displays in the Maximum length list box. Click OK or press Enter.

Text Form Field Options	? X
Type: Regular text	Default text: Insert Last Name	OK / Cancel / Add Help Text...
Maximum length: Unlimited	Text format:	

d. Key the following text in the designated cell by following steps 2a, 2b, and 2c for each:

Insert First Name and Middle Initial	First Name and Middle Initial
Insert Job Title	Position/Job Title
Insert Social Security Number	Social Security Number
Insert Street Address	Street Address
Insert Birth Date	Date of Birth
Insert City, State, Zip Code	City, State, Zip Code
Insert Area Code + Phone Number	Home Phone Number
Insert Area Code + Phone Number/Ext.	Business Phone Number
Insert Dental Location Number	Dental Location Number

3. Create the check boxes for the empty cells, as shown in figure 7.5, by completing the following steps:
   a. Position the insertion point on the line below *Coverage Type*, click the Check Box Form Field button (second button) on the Forms toolbar, press the spacebar once, and then key **Single**; press Ctrl + Tab, create another check box, press the spacebar once, and then key **Single + 1**; press Ctrl + Tab, insert another check box, press the spacebar once, and then key **Family**.
   b. Position the insertion point below *Gender*, create a check box, press the spacebar once, and then key **Male**; press Ctrl + Tab, create another check box, press the spacebar once, and then key **Female**.
   c. Position the insertion point below *Marital Status* and then create a drop-down list:
      1) Click the Drop-Down Form Field button (third button) on the Forms toolbar and click the Form Field Options button (fourth button) on the Forms toolbar.
      2) At the Drop-Down Form Field Options dialog box, key **Single** in the Drop-down item text box and click the Add button.
      3) Add **Married**, **Divorced**, and **Widowed** to the list, following step 3c2.
      4) Click OK or press Enter.

4. Protect the template form by clicking the Protect Form button (last button) on the Forms toolbar.
5. Save the document again with the same name (c07ex02, Dental.dot).
6. Print and then close c07ex02, Dental.dot.
7. Open c07ex02, Dental.dot and make sure <u>D</u>ocument displays in the Create New section of the New dialog box. (*Hint:* If field codes display in the fill-in form fields, click <u>T</u>ools and <u>O</u>ptions and then remove the checkmark at the left of *Field codes* at the View tab. The Field Shading option should display *Always*.)

8. Select each text form field and key the appropriate information—use your own name, etc. or make up the information.
9. Click in the appropriate check box for the desired response.
10. Save the document and name it c07ex02, Dental 2.
11. Print and then close c07ex02, Dental 2.

figure
7.5

Exercise 2

| **Long Island Dental Plan** |
| Enrollment Application Form |

| Maxwell Laboratories, Inc. | Date: 9/17/2001 |

Applicant Information

| Last Name | First Name and Middle Initial |
| Insert Last Name | Insert First Name and Middle Initial |

| Position/Job Title | Social Security Number |
| Insert Job Title | Insert Social Security Number |

| Street Address | Gender | Date of Birth |
| Insert Street Address | ☐ Male   ☐ Female | Insert Birth Date |

| City, State, Zip Code | Marital Status |
| Insert City, State, Zip Code | Single |

| Home Phone Number | Business Phone Number + Ext. |
| Insert Area Code + Phone Number | Insert Area Code + Phone Number/Ext. |

| Coverage Type | Dental Location Number |
| ☐ Single   ☐ Single + 1   ☐ Family | Insert Dental Location Number |

Creating Postcards to Promote Business

If you have a brief message to get across to prospective customers, postcards can be an appropriate means of delivering the message. Postcards are inexpensive to create and use. They can be used as appointment reminders, just-moved notes, return/reply cards, display cards, thank you cards, or invitations. You can purchase pre-designed, printed postcards with attractive borders and color combinations, in differing sizes and weights that meet U.S. Postal Service standards; and you can find blank, pre-stamped 3-1/2 inch by 5-1/2 inch postcards at any U.S. Postal

DTP POINTERS
Choose a color from within a graphic to add color to text.

Service location. Or, you can use the Word Labels feature, which provides a predefined postcard sized at 4 inches by 6 inches. Two postcards will display on a standard-sized sheet of paper when you use Word's postcard label Avery 5389.

DTP POINTERS
Be aware of physical requirements for postcards.

Most postcards are created on 100- to 110-pound uncoated cover stock paper. The paperweight or thickness should be strong enough to hold up in the mail. The front side of the postcard is used for your return address and the recipient's address along with an area reserved for the postage. On the reverse, you can create a headline and use a graphic, photo, or watermark to emphasize the message. You will need to leave room for your message and optional signature.

exercise 3

Creating Postcards Using Word's Labels Feature

1. At a clear document screen, create the two postcards in figure 7.6 by completing the following steps:
   a. Display the Drawing, Tables and Borders, and Picture toolbars.
   b. Click Tools and then click Envelopes and Labels.
   c. At the Envelopes and Labels dialog box, select the Labels tab and click the Options button.
   d. At the Labels Options dialog box, select 5389 - Post Card in the Product number list box. Click OK or press Enter.
   e. At the Envelopes and Labels dialog box click the New Document button.
   f. Click Table and Show Gridlines if the gridlines are not displayed.
   g. Click the Align Top Left button on the Tables and Borders toolbar.
   h. With the insertion point located in the first postcard, press the spacebar once, and then press Enter.
   i. Insert the world image shown in figure 7.6. Key **world** in the Search for clips: text box at the Insert ClipArt dialog box.
   j. Select the world image and change the text wrap to In Front of Text.
   k. Size and position the image similar to figure 7.6.
   l. Right-click the picture and select Edit Picture from the shortcut menu.

Step 11

m. At the Microsoft Word Picture editor, double-click on the light green color (South America) on the globe, click the down arrow at the right of Color in the Fill section of the Format AutoShape dialog box. Click the More Color button, record the color settings, and then close Microsoft Word Picture. (If necessary, ungroup the image first and then select the green area. *Hint: 85, 73, 166.*)

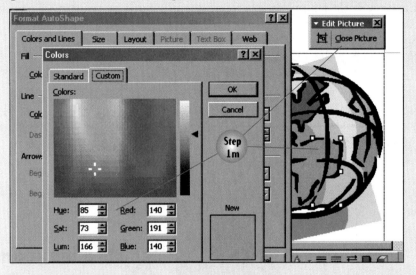

n. Insert the text by completing the following steps:
   1) Click the Text Box button on the Drawing toolbar and drag the crosshairs to draw a box approximately 2-1/2 inches square. (Verify at the Format Text Box dialog box.)
   2) Position the insertion point in the text box and key **See the world a little clearer, a little brighter with regular eye examinations.**
   3) Select *See the world* and change the font to 24-pt Bauhaus 93. Select the rest of the text and change the font to 24-pt Bradley Hand ITC bold.
   4) Right align the text and remove the borderline around the text box.
   5) Position the text box similar to figure 7.6. (If necessary, change the Fill Color to No Fill.)
o. Create the explosion shape by completing the following steps:
   1) Click the AutoShapes button on the Drawing toolbar, point to Stars and Banners, select the shape in the first row and second column *(Explosion 2),* and then drag the crosshairs to create the shape similar to figure 7.6.
   2) Select the shape and add the Fill Color that matches the light green in the picture by keying the settings you recorded in step 1m. Remove the borderline around the AutoShape.
   3) Size and position the shape similar to figure 7.6.
   4) Click the WordArt button on the Drawing toolbar and select the second style in the first row. *(Hint: You cannot rotate regular text in an AutoShape.)*

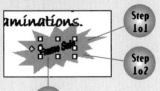

   5) At the Edit WordArt text box, key **Frame Sale** and change the font to 8 pt Arial. Click OK or press Enter. Center the text horizontally and vertically in the shape.
p. Insert the glasses image shown in figure 7.6. Key **glasses** in the Search for clips: text box at the Insert ClipArt dialog box.
q. Select the glasses and change the text wrap to In Front of Text.
r. Size and position the glasses similar to figure 7.6.

2. Copy the completed postcard to the postcard below by completing the following steps:
   a. Position the insertion point in the postcard and then select the row. *(Hint: The postcard is in a table format.)*
   b. Copy and paste the formatted postcard to the second postcard.
   c. Delete any empty rows.
3. Create a single 1/2 pt border around the postcards by selecting the entire table and clicking the All Borders button on the Tables and Borders toolbar.
4. Save the document with Save <u>A</u>s and name it c07ex03, Postcard.
5. Print two pages of postcards (4 cards in total) and then close c07ex03, Postcard.

figure

7.6   *Exercise 3*

Using Mail Merge in Promotional Documents

Mail merge is the process of combining variable information with standard text to create personalized documents. Word's Mail Merge feature enables you to create form letters, envelopes, labels, and catalogs. To do so, you merge a *main document*, which contains standard data such as the text of a form letter or the return address and picture on a postcard, with a *data source*, which contains varying data such as names and addresses. Special codes called *merge fields* in the main document direct Word to collect information from the data source and use it in the main document to create personalized documents. There are three basic processes involved in a mail merge:

1. Create a new main document or edit and designate an existing document as a main document.
2. Create a new data source or choose an existing one.
3. Perform the merge operation.

Word can create a merge from many different data sources. These sources include a Word document formatted in a table, tab, or comma-delimited format; an imported application or database such as Microsoft Access, Excel, dBASE, Paradox, etc; and a shared office file such as the Personal Address Book, Outlook, or Microsoft Network lists. You will create a data source formatted in a table.

Using the Mail Merge Helper

Figure 7.7 illustrates the Mail Merge Helper dialog box, which lays out the three stages in creating a merged document—creating a main document, creating a data source, and completing a merge. Click Tools and Mail Merge to access this dialog box. In exercise 4, you will use Mail Merge Helper to merge addresses onto the reverse side of the four postcards created in exercise 3.

Mail merge
The process of combining variable information with standard text to create personalized documents.

Main document
A form that receives the data.

Data source
Contains variable data such as names and addresses.

Merge fields
Merge fields are special codes in the main document that direct Word to collect information from the data source and use it in the main document to create personalized documents.

figure
7.7

Mail Merge Helper Dialog Box

Click the down arrow and select the type of mail merge main document you want to create.

Creating a Data Source

When creating a data source, consider the present and future uses of this information. The data source contains the variable information that will be inserted in the main document. Word provides predetermined field names for this purpose, which you may use if they represent the data you are creating.

Variable information in a data source is saved as a *record*. A record contains all the information for one unit (for example, a person, family, customer, client, or business). A series of fields makes one record, and a series of records makes a data source.

Record

Contains all the information for one unit (person, family, or business).

exercise 4

Creating a Data Source

1. At a clear document screen, create a data source containing the information shown in figure 7.8 by completing the following steps:
   a. Click Tools and Mail Merge.
   b. At the Mail Merge Helper dialog box shown in figure 7.7, click the Create button. From the drop-down list that displays, click Mailing Labels.
   c. At the dialog box asking if you want to use the active document or a new document window, select Active Window. (This is the clear document screen behind the dialog box.)
   d. Click the Get Data button and then click Create Data Source at the drop-down list.
   e. At the Create Data Source dialog box shown in figure 7.9, the fields provided by Word are shown in the Field names in header row list box. These fields are needed for the data source in this exercise: *Title, FirstName, LastName, Address1, Address 2, City, State,* and *PostalCode.*
   f. To remove *JobTitle* or any other unwanted fields, click the down arrow on the vertical scroll bar at the right of the Field names in header row list box until *JobTitle* is visible. Click *JobTitle* in the list box and then click Remove Field Name. When *Job Title* is removed, it will display in the Field name text box. Remove the following unwanted fields from the Field names in header row list box: *Job Title, Company, Country, HomePhone,* and *WorkPhone.* Click OK or press Enter.

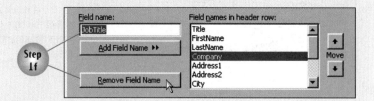

   g. Save the document with Save As and name it c07ex04, Postcard data source.

h. At the dialog box containing the warning that the data source contains no data, click Edit Data Source. This displays the Data Form dialog box shown in figure 7.10.

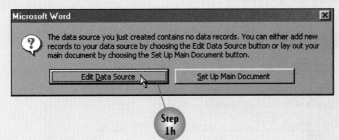

i. At the Data Form dialog box, key the title **Mrs.** for the first customer shown in figure 7.10, and then press the Enter key or the Tab key.
j. Continue keying the information in figure 7.8 for the customer, Mrs. Peggy McSherry, in the appropriate fields.
k. After entering all the information for Mrs. Peggy McSherry, click the Add New button. This saves the information and displays a blank Data Form dialog box. Continue keying the information for each person in this manner until all records shown in figure 7.8 have been created.
l. After creating the last record for the data source, click the View Source button and compare your document to figure 7.11.
2. Click the Save button on the Standard toolbar.
3. Close c07ex04, Postcard data source.
4. At the clear window, close the document without saving it.

figure

7.8

Data Source Client Information

Title	=	Mrs.	Title	=	Mr.
FirstName	=	Peggy	FirstName	=	Eric
LastName	=	McSherry	LastName	=	Gohlke
Address1	=	3055 Kinzie Court	Address1	=	3090 North Orchard
Address2	=		Address2	=	
City	=	Wheaton	City	=	Downers Grove
State	=	IL	State	=	IL
PostalCode	=	60187	PostalCode	=	60515
Title	=	Mrs.	Title	=	Ms.
FirstName	=	Kathleen	FirstName	=	Margo
LastName	=	Nixon	LastName	=	Godfrey
Address1	=	409 Highland Drive	Address1	=	Apartment 105B
Address2	=		Address2	=	993 Sandpiper Lane
City	=	Downers Grove	City	=	Westmont
State	=	IL	State	=	IL
PostalCode	=	60515	PostalCode	=	60599

Create Data Source Dialog Box

7.9

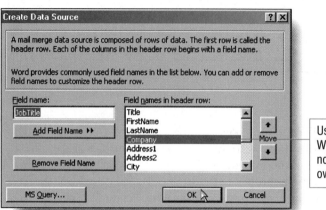

Use these fields provided by Word. Remove fields you do not need and/or add your own fields.

figure

7.10

Data Form Dialog Box

Press the Tab key to move to the next field or press Shift + Tab to move to the previous field.

Chapter Seven

figure

7.11

Postcard Data Source

Title	FirstName	LastName	Address1	Address2	City	State	PostalCode
Mrs.	Peggy	McSherry	3055 Kinzie Court		Wheaton	IL	60187
Mrs.	Kathleen	Nixon	409 Highland Drive		Downers Grove	IL	60515
Mr.	Eric	Gohlke	3090 North Orchard		Downers Grove	IL	60515
Ms.	Margo	Godfrey	Apartment 105B	993 Sandpiper Lane	Westmont	IL	60599

The header row identifies the names of the fields.

Creating the Main Document

When you have determined the fields and field names and created the data source, the next step is to create the main document. When the main document is completed and the fields have been inserted in the proper locations, it will look similar to the postcards shown in figure 7.12.

Notice in figure 7.12 that there is a space between the fields. Spaces, and any punctuation, are inserted between fields as if there were text so that when the variable information is inserted, it is spaced correctly. In addition, key a comma and space between the *<City>* field and the *<State>* field in an address. Fields can be used in a main document as often as needed.

Postcard Main Document

NAPER GROVE VISION CARE
5018 Fairview Avenue
Downers Grove, IL 60515
(630) 555-3932

JUST A FRIENDLY REMINDER...

It's time for your eye examination.
Please call our office now
for your appointment.

«Title» «FirstName» «LastName»
«Address1»
«Address2»
«City», «State» «PostalCode»

«NEXT RECORD»NAPER GROVE VISION CARE
5018 Fairview Avenue
Downers Grove, IL 60515
(630) 555-3932

JUST A FRIENDLY REMINDER...

It's time for your eye examination.
Please call our office now
for your appointment.

«Title» «FirstName» «LastName»
«Address1»
«Address2»
«City», «State» «PostalCode»

Merging Information to a Postcard

Merge to Printer

Once the data source and the main document have been created, they can be merged. Merged documents can be saved in a new document or sent directly to the printer. A main document and a data source can be merged with buttons on the Mail Merge toolbar or with options at the Mail Merge Helper dialog box.

When a main document is open, the Mail Merge toolbar shown in figure 7.13 displays. Figure 7.13 identifies each button on the Mail Merge toolbar. To merge to the printer, open the main document and then click the Merge to Printer button on the Mail Merge toolbar or select Printer at the Merge to: list box at the Merge dialog box accessed through the Mail Merge Helper. In exercise 5, place the printed postcards from exercise 3 into your printer. (Be careful to position them correctly into the printer so the merge will occur on the reverse side of each postcard.)

figure

Mail Merge Toolbar

| Insert Merge Field ▾ | Insert Word Field ▾ | «» ABC | ◀ | ◀ | 1 | ▶ | ▶◀ | | | | Merge... | | |

Insert Merge Field
Insert Word Field
View Merged Data
First Record
Previous Record
Go To Record
Next Record
Last Record
Mail Merge Helper
Check for Errors
Merge to New Document
Merge to Printer
Start Mail Merge
Find Record
Edit Data Source

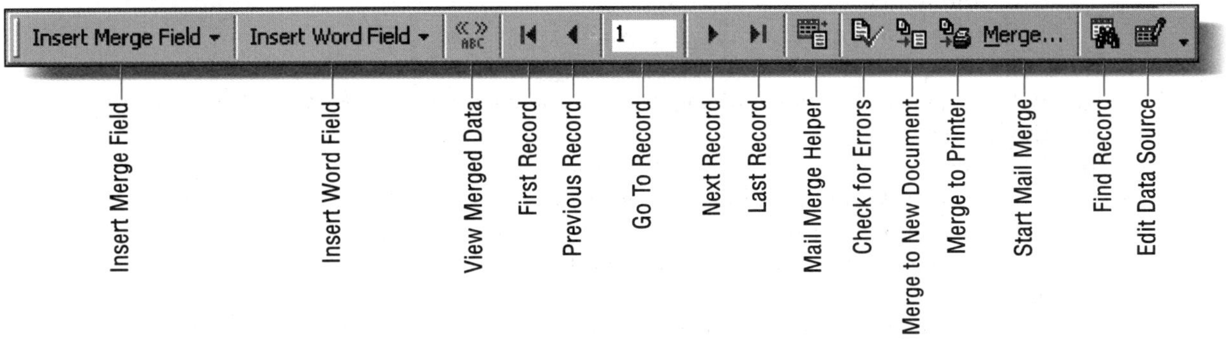

exercise 5

Creating a Main Document and Merging

1. At a clear document screen, create an AutoText entry for the main document shown in figure 7.12 by completing the following steps:
    a. Key the following return address and message in the formatting given below.

NAPER GROVE VISION CARE	(16-pt Arial in Small caps with Shadow)
5018 Fairview Avenue	(12-pt Arial)
Downers Grove, IL 60515	
(630) 555-3932	
JUST A FRIENDLY REMINDER...	(12-pt Arial bold, All caps, apply Green color—85, 72, 166.
It's time for your eye examination.	(12-pt Arial)
Please call our office now	
for your appointment.	

    b. Press Enter.
    c. Create an AutoText entry from the text in step 1a by completing the following steps:
        1) Press Ctrl + A to select all.
        2) Click Insert, point to AutoText, and then click New.
        3) At the Create AutoText dialog box, key **Postcard** in the Create AutoText entry text box.
        4) Click OK or press Enter.
        5) With the text still selected, press the Delete key.

2. Create the main document using the Mail Merge Helper by completing the following steps:
   a. Click Tools and Mail Merge.
   b. At the Mail Merge Helper dialog box, click Create (below *Main Document*).
   c. At the drop-down list that displays, click Mailing Labels.
   d. Click the Active Window button.
   e. At the Mail Merge Helper dialog box, click Get Data (below *Data source*).
   f. At the drop-down list that displays, click Open Data Source.
   g. At the Open Data Source dialog box, double-click *c07ex04, Postcard data source* in the list box.
   h. Click the Set Up Main Document button.
   i. At the Labels Options dialog box, make sure *5389 – Post Card* is selected in the Product number: list box. Click OK or press Enter.
   j. Position the insertion point in the Sample label text box.
   k. Key **Postcard** and press F3. (The return address and message should display.)
   l. Insert the merge field codes into the Sample Label by completing the following steps:
      1) From the left edge of the Sample Label, press Ctrl + Tab six times.
      2) Click the Insert Merge Field button, click *Title* from the drop-down menu, and then press the spacebar once.
      3) Click the Insert Merge Field button, click *FirstName* from the drop-down menu, and then press the spacebar once. (The merge fields may wrap to the next line—do not be concerned!)
      4) Click the Insert Merge Field button, click *LastName*, and then press Enter.
      5) Press Ctrl + Tab six times.
      6) Click the Insert Merge Field button, click *Address1*, and then press Enter.
      7) Press Ctrl + Tab six times.
      8) Click the Insert Merge Field button, click *Address2*, and then press Enter.
      9) Press Ctrl + Tab six times and continue inserting the *City*, *State*, and *PostalCode* merge fields, including a comma between the city and state and using spaces as you would in regular address text. Click OK.
3. Merge the data source to the mail document by completing the following steps:
   a. At the Mail Merge Helper dialog box, click the Merge button under *Merge the data with the document*.
   b. At the Merge dialog box, make sure you merge to a *New document*, and then click the Merge button.
4. Select all four postcards and add a borderline around each postcard.
5. Save the merged postcards and name them c07ex05, Merged.
6. Insert the four postcards created in exercise 3 into your printer, correctly, and print c07ex05, Merged to the reverse side of the postcards as shown in figure 7.14.
7. Close c07ex05, Merged.
8. Save the main document and name it c07ex05, Postcard main document.
9. Close c07ex05, Postcard main document.

figure
7.14
Merged Postcards

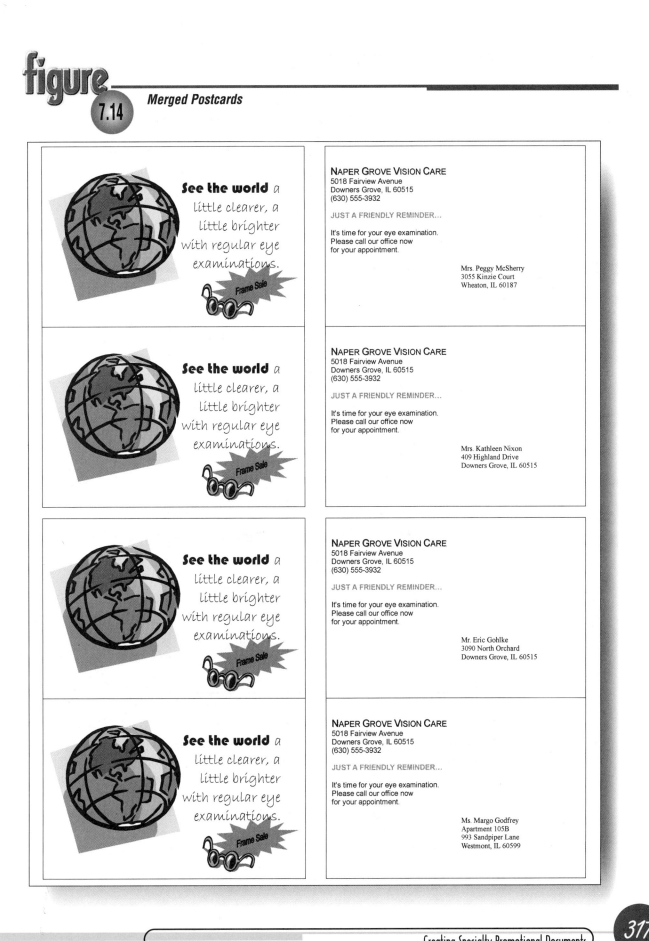

Creating Invitations and Cards

You will be using a table and the 2 pages per sheet option at Page Setup to format various cards, such as holiday cards, business or personal invitations, seminar or open house announcements, personal notes, and even birth announcements. Figure 7.15 illustrates the result of dividing a standard-sized sheet of paper into four cells using a table, which is then folded to accommodate text and graphics. Each of the four panels (cells) in figure 7.15 has been identified with a panel number and marked with instructions for rotating text and graphics.

figure 7.15

Guide for Creating Cards in Portrait Orientation

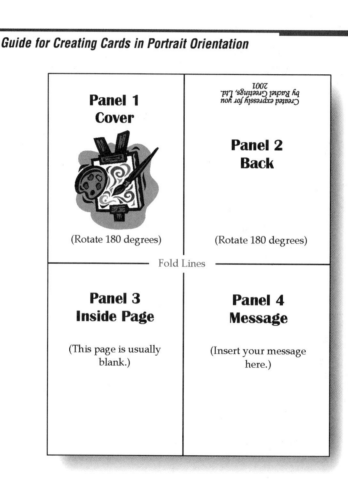

Panel 1 Cover

(Rotate 180 degrees)

Created expressly for you by Rachel Greetings, Ltd. 2001

Panel 2 Back

(Rotate 180 degrees)

Fold Lines

Panel 3 Inside Page

(This page is usually blank.)

Panel 4 Message

(Insert your message here.)

Another method produces two invitations or cards on a single sheet of landscaped paper divided into four sections. Using this method, you may key, format, and print the text on one side of a sheet of paper and then reinsert the paper into your printer and print text and/or graphics on the reverse side. The final step is then cutting the paper in half and folding the top to meet the bottom as shown in figure 7.16.

figure
7.16

Guide for Creating Cards in Landscape Orientation

As discussed in chapter 6, Word provides an option to print two half-sheet pages printed in landscape or portrait orientation on the same sheet. A page border may be added to both pages or to just one as shown in figure 7.17. This option is conducive to creating cards in varying sizes and layouts. Also consider folding a half sheet in half again and printing on card stock.

figure
7.17

Guide for Creating Cards Using Two Half-Sheet Pages

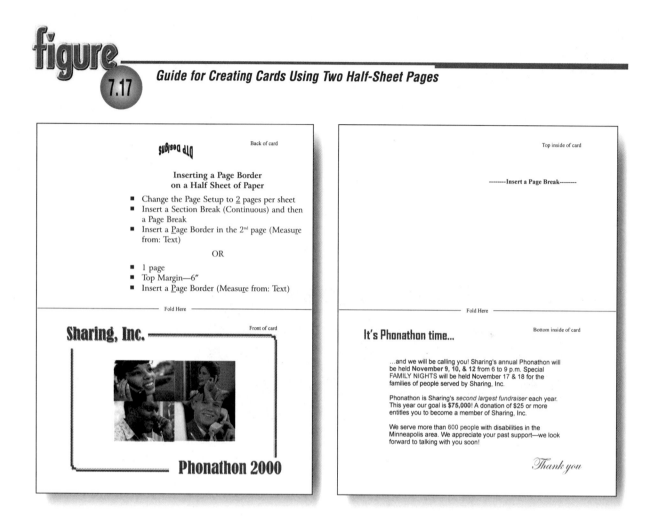

Planning and Designing Cards

In planning and designing your cards, consider focus, balance, consistency, proportion, contrast, and directional flow. Because you are working in a small area, remember to allow plenty of white space around design elements. If you are using a graphic image for focus, be sure that the image relates to the subject of the card. Promote consistency through the use of color, possibly picking out one or two colors from the graphic image used in your card and including the company logo, if one is available, to promote consistency among company documents. Select one or two fonts that match the tone of the document.

Your choice of paper is also important—consider using a heavier weight paper, such as 60- or 65-pound uncoated cover stock paper. Packaged card stock such as HP Greeting Card or HP Premium Inkjet Heavyweight may be used to produce near store-quality cards. Also consider using marbleized paper or parchment paper for invitations and other types of cards.

The envelope size used with the HP Greeting Card paper package measures 5-3/4 inches by 8-3/4 inches. To print a custom-sized envelope, key the desired dimensions at the Envelope Size dialog box as shown in figure 7.18. Refer to your printer documentation to determine the correct way to load envelopes for your specific printer. If you have a long list of recipients, consider creating a master copy of your card and taking it to a commercial printer to have it reproduced and machine folded. For a mass mailing of an invitation or a holiday card, consider creating a data source consisting of names and addresses, and then merging this information onto envelopes or mailing labels.

figure
7.18

Selecting a Custom-Sized Envelope

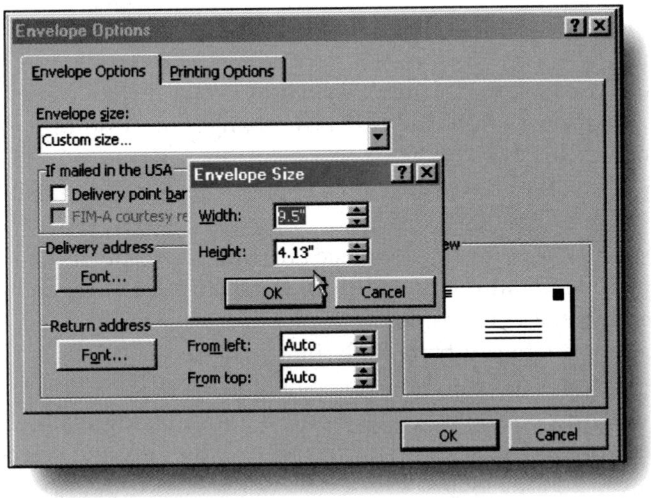

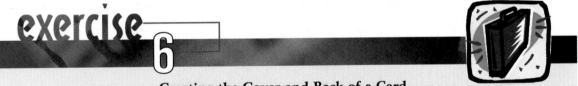

exercise
6

Creating the Cover and Back of a Card

1. At a clear document screen, create the cover and back of the card shown in figure 7.19 by completing the following steps:
   a. Click File and Page Setup.
   b. Select the Margins tab at the Page Setup dialog box and select the option for 2 pages per sheet. Click OK or press Enter.
   c. With the insertion point positioned in the first one-half sheet (page 1), insert a Next page Section break.
   d. With the insertion point now positioned in the second one-half sheet (page 2), draw one text box measuring approximately 3/4 inch by 2-3/4 inches. Double-click the box and verify the measurements at the Format Text Box dialog box at the Size tab.
   e. Choose the Layout tab and click the Advanced button.

f. For the horizontal position of the text box, change the Absolute position to 0.65 inch to the left of *Page*.

g. For the vertical position, change the Absolute position to 0.4 inch below *Page*. Click OK twice.

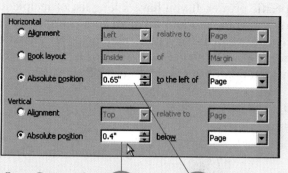

Step 1g   **Step 1f**

h. Position the insertion point in the text box, change the font to 36-pt Bernard MT Condensed in Green with Shadow, and then key **Sharing, Inc.** Center the text within the text box and remove the border around the text box.

i. Create another text box measuring 3/4 inch by 3-3/4 inches. Verify the setting.

j. For the horizontal position of the text box, change the Absolute position to 4.10 inches to the left of *Page*.

k. For the vertical position of the text box, change the Absolute position to 4.35 inches below *Page*.

l. Position the insertion point in it, change the font to 36-pt Bernard MT Condensed in Green, and then key **Phonathon 2000**. Center the text and remove the border around the text box.

m. Create the border on page 2 by completing the following steps:
   1) Click Format and then Borders and Shading.
   2) Select the Page Border tab at the Borders and Shading dialog box.
   3) Click the down arrow at the right of the Arts list box and select the border shown in the graphic below.
   4) Change the border Color to Green and the border Width to 12 pts.
   5) Click the down arrow at the right of the Apply to: list box and select *This section*.

Step 1m2

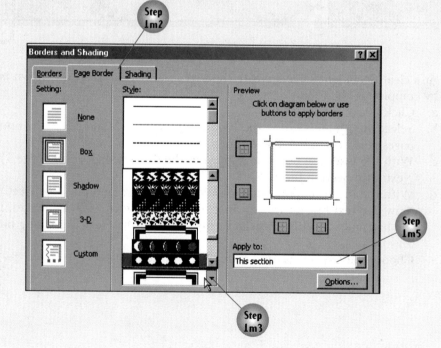

Step 1m5

Step 1m3

6) Click the <u>O</u>ptions button and at the Border and Shading Options dialog box, change the T<u>o</u>p and Botto<u>m</u> margins to 10 pts and the <u>L</u>eft and <u>R</u>ight margins to 2 pts.

7) Click the down arrow at the right of the Meas<u>u</u>re from: list box and select *Text*.

8) Be sure to deselect all the check boxes in the Options section (no checkmarks).

9) Click OK and click OK again to close the Borders and Shading dialog box.

n. Create the photo image in the center of the card by completing the following steps:

1) Insert one of the telephone images shown in figure 7.19. At the Insert ClipArt dialog box, click the *Photographs* category, scroll to find the image, and then click the Insert clip button. Resize the image to 1.25 inches by 1.88 inches, select the photo, and then change the text wrap to I<u>n</u> *Front of Text*.

2) Insert the other three telephone images shown in figure 7.19. These images are also found in the *Photographs* category. Select each of the following photos, resize each to 1.25 inches by 1.88 inches, and then select each photo again and change the text wrap to I<u>n</u> *Front of Text*.

3) Align the photos as shown in figure 7.19, hold down the Shift key and select each photo. Click the <u>D</u>raw button on the Drawing toolbar and then click <u>G</u>roup.

4) Double-click the combined photo and click <u>C</u>enter in the Horizontal alignment section of the Layout tab at the Format Object dialog box.

5) Position the photo vertically similar to figure 7.19.

o. Add the design logo to page 1 by completing the following steps:

1) Press Ctrl + Home to position the insertion point in the first page.

2) Click the Insert WordArt button on the Drawing toolbar, select the fourth style in the first row, and then click OK.

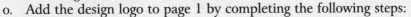

3) Key **DTP Designs** in the Edit WordArt Text text box, change the font to 18-pt Arial Black, and then click OK.

4) Select the logo and click the Free Rotate button on the Drawing toolbar. Rotate the WordArt image 180 degrees.

5) Position the logo similar to figure 7.19.

2. Save the cover and back of the card and name the document c07ex06, Cover.
3. Print and then close c07ex06, Cover.
4. Open Sharing.doc located on your student CD.
5. Save this for the inside document and name it c07ex06, Inside.
6. Place the printed cover from step 3 into your printer. (Be careful to position it correctly so the inside document will print on the reverse side of the cover.)
7. Print and then close c07ex06, Inside.

figure

7.19

Exercise 6

DTP Designs

Sharing, Inc.

Phonathon 2000

It's Phonathon time...

...and we will be calling you! Sharing's annual Phonathon will be held November 9, 10, & 12 from 6 to 9 p.m. Special FAMILY NIGHTS will be held November 17 & 18 for the families of people served by Sharing, Inc.

Phonathon is Sharing's *second largest fundraiser* each year. This year our goal is $75,000! A donation of $25 or more entitles you to become a member of Sharing, Inc.

We serve more than 600 people with disabilities in the Minneapolis area. We appreciate your past support—we look forward to talking with you soon!

Thank you

Creating Name Badges

An appropriate name badge (tag) shows your name, your title, and the company or organization with which you are affiliated. The individual's name should be easy to read and the most dominant element on the name tag. Remembering a person's name is one of the biggest compliments you can pay to that person. However, if you are in a business where you meet a lot of people, remembering names can be difficult. Name badges can definitely reduce the embarrassment of forgetting someone's name.

An alternative to choosing labels for name badges is to purchase nametag holders and insert a business card or name badge printed on heavier weight paper inside the holder. The holder is a clear plastic sleeve with a clip or pin on the reverse. Holders are usually available through mail order paper companies or office supply companies.

exercise 7

Creating Name Badges Using Merge

1. At a clear document screen, create the name badges in figure 7.20 by completing the following steps:
   a. Display the Drawing toolbar and the Tables and Borders toolbar.
   b. Click Tools and Mail Merge.
   c. At the Mail Merge Helper dialog box, click Create and select Mailing Labels from the drop-down list. At the question asking if you want to use the active document window or a new document, create Active Window.
   d. At the Mail Merge Helper dialog box, click Get Data (below Data source).
   e. At the drop-down list that displays, click Open Data Source.
   f. At the Open Data Source dialog box, double-click Floral Data Source.doc located on your student CD.
   g. At the prompt *Word needs to set up your main document*, click the Set Up Main Document button.
   h. At the Label Options dialog box, select *5095 - Name Badge* in the Product number: list box, and click OK or press Enter.
   i. At the Create Labels dialog box, click OK. (You will not key text in the Sample Label text box.)
   j. At the Mail Merge Helper dialog box, click Edit under the Main document section and click Mailing Label: Document#.

k. Format the nametag text and insert merge fields by completing the following steps:
   1) Make sure the table gridlines display.
   2) Position the insertion point in the first cell and click the Align Top Left button on the Tables and Borders toolbar.
   3) Position the insertion point on the second paragraph symbol that displays. Turn on Show/Hide ¶.
   4) Change the alignment to Center and turn on <u>K</u>erning at 14 points.
   5) Change the font to 16-point Britannic Bold in S<u>m</u>all caps. Click the Insert Merge Field button on the Mail Merge toolbar and select *Association* from the drop-down list.
   6) Press Ctrl + Tab, click <u>I</u>nsert, and then click <u>S</u>ymbol. Select the <u>S</u>ymbols tab and change the <u>F</u>ont to Wingdings. Select the symbol in the fifth row and the tenth column. Click <u>I</u>nsert and Close.

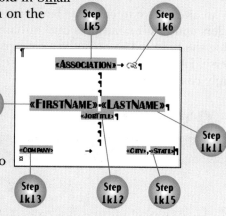

   7) Select the symbol and change the color to Teal.
   8) Deselect the symbol, change the font to 11-point Britannic Bold in Black, and then press Enter four times.
   9) Change the font to 20-point Britannic Bold.
   10) Click the Insert Merge Field button on the Mail Merge toolbar and click *FirstName*.
   11) Press the space bar once, click the Insert Merge Field button, and then click *LastName*.
   12) Change the font to 11-point Britannic Bold. Press Enter and insert the *JobTitle* field.
   13) Press Enter four times, change the alignment to Align Left, and then insert the *Company* field.
   14) Create a right tab at approximately 3-1/4 inches on the Ruler.
   15) Press Ctrl + Tab and insert the *City* and *State* fields separated by a comma and space.
   16) Select by dragging from the paragraph symbol above *FirstName* to the paragraph symbol below *JobTitle*, click F<u>o</u>rmat, click <u>B</u>orders and Shading, and then select the <u>S</u>hading tab. Click the Teal color in the fifth row of the color palette. Make sure *Paragraph* displays in the Apply to text box and click OK or press Enter.

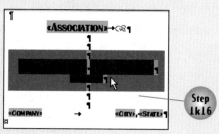

   17) Select *FirstName*, *LastName*, and *JobTitle* and change the font color to White.
l. Save the nametag text as an AutoText entry by completing the following steps:
   1) Select by dragging through the nametag text beginning with the Enter at the top of the cell and including the last line of text in the cell.
   2) With this text selected, click <u>I</u>nsert, point to <u>A</u>utoText, and then click <u>N</u>ew.

3) At the Create AutoText dialog box, key **floral** in the text box. Click OK.

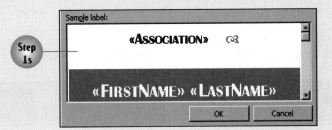

Step 113

m. Close the document window without saving.
n. At a clear document screen, click Tools and Mail Merge.
o. At the Mail Merge Helper dialog box, click Create, and select *Mailing Labels*. At the dialog box that displays, click Active Window.
p. Click Get Data and click *Open Data Source* from the drop-down menu. At the Open dialog box, double-click Floral data source.doc located on your student CD.
q. Click the Set Up Main Document button.
r. Select *5095 - Name Badge* in the Product number: list box in the Label Options dialog box and click OK or press Enter.
s. With the insertion point positioned in the Sample label text box, key **floral**, and then press F3. Click OK to close the Create Labels dialog box.

Step 1s

Sample label:

«ASSOCIATION» ⌘

«FIRSTNAME» «LASTNAME»

OK   Cancel

t. At the Mail Merge Helper dialog box, click Merge.
u. At the Merge dialog box, make sure *New document* displays in the Merge to: list box and then click Merge.
2. Save the document and name it c07ex07, Nametag.
3. Print and then close c07ex07, Nametag.
4. Save the main document and name it Floral main document.doc.
5. Close Floral main document.doc.

Optional: Add borderlines around each of the nametags by selecting the entire table; clicking Format and then Borders and Shading; select the Borders tab and then click All in the Settings: section of the Borders and Shading dialog box.

MIDWEST FLORAL ASSOCIATION ⏎	MIDWEST FLORAL ASSOCIATION ⏎
LISA WEBER DIRECTOR OF FLORAL MARKETING	**RACHEL HARTFORD** SALES REPRESENTATIVE
MAY FOODS, INC.　　　　INDIANAPOLIS, IN	J. C. DESIGNS, INC.　　　　AURORA, IL
MIDWEST FLORAL ASSOCIATION ⏎	MIDWEST FLORAL ASSOCIATION ⏎
MARCUS COLLINS BUYER	**AJAY PATEL** REGIONAL MANAGER
INTERNATIONAL PACKAGING, INC.　　CHICAGO, IL	EAST LAKE EXPORT　　　　CINCINNATI, OH
MIDWEST FLORAL ASSOCIATION ⏎	MIDWEST FLORAL ASSOCIATION ⏎
MARIE DuBOIS BUYER	**CARLOS MARTINEZ** MIDWEST SALES MANAGER
MIDWEST FOODS, INC.　　　SOUTHFIELD, MI	FLORAL INTERNATIONAL　　　CHICAGO, IL
MIDWEST FLORAL ASSOCIATION ⏎	MIDWEST FLORAL ASSOCIATION ⏎
JOSEPH CHAPLIN RETAIL SALES MANAGER	**SAMUEL WEISS** VICE-PRESIDENT
AFD LIMITED, INC.　　　SPRINGFIELD, IL	SAM'S FLORAL SUPPLIES　　SOUTH BEND, IN

chapter summary

➤ The Labels feature formats your document so that you can print on designated label sheets.

➤ Use the AutoText feature to assist you in formatting documents created in Word's Label feature.

➤ Field codes are used to format date, time, and page numbers automatically.

➤ To insert field codes in a document, you can key the field code syntax, or click the field you want in the Field names list at the Field dialog box.

➤ Syntax is a set of rules for entering field codes.

➤ The curly brackets used around field codes are called field characters.

➤ The identifier is the name you give a field.

➤ A switch is a field instruction that changes the behavior or formatting of a field.

➤ Press Ctrl + F9 to access the field characters; press Alt + F9 to toggle field codes on and off; and press F9 to update fields.

➤ To display field results instead of field codes, clear the Field codes check box at the Options dialog box.

➤ When a form template is created and then protected, the text in the template can still be changed. To make changes, you must unprotect the document.

➤ To unprotect a template document, click the Protect Form button on the Forms toolbar to deactivate it.

➤ Word includes a mail merge feature that you can use to create letters, envelopes, postcards, and much more, all with personalized information.

➤ The data source and the main document may be merged to a new document or to the printer.

➤ A data source document and a main document are needed to perform a merge. A data source document contains the variable information. The main document contains the standard text along with identifiers showing where variable information is to be inserted.

➤ A record contains all the information for one unit (person, family, customer, or client).

➤ Merge fields are special codes in the main document that direct Word to collect information from the data source and use it in the main document to create personalized documents.

➤ Unwanted field names can be removed and additional field names can be added at the Create Data Source dialog box.

➤ Any formatting codes you want applied to the merged document should be inserted in the main document.

➤ Use Word's Mail Merge Helper to assist you in creating the data source, main document, and merge.

➤ Mail merge is the process of combining variable information with standard text to create personalized documents.

➤ Text added to an AutoShape by right-clicking and selecting Add Text cannot be rotated.

➤ Use the Rotate or Flip option at the Draw menu or use the Free Rotate tool on the Drawing toolbar to rotate pictures or objects.

➤ Use Microsoft Word Picture (graphic editor) to group an image before flipping it vertically or horizontally.

➤ The 2 pages per sheet feature reduces each page to the size of a half page.

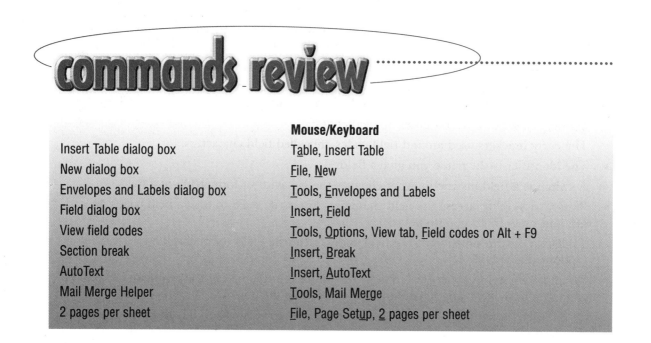

commands review

	Mouse/Keyboard
Insert Table dialog box	Table, Insert Table
New dialog box	File, New
Envelopes and Labels dialog box	Tools, Envelopes and Labels
Field dialog box	Insert, Field
View field codes	Tools, Options, View tab, Field codes or Alt + F9
Section break	Insert, Break
AutoText	Insert, AutoText
Mail Merge Helper	Tools, Mail Merge
2 pages per sheet	File, Page Setup, 2 pages per sheet

thinking offline

True/False: Circle the letter T if the statement is true; circle the letter F if the statement is false.

T F 1. A main document is a document that contains variable information about customers, clients, products, etc.

T F 2. You can insert an AutoText entry in a document by keying the AutoText entry name and then pressing Alt + F3.

T F 3. *FirstName*, *JobTitle*, and *Address1* are examples of field names.

T F 4. Field codes are used to format date, time, and page numbers automatically.

T F 5. The AutoText feature can be used to store text and graphics used to format a label.

T F 6. Text created in WordArt can be rotated.

T F 7. Press Alt + F9 to access the field characters.

T F 8. Mail merge involves two documents.

T F 9. The 2 pages per sheet feature is accessed from the Format menu.

T F 10. A watermark cannot be created inside a cell of a table.

Completion: In the spaces provided, indicate the correct term, command, or number.

1. To position a watermark below the text layer, click the Text Wrapping button on the Picture toolbar, and then select this option: _____.

2. The data source and the main document can be merged to a new document or to the _____.

3. Press _____ to access the field characters (*Hint:* This is a keyboard command.)

4. To unprotect a template document, click the _____ button on the Forms toolbar to deactivate it.

5. You can merge the source document to the main document by clicking the Merge to New Document button on the _____ toolbar.

6. To rotate text inside a table, click this button on the Tables and Borders toolbar: _____.

7. To rotate a picture 180 degrees, click this option at the Rotate or Flip menu _____.

8. The _____ button on the Forms toolbar controls shading in form fields.

9. Press _____ to insert a tab code within a table.

10. A _____ contains all the information for one unit (person, family, customer, or client).

Assessment 1

Gift certificates are excellent promotional documents that can be used for generating further purchases or used as rain checks, mini awards, "runner-up" prizes, or warranties. As an employee at Butterfield Gardens, create a gift certificate that may be purchased by customers and used for in-store shopping.

1. At a clear document screen, create a gift certificate similar to figure 7.21 by completing the following steps: (Key text from figure 7.21.)
   a. Change all the margins to 0.65 inches.
   b. Create a table with 2 columns and 1 row.
   c. Turn on the table Show Gridlines feature.
   d. With the insertion point positioned in the first cell, click Table, Table Properties, and then make the following changes at the Table Properties dialog box:
      1) At the Table tab select Center Alignment. Click Options, and then change the margins to 0.2 inch.
      2) At the Row tab, key **2.75** inches at the Specify height text box and select *Exactly* at the Row height list box.
      3) At the Column tab, key **4.75** inches for Column 1 Preferred Width and key **2.25** inches for Column 2 Preferred Width.
      4) At the Cell tab select Top Vertical alignment.
   e. Add a border around the outside of the table.
   f. With the insertion point still located in the first cell, press the spacebar once and press Enter. (This is necessary to insert an Enter code inside the first cell.)

g. Press the down-arrow key once, and key **Gift Certificate**. Press Enter twice.

h. Select *Gift Certificate* and change the font to 36-pt French Script MT.

i. At the Tab dialog box, set Left tabs at 1 inch, 1.75 inches, and 2.5 inches; set a Right tab at 4.3 inches with a line style Leader.

j. Key the text shown in figure 7.21 and press the spacebar once after keying a text label and press Ctrl + Tab to move to the next tab and to create the underline. Press Shift and the underline key to create the line between *to* and *Dollars*. Double space between each line.

k. Insert the tree image shown in figure 7.21. Key **trees** in the Search for clips: text box at the Insert ClipArt dialog box.

l. Size and position the tree image similar to figure 7.21.

2. Create two more certificates by copying and pasting the row.

3. Save the document and name it c07sa01, Certificate.

4. Print and then close c07sa01, Certificate.

figure

7.21

Assessment 1

36-pt French Script MT

12-pt Times New Roman

12-pt Times New Roman

Gift Certificate

Butterfield Gardens
29 W 036 Butterfield Road
Warrenville, IL 60555
(630) 555-1062
http://www.grower.com

Date _____

This certificate entitles _____

to _____ Dollars $ _____

Presented by _____

Authorized signature _____

Assessment 2

You are working at Tuscany Realty and have been asked to prepare an announcement for an open house advertising the sale of a custom-built home on a golf course. The announcement is to be prepared as a postcard and mailed to prospective clients and all homeowners in this neighborhood. This promotional document makes the realtor's name visible to any homeowners in the neighborhood who may be thinking of selling their home or buying a new one. The card will be reproduced at a printing company. Create two postcards similar to the ones shown in figure 7.22. Follow the guidelines given below.

1. Create the formatting and text for the postcard by completing the following steps:
    a. Choose the Avery 5389 - Post card definition at the Labels dialog box.
    b. Click the New Document button at the Labels dialog box.
    c. Create the dots in the left top corner and right bottom corner of the postcard by completing the following steps:
        1) Change the alignment in the cell to Align Top Left.
        2) Insert the Wingding symbol found in the third row and the eighth column from the right. The small dots are also in the Wingding character set, located in the fifth row and the sixteenth column from the left.
        3) Use F4, the repeat key, to save time in duplicating the dots.
    d. The vertical line in the postcard was drawn using the Line button on the Drawing toolbar (be sure to hold down the Shift key as you draw the line).
    e. Create text boxes inside the label (table format) to hold the formatted text.
    f. Key **Tuscany Realty** in WordArt. Use the Deflate (Bottom) shape in the fourth row and the fourth column of the shape palette. Select the Wide Latin font and change the font color to purple.
    g. Insert the real estate picture shown in figure 7.22. Key **houses** in the Search for clips: text box at the Insert ClipArt dialog box.
    h. Position and size the image as it appears in figure 7.22.
    i. Use Footlight MT Light for the office address and *Open House*. Use Times New Roman for the message text.
    j. Copy the first postcard text to the second postcard.
2. Save the document as c07sa02, House.
3. Print and then close c07sa02, House.

Optional: Create a data source consisting of four of your friends, neighbors, co-workers, or relatives. Create a main document using your return address, the field codes for the data source, and any graphic or symbol that attracts attention and relates to the subject matter in assessment 2. Merge the data source to the main document and print the merged document to the reverse side of the postcards created in assessment 2.

figure

7.22

Assessment 2

Assessment 3

As an employee at First Bank, one of your responsibilities is to create an invitation for an "Evening Out on the Town" to be sent to several important bank clients. Use Word's table or the <u>2</u> pages per sheet feature and create the invitation in either landscape or portrait orientation.

1. Add graphics, watermarks, lines, borders, symbols, or other enhancements to your document. Use the text below:

   > **On behalf of First Bank, we would like to cordially invite you to an "Evening Out on the Town" Thursday, May 20, 2001.**
   > **Cocktails - 5:00 p.m.–5:30 p.m.**
   > **Dinner - 5:30 p.m.–7:00 p.m.**
   > **Trattoria 8**
   > **15 North Dearborn Street**
   > **Chicago, Illinois**
   > **Theater - 7:30 p.m.**
   > **Phantom of the Opera**
   > **Chicago Theatre**
   > **175 North State Street**
   > **Chicago, Illinois**
   > **Please RSVP to Victoria Franz, (302) 555-3456 by April 24, 2001**

2. Include the following specifications:

   - Consider your audience in creating an appropriate design.
   - Prepare a thumbnail sketch.
   - Use an appropriate font and vary the type size and type style.
   - Change the character spacing in at least one occurrence.
   - Use vertical and horizontal lines, or an appropriate graphic image, graphic border, or symbols to add interest and impact.
   - Use special characters where needed—en or em dashes, bullets, etc.
   - Change the leading if necessary.

3. Save the document and name it c07sa03, Bank.
4. Print and then close c07sa03, Bank.
5. Evaluate your invitation with the Document Analysis Guide.

CREATIVE ACTIVITY

1. Create a promotional document of your own design or from an example you have saved or found in the mail, at a store, or from any other source. If you are using a sample document, first evaluate the document for good layout and design, a clear and concise message, and proper use of other desktop publishing concepts as outlined in the Document Analysis Guide. Some possible promotional documents include the following examples:

   - Invitation to a new store opening
   - Invitation to a class reunion
   - Bookmark
   - Name badge including a company or organization name or logo
   - Business greeting card
   - Postcard as a follow-up
   - Postcard used to promote a new business (coffee shop, party planner, attorney's office, computer services)
   - Membership card
   - Ticket with a company or organization name or logo
   - Gift certificate
   - Thank you card
   - Employee retirement announcement
   - Company party invitation
   - Postcard advertising a sample sale
   - Raffle ticket for a charity
   - Postcard announcing the opening of a golf course
   - Postcard advertising services at a travel agency

2. Create a copy of the document with any necessary improvements. Try to find unusual, creative documents that were used to promote a business, organization, item, or event.

3. If the sample document was created on odd-sized paper, check to see if your printer can accommodate the paper size. You may need to recreate the document on standard-sized paper and trim it to size.

4. Save the completed document and name it c07ca01, Promotional.

5. Print and then close c07ca01, Promotional—attach the original document if one was used.

Chapter 08

Creating Web Pages

PERFORMANCE OBJECTIVES

Upon successful completion of chapter 8, you will be able to create a Web home page with hyperlinks using Word 2000 and apply basic desktop publishing concepts to the layout and design of the Web page.

DESKTOP PUBLISHING TERMS

Bookmark	Hyperlink	Theme
Frame	Internet	URL
Frameset	Intranet	Web page
GIF and JPEG file	Internet Service	World Wide Web
formats	Provider (ISP)	(WWW)
HTTP	Marquee	WYSIWYG

WORD FEATURES USED

Alternative text	Forms	Scrolling text
AutoShapes	Frames	Sound clips
Background color	Graphics	Tables
Blank Web Page	Heading styles	Templates
template	Horizontal lines	Themes
Bookmarks	Hyperlinks	Web toolbar
Bullets	Microsoft Word Web	Web Tools toolbar
Clip Art	site	Web Page Preview
Document Map	Objects	Web Page Wizard
Font colors	Pictures	WordArt

In this chapter, Word is used to create Web pages. Web pages provide promotional information about a company's or organization's products, resources, or services. Increasingly, businesses, organizations, and individuals are accessing the Internet to conduct research, publish product or catalog information, communicate, and market products globally. In addition, companies are using intranets to efficiently share information among employees.

Users access the Internet for several purposes: to communicate using e-mail; to subscribe to news groups; to transfer files; to socialize with other users; and to access virtually any kind of information imaginable.

What is a *Web page*? It is a computer file containing information in the form of text or graphics along with commands in a language called Hypertext Markup Language (HTML). When one of these pages is placed on a server, which is a computer hooked up to the Internet, it receives an address that other users will key in to call up the page.

Web Page

A computer file created in HTML and used on the Web.

Understanding Internet and Intranet Terminology

Internet

Worldwide network of computers connected together to share information.

The *Internet* is a worldwide network of commercial, educational, governmental, and personal computers connected together for the purpose of sharing information. The *World Wide Web (WWW)* is the most commonly used application on the Internet and is a set of standards and protocols used to access information available on the Internet. An *intranet* is an "internal Internet" within an organization that uses the same Web technology and tools as the Internet and is also used to share information. Intranets are many times only accessible to the employees within an organization. An intranet may provide employees with on-line access to reference material, job postings, phone and address lists, company policies and procedures, enrollment in and updates on benefit plans, company newsletters, and other human resource information.

World Wide Web (WWW)

A set of standards and protocols used to access information on the Internet.

Throughout this chapter, you will simulate creating Web pages for both the Internet and an organization's intranet. These Web pages will be saved as HTML files to a floppy disk or hard drive. You will view each Web page in the Internet Explorer screen.

Intranet

An "internal Internet" within an organization that uses Internet technology and tools.

Using the Web Toolbar

URL

A Uniform Resource Locator is the address used to identify locations on the Internet.

The *Uniform Resource Locator*, referred to as URL, is the method used to identify locations on the Internet. It is the address that you key in to call up a Web page or site. A typical URL is *http://www.microsoft.com*. The first part of the URL, *http://*, identifies the protocol. The letters *http* stand for *Hypertext Transfer Protocol*, which is one of the protocols or languages used to transfer data within the World Wide Web. The colon and slashes separate the protocol from the server name. The server name is the second component of the URL. For example, in *http://www.microsoft.com*, the server name is identified as *www.microsoft*. The last part of the URL specifies the domain to which the server belongs—for example, *.com* refers to "commercial," *.edu* refers to "educational," *.gov* stands for "government," and *.mil* refers to "military."

HTTP

Hypertext Transfer Protocol is one of the languages used to transfer data within the WWW.

If you know the URL for a specific Web site and would like to visit that site, key the URL in the Address section of the Web toolbar. To display the Web toolbar as shown in figure 8.1, click <u>V</u>iew, point to <u>T</u>oolbars, and then click *Web* at the drop-down list. You can also display the Web toolbar by positioning the mouse pointer on a toolbar, clicking the *right* mouse button, and then clicking *Web* at the drop-down list.

figure

8.1   *Web Toolbar*

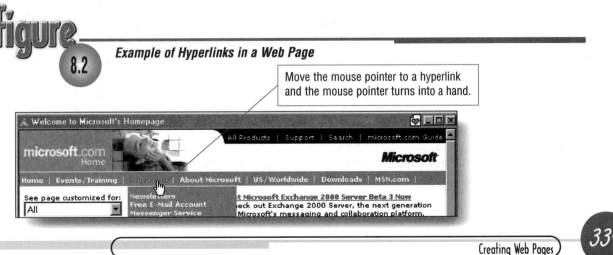

Back Forward Stop Current Jump Refresh Current Page Start Page Search the Web Favorites Go Show Only Web Toolbar Address More Buttons

Before keying a URL in the Address text box on the Web toolbar, make sure you are connected to the Internet. Key the URL exactly as written, including any colons (:) or slashes (/).

When you are connected to a URL (Web site address), the home page for the specific URL (Web site) displays. (Web pages are constantly changing. If a particular Web page asked for in an exercise is no longer available, you will need to substitute a different one.) The home page is the starting point for viewing any Web site. At the home page you can "branch off" to other pages within the Web site or jump to other Web sites. You do this with hyperlinks that are embedded in the home page, as shown in figure 8.2. *Hyperlinks* are colored and underlined text or a graphic that you click to go to a file, a location in a file, an HTML page on the World Wide Web, or an HTML page on an intranet. Move the mouse pointer on a hyperlink and the mouse pointer becomes a hand. This is one method for determining if something is a hyperlink. Most pages contain a variety of hyperlinks. Using these links, you can zero in on the exact information for which you are searching.

Hyperlink
Text or graphic in a Web page that will connect you to other pages or Web sites in different locations.

Using the Internet Explorer toolbar, you can jump forward or backward among the documents you have opened and you can add interesting documents you find on the Web to the Favorites folder to return to them later more easily. To do this, display the site, and then click the Favorites button on the toolbar. This causes a side bar to display. To add a favorite site, click the Add button located at the top of the Favorites side bar. Make sure the information in the Name text box is correct, and then click OK.

figure

8.2   *Example of Hyperlinks in a Web Page*

Move the mouse pointer to a hyperlink and the mouse pointer turns into a hand.

Planning and Designing a Web Page

You can build a Web site yourself, or hire a freelancer or Web access provider. Some advertising consultants develop Web sites for a fee. However, with the help of Word's Web Page Wizard or Word's Blank Web Page template, you can easily create your own Web pages.

Where do you start? Planning is a basic desktop publishing concept that applies to Web pages as well as any other documents created in Word. During the planning stage of your Web page, consider the following Web page design tips:

- Determine the goal of your Web site.

DTP POINTERS
Look at other Web pages for layout and design ideas.

- Identify and focus on your intended audience.
- Review and critique other sites.
- Determine elements to be emphasized and used. Keep the design simple. Use white space effectively.
- Determine links. Be consistent with hyperlinks so that the visitor knows where they are, where they came from, and where they can go. Be sure all links are current.
- Create a storyboard.
- Maintain consistent color scheme.

DTP POINTERS
Keep the background simple.

- Keep the background simple, making sure the text can be seen clearly. Make sure there is enough contrast between the text and background.
- Avoid small text.
- For bulleted text, avoid using a single bullet. Don't use more than two levels of bullets.
- Use consistent wording in bulleted text.

DTP POINTERS
Use consistency in design elements.

- Use graphics that relate to the content. Graphics should not distract from the message.
- Keep graphs simple. The most effective graphs are pie charts with three or four slices and column charts with three or four columns.
- Remember that a Web page is the first impression you're giving the world about your product, information, or yourself. A poor Web page can be worse for your business than having none at all.
- Maintain and keep your Web site current.

Consider using a thumbnail sketch and a storyboard to organize your page layout before actually creating it. Include space for text, photographs, graphics, headlines, divider lines, etc. Instead of including everything on one huge Web front page, use hyperlinks to other pages.

Remember that the Web site's front door is its home page. This page should contain the elements to achieve the goals an organization (or individual) has set for the Web site. Understand what your goals are before you design the site. Are you creating a Web site on an intranet to share information among employees or a Web page on the Internet to market a product or service? Know your budget before starting. There are things you can do on any budget, but some things (such as videos and animation) may cost more than you can afford.

DTP POINTERS
Use a company logo to reinforce company recognition.

Some Web designers suggest that you create a nameplate or banner to display a logo and company name in an interesting way. Include your company logo to reinforce your company's identity. The site should also include alternative ways to reach the company such as an address, telephone number, e-mail address, and fax number.

Graphics are probably the simplest way to make your Web page look better. Be sure to choose a graphic that is appropriate to the subject of the page. Animation, video, and scrolling words are eye-catching devices to entice your audience to return to your Web site. They can take a while to load. You may want to avoid using a graphic that takes longer than 15 to 20 seconds to load. Use small graphics that are less than 30K in size. When in doubt, keep the basic design simple. The main point in designing a Web page is to get the message across! In addition, remember that everything you want to use on your home page must be transferred into computer files. If you want to use a photograph, you must scan the photo to convert it to a graphic file. Format main headings with HTML heading styles so a reader can more quickly browse through a document when using the document map in Word's Online Layout view.

DTP POINTERS
Too many graphics or large graphics can slow down your Web page.

In exercise 1, you will take a look at a few Web home pages using URLs. As you view each of the Web sites listed in the exercise, pay attention to the layout and design of each home page. For instance, when viewing *http://www.umich.edu*, notice the banner. It repeats the blue and maize color scheme used by the school, the watermark of the school emblem reinforces tradition, the circle photo shapes provide variety in design, and the generous amount of white space organizes the text and makes it easy to read.

exercise 1

Viewing Web Site Home Pages for Design and Layout Ideas

1. Make sure you are connected to the Internet.
2. Explore several locations on the World Wide Web from within Word by completing the following steps:
   a. Display the Web toolbar.
   b. Click in the Address text box located on the Web Toolbar.
   c. Key **http://www.umich.edu** and then press Enter.
   d. The home page will display similar to the one shown in figure 8.3. Home pages are frequently updated, so the University of Michigan home page you are viewing may vary slightly from what you see in figure 8.3. Scroll down the home page, studying the layout.
   e. After viewing the University of Michigan, view the Web site for the Chicago Convention and Tourism Bureau. To do this, click the current address located in the Address text box, key **http://www.chicago.il.org**, and then press Enter. Scroll down the home page, studying the layout and design elements.
   f. View the Web site for Eastman Kodak. Key **http://kodak.com** and then press Enter. (Notice the hyperlinks to send multimedia postcards, pictures on CDs, and digital cameras and technology.)
   g. Display the Kodak Picture CD page and then print the page by clicking the Print button on the Internet Explorer toolbar. (If this page is no longer available, print another page of interest to you.)
3. After printing the Kodak Picture CD page, click File and then Close.

University of Michigan Home Page

Using Internet Explorer

In exercise 1, you visited the first Web site by keying the URL in the Address text box in the Web Toolbar. This opened the Internet Explorer program window and also displayed the home page for the Web site. The Internet Explorer program window contains many features similar to the Word window. The Internet Explorer toolbar contains buttons for accessing a variety of commands, which are shown and described in figure 8.4.

figure

8.4

Internet Explorer Toolbar Buttons

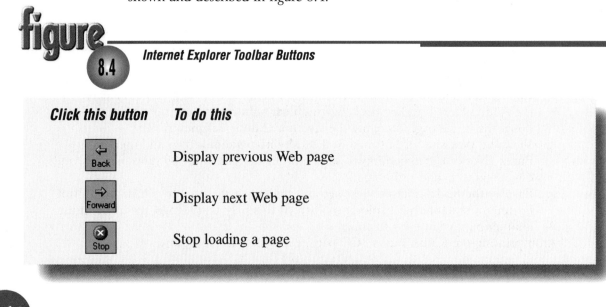

Click this button	To do this
⇐ Back	Display previous Web page
⇒ Forward	Display next Web page
⊗ Stop	Stop loading a page

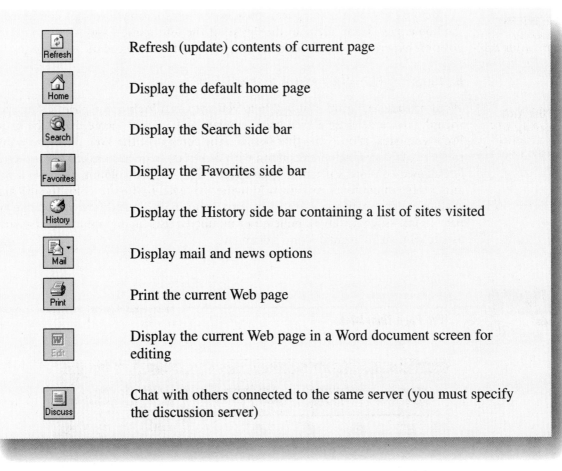

Refresh	Refresh (update) contents of current page
Home	Display the default home page
Search	Display the Search side bar
Favorites	Display the Favorites side bar
History	Display the History side bar containing a list of sites visited
Mail	Display mail and news options
Print	Print the current Web page
Edit	Display the current Web page in a Word document screen for editing
Discuss	Chat with others connected to the same server (you must specify the discussion server)

If you click on a hyperlink in a Web page, you can then click the Back button on the Internet Explorer toolbar to display a previous page or location. If you clicked the Back button and then want to go back to the hyperlink, click the Forward button. By clicking the Back button, you can back your way out of any hyperlinks and return to the default Web home page.

As you visit different Web sites, Internet Explorer keeps track of the sites. Click the History button on the Internet Explorer toolbar. The History side bar displays.

Creating a Web Home Page Using the Web Page Wizard

Now that you have spent some time viewing several Web site home pages, you may have a few ideas on how to design an appealing home page. The pages were designed using a language called Hypertext Markup Language (HTML). This is a language that Web browsers use to read hypertext documents. In the past, a person needed knowledge of HTML to design a Web page. Now, a Web page can be created in Word with the Web Page Wizard or Blank Web Page template, or a Word document can be converted to HTML. (To convert an existing Word document to a Web page, click File and then Save as Web Page.) Several additional Web templates are available for downloading from the Microsoft World Wide Web site. When you download these templates, they are installed in the same folder as the existing Web templates.

Before creating a home page, consider the information you want contained in the home page. Carefully plan the layout of the information and where to position hyperlinks. Good design is a key element to a successful home page.

Accessing the Web Page Wizard

Word provides a wizard that will help you prepare a Web home page. Using the wizard, you can choose a Web page template and a visual theme. From the list of Web templates, choose one that best fits the content of the Web page you want to create. Choices include a column with contents, frequently asked questions, a left-aligned column, a personal Web Page, a right-aligned column, a simple layout, and a table of contents, as shown in figure 8.5. Many different color themes are available. When you use a Web template, you can create and format popular Web page items—such as tables, bulleted or numbered lists, and graphic objects—just as you can with a regular Word document.

figure
8.5

Web Page Templates

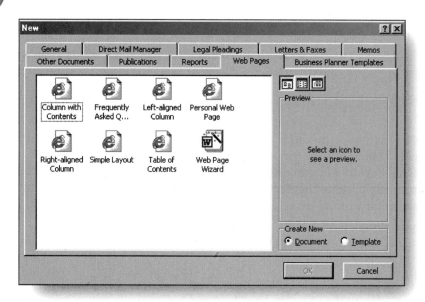

Access the Web Page Wizard at the New dialog box with the Web Pages tab selected. To use the Web Page Wizard, double-click the Web Page Wizard icon. At the first Web Page Wizard dialog box, choose options to customize your Web page at each of the screens and continue clicking the Next> button to advance to the next screen. At the Theme dialog box, choose a coordinated visual theme, as shown in figure 8.6, and then click the Finish button. With the Web site home page displayed, key the desired information.

figure

8.6

Web Page Themes

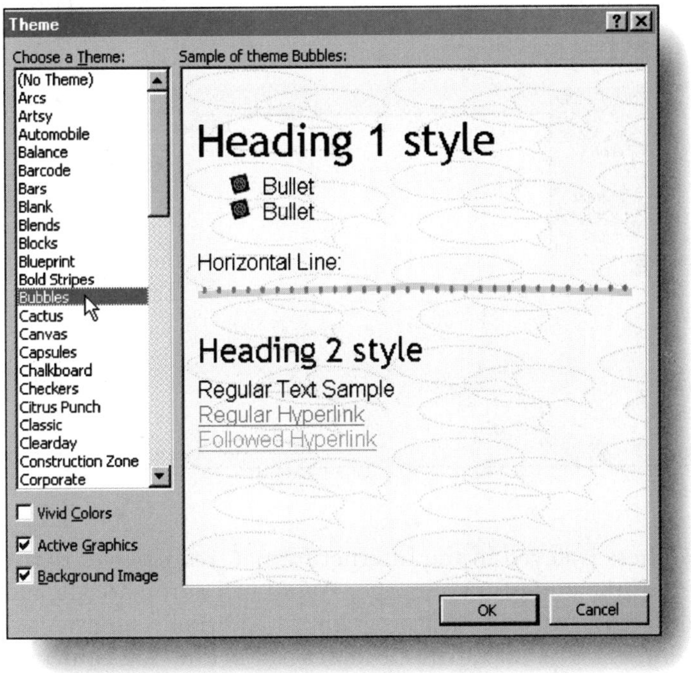

Creating Hyperlinks in a Web Home Page

The Web sites you visited in exercise 1 included hyperlinks to connect you to other pages or Web sites in different locations. The reader of your document can jump to a location in that document, a different Word document, or a file created in a different program such as an Excel spreadsheet. The destination document or file can be on your hard drive, on your organization's network (intranet), or on the Internet, such as a page on the World Wide Web. You can create hyperlinks from selected text or graphic objects—such as buttons and pictures. By default, the hyperlink text displays in blue and is underlined. When you return to the document after following a hyperlink, the hyperlink text color changes to dark red. You do not have to be on the Internet to use hyperlinks in Word documents.

You can create a hyperlink in your own home page. To do this, select the text you want specified as the hyperlink and then click the Insert Hyperlink button on the Standard toolbar. You can also click Insert and then Hyperlink. At the Insert Hyperlink dialog box shown in figure 8.7, key the Web site URL or page name in the Type the file or Web page name text box and click the OK button.

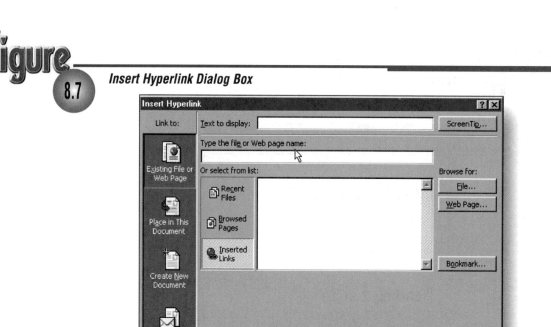

figure
8.7

Insert Hyperlink Dialog Box

If an e-mail address is keyed in the Internet format, *yourname@servername.com* (it is usually typed at the end of a Web page), Word will automatically create a hyperlink to your default Internet mail program. In addition, you can create hyperlinks to bookmarks in a document, as described below. You can create a bookmark in a document by selecting a word or sentence, then clicking Insert and then Bookmark. At the Bookmark dialog box, key a short description in the text box, click Add, and then click OK. You can then create a hyperlink from another section in the document to the bookmark or from any other document to the bookmark. Bookmarks are frequently used in Web pages to move the reader quickly from the bottom of a page to the top of a page.

Editing or Deleting a Hyperlink

To edit an existing link, right-click the hyperlink and then choose Hyperlink at the shortcut menu. Select the Edit Hyperlink option at the shortcut menu. To delete a hyperlink (but not the document text), click the Remove Link button located in the bottom left corner of the Edit Hyperlink dialog box.

Creating Bookmarks

Bookmark

Links that are used to move your cursor to another location within a document.

A *bookmark* can be used to move your cursor to another location within the same document. It creates a link within the same page. You must first create a bookmark and then connect it to another location within your page by creating a hyperlink to it. Create a bookmark from the top of a page to a location within the page by completing the following steps:

1. Insert Bookmarks:
   a. Position your insertion point at the location you would like to make a bookmark, or select (highlight) text within your document. The text can be headings. Click Insert and then Bookmark.

b. At the <u>B</u>ookmark dialog box, key in a name for your bookmark. Bookmark names must begin with a letter and can contain numbers. You cannot include spaces. You can, however, use the underscore character to separate words (i.e., first_heading). Click the <u>A</u>dd button.

2. Hyperlink the text at the top of your document to your bookmarks:
   a. Select the text at the top of your page. Do not include the space after the word.
   b. Click the Insert Hyperlink button on your Standard toolbar.
   c. Click the <u>B</u>ookmark command button at the Insert Hyperlink dialog box. Click on the bookmark name and then click the OK button. Click the OK button to close the dialog box.

Adding Bullets and Lines to a Web Page

Bullets can be added to your document lists by clicking the Bullet button on the Formatting toolbar. You also can change regular bullets to special graphical bullets for your Web page. Select the bulleted list in your document. Click F<u>o</u>rmat and then Bullets and <u>N</u>umbering. At the <u>B</u>ulleted tab, click <u>P</u>icture. Scroll through the clips and make a choice. Click on your choice and then click Insert Clip.

You can use horizontal lines to separate sections of a Web page. Click F<u>o</u>rmat and then <u>B</u>orders and Shading. At the <u>B</u>orders tab, click the <u>H</u>orizontal Line button. At the Pictures tab, scroll and click the desired line type. Click the Insert Clip button at the pop-up menu.

DTP POINTERS
Horizontal lines are used to separate sections of a Web page.

You can also insert Web Bullets and Web Dividers (lines) at the Insert ClipArt dialog box. To do this, Click <u>I</u>nsert, <u>P</u>icture, and then <u>C</u>lip Art. At the Pictures tab, scroll down to Web Bullets and Buttons or the Web Dividers (for lines). Many exciting choices are available. Click the *Keep Looking* hyperlink to view additional clips. Click on your choice and then click Insert Clip. Close the Insert ClipArt dialog box.

8.8 *Insert ClipArt Dialog Box, Web Dividers Category*

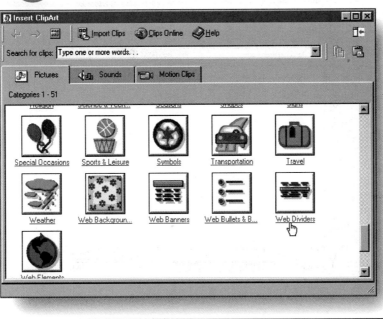

You may also insert a clip from the Web. Some good Web sites for free backgrounds, graphics, and links to other pages include *http://www.geocities.com/ginis* and *http://www.clipart.com*.

In this chapter, you will be saving your Web pages onto a floppy disk or hard drive. For a home page to be available on the Web, however, you must have access to a Web server. Consult your instructor if you are a student. Large businesses usually have their own server and you should contact the Information Systems department of the company to arrange for space on the server to store your HTML documents (home pages). An option for an individual is to rent space from an *Internet Service Provider (ISP)*, a company that sells access to the Internet. The ISP you use to access the Web will also arrange to store your Web page. Check out all the fees involved, as there are many different fee structures in existence.

ISP
An Internet Service Provider (ISP) sells access to the Internet.

Saving Web Pages

When you save your document, the graphical images are saved to your default folder in a subfolder, separate from your HTML document. The images are not saved within the HTML file. For example, a graphical bullet may display in the subfolder as image001.gif. There is also an .xml file added to the subfolder.

DTP POINTERS
Create a folder to save your Web page.

It is recommended that before you save your document, you create a folder on the disk or hard drive and save your Web page in the folder. When your page is in final form and you are ready to place it on the Internet, you will need to move the folder and subfolders (Word creates these to store images you have used in your document) to the server or "space" you have been given.

To save a regular Word document as a Web page (Word gives it the .htm extension), click File and Save as Web Page. At the Save As dialog box, change the Save in to the A drive or the drive where you intend to save your work. Key in your File name. The Save as type box will say Web Page. Click the Save button. Keep in mind that not all formatting will be able to be transferred into Hypertext Markup Language. (.htm or .html). The file extensions .htm and .html are basically the same, except the "l" is dropped from some operating systems.

figure
8.9

Save As Dialog Box, Showing Save as type: Web Page

If you know ahead of time that you wish to create a Web page, click File and New. At the New dialog box, click the General tab. Double-click the Web Page icon. When you save this document, the document will automatically be saved with an .htm extension. An advantage of beginning your page as a Web page is that as you preview your page at your browser, you will know right away what formatting works.

Previewing a Web Page

After creating a Web page or converting a Word document to a Web page, you should preview the page as it will appear on the Internet Explorer screen. To do this, make sure you saved the document and then click the Web Page Preview button on the Standard toolbar, or click File and Web Page Preview.

exercise 2

Creating a Personal Web Home Page

1. At a clear document screen, create your personal home page in Word based on the Web Page template by completing the following steps:
   a. Click File and then New.
   b. At the General tab, double-click the Web Page icon.
   c. Click File and then Save as Web Page. Create a New Folder named *Personal Web Page*. Double-click the *Personal Web Page* folder. Key in the File name **c08ex02, Personal Web Page**. (Word will automatically insert an .htm or .html extension.) Click the Save button. (Save and preview your document often at your browser.)
   d. Click Insert, point to Picture, and then click Clip Art.
      1) At the Insert ClipArt dialog box, select the Pictures tab, choose a category, scroll to find an image that interests you, and then insert the clip. Close the Insert ClipArt dialog box. (See figure 8.10 for a sample document.)
      2) Resize the image by dragging the corner sizing handles.
      3) Deselect the image and then press the spacebar four times and press the Enter key twice. Position your insertion point after the four spaces.
   e. Display the Drawing toolbar. Click the Insert WordArt button on the Drawing toolbar; choose a WordArt style, font, and font size; and then key your name in the Edit WordArt text box. Click the OK button. Move the WordArt text to the right of the picture image.
   f. Position your insertion point at the end of your document by pressing Ctrl + End.
   g. Insert scrolling text by completing the following steps:
      1) Display the Web Tools toolbar.
      2) Click the Scrolling Text button.
      3) Click the down arrow at the right of Background color and select yellow or an appropriate color for your page.

Step 1g2

Scrolling Text

      4) Select *Scrolling Text* in the Type the scrolling text here box.
      5) Key in a sentence about yourself. Click OK or press the Enter key.
      6) Center the scrolling text. To do this, deselect the scrolling text box by clicking to the right of the box. Click the Center align button on the Formatting toolbar. Press the Enter key twice. *(Hint: Another way to access the Scrolling Text dialog box is to right-click on the scrolling text and then click Properties while at the Word document screen—not in the browser.)*

h. Key **Experience | Education | Contact** and then press Enter.
i. Position the insertion point on *Experience | Education | Contact,* click the down arrow at the right of the Style list box on the Formatting toolbar, and then click *Heading 3.* Make sure the line is centered horizontally. Press Ctrl + End

> **Heading 3** 13 pt
>
> Step 1i

j. Change the alignment to Align Left, apply Heading 2, key **Professional Experience**, and then press Enter.
k. Click F~o~rmat, Bullets and ~N~umbering, and then select a bullet. Click OK or press Enter.
l. Key information about your professional experience and press Enter for each item in the list. Press the Enter key twice (to add extra white space and the second enter will turn off bullets). Change the font if desired.

> Step 1m2

m. Insert a horizontal line by completing the following steps:
   1) Click F~o~rmat and then ~B~orders and Shading.
   2) Click ~H~orizontal Line at the ~B~orders tab.

   > Horizontal Line...

   3) At the Pictures tab, scroll and select an appropriate line style. Click the Insert clip button. Press Enter.

   > **Horizontal Line** ? X
   > ← → ▦ Import Clips Clips Online Help
   > Pictures Motion Clips
   > Clips 1 - 60

n. Apply the Heading 2 style, key **Educational Background**, and then press Enter.
o. To add another bulleted list using the same bullet as above, click the Bullets button on the Formatting toolbar.

> Step 1m3

p. Key information about your educational background and then press the Enter key twice.
q. Insert the same horizontal line as above by selecting it and copying it to the Clipboard, pressing Ctrl + End to position your insertion point at the end of the document, and then clicking Paste. Press the Enter key twice.
r. Apply the Heading 2 style, key **Contact**, and then press the Enter key.
s. To insert symbols, click ~I~nsert and then ~S~ymbol.
   1) At the Symbols tab, change the Font to Wingdings.
   2) Click the phone located in the ninth column from the left in the first row.
   3) Click ~I~nsert and then close the Symbol dialog box. Press the space bar and key in your phone number with your area code. Press the Enter key.
   4) Insert the mailbox symbol in the Wingdings font located in the fourteenth column from the left in the first row. Press the space bar and key in your mailing address. Press the Enter key twice.
   5) Insert the computer symbol in the Wingdings font located in the second column from the right in the first row. Key in your e-mail address and then press Enter.
   6) Enlarge the symbols as desired by selecting the symbol (but not the space) individually and clicking the Font Size button on the Formatting toolbar. Select a larger font size. While the symbol is still selected, click the Font Color button on the Formatting toolbar and select an appropriate color.
t. Insert the same horizontal line as in the sections above as a section divider (use copy and paste) and then press Enter.

u. Click the Center align button on the Formatting toolbar and key **Top of Page**.

v. Insert hyperlinks to employers, colleges, etc. where appropriate by selecting the text and then clicking on the Insert Hyperlink button on the Standard toolbar. Key the appropriate text in the Type the file or Web page name box. Key in a ScreenTip to display. Click the OK button.

w. Insert bookmarks to link each section from the top of the page *and* to link the bottom of the page to the top of the page by completing the following steps:

    1) Select the image at the top of your page. Click Insert and then Bookmark.

    2) At the Bookmark dialog box, key **Top_of_Page** as the Bookmark name and then click Add.

    3) Position your insertion point anywhere in the text *Professional Experience*. Click Insert and then Bookmark.

    4) At the Bookmark dialog box, key **Experience** and then click Add.

    5) Position your insertion point anywhere in the text *Educational Background*. Click Insert and then Bookmark.

    6) At the Bookmark dialog box, key **Education** and then click Add.

    7) Position your insertion point anywhere in the text *Contact*. Click Insert and then Bookmark.

    8) At the Bookmark dialog box, key **Contact** and then click Add.

x. Hyperlink the bookmarks to the headings at the top and bottom of your page.

    1) Select *Experience* at the top of your page (do not include the space after the word) and then click the Insert Hyperlink button on the Standard toolbar.

    2) Click the Bookmark command button at the Insert Hyperlink dialog box.

    3) Click on the bookmark name, *Experience*, and then click the OK button. Click the OK button to close the dialog box.

    4) Follow the procedure above to hyperlink the bookmarks *Education* and *Contact*.

    5) Select the text at the bottom of your document, *Top of Page*, click the Insert Hyperlink button on the Standard toolbar, and then complete the following steps:

       a) Click the Bookmark command button at the Insert Hyperlink dialog box.

       b) Click on the bookmark name, *Top_of_Page*, and then click OK.

       c) Click the OK button to close the dialog box.

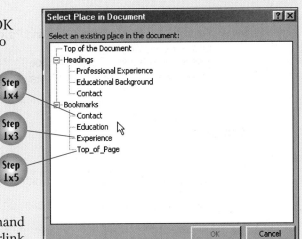

2. Save your personal Web page with the same name, c08ex02, Personal Web Page.
3. Click File and then Web Page Preview to view your Web page in a browser.
4. If necessary, adjust the top and bottom margins to fit on one page from your browser. (To change margins in a browser, click File, Page Setup, and then key settings in the Margin section in the Page Setup dialog box. Print c08ex02, Personal Web Page at the Web Page Preview by clicking the Print button on the Internet Explorer toolbar.
5. Close c08ex02, Personal Web Page.

figure
8.10

Exercise 2, Sample Web Page

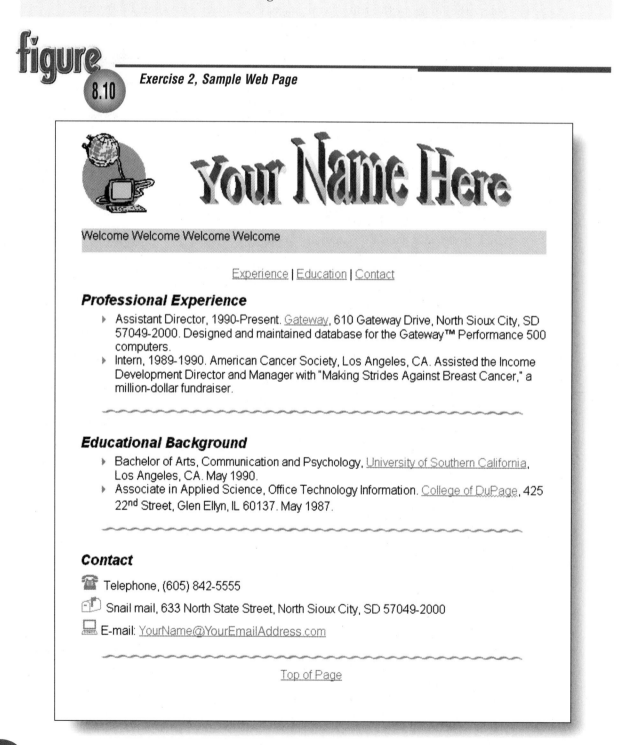

Designing a Web Page Using a Table

Working with tables on Web pages is similar to working with tables in Word documents. You can use the Draw Table option to create and modify the structure of the table. Tables are often used as a behind-the-scenes layout tool on Web pages—for instance, to arrange text and graphics. You can add borders, background color, or shading to tables on Web pages by using the Tables and Borders toolbar, or at the Borders and Shading dialog box.

To turn all the borders off, click inside the table. Click Table and then Table Properties. At the Table tab, click Borders and Shading. At the Borders tab, click None. Click the OK button at the Borders and Shading dialog box and then click the OK button on the Table Properties dialog box.

Creating Forms in a Web Page

You can use Word to create an interactive form that is used on the Web and that provides the viewer options to give input or answer questions. Users view and complete the form in a browser. The completed form is submitted to a database on an HTTP server. Web (HTML) forms use ActiveX controls, which can be created using the Web Tools toolbar (see figure 8.11). Because forms require additional support files and server support, it is recommended that you work with your network or Web administrator when planning your form. Figure 8.12 describes the form controls that are available on the Web Tools toolbar.

DTP POINTERS
Users view and complete a Web form in their browser.

DTP POINTERS
A check box is used when you wish to give the user more than one choice.

DTP POINTERS
An option button is used when you wish to give the user only one choice.

figure 8.11

Web Tools Toolbar

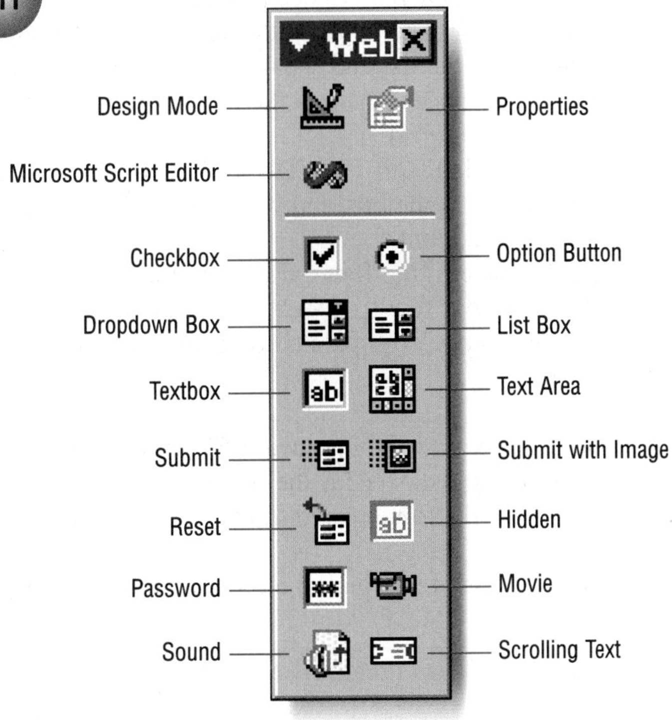

Design Mode	Properties
Microsoft Script Editor	
Checkbox	Option Button
Dropdown Box	List Box
Textbox	Text Area
Submit	Submit with Image
Reset	Hidden
Password	Movie
Sound	Scrolling Text

figure

8.12

Individual Form Control Button Descriptions

 Checkbox

Inserts a check box that can be selected or cleared that is located next to an independent option. Also inserts a check box next to each item in a group of choices that are not mutually exclusive—that is, you can select more than one check box at a time.

Checked: Determines whether the check box is selected by default.

Option Button

Inserts an option button next to each item in a group of two or more choices that are mutually exclusive—that is, you can select only one option button at a time. To place text beside this option button, type it on the form.

Checked: Determines whether the option button is selected by default.

HTMLName: The internal name you assign to the control. The name is used to identify the field name when the information is sent to a Web server.

Dropdown Box

Inserts a box that displays available choices in a drop-down list box. Enter the items you want to appear in the list box in the DisplayValues property.

DisplayValues: The items to display in the list. Enter all the items for the list and separate them with a semicolon; do not type spaces between the items. (For example: Item1;Item2;Item3)

Selected: Defaults to True. Determines whether the first item appears in the box and whether the first item is selected by default.

Size: The size of the font—defaults to l.

Value: The text sent to a Web server for each item in the list. Values are also separated by semicolon and do not use spaces.

List Box

Inserts a box that displays available choices in a list format. If the list exceeds the box size, the user can scroll through the list to view additional choices.

 Textbox

Inserts a control in which the user can enter one line of text.

Continued on next page

▦	Text Area	Inserts a control in which the user can enter multiple lines of text.
▦	Submit	Submits the data that the user filled out. Every form must have one Submit button or one Submit with Image button.
▦	Submit with Image	Displays a graphic the user clicks to submit data. When you insert this control, the Picture dialog box appears. Select the image you want. When you copy the Web page to a Web server, you must also copy the button image.
▦	Reset	Resets the form controls to their default settings, and removes data the user has entered into the form.
ab	Hidden	Inserts a hidden control that is used to pass information to a Web server—such as information about the user's operating environment—when the user submits the form.
▦	Password	Inserts a text box that displays an asterisk (*) to mask each character that the user types.

Adding Background Color to a Web Page

You can add background colors and textures to make your document more visually appealing to read online. The backgrounds will be visible on the screen, but they will not display when the page is printed, unless your browser supports background printing.

DTP POINTERS
Enhance your document with a background.

To enhance your document with a background, point to Background on the Format menu. Click the color you want. Click More Colors for the standard and custom color hues, or Fill Effects to select a gradient, textured, or patterned background. You can also add a picture to the background.

Printing a Background from Your Browser

To print a background or theme in Microsoft Internet Explorer, at the Microsoft Internet Explorer window click Tools, and then Internet Options. At the Advanced tab, scroll down to Printing and click in the Print background colors and images check box to turn this feature on. Click the OK button to close the dialog box. When you print from Explorer, your background and theme colors will print.

DTP POINTERS
Backgrounds can print from your browser.

In other browsers such as Netscape Navigator version 4.0 or later, you may find this option under File and Page Setup. At the Page Setup dialog box, click to add the checkmark Print background. Click the OK button.

In exercise 3, you will create a form requesting users to evaluate Web sites according to Web page design principles discussed earlier in this chapter. You will add a background effect to the document.

exercise 3

Creating a Web Page Survey Form

1. Create a Web page form (as shown in figure 8.13) using a table and the form control tools by completing the following steps:
   a. Click File and New. At the General tab, double-click the Web Page icon.
   b. Turn on the Web Tools, Tables and Borders, and Drawing toolbars.
   c. Create a new folder named *Survey Form* on a floppy disk or hard drive and name the document c08ex03, Web Page Survey Form. *(Hint: Save your document often.)*
2. Add a background by completing the following steps:
   a. Click Format, Background, and then Fill Effects.
   b. At the Texture tab, choose Blue tissue paper and then click OK.
3. Change the font to 12-point Garamond.
4. Create a table with 3 columns and 12 rows.
5. Turn off all borders in the table, but display the table gridlines.
6. Merge the cells in the first row by selecting the first row, clicking Table, and then clicking Merge cells.
7. Position the insertion point in the merged cell, key **Web Page Survey**, and then apply the Heading 1 style. Center the heading horizontally.
8. Merge the cells in the second row.
9. Click inside the row and key **Please complete the following survey so we may encourage professional development of Web pages. Your input is valuable to us; we appreciate your time.** Press Enter.
10. Merge the cells in the third row.
11. Click inside the row and key **Which Web page will you evaluate?**
12. Position your insertion point in the first column and the fourth row and then add a drop-down box by completing the following steps:
    a. Turn on the Design Mode from the Web Tools toolbar by clicking on the Design Mode button.
    b. Click the Dropdown Box button.
    c. Add the choices in the box that you will view and select from your browser by completing the following steps:
       1) While the box is selected, click on the Properties button from the Web Tools toolbar.
       2) At the Alphabetic tab, click in the right column beside DisplayValues and key **ty.com;coke.com;ual.com**. Do not add spaces after the semicolons.
       3) Close the Properties dialog box by clicking on the X at the top right corner of the dialog box.
       4) Click to the right of the button and press the Enter key to add white space.
13. Select the fifth row and merge the cells, and then key **What is the goal of the Web page?**
14. Position your insertion point in the first column and the sixth row and add the first Option Button by clicking on the Option Button on the Web Tools toolbar.

356

15. Click to the right of the Option Button, press the space bar once, and then key **Make money**.
16. Click inside the second column and add the second Option Button.
17. Click to the right of the Option Button, press the space bar once, and then key **Distribute information**.
18. Click inside the third column and add the third Option Button.
19. Click to the right of the Option Button, press the space bar once, and then key **Stroke an ego**. Press Enter.
20. When a person is filling out this form in a browser, you will only want them to select one choice from an Option Button. You also need to decide which choice will be the "default" choice when the page is opened. We will make the first button the default. To change the Option Buttons to only allow one choice, each Option Button must have the same HTMLName in the Properties dialog box. To change the default setting, complete the following steps:
    a. Click the first Option Button to select it.
    b. Click the Properties button on the Web Tools toolbar.
    c. At the Alphabetic tab, click in the right column beside HTMLName and then key **goal1**.
    d. To make this Option Button the default choice, click in the right column beside the word *Checked* (which shows *False*).

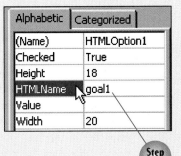

Step 20c

    e. Click the down arrow and then click *True*.
    f. You can leave the Properties dialog box open.
    g. Select the second Option Button.
    h. Click inside the Properties dialog box at the right of HTMLName and then key **goal1**. The Checked column will say *False*.
    i. Select the third Option Button.
    j. Click inside the Properties dialog box to the right of HTMLName, and then key **goal1**. The Checked column will say *False*.
    k. Close the Properties dialog box.
21. Select the seventh row and merge the cells, and then key **Who is the intended audience of the Web page?**
22. Position your insertion point in the first column and the eighth row and add a check box by completing the following steps:
    a. Click the Checkbox button on the Web Tools toolbar.
    b. Click to the right of the Checkbox button, press the space bar once, and then key **7 years – 16 years** (use an en dash).

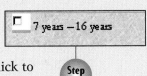

Step 22b

23. Click inside the second column, add a check box, and then click to the right of the Checkbox button, pressing the space bar once, and key **16 years – 21 years**.
24. Click inside the third column, add a check box, click to the right of the Checkbox button, press the space bar once, and then key **Over 21 years**. Press Enter.
25. Select the ninth row and merge the cells.
26. Add a Web Page Divider by completing the following steps:
    a. Click Insert, Picture, and then ClipArt.
    b. At the Insert ClipArt dialog box, Pictures tab, scroll down the list of categories, and then click the *Web Dividers* category.

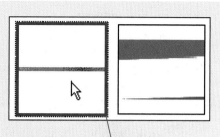

c. While in Clips 61–120, select the colorful one shown in Figure 8.13, and then click Insert clip.

d. Close the Insert ClipArt dialog box.

27. Position the insertion point in the tenth row, select the first two columns only, and merge the cells.

28. Click inside the cell and change the style to Heading 2, key **Design Elements**, and then press Enter.

Step 26c

29. Key **List a few of the design elements used to draw your attention, enhance the message, or encourage you to read further**. *(Hint: If your text style changes to something other than Garamond, select the text and change the font to 12-point Garamond.)* Press Enter.

30. Click inside the next column, press Enter twice, and then click the Text Area button on the Web Tools toolbar.

31. Position your insertion point in the next row, select the first two columns only, and merge the cells.

32. Add a text box by completing the following steps:

a. Click the Textbox button on the Web Tools toolbar, click to the right of it, and then press the space bar once.

b. Key **Please include your name**.

c. Press Enter to add space.

33. Many times you will want to give the viewer an opportunity to navigate around your page while viewing it from a browser. Create bookmarks and hyperlinks to locations within the page by completing the following steps:

a. Select the last row and merge the cells.

b. Click inside the cell and change to Center alignment.

c. Key **Top of Form | Goal of Home Page | Submit Information**.

d. Position the insertion point at the top of the page, click <u>I</u>nsert, Boo<u>k</u>mark, key **top**, and then click <u>A</u>dd.

e. Position your insertion point anywhere in *What is the goal of the Web page?*, click Insert, Bookmark, key **goal**, and then click <u>A</u>dd.

f. Insert hyperlinks by completing the following steps:

1) Scroll to bottom of your document and select *Top of Form*. Do not select the space after the word *Form*.

2) Click the Insert Hyperlink button on the Standard toolbar and then click the B<u>o</u>okmark button.

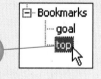

Step 33f3

3) Click the bookmark *top*. Click OK twice.

4) Select *Goal of Home Page*. (Do not select the space before or after this text.)

5) Click the Insert Hyperlink button on the Standard toolbar and then click the B<u>o</u>okmark button.

6) Click the bookmark *goal*. Click OK twice.

g. Select *Submit Information* and create a hyperlink to your e-mail address by completing the following steps:

1) Click the Insert Hyperlink button on the Standard toolbar.

2) In the left frame of the Insert Hyperlink dialog box, click the E-<u>m</u>ail Address button.

Step 33g2

3) Key in your e-mail address or use *YourName@emcp.com*.

4) Click the OK button to close the dialog box.

34. Save your document with the same name, c08ex03, Web Page Survey Form.

35. Preview the document in your browser.

36. Print c08ex03, Web Page Survey Form from your browser.

figure
8.13   *Exercise 3*

Web Page Survey

Please complete the following survey so we may encourage professional development of Web pages. Your input is valuable to us; we appreciate your time.

Which Web page will you evaluate?

`ty.com` ▼

What is the goal of the Web page?

⦿ Make money   ○ Distribute information   ○ Stroke an ego

Who is the intended audience of the Web page?

☐ 7 years - 16 years   ☐ 16 years - 21 years   ☐ Over 21 years

Design Elements

List a few of the design elements used to draw your attention, enhance the message, or encourage you to read further.

Please include your name

Top of Form | Goal of Home Page | Submit Information

Turning On or Off Features Not Supported by Web Browsers

Use the Turn On/Off Features Not Supported by Web Browsers option for creating Web pages to be viewed in Microsoft Internet Explorer version 4.0 or later, or Netscape Navigator version 4.0 or later. Click Tools and then Options, click the General tab, and then click Web Options. Click the General tab again. Select or clear the Disable features not supported by check box. In the Browser box, choose your browser.

Formatting That HTML Will Support

DTP POINTERS
HTML supports many formatting features in Word 2000.

When creating a Web page in Word, you can use many of the same formatting tools you use for Word documents. For instance, you can apply bold, italic, underline, strikethrough, superscript, and subscript formats to selected text.

You can set the colors for hyperlinks and followed hyperlinks for the entire page with the Style dialog box in the Format menu. Themes use different hyperlink colors. To change these, you must change the style at the Style dialog box. You can change colors for selected text by clicking the Font Color button on the Formatting toolbar.

You can indent text in 1/2-inch increments by clicking the Increase Indent and Decrease Indent buttons on the Formatting toolbar. In addition, you can change the alignment of text by clicking the Alignment buttons on the Formatting toolbar. A picture can be positioned on a Web page by selecting it first, then clicking an Alignment button. Drawing objects, such as WordArt and AutoShapes, can be inserted into a Web page.

Formatting That HTML Will Not Support

Formatting that is not supported by HTML at this time includes animated text (other than scrolling text), emboss, shadow, engrave, outline, and text effects. Paragraphs will automatically contain space before and after them. In addition, HTML at this time does not support margin changes at the Page Setup dialog box, columns, page borders, headers and footers, footnotes and endnotes, comments, outlines, master documents, and cross-references.

Using Word's Standard and Formatting Toolbars with HTML

The Standard and Formatting toolbars are available in Word 2000 when Word is in HTML editing mode. The features that are not available on these toolbars are deselected. To make formatting changes to an HTML document, click the Format option on the Menu bar, and a drop-down menu displays with options for changing the font, adding bullets or numbering, changing case, style, and adding a background or theme.

WYSIWYG
What You See Is What You Get.

Word is in HTML editing mode when you open an HTML document, save a document with an HTML extension, or choose the Web Page template. When a file is saved in HTML, the basic HTML page structure is in place. Word provides *WYSIWYG* (What You See Is What You Get) support for Web pages with commonly used tags, such as tables, fonts, and background sounds. If you want to view the HTML source code associated with the Web page you have created, click

<u>V</u>iew and then HTML Sourc<u>e</u>. At the HTML Source editor you can make changes. To return to the Web page in Word, click <u>F</u>ile and then E<u>x</u>it. An example of an HTML Source, the Microsoft Development Environment [design] dialog box, is shown in figure 8.14.

figure 8.14

An HTML Source, The Microsoft Development Environment [design] Dialog Box

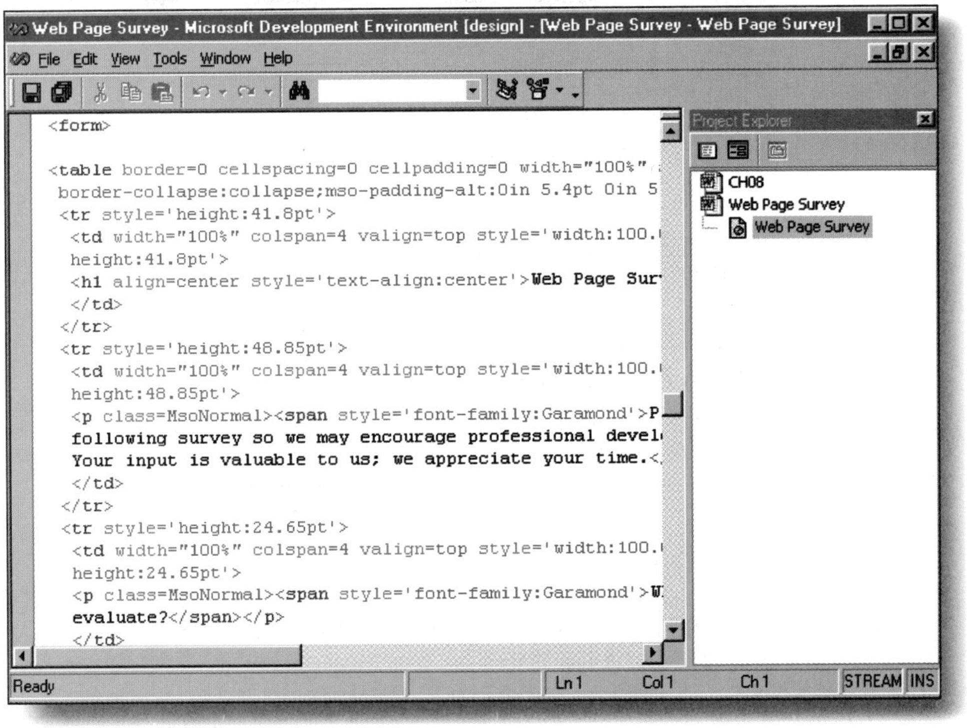

Using Font Colors

Font formats are more limited in HTML pages than in Word documents. At the Font dialog box, you can select from many font colors, which are also available on the Font Color button on the Formatting toolbar. You can also modify the color by going into the HTML source code and replacing the color code with a color you prefer.

Adding Scrolling Text to a Web Page

You can enhance your Web page with scrolling text, also known as a *marquee*, which travels across a page. Scrolling text is supported in all versions of Microsoft Internet Explorer 2.0 or later. Some other Web browsers (such as Netscape Navigator) may not support this feature. At the Web Tools toolbar, click the Scrolling Text button. Type the text that you want to scroll in the Type the scrolling text here text box. Select any other options you want—Behavior, Direction, Background color, Loop, or Speed, and then click the OK button to add the scrolling text to the page.

Marquee
Animated text that travels across the page.

DTP POINTERS
Use scrolling text to grab your viewer's attention.

To change the font size and color of scrolling text, select the text box containing the scrolling text and then change the size at the Font Size or Font Color buttons on the Formatting toolbar. To add bold and/or italic, click the corresponding buttons on the Formatting toolbar while the text box is selected.

figure
8.15

Scrolling Text Dialog Box

Scrolling Text	✕

Behavior: `Scroll ▼` Background color: `☐ Yellow ▼`

Direction: `Left ▼` Loop: `8 ▼`

Speed

Slow ──────────────●──────────── Fast

Type the scrolling text here:

`Web Page Survey`

Preview

Web Page Survey

`OK` `Cancel`

If you want to delete the scrolling text from your Web page, complete the following steps:

1. At the Web Tools toolbar, click the Design Mode button.
2. Right-click on the scrolling text.
3. Press Delete.
4. Click Exit Design Mode.

Using Themes

Theme

A set of design elements and color schemes.

A theme helps you create professional and well-designed documents. A *theme* is a set of design elements and color schemes. It provides a design for your document by using color, fonts, and graphics. A theme customizes the following elements: background color or graphics, body and heading styles, bullets, horizontal lines, hyperlink colors, and table border colors. You can apply a theme by using the Theme command on the Format menu, as shown earlier in this chapter in Figure 8.6. Select a theme and a sample displays. You may also wish to click the check mark to add Vivid Colors and then click the OK button.

DTP POINTERS

Change hyperlink formatting at the Styles dialog box.

Many times the default hyperlink color is changed when a theme is chosen. You may wish to change the hyperlink colors to the default color of blue. The default visited hyperlink (referred to as FollowedHyperlink) color is dark red. To do this, you must change the hyperlink formatting at the Styles dialog box. Click Format and Style. At the Style dialog box, click the Hyperlink style and click on the Modify button. At the Modify Style dialog box, click Format and Font. At the Font dialog box, Font tab, select the Blue Font color. Click OK and then OK. Click Apply.

To change the FollowedHyperlink color to dark red, follow the same procedures given in the preceding paragraph, except choose the FollowedHyperlink style at the Style dialog box. Change to the Dark Red Font color at the Font dialog box.

In exercise 4, you will create a table for the underlying structure of a form. A theme and an animated .gif are included to quickly create a professional-looking document. When you print the document, the animated .gif should print in a static format.

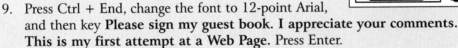

exercise 4

Creating a Guest Book Form

1. Create a Web page form as shown in figure 8.16 using a table, the control tools, a theme, and an animated .gif by completing the following steps:
2. Click File and New. At the General tab, double-click Web Page.
3. Turn on the Web Tools, Tables and Borders, and Drawing toolbars.
4. Create a new folder named *Guest Book* on a floppy disk or hard drive and name the document c08ex04, Guest Book Form. *(Hint: Save your document often.)*
5. Add a theme to your form by completing the following steps:
   a. Click Format and Theme.
   b. Choose Citrus Punch and then click OK.
6. Change the font to 22-point Lucida Calligraphy.
7. Key **Please sign my Guest Book** and then press Enter.
8. Add an animated .gif by completing the following steps:
   a. Position the insertion point to the left of the word *Please* and click Insert, Picture, and then ClipArt.
   b. Click the Motion Clips tab.
   c. Click the *Business* category and scroll until you locate the picture shown at the right.
   d. Click Insert clip and then close the ClipArt dialog box.

Step 8c

9. Press Ctrl + End, change the font to 12-point Arial, and then key **Please sign my guest book. I appreciate your comments. This is my first attempt at a Web Page.** Press Enter.
10. Change the font style to Heading 1 and key **Personal Information**. Press Enter.
11. Create a table with 2 columns and 12 rows.
12. Change the first column size to about 2 inches.
13. Change the second column size to about 2-1/2 inches.
14. Turn off all borders in the table, but display the table gridlines.
15. Create the text in the first column by completing the following steps (at this point, key the text for this column only):
    a. Key **First Name**.
    b. Position your insertion point in the next row and then key **Last Name**.
    c. Position your insertion point in the next row and then key **Street Address**.
    d. Continue keying the text in the first column as shown in figure 8.16 (until the Submit Query button).

16. Insert the Submit Query button by completing the following steps:
    a. Position your insertion point in the first column and eleventh row.
    b. Click the Design Mode button on the Web Tools toolbar. (Design Mode is now on.)
    c. Click the Submit button on the Web Tools toolbar.
17. Insert the Reset button by completing the following steps:
    a. Position your insertion point in the second column and eleventh row.
    b. Click the Reset button on the Web Tools toolbar.
18. To add the hyperlink *Back to my Home Page*, select the last row and complete the following steps:
    a. Merge the cells.
    b. Center align the cell.
    c. Press Enter and key **Back to my Home Page**.
    d. Select *Back to my Home Page*, click the down arrow at the Style list box on the Formatting toolbar, and then click Hyperlink.

Step 18d

19. To add the text boxes for the viewers to insert information, complete the following steps (the text boxes may appear short, but they will display correctly in the browser):
    a. Position the insertion point in column 2 and row 1.
    b. Click the Textbox button on the Web Tools toolbar.
    c. Continue adding eight more textboxes in the next seven rows by positioning your insertion point in the cell and clicking the Textbox button on the Web Tools toolbar.
20. Add a text area in the second column and tenth row. To do this, click the Text Area button on the Web Tools toolbar.
21. Save your document again with the same name, c08ex04, Guest Book Form.
22. Preview your document in your browser.
23. Print c08ex04, Guest Book Form from your browser.

figure
8.16
Exercise 4

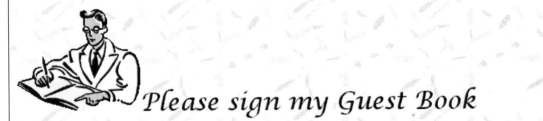

Please sign my guest book. I appreciate your comments. This is my first attempt at a Web Page.

Personal Information

First Name

Last Name

Street Address

City

State

Zip Code

Country

Phone

E-Mail

Comments

[Submit Query]   [Reset]

Back to my Home Page

Editing in Web Layout View

DTP POINTERS

The Document Map feature is helpful to jump between locations in a large document.

Web Layout View enables you to view your document as it might appear online. The Document Map feature is available and it displays to the left of the screen in Web Layout View. Document Map is helpful in jumping between locations in large documents. In order for the Document Map to display the main headings, you must apply HTML heading styles to your heading text.

figure
8.17

Document Map Displaying Main Headings

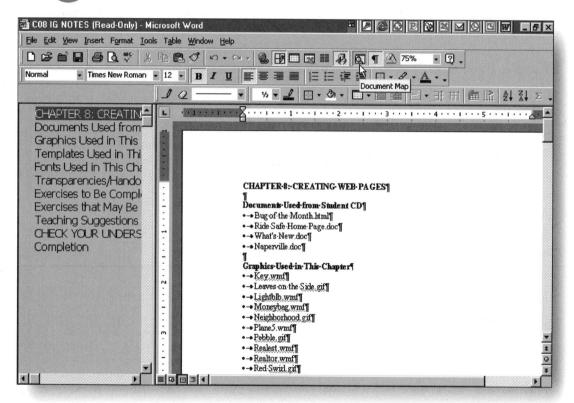

NaperV and Associates is a large corporation located in Lisle, IL. It is sponsoring a conference and has decided to put the conference agenda and evaluation form on its company intranet. In the following exercise, you will create the evaluation form. In the assessments at the end of the chapter, you will work with the agenda.

exercise 5

Creating an Evaluation Form Online

1. Open Evaluation Form.doc located on your student CD.
2. Create a new folder on a floppy disk and name it *Evaluation*.
3. Click File, Save as Web Page, and name the document c08ex05, Evaluation Form. *(Hint: Save often while creating this Web page.)*
4. Click Ctrl + End to move the insertion point below the banner.
5. Display the Web Tools, Tables and Borders, and Drawing toolbars.
6. Press the Center align button on the Formatting toolbar.
7. Change the font to 10-point Arial bold and key **Please tell us what you think about the conference. Use the following scale:**. *(Hint: The text may not appear centered under the banner.)* Press Enter.
8. Create a table by completing the following steps:
   a. Click Table, point to Insert, and then click Table.
   b. At the Insert Table dialog box, create a table with 1 column and 1 row.
   c. In the AutoFit behavior section of the Insert Table dialog box, click the AutoFormat button, select the *List 1* format in the Formats list box, and then remove the check mark next to Shading in the Formats to apply section. Click OK twice.
   d. Center the table horizontally by clicking Table, Table Properties, and then Center in the Alignment section of the Table tab. Click OK or press Enter.
   e. Change the font to 9-point Arial bold italic in Dark Red, key **3 Strongly Agree/Excellent**, and press the space bar five times; key **2 Agree/Good**, press the space bar five times; key **1 Disagree/Needs Improvement**, press the space bar five times; and then key **NA Not Applicable**. (The text may wrap to the next line, but it will display on one line in Web Page Preview.)
9. Deselect the table, click the Align Left button on the Formatting toolbar, and then press Enter twice.
10. Save the document again and view at Web Page Preview.
11. Click the Edit button on the Internet Explorer toolbar, and create another table for the remainder of the document by completing the following steps:
    a. Click Table, point to Insert, and then click Table.
    b. At the Insert Table dialog box, create a table with 3 columns and 20 rows.
    c. In the AutoFit behavior section of the Insert Table dialog box, click the AutoFormat button and select the *3D effects 3* format. (Make sure a check mark displays in the check box next to Shading.) Click OK twice.
    d. Click Table and then Table Properties.
    e. Select the Table tab and click Center in the Alignment section.
    f. Select the Column tab and change the width of column 1 to 0.25 inch, column 2 to 3.25 inches, and column 3 to 2.6 inches. Click OK.
    g. Select the entire table and then change the font to 12-point Arial and make sure bold is turned off.
    h. Position the insertion point in column 2, row 1, turn on bold, and then key **Questions**.
    i. Press Tab, make sure bold is on, and then key **Evaluation**.
    j. Select column 1 and click the Align Right button on the Formatting toolbar.
    k. Select column 2 (except for the heading, Questions) and click the Align Left button on the Formatting toolbar.

l. Position the insertion point in column 1, row 2, and key **1** (without the period and make sure bold is turned off). Press the tab key. Key **The conference was interesting** again, with bold turned off.

m. Continue keying the number of the questions in the first column and the questions in the second column until you reach the heading *Topics*. Refer to Figure 8.18 for the text.

12. After question 5, select the next row and merge the cells.

13. Change the alignment to Align Left, key **Topics**, and then press Enter.

14. Press the Ctrl + Tab to move the insertion point to the default tab.

15. Create the check boxes by completing the following steps:

a. Click the Design Mode button on the Web Tools toolbar.

b. Click the Checkbox button on the Web Tools toolbar.

c. Click to the right of the box, press the space bar once, key **Getting Organized**, and then press Enter.

d. Press Ctrl + Tab and then click the Checkbox button.

e. Click to the right of the box, press the space bar once, key **How Far is Too Far?**, and then press Enter.

f. Press Ctrl + Tab and then click the Checkbox button.

g. Click to the right of the box, press the space bar once, key **Communicate with Confidence**.

16. Continue keying the numbers and questions for 6, 7, and 8.

17. After question 8 select the next row and merge the cells.

18. Change the alignment to Align Left, key **Facilities**, and then press Tab.

19. Continue keying the numbers and questions for 9–12.

20. After question 12, select the next row and merge the cells.

21. Change the alignment to Align Left, key **Additional Comments**, and then press Tab.

22. Continue keying the numbers and questions for 13–15. (Refer to figure 8.18 for the text.)

23. To insert the text areas for questions 13–15, complete the following steps:

a. Position the insertion point in the third column and seventeenth row and click the Text Area button on the Web Tools toolbar.

Step 23a

> 13 What was the most useful thing you learned in this conference?

b. Copy and paste the text area box to the eighteenth and nineteenth rows.

24. To add the Submit Query and Reset buttons to the form, complete the following steps:

a. Click inside the second column and the last row.

b. Press the Enter key to add extra space.

c. Click the Submit button on the Web Tools toolbar.

d. Click to the right of the image to get the flashing insertion point, press the spacebar about ten times, and then click the Reset button on the Web Tools toolbar.

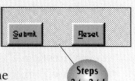

Steps 24c-24d

25. You are now ready to create the *Evaluation* column. Complete the following steps:

a. Position the insertion point in the third column and second row.

b. Key **3** and then press the space bar once.

c. Click the Option Button on the Web Tools toolbar.
d. Click to the right of the Option Button and then press the space bar five times.
e. Key **2** and then press the space bar.
f. Click the Option Button on the Web Tools toolbar.
g. Click to the right of the Option Button and then press the space bar five times.
h. Key **1** and then press the space bar.
i. Click the Option Button on the Web Tools toolbar.
j. Click to the right of the Option Button and then press the space bar five times.
k. Key **NA** and then press the space bar.
l. Click the Option Button on the Web Tools toolbar.
m. Select the cell containing the four option buttons, click Copy on the Standard toolbar, and then paste this information to the appropriate rows.

26. The Option Buttons will need to be changed so that the first button in each row is the default. Each row of buttons will have the same HTMLName. Complete the following steps (Design Mode must be on):

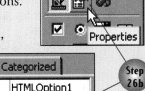

a. Position the insertion point in the first row of Option Buttons. This is the third column and second row of the table.
b. Click on the first Option Button. With the button selected, click on the Properties button on the Web Tools toolbar. In the Alphabetic tab, click to the right of Checked. Click on the down arrow to change to *True*. Click to the right of *HTMLName* and key **1** for the *HTMLName*.
c. Click the Option Button to the right of the *2*.
d. At the Properties dialog box, change the *HTMLName* to **1**. The *Checked* column will indicate *False*. (You do not have to change this.)
e. Click the Option Button to the right of the *1*. At the Properties dialog box, change the *HTMLName* to **1**. The *Checked* column will indicate *False*. (You do not have to change this.)
f. Click on the Option Button at the right of *NA*. At the Properties dialog box, change the *HTMLName* to **1**. The *Checked* column will indicate *False*. (You do not have to change this.)
g. Click on the Option Button to the right of the *3* for the second question. (If the Properties box isn't open, click the Properties button.) At the Properties dialog box, change the *Checked* column to *True*. Change the *HTMLName* to **2**.

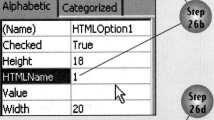

h. Continue changing the remainder of the rows of Option Buttons so that the first Option Button is *True* and each row of Option Buttons has the same HTMLName.
i. Click the Design Mode button to turn this feature off.
j. Make sure all border lines have been removed from the table.

27. Save the document again with the same name, c08ex05, Evaluation Form.
28. View c08ex05, Evaluation Form at Web Page Preview. (Compare the document to figure 8.18.)
29. Print c08ex05, Evaluation Form at Web Page Preview and then close.

figure
8.18
Exercise 5

NaperV and Associates

CONFERENCE: PRIDE AND PROFESSIONALISM

Evaluation Form

Please tell us what you think about the conference. Use the following scale:

3 Strongly Agree/Excellent	2 Agree/Good	1 Disagree/Needs Improvement	NA Not Applicable

	Questions	Evaluation			
1	The conference was interesting	3 ⊙	2 ○	1 ○	NA ○
2	The topics and subjects covered were relevant	3 ⊙	2 ○	1 ○	NA ○
3	I was energized or stimulated by the conference	3 ⊙	2 ○	1 ○	NA ○
4	I would recommend this format for future events	3 ⊙	2 ○	1 ○	NA ○
5	Overall quality of the conference	3 ⊙	2 ○	1 ○	NA ○

Topics

☐ Getting Organized
☐ How Far is Too Far?
☐ Communicate with Confidence

6	The presenter was well informed and interesting	3 ⊙	2 ○	1 ○	NA ○
7	I am interested in another presentation on this topic with more information	3 ⊙	2 ○	1 ○	NA ○
8	Overall quality of the presentation	3 ⊙	2 ○	1 ○	NA ○

Facilities

9	The meeting events were well organized	3 ⊙	2 ○	1 ○	NA ○
10	The facilities were satisfactory	3 ⊙	2 ○	1 ○	NA ○
11	The meeting room arrangements were comfortable	3 ⊙	2 ○	1 ○	NA ○
12	The quality of the luncheon was good	3 ⊙	2 ○	1 ○	NA ○

Additional Comments

13 What was the most useful thing you learned in this conference?

14 What other topics are you interested in having presented?

15 Comments and suggestions on this conference

[Submit Query]   [Reset]

Inserting Graphics and Objects in a Web Page

HTML supports two main graphic file formats: .gif and .jpg. However, with Word 2000, you can use many other graphic file formats—such as .wmf, .tif, .cgm, and .bmp—and Word will automatically convert the graphic image to a format suitable for HTML pages when you save the Word document with Save as Web Page. Word will save each graphic file as image001.gif, image002.gif, and so on in a subfolder in your Word document folder.

Resize your image in Word before saving the document as an HTML file. If you have problems resizing a particular graphic, you may need to load the image into a graphic-editing program such as Microsoft Word Picture, Microsoft Photo Editor, or Microsoft PhotoDraw 2000. To change to a different editor, click Tools, Options, select the Edit tab, and then select the desired editor in the Picture editor list box. To access the editor, right-click on the image and select Edit Picture from the pop-up menu; or double-click on the image, or click Insert, Object, and then select the editor.

You can change the position of an image on a Web page by selecting the image, then clicking one of the alignment buttons on the Formatting toolbar. You also can change text-wrapping options on the Picture toolbar.

Using Alternative Text in Place of Graphics

You may want to create alternative text that displays when graphics or hyperlinked graphics cannot display. Graphics, photos, and visuals create large files and slow down performance of the Web page. As an alternative, many Web pages will include text in place of the graphic image.

Understanding .GIF and .JPG File Formats in HTML

When a graphical bullet or line or a clip art image is added to an HTML document, Word automatically saves the bullet, line, or graphic as a *.gif* (Graphics Interchange Format, GIF) or *.jpg* (Joint Picture Experts Group, JPEG) file. The file is saved separately from the document HTML file. At this time, HTML does not have the capability to save a graphic file within its format. Therefore, the two file formats that HTML will recognize, .gif and .jpg, are saved separately from the HTML document in the default folder in a subfolder. The .gif extension is used for clip art and objects, and the .jpg extension is used for photographic pictures. Files are saved in this manner in order to display the images in the HTML document when you open it. For instance, if you add a clip art image, it will appear as image001.gif in the subfolder of the document file, but not within the document file. Do not delete the .gif or .jpg files from your subfolder thinking that they are taking up too much space on your drive or disk. They must remain in the subfolder in which they are connected in order for them to display at your browser.

DTP POINTERS
Photos, videos, and background sounds add impact to a Web page, but they create large files and slow down performance.

DTP POINTERS
Word automatically saves images as .gif or .jpg files.

figure
8.19

Subfolder Opened Showing Image Files

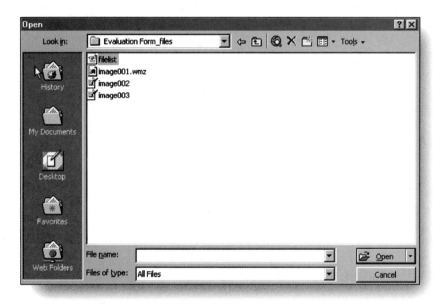

Downloading More Graphics and Images

Additional images for Web pages are available on the World Wide Web. Click Insert, Picture, and Clip Art. Click Clips Online to access the Internet menu, and then click Browse Web Art Page. Follow the directions to download the images that you want. One valuable Web URL that contains many images, icons, backgrounds, sounds, fonts, and more is *http://msdn.microsoft.com/downloads*.

Scanning Pictures for a Web Page

DTP POINTERS
In Web pages, clip art and objects are usually saved as .gif files and photographs are usually saved as .jpg files.

If a scanner is attached to your computer, you can use Word and Microsoft Photo Editor to scan and edit your images into Word documents or into documents saved in HTML. Consider scanning pictures of relatives, vacation spots, or special events for a personal Web site. Scan pictures of new employees, award winners, or new products for a company Web site.

Adding AutoShapes and Other Drawing Objects to a Web Page

Drawing objects, such as AutoShapes, text boxes, and WordArt objects, can be inserted into Web pages. When you save your document with Save as Web Page, Word converts the drawing object into a .gif image.

Using Graphics as Hyperlinks

DTP POINTERS
Graphics break up text-intensive areas on a Web page.

As you browsed the Web sites in exercise 1, did you notice that graphics were sometimes used as hyperlinks to other Web sites or documents? You can hyperlink your graphics just as easily as you created text hyperlinks earlier in this chapter. To hyperlink a graphic to a Web page or document, complete the following steps:

1. Insert the graphic.
2. Select the graphic.
3. Click Insert and Hyperlink to display the Insert Hyperlink dialog box.
4. Type the file or Web page name in the text box. If you do not know the path or URL, click Browse for File, Web page, or Bookmark.
5. Add a ScreenTip.
6. Click the OK button.
7. If the graphic is too large and seems to slow down the Web page, create alternative text to substitute for the image.

Using Frames in Web Pages

When a single Web page is divided into sections that can display separate Web pages, each section is referred to as a *frame*. This feature allows you to display a new page in one frame while other frames stay unchanged. Hyperlinks in one frame can be used to change what is being displayed in another frame. For instance, the banner frame and the contents frame may remain constant, whereas the main frame may display different Web pages accessed by hyperlinks in the contents frame, as shown in figure 8.20. A Web page that contains frames may be referred to as a *frameset* (sometimes referred to as a *frames page* or *container page*). You may have as many frames as you want in a frames page and in varying designs; however, the more frames you have, the more complicated navigation becomes.

Use the Frames toolbar to add frames to your Web page. Save the new frames page just as you would save a Word document or a Web page without frames. Once you add frames to a frames page, you can set the Web page that appears initially in each frame. Then you can add hyperlinks to other Web pages, which will then display in each frame.

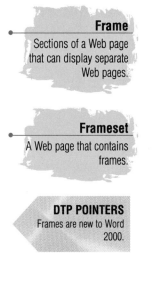

Frame
Sections of a Web page that can display separate Web pages.

Frameset
A Web page that contains frames.

DTP POINTERS
Frames are new to Word 2000.

figure
8.20   *Frames in a Web Page*

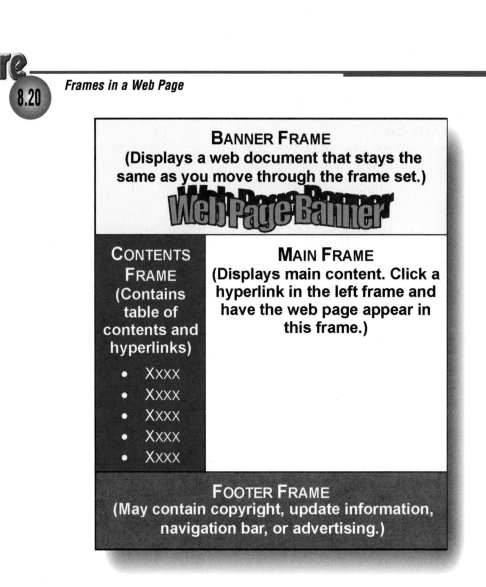

To change characteristics of a frame or frameset, such as the size and borders, click the Frame Properties button on the Frames toolbar. At the Frame Properties dialog box, select the Borders tab as shown in figure 8.21 or select the Frame tab as shown in figure 8.22. At these two tabs you will find options to display or hide the frame border and the scrollbar, size the frame, name the frame, update the frame, and adjust the flexibility of the frame in a browser. Many times you may think you are looking at a Web page without frames, when in reality there are frames in the page but the frames are hidden.

To add new frames to a Web page, click the New Frame Left (Right, Above, Below) button on the Frames toolbar as shown in figure 8.23.

figure

8.21

Borders Tab at the Frame Properties Dialog Box

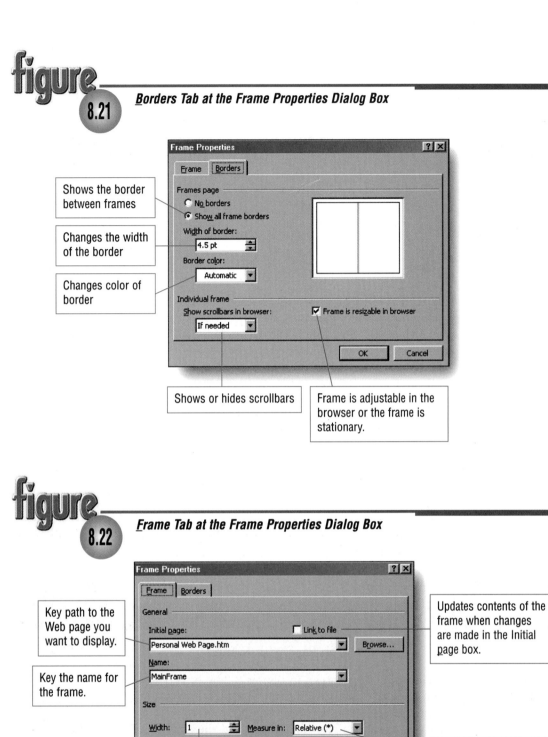

Shows the border between frames

Changes the width of the border

Changes color of border

Shows or hides scrollbars

Frame is adjustable in the browser or the frame is stationary.

figure

8.22

Frame Tab at the Frame Properties Dialog Box

Key path to the Web page you want to display.

Key the name for the frame.

Updates contents of the frame when changes are made in the Initial page box.

Choose how the width should be measured.

Key width you want for the frame.

figure

8.23 *Frames Toolbar*

| Table of Contents in Frame | New Frame Left | New Frame Right | New Frame Above | New Frame Below | Delete Frame | Frame Properties |

You create links to other Web sites or documents by inserting hyperlinks. In the Insert Hyperlink dialog box, you can pick the frame you want the Web page to appear in. When you click a hyperlink, the Web page is displayed in the designated frame. Assign a unique name to each frame if you want to control where a Web page will appear when you click a hyperlink. Frame names are case sensitive and can use both letters and numbers. Word provides a default name for each frame—*file 1, file 2,* etc. For instance, if you have three frames in a Web page, you are actually working with four separate documents. The frameset is one document, which defines the contents, and each of the three frames is considered a separate Web page. Each of the four files must be saved as a separate Web page. To save the container page, use File, Save as Web Page from the menu. To save each frame page, right-click in any blank area of the frame, and then choose Save Current Frame As.

In exercise 6, you will create a Web page using frames for Ride Safe, Inc. You will include hyperlinks to other Web pages saved on your student CD and links to Web sites on the Internet.

exercise 6

Creating a Web Page with Frames

1. Create a Web page with frames (as shown in figures 8.24a, b, and c) using the Web Page Wizard by completing the following steps:
   a. At a clear document screen, click File and then New.
   b. Select the Web Pages tab at the New dialog box and then double-click the Web Page Wizard icon.
   c. At the Start screen, click Next>.
   d. At the Title and Location screen, key **Ride Safe Web Page** in the Web site title text box and then key **A:\Ride Safe Web Page** in the Web site location text box. Click Next>.
   e. At the Navigation screen, select the Vertical frame, and then click Next>.
   f. At the Add Pages screen, complete the following steps:

1) Click the Add Existing File button and select *RS Helmet Safety Links.doc* located in the *Ride Safe* folder on your student CD. *(Hint: Click the Up One Level and Back arrow to locate the documents.)* Click Open to add the file.

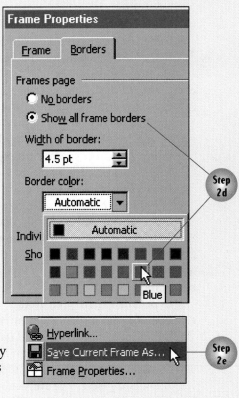

2) Click the Add Existing File button and then select *Frequently Asked Questions.doc* located in the *Ride Safe* folder on your student CD. Select *Blank Page 1* in the Current Pages in Web site list box and click the Remove Page button.

3) Select *Blank Page 2* in the Current Pages in Web site list box and click the Remove Page button.

4) Click Next>.

g. At the Organize Pages screen, select *Personal Web Page*, click the Rename button, key **Ride Safe Home Page**, and then click OK. Click Next>.

h. At the Visual Theme screen, make sure Add a visual theme is selected, click the Browse Themes button, and select *Fiesta* in the Choose a Theme list box. Click OK and then click Next>. (If Fiesta is not available, select a similar theme.)

i. Click Finish.

2. Customize the frames in the Web page by completing the following steps:

a. Position the insertion point on the line above *Main Heading Goes Here* and click the New Frame Above button on the Frames toolbar.

b. With the insertion point in the top frame, click Insert, File, select *RS Banner.doc*, which is in the *Ride Safe* folder on your student CD, and then click Insert.

c. Click Format, Theme, and then select the *Fiesta* theme. Click OK.

d. Click the Frame Properties button on the Frames toolbar, select the Borders tab, and then click Show all frame borders. Change the Border color to Blue. Click OK.

e. Right-click in any blank area of the top frame and choose Save Current Frame As, make sure the folder *Ride Safe Web Page* displays in the Save in list box, and then key **RS Banner**. (Make sure .htm/.html displays in the Save as type list box.) Click Save.

f. Save the frameset by clicking File and Save as Web Page. Make sure *Ride Safe Web Page* displays in the Save in list box, key **c08ex06, Ride Safe Web Page** in the File name text box, and then click Save. (Word automatically assigns an .htm or .html extension.)

g. Position the insertion point in the main frame, select *Main Heading Goes Here*, key **Ride Safe Home Page**, and apply the Heading 2 style.

h. Delete any hard returns above *Ride Safe Home Page* and then click Format, Paragraph, and make sure *0 pt* displays in the Before text box in the Spacing section. Click OK.

i. Delete all the text beginning with Contents up to the last hyperlink, *Back to top*. Delete *Last Revised: Date,* but do not delete *Back to top*.

j. Position the insertion point below *Ride Safe Home Page* and insert Our Goal.doc located in the *Ride Safe* folder on your student CD.

k. Select the headings, *Our Goal, Our Program,* and *Our Commitment* and apply the Heading 3 style. (*Hint: Use the Format Painter.*) (If needed, press Enter before *Our* to force the text to the next line.)

l. Click anywhere in the body text in each paragraph and apply the Normal style.

m. Right-click in any blank area of the main frame and choose Save Current Frame As and key **Ride Safe Home Page** in the File name text box in the Save As dialog box, and then click Save. (Word should automatically assign an .htm extension, and the correct file name may already display.) Make sure you are saving to the *Ride Safe Web Page* folder.

n. Click File and then Web Page Preview. Scroll through the document and click the hyperlink at the bottom of the page.

3. Add a graphic image to the left frame by completing the following steps:

   a. Click the Edit button to return to Word and position the insertion point in the left frame.

   b. Click Insert, Picture, From File, and insert RSBiker.gif located in the *Ride Safe* folder on your student CD. Click Insert.

   c. Select the image, click the Text Wrapping button on the Picture toolbar, and then click In Front of Text.

   d. Size and position the image as in figure 8.24a.

   e. Press Enter until the insertion point is positioned below the image (if needed, drag the image back to the desired position), change the font to 11-point Verdana, and then key **"About 30% of car/bike collisions involving kids under 15 occur when children swerve unexpectedly into the path of a faster moving vehicle."**

   f. Right-click in any blank area of the left frame and choose Save Current Frame As. Make sure you are saving to the *Ride Safe Web Page* folder, key **TOCFrame** in the File name text box in the Save As dialog box, and then click Save. (The extension .htm should automatically display.)

4. Add a hyperlink to the RS Helmet Safety Links Web page shown in figure 8.24b by completing the following steps:

   a. Click the hyperlink *RS Helmet Safety Links* located in the left frame.

   b. Scroll through the Links Web page and test the hyperlinks already created.

   c. Position the insertion point between the last bullet and *International In-Line Skating Association* and insert the image shown at the right by completing the following steps:

      1) Click Insert, Picture, and then Clip Art.

Step 4c

2) At the Insert ClipArt dialog box, select the Motion Clips tab.
3) Key **skating** in the Search for clips text box and press Enter.
4) Click on the rollerblade image, click Insert clip at the pop-up menu, and then close the dialog box.
5) Size the image similar to the other hyperlink graphics in this Web page.
6) Select the rollerblade image, click the Insert Hyperlink button on the Standard toolbar, click E_xisting File or Web Page, and then key **http://www.iisa.org/index.html** in the Type the fil_e or Web page name text box. Click OK. (To test this hyperlink, make sure you are connected to the Web.)
7) Click the Save button on the Standard toolbar and then view the page in Web Page Preview. Scroll through the page and then click the Edit button to return to Word.

5. Click _File, Save as Web Page, make sure _c08ex06, Ride Safe Web Page_ displays in the File _name text box and _Ride Safe Web Page_ displays in the Save _in list box, and then click S_ave.

6. Click _Frequently Asked Questions_ in the left frame and scroll through the Web page and test the existing hyperlink as shown in figure 8.24c.

7. View the _Frequently Asked Questions_ Web page in Web Page Preview.

8. Position the insertion point in each frame and print each page separately.

9. Close c08ex06, Ride Safe Web Page.htm.

figure
8.24a

Exercise 6, Ride Safe Home Page

figure
8.24b

Exercise 6, RS Helmet Safety Links.htm

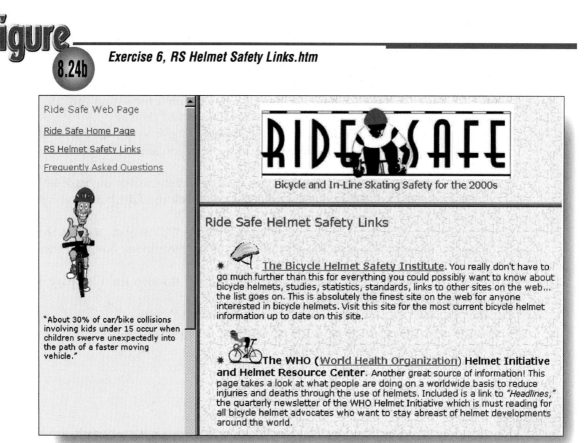

figure
8.24c

Exercise 6, Frequently Asked Questions.htm

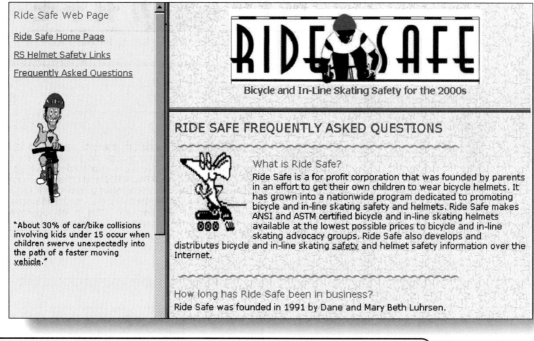

chapter summary

➤ The Internet is a worldwide network of commercial, educational, governmental, and personal computers connected together for the purpose of sharing information.

➤ The World Wide Web (WWW) is the most commonly used application on the Internet and is a set of standards and protocols used to access information available on the Internet.

➤ An intranet is an "internal Internet" within an organization that uses the same Web technology and tools as the Internet and is also used for sharing information.

➤ Word provides the ability to jump to the Internet from the Word document screen.

➤ An Internet Service Provider (ISP) sells access to the Internet.

➤ The Uniform Resource Locator, referred to as URL, is the method used to identify locations on the Internet.

➤ Home pages are the starting point for viewing Web sites. Home pages are also documents that describe a company, school, government, or individual and are created using a language called Hypertext Markup Language (HTML).

➤ You can create a home page in Word and then convert it to an HTML document, or you can create a Web page using the Web Page Wizard or the Blank Web Page template.

➤ Plan and design your Web page with a purpose in mind. Review other Web pages on the Internet or an intranet for design ideas.

➤ Hyperlinks are colored and underlined text or a graphic that you click to go to a file, a location in a file, an HTML page on the WWW, or an HTML page on an intranet.

➤ One method for creating a hyperlink is to select the text and then click the Insert Hyperlink button on the Standard toolbar. At the Insert Hyperlink dialog box, key the URL and then click OK.

➤ Bookmarks are created and used to move to another location within a document.

➤ Format a Web page with Menu bar options as well as buttons on the toolbars.

➤ The Web Page Wizard includes several different types of Web page layouts in addition to many visual styles.

➤ Lines are added to a Web page through the Clip Art dialog box.

➤ Preview a Web page document by clicking File and then Web Page Preview.

➤ HTML does not support all of the Word formatting features.

➤ HTML does not support all graphic formats. Word automatically converts various graphic files into .gif or .jpg formats, which are suitable for HTML pages.

➤ Graphical images are saved to your default folder in a subfolder, separate from your HTML document.

➤ Tables can be used to control the layout of a Web page.

➤ Forms can be used to collect and present data on a Web page.

➤ You can create and use form controls from the Web Tools toolbar.

➤ A checkbox control is used when the user can select more than one choice at once.

➤ An option button control is used when the user should select only one option.

➤ Many design themes are available to help you create professional and well-designed documents.

➤ A frame is a Web page that is divided into sections that can display separate Web pages.

commands review

	Mouse/Keyboard
Bookmark	Click Insert, Bookmark
Display the Web toolbar	Click Web toolbar button on Standard toolbar; or right-click any toolbar and click Web
Display Internet Explorer Search page	Click Search the Web button on the Web toolbar
Save Word document in HTML format	Click File, Save as Web Page
Display the Web Page Wizard	Click File, New, select the Web Pages tab, and then double-click the Web Page Wizard icon
Display a Blank Web page	Click File, New, select the General tab, and then double-click the Web Page icon
Insert graphics	Click Insert, point to Picture, and then click Clip Art
Insert Alternative text	Right-click on image, click Format, Picture, Web tab
Insert a hyperlink	Click Insert Hyperlink button on the Standard toolbar, or click Insert, then Hyperlink
Preview a Web page	Click File, then Web Page Preview
Edit a hyperlink	Select the hyperlink, right-click and select Hyperlink, then click Edit Hyperlink
Display Lines	Click Format, Borders and Shading, Horizontal Line
Display Bullets and Numbering dialog box	Click Format, Bullets and Numbering
Display Scroll Text dialog box	Click Scrolling Text at the Web Tools toolbar
Display Background color	Click Format, point to Background, then select a color or fill effect
Tables	Click Table, Insert, Table; or click the Draw Table button on the Tables and Borders toolbar
Themes	Format, Themes
Forms	Display the Web Tools toolbar
Frames	Display the Forms toolbar

Completion: In the space provided at the right, indicate the correct term or command.

1. List three reasons why users access the Internet.   _____

    _____

2. The letters ISP stand for this.   _____

3. This is a method used to identify locations on the Internet.   _____

4. This is an "internal Internet" used to share information within an organization.   _____

5. Insert this button control in a form when the user should select only one option.   _____

6. Click this button in the Internet Explorer program window to display the previous page or location.   _____

7. Click this in a home page to link to another page or location.   _____

8. This is used to move to another location within a document.   _____

9. A home page on the Web is created using this language.   _____

10. A home page can be created in Word and then converted to HTML or created with this feature.   _____

11. Click this button on the Standard toolbar to add a hyperlink to selected text.   _____

12. Apply background shading to a Web document by clicking Background at this drop-down menu.   _____

13. This Word feature is used to control the layout of a Web page.   _____

14. This HTML feature displays text like a marquee traveling across the page.   _____

15. Center a graphic horizontally on a Web page by clicking this button on the Formatting toolbar.   _____

16. To create a transparent area in a picture, use this Microsoft graphic editor.   _____

17. Themes are available at this dialog box.   _____

18. This feature is used to divide Web pages into sections that can display separate Web pages.   _____

Assessment 1

NaperV and Associates has asked you to create an agenda for the Pride and Professionalism conference to be held in Lisle, IL. The agenda will be placed on the intranet of NaperV and Associates, so you must create the agenda as a Web page. Include the following specifications:

1. Create a table so that you will have better control over the layout. Insert a banner at the top of the page. The banner has been created already and is located on your student CD as NaperV Banner.htm.
2. Use appropriate heading styles, color, font types and sizes for the heading information.
3. In the sample shown in Figure 8.25 the first column was right aligned. Right alignment was also used for the second lines in the second column.
4. Be sure to turn the table lines off, but the gridlines are helpful.
5. An image was added that was changed to a watermark by completing the following steps:
    a. Position your insertion point in the *Getting Organized* cell.
    b. To add the watermark, click <u>I</u>nsert, <u>P</u>icture, and <u>C</u>lipArt. At the Pictures tab, click the *People at Work* category.
    c. Select the lady with the brief case image as shown in figure 8.25 (in the clips 241–300 section).
    d. Click Insert clip. Close the Insert ClipArt dialog box.
    e. Select the image, click the Text Wrapping button on the Picture toolbar, and then click I<u>n</u> Front of Text so you can move and resize the image.
    f. Click the Image Control button and then click <u>W</u>atermark.
    g. Change the Text Wrapping to Behin<u>d</u> Text. *(Hint: You may need to reduce the size of the right column of your table drastically to resize and place the image where you want it on your page. Then, resize your column.)*
6. Save your document by clicking <u>F</u>ile, Save as Web Pa<u>g</u>e, and then name the Web page c08sa01, Agenda.
7. View c08sa01, Agenda at Web Page Preview.
8. Print at the browser and then close c08sa01, Agenda.

figure

8.25

Assessment 1

NaperV and Associates

Conference Agenda

Pride and Professionalism
» **Wednesday, April 28, 2001** «
8:30 a.m. - 3:30 p.m.

Holiday Hotel
Room 327
12 East State Street
Lisle, IL 60333

8:30 a.m. - 9:00 a.m.	Continental Breakfast
9:00 a.m. - 9:30 a.m.	**Opening Remarks**
	Gail Lacey, President, NaperV and Associates
9:30 a.m. - 10:30 a.m.	**Getting Organized**
	Speaker: *Janice Bianco*, Author
10:30 a.m. - 11:00 a.m.	Break
11:00 a.m. - 12 noon	**How Far is Too Far?**
	Speaker: *Cynthia Nielsen*, Human Resources Director
12 noon - 1:30 p.m.	Lunch/Networking
1:45 p.m. - 2:45 p.m.	**Communicate with Confidence**
	Speaker: *Alexander Kemper*, Ph.D.
2:45 p.m. - 3:00 p.m.	Break
3:00 p.m. - 3:30 p.m.	**Closing Remarks, Questions, Answers**
	Gail Lacey, President, NaperV and Associates

Assessment 2

Assume you are working for a travel vacation company named Paradise Vacations that specializes in selling vacation packages to tropical locations. Your company is setting up a Web page to advertise its travel services, which have recently expanded to include travel packages for corporate clients. Figure 8.26 is a sample Web page; use your own design ideas to create Paradise Vacations' Web page using Word Web templates, a Blank Web Page, a table, or frames. Include the following specifications:

1. Plan what you want to accomplish in this Web page. Do you want to include an introductory paragraph, a table of contents, hyperlinks, a consistent theme, a logo, motion clips, or a navigation bar with hyperlinks to different sections in the Web page or to an e-mail address? View other travel sites on the Web for design ideas.
2. Once you have a basic plan, create a thumbnail sketch of the design and layout of the Web page.
3. Create a folder on a floppy disk or the hard drive and name the folder *Travel*.
4. Add an appropriate design theme using consistent background, font colors, and design elements.
5. Include at least two graphical elements—pictures, photographs, scanned images, or motion clips.
6. If sound is available, include a sound clip with a tropical overtone.
7. Save your document in HTML and name it c08sa02, Travel. (Be sure to save often.)
8. Include the text in figure 8.26, although you may rearrange and reword the text if desired.
9. View the Web page frequently in Web Page Preview to arrange the text and design elements properly.
10. Include the following hyperlinks (first try out each of the links to make sure they are operating properly):

> Car Rental—*http://www.hertz.com*
> Cruises—*http://www.cruise.com*
> Site Maps—*http://www.mapquest.com*
> Hotel Reservations—*http://www.marriott.com*
> Air Reservations—*http://www.ual.com*
> Golf—*http://www.seasidegolf.com*

11. Create a bookmark and hyperlink from the bottom of the page to the top of the page.
12. Save the Web page again with the same name (c08sa02, Travel).
13. View the document at Web Page Preview and make any necessary adjustments.
14. Close c08sa02, Travel.

figure
8.26

Assessment 2, Sample Solution

PARADISE VACATIONS

Scrolling Text

:kages for 2001...

All About Paradise Vacations

Paradise Vacations is a leading travel agency in the Chicago area specializing in tropical vacation packages and now offering up-to-date travel information via e-mail, in person, and online. Our new Website, http://www.paradisev.com, is a one-stop travel site on the Internet providing secure online reservation capabilities for air, car, hotel and vacation reservations, plus access to other travel information.

Fabulous Vacation Destinations

Take a dream vacation to any one of the following locations or talk to one of our travel consultants and we can suggest other locations based on your desires and needs. Contact our corporate travel consultants for all your business needs.

- Florida—Sanibel Island, Miami, Key Biscayne, Orlando
- Hawaii, Maui, Oahu, Kauai
- Mexico—Cancun, Cozumel
- Bahamas & Caribbean— Nassau, Bermuda, Grand Cayman, Jamaica, Virgin Islands, St. Croix

Return to Top

Contact Us At...

- 100 West Monroe, Chicago, IL 60601
- (606) 555-2389
- http://www.paradisev.com
- E-mail: paradisv@aol.com

Car Rental   Cruises   Site Maps

Hotel Reservations   Air Reservations   Golf

Last Updated: October 14, 2001

You will create a Web home page for NaperV and Associates and use the Web Page Wizard to format this page with frames. At the home page you will hyperlink to the guest book form created in exercise 4 and to the evaluation form created in exercise 5 of this chapter. Include the following specifications:

1. Open the Web Page Wizard.
2. Decide on the type of navigation to be used—Vertical frame, Horizontal frame, or Separate page.
3. Add the guest book form from exercise 4 and the evaluation form from exercise 5 to the NaperV Web site and remove any blank pages at the Add Pages screen.
4. Rename the Personal Web Page to NaperV Web Page.
5. Choose an appropriate theme.
6. Insert NaperV Banner.htm located in your student CD. You will decide in which frame you will place the banner.
7. Include a frame for the hyperlinks.
8. Include the text below in the main frame of the home page (rewrite and rearrange the text as you desire):
   NaperV and Associates is a large consulting firm located in Lisle, IL. NaperV specializes in computer-training workshops, team-building seminars, motivational workshops, presentation skills sessions, professional communication programs, partnership building workshops, global awareness presentations, and networking workshops. New topics are our challenge—we pride ourselves on our current programs. We provide training at our facility at 325 Short Drive, Lisle, IL 60532 or at your business location. We are flexible and concerned with our clients' needs. Our qualified trainers and presenters will customize their programs to fit your specific goals.

   > **To contact NaperV and Associates:**
   > **Call for information at: (630) 555-8987**
   > **Fax: (630) 555-3888**
   > **E-mail:** NaperV@msn.com
   > **Web site:** http://www.naperv.com

9. Use any appropriate graphics, bullets, banner, or dividers.
10. Optional: Include a map to the location or a hyperlink to a Web site that will provide a map to Lisle, IL from Chicago.
11. Save each of the Web pages in each of the frames often.
12. View each page in Web Page Preview.
13. Print each page in the browser. Make sure that background printing is turned on.

CREATIVE ACTIVITY

Create a Web page on a topic of your choosing. Suggested topics include: gardening, a favorite sport or team, community project, volunteer project, hobby, or vacation spot. Look at other Web sites for ideas and layout. Research your topic on the Internet and include at least three hyperlinks. Use appropriate graphics, borders, buttons, dividers, and background. Designate a folder on a floppy disk for your Web files. You may use frames, a blank Web page, or any Word Web templates. Optional: Include a sound clip if you have sound available on your computer.

Chapter 09

Creating Presentations Using PowerPoint

PERFORMANCE OBJECTIVES

Upon successful completion of chapter 9, you will be able to create onscreen presentations, overhead transparencies, paper printouts, 35mm slides, notes, handouts, and outlines using PowerPoint's AutoContent Wizard and presentation designs.

DESKTOP PUBLISHING TERMS

Real time	AutoLayouts	Effect
HTML	Placeholder	Build
Published presentation	Slide indicator	Hyperlink
Storyboard	Transition	Broadcast

WORD AND POWERPOINT FEATURES USED

Animation effects	Microsoft Clip Gallery	Slide Sorter view
AutoContent Wizard	Online meetings	Slide transitions
Design templates	Online broadcasts	Slide view
Hyperlinks	Outline view	Transitions
Importing from Word	Slide Show view	TriPane view

Using PowerPoint to Create a Presentation

What is a presentation? A presentation communicates information using visual images to convey your message to an audience. Microsoft PowerPoint 2000 is a complete graphic presentation program, which allows you to create the following:

- **Onscreen presentations.** Onscreen presentations are popular because of their many special effects and features. The ability to add animation, movies, sound, and hyperlinks make this form of presentation very attractive and effective. To conduct an on-screen presentation you must have a computer and a compatible projecting device. You may find that an onscreen presentation does not fit on a floppy disk, in which case, you may need to store it on a zip disk or CD-RW disk. PowerPoint has a Projector Wizard that automatically sets and restores screen resolution for the target projection system.

- **Self-running presentations.** Self-running presentations allow the user to set up a presentation to run unattended in a booth or kiosk. A self-running presentation restarts when it is finished and also when it has been idle on a manually advanced slide for longer than 5 minutes.

- **Online meetings.** Online meetings use Microsoft's NetMeeting program with PowerPoint, allowing you to share presentations and exchange information with people at different sites in *real time* as if everyone were in the same room.

- **Presentation broadcasting.** Presentation broadcasting allows you to broadcast a presentation, including video and audio, over the Web. By using Microsoft Outlook or another e-mail program, you schedule the broadcast. The presentation is saved in *HTML* and your audience can view the presentation using Microsoft Internet Explorer 4.0 or later.

- **Presentations on the Web.** These presentations are published on the Web. A *published* presentation means a copy of your PowerPoint presentation in HTML format is placed onto the World Wide Web. Because navigation is a critical element, PowerPoint presentations in HTML format include a navigation bar enabling you to advance slides using the Outline pane.

- **Overhead transparencies.** Overhead transparencies are created by printing the slides as black-and-white or color transparencies. Transparencies are the most commonly used visual format for formal and informal presentations. They work well with small- to medium-sized groups. They allow for more interaction between audience and presenter; equipment is usually readily available; overhead projectors are easy to use; additional points can be added or highlighted with a transparency marker; and they are fairly easy and inexpensive to produce. Laser and ink jet printers can print files that you create on transparency film.

- **35mm slides.** PowerPoint allows you to convert the slides to a 35mm format, and offers a wizard that will send your file to an external service for development. Slides maintain high-quality color and can add visual impact. Slide presentations work well with medium- to large-sized audiences.

- **Handouts, Notes Pages, and Outlines.** Handouts, Notes Pages and Outlines can be printed to assist your audience during a presentation. Handouts are mini versions of the slides with an area for the audience to make notes; notes pages are the speaker's notes; and outlines contain the slide titles and main points of the presentation.

In addition to saving production costs by creating your own presentations, there are other advantages. First, you can maintain control over designing and producing them. Since you can easily make last-minute changes, you can produce a top-quality product right up to the last minute. Second, you have the flexibility of working around your own schedule. Third, creating presentation materials on your own, as with other desktop-published documents, just takes some time, practice, effort, and patience.

Planning the Presentation

The planning process for a presentation is basically the same as for other documents you have created. In the planning stages you must:

- **Establish a purpose.** Do you want to inform, educate, sell, motivate, persuade, or entertain?

- **Evaluate your audience.** Who will listen to and watch your presentation? What is the age range? What is their education and economic levels? What knowledge do they have of the topic beforehand? What image do you want to project to your audience?

- **Decide on content.** Decide on the content and organization of your message. Do not try to cover too many topics—this may strain the audience's attention or cause confusion. Identify the main point,

- **Determine the medium to be used to convey your message**. To help decide the type of medium to be used, consider such items as topic, equipment availability, location, lighting, audience size, and so on.

Designing the Presentation

When choosing a design for the slides, consider your audience, topic, and method of delivery. You would not want to select a design with bright vibrant colors for an audience of conservative bankers. Nor would you use a design with dark colors or patterns if you plan to photocopy printouts—the contrast of colors and patterns may blur. In addition to design, consider the following items when determining layout:

- **Continuity.** Assure consistency, avoid redundancy, and use forceful expressions in the design and layout. Repeat specific design elements such as company logos, color, font, and type of bullets used. Consistent elements help to connect one slide to the next and contribute to a cohesive presentation.

- **Color.** Use restraint with color to enhance the message, not detract from it. Colors must look good together. Studies on the psychology of color suggest that certain colors elicit certain feelings in an audience. For example, blue backgrounds promote a conservative approach to the information presented and provide general feelings of calmness, loyalty, and security. Yellow or white text against a dark blue or indigo background is a good combination. Black backgrounds are effective in financial presentations. Black also seems to show directness or forcefulness. Green backgrounds project an image of being direct, social, or intelligent. Green acts to stimulate interaction and is a good choice for use in training and educational presentations. Purple or magenta is appropriate in presentations that tend to entertain or represent less conservative or serious topics.

- **Create an outline.** An outline is a list of headings in the chronological order of the presentation. Follow basic outlining rules such as "Every A needs a B," meaning that you should have at least two supporting points for each main point.

- **Create a storyboard.** A *storyboard* is a visual example of the headings in the outline. When creating a storyboard, your information should not exceed what will fit on a 5 × 7″ index card to avoid filling an entire 8 1/2 × 11″ sheet of paper. The goal is to limit the amount of information the audience must read so that they can focus on what is being said and visually presented.

DTP POINTERS
Good presentational strategy includes attention to message, visuals, and delivery.

DTP POINTERS
Introduce one concept per slide.

DTP POINTERS
Consistency is important in maintaining a uniform appearance.

DTP POINTERS
Think about how your audience will respond to the colors in your presentation.

DTP POINTERS
Be consistent when using color to present facts in a presentation.

Storyboard
A visual example of the headings in an outline.

- **Consider the medium.** In addition to careful planning and preparation for your presentation, consider the actual delivery of the presentation. Be sure that the medium that you select fits the audience and available equipment.

- **Prepare fully.** Be ready for the unexpected. If you are providing the audience with handouts, know how many you will need. Have a backup plan for equipment failures or if you forget the materials. Be prepared for all logical possibilities. You can feel at ease in front of an audience by being fully prepared and practicing the presentation.

Creating Transparencies and Slides

When creating overhead transparencies or slides, consider these guidelines:

- **Typeface.** One typeface is fine; use two at the most. Instead of changing typefaces, try varying the type style, such as bold or italics. Legibility is of utmost importance.

- **Type size.** Eighteen points is the minimum. You want everyone in the room to be able to read what you have taken the time to prepare. Choose a thicker font or apply bold to increase the readability of the text.

- **Headings.** Keep titles short if possible; long headings are harder to read. Kern and track if necessary.

- **Organization.** Keep transparencies and slides simple and easy to read. Outline your message to organize ideas and then introduce one main topic or major point per transparency or slide. Each idea or supporting point needs its own line. Limit the number of words per line and the number of lines on a transparency to approximately seven.

Creating a PowerPoint Presentation

PowerPoint provides various methods for creating a presentation (see figure 9.1). To create a presentation, choose one of the following:

- **AutoContent Wizard.** Creates a new presentation by prompting you for information about content, purpose, style, handouts, and output. You choose from a variety of presentations in specific category groups as shown in figure 9.2. PowerPoint chooses a background and color scheme based on your responses. The AutoContent Wizard may be accessed at the PowerPoint dialog box or by clicking File and then New. At the New Presentation dialog box with the General tab selected, double-click AutoContent Wizard.

- **Design Template.** A design template includes preformatted layouts, fonts, and colors that blend together to create a consistent look. A conservative design template such as Soaring may be used for a team building presentation. Whereas, the Notebook template would be appropriate for a new course presentation at a college. Various Design Templates are shown in figure 9.3.

- **Blank presentation.** Creates a new, blank presentation using the default settings for text and colors. To begin your presentation at a blank screen, choose the Blank presentation option at the PowerPoint dialog box; click File, New, and then double-click Blank Presentation; or press the New button on the Standard toolbar. The New Slide dialog box will automatically display at the Blank presentation screen as shown in figure 9.4.

DTP POINTERS
Use no more than two fonts per slide—use a serif typeface for the title and sans serif for the body. Serif typefaces are generally used where there is more text.

DTP POINTERS
Keep headings short in transparencies and slides.

DTP POINTERS
ALL CAPS does not leave room for further emphasis.

DTP POINTERS
Keep text parallel; if the first word in a bulleted list ends in *ing*, make sure all the bulleted items end with *ing*. Example: Offering, Preparing, Organizing, etc.

DTP POINTERS
Use the Blank Presentation template if you want complete control over the presentation design.

- **Open an existing presentation.** Opens an existing presentation so that you can edit or show it. Simply begin by clicking the Open button on the Standard toolbar or click Open an existing presentation at the PowerPoint dialog box.

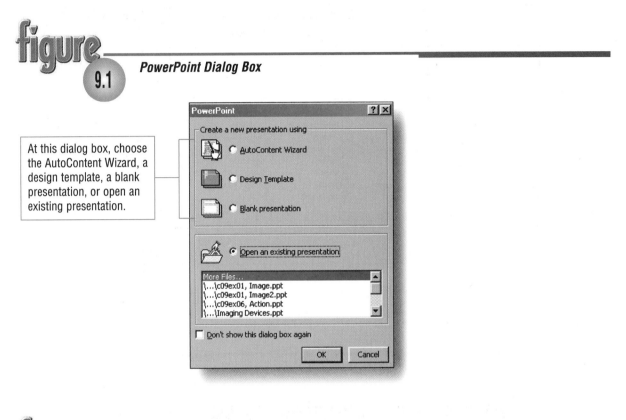

figure
9.1

PowerPoint Dialog Box

At this dialog box, choose the AutoContent Wizard, a design template, a blank presentation, or open an existing presentation.

figure
9.2

AutoContent Wizard—Presentation Types

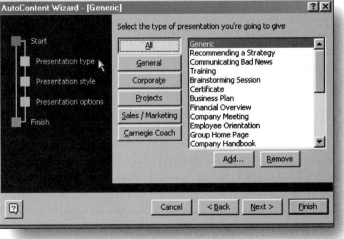

figure
9.3

New Presentation Dialog Box—Design Templates Tab

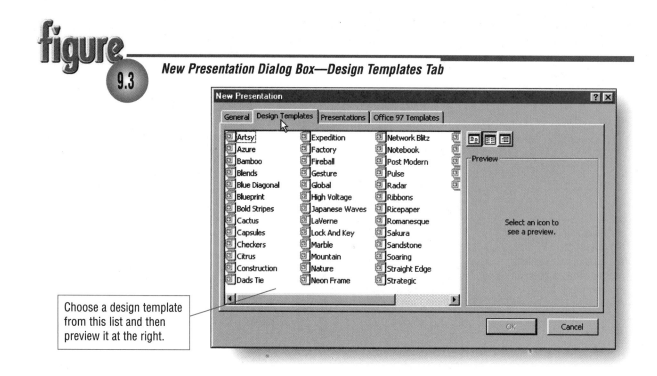

Choose a design template
from this list and then
preview it at the right.

figure
9.4

New Slide Dialog Box

Click the desired
AutoLayout and then
click OK, or double-click
the desired AutoLayout.

AutoLayouts

PowerPoint's
predesigned slide layouts
(e.g., Chart & Text,
Blank, and Bulleted List).

Placeholder

A location on a slide
where information is to
be entered.

Choosing an AutoLayout

PowerPoint includes 24 different types of pre-designed slide layouts, called
AutoLayouts. When you choose an AutoLayout, each slide layout will contain
placeholders. A *placeholder* is a location on the slide where information is to be
entered. For example, you would click in the title placeholder and key text in it.
When text is entered, the placeholder turns into a text object. Each AutoLayout
may contain one or more of the following placeholders:

- Title: Used to hold the title of the slide.
- Bulleted List: Used for a bulleted list of related points or topics.
- 2-Column Text: Bulleted list in two columns.
- Table: Used for a table that is inserted from Microsoft Word.
- Organization Chart: Used to display an organization chart in a slide.
- Chart: Holds a chart, which is a visual representation of data.
- Clip Art: Holds a picture in a slide such as a clip art picture.
- Media Clip: Inserts a media clip such as a sound or movie file.
- Object: Holds an external object such as a picture, text box, movie, or sound.

You can replace an AutoLayout format previously selected for a slide by clicking Format and Slide Layout. Make a selection from the Slide Layout dialog box and then click the Apply button.

Understanding the PowerPoint Window

When PowerPoint has been loaded and you have chosen the specific type of presentation you want to create, you are presented with the PowerPoint window as shown in figure 9.5. What displays in the presentation window will vary depending on what type of presentation you are creating. However, the PowerPoint window contains some consistent elements.

figure 9.5

PowerPoint Window—Normal View (TriPane Screen)

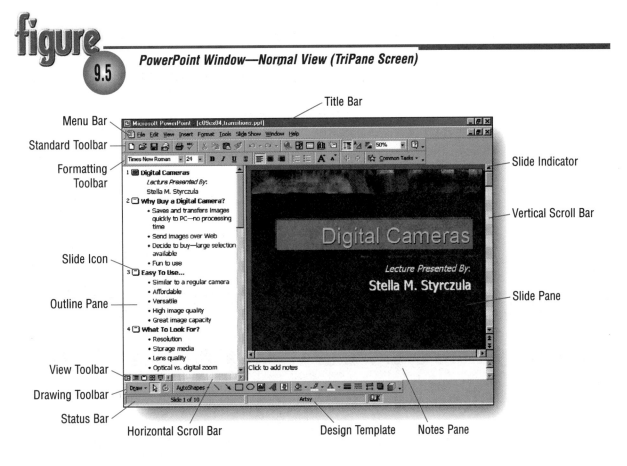

Understanding PowerPoint's Standard and Formatting Toolbars

Many buttons on PowerPoint's Standard toolbar remain consistent with Word and other Microsoft applications. However, as shown in figure 9.6, some buttons differ to represent specific PowerPoint features.

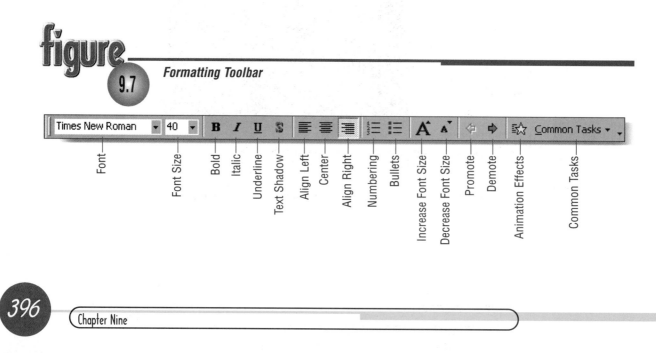

figure 9.6 — *Standard Toolbar*

The following buttons appear on the PowerPoint Standard toolbar:

Select this button	To perform this action
Insert Chart	Embed a chart in a slide using specified data
New Slide	Add a new slide to the open presentation
Expand All	Expand the Outline pane, displaying all titles and body text for each slide
Show Formatting	Display text formatting in the Outline pane
Grayscale Preview	Preview presentation in grayscale

PowerPoint's Formatting toolbar (shown in figure 9.7) includes a variety of options such as changing typeface, type size, and style (bold, italics, and underline).

figure 9.7 — *Formatting Toolbar*

The following buttons on the Formatting toolbar activate specific PowerPoint features:

Select this button	To perform this action
Text Shadow	Add or remove a shadow to or from selected text
Increase Font Size	Increase font size by approximately 4 points
Decrease Font Size	Decrease font size by approximately 4 points
Promote (Indent less)	Move selected text to the previous level (left) in an outline
Demote (Indent more)	Move selected text to the next level (right) in an outline
Animation Effects	Display transitions and effects
Common Tasks button	Display a shortcut menu listing the following options: New Slide (Ctrl-M), Slide Layout, or Apply Design Template

Spell Checking, Saving, and Closing a Presentation

Like Microsoft Word 2000, PowerPoint 2000 automatically spell checks text keyed into the presentation. In addition, the Save, Save As, and Close features are similar to Word.

Viewing a Presentation

PowerPoint provides a variety of presentation viewing options. The view can be changed with options from the View drop-down menu or with viewing buttons that display on the View toolbar located at the left side of the horizontal scroll bar, as shown in figure 9.8:

Normal View	This default view displays three panes: outline, slide and notes.
Outline View	Displays the organization of the presentation by headings and subheadings. Used when modifying text elements.
Slide View	Displays individual slides. Used for determining effectiveness of individual elements, not text, on slides.
Slide Sorter View	Displays all slides in the presentation in slide miniatures. You can easily add, move, rearrange, and delete slides.
Slide Show	Used to run a presentation.

DTP POINTERS
Key and edit text in individual slides in Slide view.

DTP POINTERS
Quickly and easily reorganize slides in Slide Sorter view.

figure 9.8

View Toolbar

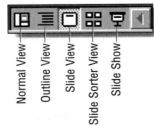

Normal View
Outline View
Slide View
Slide Sorter View
Slide Show

In Normal/Slide view, change slides by clicking the Previous Slide button or Next Slide button located at the bottom of the vertical scroll bar. You can also change to a different slide by using the arrow pointer on the scroll box (called the *slide indicator*) on the vertical scroll bar. To do this, position the arrow pointer on the slide indicator, hold down the left mouse button, drag up or down until a box displays with the desired slide number, and then release the mouse button.

Printing a Presentation

A presentation may be printed in a variety of formats. You may print each slide on a separate piece of paper; print each slide at the top of a page, leaving the bottom of the page for notes; print all or a specific number of slides on a single piece of paper; or print the slide titles and topics in outline form. Use the Print what option at the Print dialog box to specify what you want printed, as shown in figure 9.9.

figure 9.9

Print Dialog Box and Print what: List Box

You can specify several print parameters in the Print dialog box.

Your department is updating and purchasing new hardware and software, and you are responsible for researching the market for the latest technology. Prepare a short PowerPoint presentation on scanners, which will be given at the next departmental meeting.

Creating, Saving, and Printing a Presentation

1. Prepare the slides for a presentation on scanners as shown in figure 9.10 by completing the following steps:
   a. Load PowerPoint by clicking the Start button on the Windows taskbar, pointing to Programs, and then clicking Microsoft PowerPoint.
   b. At the PowerPoint dialog box, select Design Template, and then click OK.
   c. At the New Presentation dialog box with the Design Templates tab selected, double-click the *Fireball.pot* design.
   d. At the New Slide dialog box, double-click the first AutoLayout in the list box (Title Slide).

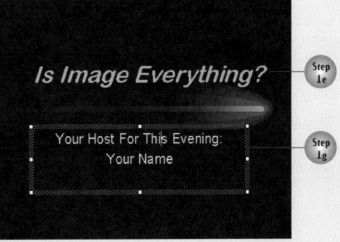

   e. At slide 1, click the text *Click to add title,* and then key **Is Image Everything?**.
   f. Select *Is Image Everything?* and change the font to 54-point Arial Rounded MT Bold italic. (Use the Increase Font Size button on the Formatting toolbar.)
   g. Click the text *Click to add subtitle,* key **Your Host For This Evening:**, press Enter, and then key **Your Name**.
   h. Select *Your Host...*and *Your Name* and change the font to 32-Arial.
2. Create slide 2 by completing the following steps:
   a. Click the Common Tasks button and click New Slide. (Or use the shortcut key Ctrl + M.)
   b. At the New Slide dialog box, double-click the second AutoLayout in the first row (Bulleted List).
   c. Click the text *Click to add title* and key **To Buy or Not to Buy?**.
   d. Select *To Buy or Not to Buy?* and change the font to 44-point Arial Rounded MT Bold italic.

e. Click the text *Click to add text* and key the following in 32-point Arial.

1st bulleted item   **As you know with technology, the longer it has been around, the cheaper it becomes.** Press Enter.

2nd bulleted item   **With scanners and other imaging devices becoming so affordable, now is the time to buy.**

3. Create slides 3-7 by completing steps as in steps 2a through 2e for each slide. Key the text in each slide as shown in figure 9.10.
4. Use Format Painter to apply the consistent formatting.
5. Save the presentation to your hard drive or floppy disk and name it c09ex01, Image. *(Hint: PowerPoint automatically inserts the .ppt extension.)*
6. View the presentation in various views by completing the following steps:
   a. Press Ctrl + Home or drag the slide indicator until the first slide displays.
   b. Click the Outline View button on the View toolbar.
   c. Change the Zoom to 50%.
   d. Click the Slide View button on the View toolbar.
   e. Click the Grayscale Preview button (third button from the right) on the Standard toolbar. Click it again to toggle the feature off.
   f. Click the Slide Sorter View button on the View toolbar.
   g. Click the Slide Show View button on the View toolbar.
7. Print all seven slides on one page by completing the following steps:
   a. Click File, Print.
   b. At the Print dialog box, click the down arrow at the right of the Print what: drop-down list box and select *Handouts*.
   c. At the Handouts section, click the down arrow at the right of the Slides per page drop-down list box, and select *9*.

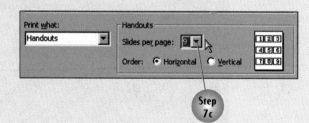

Step 7c

8. Close c09ex01, Image.ppt by clicking File and Close.

figure
9.10   *Exercise 1*

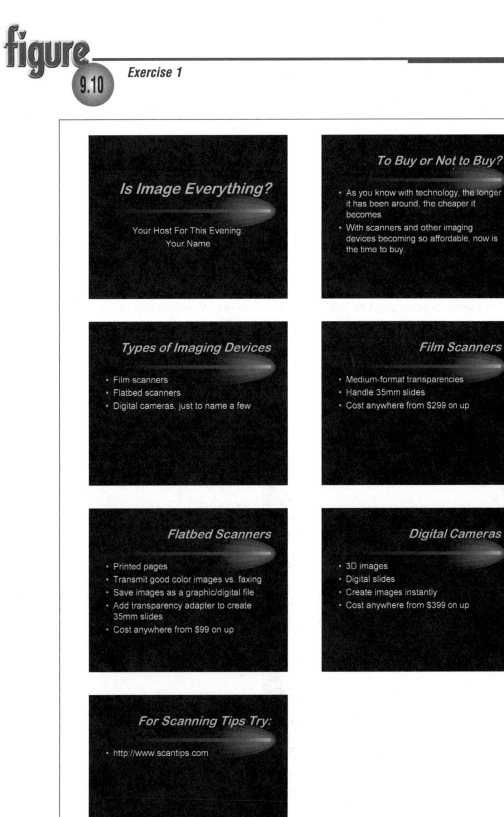

Preparing a Presentation in Outline View

In exercise 1, you created a short slide presentation using a PowerPoint design template in which you inserted a small amount of text on each slide. If you are creating a longer presentation with more slides or more text, consider using the Outline view to help organize the topics for the slides without the distractions of colorful designs, clip art, transition effects, or sound. You can create an outline in PowerPoint, or import an outline from other applications, such as Microsoft Word and Excel.

Organizing Content

Demote

Promote

When creating a presentation in Outline view, the slide title appears next to a number followed by an icon, this is the first level of your outline. Body text and bulleted items follow as levels 2 to 5. Navigate up or down with the assistance of the Outlining toolbar located on the left as shown in figure 9.11.

The Outline pane appears in Normal view and Outline view, the difference being the size of the Outline pane. To move down one level you would use the Demote button or press Alt + Shift + Right (arrow). To move up one level you would use the Promote button or press Alt + Shift + Left (arrow).

9.11 *Outlining Toolbar*

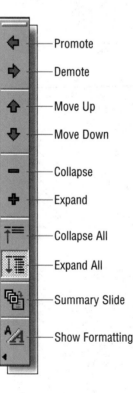

Inserting and Deleting Slides

To insert a slide(s) in Outline view or Normal view, position the insertion point to the left of the slide that will immediately precede the new slide. Click the New Slide button located on the Standard toolbar, then double-click an AutoLayout.

New Slide

To delete a slide(s), position the arrow pointer on the slide icon located next to the slide text you want to delete until the arrow pointer turns into a four-headed arrow, then click the left mouse button to select all of the text for the slide. With the text for the slide selected, press the Delete key.

Rearranging Slides

To move a slide, collapse the outline first. Click the Collapse button on the Outlining toolbar, and the title of each slide will display. A gray line below the text represents the rest of the text. Click anywhere in the title of the slide you want to move. Click the Move Down button to move the slide down or click the Move Up button to move the slide up. To expand the outline, click the Expand button on the Outlining toolbar and the levels of the selected slide will display.

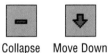

Collapse   Move Down

Move Up   Expand

You may also rearrange, delete, and add slides in the Slide Sorter View. To move, select the slide and drag it to a new location. To delete a slide, select it and press the Delete key. To add a slide, position the insertion point (vertical line) to the left of the location where you want to add a slide and then click the New Slide button on the Standard toolbar.

Applying Formatting Using the Slide Master

The Slide Master is a PowerPoint feature that promotes consistency from one slide to the next. Changes made at the Slide Master apply to *all* slides except the Title Master slide. The title slide differs from the other slides so a Title Master is available. There is also a master slide for handouts and notes.

In exercise 1, you achieved consistency by using a design template; however, you changed the font and font size on each of the slides by using the Format Painter. A more efficient way to change all the slides at once is to use the Slide Master. The Slide Master screen is shown in figure 9.12.

Format Painter

Access the Slide Master by clicking <u>V</u>iew, pointing to <u>M</u>aster, and then selecting an appropriate Slide Master. Alternatively, you may display the Slide Master by positioning the insertion point on the Slide View button, holding down the Shift key, and clicking the left mouse. Make the desired changes and then click the Slide View button (without holding down the Shift key) to exit the Slide Master, or click <u>C</u>lose on the Master toolbar.

If your presentation includes a title slide, make sure you have modified the Slide Master before changing the Title Master. Changes made at the Slide Master will be reflected in the current slide displayed as well as in the remaining slides.

figure
9.12

Slide Master

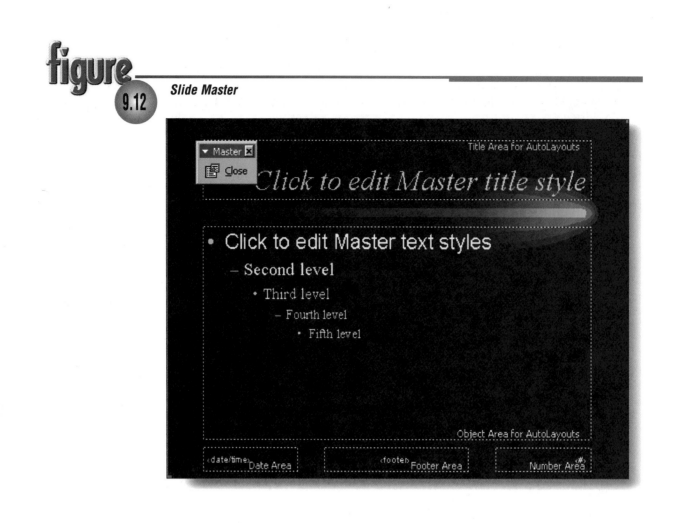

In exercise 2, you will organize your ideas for a new course presentation by using PowerPoint's Outline View. In addition, you will make consistent formatting changes by using the Slide Master.

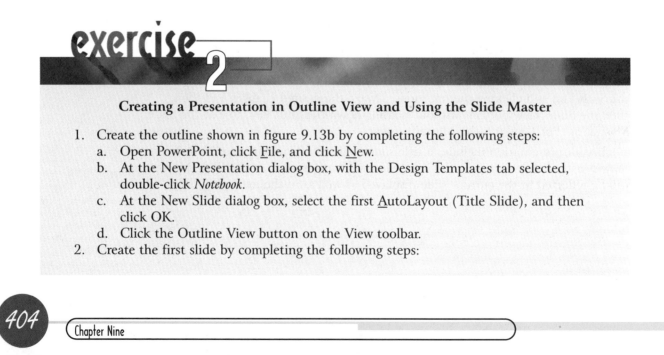

Creating a Presentation in Outline View and Using the Slide Master

1. Create the outline shown in figure 9.13b by completing the following steps:
   a. Open PowerPoint, click File, and click New.
   b. At the New Presentation dialog box, with the Design Templates tab selected, double-click *Notebook*.
   c. At the New Slide dialog box, select the first AutoLayout (Title Slide), and then click OK.
   d. Click the Outline View button on the View toolbar.
2. Create the first slide by completing the following steps:

a. At slide 1 (you will see the slide number and a slide icon), key **College of Office Technology** and press Enter (you will be prompted to enter the title for slide 2). To advance to the next level, click the Demote button on the Outlining toolbar. Display the Outlining toolbar if necessary. *(Hint: This will take you forward to level 2, which is the subtitle.)*

b. At the subtitle, key **Program/Course Outline**, press Enter (you will remain on level 2), and then key **January 2, 2001** and press Enter. To return to the first level, click the Promote button. This will take you back to level 1, which is the title of slide 2.

3. At slide 2, complete the following steps:

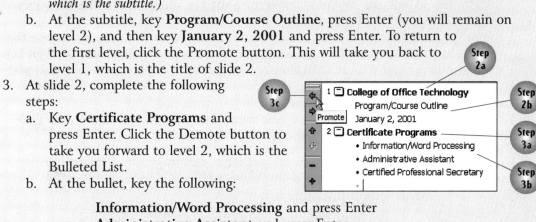

a. Key **Certificate Programs** and press Enter. Click the Demote button to take you forward to level 2, which is the Bulleted List.

b. At the bullet, key the following:

> **Information/Word Processing** and press Enter
> **Administrative Assistant** and press Enter
> **Certified Professional Secretary** and press Enter

c. Click the Promote button.

4. Complete steps 3a–c for each of the remaining slides as shown in figure 9.13a.

5. Rearrange and edit the slides by completing the following steps:

a. Change to Slide Sorter View.

b. Move slide 7 (Courses) before slide 3 (Business Correspondence). To do this, position the arrow pointer on slide 7, hold down the left mouse button, drag the arrow pointer (with a square attached) between slides 2 and 3, and then release the mouse button. A vertical line will display between the two slides.

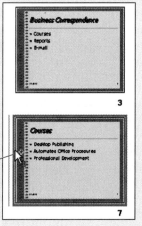

c. Move text within a slide by completing the following steps:
   1) Change to Outline View.
   2) Select *Flyers* in slide 5 and click the Move Up button 4 times.

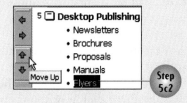

   3) Click *Newsletters* and then click the Move Down button 3 times.

d. Delete one of the slides by completing the following steps:
   1) In Outline View, click the Collapse All button on the Outlining toolbar.
   2) Position the arrow pointer on the slide icon located next to slide 4 (Business Correspondence) and the arrow pointer displays as a four-headed arrow; then select slide 4 and press Delete.

6. Save the presentation with Save <u>A</u>s to your hard drive or a floppy disk and name it c09ex02, College.
7. Change the formatting at the Master Slide by completing the following steps:
   a. Click the Slide View button.
   b. Display Slide 2 and then hold down the Shift key while clicking the Slide View button on the View toolbar.
   c. At the Slide Master, click on the text *Click to edit Master title style* and change the font to 40-point Tahoma, italic, and Shado<u>w</u>. Change the alignment to Align Left.
   d. Click on the text *Click to edit Master text styles* (this is the first bulleted level) and change the font to 32-point Tahoma.
   e. Click <u>V</u>iew and then <u>H</u>eader and Footer.
   f. At the Header and Footer dialog box, select the Slide tab and turn on the <u>D</u>ate and time and Slide <u>n</u>umber options. Click Appl<u>y</u> to All.

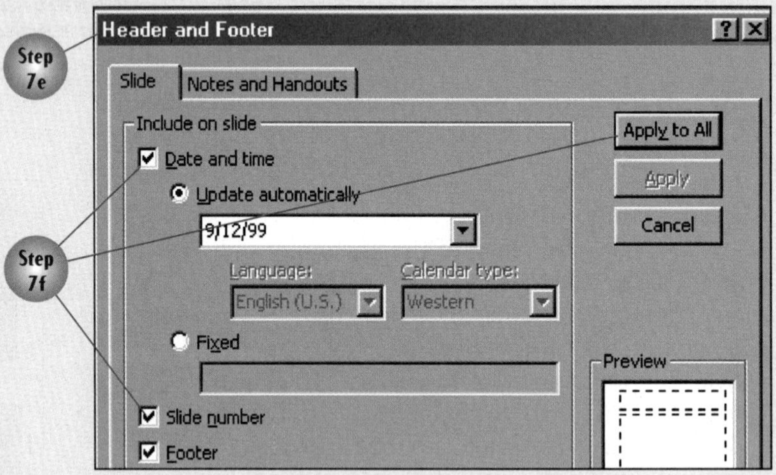

Step 7e

Step 7f

   g. Delete the remaining levels and then click the Slide View button without the Shift key. (This closes the Slide Master.)
   h. Display slide 1 and hold down the Shift key while clicking the Slide View button.
   i. At the Title Master, click on the text *Click to edit Master title style* and change the font to 44-point Tahoma, italic, and Shado<u>w</u>.
   j. Click on the text *Click to edit Master subtitle style* and change the font to 32-point Tahoma.
   k. Close the Title Master.
8. Click the Outline View button on the View toolbar, delete *Business Correspondence* from slide 3, and then click Expand All.
9. Save the presentation with the same name (c09ex02, College).
10. Print the outline by displaying the Print dialog box and changing the Print <u>w</u>hat option to Outline View, and then close c09ex02, College.

figure

9.13   *Exercise 2*

a. Text for Slide Presentation

1 🖵 ***College of Office Technology***
   Program/Course Outline
   January 2, 2001
2 🖵 ***Certificate Programs***
   • Information/Word Processing
   • Administrative Assistant
   • Certified Professional Secretary
3 🖵 ***Business Correspondence***
   • Letters
   • Reports
   • E-mail
4 🖵 ***Desktop Publishing***
   • Newsletters
   • Brochures
   • Proposals
   • Manuals
   • Flyers
5 🖵 ***Automated Office Procedures***
   • Scheduling
   • Travel itineraries
   • Organizing conferences
   • Telephone techniques
   • Records management
6 🖵 ***Professional Development***
   • Stress management
   • Human relations
   • Communication skills
   • Job search/networking
   • Mock interviews
7 🖵 ***Courses***
   • Business Correspondence
   • Desktop Publishing
   • Automated Office Procedures
   • Professional Development

b. Presentation in Outline View

1 🖵 ***College of Office Technology***
   Program/Course Outline
   January 2, 2001
2 🖵 ***Certificate Programs***
   • Information/Word Processing
   • Administrative Assistant
   • Certified Professional Secretary
3 🖵 ***Courses***
   • Desktop Publishing
   • Automated Office Procedures
   • Professional Development
4 🖵 ***Desktop Publishing***
   • Flyers
   • Brochures
   • Proposals
   • Manuals
   • Newsletters
5 🖵 ***Automated Office Procedures***
   • Scheduling
   • Travel itineraries
   • Organizing conferences
   • Telephone techniques
   • Records management
6 🖵 ***Professional Development***
   • Stress management
   • Human relations
   • Communication skills
   • Job search/networking
   • Mock interviews

Importing a Word Outline into PowerPoint

If you have an existing outline created in Word, you can import it into PowerPoint. PowerPoint will create new slides, except the Title Slide, based on the Heading levels used in Word. Paragraphs formatted with the Heading 1 style become Titles, Heading 2 styles become bulleted text, and so forth. If styles were not used, PowerPoint uses tabs or indents to place the text on slides. To import a Word outline to PowerPoint, click Insert and Slides from Outline; at the Open dialog box, double-click on the file. You will practice importing a Word outline to PowerPoint in exercise 3.

Exporting a PowerPoint Presentation into Word

You can also export a PowerPoint presentation to Word. To export a PowerPoint presentation to Word, make sure the file to be exported is opened, click File, point on Send To, and then click Microsoft Word. The Write-Up dialog box opens and there are five options to choose from, as shown in figure 9.14. Select the layout you want to use and then click OK.

figure
9.14   *Write-Up Dialog Box*

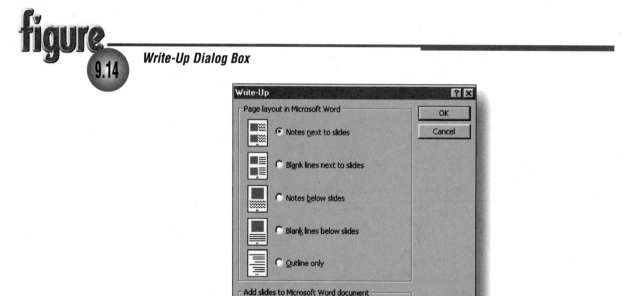

DTP POINTERS
If you change the design template for an existing presentation, check to see how the new design formatting affects text and objects in your slides. You may need to make some adjustments.

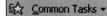

Common Tasks

Changing the Design Template

When you create a new presentation, it is based on a design template. Each design template is created differently. The background, color scheme, font, and layout of the placeholders differ from one design template to the next. To change an existing template, click on the Common Tasks button on the Formatting toolbar, select *Apply Design Template* from the drop-down menu, and double-click on the template of choice.

You can also access the design templates by clicking Format, clicking Apply Design Template, clicking the design you want from the Apply Design Template dialog box, and then clicking Apply. As with any document, when changes are made to the layout, make sure to scroll through the document to look for any inconsistencies.

You can also create a design template of your own and add it to the Templates folder on the hard drive or floppy disk.

1. Open the presentation that contains the design.
2. Delete any content you do not want included.
3. Click File and Save As.
4. At the Save As dialog box, click the down arrow at the right of *Save As type*, and then select Design Template from the drop-down list.
5. The folder automatically changes to the Templates folder.
6. Key a name for the new template in the File name text box and click Save.

Changing Color Scheme

If you are not satisfied with the colors you have been given, you can change the scheme colors of your background. You can also add text, lines, shadows, pictures, and so on. To change the color scheme, click Format, Slide Color Scheme, and select the appropriate scheme from the Color Scheme dialog box. Figure 9.15 displays the Slide Color Scheme dialog box with the Standard tab and the Custom tab displayed.

figure
9.15

Slide Color Scheme Dialog Box Showing Standard Tab and Custom Tab

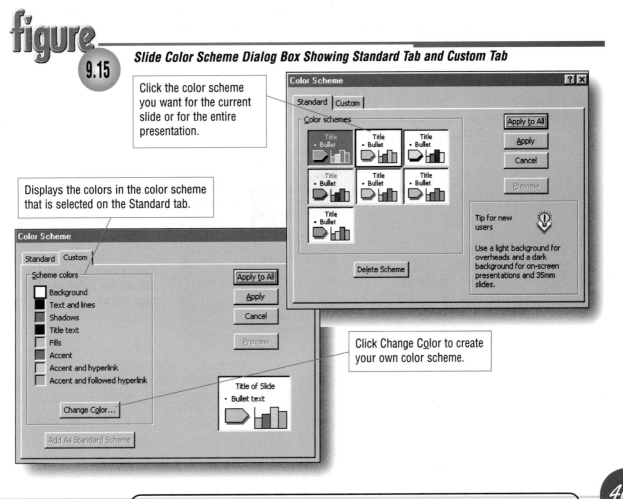

Click the color scheme you want for the current slide or for the entire presentation.

Displays the colors in the color scheme that is selected on the Standard tab.

Click Change Color to create your own color scheme.

If you change a color scheme for an individual slide and later decide you want to use the same color scheme for another slide, you can use Format Painter to copy the color scheme. Display your presentation in Slide Sorter view and use Format Painter to copy the color scheme from one slide to the next.

Changing Background

The background of a presentation is like a stage. Choose the background to correlate to the visual medium. Generally, onscreen slide shows and 35mm slides can use dark backgrounds with contrasting text and object colors, while overheads would require light-colored backgrounds.

To change the background, click Format and Background. Click the down arrow next to the current background color in the Background Fill section; a drop-down palette displays to let you select the new color. You can apply the changes to the current slide by clicking Apply, or to all slides by clicking Apply to All. Click More Colors... to select standard prism colors or create your own at the Custom tab. Click Fill Effects... to add special effects such as gradient, texture, pattern or use a picture for your background. Figure 9.16 displays the Background dialog box with Fill Palette, the Colors dialog box, and the Fill Effects dialog box, where changes may be made to a slide background.

Figure 9.17 illustrates a picture background that may be applied to a presentation by accessing the Fill Effects dialog box and choosing the Picture tab. At the Picture tab, click the Select Picture button and access the *Windows* folder where a list of pictures is available. (*Hint:* If you cannot find an image listed in the Select Picture dialog box, exit the dialog box, find the clip, and copy it to the clipboard; return to the Select Picture dialog box and paste the image in the area below the *Look in:* list box, select the clip, and then click Insert.)

figure
9.16

Background Dialog Box

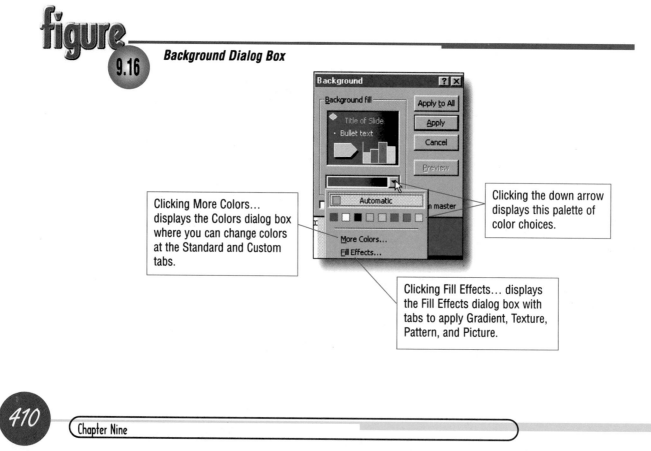

Clicking More Colors... displays the Colors dialog box where you can change colors at the Standard and Custom tabs.

Clicking the down arrow displays this palette of color choices.

Clicking Fill Effects... displays the Fill Effects dialog box with tabs to apply Gradient, Texture, Pattern, and Picture.

figure
9.17
Choosing a Picture Background

Selecting a picture background from a file in the *Windows* folder.

Using a photograph on a title slide. This photo can be found in the *Photographs* category at the Microsoft Clip Gallery.

Running a Slide Show

When running a slide show in PowerPoint, there are several methods you can choose. You can advance the slides manually or automatically, or set up a slide show to run continuously.

Running a Slide Show Manually

To run a slide show manually, open the presentation and click the Slide Show button on the View toolbar. To control the movement of slides in a slide show, refer to the following table:

To do this	Perform this action
Show next slide	Click left mouse button; or press one of the following keys: Space bar, right arrow, down arrow, or Page Down
Show previous slide	Click right mouse button; or press one of the following keys: Backspace, P, left arrow, up arrow, or Page Up
Show specific slide	Key slide number and press Enter
Toggle mouse on/off	Key A or equal sign (=)
Switch between black screen	Key B or period (.) and current slide
Switch between white screen	Key W or comma (,) and current slide
End slide show	Press one of the following keys: Esc, hyphen (-), or Ctrl + Break

exercise 3

Importing a Word Outline; Changing the Design Template, Color Scheme, and Background; and Running the Presentation

1. Open PowerPoint and import an outline created in Word by completing the following steps:
   a. Click File and New.
   b. At the New Presentation dialog box, make sure the General tab is selected, click on Blank Presentation, and then click OK.
   c. At the New Slide dialog box, make sure Title Slide is selected, and click OK.
2. Import a Word outline by completing the following steps:
   a. Display the presentation in Normal View.
   b. Click Insert and then Slides from Outline.
   c. At the Insert Outline dialog box, insert *JobsHuntingOnline.doc* (make sure you have changed to All Files in the Files of type: list box) located on your student CD. (The outline is placed in the PowerPoint window in Normal View.)
   d. Scroll through the new slides.

Step 2b

3. Change the design template by completing the following steps:
   a. Save the presentation on your hard drive or floppy disk with Save As and name it c09ex03, JobsOnline.
   b. Display slide 1 in Slide View and click the Common Tasks button on the Formatting toolbar.
   c. Click Apply Design Template.
   d. At the Apply Design Template dialog box, select Blends.pot, and then click Apply.
   e. Click the text (*Click to add title*) and key **Jobs Online**.
   f. Click the text (*Click to add subtitle*) and key **Lecturer**, press Enter, and then key **Your Name**.

Step 3c

4. Change the Color Scheme to the one shown in figure 9.18 by completing the following steps:
   a. Click Format and Slide Color Scheme.
   b. At the Color Scheme dialog box with the Custom tab selected, click Background in the Scheme colors section, and then click Change Colors.

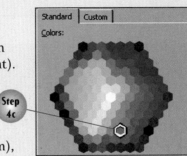

   c. At the Background Color dialog box in the Colors section, click the orange mini-hexagon (third row from bottom and fourth from right). Click OK.
   d. Click Text and lines and then Change Colors.
   e. At the Text and Line Color dialog box, click the white mini-hexagon (center of prism), and then click OK.
   f. Click Title text and then click Change Colors.
   g. At the Title Text Color dialog box, click the gold mini-hexagon (third row from bottom and fourth from left), and then click OK.
   h. At the Color Scheme dialog box, click Apply to All.
5. Change the Background by completing the following steps:
   a. Click Format and Background.
   b. At the Background dialog box, click the down arrow in the Background fill section, and then click Fill Effects.
   c. At the Fill Effects dialog box, with the Gradient tab selected, click Preset in the Colors section.

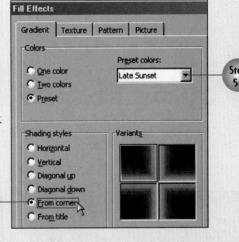

   d. Click the down arrow at the right of the Preset colors list box and select *Late Sunset*.
   e. In the Shading Styles section, click From corner, and then click OK.
   f. At the Background dialog box, click Apply to All.
6. Save the presentation with the same name c09ex03, JobsOnline.
7. Run the presentation by completing the following steps:
   a. In Slide Sorter view, click once on slide 1 or press Ctrl + Home. (This is to ensure that your slide show begins with the first slide.)
   b. Click the Slide Show button on the View toolbar. (Slide 1 will fill the entire screen.)
   c. After viewing slide 1, click the left mouse button. (Slide 2 will display.)
   d. Continue viewing and clicking until the screen returns to Slide Sorter view.
8. Print the entire presentation as Handouts with 6 slides per page and then close c09ex03, JobsOnline.

Jobs Online

Lecturer
Your Name

Job Hunting on the Web

- Forrester Research—employers spending $105 million for online advertising may expect an estimated $2.7 billion for such ads by 2003

Why Use the Internet?

- Online ads are less expensive, more dynamic, easier to manage
- Generate faster responses from job applicants and shorter hiring cycles

Job Applicants

- Free sites or nominal fee
- Sites provide search engine—job searches based on variety of criteria
- Sites offer job search "agent" that scans databases for job matches—communicate via e-mail
- Resume created and stored online

Employer Benefits

- Ad reaches wider range of applicants via the Web
- Sites offer recruiting and hiring advice
- Prescreen applicants from large database
- Sites free, small fee for recurrent ads

Online Providers

- America's Job Bank (jobsearch.org)
- CareerBuilder (careerbuilder.com)
- HeadHunter.Net (headhunter.net)
- HotJobs.com (hotjobs.com)
- JobOptions (joboptions.com)
- Monster.com (monster.com)

Running a Slide Show Automatically

Slides in a slide show can be advanced automatically after a specific number of seconds. Open a presentation, change to the Slide Sorter view, select an individual slide or select all slides in the presentation, click Slide Show, and then Slide Transition (or click the Slide Transition button on the Slide Sorter toolbar). At the Slide Transition dialog box, click Automatically after (in the Advance section), and then key the number of seconds. After making changes to the Slide Transition dialog box, click Apply to close the dialog box. You can also click Apply to All to affect all slides. A 5-second transition was added to a slide in figure 9.19.

Slide Transition

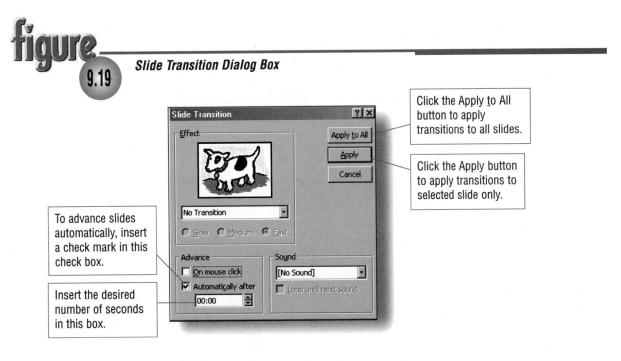

figure
9.19

Slide Transition Dialog Box

Click the Apply to All button to apply transitions to all slides.

Click the Apply button to apply transitions to selected slide only.

To advance slides automatically, insert a check mark in this check box.

Insert the desired number of seconds in this box.

To run the presentation automatically, be sure slide 1 is selected. Click the Slide Show button on the View toolbar. This runs the presentation showing each slide on the screen the specified number of seconds. When a time has been added to a slide (or slides), the time displays at the bottom of the slide (or slides) in Slide Sorter view.

Running a Slide Show in a Continuous Loop

In a continuous-loop slide show, all the slides are viewed over and over again until you stop the show. This feature is especially effective when presenting a new product or service at a trade show or at a new store opening. To run a presentation in PowerPoint in a continuous loop, click Slide Show and Set Up Show. At the Set Up Show dialog box, click the check box to the left of Loop continuously until Esc, as shown in figure 9.20. Click OK.

When you are ready to run the presentation, click the Slide Show button on the View toolbar. When you are ready to end the slide show, press the Esc key on the keyboard. You will then return to Slide Sorter view.

figure
9.20

Set Up Show Dialog Box

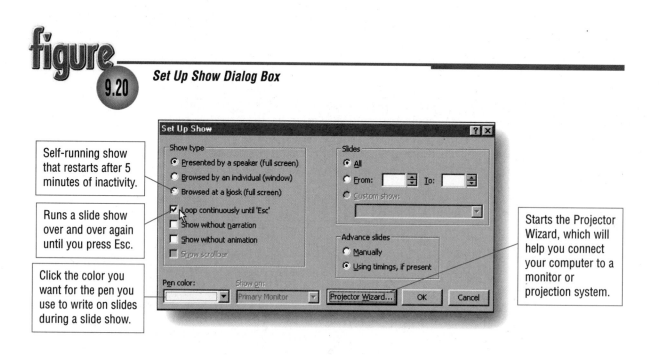

Self-running show that restarts after 5 minutes of inactivity.

Runs a slide show over and over again until you press Esc.

Click the color you want for the pen you use to write on slides during a slide show.

Starts the Projector Wizard, which will help you connect your computer to a monitor or projection system.

Setting and Rehearsing Timings for a Presentation

In some presentations, you may want to specify a different amount of time for each slide and then rehearse the presentation to ensure that the time set is appropriate. To rehearse and set a time for each slide, you would complete these steps:

1. Open the presentation.
2. Change to the Slide Sorter view.
3. Click the Rehearse Timings button on the Slide Sorter toolbar or click Sli_de_ Show and then _R_ehearse Timings. Figure 9.21 displays the Slide Sorter toolbar.
4. The first slide in the presentation displays along with a Rehearsal dialog box that appears in the top left corner of the screen as shown in figure 9.22. The Rehearsal dialog box shows the time for the current slide and the entire time for the presentation. The timer begins immediately. Click the Next Slide button when the desired time is displayed; click the Pause button to stop the timer and leave the slide on the screen; or click the Repeat button if you want the time for the current slide to start over.
5. Continue in this manner until the time for all slides in the presentation has been specified.
6. After specifying the time for the last slide, a Microsoft PowerPoint dialog box displays with the total time of the presentation and asks if you want to record the new slide timings. At this dialog box, click _Y_es to save the new timings.

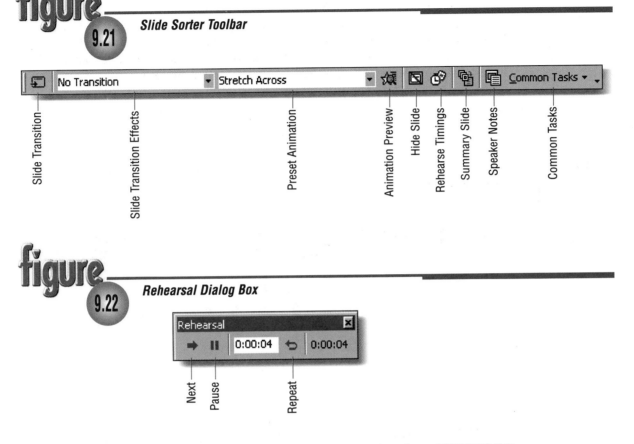

figure
9.21

Slide Sorter Toolbar

Slide Transition
Slide Transition Effects
Preset Animation
Animation Preview
Hide Slide
Rehearse Timings
Summary Slide
Speaker Notes
Common Tasks

figure
9.22

Rehearsal Dialog Box

Next
Pause
Repeat

Adding Transitions, Effects, Sounds, and Builds

If the presentation you are creating will be delivered using an on-screen slide show, the addition of transitions and effects can augment the presentation by providing movement and/or sound between slides. A *transition* is visual movement that affects an entire slide (i.e., a slide dissolving into the next slide).

In addition, you can add sound to accompany the transition, as well as apply animation effects to individual elements on your slide to create a build. An *effect* also describes movement but refers to the method used to display individual elements on the slide, such as Fly from Top, Spiral, or Swivel. A *build* is an effective tool in slide shows that helps to keep the audience on track with the major points on each slide. An example of a build is using a bulleted list to display one bullet at a time.

To apply transitions, display the presentation in Slide Sorter View, select the slide(s), click the Transition button on the Slide Sorter toolbar, and choose a transition. To apply custom animations such as builds, display the presentation in Slide View, select the slide(s), and click Custom Animation at the Slide Show menu. To select slides out of sequence, use the Ctrl key, in conjunction with the mouse; to select slides in sequence use the Shift key. Complete exercise 4 to practice applying these slides enhancements.

Transition
How one slide is removed from the screen and the next slide is displayed.

Effect
Method of displaying movement in individual elements on a slide, such as Fly from Top, Spiral, and Swivel.

Build
A feature that displays information (usually bulleted items) a little at a time.

Adding Animation Effects to a Presentation

Animation effects can be added to a presentation by using various features in PowerPoint. You may use the Slide Sorter toolbar, access commands from the View Slide menu, or select options from the Animation Effects toolbar. The Animation Effects toolbar is displayed in figure 9.23. Options on the toolbar include Flying Effect, Camera Effect, Drop In, Animation Order, and a button to access the Custom Animation toolbar.

figure 9.23

Animation Effects Toolbar

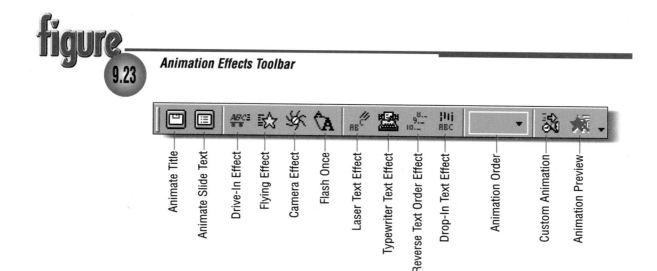

Animate Title · Animate Slide Text · Drive-In Effect · Flying Effect · Camera Effect · Flash Once · Laser Text Effect · Typewriter Text Effect · Reverse Text Order Effect · Drop-In Text Effect · Animation Order · Custom Animation · Animation Preview

Using Preset Animation

DTP POINTERS
Each slide can have a different transition effect as long as at least one element remains consistent in all the slides.

Preset Animations enables you to animate specific slide objects and text using directional effects similar to slide transitions. Objects may appear using techniques such as wiping, dissolving, flying, or flashing. Click Slide Show and then Preset Animation to use this feature.

The Animation Preview option allows you to see the animation to make sure it has the desired effect. Click the Animation Preview button (fourth button from the left) on the Slide Sorter toolbar.

Creating Custom Animations

When creating custom animation, you can perform many of the same animation tasks as you can with preset animation. However, custom animation includes more advanced animation options such as setting order and timings, as shown in the Custom Animation dialog box in figure 9.24. To access the Custom Animation dialog box you must be in Slide View. With the slide displayed in Slide View, click Slide Show and Custom Animation.

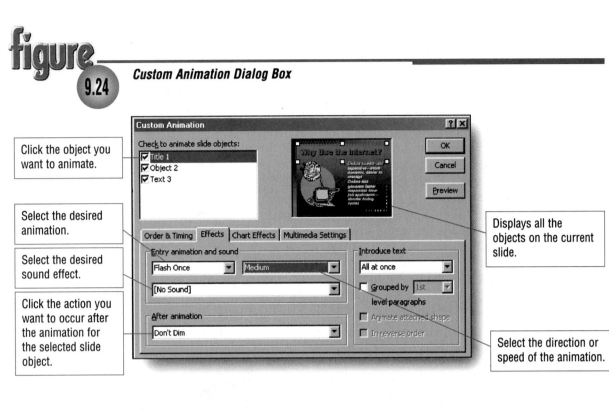

figure
9.24
Custom Animation Dialog Box

Click the object you want to animate.

Select the desired animation.

Select the desired sound effect.

Click the action you want to occur after the animation for the selected slide object.

Displays all the objects on the current slide.

Select the direction or speed of the animation.

Creating a Summary Slide

To better organize delivery of your presentation, you can create a summary slide at the beginning or closing of your presentation highlighting the main topics to be discussed. A summary slide places all or selected slide titles on one slide. Create a summary slide in Slide Sorter View by selecting the slide(s) you want and then click the Summary Slide button located on the Slide Sorter toolbar.

exercise
4

**Adding Transition, Animation Effects,
Automatic Timing, and a Summary Slide**

1. Customize the digital camera presentation in figure 9.25 by completing the following steps:
   a. Open Digital Cameras.ppt located on the student CD.
   b. Save the presentation to your hard drive or floppy disk with Save As and name it c09ex04, Transitions.
   c. Change to Slide Sorter view.
   d. Create a Summary Slide by completing the following steps:
      1) Select slides 2 through 10.
      2) Click the Summary Slide button located on the Slide Sorter toolbar. A new slide is added at the beginning of the presentation entitled "Summary Slide."
      3) Select the Summary Slide and move it to the end of the presentation.
   e. Apply a transition to slide 1 by completing the following steps:

1) Make sure you are in Slide Sorter view.
2) Select slide 1 and click the Slide Transition button on the Slide Sorter toolbar.
3) At the Slide Transition dialog box, click the down arrow at the right of the Effect list box and select *Random Bars Horizontal*, select Medium speed, and then click the down arrow at the right of the Sound list box and select *Camera*. Click Apply.

f. Animate slide 2 by completing the following steps:

1) Select slide 2 and change to Slide View.
2) Click Slide Show and then Custom Animation.
3) At the Custom Animation dialog box with the Effects tab displayed, select *Title 1* in the Check to animate slide objects: section.
4) Click the first down arrow in the Entry animation and sound section and select *Fly*, click the second down arrow and select *From Top*.

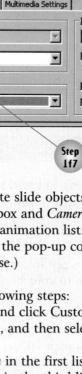

5) Click *Text 2* in the Check to animate slide objects: section.
6) Select *Spiral* in the animation list box and *Camera* in the sound list box.
7) Click the down arrow in the After animation list box and select the color *Gray* in the first row and last column of the pop-up color palette. (This is the gray you will use throughout this exercise.)
8) Click Preview and then OK.

g. Animate slide 3 by completing the following steps:

1) Display slide 3, click Slide Show, and click Custom Animation.
2) Select the Effects tab, select *Title 1*, and then select *Fly* in the first list box, *From Top* in the second list box.
3) Select *Text 2* and then select *Stretch* in the first list box, *Across* in the second list box, and *Slide Projector* (Sound) in the third list box.
4) Select *Gray* in the After animation list box.

5) Click Preview and then OK.

h. Animate slides 4 through 9 by completing the following steps:
    1) Each *Title 1* should animate with *Fly* and *From Top*.
    2) Apply the following settings to *Text 2* in Slides 4 through 9:

> Slide 4: *Stretch, Across,* with *Slide Projector* (Sound), and *Gray.*
> Slide 5: *Wipe, Right,* with *Camera* (Sound), and *Gray.*
> Slide 6: *Random Effects,* with [No Sound], and *Gray.*
> Slide 7: *Blinds, Horizontal,* with *Whoosh,* and *Gray.*
> Slide 8: *Peek, From Bottom,* with [No Sound], and *Gray.*
> Slide 9: *Strips, Left-Down,* with [No Sound], and *Gray.*

i. Animate slide 10 by clicking Slide Show, point to Preset Animation, and then click Camera.

2. Run the presentation automatically by completing the following steps:
    a. Change to Slide Sorter view and then press Ctrl + A.
    b. Click the Slide Transition button on the Slide Sorter toolbar.
    c. At the Slide Transition dialog box, click the check box next to Automatically after in the Advance section. Deselect the check box next to On mouse click.
    d. Click the spin arrows to set the timing to 8 seconds in the Automatically after text box. Click the Apply to All button.

3. Save the presentation with the same name c09ex04, Transitions.
4. Print slides 1 and 10 as Note Pages by completing the following steps:
    a. Click File and then Print.
    b. At the Print dialog box in the Print Range section, select Slides and key **1,10** in the Slides text box. Select *Notes Pages* in the Print what: section and click OK.
5. Click on the Slide View button.
6. Press Ctrl + Home to take you to the first slide.
7. Click on the Slide Show button to view the new, improved presentation.
8. Close c09ex04, Transitions.

figure

9.25

Exercise 4

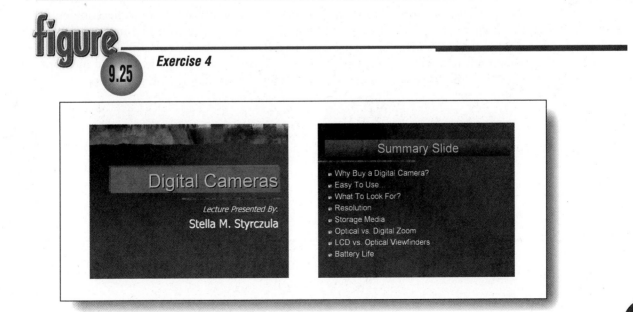

Inserting WordArt in PowerPoint

With WordArt, you can apply special effects to text. These special effects become drawing objects, meaning you can use the Drawing toolbar to change the effect. You can add a WordArt object to an individual slide or to several slides using the Slide Master. The advantage of creating WordArt in a slide master is that it will appear automatically on every slide in the presentation. WordArt is inserted into a PowerPoint slide just as it was inserted into a document. You may use WordArt to create a logo and use the Slide Master to insert the logo on each slide in the presentation.

Inserting and Manipulating Graphics in PowerPoint Slides

To enhance the visual impact of slides in a presentation, consider adding a Microsoft clip art image. Microsoft's Clip Gallery contains a variety of pictures, sounds and motion clips. Pictures include clip art, photos, bitmaps, scanned images, drawings, and other graphics. Common file name extensions are .wmf, .cgm, .gif, .jpg, .bmp, and .png. Sounds effects and music are identified by file name extensions like .wav or .mid. Motion clips such as videos are identified by .avi or animated .gif extensions.

A quick way to locate a clip you are looking for is to use the Search for clips: box, and then type one or more words that describe the clip. If you cannot find a particular clip, you can connect to the *Clip Gallery Live* Web site to preview and download additional clips. You can substitute any of the graphic files in the chapter exercises with other appropriate graphics from this site. Remember to consider your audience and the subject of your document in choosing appropriate graphics to enhance your documents.

Inserting Graphic Files

Insert Clip Art

There are several ways to insert graphic files into PowerPoint slides. If the slide layout includes an AutoLayout placeholder, click the Clip Art icon. Alternatively, an image may be inserted in a slide that does not contain a clip art placeholder. To insert an image, change to Slide View, click Insert, point to Picture, and then choose the source of your image. You may also click the Insert Clip Art button on the Drawing toolbar. Size, crop, move, and position the image as you did in Word 2000. Recoloring can be done in the Recolor Picture dialog box, shown in figure 9.26.

figure

9.26

Recolor Picture Dialog Box

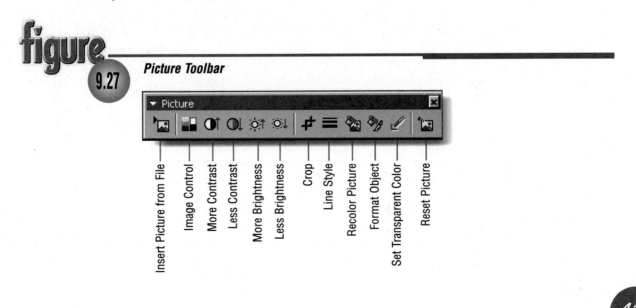

Recoloring an Image

To recolor an image, complete the following steps:

1. Display the slide in Slide View and select the image you want to recolor.
2. Click F*o*rmat, *P*icture, Picture tab, and then Recolor; or click the Recolor Picture button on the Picture toolbar. (The Picture toolbar is shown in figure 9.27.)
3. At the Recolor Picture dialog box, select the color in the Original column that you would like to change, then click the down arrow in the New column and select a new color.
4. Click Preview to see the color changes.
5. When you are satisfied with the results, click OK.

figure

9.27

Picture Toolbar

Creating Watermarks

Image Control

Draw

Create a watermark in a PowerPoint presentation by clicking the Image Control button on the Picture toolbar and then clicking <u>W</u>atermark. Move the watermark image behind the text by clicking the D<u>r</u>aw button on the Drawing toolbar, pointing to O<u>r</u>der, and then clicking Send to Bac<u>k</u>. Use the brightness and contrast button on the Picture toolbar to adjust the brightness and intensity of the image.

Adding a Logo, Inserting Clip Art, and Recoloring Clip Art in a Presentation

1. Open Technical Office.ppt located on your student CD.
2. Save the presentation using the Save <u>A</u>s and name it c09ex05, Clipart.
3. Insert a logo that displays on every slide as shown in figure 9.28 by completing the following steps:
   a. Display slide 1 in Slide View.
   b. Hold down the Shift key and click the Slide View button on the View toolbar. (The screen displays in Title Master View.)
   c. Click the WordArt button on the Drawing toolbar.
   d. Select the WordArt style in the first row and fourth column. Click OK.
   e. At the Edit WordArt Text dialog box, change the font to 32-point High Tower Text and then key **TOTI**. Click OK.
   f. Size and position the logo as in figure 9.28.
   g. Copy the logo to the clipboard, and then click <u>C</u>lose at the Slide Master.
   h. Display slide 3 in Slide Master View, insert the logo by copying it from the clipboard to the Slide Master, and then close the Slide Master.
4. Insert a clip art image in slide 3 as shown in figure 9.28 by completing the following steps:
   a. Display slide 3 in Slide View.
   b. Click the Common Tasks button and select *Slide Layout*.
   c. At the Slide Layout dialog box, select *Text & Clip Art* in the third row and first column. Click <u>A</u>pply.
   d. Double-click the Clip Art icon in the ClipArt placeholder.
   e. Select the Pictures tab at the Microsoft Clip Gallery, click in the Search for clips: text box, key **keyboard**, scroll to the image shown at the right, and then press Enter.
   f. Size and position the image if necessary.
   g. Select the bulleted text and change the font to 28-point Arial.

Step 4e

5. Insert a clip art image in slide 5 by completing the following steps:
   a. Display slide 5 in Slide View.
   b. Click the Common Tasks button and select *Slide Layout*.
   c. At the Slide Layout dialog box select *Clip Art & Text* in the third row and second column. Click <u>A</u>pply.
   d. Double-click on the ClipArt icon in the ClipArt placeholder.

e. Select the Pictures tab at the Microsoft Clip Gallery, click the Search for clips: text box, key **newsletters**, scroll to the image shown at the right, and then press Enter.

f. Size and position the image if necessary.

g. Select the bulleted text and change the font to 28-point Arial.

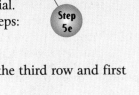

Step 5e

6. Insert a clip art image in slide 7 by completing the following steps:

a. Display slide 7 in Slide View.

b. Click the Common Tasks button and select *Slide Layout.*

c. At the Slide Layout dialog box select the *Text & ClipArt* in the third row and first column. Click Apply.

d. Double-click on the ClipArt icon in the clip art placeholder.

e. Select the Pictures tab at the Microsoft Clip Gallery, then click in the Search for clips: text box, key **computers**, scroll to the image shown at the right, and then press Enter.

f. Size and position the image if necessary.

g. Select the bulleted text and change the font to 28-point Arial.

Step 6e

7. Insert a clip art image in slide 8 by completing the following steps:

a. Display slide 8 in Slide View. (Do not change the Slide Layout.)

b. Click Insert, point to Picture, and then click Clip Art.

c. Select the Pictures tab at the Microsoft Clip Gallery, then click in the Search for clips: text box, key **meeting**, scroll to the image shown at the right, and then press Enter.

d. Size and position the image if necessary.

Step 7c

8. Recolor the clip art image in slide 3 by completing the following steps:

a. Display slide 3 in Slide View and select the clip art.

b. Click the Recolor Picture button on the Picture toolbar.

c. At the Recolor Picture dialog box, click the down arrow at the right of the ninth button below the New section.

d. At the color palette that displays, select the white color.

e. Click the tenth down arrow, select the gold color, and then click OK.

Step 8d

Step 8e

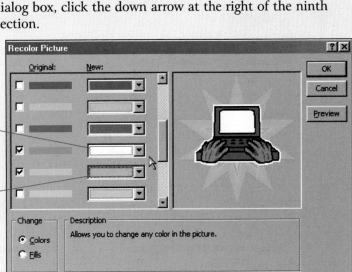

9. Create a watermark on slide 2 by completing the following steps:

a. Display slide 2 in Slide View.

b. Click Insert, point to Picture, and click Clip Art.

c. Select the Pictures tab at the Microsoft Clip Gallery, click in the Search for clips: text box, key **computers**, scroll to the image shown at the right, and then press Enter.

Step 9c

d. Make sure the image is selected and the Picture toolbar is displayed.

e. Click the Image Control button on the Picture toolbar and click <u>W</u>atermark.

f. Click the D<u>r</u>aw button on the Drawing toolbar, point to O<u>r</u>der, and then click Send to Bac<u>k</u>.

g. Move and size the image as shown in figure 9.28.

10. Insert a clip art image of your choosing to slide 4. (The image in slide 4 in figure 9.28 is a sample.)

11. Save the presentation c09ex05, Clipart.

12. Print the presentation as Handouts with 6 on a page, select Fra<u>m</u>e Slides, and then close c09ex05, Clipart.

Optional: Apply transitions, custom animations, build, and sound to the presentation.

figure
9.28
Exercise 5

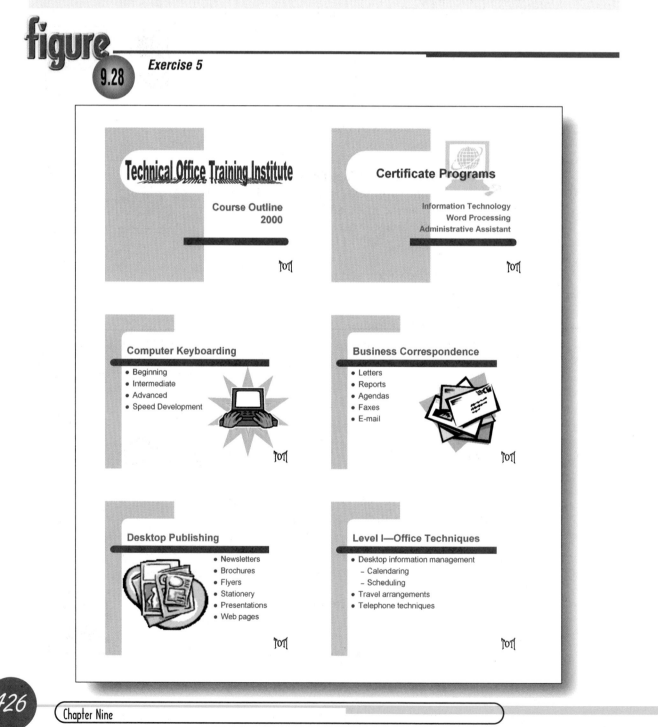

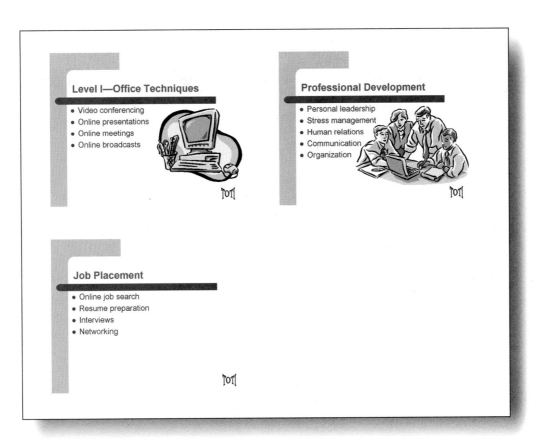

Adding Action Buttons

Action buttons are drawn objects placed on the slide that, when activated, will perform a specific action. For instance, an action button can advance to a specific slide, file, or location on the Web. When inserting action buttons, click the AutoShapes button on the Drawing toolbar, select action button from the pop-up menu, and then apply the appropriate settings. When the presenter moves the mouse over an action button, the pointer changes to a hand with an index finger, indicating that if you click the mouse some form of action will take place.

AutoShapes

AutoShapes

Using Hyperlinks

You can enrich your presentation by inserting hyperlinks. A *hyperlink* can take you to a location within the same document, a different document, or a location on the Web. You can even use hyperlinks to advance to multimedia files, such as sounds or videos. To add a hyperlink, click Insert, Hyperlink. At the Insert Hyperlink dialog box, key the address (URL) in the *Type the file or Web page name* text box and click OK. In order to run a presentation containing hyperlinks to the Web, you must be connected to the Internet.

Hyperlink
A colored and underlined text or graphic linked to a file, a location in a file, an HTML page on the Web, or an HTML page on an intranet.

exercise 6

Inserting an Action Button and Hyperlink in a Presentation

1. Add an action button and hyperlink to the presentation shown in figure 9.29 by completing the following steps:
    a. Open PowerPoint and open Imaging Devices.ppt located on your student CD.
    b. Save the presentation on your hard drive or a floppy disk with Save As and name it c09ex06, Action.
    c. Add an action button on the Slide Master that will advance you from slide to slide except from the Title Slide by completing the following steps:
        1) Display slide 2 in Slide View.
        2) Hold down the Shift key and click the Slide View button on the View toolbar.
        3) At the Slide Master, click AutoShapes on the Drawing toolbar, expand the menu, and then click Action Buttons. At the pop-up menu, select *Action Button: Forward or Next* in the second row and second column.

Step 1c3

        4) Drag the crosshairs to the bottom right corner of the slide and create an arrow shape approximately 0.5″ in height and width.

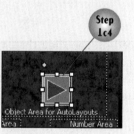

Step 1c4

        5) At the Action Settings dialog box, select the Mouse Click tab, and make sure *Next Slide* displays below Hyperlink to:.
        6) Click the check box to the left of Play sound to turn it on, and then select *Slide Projector* at the drop-down list. Click OK and close the Slide Master.
2. Add a slide number to each slide (except the title slide) by completing the following steps:
    a. Click View and then Header and Footer.
    b. At the Header and Footer dialog box, select the Slide tab, and then click the Slide number option and the Don't show on title slide option. Deselect any other options.
    c. Click Apply to All.

3. Run the presentation and click the action button to advance to slides 3, 4, 5, and 6. Click outside the button to exit the presentation.
4. Save the presentation with the same name c09ex06, Action.
5. Create a hyperlink, *http://www.scantips.com*, by completing the following steps:
   a. Display slide 5 in Slide View.
   b. At the end of the slide, *Flathed Scanners*, press the Enter key. This will give you a new bullet, then key **For more information, try Scantips.com.**
   c. Add a hyperlink to Scantips.com by completing the following steps:
      1) Select the text Scantips.com.
      2) Click the Insert Hyperlink button on the Standard toolbar.
      3) At the Insert Hyperlink dialog box, key *http://www.scantips.com* in the Type the file or Web page name: text box. Click OK.

6. Save the presentation with the same name c09ex06, Action.
7. Before you can run the slide show, the computer must be connected to the Internet. Click the Slide Show button. At slide 5, click the *Scantips.com* hyperlink.
8. When the presentation is completed, close c09ex06, Action. Exit the Internet.
9. Print the presentation as Handouts with 6 slides on a page, Scale to fit paper, and then close c09ex06, Action.

Optional: Apply clip art or photos, transitions, custom animations, build, and sound to the presentation.

figure
9.29
Exercise 6

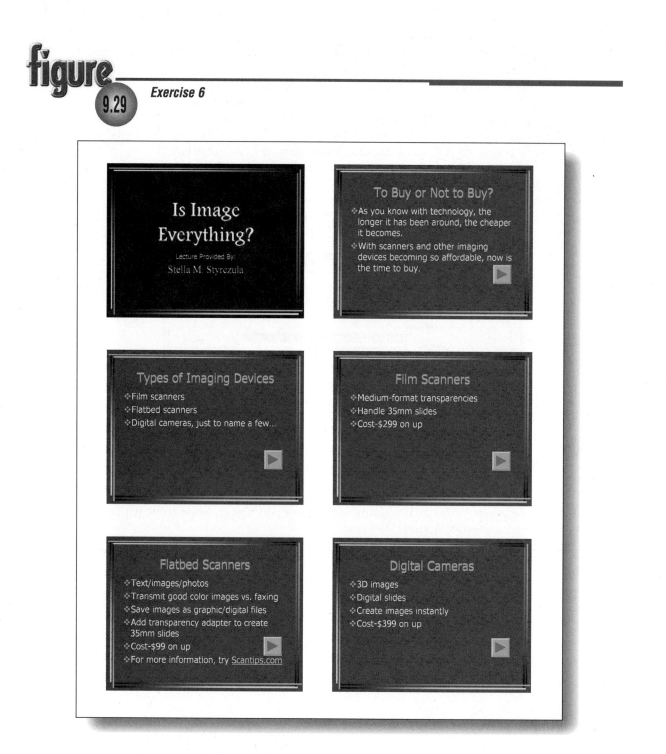

Adding Media Clips

To achieve a full multimedia effect, you can include media clips (movies and sounds) to your presentation. PowerPoint can play a clip automatically or you can play the clip on demand using the mouse. Use of these features requires your computer system to have a sound card and speakers. Media clips are inserted, resized, moved, and copied in the same way as any other image. You can modify a media clip, using the Custom Animation dialog box in the Multimedia Settings section. To add a movie or sound, click Insert, Movies and Sounds, and then select either Movie from or Sound from, and then Clip Gallery or another location.

exercise 7

**Adding a Media Clip with Sound
and an Animated Shape to an Existing Presentation**

1. Add a media clip to a presentation as shown in figure 9.30 by completing the following steps:
    a. Open JobsOnline.ppt located on your student CD.
    b. Save the presentation on your hard drive or a floppy disk with Save As and name it c09ex07, Media.
    c. Add animation to a media clip by completing the following steps:
        1) Display slide 2 in Slide View.
        2) Select the clip, click Slide show, and then click Custom Animation.
        3) At the Custom Animation dialog box with the Multimedia Settings tab selected, make sure a check mark displays in the check box next to Play using animation order, and then click More Options.
        4) At the Movie Options dialog box, click the Loop until stopped check box in the Play options section. Click OK.
        5) Select the Effects tab and change the Entry animation and sound to *Appear* for the effect and *Cash Register* for the sound. Click OK.

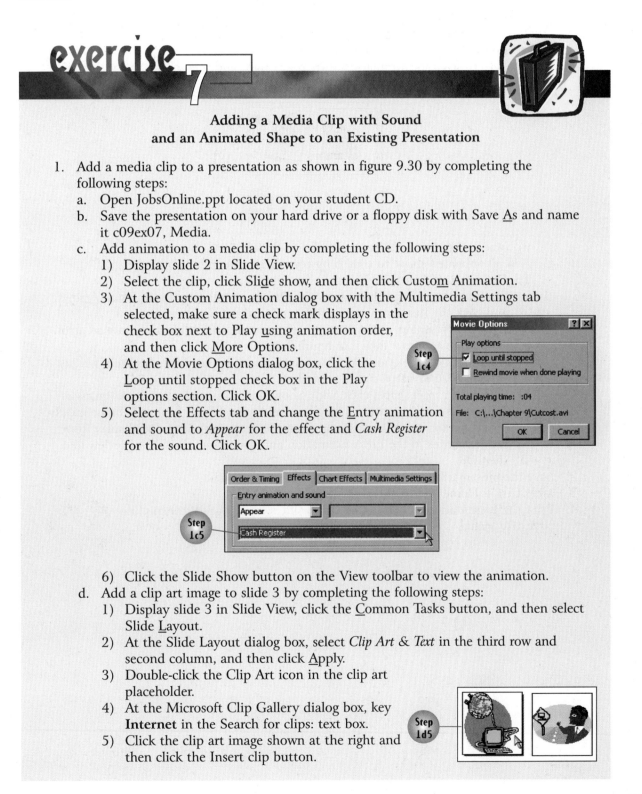

        6) Click the Slide Show button on the View toolbar to view the animation.
    d. Add a clip art image to slide 3 by completing the following steps:
        1) Display slide 3 in Slide View, click the Common Tasks button, and then select Slide Layout.
        2) At the Slide Layout dialog box, select *Clip Art & Text* in the third row and second column, and then click Apply.
        3) Double-click the Clip Art icon in the clip art placeholder.
        4) At the Microsoft Clip Gallery dialog box, key **Internet** in the Search for clips: text box.
        5) Click the clip art image shown at the right and then click the Insert clip button.

e. Add an animated graphic file (.gif) to slide 5 by completing the following steps:
   1) Display slide 5 in Slide View, click the <u>C</u>ommon Tasks button, and select Slide <u>L</u>ayout.
   2) At the Slide Layout dialog box, select *Media Clip & Text*, and then click <u>A</u>pply.
   3) Double-click the Media Clip icon in the clip art placeholder.
   4) At the Microsoft Clip Gallery dialog box, select the Motion Clips tab and key **business** in the Search for clips: text box.
   5) Select the clipboard image shown at the right and then click the Insert clip button.

Step
1e5

   6) Size and position the image similar to figure 9.30.
f. Add an animated shape to slide 6 by completing the following steps:
   1) Display slide 6 in Slide View.
   2) Click the A<u>u</u>toShapes button on the Drawing toolbar, point to Block <u>A</u>rrows, and click the first arrow in the fifth row (Striped Right Arrow).
   3) Drag the crosshairs to the bottom right corner of the slide and draw an arrow similar to the arrow shown in figure 9.30.
   4) Right-click on the arrow, click Add Te<u>x</u>t, and then key **Use the Web**. (Adjust the font size or shape size if needed.)
   5) Select the arrow shape, click Sli<u>d</u>e Show, and then click Custo<u>m</u> Animation.
   6) At the Custom Animation dialog box, select the Effects tab, and then click *Fly, From Left,* and the *Whoosh* sound from the drop-down lists that display from the text boxes in the <u>E</u>ntry animation and sound section. Click <u>P</u>review and then OK.
2. Save the presentation with the same name, c09ex07, Media.
3. Press Ctrl + Home and then run the presentation.
4. Print the presentation as Handouts with 6 slides on a page and then close c09ex07, Media.

figure
9.30

Exercise 7

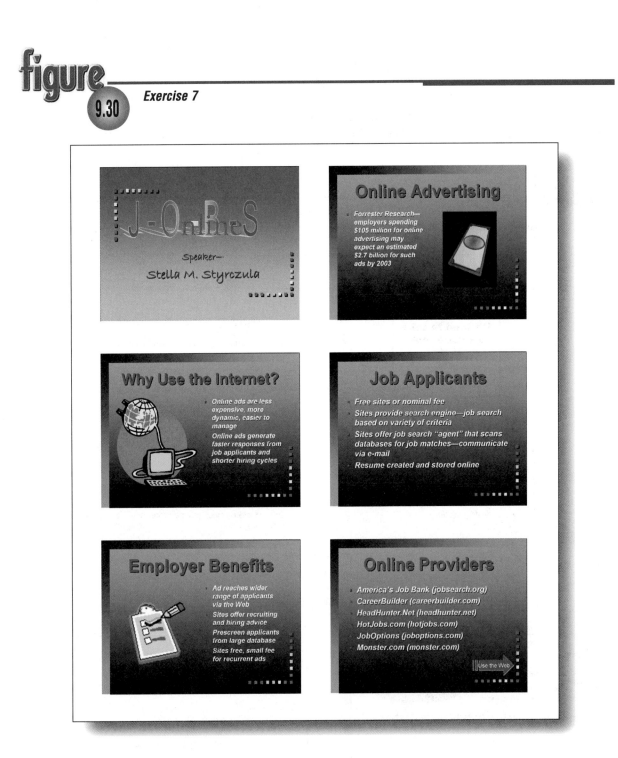

Creating Supporting Handouts for a Presentation

Presentation materials often include handouts for the audience. Handouts might contain an outline of the presentation topics and other supplementary information. Very often supplementary materials include some type of a reply/response card, a fact sheet, a brochure, and a business card. The company or individual making the presentation may even provide a special folder for all of

DTP POINTERS
Audiences appreciate handouts. The handout should say more than the speaker and the speaker should say more than the slides.

these materials with the organization's name and logo on the front cover. These materials make it easy for individuals to review the materials on their own time and to contact the company or presenter after the presentation is over. Samples of supporting documents for Ride Safe, Inc. are shown in figure 9.31.

Refrain from handing out copies of materials before or during your presentation, as this can shift the listeners' attention away from your presentation.

figure 9.31

Samples of Supporting Handouts for a Presentation

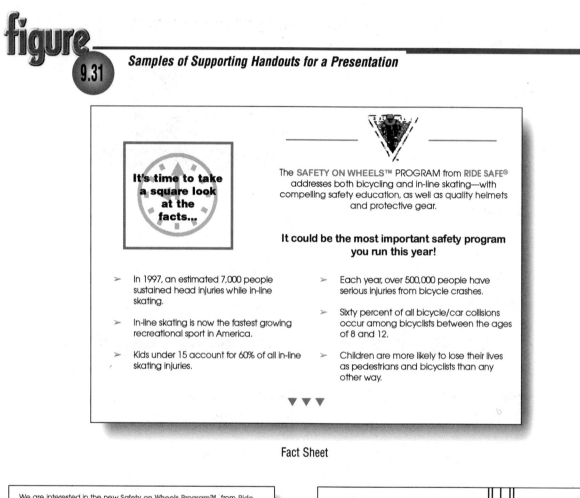

Fact Sheet

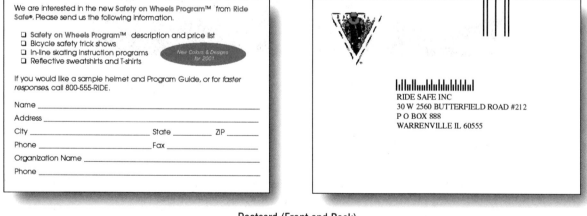

Postcard (Front and Back)

Press Release

Business Card

Certificate

E-Mailing a Presentation

E-Mail

Before you can e-mail a presentation, you must have an e-mail program such as Microsoft Outlook. To e-mail a presentation, click on the E-mail button located on the Standard toolbar. At the E-mail dialog box, you can send the entire presentation as an attachment or send the current slide. If you select *Send the entire presentation as an attachment,* your e-mail program's new message window will appear, adding the file name to the Subject line, and including it as an attachment in the message window.

Broadcasting a Presentation Online

Broadcast

To place a presentation online.

Use PowerPoint to broadcast a presentation online. An online *broadcast* places the presentation online. It is a one-way connection between you and your audience. A broadcast can be delivered to an audience in remote locations and can be transmitted to as many as 15 other people. Before you can broadcast your presentation online, you must first schedule the broadcast using an e-mail program such as Outlook, and your audience must have Internet Explorer 4.0 or later to view the presentation. Because the presentation will broadcast online, the presentation is saved as an HTML file, which allows you to store the file on a Web server for future viewing. To schedule a broadcast complete the following steps:

1. Open the presentation to be broadcast online.
2. Click Slide Show, Online Broadcast, and then Set Up and Schedule.
3. At the Broadcast Schedule dialog box, make sure the *Set Up and schedule a new broadcast* is selected by default. Click OK.
4. At the Schedule a New Broadcast dialog box with the Description tab selected, key a welcome message that will appear on the *lobby page* in the Description text box section. Key the presenter's name in the Speaker text box and the person to contact in the Contact text box. Figure 9.32 shows the Schedule a New Broadcast dialog box.

figure

9.32

Schedule a New Broadcast Dialog Box

5. To set the audio, video, audience feedback, and recording options, select the Broadcast Settings tab.
6. To view the lobby page, click the Preview Lobby Page button and a sample will display in your browser. When finished viewing the page, close the browser window.
7. To set up the members who will be participating in the broadcast use your e-mail program and then click Schedule Broadcast.
8. To begin the broadcast, click Slide Show, Online Broadcast, and then Begin Broadcast.

Online Meeting Using Microsoft NetMeeting

Online meetings are similar to online broadcasts except that the participants can participate in creating the presentation, as well as view changes as they are being made. When an online meeting has been scheduled, NetMeeting automatically starts in the background and allows you to begin sharing the contents of your file. You can host, participate, or collaborate in an online meeting.

chapter summary

➤ A presentation communicates information using visual images to convey the message to an audience.

➤ When choosing a presentation design for slides, consider the audience, the topic, and the method of delivery.

➤ Selecting a visual medium depends on many factors: the topic, your presentation style, audience size, location, equipment availability, lighting conditions, and so on.

➤ Many buttons on PowerPoint's Standard toolbar remain consistent with Word and other Microsoft applications.

➤ A PowerPoint presentation can be created by using the AutoContent Wizard, Design Template, or Blank presentation screen.

➤ PowerPoint's AutoContent Wizard provides helpful information on planning and organizing a presentation based on the topic and purpose of the presentation.

➤ Slides in PowerPoint AutoLayout templates contain placeholders where specific text or objects are inserted. Placeholders format a title, bulleted list, clip art, media clip, chart, organizational chart, table, or object.

➤ If you want changes made to a placeholder to affect all slides in a presentation, make the changes at the Slide Master.

➤ PowerPoint provides viewing options for presentations that include Normal View, Outline View, Slide View, Slide Sorter View, and Slide Show.

➤ Slides in a slide show can be advanced manually or automatically at specific time intervals, or a slide show can be set up to run continuously.

➤ Transition refers to what action takes place as one slide is removed from the screen during a presentation and the next slide is displayed.

➤ Preparing a presentation in Outline View helps to organize topics for each slide without the distractions of colorful designs, clip art, transitions, or sound. It is a good view to use when brainstorming the creation of a presentation.

➤ Sound effects and animation create impact in a slide show.

➤ PowerPoint's build technique displays important points one at a time on a slide.

➤ If you are creating a long presentation with many slides and text, use Outline View to organize the topics for the slides.

➤ You can create an outline in PowerPoint, or import an outline from another program, such as Microsoft Word.

➤ If you are not satisfied with a color scheme, you can change the scheme of colors in the background, and add text, lines, shadows, pictures, and so on.

➤ The background of a presentation should correlate to the visual medium that you are using.

➤ You can change the order of your slides in the Slide Sorter View.

➤ To better organize delivery of your presentation, you can create a Summary Slide at the beginning/closing of your presentation to highlight the main topics to be discussed.

➤ A build is an effective way to keep your audiences' attention on the topic under discussion, instead of reading the remainder of the slide.

➤ Drawing objects include AutoShapes, curves, lines, and WordArt objects and are accessible from the Drawing toolbar

➤ Microsoft's Clip Gallery contains a variety of pictures, sounds and motion clips.

➤ Action buttons are drawn objects placed on the slide that, when activated, will perform a specific action.

➤ A hyperlink can take you to a location within the same document, a different document, or a location on the Web.

➤ Presentation materials often include handouts for the audience.

➤ At PowerPoint's E-mail dialog box, you can send the entire presentation as an attachment or send the current slide.

➤ An online broadcast can be delivered to an audience in remote locations and transmitted to as many as 15 other people.

➤ Presentations can be printed with each slide on a separate piece of paper; with each slide at the top of a page, leaving room for notes; with all or a specific number of slides on a single piece of paper; or with slide titles and topics in outline form.

commands review

	Mouse/Keyboard
Start PowerPoint	Start button on Taskbar, Program, Microsoft PowerPoint
Microsoft Clip Gallery	Insert, Picture, Clip Art; Insert, Object, Microsoft Clip Gallery, OK; click Insert Clip Art button on Drawing toolbar; or double-click clip art placeholder in Slide Layout view
Run a slide show	View, Slide Show or F5; Slide Show, View Show; or click Slide Show button
WordArt	Click Insert WordArt button on Drawing toolbar; display WordArt toolbar, click Insert WordArt button; or click Insert, Picture, WordArt
Slide Master	Click Slide View button while holding down Shift key; or View, Master, Slide Master

thinking offline

True/False: Circle the letter T if the statement is true; circle the letter F if the statement is false.

T F 1. PowerPoint templates contain placeholders where specific text or objects are inserted.

T F 2. Slide View displays miniature versions of a presentation.

T F 3. Watermarks will not display on slides.

T F 4. If you want changes made to placeholders to affect all slides in a presentation, make the changes at the Slide Master.

T F 5. Click the Draw button on the Drawing toolbar to display a pop-up menu that contains the Action Buttons options.

T F 6. At Slide Sorter View, the slide fills the entire screen.

T F 7. An AutoLayout format may contain a Table placeholder.

T F 8. The Recolor picture button is found on the Drawing toolbar.

T F 9. To run a presentation, click Format and Slide Show.

T F 10. You can rearrange slides in Slide Sorter view.

Completion: In the space provided, indicate the correct term(s).

1. Display the _____ toolbar to create builds and animate text and objects for a slide show.

2. Click _____ view to display several slides on a screen at one time.

3. Click _____ view to run a presentation.

4. _____ contains formatting that gives each slide in a presentation identical properties.

5. _____ displays important points on a slide one point at a time.

6. Click the _____ button on the WordArt toolbar to display a palette of shape options.

7. In Outline View, click _____ on the Outlining toolbar to move the insertion point to the next tab stop.

8. To display the Slide Transition dialog box, click _____ on the Menu bar, and then click Slide <u>T</u>ransition.

9. Click the <u>L</u>oop continuously until 'Esc' option at the _____ dialog box to specify that a presentation run continuously.

10. A _____ can take you to a location within the same document, to a different document, or a location on the Web.

Assessment 1

You work for a travel vacation company named Paradise Vacations that specializes in selling vacation package plans to tropical locations. The company is setting up a display booth at a travel trade show. You need to create an electronic slide show to run continuously in your booth. Your target audience is travel consultants who sell vacation package plans to their clients. Your goal is to inform your audience of the travel plan benefits your company can offer to their travel clients, thereby motivating the travel consultants to promote vacation packages when selling travel plans to their clients. Using the text from figure 9.33, create an on-screen presentation in PowerPoint according to the following specifications:

1. Use a Blank presentation template and customize it to your liking; or, select a PowerPoint Design Template that meets your needs. *(Hint: Photographs make dramatic backgrounds.)*

2. When the first slide displays, change to Outline view. Utilizing the information provided in figure 9.33, Paradise Vacations Text, use the ideas supplied in the slide presentation design template to guide you in organizing your presentation. You can also edit the text to fit your needs.

3. After completing your presentation in Outline view, switch to Slide View.

4. Apply an appropriate presentation design.

5. Add any appropriate clip art, animated clips, movies, or photographs.

6. Use a build effect for the bulleted items. You decide on the bullet symbol to be used.

7. Apply transition effects to your slides. You decide if you want one type of transition for the whole presentation or if you want a different transition for each slide.
8. Time the slides to change every 8 seconds.
9. Make the slide show a continuous on-screen presentation.
10. Save the presentation and name it c09sa01, Paradise.ppt.
11. Run the on-screen presentation for a classmate or your instructor.
12. Print and then close c09sa01, Paradise. (Check with your instructor about printing this presentation. One suggestion is to print six slides per page in Black and White to save on paper and printer ink.)

Optional: Add animation and sound effects to your Paradise Presentation.

figure
9.33 *Paradise Vacations Text*

Paradise Vacations, specializing in tropical vacations, offers over 35 fabulous vacation destinations. You can select from over 225 hotels, resorts, condos, and villas at some of the most popular destinations in the Caribbean, Mexico, the Bahamas, Bermuda, Florida, and Hawaii. Choose from a range of moderate to luxurious accommodations, including several all-inclusive vacation properties.

Departing from over 50 U.S. cities, Paradise Vacations is one of the nation's leading vacation companies. We offer value, quality, variety, reliability, and superior service.

Paradise Vacations include roundtrip airfare, hotel accommodations, roundtrip airport-hotel transfers, hotel taxes, hotel service charges and surcharges, and the services of a Paradise representative at your destination.

Your Paradise Representative is professionally trained, friendly, and reliable. Your representative will direct you to your airport-hotel transfer, acquaint you with your destination, arrange optional excursions, and answer your questions.

Our own Hotel Rating Guide helps you to select the accommodations that best fit your needs. Ratings are based on property location, cleanliness, amenities, service, and room quality.

We offer a free Price Protection Guarantee. Sometimes the price of a vacation package plan changes. We guarantee that once your balance is paid in full, we will not increase the price of your vacation. In addition, we periodically offer special promotion prices on vacation package plans. If we advertise a discounted price on the exact same vacation you have booked, you will automatically receive the savings.

Travel with Paradise and travel with the best! Contact your travel consultant for vacation packages and ask for Paradise Vacations!

Assessment 2

1. Create a presentation based on the text shown in figure 9.34. You determine the template and the Autolayout.
2. Insert appropriate transitions, clip art, photographs, backgrounds, etc.
3. After creating the presentation, save it on the hard drive or a floppy disk and name it c09sa02, Telephone.
4. Print and then close c09sa02, Telephone. (Check with your instructor about printing this presentation. One suggestion is to print 6 slides per page.)

figure

9.34 **Telephone Technique Text**

Slide 1	Title	=	Telephone Techniques
	Subtitle		You have less than 10 seconds to make your first impression!
Slide 2	Title	=	Answering Calls
	Bullets		Answer on first or second ring
			Use a pleasant voice
			Identify company and office the caller has reached
			If it is a direct line, identify yourself
Slide 3	Title	=	Directing the Call
	Bullets		Gather information from the caller
			Handle the request or forward call
			Retrieve information and place call on hold or offer to call back
Slide 4	Title	=	Taking Messages
	Bullets		Use the 3 W's
			Who is to be called back?
			When is the best time to return the call?
			What information is the caller seeking?
			Write clearly and concisely
			Use message form
Slide 5	Title	=	Terminating the Call
	Bullets		Verify information in the message
			Thank caller and assure follow up on message
			Give time frame when caller can expect to be called back
			Allow caller to hang up first

CREATIVE ACTIVITY

Create a PowerPoint presentation on a topic of your choosing. Include between 6 to 10 slides. Select a topic that is of interest to you. Possibly research a vacation; a college you would like to attend; a health club; hobby; special interest group; a gardening project; a new computer, scanner, digital camera, etc. and use the Internet to aid in your search for information. Include the following specifications:

1. Be creative and have fun!
2. Select a Blank Presentation, the AutoContent Wizard, or a Design Template.
3. Insert at least one hyperlink to the World Wide Web.
4. Use at least one action button.
5. Use a build for your bulleted items.
6. Insert at least one animated graphic or movie.
7. Use consistency in color and design.
8. Use at least one consistent transition in your presentation.
9. Save your presentation to the hard drive or a floppy disk and name it c09ca01, Creative.
10. Print the entire presentation as Handouts with 6 slides per page and then close c09ca01, Creative.
11. Give your presentation in class and ask your peers to evaluate your presentation and how you presented it. Write a short evaluation on a note card for each presentation and give the cards to the presenter at the end of class. Use the following criteria in evaluating the presentations:
    a. Presenter introduced herself (himself)
    b. Presenter was poised and confident
    c. Use of equipment
    d. Presenter did not read the presentation
    e. Use of clip art
    f. Did not over decorate (too many bells and whistles)
    g. Number of words per slide
    h. Logical order
    i. Choice of background and colors
    j. Wording, punctuation, and grammar
    k. Conclusion

Performance Assessments

Unit 02 PA

PREPARING PROMOTIONAL DOCUMENTS, WEB PAGES, AND POWERPOINT PRESENTATIONS

Assume you are working for a well-known certified public accounting firm named Winston & McKenzie, CPA. A relatively new department in your firm, Executive Search Services, offers other companies assistance in searching for individuals to fill executive positions. You have been asked to prepare various presentation materials that will be used to inform other partners (owners), staff members, and clients of the scope of this department.

First, you will create a fact sheet (similar formatting to a flyer) highlighting the services of the Executive Search Department and the qualifications of its consultants. Second, you will prepare a self-mailing brochure that lists the services of the Executive Search Department, the benefits to the reader, the way to obtain more information, and a mailing label section. You will then create a PowerPoint presentation highlighting the offerings of a local non-profit organization for which you, as a representative of your company, are an active volunteer. Finally, you will create a Web home page highlighting the services of the Executive Search Department.

Think about the audience of an accounting firm in general, and then think more specifically about the audience that might use Executive Search Services. Before you begin, print Fact Sheet Text.doc, W&McK Text1.doc, W&McK Text2.doc, and W&McK Text3.doc located on your student CD. Read the text in these documents to familiarize yourself with the services offered by this company. Include some consistent elements in all of the documents. Use a logo, a graphic image, a special character, text boxes, ruled lines, borders, fill, or color to create unity among the documents. Incorporate design concepts of focus, balance, proportion, contrast, directional flow, color, and appropriate use of white space.

Assessment 1

Using the text in Fact Sheet Text.doc, create a fact sheet highlighting the services offered by Winston & McKenzie's Executive Services Department according to the following specifications:

1. Create a thumbnail sketch of your proposed page layout and design. You will need to experiment with the layout and design!
2. Create styles for repetitive formatting, such as for bulleted text or headings.

3. Design a simple logo using the Drawing toolbar, WordArt, clip art, or other Word features.
4. Vary the fonts, type sizes, and type styles to emphasize the relative importance of items.
5. Use bullets to list the services offered. You decide on the character to use as a bullet.
6. You may use any relevant picture, symbols, borders, colors, etc. in your fact sheet. You decide on the position, size, shading, border/fill, spacing, alignment, and so on.
7. Save the document and name it u02pa01, Facts.
8. Print and then close u02pa01, Facts.
9. Print a copy of the Document Evaluation Checklist. Use the checklist to evaluate your fact sheet. Hand in both items.

Assessment 2 two

Using the text in W&McK Text1.doc; W&McK Text2.doc; and W&McK Text3.doc located on your student CD, create a three-panel brochure according to the following specifications: *(Hint: Save periodically as you work through this assessment.)*

1. Create a dummy of the brochure layout so you know exactly which panel will be used for each section of text. Use W&McK Text1.doc as the text in panel 1, W&McK Text2.doc as the text in panel 2, and W&McK Text3.doc as the text in panel 3. (Panel 3 is actually the information request side of a card the reader can send to the company for more information. The mailing address side, which is panel 4, will be created in step 5.)
2. Prepare a thumbnail sketch of your proposed layout and design.
3. Include the following formatting:
   a. Change the paper size to Letter Landscape.
   b. Change the top and bottom margins to 0.5 inch, and the left and right margins to 0.55 inch (or as close to this as possible).
   c. Turn on kerning at 14 points.
4. Create the inside panels of the brochure according to the following specifications:
   a. Use the column feature to divide the page into panels using uneven columns.
   b. You decide on appropriate typeface, type size, and type style selections that best reflect the mood or tone of this document and the company or business it represents.
   c. Create a customized drop cap to be used at the beginning of each paragraph in panel 1. You decide on the color, position, the typeface, the number of lines to drop, and the distance from the text.
   d. Create any styles that will save you time and keystrokes, such as styles for headings, body text, and bulleted items.
   e. Itemize any lists with bullets. You decide on the bullet symbol, size, color, spacing, etc.
   f. Use text boxes to specifically position text if necessary or to highlight text in a unique way.

g. Include ruled lines. You decide on the line style, thickness, placement, color, etc.

5. To make the brochure self-mailing, create the mailing address side of the request for information (created in panel 3) by completing the following steps in panel 4:

a. Insert the mailing address into a text box, then use Word's Text Direction feature to rotate the mailing address 90 degrees. You decide on an appropriate font, type size, and color. Key the following address:

Winston & McKenzie, CPA
Executive Search Services
4600 North Meridian Street
Indianapolis, IN 46240

b. Use the mouse to size and position the text box containing the mailing address to an appropriate mailing address position. You can also use the Format Text Box dialog box to position the text box more precisely.

c. Create a vertical dotted line representing a cutting line or perforated line at the right edge of panel 4. Draw the line from the top of the page to the bottom of the page. Pay attention to the placement of this dotted line. If the reader were to cut the reply/request card on this line, are the items on the reverse side of the card (panel 3) placed appropriately? If not, make adjustments.

6. Create the return address on panel 5 by following steps 5a and 5b to create the return address. Use the same address as in step 5a. Position the return address text box into an appropriate return address position.

7. Create the cover of the brochure by completing the following steps in panel 6:

a. Key **You Can't Afford to Make the Wrong Hiring Decision!** as the title of the brochure.

b. Use any appropriate graphic image that is available. A large selection of graphics is available by searching for clips using the keyword *business*. You may also consider creating your own logo on the front cover of the brochure. You decide on the position, size, and border/fill, if any.

c. Decide on an appropriate location and include the company name, address, and the following phone and fax numbers:

Phone: **(317) 555-8900**
Fax: **(317) 555-8901**

8. Save the brochure and name it u02pa02, Brochure.
9. Print and then close u02pa02, Brochure.
10. Print a copy of Document Evaluation Checklist.doc. Use the checklist to evaluate your brochure. Make any changes, if necessary. Hand in both items.

Optional: To save on mailing costs, you have to send out postcards to prospective clients. Rewrite and shorten the text in W&McK Text1.doc so it highlights the pertinent points, but fits onto a 4-by-6-inch postcard. Include the company's name, address, phone, and fax numbers.

Assessment three

In addition to being an employee at Winston & McKenzie, you represent the company as an active volunteer for the Metropolitan Art League. One of your responsibilities is to create an on-screen presentation highlighting important aspects of the Art League. Create the presentation by completing the following steps:

1. Open Spotlight.ppt located on your student CD.
2. Apply an appropriate presentation design.
3. Use a build effect for bulleted items. You decide on the bullet symbol to be used.
4. Apply transition effects to your slides.
5. Make the slide show a continuous on-screen presentation. You decide the time increments for the slides.
6. Enhance the presentation with varying fonts, font sizes, and colors.
7. Use any appropriate clip art images, symbols, pictures, etc.
8. Save the presentation and name it u02pa03, Spotlight.ppt.
9. Print and then close u02pa03, Spotlight.ppt.

Optional: Add an appropriate sound—click Insert, point to Movies and Sounds, and then click Sound from Gallery or Play CD Audio Track.

Assessment four

Use the text in the brochure in Assessment 2 (the text is also located on your student CD as W&McK Text1.doc, W&McK Text2.doc, and W&McK Text 3.doc) to create a Web home page for Winston & McKenzie, CPA. The Web page should highlight the services of the Executive Search Department. Include the following specifications:

1. Create a thumbnail of the Web home page.
2. Use the Web Page Wizard, the Blank Web Page template, or create the home page as a Word document and save it in HTML.
3. Use appropriate graphical bullets.
4. Use a graphic horizontal line—choose an appropriate line style.
5. Enhance the text with bold, italic, varying fonts, font sizes, and color.
6. Use a background color or fill effect.
7. Include a graphic or photo. (Consider downloading a clip from the Internet.)
8. Insert two hyperlinks (graphic links or text links).
9. Include an address, phone number, fax number, and an E-mail address.
10. View the Web page in Web Page Preview.
11. Save the document and name it u02pa04, Web Page.html.
12. Print and then close u02pa04, Web Page.html.

Optional: Include scrolling text or sound.

Unit three

PREPARING PUBLICATIONS

Chapter 10

Creating Basic Elements of a Newsletter

PERFORMANCE OBJECTIVES

Upon successful completion of chapter 10, you will be able to create newsletters using your own designs based on desktop publishing concepts and Word features such as columns and styles. You will also be able to improve the readability of your newsletters by specifying line spacing, using kerning, adjusting character spacing, and changing alignment.

DESKTOP PUBLISHING TERMS

Byline	Leading	Subhead
Folio	Nameplate	Subtitle
Gutter	Orphan	Tombstoning
Headline	Picas	Widow

WORD FEATURES USED

Balanced and unbalanced columns	Graphic images	Paragraph indent
	Line spacing	Styles
Character spacing	Newspaper columns	WordArt

Designing a newsletter may appear to be a simple task, but newsletters are more complex than they appear. Newsletters can be the ultimate test of your desktop publishing skills. Remember that your goal is to get the message across. Design is important because it increases the overall appeal of your newsletter, but content is still the most crucial consideration. Whether your purpose for creating a newsletter is to develop better communication within a company or to develop awareness of a product or service, your newsletter must give the appearance of being well planned, orderly, and consistent. In order to establish consistency from one issue of a newsletter to the next, you must plan your document carefully.

Defining Basic Newsletter Elements

Successful newsletters contain consistent elements in every issue. Basic newsletter elements divide the newsletter into organized sections to help the reader understand the text, as well as to entice the reader to continue reading. Basic elements usually include the items described in figure 10.1; figure 10.2 shows their location on a newsletter page. Additional newsletter enhancements and elements are presented in chapter 11.

Basic Newsletter Elements

- **Nameplate:** The nameplate, or banner, consists of the newsletter's title and is usually located on the front page. Nameplates can include the company logo, a unique typeface, or a graphic image to help create or reinforce an organization's identity. A logo is a distinct graphic symbol representing a company.

- **Subtitle:** A subtitle is a short phrase describing the purpose or audience of the newsletter. A subtitle can also be called a tagline. The information in the subtitle is usually located below the nameplate near the folio.

- **Folio:** A folio is the publication information, including the volume number, issue number, and the current date of the newsletter. The folio usually appears near the nameplate, but it can also be displayed at the bottom or side of a page. In desktop publishing, folio can also mean page number.

- **Headlines:** Headlines are titles to articles and are frequently created to attract the reader's attention. The headline can be set in 22- to 72-point type or larger and is generally keyed in a sans serif typeface.

- **Subheads:** Subheads are secondary headings that provide the transition from headlines to body copy. Subheads can also be referred to as *section headings* because they can also break up the text into organized sections. Subheads are usually bolded and sometimes keyed in larger type sizes. There may be more space above a subhead than below.

- **Byline:** The byline identifies the author of an article.

- **Body Copy:** The main part of the newsletter is the body copy or text.

- **Graphic Image:** Graphic images are added to newsletters to help stimulate ideas and add interest to the document. They provide visual clues and visual relief from text-intensive copy.

figure
10.2

Locating Basic Elements in a Newsletter Page

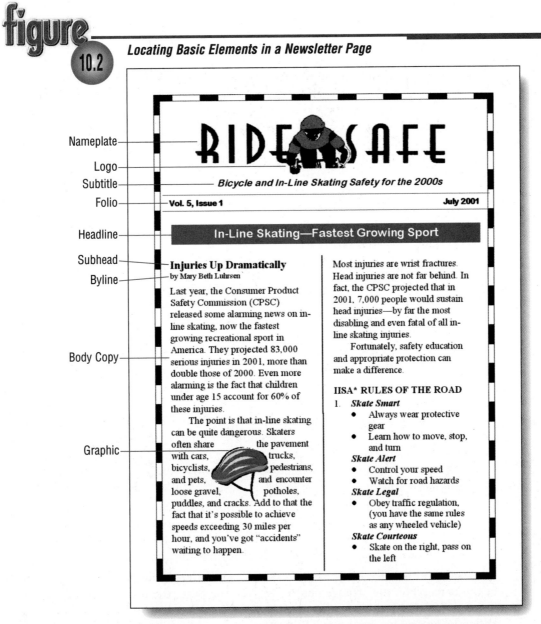

Nameplate
Logo
Subtitle
Folio
Headline
Subhead
Byline
Body Copy
Graphic

Planning a Newsletter

Before creating a newsletter, consider the target audience and the objective for providing the information. Is the goal of the newsletter to sell, inform, explain, or announce? What is the purpose of the newsletter? Companies and organizations often use newsletters to convey a sense of pride and teamwork among employees or members. When planning a company newsletter, consider the following suggestions:

- If a scanner is available, use pictures of different people from your organization in each issue.
- Provide contributor forms requesting information from employees.
- Keep the focus of the newsletter on issues of interest to the majority of employees.

- Make sure you include articles of interest to varying levels of employment.
- Hand out regular surveys to evaluate newsletter relevancy.

If the aim of your newsletter is to promote a product, the focal point may be a graphic image or photograph of the product rather than more general company news. Your aim can also influence the selection of typefaces, type sizes, visual elements, and the placement of elements. Also consider the following questions when planning the newsletter: What is the image you want to project? How often will the newsletter appear? What is your budget? How much time can you devote to its creation? What items are likely to be repeated from issue to issue? And, will your newsletter accommodate ads, photographs, or clip art? After answering these questions, you are ready to begin designing the newsletter.

Designing a Newsletter

DTP POINTERS
Look at as many publications as you can to get ideas for design.

Desktop publishing concepts and guidelines discussed in previous chapters provide you with good starting points for your newsletter. These guidelines emphasize the use of consistency, balance, proportion, contrast, white space, focus, directional flow, and color. If you are designing a newsletter for a company or organization, make sure the design coordinates with their design identity by using the same logo, typefaces, type sizes, column arrangements, and color choices that are used in other correspondence.

DTP POINTERS
Newsletter design should be consistent from issue to issue.

One of the biggest challenges in creating a newsletter is balancing change with consistency. A newsletter is a document that is typically reproduced on a regular basis, whether monthly, bimonthly, or quarterly. With each issue, new ideas can be presented, new text created, and new graphics or photos used. However, for your newsletter to be effective, each issue must also maintain a consistent appearance. Consistency contributes to your publication's identity and gives your readers a feeling of familiarity.

DTP POINTERS
Many logos are trademarks—before using them, find out whether you need permission.

Consistent newsletter features and elements may include the following: size of margins, column layout, nameplate formatting and location, logos, color, ruled lines, formatting of headlines, subheads, and body text. Later in the chapter, you will create styles to automate the process of formatting consistent elements.

DTP POINTERS
Use graphic accents with discretion.

Focus and balance can be achieved in a newsletter through the design and size of the nameplate, the arrangement of text on the page, the use of graphic images or scanned photographs, or the careful use of lines, borders, and backgrounds. When using graphic images or photos, use restraint and consider the appropriateness of the image. A single, large illustration is usually preferred over many small images scattered throughout the document. Size graphic images or photos according to their relative importance to the content. Headlines and subheads can serve as secondary focal points as well as provide balance to the total document.

White space around a headline creates contrast and attracts the reader's eyes to the headline. Surround text with white space if you want the text to stand out. If you want to draw attention to the nameplate or headline of the newsletter, you may want to choose a bold type style and a larger type size. Another option is to use WordArt to emphasize the nameplate title. Use sufficient white space throughout your newsletter to break up gray areas of text and to offer the reader visual relief.

Good directional flow can be achieved by using ruled lines that lead the reader's eyes through the document. Graphic elements, placed strategically throughout a newsletter, can provide a pattern for the reader's eyes to follow.

In figure 10.2, focus, balance, contrast, and directional flow were achieved through the placement of graphic images at the top and bottom of the document, the blue shaded text box with reverse text, and bolded headings.

If you decide to use color in a newsletter, do so sparingly. Establish focus and directional flow with color to highlight key information or elements in your publication.

Creating a Newsletter Page Layout

Typically, page layout begins with choosing the size and orientation of the paper and determining the margins desired for the newsletter. Next, decisions on the number, length, and width of columns become imperative. Typefaces, type sizes, and type styles must also be considered, as well as graphic images, ruled lines, and shading and coloring.

Choosing Paper Size and Type

The first considerations in designing a newsletter page layout are the paper size and type. The number of copies needed and the equipment available for creating, printing, and distributing the newsletter can affect this decision. Most newsletters are created on standard 8-1/2 by 11 inch paper, although some are printed on larger sheets such as 8-1/2 by 14 inches. The most economical choice for printing is the standard 8-1/2 by 11 inch paper and it is easier to hold and read, cheaper to mail, and fits easily in standard file folders.

Paper weight is determined by the cost, the quality desired, and the graphics or photographs included. The heavier the stock, the more expensive the paper. In addition, pure white paper is more difficult to read because of glare. If possible, investigate other, more subtle colors. Another option is to purchase predesigned newsletter paper from a paper supply company. These papers come in many colors and designs. Several have different blocks of color created on a page to help separate and organize your text.

Creating Margins for Newsletters

After considering the paper size and type, determine the margins of your newsletter pages. The margin size is linked to the number of columns needed, the formality desired, the visual elements used, the amount of text available, and the type of binding. Keep your margins consistent throughout your newsletter. Listed here are a few generalizations about margins in newsletters:

DTP POINTERS
Be generous with your margins; do not crowd text.

- A wide right margin is considered formal. This approach positions the text at the left side of the page—the side where most readers tend to look first. If the justification is set at full, the newsletter will appear even more formal.

- A wide left margin is less formal. A table of contents or marginal subheads can be placed in the left margin giving the newsletter an airy, open appearance.

- Equal margins tend to create an informal look.

If you plan to create a multipage newsletter with facing pages, you may want to use Word's mirror margin feature, which accommodates wider inside or outside margins. Figures 10.3 and 10.4 illustrate mirror margins in a newsletter. Often the inside margin is wider than the outside margin; however, this may depend on the amount of space the binding takes up. To create facing pages with mirror margins, click File, then Page Setup. At the Page Setup dialog box, select the Margins tab, and then select the Mirror margins option. If you plan to include page numbering, position the numbers on the outside edges of each page.

Also consider increasing the *gutter* space to accommodate the binding on a multipage newsletter. To add gutter space on facing pages, add the extra space to the inside edges; on regular pages, add space to the left edges. To add gutters, display the Page Setup dialog box with the Margins tab selected, then select or key a gutter width at the Gutter option. Gutters do not change the margins, but rather add extra space to the margins. However, gutters make the printing area of your page narrower. Gutter space may be added to the left side of your page, to the left and right sides if the mirrored margin feature is chosen, or to the top of a sheet.

DTP POINTERS
Place page numbers on the outside edges when using mirror margins.

Gutter
Extra space added to the inside margin to accommodate the binding.

figure
10.3

Outside Mirror Margins on Facing Pages of a Newsletter

Binding or Fold

Page 2   Dancing   Art & Theatre   Page 3

Art Happenings

Dancing lessons will be available at the Elite Dance Studio beginning March 1. Sign up early to guarantee that you will get the class you've been waiting for. Ballroom dancing and modern dance are popular classes.
     Classes will be limited to twenty dancers. Come alone or sign up with a friend.

View artwork of open campus faculty—drawings, paintings, photographs, jewelry, and computer animation. Discuss available classes with faculty.

Theatre
"Phantom of the Opera" will be playing

Outside Mirror Margins

figure
10.4
Inside Mirror Margins on Facing Pages, with Gutter Space

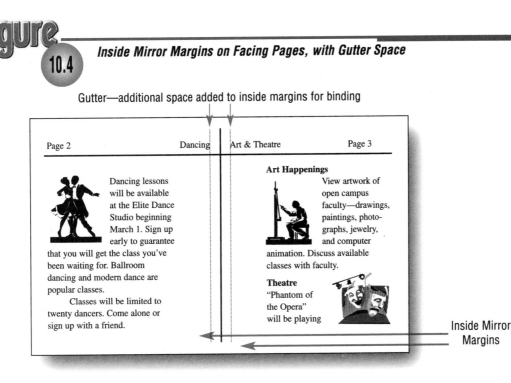

Gutter—additional space added to inside margins for binding

Creating Newspaper Columns for Newsletters

When preparing newsletters, an important consideration is the readability of the document. The line length of text can enhance or detract from the readability of text. Setting the text in columns can make it easier for your readers.

Newspaper columns in a newsletter promote the smooth flow of text and guide the reader's eyes. As discussed earlier in chapter 6, Word's Newspaper Columns feature allows text to flow from column to column in the document. In order to work with columns, Word must be set to Print Layout view. When the first column on the page is filled with text, the insertion point moves to the top of the next column on the same page. When the last column on the page is filled, the insertion point moves to the beginning of the first column on the next page.

> **DTP POINTERS**
> Columns added to newsletters improve readability.

Newspaper columns can be created using the Columns button on the Standard toolbar or with options from the Columns dialog box. Columns of equal width are created with the Columns button on the Standard toolbar. To create columns of unequal width, use the Columns dialog box, click Format, then Columns. Generally, keying text first and then formatting the text into newspaper columns is considered faster.

Columns

Using Balanced and Unbalanced Columns

Word automatically lines up (balances) the last line of text at the bottom of each column. On the last page of a newsletter, the text is often not balanced between columns. Text in the first column may flow to the bottom of the page, while the text in the second column may end far short of the bottom of the page. Columns can be balanced by inserting a section break at the end of the text by completing the following steps:

1. Position the insertion point at the end of the text in the last column of the section you want to balance.
2. Click Insert and then Break.
3. At the Break dialog box, click Continuous and then click OK or press Enter.

Figure 10.5 shows the last page of a document containing unbalanced columns and also a page where the columns have been balanced. If you want to force a new page to start after the balanced columns, click after the continuous break and then insert a manual page break.

figure

10.5 *Unbalanced and Balanced Columns*

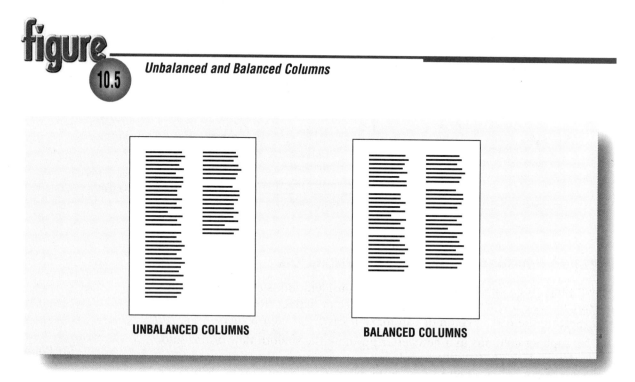

UNBALANCED COLUMNS   BALANCED COLUMNS

Determining Number of Columns

The number of columns used in newsletters may vary from one column to four or more columns. The size of the paper used, the font and type size selected, the content and amount of text available, and many other design considerations affect this decision.

One-column newsletters are easy to produce because the articles simply follow each other. If you do not have much time to work on your newsletter, this format is the one to use. The one-column format is the simplest to design and work with because it allows you to make changes and additions easily. You will want to use a large type size—usually 12 points—to accommodate the long line length of a one-column design. Be sure to use wide margins with this column layout. Also, keep in mind that an asymmetrically designed page is more interesting to look at than a symmetrical one, as shown in figure 10.6.

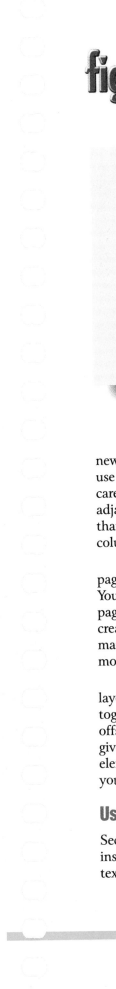

figure
10.6
Asymmetrical and Symmetrical Design in Newsletters

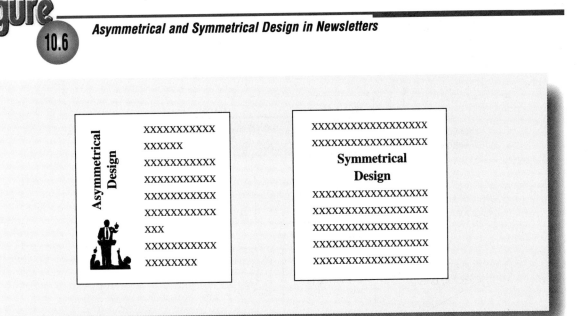

The two-column newspaper format is the most frequently used selection for newsletters. It gives a formal look, especially if used with justified text. Generally, use type sizes between 10 and 12 points when using a two-column layout. Be careful to avoid *tombstoning*, which occurs when headings display side by side in adjacent columns. Using an asymmetrical design in which one column is wider than the other and adding graphic enhancements will make this classic two-column format more interesting.

A three-column format is successful if you avoid using too much text on the page. This popular format is more flexible for adding interesting design elements. You may use a smaller type size (9 to 11 points) and fit more information on a page. Placing headings, text, or graphics across one, two, or three columns can create a distinctive flow. Often, one column is reserved for a table of contents, marginal subheads, or a masthead (publication information), thus allowing for more white space in the document and more visual interest.

A four-column design gives you even more flexibility than the three-column layout; however, more time may be spent in putting this newsletter layout together. Leaving one column fairly empty with a great deal of white space to offset more text-intensive columns is a visually appealing solution. This format gives you many opportunities to display headings, graphics, and other design elements across one or more columns. You will need to use a small type size for your text—9 to 10 points.

Tombstoning
When headings display side by side in adjacent columns.

Using Varying Numbers of Columns in a Newsletter

Section breaks can be used to vary the page layout within a single newsletter. For instance, you can use a section break to separate a one-column nameplate from text that can be created in three-columns, as shown in figure 10.7.

figure
10.7
Section Breaks in Newsletters

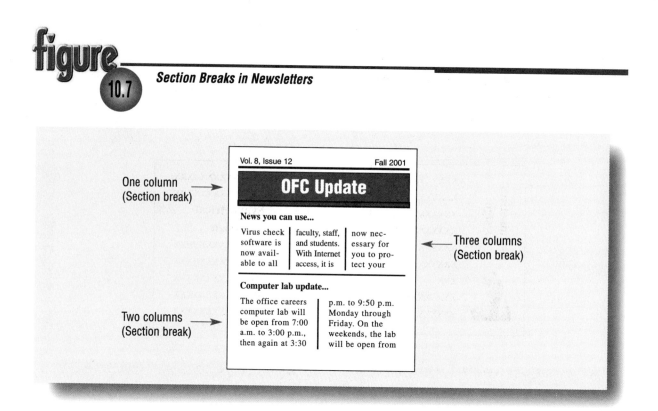

There are basically three methods for inserting section breaks in documents. One method uses the Break dialog box. Another method automatically inserts a section break if you select the option *This Point forward* in the A̲pply to section of the Columns dialog box. In the third method, select the text first and then apply column formatting.

To move the insertion point between columns, use the mouse or press Alt + up arrow to move the insertion point to the top of the previous column, or press Alt + down arrow to move the insertion point to the top of the next column.

In addition, when formatting text into columns, Word automatically breaks the columns to fit the page. If a column breaks in an undesirable location, you can insert a column break in the document to control where the columns end and begin on the page. To insert a column break, position the insertion point where you want the new column to begin, then press Ctrl + Shift + Enter or click I̲nsert, B̲reak, then C̲olumn break.

Changing the Number of Columns

To change the number of columns for an entire newsletter, click E̲dit, then Select Al̲l; to change the number of columns for part of a document, select the affected text only; to change the number of columns in several existing sections, click to select the multiple sections. After selecting the areas you want to change, click Fo̲rmat, C̲olumns, and then enter the number of columns desired.

If you want to remove columns in your newsletter, click in the section or select multiple sections you want to change, then click Fo̲rmat, then C̲olumns, and then click O̲ne in the Presets section.

Determining Column Width

Column width, type size, and leading are related, in that altering one setting affects the settings of the others. As a general rule, narrow columns are easier to read than wide ones, but the number of words is important. Typically, columns contain 5 to 15 words per line. In typesetting, the vertical line spacing, measured from the baseline of one line of text to the baseline of the next line of text, is referred to as *leading*. In general, short lines use minimal leading, whereas long lines require more leading.

One method for determining column width is based on the typeface and point size used. Choose a typeface and type size you intend to use in the body text (choose a serif font in a type size between 10 and 12 points). Type a complete lowercase alphabet, print it, measure the length of the alphabet with a ruler, and multiply by 1.5 to determine the column width, as shown in figure 10.8. Generally, line length should be approximately 1.5 to 2 alphabets or 39 to 52 characters.

Line length in typesetting is usually measured in *picas*. Since 6 picas equal 1 inch, a line length of 5 inches would be measured as 30 picas. A guideline in typesetting is that the line length measured in picas does not exceed twice the point size of the type. For instance, 12-point type looks best in a 20- to 23-pica column.

Leading
Vertical line spacing measured from the baseline of one line to the baseline of the next line.

Picas
Line length in typesetting—6 picas equal 1 inch.

figure
10.8 *Determining Column Width*

12-point Times New Roman	**12-point Palatia**
abcdefghijklmnopqrstuvwxyz	abcdefghijklmnopqrstuvwxyz
Measures: **2 inches**	Measures: **2.25 inches**
$2 \times 1.5 = 3$ **inches**	$2.25 \times 1.5 = 3.38$ **inches**
3 inches = 18 picas	**3.38 inches = 22.8 picas**

Changing Column Widths

If your newsletter is divided into sections, click in the section you want to change, then drag the column marker on the horizontal ruler. If an adjacent column is hampering your efforts to change a column width, reduce the width of the adjacent column first. If the column widths are equal, all of the columns will change. If the column widths are unequal, only the column you are adjusting changes. To specify exact measurements for column widths, use the Columns dialog box.

Adding Vertical Lines between Columns

Click in the section where you want to add a vertical line and then click Format, Columns. At the Columns dialog box, turn on the Line between check box and then close the dialog box.

Adding Borders to Newsletter Pages

You can add page borders and text box borders to change the appearance of your newsletters. Borders help separate different articles. To add a page border, click Format, Borders and Shading, select the Page Border tab, and then select a particular line Style, Width, and Color, or select a predesigned Art border.

To change a text box border, select it, double-click its edge, select the Colors and Lines tab, and then select various options at the Format Text Box dialog box.

Creating Your Own Newsletter

A thumbnail sketch is an excellent way to experiment with different layouts and designs. Look at the work of others for hints and suggestions on different layouts. Creating a thumbnail is like "thinking" on paper. See figure 10.9.

figure
10.9   *Thumbnail Sketch of a Newsletter*

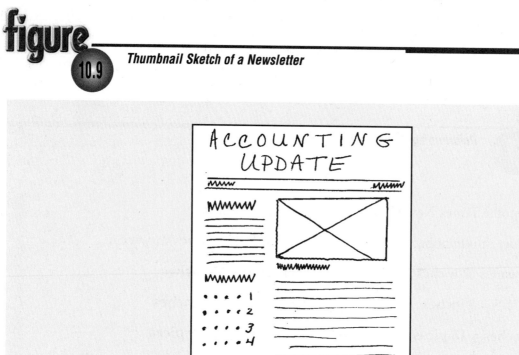

Using Styles in Newsletters

Styles are especially valuable for saving time, effort, and keystrokes in creating newsletters. Newsletters are typically one of the most frequently created desktop publishing documents, and they contain elements that must remain consistent from page to page as well as from issue to issue. Styles reinforce consistency in documents by saving repetitive formatting instructions with a name so they can be applied over and over.

In addition to predesigned system styles included in many Word template or wizards, you have the option to create your own customized styles either based on system styles or created from scratch. Throughout the creation of the newsletter in figure 10.10, you will use various predesigned system styles and customize them to certain specifications as well as create your own styles based on existing styles.

Adjusting Leading in Newsletters

While creating newsletters, you may find areas where adjustments should be made to increase or decrease white space between lines. This may occur when creating a nameplate, headline, subhead, or body text. Insufficient leading makes the text difficult to read; extra leading makes a page look less gray. However, too much leading or too little leading can make it difficult to find the beginning of the next line.

In Word, you can adjust leading by adjusting the line spacing—single, 1.5 lines, or double—or by specifying an exact amount at the *At Least* or *Exactly* settings. Or you can adjust line and paragraph spacing at the Paragraph dialog box. To adjust line and paragraph spacing, click F*o*rmat, then *P*aragraph. At the Paragraph dialog box, select the *I*ndents and Spacing tab. Make selections at the Spacing section by selecting or keying a measurement *B*efore or Aft*e*r your line of text.

Normal leading in Word is 120% of the type size being used. For example, a 10-point type has 12 points of leading. Large type size may require an adjustment from the normal leading. For instance, if a headline contains two lines both keyed at 30 points, the space between the two lines may be too wide. Reducing the leading will improve the appearance of the heading. Consider the following guidelines when determining leading:

- Large type requires more leading.
- Longer lines need more leading to make them easier to read.
- Sans serif type requires more leading because it does not have serifs that guide the eye along the line.
- Use styles to apply line spacing consistently in newsletters.

Reducing the Size of Graphic Files

The logo used in figure 10.10, which is a graphic file located on your student CD (Ridesf1blue.bmp), is a fairly large file. Therefore, you will need to consult with your instructor on how best to manage large files, particularly in this chapter.

To speed up scrolling in your document, you may replace the graphic at the document screen with a picture placeholder. On the T*o*ols menu, click *O*ptions, and then click the View tab. To hide pictures, select the *P*icture placeholders check box. Word displays an outline instead of the picture. If you view the document at Print Preview, the picture will display and it should print properly.

Creating a Folio

Throughout the exercises in this chapter, you will continually build the newsletter shown in figure 10.10. Each exercise involves creating a style for a specific newsletter element. Each exercise builds on the previous one, finally resulting in a completed newsletter with embedded styles and saved as a template to help you create the next issue.

Creating a folio for your newsletter will be the first step in building the Ride Safe newsletter. The *folio* will consist of publishing information that will change from issue to issue, such as the volume number, issue number, and date. However, the formatting applied to the folio will remain consistent with each issue. To ensure this consistency, prepare a folio style and apply it to the new information keyed into the folio each month. Using this style will reduce time and effort.

Frequently, the folio is preceded or followed by a graphic line that sets the folio information apart from the rest of the nameplate. The folio can appear at the top of the nameplate as in this exercise, although it is more commonly placed below the nameplate. Reverse text can be added for emphasis and interest and text set in italic is often used.

figure 10.10 Ride Safe Newsletter with Elements and Styles Marked

exercise 1

Creating a Folio Style for a Newsletter

1. At a clear document screen, create the folio for the newsletter in figure 10.10 by completing the following steps:
    a. Change all the margins to 0.75 inch.
    b. Change to Print Layout View, change the Zoom Control to 75%, and click the Show/Hide ¶ button to display nonprinting characters.
    c. Change the font to 13-point Impact, key **Volume 5, Issue 1**, and then press the space bar three times.
    d. Insert the bullet symbol (•) in the folio by clicking <u>I</u>nsert and then <u>S</u>ymbol.
    e. At the Symbol dialog box, select the <u>S</u>ymbols tab, select the Wingdings font, and then select the symbol in the fifth row and the sixteenth column.
    f. Click <u>I</u>nsert and then Close.
    g. Press the space bar three times, key **June 2001**, and then press Enter.
    h. Select the line you have just typed and change the character spacing to Expanded <u>B</u>y 1 pt and turn on kerning at 13 points at the Font dialog box. Click OK or press Enter.
    i. With the text still selected, click F<u>o</u>rmat and then <u>P</u>aragraph.
    j. At the Paragraph dialog box, select the <u>I</u>ndents and Spacing tab.
    k. Change the <u>L</u>eft Indentation to 0.25 inch and then key **6 pt** in the Aft<u>e</u>r text box located in the Spacing section. Click OK or press Enter.
    l. Select the symbol between the issue number and date and change the font color to Blue (second row and third color from the right in the color palette).
    m. Create a style from existing text by completing the following steps:
        1) Position the insertion point anywhere in the folio text.
        2) Click inside the Style list box on the Formatting toolbar to select the current style name.
        3) Key **Folio** and press Enter. (The Folio style is then added to the list of styles available in this document.)

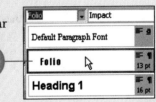

Step 1m3

2. Save the document on your hard drive or to a floppy disk and name it c10ex01, Folio. (You may want to save this exercise and the following Ride Safe newsletter exercises under one file name to reduce disk space.)
3. Close c10ex01, Folio. (You will not print until the entire newsletter has been created.)

Creating a Nameplate

A *nameplate* or banner is the first thing that captures the reader's eyes; it provides immediate identification of the newsletter. A nameplate is the artwork (graphic, logo, scanned image, cropped image, etc.) or type that includes the name of the publication and is usually placed at the top of the first page of a newsletter. The choice of fonts, type sizes, and the designs of the name are important because the reader sees them repeatedly.

Nameplate
A newsletter element, also known as a banner, that first captures the reader's eyes and immediately identifies the newsletter.

The nameplate in exercise 2 consists of the company's name and a logo bordered by two dotted lines created in the same color as that used in the logo. Ride Safe, Inc., uses two different logo designs in most of their publications. The Ride Safe logos, however, may display in several different colors, such as blue, red, teal, orange, yellow, or purple. Most nameplates remain unchanged from issue to issue; therefore, saving it as a style is not necessary. But the nameplate should be saved to a newsletter template.

Figure 10.11 illustrates several examples of nameplates. Examine them for the use and different location of elements. Looking at the work of others can help you develop your own skills in design and layout.

figure
10.11

Sample Nameplates

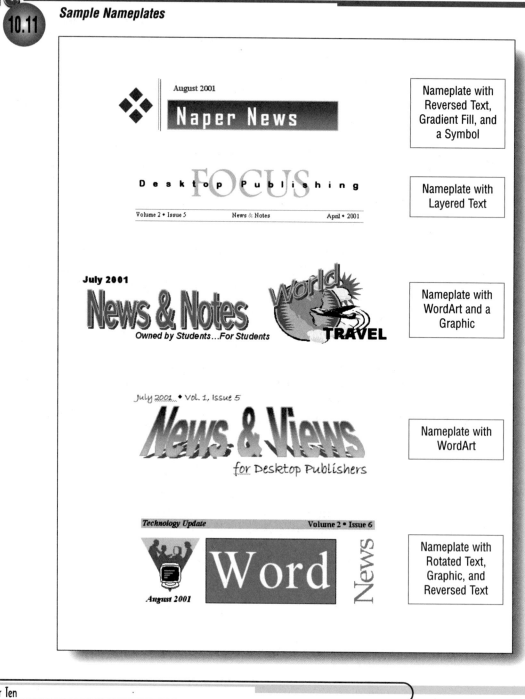

exercise 2

Creating a Nameplate for a Newsletter

1. At a clear document screen, create the nameplate shown in figure 10.10 by completing the following steps:
   a. Open c10ex01, Folio.
   b. Save the document on the hard drive or to a floppy disk with Save As and name it c10ex02, Nameplate.
   c. Format the nameplate by completing the following steps:
      1) Position the insertion point on the paragraph symbol below the folio and make sure Normal displays in the Style list box on the Formatting toolbar.
      2) Change the font to 13-point Impact in Blue.
      3) Click Format, Paragraph, and make sure 0 inches displays in the Left Indentation text box. Click OK or press Enter.
      4) Click Insert and then Symbol.
      5) At the Symbol dialog box, select the Symbols tab, change the font to Wingdings, and then select the bullet symbol in the fifth row and the sixteenth column.
      6) Click Insert and then Close.
      7) Continue pressing the F4 key until you have created an entire row of blue symbols, and then press Enter.

Volume·5,·Issue·1···•···June·2001¶

   d. Insert the Ride Safe logo by completing the following steps:
      1) Position the insertion point on the paragraph below the dotted line, click Insert, point to Picture, and then click From File.
      2) Insert Ridesf1blue.bmp located on your student CD.
      3) Select the image and then click the Center Align button on the Formatting toolbar.
      4) Deselect the image, position the insertion point on the paragraph symbol below the image, press Enter, and then change the alignment to Align Left.
   e. Select the blue dotted line (do not select the paragraph symbol at the end of the dotted line).
   f. Click the Copy button on the Standard toolbar.
   g. Position the insertion point on the second paragraph symbol below the logo, click the Paste button on the Standard toolbar, and then press Enter.
2. Save the document again with the same name, c10ex02, Nameplate.
3. Close c10ex02, Nameplate. (You may want to wait to print the entire newsletter when it is completed.)

Creating a Subtitle

Subtitle

A newsletter element that emphasizes the purpose of the newsletter and identifies the intended audience.

As the third step in building a newsletter, you will create a subtitle. The text in the subtitle will remain consistent from issue to issue, so creating a style is not necessary. A *subtitle* emphasizes the purpose of the newsletter and identifies the intended audience. It is usually keyed in a sans serif typeface in 14 to 24 points, and kerning should be turned on.

exercise 3

Creating a Subtitle in a Newsletter

1. At a clear document screen, add a subtitle to the newsletter shown in figure 10.10 by completing the following steps:
   a. Open c10ex02, Nameplate.
   b. Save the document on the hard drive or to a floppy disk with Save As and name it c10ex03, Subtitle.
   c. Format the subtitle by completing the following steps:
      1) Position the insertion point on the paragraph symbol below the dotted line and change the font to 13-point Impact italic, making sure the font color displays in Black.
      2) Change the character spacing to Expanded By 1 pt and then turn on kerning at 13 pt. Choose OK or press Enter.
      3) Click Format and then Paragraph.
      4) At the Paragraph dialog box, select the Indents and Spacing tab, change the Spacing Before to 0 pt, change the Spacing After to 12 pt, and then click the Tabs button.
      5) At the Tabs dialog box, key **6.75** inches in the Tab stop position text box, select Right Alignment, click the Set button, and then click OK or press Enter.
      6) Press Tab and key **Bicycle and In-Line Skating Safety News.**

         Bicycle and In-Line Skating Safety News •

         Step 1c6
      7) Press the space bar three times and then click the Italic button on the Formatting toolbar to turn this feature off.
      8) Insert the same bullet symbol used in creating the dotted lines in the nameplate.
      9) Press Enter.
      10) Select the symbol and change the font color to Blue.
2. Save the document again with the same name, c10ex03, Subtitle.
3. Close c10ex03, Subtitle. (You will print when the newsletter is complete.)

Creating a Headline

DTP POINTERS

Avoid using underlining in a headline or subhead.

After completing the folio, nameplate, and subtitle, you will now create a headline in exercise 4. *Headlines* organize text and help readers decide whether they want to read the article. To set the headline apart from the text, use a larger type size, heavier weight, and a different typeface than the body. When determining a type size for a headline, start with 18 points and increase the size until you find an appropriate one. As a general rule, choose a sans serif typeface for a headline; but this is not a hard-and-fast rule. Because the headline consists of text that will change with each issue of the newsletter, consider creating a style to format the headline.

Headlines of more than one line often improve in readability and appearance if leading is reduced. The leading in a headline should be about the same size as the type used. Using all caps (sparingly) or small caps substantially reduces leading automatically, because capital letters lack descenders.

Headlines and subheads should have more space above than below. This indicates that the heading goes with the text that follows rather than the text that precedes the heading.

exercise 4

Creating a Headline Style for a Newsletter

1. At a clear document screen, create a headline style for the newsletter in figure 10.10 by completing the following steps:
   a. Open c10ex03, Subtitle.
   b. Save the document on the hard drive or a floppy disk with Save As and name it c10ex04, Headline.
   c. Format the headline in figure 10.10 by completing the following steps:
      1) Position the insertion point on the paragraph symbol below the subtitle. (Press Ctrl + End.)
      2) Change the font to 24-point Britannic Bold. (Make sure italic is turned off.)
      3) Change the font color to Gray-50% and turn on Small caps (Ctrl + Shift + K).
      4) Select the Character Spacing tab in the Font dialog box, change character spacing to Expanded By 1.5 pt and make sure kerning is turned on at 13 pt. Click OK or press Enter.
   d. Key **In-Line Skating—Fastest Growing Sport**. (Use an em dash.)
   e. Format the headline by completing the following steps:
      1) Select *In-Line Skating...*, click Format, and then Paragraph.
      2) At the Paragraph dialog box, select the Indents and Spacing tab.
      3) Change the Spacing Before to 6 pt and the Spacing After to 18 pt, and then click OK or press Enter.
      4) Deselect the text, position the insertion point at the end of the line, and then press Enter.
   f. Create a style from existing text by completing the following steps:
      1) Position the insertion point anywhere in the headline text.
      2) Click inside the Style list box on the Formatting toolbar to select the current style name.
      3) Key **Headline** and then press Enter. (The Headline style is then added to the list of styles available in this document.)
2. Save the document again with the same name c10ex04, Headline.
3. Close c10ex04, Headline. (You will print when the newsletter is complete.)

Step 1f3

Headline	▾	Britannic Bold
Default Paragraph Font		≡ a
Folio		≡ ¶ 13 pt
Heading 1		≡ ¶ 16 pt
Heading 2		≡ ¶ 14 pt
Heading 3		≡ ¶ 13 pt
HEADLINE	▷	≡ ¶ 24 pt

Formatting Body Text in a Newsletter

In exercise 5, you will format the body text for the newsletter you are building in this chapter. You will change the font and type size, create em spaces for paragraph indentations, and turn on the Columns feature. Before doing so, take a look at some of the formatting options that apply to body text.

Applying the Widow/Orphan Feature

Word's Widow/Orphan control feature is on by default. This feature prevents the first and last lines of paragraphs from being separated across pages. A *widow* is a single line of a paragraph or heading that is pushed to the top of the next page. A single line of text (whether part of a paragraph or heading) appearing by itself at the end of a page is called an *orphan*. This option is located in the Paragraph dialog box at the Line and Page Breaks tab.

Even with this feature on, you should still watch for subheadings that are inappropriately separated from text at the end of a column or page. If a heading displays inappropriately, insert a column break. To insert a column break, position the insertion point where you want a new column to begin, then press Ctrl + Shift + Enter, or click Insert, Break, and then Column break.

Aligning Text in Paragraphs in Newsletters

Align Left

Center

Align Right

Justify

The type of alignment you choose for a newsletter influences the tone of your publication. Text within a paragraph can be aligned in a variety of ways: at both the left and right margins (justified); at the left or right; or on the center of the text body, causing both the left and right margins to be ragged.

Justified text is common in publications such as textbooks, newspapers, newsletters, and magazines. It is more formal than left-aligned text. For justified text to convey a professional appearance, there must be an appropriate line length. If the line length is too short, the words and/or characters in a paragraph may be widely spaced, causing "rivers" of white space. Remedying this situation requires increasing the line length, changing to a smaller type size, and/or hyphenating long words. Text aligned at the left is the easiest to read. This alignment has become popular with designers for publications of all kinds. Center alignment should be used on small amounts of text.

Indenting Paragraphs with Em Spaces

In typesetting, tabs are generally measured by em spaces rather than inch measurements. An em space is a space as wide as the point size of the type. For example, if the type size is 12 points, an em space is 12 points wide. Generally, you will want to indent newsletter text one or two em spaces.

Em space indentations can be created in two ways. One way is to display the Paragraph dialog box with the Indents and Spacing tab selected, and then select or key an inch or point increment at the Left or Right Indentation text boxes (be sure to include **pt** when keying a point increment). Or, you can create an em space at the Tabs dialog box. In exercise 5, you will change the default tab setting to 0.25 inches to create an em space indentation for each paragraph preceded with a tab code (0.25 inches is approximately 24 points or 2 em spaces for text keyed in 12-point type size).

Be sure to use em spaces for any paragraph indentations used in newsletters. Also, use em spaces for spacing around bullets and any other indented text in newsletters.

Generally, the first paragraph after a headline or subhead is not indented even though all remaining paragraphs will have an em space paragraph indentation. In figure 10.10, notice the paragraph formatting in the newsletter.

Creating a Body Text Style in a Newsletter

1. At a clear document screen, create a body text style for the newsletter in figure 10.10 by completing the following steps:
   a. Open c10ex04, Headline.
   b. Save the document on the hard drive or a floppy disk with Save <u>A</u>s and name it c10ex05, Body.
   c. Position the insertion point on the paragraph symbol below the headline text. (Make sure the style is Normal.)
   d. Insert Ride Safe.doc located on your student CD and then delete the paragraph symbol at the end of the document.
   e. Create a section break between the headline and the body text by completing the following steps:
      1) Position the insertion point at the beginning of *Injuries Up Dramatically*.
      2) Click <u>I</u>nsert and then <u>B</u>reak.
      3) At the Break dialog box, select Con<u>t</u>inuous in the Section break types section, and then click OK or press Enter.
   f. Turn on the columns feature by completing the following steps:
      1) With the insertion point still positioned at the beginning of *Injuries Up Dramatically*, click F<u>o</u>rmat and then <u>C</u>olumns.
      2) At the Columns dialog box, select *Three* in the Presets section.
      3) Click the Line <u>b</u>etween option (this inserts a line between the columns), and make sure the <u>E</u>qual column width option is on.
      4) Make sure This section displays in the <u>A</u>pply to list box, and then click OK or press Enter.

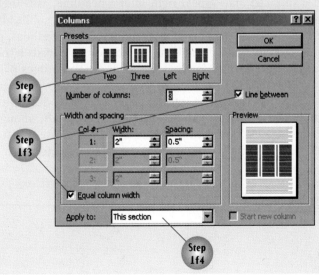

g. Format the body text by completing the following steps:
1) Select all the text in the three columns beginning with *Injuries Up Dramatically* by pressing Ctrl + Shift + End and then change the font to 11-point Garamond.
2) With the text still selected, click Format and then Paragraph.
3) At the Paragraph dialog box, select the Indents and Spacing tab, change Line spacing to At least, key **11 pt** in the At text box, and then change the Spacing After to 4 pt.

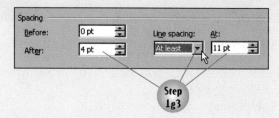

4) To change the paragraph indentions to an em space, click the Tabs button at the Paragraph dialog box.
5) At the Tabs dialog box, key **0.25** inches in the Tab stop position text box, make sure Left is selected in the Alignment section, and then click the Set button.
6) Click OK or press Enter to close the Tabs dialog box.
h. Create a style to format the body text by completing the following steps:
1) Position the insertion point in one of the paragraphs in the body of the newsletter.
2) Click the Style box on the Formatting toolbar to select the current name, key **RS Body**, and then press Enter. (The RS Body style is then added to the list of styles available in this document.)
2. Save the document with the same name c10ex05, Body.
3. Close c10ex05, Body. (You will print when the newsletter is complete.)

Creating Subheads for Newsletters

Subhead

A newsletter element that organizes text and expands on headlines.

At times a subhead may appear right after a headline, as is the case with this chapter's newsletter. Refer to figure 10.10 to view the subheads you will create in this exercise. *Subheads* organize text and expand on headlines, giving readers more information or clues about the text. In addition, subheads also provide contrast to text-intensive body copy. Marginal subheads are sometimes placed in the left margin or in a narrow column to the left of the body text, providing an airy, open appearance. Subheads can be set in a larger type size, different typeface, or heavier weight than the text. They can be centered, aligned left, or aligned right and formatted in shaded boxes. In exercise 6, you will create a customized style based on an existing style. Figure 10.12 shows a newsletter created with marginal subheads.

figure

10.12

Marginal Subheads

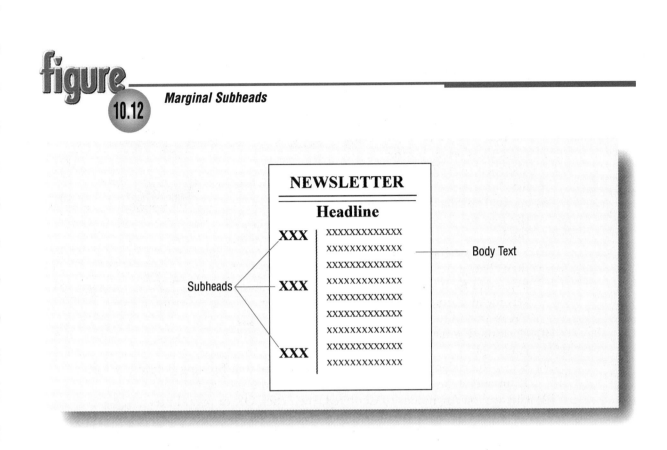

exercise

6

Creating a Subhead Style

1. At a clear document screen, create a subhead style for the newsletter in figure 10.10 by completing the following steps:

    a. Open c10ex05, Body.

    b. Save the document on the hard drive or a floppy disk with Save As and name it c10ex06, Subhead.

    c. Create a style to format the subheads in the newsletter in figure 10.10 based on an existing style by completing the following steps:

        1) Select *Injuries Up Dramatically* and then select the *Heading 3* style at the Style list box on the Formatting toolbar. (This will apply the Heading 3 style to the selected text.)

        2) With *Injuries Up Dramatically* still selected, click Format, and then Style.

        3) At the Style dialog box, make sure *Heading 3* is selected in the Styles list box. Make sure Styles in use displays in the List box. Read the description of the style formatting.

        4) Click the New button at the Style dialog box.

5) At the New Style dialog box, key **Subhead** in the Name list box.

6) Make sure that Heading 3 displays in the Based on list box.

7) Click the Format button and then select *Font* at the pop-up list.

8) At the Font dialog box, change the font to 13-point Britannic Bold.

9) Select the Character Spacing tab, then change the Spacing to Expanded By 0.5 pt and turn on kerning at 13 pt, and then click OK or press Enter.

10) Click the Format button and then Paragraph.

11) Select the Indents and Spacing tab, make sure that Spacing Before is set at 12 pt and change the Spacing After setting to 6 pt.

12) Change the Alignment to Centered, then click OK or press Enter.

13) Click the Format button, click Border, and then select the Shading tab.

14) Select the fourth fill in the first row of the Fill palette (Gray-12.5%). Make sure Paragraph displays in the Apply to list box. Click OK or press Enter.

15) Click OK or press Enter at the New Style dialog box.

16) Click Apply at the Style dialog box.

2. Apply the Subhead style to the other subheadings in the newsletter by completing the following steps:

a. Position the insertion point on the heading *A Message to Parents*, located in the second column, then select *Subhead* in the Style list box on the Formatting toolbar. Delete the paragraph symbol before the subheading.

b. Position the insertion point in the first subhead *Injuries Up Dramatically*, click Format, and then Paragraph. Select the Indents and Spacing tab and then change the Spacing Before to 0 pt. Click OK or press Enter. (This will eliminate the space before the first subhead at the beginning of the body text. The Subhead style remains unchanged.)

3. Save the document again with the same name, c10ex06, Subhead.

4. Close c10ex06, Subhead. (You will print when the newsletter is complete.)

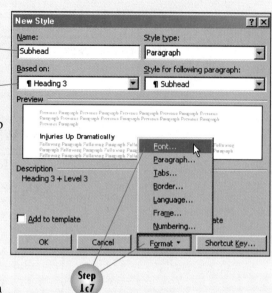

Step 1c5

Step 1c6

Step 1c7

Creating a Byline

The next step is to create the byline. The *byline* identifies the author of the article and is generally keyed in italic using the same typeface as the body text. The byline may be the same size as the body typeface, but it may also be set in a type size one or two points smaller.

The byline may appear below the headline or subhead, depending on which is the title of the article, or it may appear as the first line of the body text if it follows a headline or subhead that spans two or more columns. The byline may be placed at the left margin of a column or flush right in a column.

Byline

A newsletter element that identifies the author of the article.

exercise 7

Creating a Byline Style in a Newsletter

1. At a clear document screen, create a byline style for the newsletter in figure 10.10 by completing the following steps:
    a. Open c10ex06, Subhead.
    b. Save the document on the hard drive or to a floppy disk with Save <u>A</u>s and name it c10ex07, Byline.
    c. Create a style to format the byline in the newsletter in figure 10.10 by completing the following steps:
        1) Select the byline *by Mary Beth Luhrsen* below the first subhead *Injuries Up Dramatically*.
        2) Change the font to 10-point Garamond italic.
        3) At the Paragraph dialog box, change the Spacing <u>B</u>efore to 0 pt and the Spacing Aft<u>e</u>r to 6 pt. Click OK or press Enter.
    d. Create a style from existing text by completing the following steps:
        1) Position the insertion point anywhere in the byline text.
        2) Click inside the Style list box on the Formatting toolbar to select the current style name.
        3) Key **Byline** and then press Enter. (The Byline style is then added to the list of styles available in this document.)

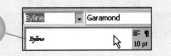

Step 1d3

        4) Apply the Byline style to the byline below *A Message to Parents*.
2. Save the document again with the same name, c10ex07, Byline.
3. Close c10ex07, Byline. (You will print when the newsletter is complete.)

Inserting Graphic Images in Newsletters

Clip art added to a newsletter should support or expand points made in the text. Use clip art so that it will give the newsletter the appearance of being well planned, inviting, and consistent. You can modify clip art by using Word's Draw program and Microsoft Word Picture graphic editor. Large and relatively inexpensive selections of clip art can be purchased on CD-ROM. In addition, you may want to scan predesigned company logos (with permission) or photographs that relate to the subject of your newsletter.

DTP POINTERS
Position illustrations close to the text they illustrate.

The image used in the nameplate in figure 10.10 was scanned professionally and copied to your student CD in a file format that was compatible with Word 2000. Because of the bitmap file format in which it was saved, you cannot alter this image in Microsoft Word Picture. To change the color of the scanned image, you may access Windows Paint or alter the bitmapped image by using the Set Transparent Color tool on the Picture toolbar as shown in figure 10.13. Complete the following steps to use the Set Transparent Color tool on a bitmapped graphic:

Set Transparent Color

1. Display the Picture toolbar.
2. Select the bitmapped image.
3. Click the Set Transparent Color button (second from the right) on the Picture toolbar.

4. Drag the transparency tool (mouse pointer) into the area you want to change and then click the left mouse.
5. Click the Fill Color button on the Drawing toolbar and select a color. Optional steps for using Paint are provided at the end of exercise 8.

figure
10.13

Using the Set Transparent Color Tool to Change Color in a Bitmapped Graphic

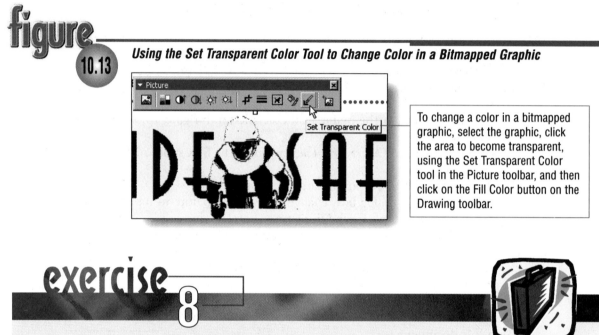

To change a color in a bitmapped graphic, select the graphic, click the area to become transparent, using the Set Transparent Color tool in the Picture toolbar, and then click on the Fill Color button on the Drawing toolbar.

exercise 8

Inserting Graphic Images into a Newsletter

1. At a clear document window, insert two graphics in the newsletter shown in figure 10.10 by completing the following steps:
   a. Open c10ex07, Byline.
   b. Save the document on the hard drive or a floppy disk with Save As and name it c10ex08, Newsletter.
   c. Display the Picture toolbar.
   d. Position the insertion point in the second sentence in the second paragraph, near the text referring to *pedestrians, and pets*.
   e. Insert the family graphic shown in figure 10.10 by completing the following steps:
      1) Click Insert, point to Picture, and then click Clip Art.
      2) At the Insert ClipArt dialog box, key **bicycling** in the Search for clips text box and press Enter.
      3) Scroll to find the image in figure 10.10, click the Insert clip button, and then close the dialog box.
      4) Select the image, click the Text Wrapping button on the Picture toolbar, and click Square.
      5) Size and position the image as in figure 10.10.
      6) Add the gray background to the image by selecting the image, clicking the down arrow at the right of the Fill Color button on the Drawing toolbar, and then selecting *Gray-25%* in the fourth row and last column.

      Step 1e3

   f. Insert the helmet graphic shown in figure 10.10 by completing the following steps:
      1) Position the insertion point near the beginning of the third column.
      2) Click Insert, point to Picture, and then click Clip Art.

3) At the Insert ClipArt dialog box, key **bicycling** in the Search for clips text box, and press Enter.

4) Scroll to find the helmet in figure 10.10 (the color is different), click the Insert clip button, and then close the dialog box.

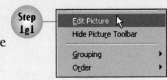

5) Select the image and change the text wrap to Tight.

6) Size and position the image as in figure 10.10.

g. Change the color of the helmet by completing the following steps:

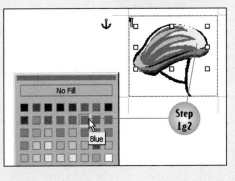

1) Right-click on the image and then click E*d*it Picture at the pop-up menu.

2) At the Microsoft Word Picture editor screen, click on any part of the helmet where you want to change the color (your helmet may vary from the one shown in figure 10.10—use your own design ideas!). Click the Fill Color button on the Drawing toolbar and select a color. Click on any other areas of the helmet if you want to change it further.

3) Click the *C*lose Picture button on the Edit Picture toolbar.

2. View your newsletter in Print Preview.

3. Save the document again with the same name c10ex08, Newsletter.

4. Print and then close c10ex08, Newsletter.

Accessing the Windows Paint Program to Customize a Graphic

You can customize a graphic while in a Word file by accessing Windows Paint.

1. Click the Start button on the Taskbar, point to *P*rograms, point to Accessories, and then click Paint.

2. At the Paint screen, click *F*ile and *O*pen.

3. At the Open dialog box, click the down arrow at the right of the Files of *t*ype text box and select *All Files*.

4. Click the down arrow at the right of the Look *i*n text box and select the drive where your graphic is located; then click the Open button.

5. At the Paint dialog box, click *I*mage and then *A*ttributes.

6. At the Attributes dialog box, select Co*l*ors in the Colors section. Click OK or press Enter. (A color palette should display at the bottom of the screen.)

7. Click the Fill with Color button (jar of paint spilling) on the Paint tool palette. Click any color on the color palette. Position the insertion point inside the image and left-click. (The area should display in your chosen color.)

8. Save the picture on your hard drive or to a floppy disk with Save *A*s and give the file a name.

9. Click *F*ile and E*x*it.

Saving the Newsletter as a Template

To save time in creating future issues of your newsletter, save your newsletter as a template. To do this, delete all text, pictures, objects, etc., that will not stay the same for future issues. Likewise, leave the nameplate and all text, pictures, symbols, etc., that will remain (or use the same style) in each issue of your newsletter. For example, to save the Ride Safe newsletter in exercise 8 as a template as shown in figure 10.14, leave the following items and delete the rest:

- Folio (the month and volume/issue numbers will change, but the titles will remain—use the folio text as placeholder text)
- Nameplate
- Subtitle
- Headline (the headline text will change, but the position and formatting will remain—use the headline text as placeholder text)
- Subheads (the subhead text will change, but the formatting will remain—use the subhead text as placeholder text)
- Byline (the byline text will change, but the position and formatting will remain—use the byline text as placeholder text)
- Body Text (the body text will change, but the formatting will remain—leave a paragraph as placeholder text)

exercise 9

Saving a Newsletter as a Template

1. Open c10ex08, Newsletter and complete the following steps to save it as a template.
2. Delete all text and newsletter elements that will change with each issue (refer to the bulleted items above).
3. Click File and then Save As.
4. At the Save As dialog box, select Document Template (*.dot) at the Save as type text box, key **Ride Safe Newsletter** in the File name text box, click Save, and then close the dialog box.
5. To use the template, click File, New, and then double-click *Ride Safe Newsletter.dot* at the General tab.
6. Select and replace text that needs to be updated. Delete any placeholder text when necessary.

figure
10.14

Exercise 9, Ride Safe Newsletter Template

Volume 5, Issue 1 • June 2001

RIDE SAFE

Bicycle and In-Line Skating Safety News •

IN-LINE SKATING—FASTEST GROWING SPORT

Injuries Up Dramatically

by Mary Beth Luhrsen

Last year, the Consumer Product Safety Commission (CPSC) released some alarming news on in-line skating, now the fastest growing recreational sport in America. They projected 83,000 serious injuries in 2001, more than double those of 2000. Even more alarming is the fact that children under age 15 account for 60% of these injuries.

chapter summary

➤ Newsletter elements divide the newsletter into organized sections to help the reader understand the text. Basic newsletter elements include nameplate, subtitle, folio, headline, subhead, byline, and body copy.

➤ Focus and balance can be achieved in a newsletter through the design and size of the nameplate, through the use of graphic images, and through careful use of lines, borders, and backgrounds.

➤ The margin size for a newsletter is linked to the number of columns needed, the formality desired, the visual elements used, and the amount of text available. Keep margins consistent in a newsletter.

➤ The line length of text in a newsletter can enhance or detract from the readability of the text.

➤ Section breaks are used to vary the page layout within a single newsletter.

➤ Typesetters and professional designers measure horizontal space on a page using picas: a pica is equal to 12 points; one inch is equal to 6 picas.

➤ Setting text in columns may improve the readability of newsletters.

➤ Word's default leading is equal to approximately 120% of the type size used.

➤ Headlines and subheads should have more leading above than below.

➤ Word automatically lines up (balances) the last line of text at the bottom of each column. The last page of columns can be balanced by inserting a continuous section break at the end of the text.

➤ Set tabs in a typeset document by em spaces rather than inch measurements.

➤ An em space is a space as wide as the point size of the type.

➤ A challenge in creating a newsletter is how to balance change with consistency. Styles assist in maintaining consistency in recurring elements.

➤ When formatting instructions contained within a style are changed, all the text to which the style has been applied is automatically updated.

➤ Styles are created for a particular document and are saved with the document.

➤ A style can be applied using the Style button on the Formatting toolbar or the Style dialog box.

➤ Clip art added to a newsletter should support or expand points made in the text. Use clip art so that it will give the newsletter the appearance of being well planned, inviting, and consistent.

commands review

	Mouse/Keyboard
Columns dialog box	Format, Columns; or click the Columns button on the Standard toolbar
Character Spacing dialog box	Format, Font, Character Spacing tab

	Mouse/Keyboard
Kerning	Format, Font, Character Spacing tab
Insert a column break	Insert, Break, Column break; or Ctrl + Shift + Enter
Insert a section break	Insert, Break, Continuous (Next page, Even page, or Odd page)
Insert symbols	Insert, Symbols, Symbols tab
Insert Picture dialog box	Insert, Picture, From File
Leading	Format, Paragraph, Indents and Spacing tab, Spacing Before and Spacing After
Style dialog box	Format, Style
Widow/Orphan	Format, Paragraph, Line and Page Breaks
Windows Paint program	Start, Program, Accessories, Paint

thinking offline

True/False: Circle the letter T if the statement is true; circle the letter F if the statement is false.

T F 1. A folio provides information that describes the purpose of the newsletter and/or the intended audience of the newsletter.

T F 2. Column formatting affects the entire document unless your document is divided into sections.

T F 3. Columns are separated by a default setting of 0.25 inches of space.

T F 4. If one column is longer than another, you can balance the text within the columns by inserting a Text wrapping break.

T F 5. A guideline in typesetting is that line length measured in picas does not exceed two times the point size used in the body text of a newsletter.

T F 6. An em space indentation can be created at the Tabs dialog box and keyed in a point or inch increment.

T F 7. Extra leading can make a page look less gray.

T F 8. If a headline contains two lines both keyed in 36 points, the default spacing between the two lines (leading) should be increased to improve readability.

T F 9. One advantage of using styles in formatting a newsletter is that when formatting within a style is changed, the text to which it has been applied changes also.

T F 10. Once a style has been created, the only way to change the style is to rename it and create it again.

Terms: In the space provided, indicate the correct term, command, or number.

1. Insert this (or these) into a document to control where columns end and begin on a page. _____

2. A set of formatting instructions that is saved with a name and can be used over and over is called this. _____

3. This feature prevents the first and last lines of paragraphs from being separated across pages.

4. This newsletter element identifies the author of an article.

5. If you create a multipage newsletter with facing pages, you may want to use this margin feature to accommodate wider inside or outside margins.

6. This Word feature marks the end of a section and stores the section's formatting.

7. This newsletter element may include a logo, a unique typeface, or a graphic image to help create or reinforce an organization's identity.

8. This newsletter element includes a short phrase describing the purpose or audience of the newsletter.

Assessment 1

1. Design and create two nameplates (including subtitle, folio, graphics, etc.) for two newsletters for organizations, schools, or a neighborhood to which you belong (real or fictional). Prepare thumbnail sketches of your designs and attach them to the back of your nameplates. Prepare one nameplate using an asymmetrical design. Also, include a graphic image, scanned image, WordArt, or special character symbol in at least one of the nameplates.

2. Save the documents on your hard drive or to a floppy disk and name them c10sa01a, Nameplate and c10sa01b, Nameplate.

3. Print and then close c10sa01a, Nameplate and c10sa01b, Nameplate.

Assessment 2

Besides taking classes, you also work part-time creating desktop documents for several offices and stores in your town. Naper Grove Vision Care recently hired you to design and produce their quarterly newsletter, which is distributed to patients in their offices in Naperville and Downers Grove. Figure 10.15 is provided as a sample newsletter. Create a newsletter using your own design ideas and knowledge of newsletter concepts and Word features presented in chapter 10. (*Hint: Key* **eyes** *at the Insert ClipArt dialog box for appropriate graphics.*) Include the following specifications:

1. Prepare a thumbnail sketch of your design.
2. Create an attention-getting nameplate.
3. Use a sans serif font in an appropriate size for the heading for the newsletter.
4. Open Focal Point.doc located on your student CD.
5. Use either a symmetrical or asymmetrical design.
6. Consider using a graphic from the Internet.

7. Optional: Include an inspirational, popular, or thought-provoking quotation at the end of your newsletter. There may be books of popular quotations at your public library, school library, or on the Internet (search for **quotes**).
8. Save your newsletter on your hard drive or to a floppy disk as c10sa02, Eyes.
9. Print and then close c10sa02, Eyes. (Attach your thumbnail sketch.)

figure 10.15

Sample Focal Point Newsletter

Open and then print a copy of Butterfield Gardens.doc located on your student CD. Assume you received this newsletter in the mail as a marketing device. The newsletter looks relatively neat and organized, but with closer inspection, you notice there are a few errors in spelling, formatting, and layout and design. Re-create the newsletter according to the following specifications, using your own ideas for an interesting newsletter layout and design:

1. Prepare a thumbnail sketch of your design.
2. Re-create the nameplate or create a nameplate (logo, subtitle, folio) of your own for this company; consider using WordArt in your nameplate design.
3. Create a different layout and design for the newsletter using newspaper columns. Use more than one column. Use an asymmetrical design.
4. Correct all spelling and formatting errors.
5. Use any graphics or scanned images that seem appropriate.
6. Consider using a graphic or photo from the Internet.
7. Use any newsletter elements and enhancements that will improve the effectiveness and appeal of this newsletter. *(Remember: Kern character pairs and condense or expand characters.)*
8. Save your publication on the hard drive or a floppy disk and name it c10sa03, Butterfield.
9. Print and then close c10sa03, Butterfield. Attach the thumbnail sketch to the back of the newsletter.

CREATIVE ACTIVITY

1. Bring in an example of a newsletter you have collected, received in the mail, picked up at a local business, or received from an organization of which you are a member. Use the Document Evaluation Checklist (Document Evaluation Checklist.doc) to evaluate the newsletter. Revise this newsletter using a completely different layout and design. Incorporate your own ideas and use graphics or scanned images if available. Remember to use consistent elements throughout the document. Create your own styles or use the system styles included in Word to aid in formatting your document. You may want to include this revision in your portfolio along with the original.
2. Save your publication on your hard drive or to a floppy disk and name it c10ca01, Newsletter.
3. Print and then close c10ca01, Newsletter. Attach the Document Evaluation Checklist and the original document to the back of your revised version.
4. Optional: Draw a thumbnail sketch of a different nameplate for this publication. Include the folio and subtitle in the sketch. Add specifications as to which typeface, colors, clip art, etc., should be used in this design.

Chapter 11

Incorporating Newsletter Design Elements

Chapter 10 introduced you to the basic elements of a newsletter. Additional elements can be used to enhance the visual impact of a newsletter and to provide the reader with clues to the newsletter content. Newsletter-enhancing elements such as a table of contents, headers/footers, masthead, pull quotes, kickers, sidebars, captions, ruled lines, jump lines, graphics, illustrations, photos, and end signs are discussed in this chapter.

Adding Visually Enhancing Elements to a Newsletter

The most effective newsletters contain an appealing blend of text and visual elements. As illustrated in figure 11.1, visual elements such as a table of contents, pull quote, kicker, and sidebar can be used as focal points to tempt the intended audience into reading more than just the nameplate. Visual elements such as headings, subheadings, table of contents, headers/footers, ruled lines, jump lines, and end signs can be used to indicate the directional flow of information in the document. Visual elements such as headings, subheadings, headers/footers, pull quotes, sidebars, and page borders can be used to provide balance, proportion, and contrast in a newsletter. All of these elements, if used in a consistent format and manner, can create unity within a single newsletter and among different issues of a newsletter.

Formatting a Newsletter Using Columns, Text Boxes, and Tables

The majority of newsletters are formatted in a two- or three-column page layout. As discussed in Chapter 10, columns may be equal in width, providing a symmetrical design, or they may be unequal in width, providing an asymmetrical design. There are three ways to create the appearance of columns in a newsletter page layout—newspaper columns, text boxes, or tables. Your challenge is to determine which method will work best to achieve the desired results in your newsletter.

Using the Columns feature may seem like an obvious choice, especially when creating newsletters similar to those displayed and created in Chapter 10. However, placing text within text boxes or tables allows you more easily to change the position or shape (height and width) of an article, as is so often required when trying to copy-fit text in a newsletter. For example, in the newsletter in figure 11.1, the first column was created by using a text box and a table. A text box with a shadow border was used to create the sidebar; a table with a top border was used to create the table of contents. The second column was created by placing each article within separate tables. The dark blue line was drawn using the Line button on the Drawing toolbar to act as a visual separator between the two articles (tables). In this case, tables were the preferred method because of the graphic and pull quote that were contained in the articles. In a table, text will wrap around a graphic or text box, whereas text will not wrap around these elements if the original text is also contained within a text box. As compared to text boxes, however, tables are not as easy to position and may produce unpredictable results when inserting text boxes within the table.

As another example, look at figure 11.17. To accommodate the "Bicycle Safety" article (on page 1) and the text wrapping around the pull quote, the Columns feature was used to format the page into two uneven columns. All of the remaining articles and features are contained in text boxes. When using any of these methods to format a newsletter, pay special attention to the alignment of these elements in relation to the columns you are trying to visually create.

figure
11.1

Visually Enhancing Elements in a Newsletter

From the Desktop

Volume 2, Issue 3   **March 2001**

✍ Mark Your Calendar:

Workshop:

Desktop Publishing Using Microsoft Word 2000

This workshop will help you learn how your students can meet today's demand for desktop publishing skills on the job using Microsoft Word 2000

Presenter:
Nancy Stanko
College of DuPage

When:
December 3, 2001
1–4 p.m.

Where:
Okemos Community College
Room 3067
2040 Mount Hope Road
Okemos, MI 47851

Cost:
$50 — includes materials and disk
To reserve your place, call:
(800) 555-6018

— Sidebar

INSIDE THIS ISSUE

— Table of Contents

TWO WAYS TO LEARN . . . — Kicker

Training Techniques

Two types of training are available for those just beginning in desktop publishing.

The first type is a content-based program. This program is based on a typical college program and the information is presented in a classroom situation. Classroom time is usually divided between the presentation of concepts or theory and directed hands-on training. Instructional books and videos are frequently utilized.

Skill-based training is another type of training. This training is useful to businesses because skill-based training produces capable people quickly. Productive skills are put to use on the type of job the person will be expected to fulfill.

Both types of training can produce workers with equal productivity and confidence. The best equipment is wasted if people are not trained to use it efficiently. Good training, regardless of which type, is essential to desktop publishing. ■ — End Sign

DESKTOP RESOURCES . . .

Knowledge Is Power

How can one have the up-to-date knowledge needed to keep on the cutting edge of desktop publishing? One way to gain desktop publishing knowledge is to read, read, read! Read some of the periodicals, newsletters, and books now available that address all aspects of desktop publishing.

Two basic types of periodicals are available. The first type is based on technological development and communication arts. These periodicals contain useful information about current products. The second type contains knowledge of technique, style, and applications.

> *One way to gain desktop publishing knowledge is to read, read, read!* — Pull Quote

Many newsletters and books are available. Your local library and bookstores can be good sources for resource material.

(See *Knowledge Is Power* on page 2) — Jump Line

Creating Headers and Footers

Headers and/or footers are commonly used in newsletters, manuscripts, textbooks, reports, and other publications. The term *header* refers to text that is repeated at the top of every page. Alternately, the term *footer* refers to text that repeats at the bottom of every page. In figure 11.1, a horizontal, dark blue ruled line, the name of the newsletter, and the page number are included in a footer at the bottom of the page. In a newsletter, information such as a page number, the name of the newsletter, the issue or date of the newsletter, and the name of the organization producing the newsletter are often included in a header or footer, as illustrated in the header and footer examples in figure 11.2.

figure

11.2   *Examples of Headers and Footers*

TRAINING NEWS

Header Example

FINANCIAL SPOTLIGHT   NOVEMBER 2001

Header Example

Winners wear helmets!

Header Example

Footer Example

Page 2   *Fly with Sunshine Air*

Footer Example

Community News   **3**

Footer Example

3

Since a header or footer is commonly repeated on every page starting with the second page, it provides the perfect place to reinforce the identity of a company or organization. For example, including the company or organization name, a very small version of the nameplate, or a logo in a header or footer can increase a reader's awareness of your identity. In figure 11.2, the Ride Safe header (the third header example) includes both the company logo and slogan, while the Community News footer includes the newsletter name and the page number.

Headers or footers, consistently formatted, help to establish unity among the pages of a newsletter, as well as among different issues of a newsletter. In addition, they serve as landmarks for the reader, adding to the directional flow of the document.

Horizontal ruled lines are frequently placed in headers or footers. These serve as a visually contrasting element that clearly identifies the top or bottom of each page. Different effects can be achieved by varying the weight (thickness) of the line, the number of lines, and the arrangement of the lines.

To create a header or footer, click View and then click Header and Footer. Key the desired header text in the header pane. If you are creating a footer, click the Switch Between Header and Footer button on the Header and Footer toolbar, then key the desired footer text in the footer pane. Click Close on the Header and Footer toolbar.

When you access the Header and Footer feature, Word automatically changes the viewing mode to Print Layout, and your document text is dimmed in the background. After you insert text in the header and/or footer panes and then click Close on the Header and Footer toolbar, the document text is displayed in black and the header and/or footer is dimmed. If the Normal viewing mode was selected before the header and/or footer was created, you are returned to the Normal viewing mode. In the Normal viewing mode, a header or footer does not display on the screen. Change to Print Layout viewing mode to view the header or footer text dimmed in the background, or use Print Preview to view how a header and/or footer will print.

Placing Headers/Footers on Different Pages

By default, Word will insert a header and/or footer on every page in the document. You can create different headers and footers in a document. For example, you can do the following:

- Create a unique header or footer on the first page.
- Omit a header or footer on the first page.
- Create different headers or footers for odd and even pages.
- Create different headers or footers for sections in a document.

A different header or footer can be created on the first page of a document. To do this, position the insertion point anywhere in the first page, choose View, then Header and Footer. (If you are creating a footer, click the Switch Between Header and Footer button.) Click the Page Setup button on the Header and Footer toolbar. Make sure the Layout tab is selected, choose Different first page, then choose OK or press Enter. The header/footer pane will be labeled *First Page Header (or Footer)*. Key the desired text for the first page header or footer, then click the Show Next button on the Header and Footer toolbar to open another header or footer pane labeled *Header (or Footer)*. Key the text for the header or footer that will print on all but the first page, then choose Close at the Header and Footer toolbar. You can follow similar steps to omit a header or footer on the first page. Simply do not key any text when the first header or footer pane is opened.

Switch Between Header/Footer

Page Setup

Show Next

The ability to place different headers and footers on odd and even pages is useful when numbering pages in a multipage newsletter. Odd page numbers can be placed on the right side of the page and even page numbers can be placed on the left side of the page. For example, in a four-page newsletter, a footer can be created that includes right-aligned page numbering that will appear on the odd pages only. Alternately, another footer can be created that contains left-aligned page numbering that will appear on even pages only.

To create a different header and/or footer on odd and even pages, choose View, then Header and Footer. (If you are creating a footer, click the Switch Between Header and Footer button.) Click the Page Setup button on the Header and Footer toolbar, and then select the Layout tab. Make sure there is no check mark in the Different first page option. Choose Different odd and even, then choose OK or press Enter. The header/footer pane will be labeled *Odd Page Header (or Footer)*. Key the desired text at the header or footer pane. Click the Show Next button on the Header and Footer toolbar. At the next header/footer pane, labeled *Even Page Header (or Footer),* key the desired text, then click the Close button on the Header and Footer toolbar.

Using Spot Color

Spot color refers to using one other color, in addition to black, as an accent color in a publication. Using spot color can make a black-and-white publication more appealing. If you have a color printer, you can see the results of using a second color immediately. You can then take the newsletter to be professionally printed on high-quality paper. Using color always adds to the cost of a publication, so be sure to price this out in the planning stages of your document. The more colors used in a publication, the more expensive it is to produce.

Spot color can be applied to such elements as graphic lines, graphic images, borders, background fill, headings, special characters, and end signs. If your logo or organizational seal contains a particular color, use that color as a unifying element throughout your publication. You can also apply spot color to the background in a reverse text box or to a drop cap. Variations of a spot color can be obtained by *screening*, or producing a lighter shade of the same color. Just as an all black-and-white page may have a gray look to it, using too much spot color can change the whole "color" of the document, defeating the purpose of using spot color for emphasis, contrast, and/or directional flow. Refer to the two newsletter samples in figure 11.3 to see how spot color can really add to the visual appeal of a publication.

Spot color

Using another color in addition to black as an accent color in a publication.

Screening

Decreasing the intensity of a color to produce a lighter shade.

figure
11.3
Newsletter with and without Spot Color

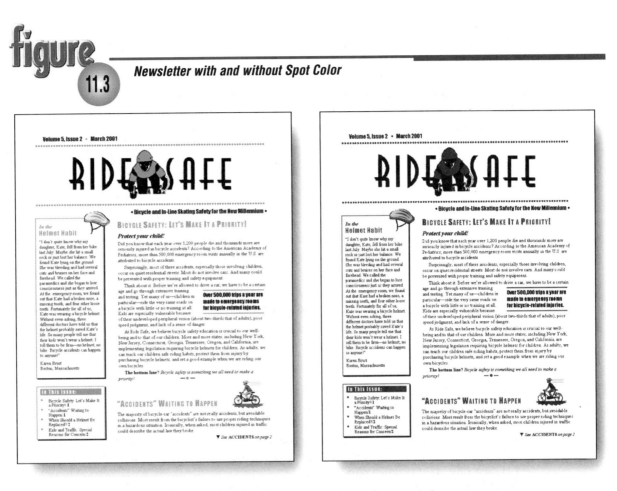

In exercises 1 through 9, you will build a two-page newsletter, as shown in figure 11.17, adding visual enhancements as you proceed. In addition, you will use copy-fitting techniques and add spot color to the newsletter throughout the range of exercises. First, in exercise 1, you will create a header and footer that will begin on the second page of the newsletter. You will also create a blank different first page header/footer so that the header and footer text will not print on the first page.

exercise 1

Creating a Header and Footer in a Newsletter

1. Add a header and footer to the beginning stages of a newsletter, as shown on the second page of the *Ride Safe* newsletter in figure 11.4, by completing the following steps:
   a. Open Newsletter Banner.doc located on your student CD.
   b. Save the document on the hard drive or to a floppy disk with Save As and name it c11ex01, Header&footer.
   c. Change the Zoom viewing mode to 75% and turn on the display of nonprinting characters.

d. Select the month and year in the folio and key the current month and year.

e. Select one of the dotted lines in the banner, display the Clipboard toolbar, and then click the Copy button on the Clipboard toolbar. (This line will be pasted in the header later.)

f. Create two uneven columns using the Columns feature by completing the following steps (these columns are being set up for some steps in future exercises and to avoid some potential problems):

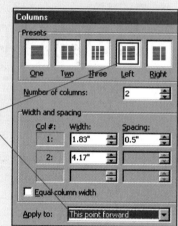

1) Press Ctrl + End to position the insertion point below the newsletter banner, then click Format, then Columns.

2) At the Columns dialog box, select Left in the Presets section, and then select *This point forward* in the Apply to list box.

3) Click OK.

4) Click Insert, Break, and then select Column break. Click OK.

5) With the insertion point at the top of the second column, repeat the previous step to insert one more column break. This will produce a second page, which is necessary to produce the header and footer.

g. Press Ctrl+Home to position the insertion point at the beginning of the document.

h. Create a different first page header/footer by completing the following steps:

1) Click View and then Header and Footer.

2) Click the Page Setup button on the Header and Footer toolbar, make sure the Layout tab is selected, and then click the Different first page check box.

3) Click OK. The Header pane should display *First Page Header*.

4) Leave the Header pane blank so header/footer text will not print on the first page.

i. Create the header for the rest of the newsletter by completing the following steps:

1) Click the Show Next button on the Header and Footer toolbar. The Header pane should be labeled *Header*.

2) With the insertion point in the Header pane, choose Insert, point to Picture, and then click From File.

3) At the Insert Picture dialog box, change the Look in list box to display the location of your student CD files, and then double-click *Ridesf2teal.bmp*.

4) Format the picture by completing the following steps:

   a) Select the image, select Format, and then Picture.

   b) At the Format Picture dialog box, select the Size tab and change the height and width in the Scale section to 35%.

   c) Click OK or press Enter.

   d) Click once to the right of the image to deselect it.

5) Click the Text Box button on the Drawing toolbar and draw a text box to the right of the Ride Safe logo that will accommodate the dotted line and slogan shown on page 2 of the newsletter in figure 11.4.

6) Double-click the text box border to display the Format Text Box dialog box and make the following changes:

a) Select the Colors and Lines tab and change the line color to No Line.
b) Select the Size tab, then change the height to 0.3 inch and the width to 7.1 inches.
c) Select the Layout tab and then click <u>A</u>dvanced. Change the horizontal position to 0.9 inch to the left of page, and change the vertical position to 0.7 inch below page. *(Hint: Remember to set the <u>to</u> the left of and belo<u>w</u> options first.)*
d) Click OK to close the Advanced Layout dialog box.
e) Click the Text Box tab and change the left and right internal margins to 0 inches.
f) Click OK or press Enter.
7) Insert the dotted line and slogan by completing the following steps:
a) Click once inside the text box to position the insertion point.
b) Display the Clipboard toolbar and click the item on the Clipboard toolbar that represents the dotted line. (See the illustration to the right for clarification.) The line length will be adjusted in the following steps.

c) Position the insertion point in the middle of the dotted line, then press the Delete key until the paragraph symbol displays at the end of the dotted line within the text box. Continue pressing the Delete key until there is approximately enough space at the end of the line to key the slogan within the text box.
d) Position the insertion point at the end of the dotted line, then key **Winners wear helmets!**. (If some of the text disappears, delete more of the dotted line until the entire slogan is visible.)
8) Select the slogan, display the Font dialog box, and then make the following changes:
a) Click the Fo<u>n</u>t tab and change the font to 12-point Times New Roman Bold Italic and the color to Black.
b) Click the Cha<u>r</u>acter Spacing tab, click the down arrow in the <u>P</u>osition list box, and select Raised. Make sure *3 pt* displays in the B<u>y</u> box. (This raises the slogan to be in alignment with the dotted line.)
c) Click OK or press Enter.
d) If the slogan wraps to the next line, delete more of the dotted line until the slogan fits in the text box. If you delete more than necessary, click the Undo button on the Standard toolbar. If the slogan does not extend to the right margin, select a section of the line, and copy and paste it to the existing line.
j. Create the footer that will begin on the second page by completing the following steps:
1) Click the Switch Between Header and Footer button on the Header and Footer toolbar to switch to the Footer pane.
2) Insert the round bullets by completing the following steps:
a) Change the alignment to center.
b) Click <u>I</u>nsert, <u>S</u>ymbol, then make sure the <u>S</u>ymbols tab is selected.
c) Change the <u>F</u>ont to Wingdings and select the round bullet in the third row, twenty-first column.
d) Click <u>I</u>nsert six times to insert six bullets, and then click Close.
e) Select the six bullets, then change the font to 11-point Impact, Teal.

      f) Insert a space between each pair of bullets, with the exception of inserting two spaces between the third and fourth bullet.

   3) Insert and format automatic page numbering by completing the following steps:

      a) Position the insertion point between the two spaces following the third bullet.

      b) Click the Insert Page Number button on the Header and Footer toolbar to automatically insert a page number.

      c) Select the page number and change the font size to 12-point Impact.

   4) Click the Page Setup button on the Header and Footer toolbar and select the Margins tab. In the From Edge section, change the distance from the bottom edge of the page to the footer to 0.6 inch. (Within the existing bottom margin setting, the footer would be partially cut off when printed, making this adjustment necessary. Increase this distance if the footer is only partially visible when viewing the document in Print Preview.) Click OK or press Enter.

   5) Insert the horizontal lines on each side of the bullets by completing the following steps:

      a) Display the Drawing toolbar and double-click the Line button on the Drawing toolbar.

      b) Hold the Shift key down and draw a line to the left of the three bullets that is the same approximate length and in the same approximate location as shown in figure 11.4 (second page).

      c) With the cross hairs still displayed, draw a horizontal line to the right of the bullets as shown in figure 11.4.

      d) Click the Line button to turn this feature off.

   6) Double-click the horizontal line on the left and make the following changes at the Format AutoShape dialog box:

      a) Select the Colors and Lines tab and change the line weight to 2 points.

      b) Select the Size tab and change the width of the line to 3.14 inches.

      c) Select the Layout tab and click Advanced. At the Advanced Layout dialog box, select the Picture Position tab and then change the horizontal alignment to left margin. Change the vertical position to 10.3 inches below page. *(Hint: Remember to change the relative to and below options first.)*

      d) Click OK two times.

   7) Double-click the horizontal line on the right and repeat steps 6a through 6d above, except change the horizontal position of the line to 4.89 inches from the left edge of the page.

   8) Click Close on the Header and Footer toolbar.

  k. View the newsletter in Print Preview. Make sure no header or footer text displays on page 1 and the header and footer text correctly displays on page 2.

2. Save c11ex01, Header&footer.

3. Position the insertion point on page 2 to print the page displaying the header and footer. Display the Print dialog box and select Current page in the Page range section of the Print dialog box. Click OK or press Enter.

4. Close c11ex01, Header&footer.

figure
11.4
Exercise 1, Page 1

Volume 5, Issue 2 • March 2001

RIDE SAFE

• Bicycle and In-Line Skating Safety for the New Millennium •

figure
11.4

Exercise 1, Page 2

Winners wear helmets!

•••2•••

Look at a hard copy of c11ex01, header&footer, and notice how the triangular logo in the header repeats the image of the bicyclist in the nameplate. In addition, the dotted line in the header on page 2 is consistent in style and color with the dotted lines located within the nameplate on page 1. The typeface used for the slogan is the same that will be used for the body text. The footer repeats the round bullet symbols found in the nameplate, the header, and the end signs which will later be used within the body copy to indicate the end of an article. As you can see, headers and footers can provide a visual connection between the separate pages in a multipage publication.

Creating Sidebars in a Newsletter

A *sidebar* is a block of information or a related story that is set off from the body text in some type of a graphics box. In figure 11.1, a sidebar is included in the first column. A sidebar can also include a photograph or a graphic image along with the text. Frequently, the sidebar contains a shaded or screened background. A screened (lighter) version of the main color used in a newsletter can serve as the background screen. The sidebar can be set in any position relative to the body text. In Word, sidebars can easily be created by creating a text box and inserting text.

Sidebar
Information or a related story set off from the body text in a graphics box.

In exercise 2, you will create a sidebar using a text box and then position the text box at the left margin to set up the boundaries for the first column. The newsletter page layout will include two columns based on an underlying three-column grid. In later exercises, you will add more visually enhancing elements to the same newsletter.

exercise 2

Inserting a Sidebar in a Newsletter

1. Insert a sidebar (containing the "In the Helmet Habit" feature) in the newsletter from exercise 1, as shown in figure 11.5, by completing the following steps:
    a. Open c11ex01, Header&footer.
    b. Save the document on the hard drive or to a floppy disk with Save As and name it c11ex02, Sidebar.
    c. Change the Zoom viewing mode to 75%, then turn on the display of nonprinting characters.
    d. Turn on Kerning for fonts 14 Points and above.
    e. Position the insertion point to the left of the first column break in the first column on page 1.
    f. Click the Text Box button on the Drawing toolbar and draw a text box that is approximately the same size and in the same position as the sidebar (see "In the Helmet Habit") shown in figure 11.5.
    g. Make sure the insertion point is positioned within the text box, and then insert the Helmet Habit Text.doc located on your student CD. Do not be concerned if all the text is not visible at this point.

h. Make sure the font size of the sidebar text is 10 points. If not, click the text box border one time so the border displays as closely spaced dots, and then change the font size to 10 points.

i. Double-click the text box border and make the following changes at the Format Text Box dialog box:
1) Select the Colors and Lines tab and change the line color to Teal and the line style to *1 1/2 pt*.
2) Select the Size tab and change the height to 5.03 inches and the width to 2.2 inches.
3) Select the Layout tab and click <u>A</u>dvanced. At the Advanced Layout dialog box, select the Picture Position tab and change the horizontal alignment to left margin. Change the vertical position to 3.11 inches below page. *(Hint: Remember to change the <u>r</u>elative to and belo<u>w</u> options first.)*
4) Click OK twice.

j. Add a shadow to the text box border by completing the following steps:
1) With the text box still selected, click the Shadow button on the Drawing toolbar, and then click <u>S</u>hadow Settings.
2) Change the shadow color to Black using the Shadow Color button on the Shadow Settings toolbar. The shadow will automatically be added to the text box border.
3) Close the Shadow Settings toolbar.

k. Format the title of the sidebar text by completing the following steps:
1) Change the Zoom viewing mode to 100%.
2) Position the insertion point at the beginning of the title, *In the Helmet Habit*, and press Enter.
3) Select *In the*, then change the font to 12-point Times New Roman Bold Italic and the color to Teal.
4) Position the insertion point after *In the*, delete the space, and then press Enter.
5) Select *Helmet Habit* and make the following changes:
   a) Change the font to 14-point Impact and the color to Teal, and expand the character spacing by 1.2 points.
   b) Position the insertion point within *In the*, display the Paragraph dialog box, and then change the Line spacing to Exactly At 10 points.
   c) Position the insertion point within the words *Helmet Habit* and change the spacing after the paragraph to 6 points.

l. For use in future issues, create styles for the sidebar heading by completing the following steps:
1) Position the insertion point within *In the* and click inside the Style list box on the Formatting toolbar.
2) Key **Sidebar Heading-1** and press Enter.
3) Position the insertion point anywhere within *Helmet Habit* and follow the preceding two steps and name this style **Sidebar Heading-2**.

m. Position the insertion point after ...*anyone!"* in the last line of the article text, press Delete to eliminate the extra hard return, and change the spacing after the paragraph to 6 points.

n. Insert the helmet image by completing the following steps:
1) Deselect the text box.
2) Display the Insert ClipArt dialog box and then search for clips using the keyword *helmet*.

3) Insert the helmet clip art that matches the helmet in figure 11.5.
4) Do not be concerned if parts of your newsletter move out of place. Adjustments will be made in the next step.

o. Format the helmet image by completing the following steps:

1) Select the helmet, click the Text Wrapping button on the Picture toolbar, and then In Front of Text.
2) Right-click the image and click Edit Picture.
3) At the Microsoft Word Picture editing screen, click the front part of the helmet to select it, and then change the fill color to Yellow.
4) Click the back part of the helmet and change the fill color to Yellow.
5) Click each of the striped segments on the helmet and change the fill color to Teal.
6) Click the Select Objects button on the Drawing toolbar and draw a box around the entire helmet to select all of the picture segments.

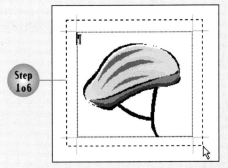

Step 1o6

7) Click Draw on the Drawing toolbar and click Group.
8) With the helmet still selected, click Draw again, point to Rotate or Flip, and then click Flip Horizontal.
9) Click Close Picture on the Edit Picture toolbar to return to your document.
10) Use the corner sizing handles and reduce the size of the helmet so that it is similar to the helmet shown in figure 11.5.

p. Click and drag the helmet so that it is overlapping the upper right corner of the sidebar text box as shown in figure 11.5.

2. Save c11ex02, Sidebar.
3. Print the first page only and then close c11ex02, Sidebar. *(Hint: This newsletter continues to build throughout the remaining chapter exercises. Saving each exercise as a separate document takes up a tremendous amount of disk space. As an alternative, open c11ex02, Sidebar; save the document with Save As; and name the document c11newsletter. Continue completing the remaining exercises and save each exercise with the same name, c11newsletter, as you progress through the exercises. Consult with your instructor about this recommendation.)*

figure

11.5

Exercise 2, Page 1

Volume 5, Issue 2 · March 2001

RIDE SAFE

• Bicycle and In-Line Skating Safety for the New Millennium •

In the
Helmet Habit

"I don't quite know why my daughter, Kate, fell from her bike last July. Maybe she hit a small rock or just lost her balance. We found Kate lying on the ground. She was bleeding and had several cuts and bruises on her face and forehead. We called the paramedics and she began to lose consciousness just as they arrived. At the emergency room, we found out that Kate had a broken nose, a missing tooth, and four other loose teeth. Fortunately for all of us, Kate was wearing a bicycle helmet. Without even asking, three different doctors have told us that the helmet probably saved Kate's life. So many people tell me that their kids won't wear a helmet. I tell them to be firm—no helmet, no bike. Bicycle accidents can happen to anyone!"

Karen Brust
Boston, Massachusetts

Creating a Newsletter Table of Contents

A table of contents is optional in a one- or two-page newsletter. However, in multipage newsletters, a table of contents is an important and necessary element. A *table of contents* lists the names of articles and features in the newsletter, along with their page numbers. The information in the table of contents greatly influences whether the reader moves beyond the front page. Consequently, the table of contents needs to stand out from the surrounding information. It must also be legible and easy to follow.

A table of contents is usually located on the front page of a newsletter. It is often placed in the lower-left or -right corner of the page. It can, however, be placed closer to the top of the page on either side or even within an asymmetrically designed nameplate. If a newsletter is designed to be a self-mailer, the table of contents can be placed in the mailing section so the reader is invited into the newsletter before it is even opened.

The table of contents in figure 11.1 is located in the lower-left corner. The dark blue top border and the bold title and numbers make the table of contents easily identifiable while adding visual interest to the page. The table of contents, along with the shadow box above it, also adds weight to the left side of the page and balance to the page as a whole.

There are many ways to format a table of contents to make it easy to find and visually interesting. As illustrated in figure 11.6, a table of contents can easily be made by inserting text in a text box and then adding various borders, screened backgrounds, fonts, graphics, lines, reverse text, and special characters. You can also use paragraph borders and shading to highlight text in a table of contents.

Table of contents
A list of articles and features and their page numbers.

DTP POINTERS
The table of contents must stand out from surrounding text, be legible, and have a consistent design from issue to issue.

figure 11.6 — Examples of Tables of Contents

Inside! 📖
Strong Performance on Standardized Tests 2
National Merit Scholars Named 2
District Reaffirms Long-Range Plans 3
Districtwide Cleaning Service Contract 4
Volunteers Needed 4
Board of Education 4

In This Issue:
Who's Using Desktop Publishing?/1
From the Director's Desk/1
Academic News/2
Administrative News/3
In the Future/4
Training News/4

Inside This Issue:
▲ Fitness and Family Fun 2
▲ Runner's Training Program 3
▲ Fitness and Pregnancy 3
▲ Fitness and Weight Control 4

IN THIS ISSUE:
➤ Announcing PC Help Version 4.0— Coming Soon! (**Page 1**)
➤ From the Editor's Desk (**Page 2**)
➤ The Technical Advisor (**Page 2**)

Inserting a Table of Contents in a Newsletter

1. Add a table of contents, as shown in figure 11.7, to the newsletter from exercise 2 by completing the following steps:
   a. Open c11ex02, Sidebar.
   b. Save the document on the hard drive or to a floppy disk with Save As and name it c11ex03, Table of contents.
   c. Change the Zoom viewing mode to 75% and turn on the display of nonprinting characters.
   d. Insert the table of contents text in a text box by completing the following steps:
      1) Draw a text box that is approximately the same size and in the same position as the table of contents text box shown in figure 11.7.
      2) Position the insertion point within the text box and insert the file Table of Contents Text.doc located on your student CD.
   e. Double-click the text box border and make the following changes at the Format Text Box dialog box:
      1) Select the Colors and Lines tab, change the line color to Teal, and change the line style to *1 1/2 pt*.
      2) Select the Size tab, change the height to 1.9 inches, and change the width to 2.2 inches.
      3) Select the Layout tab and click Advanced. At the Advanced Layout dialog box, select the Picture Position tab, and then change the horizontal alignment to left margin. Change the vertical alignment to bottom margin. *(Hint: Remember to change the relative to options first.)*
      4) Click OK twice.
   f. Add a black shadow border to the text box by using the Shadow button on the Drawing toolbar. Follow the same steps to create the shadow as listed in exercise 2, steps 1j1–1j3.
   g. Format the table of contents title by completing the following steps:
      1) Change the Zoom viewing mode to 100%.
      2) Position the insertion point to the left of *In This Issue:*, then press the space bar once.
      3) Select *In This Issue:* and make the following changes at the Font dialog box:
         a) Click the Font tab and change the font to 12-point Impact.
         b) Click the Character Spacing tab and change the Spacing to Expanded By 1.2 points.
         c) Click OK or press Enter.
      4) Position the insertion point to the right of the colon in the title, display the Paragraph dialog box, and then change the spacing after the paragraph to 8 points. Click OK or press Enter.
      5) Position the insertion point anywhere within the title, then create the shaded background by completing the following steps:
         a) Click Format, Borders and Shading, and then select the Shading tab.
         b) Select Teal in the fifth row, fifth column of the Fill section.
         c) Click OK or press Enter.
      6) Select *In This Issue:* and change the text color to white.

h. For use in future issues, create a style from the formatted title by completing the following steps:
  1) Position the insertion point within *In This Issue:* and click inside the Style list box on the Formatting toolbar.
  2) Key **ToC Heading** and press Enter.
i. Format the bulleted text in the table of contents by completing the following steps:
  1) Select the remaining text below the title and change the font to 11-point Times New Roman. *(Hint: Do not be concerned if some of the text is not visible at this point.)*
  2) With the text still selected, display the Paragraph dialog box, and then make the following changes:
    a) Change the spacing after the paragraph to 2 points.
    b) Change the Line Spacing to Exactly 12 points.
    c) Click OK to close the Paragraph dialog box.
  3) With the text still selected, add a bullet to each article name by completing the following steps:
    a) Select Format, Bullets and Numbering, and then select the Bulleted tab.
    b) Click the first bulleted selection and then click Customize.
    c) At the Customize Bulleted List dialog box, click Font, then change the font size to 14 points and the color to Teal.
    d) Click OK or press Enter.
    e) Click Bullet, then change the Font to Wingdings. Select the round bullet in the fifth row, sixteenth column.
    f) Click OK or press Enter to close the Symbol dialog box and then click OK again to close the Customize Bulleted List dialog box.
  4) Select the slash mark in each table of contents item, change the color to Teal, and apply bold. *(Hint: Use Format Painter to repeat the formatting.)*
  5) Select each page number and change the font to Impact, Bold.
j. For use in future issues, create a style for the bulleted items in the table of contents by completing the following steps:
  1) Position the insertion point anywhere within the first bulleted item.
  2) Click once in the Style list box on the Formatting toolbar to select the current style name.
  3) Key **ToC bullets** as the new style name and press Enter.
2. Save c11ex03, Table of contents.
3. Print the first page only and then close c11ex03, Table of contents. (You may want to wait and print the whole newsletter when it is completed in exercise 9.)

figure
11.7

Exercise 3, Page 1

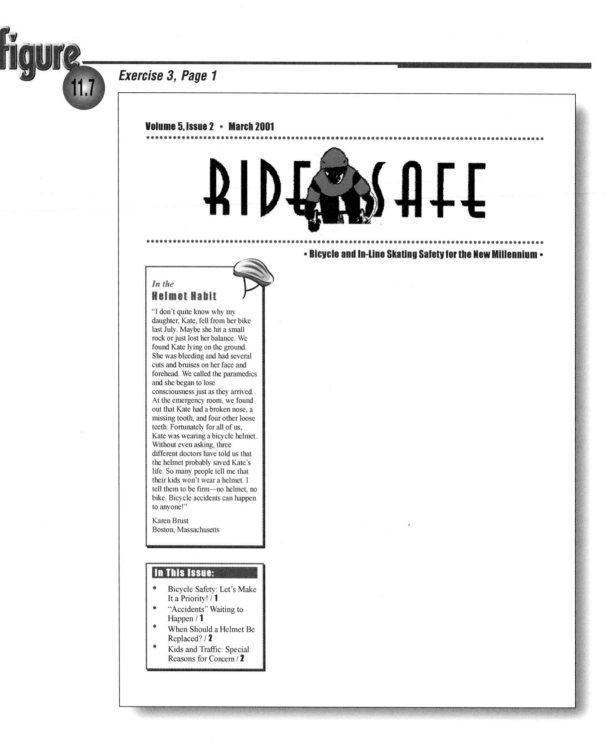

Volume 5, Issue 2 • March 2001

RIDE SAFE

• Bicycle and In-Line Skating Safety for the New Millennium •

In the
Helmet Habit

"I don't quite know why my daughter, Kate, fell from her bike last July. Maybe she hit a small rock or just lost her balance. We found Kate lying on the ground. She was bleeding and had several cuts and bruises on her face and forehead. We called the paramedics and she began to lose consciousness just as they arrived. At the emergency room, we found out that Kate had a broken nose, a missing tooth, and four other loose teeth. Fortunately for all of us, Kate was wearing a bicycle helmet. Without even asking, three different doctors have told us that the helmet probably saved Kate's life. So many people tell me that their kids won't wear a helmet. I tell them to be firm—no helmet, no bike. Bicycle accidents can happen to anyone!"

Karen Brust
Boston, Massachusetts

In This Issue:

- Bicycle Safety: Let's Make It a Priority! / **1**
- "Accidents" Waiting to Happen / **1**
- When Should a Helmet Be Replaced? / **2**
- Kids and Traffic: Special Reasons for Concern / **2**

Creating Pull Quotes

Pull quote

A short, direct phrase, statement, or important point formatted to stand out from the rest of the body copy.

A pull quote, as illustrated in figure 11.1, acts as a focal point, helps to break up lengthy blocks of text, and provides visual contrast. A *pull quote* (also called a *pull out* or *call out*) is a direct phrase, summarizing statement, or important point associated with the body copy of a newsletter. Using pull quotes is an excellent way to draw readers into an article.

Effective pull quotes are interesting, brief, and formatted to stand out from the rest of the body copy. Keep in mind the following tips when creating pull quotes for a newsletter:

- Include relevant and interesting text in a pull quote. Edit any direct quotes so they will not be taken out of context when read individually as a pull quote.
- Pull quotes should be brief—approximately 10 to 15 words and never longer than a few lines.
- Choose a font or font style that contrasts with the font used for the article text.
- Increase the type size.
- Vary the type style by bolding and/or italicizing the pull quote text.
- Set the pull quote off from the rest of the body text with ruled lines or a graphics box.
- Use at least one element in your pull quote design that establishes a visual connection with the rest of your newsletter.
- Be consistent. Use the same format for other pull quotes throughout the newsletter and throughout future issues of the same newsletter.

The pull quotes displayed in figure 11.8 show some different ways that pull quote formatting can be customized to attract the reader's attention. The rectangular pull quote examples were created using text boxes. The oval and round rectangle were created using AutoShapes. Various background fills were used including solid fill, textured fill, and gradient fill. Additional effects such as borders, shadows, and 3-D were also used. These pull quote examples are only a small representation of the many ways that pull quotes can be customized.

figure
11.8

Examples of Various Pull Quote Formats

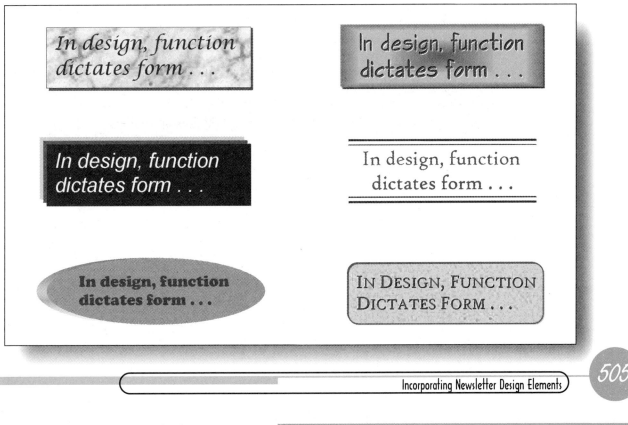

DTP POINTERS
Create styles for repetitive formatting.

In exercise 4, you will insert the first newsletter article, format the article heading and article text, and create a pull quote. Since these particular elements may be repeated throughout the newsletter, you will then create styles for these elements.

Creating Styles and a Pull Quote in a Newsletter

1. Insert and format the first article, create a pull quote, and create styles, as shown in figure 11.9, by completing the following steps:
    a. Open c11ex03, Table of contents.
    b. Save the document on the hard drive or to a floppy disk with Save As and name it c11ex04, Pull quote.
    c. Change the Zoom viewing mode to 75% and turn on the display of nonprinting characters.
    d. Position the insertion point to the left of the column break in the second column and then insert Bicycle Safety Text.doc from your student CD.
    e. Select the article heading *Bicycle Safety: Let's Make It a Priority!* and make the following changes:
        1) Change the font to 18-point Impact, change the color to Teal, and apply S<u>m</u>all caps.
        2) Expand the character spacing by *1.2 pt.*
        3) Change the spacing after the paragraph to 6 points.
    f. Create a style for future article headings by completing the following steps:
        1) Make sure the insertion point is positioned within the article heading.
        2) Click once in the Style list box located on the Formatting toolbar to select the current style name.
        3) Key **Article Head** as the new style name and press Enter.
    g. Format the article text by completing the following steps:
        1) Position the insertion point at the beginning of the line *Did you know...* and select all of the article text.
        2) Change the font to 11-point Times New Roman.
        3) Display the Paragraph dialog box and make the following changes:

a) At the <u>I</u>ndents and Spacing tab, change the spacing after the paragraph to 3 points.

b) In the Indentation section, change the <u>S</u>pecial option to First line B<u>y</u> 0.2 inch to indent the first line of each paragraph.

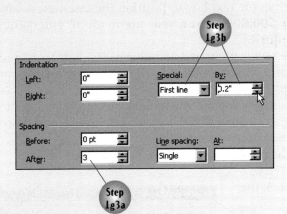

c) Click OK or press Enter.

h. Create a style for the article text by completing the following steps:

1) With the article text still selected, click once in the Style list box located on the Formatting toolbar to select the current style name.

2) Key **Article Text** as the style name and press Enter.

i. Create a style for the first paragraph of the article that eliminates the first line indentation by completing the following steps:

1) Position the insertion point within the first paragraph of article text.

2) Display the Paragraph dialog box, make sure the Indents and Spacing tab is selected, then change the <u>S</u>pecial option to (none) in the Indentation section.

3) Click OK or press Enter.

4) Click once in the Style list box on the Formatting toolbar to select the current style name.

5) Key **1st Paragraph** as the style name, press Enter, and then deselect the text.

j. Insert and format a text box to hold the pull quote by completing the following steps:

1) Click the Text Box button on the Drawing toolbar, and then draw a text box that is approximately the same size and in the same location as the pull quote shown in figure 11.9.

2) Double-click the text box border and make the following changes at the Format Text Box dialog box:

a) Select the Colors and Lines tab and change the line color to No Line.

b) Select the Size tab and then change the height to 0.78 inch and the width to 2.01 inches.

c) Select the Layout tab, change the Wrapping style to <u>T</u>ight, and then click <u>A</u>dvanced.

d) At the Advanced Layout dialog box, select the Picture Position tab, and then change the horizontal position to 5.84 to the left of page. Change the vertical position to 5.12 inches below the page and click OK.

e) Select the Text Box tab, and then change the right, top, and bottom internal margins to 0 inches. Leave the left internal margin at 0.05 inch.

f) Click OK.

k. Insert and format the pull quote text by completing the following steps:

1) Click once in the text box to position the insertion point.

2) Key **Over 500,000 trips a year are made to emergency rooms for bicycle-related injuries**.

3) Select the text just entered and change the font to 12-point Impact.

l. Add the top and bottom borders to the pull quote text by completing the following steps:

1) With the insertion point positioned within the pull quote text, display the Borders and Shading dialog box, and then select the <u>B</u>orders tab.

2) Change the border color to Teal.

3) Change the border line width to 2-1/4 points.

4) In the Preview section, click the top and bottom of the diagram to insert borders in these areas; the left and right sides of the diagram should be borderless.

5) Click <u>O</u>ptions to display the Borders and Shading Options dialog box. Adjust the distance from the top border to the text to 2 points, and then click OK.

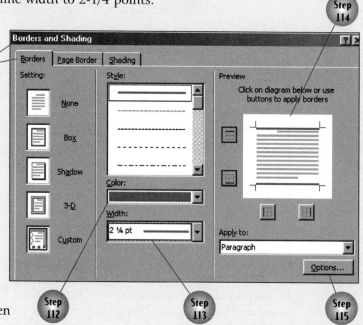

6) Click OK again to close the Borders and Shading dialog box.

m. Create a style for the pull quote by completing the following steps:

1) With the insertion point located within the pull quote text, click once in the Style list box on the Formatting toolbar to select the current style name.

2) Key **Pull Quote** as the new style name and press Enter.

n. In the last paragraph, select and bold *The bottom line?*. Then select and italicize the last sentence, *Bicycle safety is something we all need to make a priority!*

2. Save c11ex04, pull quote.

3. Print the first page only and then close c11ex04, Pull quote. (You may want to wait and print the whole newsletter when it is completed in exercise 9.)

figure

11.9

Exercise 4, Page 1

Volume 5, Issue 2 • March 2001

RIDE SAFE

• Bicycle and In-Line Skating Safety for the New Millennium •

BICYCLE SAFETY: LET'S MAKE IT A PRIORITY!

Did you know that each year over 1,200 people die and thousands more are seriously injured in bicycle accidents? According to the American Academy of Pediatrics, more than 500,000 emergency room visits annually in the U.S. are attributed to bicycle accidents.

Surprisingly, most of these accidents, especially those involving children, occur on quiet residential streets. Most do not involve cars. And many could be prevented with proper training and safety equipment.

Think about it. Before we're allowed to drive a car, we have to be a certain age and go through extensive training and testing. Yet many of us—children in particular—ride the very same roads on a bicycle with little or no training at all. Kids are especially vulnerable because of their undeveloped peripheral vision (about two-thirds that of adults), poor speed judgment, and lack of a sense of danger.

> **Over 500,000 trips a year are made to emergency rooms for bicycle-related injuries.**

At Ride Safe, we believe bicycle safety education is crucial to our well-being and to that of our children. More and more states, including New York, New Jersey, Connecticut, Georgia, Tennessee, Oregon, and California, are implementing legislation requiring bicycle helmets for children. As adults, we can teach our children safe riding habits, protect them from injury by purchasing bicycle helmets, and set a good example when we are riding our own bicycles.

The bottom line? *Bicycle safety is something we all need to make a priority!*

In the Helmet Habit

"I don't quite know why my daughter, Kate, fell from her bike last July. Maybe she hit a small rock or just lost her balance. We found Kate lying on the ground. She was bleeding and had several cuts and bruises on her face and forehead. We called the paramedics and she began to lose consciousness just as they arrived. At the emergency room, we found out that Kate had a broken nose, a missing tooth, and four other loose teeth. Fortunately for all of us, Kate was wearing a bicycle helmet. Without even asking, three different doctors have told us that the helmet probably saved Kate's life. So many people tell me that their kids won't wear a helmet. I tell them to be firm—no helmet, no bike. Bicycle accidents can happen to anyone!"

Karen Brust
Boston, Massachusetts

In This Issue:

* Bicycle Safety: Let's Make It a Priority! / **1**
* "Accidents" Waiting to Happen / **1**
* When Should a Helmet Be Replaced? / **2**
* Kids and Traffic: Special Reasons for Concern / **2**

Creating Kickers and End Signs

Additional elements, such as kickers and end signs, can also be used in a newsletter. A *kicker* is a brief sentence or phrase that is a lead-in to an article. Generally, it is set in a size smaller than the headline but larger than the body text. It is often stylistically distinct from both the headline and the body text. Kickers can be placed above or below the headline or article heading. In figure 11.1, a kicker is placed above the first article heading and serves as a lead-in to the first article.

Kicker
A lead-in phrase or sentence that precedes the beginning of an article.

Symbols or special characters used to indicate the end of a section of text, such as the end of an article, are known as *end signs*. In figure 11.1, an end sign follows the last paragraph in the first article. The end sign is the same color as the accent color in the newsletter to contribute to the unified appearance of this newsletter. The end sign in the *Ride Safe* newsletter, shown in figure 11.10, mimics the dots in the nameplate and the footer and the colors coordinate with the newsletter's color scheme. Appropriate special characters or combinations of these characters—such as •, ■, ❑, ◆, ❖, ☬, ✂, ■, and ✗, from the Wingdings, Webdings, or Monotype Sorts font selection—may be used as end signs.

In exercise 5, you will add a kicker and an end sign to the *Ride Safe* newsletter from exercise 4.

exercise 5

Creating a Kicker and an End Sign in a Newsletter

1. Insert the kicker and end sign shown in figure 11.10 to the newsletter from exercise 4 by completing the following steps:
   a. Open c11ex04, Pull quote.
   b. Save the document on the hard drive or to a floppy disk with Save As and name it c11ex05, End sign.
   c. Change the Zoom viewing mode to 75% and turn on the display of nonprinting characters.
   d. Create the kicker by completing the following steps:
      1) Position the insertion point at the beginning of the first paragraph below the article heading.
      2) Key **Protect your child!** and then press Enter.
      3) Select *Protect your child!* and change the font to 14-point Times New Roman Bold Italic.
   e. Create a style for the kicker formatting by completing the following steps:
      1) Position the insertion point anywhere within the kicker.
      2) Click once in the Style list box on the Formatting toolbar to select the current Style name.
      3) Key **Kicker** and press Enter.
   f. Create the end sign by completing the following steps:
      1) Position the insertion point at the end of the first article and press the Tab key three times. *(Hint: Make sure Italic formatting is turned off.)*
      2) Display the Symbol dialog box and select the Special Characters tab.
      3) Double-click the *Em Dash* selection and select the Symbols tab.
      4) Change the Font selection to Wingdings and double-click the round bullet in the third row, twenty-first column.
      5) Click the Special Characters tab again, double-click the *Em Dash* selection, and then click Close.
      6) Insert one space on each side of the bullet.
      7) Select the end sign and change the font to 11-point Impact. Select the round bullet and change the color to Teal.

g. Check the position of the pull quote. Move the text box down to its approximate previous position.

2. Save c11ex05, End sign (or save as c11newsletter as suggested in exercise 2, step 3).

3. Print the first page only and then close c11ex05, End sign. (You may want to wait and print the whole newsletter when it is completed in exercise 9.)

figure
11.10   *Exercise 5, Page 1*

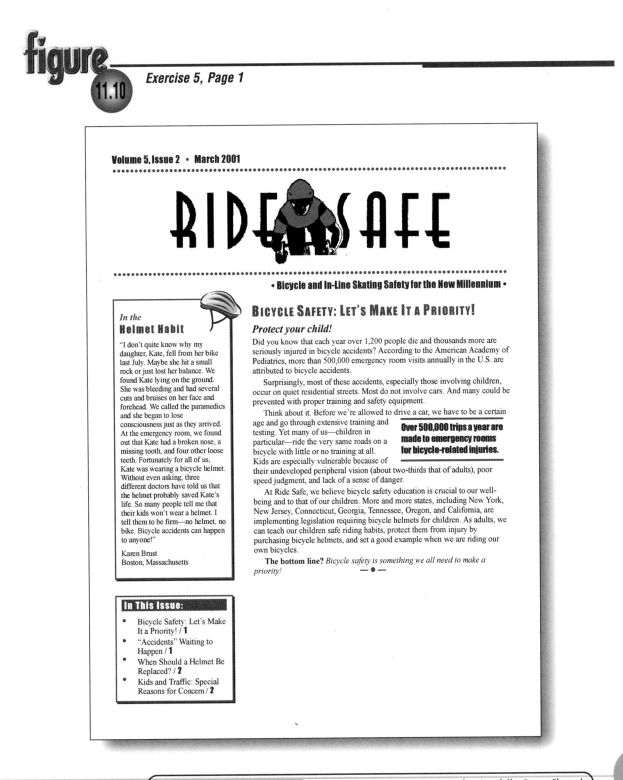

Using Linked Text Boxes in Newsletters

Newsletters routinely contain articles that start on one page and are continued onto another page. Word's text box linking feature makes your job of creating articles that are continued on to subsequent pages easier. This feature allows text to flow from one text box to another even if the text boxes are not adjacent or on the same page. Any text box can be linked with any other text box. You need at least two text boxes to create a link; however, any number of text boxes can be used to create a chain of linked text boxes. For example, if your article starts on page 1, is continued on page 2, and then finishes on page 4, you can create a chain of three linked text boxes that will contain the article text. When the first text box is filled, the text automatically flows into the second text box, and then into the third text box in the chain. This is especially useful in editing and positioning an article that is continued on another page. If you add or delete text in one of the text boxes, the remaining text in the article in the other text boxes adjusts to the change also. Furthermore, you can establish more than one chain of linked text boxes in a document. For example, you can create a chain of linked text boxes for an article that begins on page 1, and then continues on pages 3 and 4. In the same newsletter, you can create another chain of linked text boxes for another article that begins on page 2 and then continues on page 4.

Creating the Link

To link text boxes, you must first create two or more text boxes. For example, if you have an article that begins on page 1 and is to be continued on page 2 of a newsletter, create a text box on page 1 and then create another text box on page 2. Size the text boxes to fit appropriately within the allotted column width, then position the text boxes as desired. If necessary, additional size and position adjustments can be made after the text is added to the text boxes. To create a link between the two text boxes, complete these steps:

1. Click the text box that is to be the first text box in the chain of linked text boxes.
2. If the Text Box toolbar does not automatically display, right-click anywhere within the Standard toolbar and select Text Box, or click View, Toolbars, and then select Text Box.
3. Click the Create Text Box Link button on the Text Box toolbar as displayed in figure 11.11. The mouse will display as a small upright pitcher.
4. Position the pitcher in the text box to be linked. The pitcher appears tipped with letters spilling out of it when it is over a text box that can receive the link. Click once to complete the link.
5. To create a link from the second text box to a third text box, click the second text box, and then repeat steps 3 and 4 above. Repeat these steps to add more links to the chain.

figure

11.11

Text Box Toolbar

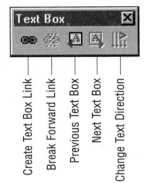

Create Text Box Link
Break Forward Link
Previous Text Box
Next Text Box
Change Text Direction

Moving Between Linked Text Boxes

You can use the Next Text Box and the Previous Text Box buttons on the Text Box toolbar, as displayed in figure 11.11, to move between linked text boxes. If you select a text box that is at the beginning of a chain of linked text boxes, the Next Text Box button is active and the Previous Text Box button is dimmed. If you select a text box that is at the end of a chain of linked text boxes, only the Previous Text Box button is active. If you select a text box that is in the middle of a chain of linked text boxes, both the Next Text Box and the Previous Text Box buttons will be available. If one or both of these buttons are active, you know that the currently selected text box is linked to another text box. If neither of these buttons is active, then the currently selected text box is not linked to any other text box.

Creating Jump Lines

Featuring the beginning of several articles on the front page of a newsletter increases the chances of attracting readers. Also, some articles may just be too lengthy to fit on one page. You must, therefore, provide a way for your readers to know where to find the remainder of an article. A *jump line* in a newsletter is used to indicate that an article or feature continues on another page.

As an aid in the directional flow of information in a document, a jump line must be distinguishable from surrounding text so the reader can easily find it. A jump line is commonly set in small italic type, approximately two points smaller than the body copy type. As an option, jump lines can also be enclosed in parentheses.

Jump line
Text telling the reader that an article continues on another page or is being continued from another page.

exercise

6

Creating Linked Text Boxes and a Jump Line in a Newsletter

1. Add an article and a jump line to the newsletter from exercise 5, as shown in figure 11.12, by completing the following steps:
    a. Open c11ex05, End sign. Save the document on the hard drive or to a floppy disk with Save As and name it c11ex06, Jump line.

b. Change the Zoom viewing mode to 75% and turn on the display of nonprinting characters.

c. Insert text boxes to hold the second article on page 1, which will be continued on page 2, by completing the following steps:
1) Scroll to the bottom of page 1.
2) Click the Text Box button on the Drawing toolbar, then draw a text box below the column break to hold the beginning of the second article. Adjustments will be made to the size and position of the text box in future steps.
3) Scroll to the top of the first column on page 2, click the Text Box button again, and draw a second text box to hold the remaining article text. Using the horizontal ruler as a guide, limit the width of the text box to the column width. Adjustments will be made to the size and position of this text box in an upcoming exercise.

d. Create a link between the two text boxes so that text will automatically flow from one text box to another by completing the following steps:
1) Select the first text box and click the Create Text Box Link button on the Text Box toolbar. If the toolbar is not displayed, right-click anywhere within the Standard toolbar, then select Text Box from the list of toolbars.
2) Position the mouse, which now displays as an upright pitcher, in the second text box until it displays as a pouring pitcher, and then click once to complete the link.

e. Double-click the border of the first text box in the link (at the bottom of page 1, second column) and make the following changes at the Format Text Box dialog box:
1) Click the Colors and Lines tab and change the line color to No Line.
2) Select the Size tab, change the height of the text box to 1.6 inches, and change the width to 5 inches.
3) Select the Layout tab and click Advanced. At the Advanced Layout dialog box, select the Picture Position tab, and then change the horizontal position to 3.15 inches to the left of the page. Change the vertical position to 8.8 inches from the top edge of the page. (Hint: Remember to change the to the left of and below options first.)
4) Click OK to return to the Format Text Box dialog box.
5) Click the Text Box tab, change the left, right, top, and bottom internal margins to 0 inches, and then click OK.

f. Click once inside the first text box to position the insertion point and insert the file Accident Text.doc located on your student CD.

g. Check the text box on page 2 and make sure the remaining article text is visible. If not, use the sizing handles to enlarge the box.

h. Format the title of the second article by completing the following steps:
1) Position the insertion point anywhere within the title "Accidents" Waiting to Happen.
2) Click the down arrow to the right of the Style list box located on the Formatting toolbar and select Article Head from the Style drop-down list.

i. Format the article text by completing the following steps:
1) Position the insertion point at the beginning of the line The majority of bicycle/car "accidents"..., hold the Shift key down, and press Ctrl + End to select all of the article text in both text boxes. (The text in the second text box will not be highlighted even though it is really selected.)
2) Click the down arrow to the right of the Style list box located on the Formatting toolbar and select Article Text from the Style drop-down list.

3) Position the insertion point anywhere within the first paragraph and apply the 1st Paragraph style from the Style list box on the Formatting toolbar.

j. Insert and format the jump line by completing the following steps:
 1) Position the insertion point at the end of the first paragraph and press Enter once.
 2) Change the paragraph alignment to right.
 3) Access the Symbol dialog box, change the font to Monotype Sorts, and then insert the triangle symbol in the fourth row, first column.
 4) Press the space bar once, key **See ACCIDENTS on page 2**, and then press Enter. If the beginning of the second paragraph is still visible below the jump line, press Enter again to force this text to appear at the beginning of the linked text box on page 2.
 5) Select *See* and apply italics.
 6) Select *ACCIDENTS* and apply bold.
 7) Select *on page 2,* and then apply italics.
 8) Select the entire jump line and change the font to 10-point Times New Roman.
 9) Make sure the spacing after the paragraph is set to 3 points.

k. Create an AutoText entry out of the formatted jump line by completing the following steps (an AutoText entry is created here instead of a style because the jump line contains mixed formatting and text that can be used in other jump lines):
 1) Select the entire jump line, including the triangle symbol.
 2) Click Insert, point to AutoText, and then click New.
 3) At the Create AutoText dialog box, key **jump line** as the AutoText entry name.
 4) Click OK or press Enter.

l. Insert the image of the boy riding a bicycle by completing the following steps:
 1) Position the insertion point to the left of the column break.
 2) Display the Insert ClipArt dialog box and search for clips using the keyword *bike*.
 3) Find and insert the image of the boy riding a bicycle (without a helmet). Part of the image will be hidden by the text box.
 4) Select the image, click the Text Wrapping button on the Picture toolbar, and then click In Front of Text.

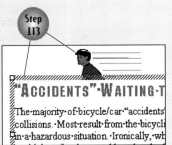

m. Format the image by completing the following steps:
 1) Right-click the image and click Format Picture.
 2) At the Format Picture dialog box, select the Size tab and change the height to 0.88 inch and the width to 1.04 inches.
 3) Click OK.

n. Use the mouse to move the image into the same approximate position as displayed in figure 11.12.

o. Place a helmet on the bicyclist's head by completing the following steps:
 1) Select the helmet image located on the top right corner of the sidebar text box.
 2) Hold down the Ctrl key, hold down the left mouse button, and then drag a copy of the image down near the bicyclist image.

p. Format the helmet image by completing the following steps:
 1) Right-click the helmet image just copied and select Format Picture.
 2) At the Format Picture dialog box, select the Size tab, and then change the height to 0.16 inch and the width to 0.17 inch.
 3) Click OK.
 4) Change the Zoom on the Standard toolbar to 200%.

5) Use the mouse to move the helmet onto the bicyclist's head as displayed in figure 11.12

Step 1p5

6) Use Print Preview to check the accuracy of the helmet position.

2. Save c11ex06, Jump line.

3. Print the first page only and then close c11ex06, Jump line. (You may want to wait and print the whole newsletter when it is completed in exercise 9.)

figure

11.12

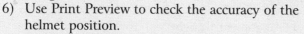

Exercise 6, Page 1

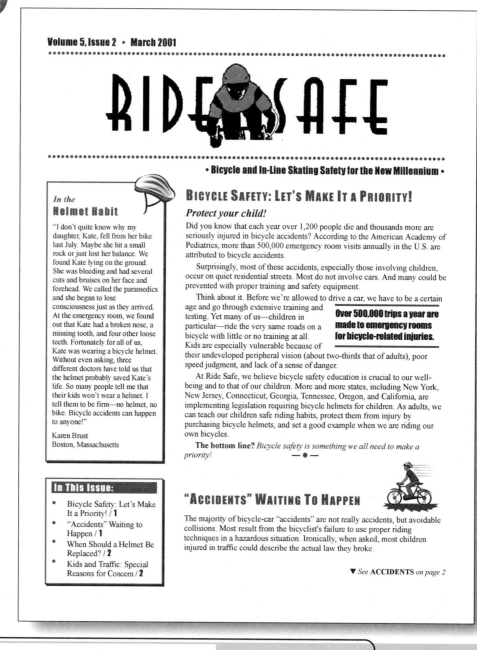

Volume 5, Issue 2 • March 2001

RIDE SAFE

• Bicycle and In-Line Skating Safety for the New Millennium •

In the Helmet Habit

"I don't quite know why my daughter, Kate, fell from her bike last July. Maybe she hit a small rock or just lost her balance. We found Kate lying on the ground. She was bleeding and had several cuts and bruises on her face and forehead. We called the paramedics and she began to lose consciousness just as they arrived. At the emergency room, we found out that Kate had a broken nose, a missing tooth, and four other loose teeth. Fortunately for all of us, Kate was wearing a bicycle helmet. Without even asking, three different doctors have told us that the helmet probably saved Kate's life. So many people tell me that their kids won't wear a helmet. I tell them to be firm—no helmet, no bike. Bicycle accidents can happen to anyone!"

Karen Brust
Boston, Massachusetts

In This Issue:

- Bicycle Safety: Let's Make It a Priority! / **1**
- "Accidents" Waiting to Happen / **1**
- When Should a Helmet Be Replaced? / **2**
- Kids and Traffic: Special Reasons for Concern / **2**

BICYCLE SAFETY: LET'S MAKE IT A PRIORITY!

Protect your child!

Did you know that each year over 1,200 people die and thousands more are seriously injured in bicycle accidents? According to the American Academy of Pediatrics, more than 500,000 emergency room visits annually in the U.S. are attributed to bicycle accidents.

Surprisingly, most of these accidents, especially those involving children, occur on quiet residential streets. Most do not involve cars. And many could be prevented with proper training and safety equipment.

Think about it. Before we're allowed to drive a car, we have to be a certain age and go through extensive training and testing. Yet many of us—children in particular—ride the very same roads on a bicycle with little or no training at all. Kids are especially vulnerable because of their undeveloped peripheral vision (about two-thirds that of adults), poor speed judgment, and lack of a sense of danger.

Over 500,000 trips a year are made to emergency rooms for bicycle-related injuries.

At Ride Safe, we believe bicycle safety education is crucial to our well-being and to that of our children. More and more states, including New York, New Jersey, Connecticut, Georgia, Tennessee, Oregon, and California, are implementing legislation requiring bicycle helmets for children. As adults, we can teach our children safe riding habits, protect them from injury by purchasing bicycle helmets, and set a good example when we are riding our own bicycles.

The bottom line? *Bicycle safety is something we all need to make a priority!*

— • —

"ACCIDENTS" WAITING TO HAPPEN

The majority of bicycle-car "accidents" are not really accidents, but avoidable collisions. Most result from the bicyclist's failure to use proper riding techniques in a hazardous situation. Ironically, when asked, most children injured in traffic could describe the actual law they broke.

▼ *See* **ACCIDENTS** *on page 2*

Using Different Graphics File Formats

If used appropriately, headers, footers, sidebars, tables of contents, pull quotes, kickers, end signs, and jump lines can help to achieve focus, balance, proportion, contrast, directional flow, and consistency within a newsletter. Graphic images, illustrations, charts, diagrams, and photographs can help to achieve these same goals.

Word includes a very large selection of predesigned graphic images in its program that you can insert into any document through the Insert ClipArt dialog box. You may also import graphics from the World Wide Web. For example, you can click Import Clips at the Insert ClipArt dialog box and directly download free graphics from Microsoft's Web page. In addition, a variety of clip art is available on the market that includes thousands of ready-made illustrations, in both color and black and white, for almost any subject area. You can also insert graphic images created in draw programs, such as Corel Draw or Windows Paint.

Just as text and programs are stored in files, graphic images (or computer art) are also stored in files on disk. Just like software, graphic files are created by many different companies. For a variety of historic, competitive, and practical reasons, graphic files are created in many different *file formats*. In Word, you can insert many popular graphics file formats directly, or with the use of specific graphics filters. The following graphic file formats do not require a separate graphic filter to be installed:

Graphic file format
The format in which a specific graphic product is stored often determined by vendors, size of files, quality, and editing capabilities.

> Enhanced Metafile (.emf)
> Graphics Interchange Format (.gif)
> JPEG File Interchange Format (.jpg)
> Portable Network Graphics (.png)
> Windows Bitmap (.bmp, .rle, .dib)
> Windows Metafile (.wmf)

A separate *graphic filter* is necessary to install the graphic file formats listed below. If you didn't install the necessary filter(s) when you installed Word, you can add the filter(s) by displaying the Windows Control Panel, and then using the Add/Remove Programs feature.

Graphic filter
A graphic translator that allows you to insert images stored in various graphic file formats.

> Computer Graphics Metafile (.cgm)
> CorelDRAW (.cdr)
> Encapsulated PostScript (.eps)
> FlashPix (.fpx)
> Hanako (.jsh, .jah, .jbh)
> Kodak Photo CD (.pcd)
> Macintosh PICT (.pct)
> PC Paintbrush (.pcx)
> Tagged Image File Format (.tif)
> WordPerfect Graphics (.wpg)

If the required graphic filter is installed, you can insert any of the previously listed graphic file formats by choosing Insert, pointing to Picture, and then selecting From File. Change to the directory location of the desired graphic files and then select the desired file name.

If you cannot import a graphic file with any of the above extensions, your system may be missing some graphic file filters. To determine which filters have been installed, click Insert, point to Picture, and then select From File. In the

Insert Picture dialog box, click the Files of type list box. If all the file extensions listed above are not displayed, you need to install a separate graphics filter for each desired file type. Refer to the Word Help or to the Word 2000 reference manual to add additional filters.

However, you may want to import a graphic that is not supported by any of the graphic filters provided with Word. In order to import an unsupported graphic file format, open the graphic file in the program from which the graphic file originated or in a drawing program such as Windows Paint, then save the graphic in an acceptable Word graphic file format. Or you can select the graphic, copy it, and paste it into your document. The graphic then becomes a Windows metafile (.wmf).

You may also download other graphics filters from the Microsoft Office Update Web site. For information on graphics filters that you can download, click Office on the Web on the Help menu to connect to the Microsoft Office Update Web site.

Photographs can also be added to a newsletter. As the old saying goes, a picture is worth a thousand words, and sometimes just saying the words is not enough. Readers relate to the "realness" of photographs as opposed to clip art or computer-generated images. Photos best describe events or people because they can accurately depict a scene or an expressed emotion. Select only those photos that are clearly defined, in focus, and correctly exposed.

Some information is better understood in a visual format. Whenever possible, include illustrations, charts, tables, and diagrams when presenting technical, numerical, and detailed information.

Using Scanned Images in a Newsletter

Scanner

Equipment that converts a photograph, drawing, or text into a compatible digital file format that can be retrieved into specific programs.

Noncomputer-generated images, such as photographs, illustrations, and diagrams, can be included in a newsletter through the use of a scanner and compatible scanner software. A *scanner* and its associated software convert a photograph, drawing, or text into a compatible digital file format that can be retrieved into a program such as Word. You may also use a digital camera and compatible digital camera software to convert photographs into compatible file formats that may be inserted into Word. See chapter 5 for a brief discussion of this process.

One very important factor to keep in mind is that you must get permission to use artwork, photos, or illustrations before you can legally scan them into a document. This includes artwork from the Web, even though you do not see the traditional copyright symbol. You may use the keywords *free graphics* in a Web search engine to find an extremely large selection of graphics that you are free to use. When you purchase clip art and stock photography, you generally buy the right to use it and even modify it, but you may not resell the images themselves as hard copy or computer images. When purchasing these items, read the copyright information provided in the front of the accompanying documentation.

DTP POINTERS

Find out about copyright restrictions on any images you want to scan and request permission, if necessary.

If you want to include a photograph in a newsletter and a scanner is not available, you can insert a placeholder, such as a text box, in your newsletter. You can then print your newsletter, paste a photograph into the area reserved by the text box, and have a commercial printer duplicate your newsletter.

When trying to determine if your photographs should be scanned professionally, keep the following two points in mind:

- If you do not need high-quality output, using images scanned from a desk model scanner is acceptable.
- If you need high-quality output, use a service bureau to have your photos professionally scanned into your newsletter.

Using Captions

Think of all the times you pick up a newspaper, newsletter, or magazine. How many times do you look at a photograph and immediately read the accompanying explanation? Many graphics images can stand on their own; however, most photographs, illustrations, and charts need to be explained to the reader. Remember that your reader's eyes are automatically drawn to images or elements that stand out on the page. Adding an explanation to your image or photo quickly gives your reader an idea of what is going on. It may even entice your reader to read the corresponding article. Accompanying descriptions or explanations of graphic images, illustrations, or photographs are referred to as *captions*.

Caption

An accompanying description or explanation of a graphic image, illustration, or photograph.

Captions should explain their associated images while at the same time establish a connection to the body copy. Make the caption text different from the body text by bolding and decreasing the type size slightly. Legibility is still the key. Keep captions as short as possible and consistent throughout your document.

Elements, such as a Word picture, Word table, Excel worksheet, PowerPoint presentation, PowerPoint slide, or graph, etc., can be labeled and numbered using Word's Caption feature. (See Word Help or a Word reference manual for more information on this feature.) This type of captioning is very useful when creating detailed reports or publications such as a year-end financial statement, technical instructional manual, or research analysis. If elements do not have to be numbered, such as photographs in a newsletter, the easiest way to create a caption is to position the insertion point below the element, and then key and format the desired caption.

figure

11.13

Caption Examples

July 4th Balloon Launch

Leave the selling to us!

Do you need a technological checkup? See our new course offerings on page 3.

The Eiffel Tower

exercise 7

Inserting a Picture Placeholder and Caption in a Newsletter

1. Add a placeholder for a photograph and caption text to the second page of the newsletter from exercise 6, as shown in figure 11.14, by completing the following steps:
   a. Open c11ex06, Jump line.
   b. Save the document on the hard drive or to a floppy disk with Save As and name it c11ex07, Picture.
   c. Change the Zoom viewing mode to 75% and then turn on the display of nonprinting characters.
   d. Insert a text box that will contain the title, the picture placeholder box, and the caption text by completing the following steps:
      1) Press Ctrl + End to position the insertion point at the top of page 2.
      2) Click the Text Box button on the Drawing toolbar, then draw a text box at the top of the second column that is approximately the same size as the placeholder box shown in figure 11.14.
   e. Double-click the text box border and make the following changes at the Format Text Box dialog box:
      1) Click the Colors and Lines tab, then change the line color to No Line.
      2) Click the Size tab, then change the height of the text box to 4.2 inches and the width to 4.7 inches.
      3) Select the Layout tab, then click Advanced. At the Advanced Layout dialog box, select the Picture Position tab, then change the horizontal position to 3.1 inches to the left of the page. Change the vertical position to 1.1 inches from the top of the page.
      4) Click OK to return to the Format Text Box dialog box.
      5) Click the Text Box tab, change the left and right internal margins to 0 inch, change the top internal margin to 0.03 inch, and change the bottom internal margin to 0 inch.
      6) Click OK or Press Enter.
   f. If the text box in column 1 and the text box just inserted in column 2 overlap each other, reduce the width of the text box in the first column so that it is approximately the same width as the column width. Use the horizontal ruler as a guide.
   g. Insert and format the title by completing the following steps:
      1) Click once in the text box to position the insertion point.
      2) Key ✍Who Says Helmets Aren't Cool?✌ (use the arrow symbols from the Wingdings font, seventh row, second and third columns) and press Enter.
      3) Position the insertion point within the title just keyed, then apply the *Article Head* style.
      4) Select each of the arrow symbols, change the color to black, and then apply bold.
   h. Insert the placeholder text by completing the following steps:
      1) Click once below the title to position the insertion point.

       2) Press Enter eight times and change the alignment to center.

       3) Key **Insert picture of children from Silverton, Oregon here.**, then press Enter.

       4) Change the paragraph alignment to left and press Enter six times.

  i. Create the border that defines the photograph placeholder by completing the following steps:

       1) Position the insertion point to the left of the first paragraph symbol below the title.

       2) Select from the first paragraph symbol downward, excluding the last paragraph symbol in the text box.

       3) Display the Borders and Shading dialog box, then select the <u>B</u>orders tab.

       4) In the Setting section, click Bo<u>x</u>, and then change the border color to Teal and the border line width to *1 1/2 pt*.

       5) Click OK or press Enter.

  j. Insert and format the caption under the placeholder box by completing the following steps:

       1) Position the insertion point to the left of the last paragraph symbol.

       2) Insert the file Picture Text.doc located on your student CD.

       3) Select the text just inserted and change the font to 10.5-point Times New Roman Bold Italic.

       4) With the insertion point within the caption text, display the Paragraph dialog box, and change the spacing before the paragraph to 4 points.

2. Save c11ex07, Picture.

3. Position the insertion point on page 2. Print page 2 only and close c11ex07, Picture. (You may want to wait and print the whole newsletter when it is completed in exercise 9.)

figure
11.14

Exercise 7, Page 2

....*Winners wear helmets!*

⟨WHO SAYS HELMETS AREN'T COOL?⟩

Research indicates that 60% of all U.S. bicycle-car collisions occur among bicyclists between the ages of 8 and 12. Still, an average of only $1 is spent per child between birth and age 15 teaching traffic education. Children are permitted to travel with only *"look both ways before you cross the street"* and *"make sure you stop at all stop signs"* warnings. Obviously these "warnings" are not enough.

Insert picture of children from Silverton, Oregon here.

Certainly not the children of Silverton, Oregon! One of the biggest reasons children don't wear bicycle helmets is because their friends don't wear them. By getting all the children in your school or neighborhood to order bicycle helmets at the same time, you can help turn this peer pressure from negative to positive. Suddenly, wearing a bicycle helmet becomes the "cool" thing to do.

•••2•••

Creating a Newsletter Masthead

The *masthead* is a newsletter element that contains the newsletter's publication information. A masthead (see figure 11.15) usually contains the following items:

Masthead
A list of persons contributing to the production of a newsletter and other general publication information.

- the company or organization (producing the newsletter) name and address
- the newsletter's publication schedule, such as weekly, monthly, or biannually
- the names of those contributing to the production of the newsletter, such as editor, authors, and graphic designers
- copyright information

The masthead may also contain a small logo, seal, or other graphic identifier. Although a masthead is commonly located on the back page of a newsletter, you will sometimes find it on the first page. Wherever you decide to place the masthead, be consistent from issue to issue in the masthead's design, layout, and location.

figure

11.15 *Examples of Masthead Designs*

From the ◻◻◻ Desktop

Editor: **Martha Ridoux**
Design and Layout:
            Grace Shevick
Contributing Authors:
            Jonathan Dwyer
            Nancy Shipley
            Christine Johnson
Published Monthly by:
            DTP Training, Inc.
            4550 North Wabash St.
            Chicago, IL 60155
            312 555-6840
            Fax: 312 555-9366
            http://www.dtp.com
©Copyright 2001 by:
            DTP Training, Inc.
            All rights reserved.

From the ◻◻◻ Desktop

Editor:
Martha Ridoux

Design and Layout:
Grace Shevick

Authors:
Jonathan Dwyer
Nancy Shipley
Christine Johnson

Published Monthly by:
DTP Training, Inc.
4550 North Wabash St.
Chicago, IL 60155
312 555-6840
Fax: 312 555-9366
http://www.dtp.com

©**Copyright 2001 by:**
DTP Training, Inc.
All rights reserved.

exercise 8

Creating a Newsletter Masthead

1. At a clear document window, add a masthead to the second page of the newsletter from exercise 7, as shown in figure 11.16, by completing the following steps:
   a. Open c11ex07, Picture.
   b. Save the document on the hard drive or to a floppy disk with Save As and name it c11ex08, Masthead.

c. Change the Zoom viewing mode to Whole Page and turn on the display of nonprinting characters.
d. Insert a text box to hold the masthead text by completing the following steps:
   1) Click the Text Box button on the Drawing toolbar.
   2) Position the cross hairs toward the bottom half of the first column on page 2 and draw a text box of the approximate size and location as shown in figure 11.16.
e. Double-click the text box border and make the following changes at the Format Text Box dialog box:
   1) Select the Colors and Lines tab and change the line color to Teal, and change the line style to *1 1/2 pt.*
   2) Select the Size tab, change the height of the text box to 2.86 inches, and change the width to 2.2 inches.
   3) Select the Layout tab and click Advanced. At the Advanced Layout dialog box, select the Picture Position tab and change the horizontal alignment to left margin. Change the vertical position to 7.2 inches below the top of the page. *(Hint: Remember to change the relative to and below options first.)*
   4) Click OK twice.
f. Change the Zoom viewing mode to 100%.
g. Click once inside the text box to position the insertion point, then insert the file Masthead Text.doc located on your student CD. (All of the text will be visible after formatting is completed in the following steps.)
h. Format the masthead title by completing the following steps:
   1) Position the insertion point within *Ride Safe* and apply the ToC Heading style from the Style list box on the Formatting toolbar.
   2) Change the alignment to center.
   3) Change the spacing after the paragraph to 6 points.
i. Format the remaining masthead text by completing the following steps:
   1) Select the remaining masthead text and change the alignment to center. *(Hint: Hold down the Shift key and press Ctrl + End to select the remaining text in the text box, even if some of the text is not completely visible.)*
   2) With the text still selected, change the font to 9-point Times New Roman.
   3) Bold the following: *Editor:, Design and Layout:, Authors:, Published quarterly by:,* and © *Copyright 2001 by:.*
   4) Apply italics to the remaining text that was not bolded.
   5) Adjust the paragraph spacing and line spacing (leading) by completing the following steps:
      a) Position the insertion point after the following items and change the spacing after the paragraph to 1 point at the Paragraph dialog box: *Brandon Keith, Cassie Lizbeth, Amanda Knicker,* and *Fax: .... (Hint: Use F4 after you have formatted the first item to quickly repeat the formatting.)*
      b) Select all of the masthead text, except for the heading, and change the Line Spacing to Exactly At 10 points at the Paragraph dialog box.
j. Save c11ex08, Masthead.
k. Print page 2 only and then close c11ex08, Masthead. (You may want to wait and print the whole newsletter when it is completed in exercise 9.)

figure
11.16

Exercise 8, Page 2

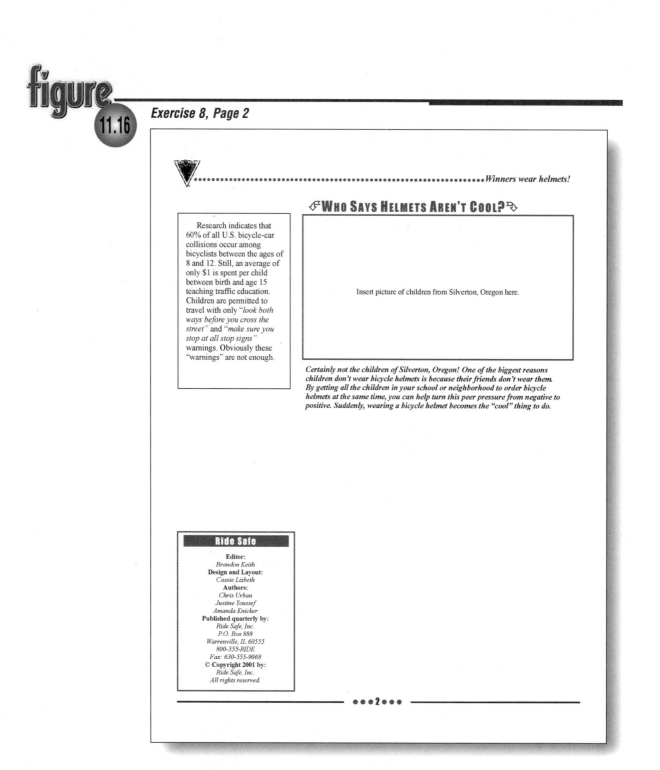

....*Winners wear helmets!*

☞WHO SAYS HELMETS AREN'T COOL?☜

Research indicates that 60% of all U.S. bicycle-car collisions occur among bicyclists between the ages of 8 and 12. Still, an average of only $1 is spent per child between birth and age 15 teaching traffic education. Children are permitted to travel with only *"look both ways before you cross the street"* and *"make sure you stop at all stop signs"* warnings. Obviously these "warnings" are not enough.

Insert picture of children from Silverton, Oregon here.

Certainly not the children of Silverton, Oregon! One of the biggest reasons children don't wear bicycle helmets is because their friends don't wear them. By getting all the children in your school or neighborhood to order bicycle helmets at the same time, you can help turn this peer pressure from negative to positive. Suddenly, wearing a bicycle helmet becomes the "cool" thing to do.

Ride Safe

Editor:
Brandon Keith
Design and Layout:
Cassie Lizbeth
Authors:
Chris Urban
Justine Youssef
Amanda Knicker
Published quarterly by:
Ride Safe, Inc.
P.O. Box 888
Warrenville, IL 60555
800-555-RIDE
Fax: 630-555-9068
© **Copyright 2001 by:**
Ride Safe, Inc.
All rights reserved.

•••2•••

Using Additional Enhancements for Starting Paragraphs

In chapter 6, you learned about the Drop Cap feature. This design element is often used to indicate the beginning paragraph of a new article. Other types of paragraph enhancements can also be included in a newsletter. The following is a short list of paragraph enhancements—you may think of many more:

- Set the first few words of the beginning paragraph in all caps.
- Set the first line of the beginning paragraph in all caps.
- Set the first word of the beginning paragraph in small caps.
- Set the first line of the beginning paragraph in color.
- Use a larger type size with more leading in the first line of the beginning paragraph.

Understanding Copy Fitting

Publications such as magazines and newsletters contain information that varies from issue to issue. Though there is structure in how the articles or stories are laid out on the page (such as the unequal two-column format in the *Ride Safe* newsletter), there may be times when more or less text is needed to fill the page. Making varying amounts of text or typographical enhancements fit in a fixed amount of space is referred to as *copy fitting*. Many copy-fitting techniques have been used in the exercises throughout this textbook. Some copy-fitting suggestions include the following:

To create more space:

- Reduce the margins.
- Change the justification.
- Change the typeface, type size, or style, but limit body type size to a minimum of 9 points, preferably 10 points.
- Reduce the spacing before and after paragraphs (or hard returns) to reduce the spacing around the nameplate, headlines, subheads, frames, or text boxes.
- Reduce the spacing between paragraphs.
- Use hyphenation.
- Condense the spacing between characters.
- Reduce the leading (line spacing) in the body copy.
- Remove a sidebar, pull quote, kicker, or end sign.
- Edit the text, including rewriting and eliminating sections.

To fill extra space:

- Increase the margins.
- Change the justification.
- Change font size but limit body type size to a maximum of 12 points.
- Increase the spacing between paragraphs.
- Adjust the character spacing.
- Increase the leading (line spacing) in the body copy.
- Increase the spacing around the nameplate, headlines, subheads, text boxes or graphic images.
- Add a sidebar, pull quote, kicker, end sign, graphic lines, clip art, photo, etc.
- Add text.

Be consistent when making any copy-fitting adjustments. For example, if you increase the white space after a headline, increase the white space after all headlines. Or, if you decrease the type size of the body copy in an article, decrease the point size of all body copy in all articles. Adjustments are less noticeable when done uniformly. Also, adjustments often can be very small. For instance, rather than reducing type size by a whole point, try reducing it a half or quarter point. In addition, Word includes a Shrink to Fit feature that automatically "shrinks"

> **Copy fitting**
> Fitting varying amounts of text or typographical enhancements into a fixed amount of space.

> **DTP POINTERS**
> Copy-fitting adjustments are less noticeable when done uniformly throughout the whole document.

the contents of the last page in a document on the previous page if there is only a small amount of text on the last page. To access this copy-fitting feature, click the Print Preview button on the Standard toolbar (or click File, then Print Preview), then click the Shrink to Fit button (seventh button from the left) on the Print Preview toolbar. Word will automatically reduce the point size in order to fit the text on the previous page. Carefully check your document after using the Shrink to Fit feature, as the results are not always desirable.

In the *Ride Safe* newsletter created in the previous exercises, adjustments were made to the typeface, type size, type style, spacing above and below the article headings, spacing between paragraphs, spacing within the paragraphs (leading), and size and position of text boxes.

In the next exercise, you will position the linked text box and add two more articles to the second page of the *Ride Safe* newsletter. You will also apply styles and insert a clip art image. These articles are selected and adjusted to "fit" into the remaining space.

exercise 9

Adding Articles, Applying Styles, and Using Copy-Fitting Techniques

1. Add two articles and complete the "continued" article on the second page of the newsletter from exercise 8, as shown in figure 11.17, by completing the following steps (make your own minor adjustments if necessary to fit the articles in their respective locations):

   a. Open c11ex08, Masthead.

   b. Save the document on the hard drive or to a floppy disk with Save As and name it c11ex09, Newsletter.

   c. Change the Zoom viewing mode to Whole Page and turn on the display of nonprinting characters.

   d. To make room for "The Light Bulb Test" article at the beginning of page 2, click and drag the linked text box located on page 2 that contains the remaining text from the "Accidents" article to the open space in the second column. This text box will be formatted in future steps.

   e. Position the insertion point at the top of page 2, then click the Text Box button on the Drawing toolbar. Draw a text box to hold "The Light Bulb Test" article that is approximately the same size and in the same location as shown in figure 11.17.

   f. Double-click the text box border and make the following changes at the Format Text Box dialog box:

      1) Click the Colors and Lines tab and change the line color to No Line.

      2) Click the Size tab, change the height to 3.65 inches, and change the width to 2.4 inches.

      3) Select the Layout tab and click Advanced. At the Advanced Layout dialog box, select the Picture Position tab, then change the horizontal alignment to left margin. Change the vertical position to 1.1 inches from the top of the page. *(Hint: Remember to set the relative to and below options first.)*

      4) Click OK to return to the Format Text Box dialog box.

5) Click the Text Box tab, and then change the left, right, top, and bottom internal margins to 0 inch.

6) Click OK or press Enter.

g. Change the Zoom viewing mode to 100%.

h. Click once inside the text box to position the insertion point and insert the file Light Bulb Text.doc located on your student CD.

i. Position the insertion point within the heading *The Light Bulb Test* and apply the Article Head style.

j. Insert the light bulb image by completing the following steps:

1) Position the insertion point between *Light* and *Bulb* in the heading and press the space bar one time.

2) Make sure the insertion point is positioned between the two spaces and display the Insert ClipArt dialog box.

Step 1j4

3) At the Insert ClipArt dialog box, search for clips using the keywords *light bulb*.

4) Find and insert the light bulb image that matches the image in figure 11.17. The image will be quite large and it will appear that your article text has disappeared. This will be corrected in the next step.

k. Click the light bulb image to select it (black sizing handles should appear), and then use one of the corner sizing handles to size the light bulb image so that it resembles the image shown in figure 11.17. Make sure the light bulb is small enough so that your article heading fits all on the same line and all the article text fits within the text box.

l. Position the insertion point within the first paragraph and apply the 1st Paragraph style.

m. Position the insertion point within the second paragraph and apply the Article Text style.

n. Create the end sign at the end of the article by completing the following steps:

1) On page 1, select the end sign at the end of the first article.

2) Click the Copy button on the Standard toolbar.

3) Position the insertion point at the end of "The Light Bulb Test" article, press the space bar three times, and then click the Paste button on the Standard toolbar.

o. Double-click the border of the linked text box that contains the remaining text from the "Accidents" article and make the following changes at the Format Text Box dialog box:

1) Click the Colors and Lines tab and change the line color to No Line.

2) Click the Size tab, change the height of the text box to 2.3 inches, and change the width to 2.4 inches.

3) Select the Layout tab and click <u>A</u>dvanced. At the Advanced Layout dialog box, select the Picture Position tab, and then change the horizontal alignment to left margin. Change the vertical position to 4.78 inches below the top of the page. *(Hint: Remember to set the <u>r</u>elative to and belo<u>w</u> options first.)*

4) Click OK to return to the Format Text Box dialog box.

5) Click the Text Box tab, and then change the left, right, top, and bottom internal margins to 0 inches.

6) Click OK or press Enter.

p. Insert and format the "continued" jump line at the beginning of the text in the linked text box by completing the following steps:
1) Position the insertion point at the beginning of the text in the linked text box.
2) Click Insert, point to AutoText, and then select AutoText. Select *jump line* from the AutoText entry list box at the AutoText tab located in the AutoCorrect dialog box.)
3) Press Enter once.
4) With the insertion point within the jump line, display the Paragraph dialog box, and then change the Special option in the Indentation section to (none). Click OK.
5) Delete the word *See*.
6) Select the word *on* and key **from**.
7) Select the number *2* and key **1**.

q. Insert the line above the jump line by completing the following steps:
1) With the insertion point still within the jump line, display the Borders and Shading dialog box, and make sure the Borders tab is selected.
2) Make sure the border color is Teal, change the border line width to *1 pt*, and then click the top of the diagram in the Preview section to insert a top border. Make sure no borders display on the remaining sides of the diagram. Click OK.

r. Copy and paste the end sign from "The Light Bulb Test" article to the end of this article.

s. Save c11ex09, Newsletter.

t. Insert an article in the remaining space in the second column by completing the following steps:
1) Click the Text Box button on the Drawing toolbar and draw a text box to hold the "When Should a Helmet Be Replaced?" article that is approximately the same size and in the same location as shown in figure 11.17.
2) Double-click the border of the text box and make the following changes at the Format Text Box dialog box:
   a) Select the Colors and Lines tab and change line color to No Line.
   b) Select the Size tab, then change the height of the text box to 4.7 inches and the width to 4.7 inches.
   c) Select the Layout tab and click Advanced. At the Advanced Layout dialog box, select the Picture Position tab, then change the horizontal position to 3.1 inches to the left of the page. Change the vertical position to 5.4 inches from the top edge of the page. *(Hint: Remember to set the to the left of and below options first.)*
   d) Click OK to return to the Format Text Box dialog box.
   e) Select the Text Box tab, and then change the left, right, top, and bottom internal margins to 0 inch. Click OK.

u. Click once inside the text box to position the insertion point and insert the file Replace Helmet Text.doc from your student CD.

v. Apply styles to the article text just inserted by completing the following steps:
1) Position the insertion point within the title *When Should a Helmet Be Replaced?*, then apply the Article Head style.
2) Select all the paragraph text and apply the 1st Paragraph style.

w. Insert the bullet and emphasize the text at the beginning of each paragraph by completing the following steps:

1) With the insertion point positioned at the beginning of the first paragraph, select all of the article text.
2) Click Format, Bullets and Numbering, and then select the Bulleted tab.
3) Select the first bulleted example and click Customize.
4) In the Bullet character section, click Font, change the font size to 11 points and the bullet color to Teal, and then click OK.
5) Click Bullet, change the Font to Wingdings, and then select the round bullet in the third row, twenty-first column.
6) Click OK twice to return to your newsletter.
7) Select the phrase *After a crash.* and change the font to 11-point Impact.
8) Repeat step 7 to format the three remaining phrases at the beginning of each bulleted item. (A style could be created for this formatting, if desired; otherwise, press F4 to repeat the formatting.)

x. Insert the helmet image by completing the following steps:
   1) Click the Zoom arrow on the Standard toolbar and change the viewing mode to Two Pages.
   2) Position the insertion point anywhere within the *Bicycle Safety* article on page 1, and then display the Insert ClipArt dialog box. *(Hint: The helmet image is being inserted in this location so that it can be floated above the text and dragged into position. Word will not let you float an image in front of text if you try to insert the image into a text box, as exists on page 2.)*
   3) At the Insert ClipArt dialog box, search for clips using the keyword *helmet.*
   4) Find and insert the helmet image that matches the image in figure 11.7.
   5) Click the helmet image to select it (black sizing handles should appear), click the Text Wrapping button on the Picture toolbar, and then click In Front of Text.
   6) Change the helmet colors by completing the following steps:
      a) Right-click the image and click Edit Picture.
      b) At Word's Picture editor screen, select the back part of the helmet, and then change the fill color to Teal.
      c) Click each of the stripes on the helmet and change the fill color to Yellow.
      d) Click Close Picture on the Edit Picture toolbar.
   7) Drag the helmet to its approximate position as displayed in figure 11.17.
   8) Change the viewing mode to 100%.
   9) Use one of the corner sizing handles to size the helmet image so that it resembles the image shown in figure 11.17.
   10) Adjust the position of the helmet, if necessary.
y. Scroll through the newsletter and make any copy-fitting adjustments that may be necessary.
2. Save c11ex09, Newsletter.
3. Print both pages of the *Ride Safe* newsletter and then close c11ex09, Newsletter.

figure
11.17
Exercise 9

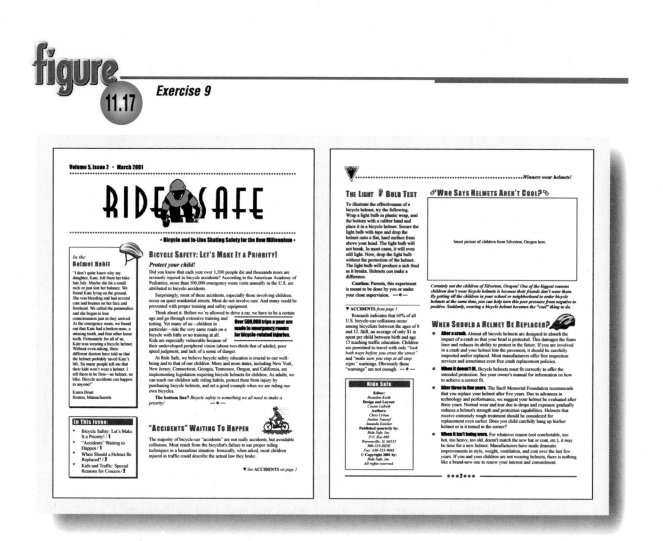

Saving Your Newsletter as a Template

To save time when creating future issues of your newsletter, save it as a template document. To save it as a template, delete all text, text boxes, pictures, objects, etc. that will not stay the same for future issues. Likewise, leave all text, pictures, symbols, text boxes, headers and footers, etc. that will remain the same in each issue of your newsletter. All styles created for the newsletter will remain with the template. For example, to save the *Ride Safe* newsletter as a template, leave the following items and delete the rest:

- Folio
- Nameplate
- Headers and footers
- Sidebar with the title because this will be a feature article every month; delete the sidebar article text only
- Table of contents and heading; delete the table of contents text only
- Masthead
- Remaining text boxes; delete the articles within each text box. (The text boxes will most likely need to be reformatted each time you create a new issue of your newsletter; however, they serve as a basic framework for future issues.)

Once you have deleted the text and elements that will change every month, add placeholder text if desired, and then save the newsletter on the hard drive or to a floppy disk with Save As. At the Save As dialog box, click the down arrow to the right of the Save as type list box and select *Document Template* as the file type. Double-click the template folder in which you want to save your newsletter template, key a name for your newsletter template, and then click OK. See figure 11.18 for an example of how the *Ride Safe* newsletter might look if saved as a template.

figure 11.18   *Sample Newsletter Template*

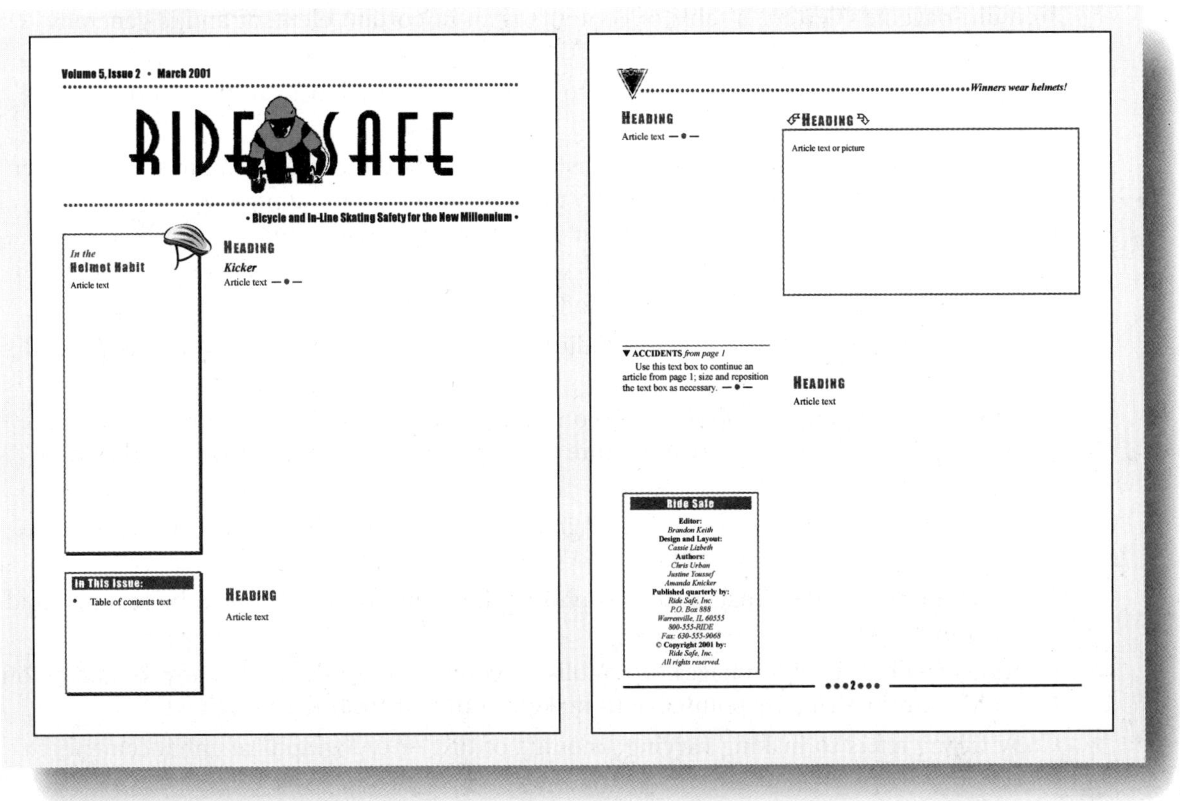

chapter summary

➤ Elements can be added to a newsletter to enhance the visual impact, including table of contents, headers and/or footers, masthead, pull quotes, kickers, sidebars, captions, ruled lines, jump lines, page borders, and end signs.

➤ Use spot color—a color in addition to black—in a newsletter as an accent to such features as graphics lines, graphics images, borders, backgrounds, headings, and end signs.

➤ Headers and footers are commonly used in newsletters. Headers/footers can be placed on specific pages, only odd pages, or only even pages and can include page numbering, a slogan, a logo, or a horizontal ruled line.

➤ A sidebar is set off from the body text in a text box and can include a photograph or graphics image along with text.

➤ In multi-page newsletters, a table of contents is an important element and is generally located on the front page in the lower left or right corner.

➤ A pull quote acts as a focal point, helps to break up lengthy blocks of text, and provides visual contrast.

➤ A masthead is a repeating element that usually contains the company address, newsletter publication schedule, names of those contributing to the production, and copyright information. It is generally located on the back page of a newsletter.

➤ A kicker is generally set in a smaller type size than the headline but larger than the body text and is placed above or below the headline or article heading.

➤ Symbols or special characters used to indicate the end of a section of text are called end signs.

➤ In a newsletter, a jump line indicates a continuation of an article or feature to another page and enables the newsletter to feature the beginning of several articles on the front page.

➤ Graphics images, illustrations, charts, diagrams, and photographs can add focus, balance, proportion, contrast, directional flow, and consistency to a newsletter.

➤ Noncomputer-generated images such as photographs and illustrations can be scanned and inserted in a newsletter.

➤ Captions can be added to images to establish a connection to the body copy. Bold caption text and set it in a smaller point size to make it different from the body text.

➤ Copy fitting refers to making varying amounts of text or typographical enhancements fit in a fixed amount of space.

commands review

	Mouse/Keyboard
Insert File dialog box	Click Insert, File
Insert Picture dialog box	Click Insert, point to Picture, then click From File or ClipArt
Format Picture dialog box	Select picture, click Format, then Picture
Headers and footers	Click View, Header and Footer; click Switch Between Header and Footer button to display Header or Footer pane
Display Drawing toolbar	Click Drawing button on Standard toolbar or right-click in the Standard toolbar, select Drawing
Draw a text box	Click the Text Box button on the Drawing toolbar or click Insert, then Text Box
Insert a text box around selected text	Select text, click Text Box button on Drawing toolbar
Format Text Box dialog box	Select text box, Format, Text Box
Format Object dialog box	Select object, Format, Object
Paragraph Borders and Shading dialog box	Click Format, Borders and Shading dialog box
Kerning (spacing of specific pairs of characters)	Click Format, Font, Character Spacing tab, Kerning for fonts, enter specific amount of Points and above to be kerned
Tracking (spacing of all characters)	Click Format, Font, Character Spacing tab, Spacing, Expand or Condense or Normal, enter point By: amount in point increments
Paragraph spacing	Click Format, Paragraph
Insert special characters	Click Insert, Symbol
Style dialog box	Click Format, Style
Columns dialog box	Click Format, Columns
Insert a column break	Click Insert, Break, Column Break
Bullets and Numbering dialog box	Click Format, Bullets and Numbering

thinking offline

Matching: Match the terms with the correct definitions by writing the letter of the term on the blank line in front of the correct definition.

Ⓐ Caption   Ⓔ Header   Ⓘ Pull quote
Ⓑ Copy fitting   Ⓕ Jump line   Ⓙ Scanner
Ⓒ End sign   Ⓖ Kicker   Ⓚ Sidebar
Ⓓ Footer   Ⓗ Masthead   Ⓛ Spot color

_____ 1. A repeating element that can add consistency among newsletter issues and that contains the company address, newsletter publication schedule, names of those contributing to the production of the newsletter, and copyright information.

_____ 2. Description or explanation of a graphics image, illustration, or photograph.

_____ 3. Text that is repeated at the top of every page.

_____ 4. A block of information or a related story that is set off from the body text in a graphics box.

_____ 5. A color in a newsletter, other than black, used as an accent.

_____ 6. A brief direct phrase, summarizing statement, or important point associated with the body copy of a newsletter.

_____ 7. A symbol or special character used to indicate the end of a section of text.

_____ 8. Indication that an article or feature continues to another page.

_____ 9. A brief sentence or phrase that is a lead-in to an article.

_____ 10. A device that converts a photograph, drawing, or text into a compatible digital file format.

Concepts: Write your answers to the following questions in the space provided.

1. List at least five tips to consider when creating a pull quote.

2. Why is it important to have some knowledge of graphic file formats?

3. List at least six copy-fitting ideas to create more space in a document.

4. What is the purpose of linking text boxes and why is this feature advantageous to use in a newsletter?

5. List at least four paragraph enhancements that can be included in a newsletter.

Assessment 1

1. Find two newsletters from two different sources. Review the newsletters for the items listed below. Label those items that you find in each newsletter.

> Nameplate
> Subtitle
> Folio
> Headlines
> Subheads
> Table of contents
> Masthead
> Header
> Footer
> Sidebar
> Pull quote
> Kicker
> End sign
> Jump line
> Caption
> Spot color

Optional: Write a summary explaining which of the two newsletters is the most appealing and why.

Assessment 2

In this assessment, you are to redesign the first page of a newsletter located on your student CD. Two pages of text are provided. You only need to redesign the first page, but you may use any of the text on the second page for copy-fitting purposes.

1. Redesign a basic newsletter named Redesign Text.doc located on your student CD according to the following specifications:
   a. Create a new nameplate, subtitle, and folio. Experiment with thumbnail sketches.
   b. Create the body of the newsletter using an asymmetrical column layout.
   c. Include the following:

   > Header and footer
   > Table of contents
   > Sidebar
   > Pull quote
   > Graphic with caption
   > Spot color (or varying shades of gray)

   d. Use a kicker, end signs, jump line, clip art, text box placeholder for a photo, etc., for visual effect or copy fitting.
   e. Use tracking (character spacing), leading (line spacing), paragraph spacing before and after, text boxes, etc., to set the body copy attractively on the page.
2. Save the new newsletter on the hard drive or to a floppy disk and name it c11sa02, Redesign newsletter.
3. Print and then close c11sa02, Redesign newsletter.
4. In class, edit each other's newsletters by completing the following steps:
   a. Independently choose an editor's name for yourself and do not share it with the rest of the class. (This is your chance to be famous!)
   b. Your instructor will collect all the newsletters and randomly distribute a newsletter to each class participant.
   c. Sign your individual editor's "name" on the back of the newsletter and make editorial comments addressing such items as target audience, visual appeal, overall layout and design, font selection, graphics image selection, focus, balance, proportion, contrast, directional flow, consistency, and use of color.
   d. Rotate the newsletters so that you have an opportunity to write editor's comments on the back of each newsletter, identified by your individual editor's name only.
   e. Review the editors' comments on the back of your own newsletter, and revise your newsletter keeping your editorial staff's comments in mind.
   f. Save and name the revised version of your newsletter c11sa02, Revised.
   g. Print c11sa02, Revised.
   h. Evaluate your revised newsletter with the Document Evaluation Checklist (Document Evaluation Checklist.doc) located on your student CD.

Assessment 3

Assume that you are an employee of Ride Safe, Inc., and are responsible for creating their newsletter. You have already completed an issue of this newsletter in c11ex09, and now you have to create the next issue using articles that other employees have submitted to you. Using text (articles) from your student CD and the *Ride Safe* newsletter already created, create the next issue of the *Ride Safe* newsletter according to the following specifications:

1. Print RideSafe Issue2 Text.doc located on your student CD.
2. Review the printout of possible articles to be used for the second issue of your newsletter. Decide what articles you would like to include. Save the rest for possible fillers.
3. Make a thumbnail sketch of a possible layout and design. You can open c11ex09, Newsletter.doc and use the framework of that newsletter to create this second issue. Be consistent in column layout and design elements used. Include the following items:

   > Masthead
   > Sidebar
   > Pull quote
   > End sign
   > Caption
   > Picture
   > Spot color

4. For the masthead, use your instructor's name as the editor and your name for the design and layout.
5. Create a style for the article headings.
6. You decide on the order and placement of articles. Use bullets, bold, italics, reverse text, etc., if appropriate to the design and layout of this new issue of your newsletter.
7. Make any copy-fitting adjustments as necessary.
8. Save the document on the hard drive or to a floppy disk and name it c11sa03, Ride safe issue2.
9. Print and then close c11sa03, Ride safe issue2.
10. Evaluate your newsletter with the Document Evaluation Checklist.

Optional: Rewrite and redesign all the article heads to be more clever, interesting, and eye-catching.

CREATIVE ACTIVITY

With a partner, find a poor example of a newsletter and redesign the first page, including the nameplate. Use a different column layout and copy-fitting techniques to produce a newsletter that entices people to actually read your publication. Rewrite the text copy to make it more interesting. Re-create, save on the hard drive or to a floppy disk, and print c11ca01, and then close it. In class, break up into small groups of four to six students and present the before and after versions of your newsletter. Give a brief explanation of the changes made, problems encountered, and solutions found. Vote on the most creative copy and the most creative design separately.

Performance Assessments

Unit 03 PA

PREPARING PUBLICATIONS

Assessment 1

At a clear document window, create a one-page newsletter by completing the following instructions. This newsletter may be a holiday, personal, or family newsletter that you would like to duplicate and mail to your friends or relatives. Write four or five short paragraphs describing the highlights of this year and your expectations for next year. You may include items about your accomplishments, awards, talents, skills, hobbies, or any vacations you may have taken. Use the Thesaurus and Spelling features to assist you. Also, be sure to create your own styles, use any appropriate built-in styles, or use the Format Painter to assist you in repetitive formatting.

1. Create a thumbnail sketch of your newsletter.
2. Incorporate the following in your newsletter:
   a. Use appropriate typefaces and type sizes for all of the elements in your newsletter.
   b. Use em spaces for any indented text.
   c. The nameplate should include your last name (e.g., Smith Family Newsletter).
   d. Create a subtitle.
   e. Create a folio.
   f. Use appropriate column numbers and widths.
   g. Apply the desktop publishing concepts of focus, balance, proportion, contrast, directional flow, and consistency to your newsletter design and layout.
   h. Use kerning and character spacing.
   i. Use appropriate leading (paragraph spacing) before and after the headline and all subheads.
   j. Use a graphic, symbol, WordArt object, clip art, or a scanned picture. (A photograph would add a nice personal touch!)
   k. Be creative.
3. Save the newsletter to the hard drive or a floppy disk and name it u03pa01, Newsletter.
4. After completing u03pa01, Newsletter, print and exchange newsletters in the classroom and evaluate them using the Document Evaluation Checklist (Document Evaluation Checklist.doc) located on your student CD. Write any additional comments or suggestions, discussing weaknesses and strengths, on the bottom of the second page of the evaluation form.

Optional: Write and create a newsletter about the program in your major area of study. Research your program and include course descriptions, course learning objectives, certificate and degree options, prerequisites, etc. Relate your program's course of study to current trends in business.

Assessment **two** 2

In this assessment, you will create a two-page newsletter.

1. At a clear document window, open Redesign Text.doc, located on your CD.
2. Save the document with Save <u>A</u>s to the hard drive or a floppy disk and name it u03pa02, Disclosures.
3. Redesign both pages of the newsletter and include the following elements and techniques:
    a. Nameplate
    b. Folio
    c. Heading and subheading styles
    d. Header and footer
    e. Table of contents
    f. Sidebar
    g. Pull quote
    h. Graphic image with caption
    i. Spot color
    j. A kicker, end signs, jump lines, and/or graphic images if desired or needed for copy fitting.
    k. Tracking, leading, paragraph spacing, and so on, to set the body copy attractively on the page.
    l. Any design elements necessary to achieve consistency and unity between the two pages.
4. When completed, save the document again with the same name, u03pa02, Disclosures.
5. Print and then close u03pa02, Disclosures. (Ask your instructor about printing each page separately or printing the pages back to back.)
6. Evaluate your own work using the Document Evaluation Checklist (Document Evaluation Checklist.doc.) located on your student CD. Revise your document if any areas need improvement.

Assessment **three** 3

At a clear document window, create a cover for your portfolio with the following specifications:

1. Create a thumbnail sketch of your cover.
2. Use at least one graphic element such as WordArt, a watermark, ruled lines, a graphic image, or a scanned image.
3. Consider balance, focus, contrast, directional flow, and proportion when creating the cover.
4. Save the completed cover to the hard drive or a floppy disk and name it u03pa03, Cover.
5. Print and then close u03pa03, Cover.

Optional: Create another cover for your portfolio. Assume you are applying for a government position or for a job in a comedy gallery and try to convey a tone that is appropriate to your purpose.

Index